Regulating Coastal Zones

Regulating Coastal Zones addresses the knowledge gap concerning the legal and regulatory challenges of managing land in coastal zones across a broad range of political and socio-economic contexts.

In recent years, coastal zone management has gained increasing attention from environmentalists, land use planners, and decision-makers across a broad spectrum of fields. Development pressures along coasts such as high-end tourism projects, luxury housing, ports, energy generation, military outposts, heavy industry, and large-scale enterprise compete with landscape preservation and threaten local history and culture. Leading experts present fifteen case studies among advanced-economy countries, selected to represent three groups of legal contexts: Signatories to the 2008 Mediterranean ICZM Protocol, parties to the 2002 EU Recommendation on Integrated Coastal Zone Management, and the USA and Australia.

This book is the first to address the legal-regulatory aspects of coastal land management from a systematic cross-national comparative perspective. By including both successful and less effective strategies, it aims to inform professionals, graduate students, policymakers, and NGOs of the legal and socio-political challenges as well as the better practices from which others could learn.

Rachelle Alterman is a Professor (emerita) of urban planning and law at the Technion – Israel Institute of Technology and Senior Researcher at the Neaman Institute for National Policy Research. She heads the Laboratory on Comparative Planning Law and Property Rights. Alterman is the founding president of the International Academic Association on Planning, Law and Property Rights (PLPR). Her research interests include comparative planning law and land use regulation, comparative land policy and property rights, housing policy, and implementation of public policy. For her pioneering contribution to the field, she was awarded Honorary Member status by the Association of European Schools of Planning (among only six awarded this distinction, and the only non-European), and has been selected as one of sixteen global "leaders in planning thought" whose academic autobiographies are compiled in the book *Encounters in Planning Thought* (Routledge, 2017).

Cygal Pellach holds a Bachelor of Planning from the University of New South Wales, Sydney, Australia, and a MSc in Urban and Regional Planning from the Technion – Israel Institute of Technology. She is currently completing a doctoral degree, also at the Technion, under Rachelle Alterman's supervision. Between her M.Sc. and her PhD studies, Cygal served as the team leader in the EU-funded research project, Mare Nostrum, headed by Alterman. Prior to embarking on an academic path, Cygal garnered five years' experience in urban planning practice, working in private consultancy in Melbourne (VIC), Australia.

Urban Planning and Environment
Series Editors: Donald Miller and Nicole Gurran

Maintaining and enhancing living conditions in cities through a combination of physical planning and environmental management is a newly emerging focus of governments around the world. For example, local governments seek to insulate sensitive land uses such as residential areas from environmentally intrusive activities such as major transport facilities and manufacturing. Regional governments protect water quality and natural habitat by enforcing pollution controls and regulating the location of growth. Some national governments fund acquisition of strategically important sites, facilitate the renewal of brown fields, and even develop integrated environmental quality plans. The aim of this series is to share information on experiments and best practices of governments at several levels. These empirically based studies present and critically assess a variety of initiatives to improve environmental quality. Although institutional and cultural contexts vary, lessons from one commonly can provide useful ideas to other communities. Each of the contributions are independently peer reviewed, and are intended to be helpful to professional planners and environmental managers, elected officials, representatives of NGOs, and researchers seeking improved ways to resolve environmental problems in urban areas and to foster sustainable urban development.

Titles in the series:

Governing for Resilience in Vulnerable Places
Edited by Elen-Maarja Trell, Britta Restemeyer, Melanie M. Bakema, Bettina van Hoven

Bicycle Urbanism
Reimagining Bicycle Friendly Cities
Edited by Rachel Berney

Instruments of Land Policy
Dealing with Scarcity of Land
Edited by Jean-David Gerber, Thomas Hartmann, Andreas Hengstermann

For more information about this series, please visit: https://www.routledge.com/Urban-Planning-and-Environment/book-series/UPE

Regulating Coastal Zones

International Perspective on Land
Management Instruments

**Edited by Rachelle Alterman
and Cygal Pellach**

Routledge
Taylor & Francis Group

LONDON AND NEW YORK

First published 2021
by Routledge
2 Park Square, Milton Park, Abingdon, Oxon OX14 4RN

and by Routledge
52 Vanderbilt Avenue, New York, NY 10017

Routledge is an imprint of the Taylor & Francis Group, an informa business

British Library Cataloguing-in-Publication Data
A catalogue record for this book is available from the British Library

Library of Congress Cataloging-in-Publication Data
Names: Alterman, Rachelle, editor. | Pellach, Cygal, editor.
Title: Regulating coastal zones : international perspectives on land-management instruments / edited by Rachelle Alterman and Cygal Pellach.
Description: New York : Routledge, 2020. | Series: Urban planning and environment | Includes bibliographical references and index.
Identifiers: LCCN 2020023948 (print) | LCCN 2020023949 (ebook) | ISBN 9781138361553 (hardback) | ISBN 9781138361560 (paperback) | ISBN 9780429432699 (ebook)
Subjects: LCSH: Coastal zone management–Case studies. | Coastal zone management–Law and legislation–Case studies.
Classification: LCC HT391 .R3854 2020 (print) | LCC HT391 (ebook) | DDC 333.91/7–dc23
LC record available at https://lccn.loc.gov/2020023948
LC ebook record available at https://lccn.loc.gov/2020023949

ISBN: 9781138361553 (hbk)
ISBN: 9781138361560 (pbk)
ISBN: 9780429432699 (ebk)

Typeset in Sabon
by KnowledgeWorks Global Ltd.

Cover images (from left):

Borkum island coast on the Wadden Sea, Germany. Available at: https://pixabay.com/photos/borkum-island-gulls-wadden-sea-4428395/

Gold Coast, Queensland, Australia. CC BY 2.0 license. Available at: https://www.flickr.com/photos/lennykphotography/15774425432/

The coast at Nice. Annie and Andrew. CC BY 2.0 license. Available at: https://www.flickr.com/photos/anwenandandrew/6065731555

Creative Commons licenses of images used in this book:

CC BY 2.0 – see: https://creativecommons.org/licenses/by/2.0/
CC BY-SA 2.0 – see: https://creativecommons.org/licenses/by-sa/2.0/
CC BY 2.5 – see: https://creativecommons.org/licenses/by/2.5/
CC BY 3.0 – see: https://creativecommons.org/licenses/by/3.0/
CC BY-SA 4.0 – see: https://creativecommons.org/licenses/by-sa/4.0/

Dedicated to the memory of my only (and younger) sister, Dr. Tzila Shamir (Leichter). She was a brilliant mathematician, whose death from juvenile diabetes cut short her research in robotics, including early contributions to autonomous vehicles and to the math of mobility of people with disabilities.

Rachelle Alterman (Leichter)

Dedicated to the memory of my maternal grandparents, who took full advantage of living on Sydney's coast, each in their own way. Geri loved to walk and swim at the beach. Justin travelled by ferry as often as he could. Both were dedicated to the pursuit of knowledge and thus surely influenced my path in life.

Cygal Pellach

Contents

Preface

The seeds of this book were planted several years ago during the Mare Nostrum project, funded through a research grant by the European Union.[1] The project, led by Rachelle as Coordinator and Cygal as Deputy Coordinator, focused on the legal-regulatory aspects of coastal zone land management in the Mediterranean area. While this book was inspired by the Mare Nostrum project, it has gone much beyond that project in scope, method, and, most importantly, in the much-expanded set of countries.

From this book's broad cross-national perspective encompassing fifteen countries, we learn that despite several decades of laws, policies, and research about Integrated Coastal Zone Management (ICZM), many countries still face persistent impediments to achieving this goal. Knowledge sharing across countries and disciplines is essential for promoting sustainable coastal conservation and for meeting the special challenges posed by climate change. We hope that this book contributes in this direction.

This is not a regular edited volume. It is a concerted team project. We have been very privileged to cooperate with a group of top experts in the various fields related to the legal-regulatory aspects of coastal zone management: Land use planning, planning law, environmental law, and planning governance. Each scholar has agreed to invest much time to analyse their country's coastal land laws and regulations according to our specially designed framework. At times, we asked the authors to go through several rounds of questions about nitty-gritty issues that needed clarification for cross-national calibration. We are immensely thankful to our colleagues for their trust in us.

---

1 Cross-border cooperation in the Mediterranean: The ENPI CBCMED programme. See http://www.enpicbcmed. eu/programme

Acknowledgements

Special thanks to two experts in water- and marine-related disciplines who kindly helped us out with some of the unavoidable concepts and terms related to shorelines:

- Dr. Dov Zviely, an expert in coastal morphology and related aspects of morphodynamics, hydrography, paleogeography, and sedimentology; Head of the M.A. program in Marine Resource Management at Ruppin Academic Center, Israel
- Dr. Roey Egozi, hydrologist, Research Station for Erosion Studies, Israel Ministry of Agriculture and Rural Development

We would also like to thank all of our partners in the Mare Nostrum project (2013–2016), but particularly Pablo Grostithas and Kostas Lalenis, for their valuable insights about the Spanish and Greek contexts respectively.

Contributors

Helle Tegner Anker is a Professor of Law at the Faculty of Science, University of Copenhagen. She has specialised in environmental and planning law, including access to justice, EIA, land use planning, nature protection, ICZM and renewable energy. She has been appointed as member of several committees established by the Danish Government.

Evangelia Balla is a Surveying Engineer and Urban and Regional Planner. She is currently a Researcher at the Department of Urban and Regional Planning and Geo-information Management at the Faculty of Geo-information Management and Earth Observation (ITC) of the University of Twente (NL).

Angela Barbanente is a Professor of Regional Planning at the Polytechnic University of Bari, Italy. She was deputy president of the regional government of Puglia from 2005 to 2015, with responsibility for spatial planning, housing, urban policy, landscape, environmentally protected areas, and cultural heritage.

Inês Calor is an architect and holds a PhD in Geography and Urban Planning. She is currently working as an urban planner in a Portuguese municipality and a researcher at CEGOT, University of Porto. Her recent research focuses on illegal development, planning enforcement, and compliance with short-term rental rules.

Dafna Carmon is an urban planner and a lawyer, holding a PhD in urban planning from the Technion – Israel Institute of Technology. She was a senior researcher in the EU Mare Nostrum project on ICZM in the Mediterranean. Dafna is a consultant to local municipalities, specializing in social planning and public participation. She is also an adjunct teacher at Tel-Aviv University.

Paulo V.D. Correia is an Associate Professor at IST, Lisbon University. He holds a PhD in Civil Engineering (Planning and Transportation) from IST and an MA in Regional Science from the University of Liverpool. He is a former General Director for Spatial Development and past President of both CEU-ECTP (European Council of Spatial Planners) and the Portuguese Association of Planners.

Enzo Falco is an Assistant Professor at Dipartimento DICAM, Università degli Studi di Trento, Italy, and Visiting Researcher, Department of Urbanism, TU Delft. He conducts research on planning law, TDR, and theories of public participation in planning.

Georgia Giannakourou is a Full Professor of Planning and Environmental Law and Policies at National and Kapodistrian University of Athens (Department of Political Science and Public Administration). She is also an Attorney at Law in the Athens Bar.

Nicole Gurran is a Professor of Urban and Regional Planning at the University of Sydney. She has led and collaborated on a series of studies on aspects of urban policy, climate change, and planning, and she has authored numerous publications and books, including *Australian Urban Land Use Planning: Principles, Policy, and Practice.*

Pieter Jong is a lecturer in Environmental Law at Delft University of Technology. In addition to his academic activities, he is employed by the Dutch Ministry of Infrastructure and Water Management. He also works as a senior policy advisor on Environmental Noise, Railway Vibrations, and Healthy Urban Environment.

Naja Marot is an Assistant Professor of Regional Planning, Tourism and Recreation at the University of Ljubljana, Slovenia. Her research focuses on (territorial) governance, policy analysis, impact assessments, regional planning, territorial cohesion, degraded urban areas, post-mining regions, and public participation. She represents Slovenia on the Council of Representatives at the Association of European Schools of Planning (AESOP).

Linda McElduff is a lecturer in planning in the Belfast School of Architecture and the Built Environment, Ulster University. Her doctoral research (completed in 2014) investigated the regeneration and resilience of coastal resorts on the island of Ireland. Linda's current research interests include coastal management, resilience, and marine social science.

Pablo Molina Alegre is a lawyer and planner. He is currently partner in the law firm J&A Garrigues, S.L.P. (Barcelona, Spain), where he deals with cases related to a variety of topics in planning, environmental law, and property law. In the course of his career, Pablo has lectured at several universities in Spain and Colombia. He is a past President of the Spanish Association of Planners (2015–2017).

Loïc Prieur holds a PhD in public law. He is a lecturer at Sorbonne University and Director of the Master of Urban Planning program. A Partner at LGP law firm, he specialises in public law and urban planning law. He has several publications on French coastal law and is regularly consulted by members of parliament on draft legislation related to the coastal zones.

Heather Ritchie is a lecturer in Spatial Planning and Energy Policy in the Belfast School of Architecture and the Built Environment, Ulster University. Since completing her PhD in 2011, Heather's research interests have developed around Marine Spatial Planning, land–sea interaction, regulation at the coast and beyond, and transboundary MSP.

Hendrik van Sandick is a legal consultant on land policy, environmental law, and spatial planning. He is currently working for the Dutch Ministry of the Interior on the new Environmental and Planning Act.

Eva Schachtner is a postgraduate researcher. After law studies in Munich, Paris, and Barcelona, she worked as a Scientific Assistant for the University of Rostock and the Leibniz Institute of Ecological Urban and Regional Development on projects for the protection of the marine environment.

A. Dan Tarlock holds an AB and LLB from Stanford University. He has taught at various universities in the United States, Europe, and China and is University Distinguished Professor Emeritus, Illinois Tech, Chicago-Kent College of Law. His principal subjects were environmental law, land use planning, and water law. He has written widely on these subjects and served on numerous US and international organizations.

Fatma Ünsal is a Professor of Urban Planning who teaches urban politics and reformist approaches in urban planning at graduate and undergraduate levels. Her research topics and publications concentrate on planning legislation, coastal development, mid-size cities in Turkey, and urban development of Istanbul. She is currently the Director of the Urbanism Application and Research Centre at the University.

Marta Lora-Tamayo Vallvé is a Full Professor of Administrative Law at the National University of Distance Education (UNED), Spain. In her teaching and research, she has focused primarily on planning law from a historical and comparative perspective. She is a member of the National College of Urban Jurisprudence (CNJUR), the International Platform of Experts in Planning Law, and the Academic Council of the City Institute.

Kurt Xerri is a Lecturer at the Faculty of Laws of the University of Malta. His research interests include property law and property rights. He also serves as an advisor to the Maltese government on housing matters.

Part I
Framing

1 Introduction

Objectives and method of comparative analysis

Rachelle Alterman and Cygal Pellach

Everyone loves a pristine beach. But almost everyone (in the Global North) also likes to own land and live near the beach, to vacation in hotels on the beach, to go to country clubs located next to the beach, or at least to be able to view the beach from their home or office. Coastal locations often have a real estate premium in many countries (see for example, Markandya et al., 2008). Coastal zones are often also attractive to government agencies constructing roads and other national or local infrastructure, and many old industries are still located near the coast.

The rationale for Integrated Coastal Zone Management

Throughout human history, coastal zones have been important for livelihood and transportation. A major portion of humanity has always resided close to the coast, and still does (about 40% live within 100 km of the coast; UN, 2017). The environmental consequences of the anthropogenic (human-generated) pressures on the coast and its landscapes are much studied and discussed, but insufficient attention is devoted to the real-property aspects of coastal land. In order to improve coastal zone conservation, the land management aspects must receive more research attention. In the era of growing awareness of climate change and its intensified impacts in coastal regions, the real-property aspects are likely to become even more acute. Adaptation measures to sea level rise or extreme storm events along the coasts inevitably come up against issues related to land property rights.

Any book on coastal zones will note that they are unique and complex environments that warrant special measures for their conservation (see for example, Schernewski, 2016; Portman, 2016). The environmental assets, including the unique landscapes, are especially threatened by the heightened development pressures in coastal zones. Therefore, coastal regions have been recognized as meriting a special decision-guidance model – Integrated Coastal Zone Management, ICZM (Portman, 2016; Kay & Alder, 2005, pp. 8–9). One of the earlier, highly cited books devoted entirely to coastal management offers this definition of ICZM:

> . . . a conscious management process that acknowledges the interrelationships among most coastal and ocean uses and the environment they potentially affect. ICM is a process by which rational decisions are made concerning the conservation and sustainable use of coastal and ocean resources and space. The process is designed to overcome the fragmentation inherent in single-sector management approaches . . . in the splits in jurisdiction among different levels of government, and in the land-water interface (Cicin-Sain et al., 1998, p.1).

The above definition of ICZM and many similar ones present an ideal that can never be fully implemented, but they do set a direction for policymakers (Garriga & Losada, 2010, p. 89; Portman, 2016, p. 69). The ICZM idea has come a long way since it was first introduced in legislation in the USA in 1972 (Belknap, 1980; Felleman, 1982). In recent decades, ICZM has become widely accepted around the world as the guiding paradigm for policymaking about coastal zones (Cullinan, 2006; Portman, 2016; Ahlhorn, 2017; Ramkumar et al., 2019). Many countries have adopted laws, regulations, and policies in that direction.

Purpose and structure of this work

Unlike much of existing literature that focuses on what *should* be done in terms of better land-management and governance norms towards ICZM, this book addresses what *is* being applied de facto, juxtaposing and comparing current practices with the ICZM norms. The focus is on the laws and regulations and how they manifest in practice. In order to help to move the ICZM ideals from books, treaties, laws, and regulations to actual practice, policymakers need a "reality check" to gauge feasibility, identify impediments, or consider alternative approaches, some based on learning from other countries. To that end, we ask, what specific land-related laws, regulations, or policies have in fact been adopted and implemented by a relatively large set of countries.

This book joins a large number of publications about ICZM, created over decades by researchers from a broad range of disciplines. In order to position our book's contribution within the current body of knowledge, we distinguish among three "pillars" of ICZM:

Pillar 1: Coastal environmental dynamics (not discussed in this book)
Pillar 2: Land demarcation and property rights
Pillar 3: Modes of governance and institutions

The first pillar is outside the scope of this book. It is grounded in environmental sciences, addressing the interrelationships among the various aspects of the marine and terrestrial environments. The purpose is to provide decision makers with a multidisciplinary understanding of the special attributes of the coastal environment, its landscapes, and their dynamics.

The second pillar, pertaining to land demarcation and property rights, could be seen as the "hardware" in the kit of tools of ICZM. In this book, we focus especially on the role of laws and regulations pertaining to coastal land and how they are practised on the ground. Topics include demarcation of zones for special protection, private and public property rights and the regulations that restrict development and direct the use of land. The literature on this topic is the least abundant among the three pillars.

The third pillar of ICZM focuses on governance. One could see this as the "software" in the kit of ICZM tools. This pillar, like the first (but unlike the second), has benefited from considerable research attention, mostly with a general institutional perspective, rather than the legal-regulatory perspective adopted here. Previous research has usually highlighted the persistent problems of high fragmentation among the many coast-related government bodies and the difficulties in reaching coordinated decisions, and proposes approaches to improve institutional set-ups and better governance (superbly explained by Portman, 2016; see other examples in Cicin-Sain et al., 1998 and Ahlhorn, 2017).

In this book, we address the third pillar from the special perspective of the second pillar – the land-related laws and regulations. Our analysis encompasses the following issues: Coordination among institutions in charge of land-related policy and implementation, especially land use planning; integration of the land-related subject areas and across the land–sea divide; public participation; and capacity to enforce infringements of land-related rules. In the era of climate change, we added questions about the degree of institutional awareness of the need for adaptation to sea level rise or other climate-related challenges. We also look at the capacity of the laws themselves to adapt to climate change (Arnold, 2013).

The book has a three-tier structure of analysis: National, cross-national, and supra-national. For each tier, we address the relevant laws, regulations, and practices of land-related ICZM. Across each of the tiers, the book makes a unique contribution to the current state of knowledge both in its subject matter and in its selection of countries. This is also the first book to address all three levels and the interrelationships among them.

At the national tier, the book encompasses a large (non-random) sample of fifteen national jurisdictions selected according to specific criteria. Each country report has been written by one or more experts from that country. The country chapters are the heart of the book. Each country chapter follows a rigorous framework based on a shared set of topics, which we call "parameters", to be introduced in detail in Chapter 2. Each individual country report stands as a unique contribution to the state of knowledge about that specific country. The picture that emerges is of a (surprisingly) high degree of variety among the laws, regulations, and practices about ICZM.

The second tier – the cross-national analysis – is made possible through the systematic structure of the country reports. At this level, we as editors collate and compare the rich information provided by the country chapters in order to offer the readers opportunities for cross-learning. There is not much previously reported analysis of land regulation in the framework of ICZM that is based on a rigorous cross-national comparative perspective. Notable research efforts to date are Boelaert-Suominen & Cullinan (1994), Cicin-Sain et al. (1998), Markandya et al. (2008), Ahlhorn (2017, pp. 23–31), and Karnauskaitė et al. (2018). These pioneering publications, however, do not delve into questions concerning implementation. This book goes beyond, both in scale and breadth.

The third tier – the supra-national level – is relevant to thirteen of the countries. They each come under one or more set of rules enunciated through international law or supra-national policy intended as guidance to improve ICZM among the signatory states. Yet, in reading the country reports, one is struck by the absence of references to these relevant supra-national documents (except occasionally, when introduced during the editorial process). Although this fact foreshadows some of our findings, it does not diminish the importance of looking at the performance of the international efforts. There is not yet much research attention to the degree of influence of the supra-national ICZM norms on national laws and policies. Among the few contributions in this category are several excellent analyses by the team of Rochette and Billé (Rochette & Billé, 2010, 2013; Billé & Rochette, 2011, 2015; see also González-Riancho et al., 2009). To date, however, researchers have addressed only a handful of countries.

Over the remainder of this chapter, we introduce the supra-national laws and their implications; present the rationales for country selection; and discuss the methodology of analysis and its limitations.

Supra-national ICZM law: Shunning intervention in land rights

In 2008, a daring leap was taken when ICZM first entered the realm of international law. After several years of consideration under UN auspices (Markandya et al., 2008; Sanò et al., 2011), the Protocol on Integrated Coastal Zone Management for the Mediterranean was adopted, henceforth, the Mediterranean ICZM Protocol (UNEP, 2008). A few years earlier, in 2002, the EU adopted a supra-national policy document on ICZM endorsed by all its member states. However, adoption of international laws or policies is easier than their implementation by national and local governments, especially where land and property rights are concerned. Throughout this book, we will learn to what extent the real-property aspects of ICZM have been amenable to legal and policy change.

The Mediterranean ICZM Protocol was not just one more international agreement on environmental issues. Such agreements go much further back, to the 1940s, and over time have addressed a growing number of environmental topics.[1] Sea-related environmental agreements also go far back, to the early 1970s. The significance of the ICZM Protocol – with twenty-two signatory nations covering almost all Mediterranean countries (PAP/RAC, n.d.) – is that it was the first attempt to intervene in the terrestrial aspects of coastal zones through international law. Although a few other conventions followed for regional seas, the Mediterranean ICZM Protocol remains the most ambitious (Rochette & Billé, 2012).

However, it turns out that the idea of direct international intervention in domestic law pertaining to *land* – as distinct from sea – is much more contentious than it may have seemed in 2008 when the Mediterranean ICZM Protocol came into effect. The indicative story is the failed attempt by the EU to upgrade its "soft law" guidance on ICZM into a binding EU Directive that would apply to both sea and land.

The intentions were clear. The EU policy document was first adopted in 2002 as *Recommendation of the European Parliament and of the Council . . . Concerning the Implementation of Integrated Coastal Zone Management in Europe* (henceforth European ICZM Recommendation). During preparation of the ICZM Recommendation, the European Council established a group of experts, which in 2000 published an unofficial document called *Model Law on Sustainable Management of Coastal Zones and European Code of Conduct for Coastal Zones* (Ahlhorn, 2017; Council of Europe, 2000). This document was to evolve into a binding Directive that would cover both sea and land. A draft Directive was prepared on "maritime spatial planning and integrated coastal management" (European Parliament, 2013). The explanatory note stressed the key importance of addressing land–**sea connectivity and interactions**.[2] One should also recall that by that time, the EU itself was already a signatory to the ICZM Protocol, in addition to the eight Mediterranean states that are also EU members (PAP/RAC, n.d.).

Nevertheless, when the draft Directive came to a vote, a majority of Members of the European Parliament (MEPs) voted to eliminate the reference to rules pertaining to land, leaving only the maritime aspects and vague references to "land-sea interactions". During the debate, Kay Swinburne, a UK member of the European Conservatives and Reformists party, submitted the following:

> . . . The final agreement should have no or minimal impact on our existing process and will not impose new or added burdens. The ICM element has been dropped from the final agreement in exchange for references to, and requirements on, land-sea interactions. The importance of this relationship between land, coast and sea is already reflected in our marine planning processes. The agreement allows the UK to move forward with the delivery of marine planning and recommend its adoption. It contains additional safeguards to preclude any overlap with or impact on land planning, and underlines that the content of the marine plans will be determined by Member States. (European Parliament, 2014a)

Interestingly, among the MEPs who objected to the inclusion of the land aspects were members from the same Mediterranean states that had signed the ICZM Protocol several years earlier, along with its binding land-related regulations. We find this story quite dramatic. It conveys a strong message that, in the eyes of most EU MEPs, land laws and policies should be immune to intervention from the outside. This message is especially stark in view of the ostensibly consensual goal to better coastal protection, which often has cross-national implications.[3]

Once all references to rules for land were eliminated, the Maritime Spatial Planning Directive was adopted in 2014 (European Parliament, 2014). Thus, today, a legally binding Directive applies to the marine zones in all EU members states, while a non-binding EU ICZM Recommendations document applies to coastal land. Yet paradoxically, those EU member states located along the Mediterranean are legally bound also by the Mediterranean ICZM Protocol, which, as noted, addresses both land and sea. Furthermore, most of these states have individually ratified the ICZM Protocol. Granted, as international law, the ICZM Protocol is not very easy to invoke for adjudication in specific countries (or internationally). Our findings will show that, at best, the Protocol functions (so far) more like a policy document than binding international law. However, in principle, once ratified, the Protocol does have domestic status in national law, should any party wish to harness its legal potential.

Selection of countries

In selecting our research countries, fifteen in total, we used two key criteria: Relationship to supra-national law or policy, and shared and differing developmental attributes.

Relationship to supra-national law or policy

We tried to include a range of countries that represent the major types of relationships with supra-national law or policy. These relationships are depicted in Figure 1.1. Seven of our eight

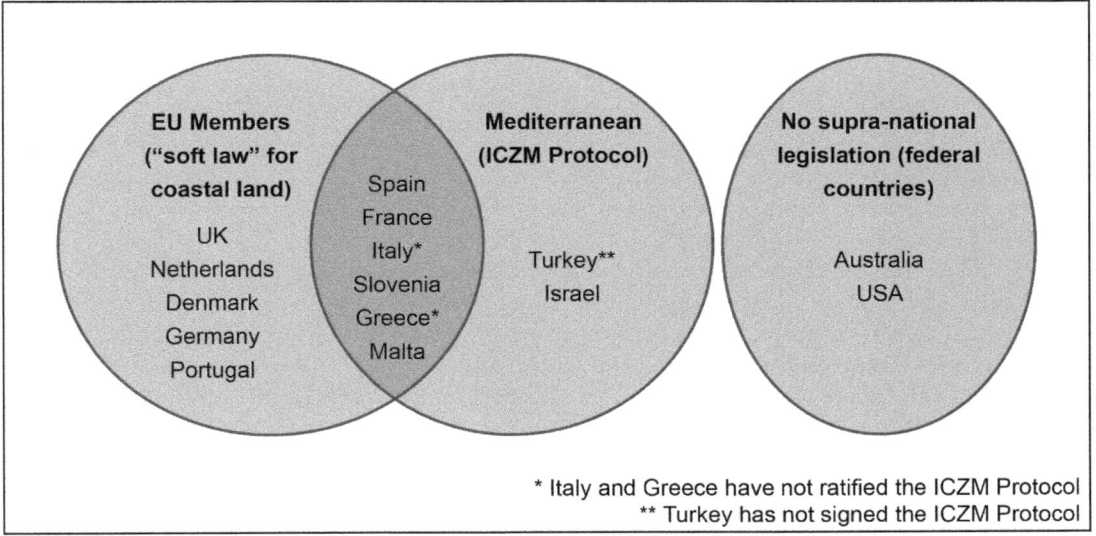

EU Members ("soft law" for coastal land)

UK
Netherlands
Denmark
Germany
Portugal

Spain
France
Italy*
Slovenia
Greece*
Malta

Mediterranean (ICZM Protocol)

Turkey**
Israel

No supra-national legislation (federal countries)

Australia
USA

* Italy and Greece have not ratified the ICZM Protocol
** Turkey has not signed the ICZM Protocol

Figure 1.1 The research countries in the context of supra-national law and policies

Mediterranean countries have signed the ICZM Protocol (Turkey has not but is eligible to do so). Five of these have already ratified the Protocol, thus rendering it part of their domestic law; Italy and Greece have not. Six of the Mediterranean countries are also members of the EU and thus come under both umbrellas – the ICZM Protocol and the EU Recommendation. One country – Israel – is bound only by the ICZM Protocol. And finally, two countries – the USA and Australia – are not legally affected by any supra-national norms for ICZM. However, both the USA and Australia are federal countries with a legal relationship between the states and the federal level that are somewhat reminiscent of the international–national relationships in the other countries. The authors for these two countries sometimes highlight important differences among the constituent states.

This book is thus well positioned to address the following question: How do the national laws and regulations in each of the relevant countries perform vis-à-vis the norms set out either by the ICZM Protocol or by the EU ICZM Recommendations?

Shared and differing developmental attributes

We sought to have an adequate common denominator to allow for comparative analysis and some cross-country learning. At the same time, we wanted to represent enough differences in relevant variables so that the findings would interest readers from a variety of countries.

The main common denominator is the level of economic development. All the selected countries have a relatively advanced economy and a good standard of living for their citizens. Except one country – Malta – all are members of the OECD – the Organisation for Economic Co-operation and Development. This organization accepts only countries with an advanced economy and a reasonably functioning (democratic) governance system. Our set of fifteen countries constitutes about 40% of all OECD members. At the same time, our sample also happens to represent 40% of the member states of the European Union (including Malta). Four of the book's countries are members of the OECD but not the EU (the US, Australia, Turkey, and Israel). The book does not encompass developing countries, with the assumption that they have an a priori weaker capacity to implement ICZM – especially its challenging norms of governance.

In selecting the countries, we also sought relevant variety. The degree of land-development pressure near the coast should be especially pertinent. This factor does not receive enough direct attention in evaluations of ICZM implementation. More attention is given to indices that assess the pressures on the natural environment (see Portman, 2016). Because our study focuses on land regulation and property rights, it is important to find a way to take development pressures on land into account.

Following an unsuccessful search for ready-made quantitative indicators of development pressures, we created our own surrogate.[4] Given limited resources, we built a simple, perhaps simplistic measure. It is based on the population density within 10 km of the coastline (persons per square kilometre), multiplied by the percentage of each country's population living within 10 km of the shoreline (see Table 1.1). The assumption is that higher population pressure is expressed in more demand for land (for housing, economic enterprises, infrastructure, recreation, etc.).

The scoring of countries using our Coastal Population Pressure Index potentially opens up an important consideration for assessing ICZM. For example, the scores for Malta and Israel, at the high end of the scale, are 70–75 times higher than those of Slovenia and Germany at the low end. Perhaps surprisingly, although the Netherlands is known for its high overall

Table 1.1 Coastal Population Pressure Index (CPPI) applied to the set of countries

	Total population	Population density within 10 km of the coast (persons per sq. km)*	Percentage of population living within 10 km of the coast**	Score on Coastal Population Pressure Index (CPPI)***
Slovenia	2,067,535	389	4%	17
Germany	80,688,538	275	7%	19
USA	321,773,631	133	20%	27
Australia	23,966,501	47	59%	28
France	64,395,347	252	16%	40
UK	64,714,995	222	34%	75
Greece	10,954,560	134	64%	85
Italy	59,799,759	352	28%	99
Denmark	5,669,093	168	73%	122
Turkey	78,665,813	465	27%	126
Portugal	10,356,070	421	31%	132
Spain	46,121,679	501	32%	161
Netherlands	16,924,927	625	45%	284
Israel	8,064,033	1984	46%	914
Malta	418,674	1288	100%	1288

* To nearest whole
** To nearest percentage point
*** Density within 10 km of coast × percentage of population living within 10 km of coast (to nearest whole)

population density, the CPPI scores show that the Netherlands' pressure along the coasts is only about one-third of Malta's or Israel's.[5] The difficulties of introducing new land regulations in densely populated high-pressure regions are likely to be greater than in low-pressure ones. When reading each of the country chapters, it is recommended to keep the Coastal Population Pressure Index in mind.

Methodology: Country-specific and comparative analysis

The research method we applied combines two levels of analysis: In-depth focus on each separate country, analogous to case-study method, and systematic cross-national comparative analysis based on shared parameters (with some minor variations). The backbone of this book is the team of leading scholars who have consented to devote their time and harness their knowledge to analyse the laws, regulations, and practices relevant to their respective countries' coastal zones. The analysis in each country report is largely descriptive, in order to provide the facts, but it also reflects each author's evaluation or criticism.

Each of the fifteen country reports, or case studies, tells a rich story, embedded in the country's unique legal, institutional, and behind-the-scenes cultural-political context. To enable systematic comparison across the countries, we articulated a framework composed of a set of parameters relevant to ICZM. These served to guide each author in writing their country reports. In order to gain reasonable consistency despite the very different legal and governance contexts, each chapter went through several iterations between the editors and the author(s).

The shared set of parameters also serves the third objective of this book: To promote cross-national learning through comparison of the laws and practices across the sample countries. Comparative legal research, in general, has both proponents and critics. The latter often note that each jurisdiction has a unique legal tradition and context and that the researcher is inevitably imbued in his or her own culture and thus cannot maintain adequate rigor for critical comparative thinking (Frankenberg, 1985, 2016; Zumbansen, 2005). Proponents argue that laws may be compared usefully cross-nationally, so long as their *functions* are shown to be similar (Zweigert & Kotz, 1998; Whytock, 2009). Proponents also note the usefulness of comparative findings in expanding the horizons of legislators and policymakers (see also Barak-Erez, 2008). The debate about the value of comparative research is paralleled among policy scientists, with arguments supporting the functional approach (Peters, 1998; Peters & Pierre, 2016). Recently, urban planning scholars have also argued in favour of comparative learning, despite the especially complex and contextualized attributes of spatial planning (van Assche at al., 2020).

This book adopts the functional approach and has a pragmatic, rather than a legal-critical, purpose: We seek to contribute to an area of law and policy that is yearning for more knowledge about ways to promote a globally essential and consensual goal of Integrated Coastal Zone Management. Systematic comparative analysis can provide a rare opportunity to observe one's own laws from an external perspective. A comparative perspective has the potential of unleashing self-critical thinking and enabling reconsideration of laws and practices that have been taken for granted.

Learning from others' experiences is especially essential in land-related laws and practices because these tend to be "home grown". One of the ways of transcending this insularity is to offer opportunities for cross-national learning (Alterman, 2001). Alterman's own prior large-scale comparative research on other topics related to planning law and to governance was also based on the functional approach (Alterman, 1997, 2001, 2011). Alterman has demonstrated that in the case of planning law and policy, identification of similar functions is possible, thus enabling fruitful cross-national comparison and learning. For example, planning laws may have similar specific functions regardless of the legal families to which the jurisdictions belong. The often-presumed cleavage among common law or civil law countries is hardly visible when it comes down to specific topics of planning law, as demonstrated in Alterman (2010) and Alterman (forthcoming). In the current book's set of countries, too, there are jurisdictions ascribed to both legal families, and, once again, one can hardly discern any significant differences along these lines.

Alongside the merits of comparative analysis of planning and law, one should also be wary of over-expectation. We agree with the criticism that comparative evaluation should shun the notion of "best practices" (Peters, 1998). Because ICZM itself is composed of a set of recommended concepts and practices, there is a temptation to harness comparative research to search for best practices. However, in reality, there is probably no set of existing laws, regulations, policies, or institutions that constitutes an optimal recipe for ICZM. Certainly, there is not any model that could be transferred intact elsewhere. Each set of laws and policies for coastal management ultimately operates within a unique country context. Cross-national learning must be fuzzy, contextual, and with a dose of scepticism. Indeed, land-related laws and policies are especially resistant to direct transfer across jurisdictions. They are always part of a thick web of legal, economic, sociocultural, and political factors that differ across space and cannot be uprooted (see also Van Assche et al., 2020). In comparative legal research as presented here, there should not be any expectation to "explain" why a specific jurisdiction has a specific set of laws and regulations and, especially, how they are applied in practice.

In the following chapter we expound upon the ten parameters for comparison.

Notes

1. For a list of international agreements, see https://en.wikipedia.org/wiki/List_of_international_ environmental_agreements. (We link to Wikipedia because, unlike the UN official sites, it presents the international environmental agreements both by topic and by date.) There are also many regional agreements.
2. See the proposed directive at https://ec.europa.eu/environment/iczm/pdf/Proposal_en.pdf. Also see discussion on the land–sea divide at https://ec.europa.eu/environment/iczm/practice.htm.
3. Strangely, we have not found any documented analysis of the significance of this story.
4. We were unable to find a ready-made set of data. We therefore used GIS (ArcGis by Esri, which supports population estimates) to extract the relevant figures, thus: Country borders were identified using the National Geographic Map from ESRI. Polygons were created for inland areas. Coastlines were manually isolated and a 10 km buffer applied (distance with linear units, end type round, and planar method). The buffer edges were manually adjusted to obtain 10 km coastal strip area. "Total population" and "Population within 10 km of the coast" were calculated using CIESIN (2018) estimates for 2015. The study considers the points contained by the 10 km coastal strip polygon, and the sum of their point information (table of contents field "UN_2015"). For islands catalogued as "small" or "very small" in the National Geographic Map, total area and population were considered. The point density provided by CIESIN (2018) is similar across most countries (usually corresponding to the smallest administrative/census units), with the exception of Turkey and Israel, where points are sparser. However, given the study scale, the point density appears to be adequate. Our thanks to Inês Calor and Mateus Magarotto for lending their time and GIS expertise.
5. Had we been able to invest in a more sophisticated index, it would have taken into account the projected population growth as well. Within such a perspective, Israel, for example, would have bypassed Malta due to Israel's much higher birth rate. According to the OECD (2020), in 2017, in Israel the rate was 3.11 children/woman; in Malta, 1.26.

References

Ahlhorn, F. (2017). *Integrated Coastal Zone Management: Status, Challenges and Prospects*. Springer Vieweg.

Alterman, R. (1997). The challenge of farmland preservation: Lessons from a six-nation comparison. *Journal of the American Planning Association* 63(2), 220–243.

Alterman, R. (2001). *National-Level Planning in Democratic Countries: An International Comparison of City and Regional Policy-Making*. Liverpool University Press.

Alterman, R. (2010). *Takings International: A comparative perspective on land use regulations and compensation rights*. American Bar Association Publishing.

Alterman, R. (2011). Comparative research at the frontier of planning law: The case of compensation rights for land use regulations. *International Journal of Law in the Built Environment* 3(2), 100–112.

Alterman, R. (Ed.). (forthcoming). *Handbook on Comparative Planning Law*. Routledge.

Arnold, C. A. (2013). Resilient cities and adaptive law. *Idaho Law Review* 50, 245–264.

Barak-Erez, D. (2008). Comparative law in practice – institutional, cultural and implementation aspects. *Din and DeVarim D*: 81–93 (in Hebrew). Available at: http://law.haifa.ac.il/images/din_udvarim/d_6.pdf

Belknap, R. K. (1980). Corporate response to coastal zone management: A case study of the Irvine coastal area. *Coastal Zone Management Journal* 8(2), 123–164.

Billé, R., & Rochette, J. (2011). Combining project-based and normative approaches for ICZM implementation. Lessons from the Mediterranean. *Littoral 2010–Adapting to Global Change at the Coast: Leadership, Innovation, and Investment*, 04002.

— (2015). The Mediterranean ICZM Protocol: Paper treaty or wind of change? *Ocean & Coastal Management* 105, 84–91.

Boelaert-Suominen, S., & Cullinan, C. (1994). *Legal and Institutional Aspects of Integrated Coastal Area Management in National Legislation*. Food and Agriculture Organization of the United Nations, Rome (Italy). Legal Office.

Cicin-Sain, B., Knecht, R. W., Knecht, R., Jang, D., & Fisk, G. W. (1998). *Integrated Coastal and Ocean Management: Concepts and Practices*. Island Press.

CIESIN (Center for International Earth Science Information Network – Columbia University). (2018). Gridded Population of the World, Version 4 (GPWv4): Population Count, Revision 11. NASA Socioeconomic Data and Applications Centre (SEDAC). Available at: https://doi.org/10.7927/H4JW8BX5

Council of Europe (2000). *Model Law on Sustainable Management of Coastal Zones and European Code of Conduct for Coastal Zones (Nature and Environment*, 101) (2000), ISBN 978-92-871-4153-8.

Cullinan, C. (2006). *Integrated Coastal Management Law: Establishing and Strengthening National Legal Frameworks for Integrated Coastal Management* (FAO Legislative Study 93). Food and Agriculture Organization of the United Nations.

European Parliament. (2014a). Debate on Maritime spatial planning and integrated coastal management. 17 April 2014. Available at: https://www.europarl.europa.eu/sides/getDoc.do?pubRef=-//EP//TEXT+CRE+20140417+ITEM-010-05+DOC+XML+V0//EN

Garriga, M., & Losada, I. J. (2010). Education and training for integrated coastal zone management in Europe. *Ocean & Coastal Management* 53(3), 89–98.

Felleman, J. P. (1982). Visibility mapping in New York's coastal zone: A case study of alternative methods. *Coastal Management* 9(3–4), 249–270.

Frankenberg, G. (1985). Critical comparisons: Re-thinking comparative law. *Harvard International Law Journal* 26, 411.

Frankenberg, G. (2016). *Comparative Law as Critique*. Edward Elgar Publishing.

Fung, A. (2006). Varieties of participation in complex governance. *Public Administration Review* 66, 66–75.

González-Riancho, P., Sanò, M., Medina, R., García-Aguilar, O., & Areizaga, J. (2009). A contribution to the implementation of ICZM in the Mediterranean developing countries. *Ocean & Coastal Management* 52(11), 545–558.

Karnauskaitė, D., Schernewski, G., Schumacher, J., Grunert, R., & Povilanskas, R. (2018). Assessing coastal management case studies around Europe using an indicator based tool. *Journal of Coastal Conservation* 22(3), 549–570.

Kay, R., & Alder, J. (2005). *Coastal Planning and Management*. Taylor and Francis.

Markandya, A., Arnold, S., Cassinelli, M., & Taylor, T. (2008). Protecting coastal zones in the Mediterranean: An economic and regulatory analysis. *Journal of Coastal Conservation* 12(3), 145–159.

OECD. (2020). Fertility rates (indicator). doi: 10.1787/8272fb01-en

PAP/RAC (n.d.). ICZM Protocol. Available at: http://paprac.org/iczm-protocol

Peters, B. G. (1998). *Comparative politics: Theory and methods*. NYU Press.

Peters, B. G., & Pierre, J. (2016). *Comparative Governance: Rediscovering the Functional Dimension of Governing*. Cambridge University Press.

Portman, M. E. (2016). *Environmental Planning for Oceans and Coasts*. Springer.

Ramkumar, M., James, R.A., Menier, D., & Kumaraswami, K. (Eds.). (2019). *Coastal Zone Management: Global Perspectives, Regional Processes, Local Issues*. Elsevier.

Rochette, J., & Billé, R. (2010). *Analysis of Mediterranean ICZM Protocol: At the crossroads between the rationality of provisions and the logic of negotiations*. Institute for Sustainable Development and International Relations (IDDRI), SciencePo. Available at: http://www.cirspe.it/gizc/Pubblicazioni/Pubblicazioni%202/4-%20ICZM_Med_IDDRI.pdf

— (2012). ICZM protocols to regional seas conventions: what? why? how?. *Marine Policy*, 36(5), 977–984.

— (2013). Bridging the gap between legal and institutional developments within regional seas frameworks. *The International Journal of Marine and Coastal Law* 28(3), 433–463.

Sanò, M., Jiménez, J. A., Medina, R., Stanica, A., Sanchez-Arcilla, A., & Trumbic, I. (2011). The role of coastal setbacks in the context of coastal erosion and climate change. *Ocean & Coastal Management*, 54(12), 943–950.

Schernewski, G. (2016). Integrated coastal zone management. In J. Harff, M. Meschede, S. Petersen & J. Thiede (Eds.), *Encyclopedia of Marine Geosciences* (pp. 363–365). Springer. Retrieved from: https://link.springer.com/referencework/10.1007/978-94-007-6238-1

UN – United Nations (2017). Factsheet: People and Oceans. The Ocean Conference. Available at: https://www.un.org/sustainabledevelopment/wp-content/uploads/2017/05/Ocean-fact-sheet-package.pdf

Van Assche, K., Beunen, R., & Verweij, S. (2020). Comparative planning research, learning, and governance: The benefits and limitations of learning policy by comparison. *Urban Planning* 5(1), 11–21.

Whytock, C. A. (2009). Legal origins, functionalism, and the future of comparative law. *BYU Law Review* 2009(6), 1879–1906.

Zumbansen, P. (2005). Comparative law's coming of age? Twenty years after critical comparisons. *German Law Journal* 6(7), 1073–1084.

Zweigert, K., & Kotz, H. (1998). *An Introduction to Comparative Law*. Translated by T. Weir. 3rd ed. Clarendon Press.

International law and policy documents (listed chronologically)

UNECE (United Nations Economic Commission for Europe) (1998). Convention on Access to Information, Public Participation in Decision-Making and Access to Justice in Environmental Matters, Aarhus, Denmark, 25 June 1998. Available at: https://www.unece.org/fileadmin/DAM/env/pp/documents/cep43e.pdf

European Parliament (2002). Recommendation of the European Parliament and of the Council of 30 May 2002 concerning the implementation of Integrated Coastal Zone Management in Europe. Official Journal L148, 06/06/2002 pp. 0024–0027. Available at: https://eur-lex.europa.eu/legal-content/EN/TXT/?uri=CELEX%3A32002H0413

UNEP (United Nations Environment Programme), MAP (Mediterranean Action Plan), PAP (Priority Actions Programme) (2008). Protocol on Integrated Coastal Zone Management in the Mediterranean. Split, Priority Actions Programme. Available at: http://iczmplatform.org//storage/documents/sewmrX-IR9gTwfvBgjJ4SAjhvqsLrBF6qB0B89xK8.pdf

European Parliament (2013). Proposal for a Directive of The European Parliament and of the Council; establishing a framework for maritime spatial planning and integrated coastal management. Brussels, 12.3.2013. 2013/0074 (COD). Available at: https://ec.europa.eu/environment/iczm/pdf/Proposal_en.pdf

European Parliament (2014). Directive 2014/89/EU of the European Parliament and of the Council of 23 July 2014; establishing a framework for maritime spatial planning. Official Journal L257, 28.8.2014, pp. 135–145. Available at: https://eur-lex.europa.eu/eli/dir/2014/89/oj

2   The parameters for comparative analysis and their expression in supra-national legislation

Rachelle Alterman and Cygal Pellach

To guide the analysis and ensure consistency across the country chapters, we translated the principles of ICZM into ten land-related parameters. These parameters also provide the backbone of the comparative analysis presented in Chapters 18–20. This chapter explains the rationale for each parameter and the degree to which it is reflected in either the Mediterranean ICZM Protocol or the EU ICZM Recommendation (or both; refer to Chapter 1). The comparative analysis in the final chapters of the book reflects back to these parameters and to the relevant supra-national rules.

Ten parameters in two sets

The ten parameters are divided into two sets:

Land demarcation and property rights
   A.   Conception of the coastal zone
   B.   Shoreline definition and delineation
   C.   Coastal public domain – extent and rules
   D.   Coastal setback zone – extent and permitted uses
   E.   Right of public access – to and along the coast

Institutions and governance
   F.   Land use planning – institutional aspects and dedicated instruments
   G.   Climate change – awareness and regulatory actions
   H.   Public participation and access to justice
    I.   Integration and coordination
   J.   Compliance and enforcement

In addition to these ten parameters, we also asked the authors to look at relevant fiscal issues related to any of them. In most country reports, there is a separate section for this aspect, but in doing the comparative analysis, we recognized that fiscal aspects are dispersed along various parameters. Thus, in the comparative analysis, we incorporated the fiscal aspects within the relevant parameters.

   The two sets of parameters probably differ in terms of their legal import vis-à-vis the two supra-national documents. The first set of parameters pertains to concrete land use limitations and clear legal distinctions about landownership and right of public access over land. If these rules are addressed in binding supra-national law, the degree of conformance could be determined, perhaps even be measurable. Thus, if the issue of compliance with international law were to be raised in legal procedures in one of the signatory countries, the court would likely be able to issue a judgement. Further, such a determination in one jurisdiction could, in principle, be of relevance in other jurisdictions (once adjusted to the local context).

By contrast, the second set of parameters deals with the normative quality of governance. There are no internationally shared criteria and standards to determine what constitutes minimally adequate levels of compliance. For example, what government actions are enough to fulfil requirements for public participation? What levels of coordination and integration are of adequate standard? What is good planning? When it comes to the parameters of the second set, we conjecture that, if ever brought before the courts, they will be regarded similarly to "soft law" – non-binding recommendations. Regarding this set of parameters, there will not be much legal difference between the Protocol and the EU recommendations.

In the following sections, we introduce each parameter and its rationale. We then look at what the two supra-national documents say on the topic. As we proceed, we also provide some "appetizers" for the comparative findings.

Parameter A: Conception of the coastal zone

What is the coastal zone? Although this term is part of the ICZM acronym, it does not have a universally agreed-upon definition (Kay & Alder, 2005; Portman, 2016). The academic and organizational literature presents a variety of approaches. Environmentalists perceive the coastal zone as characterised entirely by natural phenomena and processes that distinguish coastal zones from inland areas. One of many examples of this approach is the definition adopted by Davis and Fitzgerald (2004). They define the coastal zone as "… any part of the land that is influenced by some marine condition, such as tides, winds, biota or salinity" (p. 2). If translated into land-management policies, this description would cover an area of land where the boundaries change constantly, along with the forces of nature. In this book, we call this family of definitions "**nature-led**".

By contrast, the European Environment Agency (2006) uses a definition based on pre-determined physical distances: "The terrestrial portion of the coastal zone is defined by an area extending 10 km landwards from the coastline" (p. 11). The Agency distinguishes between "the immediate coastal strip (up to 1 km)" and "the coastal hinterland (coastal zone between 1- and 10-kilometre line)" (p. 11). Obviously, 10 km is not a nature-based criterion. Depending on the coastal biophysical system, 10 km could be a relatively good fit with land influenced by the sea (as in Davis and Fitzgerald's definition above), or the quantum could be very much "off nature". This definition was probably adopted by the EU as a convenient compromise guideline for implementing policies across the many EU member countries. We will call this type of definitions "**implementation-led**".

The Mediterranean ICZM Protocol does not offer a basic definition of what constitutes a coastal zone. It thus indicates that a formal definition is not a necessary condition for compliance with the Protocol's various rules and guidelines. Nevertheless, we were interested to know how each of the sample countries conceives of its coastal zone. In some jurisdictions, the way that the coastal zone is defined at the national level may determine the extent of land that is affected by specific coastal land regulations. We therefore asked the team of authors to answer the following questions:

- Is the coastal zone defined at the national (or state) level?
- Is the definition found in law or policy?
- What is the definition?

The findings show that most jurisdictions did adopt a formal definition of the coastal zone, with interesting variations and possible implications for further policy. Based on the evidence from the fifteen countries, we classified the definitions along scales in two dimensions: From nature-led to implementation-led and from general wording (open to interpretation) to specific wording.[1]

Parameter B: Shoreline definition and delineation

A legally based demarcation of the shoreline is usually an important benchmark for other laws and regulations for coastal land management. For the purpose of this study, we adopt Oertel's (2005) understanding of the shoreline as the boundary between land and sea at the local scale. The delimitation of the shoreline may have major implications on property rights and thus on the ease or difficulty in implementing restrictions on development in the spirit of ICZM. For example, the Mediterranean ICZM Protocol states that the parties:

> *Shall establish in coastal zones, as from **the highest winter waterline**, a zone where construction is not allowed...* (Article 8(2)(a)) (emphasis added)

This "highest winter waterline" is just one of several reference lines that may be used to define the shoreline. Our country chapter authors address these questions:

- Is the shoreline legally defined?
- What reference line is used for the delineation?
- Has the entire shoreline been demarcated in practice?

One might have thought that shoreline delineation is the most technical among our parameters, requiring expert scientific knowledge of the coastal environment and established measurement techniques, without much room for contestation. And yet, the country reports show that there is no cross-national consensus even on this parameter. While in many cases the legal definition of the shoreline is based entirely on an acknowledged hydrographic reference line with established measurement techniques, in others the legal criterion is partially administrative, and additional technical standards must be developed in order to apply it.

Parameter C: Coastal public domain – extent and rules

Public ownership of some (or all) of the coastal zone could be useful in controlling land use and protecting the coastal environment. Public landownership in coastal zones has a long philosophical and legal history – but non-uniform practice. In many jurisdictions, the legal history is tied to the "public trust doctrine" (Takacs, 2008). The well-known version of this doctrine was initially codified by Emperor Justinian in the sixth-century Byzantine Empire, based on Roman common law. The principle states:

> *By the law of nature, these things are common to mankind – the air, running water, the sea, and consequently the shores of the sea* (cited in Portman, 2016, p.3; see also Takacs, 2008, p. 711).

This ethos, with different nuances, is not exclusive to the Roman Law tradition and has been independently developed in other parts of the world, including by Indigenous cultures (Ryan, 2020).

Assertion of public ownership is not just another land-management parameter. Since it touches directly on real-property rights, this parameter is one of the most recalcitrant ones. It is likely to cause a head-on clash between environmental and private interests. In some jurisdictions, public landownership has existed in law and practice for generations. But in many countries around the globe, private landownership or other types of individual tenure are the reality along some of the coastal zones.

It may be significant that the legally binding Mediterranean ICZM Protocol refrains from addressing public landownership directly, leaving it to an indirect, non-binding land-policy recommendation –

> *… in order to ensure the sustainable management of public and private land of the coastal zones, Parties may inter alia adopt mechanisms for the acquisition, cession, donation or transfer of land to the public domain and institute easements on properties.* (Article 20(2))

The European ICZM Recommendation (2002) does address public landownership directly. It recommends that in developing ICZM strategies, Member States should consider concrete action towards public ownership, including:

> *… land purchase mechanisms and declarations of public domain to ensure public access for recreational purposes without prejudice to the protection of sensitive areas* (Chapter IV(3) (b)(ii))

Recall that almost all EU member states voted against adoption of a legally binding directive on coastal land. Perhaps this type of clause was one of the deterrents.

Regarding the public land-ownership parameter, we pose these questions:

- Does the law require that a defined area of the coastal zone be in public ownership?
- If so, how is public land defined and how is it obtained (expropriation or other means)? What legal and fiscal issues have arisen, or may arise?
- What public body owns or manages this land?
- What are the rules for the use (or development) of coastal public land?

We learn from the country reports that practices in public landownership vary greatly. The comparative analysis shows that in most jurisdictions, there have not been any major recent attempts to change the existing ownership status from private to public. Generally, only what was public, of whatever extent, remains public. In the two or three jurisdictions where private land was converted to public domain in recent decades or is slated for conversion, the process was, and still is, laden with conflicts. The stories surrounding these attempts are fascinating and may provide practical lessons for other countries.

Parameter D: Coastal setback zone – extent and permitted uses

A coastal setback zone (as we define it in this book) is a designated area within a (usually) pre-defined distance from the shoreline, where land development is prohibited or highly restricted. Setback zones should not be confused with public domain, since they may apply to privately owned land. Establishing a setback zone (sometimes referred to as "buffer zone"; Sanò et al., 2010) is seen as an important tool to protect and conserve the overall quality of the coastal zone. Setback zones are intended not only to protect the environmental values of the coast by pushing development activity further out but (depending on location) also to protect property from damage due to erosion or flooding. As sea levels rise and exceptional storm events become more frequent, setback zones should gain special importance as a land-management tool.

Coastal setback zones are used as a regulatory tool in many of the jurisdictions in our book but with great differences in functional distances. Because setback zones are usually regulated as a predetermined quantitative distance, they are ostensibly easy to compare cross-nationally. As our comparative analysis in Chapter 19 will show, reality is more complex.

The drafting of Article 8.2 of the ICZM Protocol (about the setback zone) drew the most intensive debate (Sanò et al., 2011). It is a mandatory rule for a minimum distance of 100 m from the shoreline. The debate over the setback zone is not surprising because implementation of this rule could lead to direct intervention in property rights. The setback rule is also an especially prominent part of the Protocol because it is its only quantitative norm. The Protocol specifies the reference line for the shoreline, from which the setback is calculated:

> *8.2. (a) [Parties] Shall establish in coastal zones, as from the highest winter waterline, **a zone where construction is not allowed**. Taking into account, inter alia, the areas directly and negatively affected by climate change and natural risks, **this zone may not be less than 100 meters in width**, subject to the provisions of subparagraph (b) below. Stricter national measures determining this width shall continue to apply.* (Article 8(2)(a)) (emphasis added)

The Protocol does, however, grant leeway for local conditions. Those who drafted the Protocol were probably aware that on the Mediterranean, much of the coastal zone is already built up (though with significant variations). They therefore allowed for discretionary exemptions, enumerated in the next Article:

> *8.2. (b) [The parties] May adapt, in a manner consistent with the objectives and principles of this Protocol, the provisions mentioned above:*
>
> 1 *for projects of public interest;*
> 2 *in areas having particular geographical or other local constraints, especially related to population density or social needs, where individual housing, urbanisation or development are provided for by national legal instruments.* (Article 8(2)(b))

A non-legal reading of this sub-article seems to say, "anything goes". However, in international law as adopted by the EU, the wording of these two paragraphs conveys a duty on the state to take action to implement the minimum setback as a general rule. Article 8.2 (b) should be read as allowing only justifiable exceptions to the rule (Rochette & Billé, 2010). In any case, none of our Mediterranean chapters report of any jurisprudence interpreting this Article (this topic merits separate scrutiny).

On the setback topic, our questions are:

- Is a coastal setback zone required under national (or state) regulations?
- How is the coastal setback zone defined and measured in practice?
- What restrictions on development or special permissions apply to the zone?
- In cases where establishment of a setback zone required transition from a previously permissive approach to more restrictions on development, what legal and fiscal issues have arisen? For example, are there compensation rights if unbuilt development rights are abolished?
- Are any fiscal instruments (taxes and levies) used as disincentive for development in protected zones? Or the opposite: Are fiscal tools used to incentivize development to locate or relocate in the hinterland?

The setback distances on their own should not be compared with each other. They must be analysed against the different reference lines used to define the shoreline in each jurisdiction. Furthermore, in some countries, there is more than one type of setback. With these qualifications, the variations among the setback distances are much greater than at first sight.

An obvious question is whether, more than a decade after the ICZM Protocol came into force, one can gauge its influence on the eight Mediterranean countries in this book. We address this question in our analysis in Chapter 19.

Parameter E: Right of public access – to and along the coast

Public accessibility to the coast is not just a matter of getting from place to place. The legal right to access the coastal zone (physically or as open view) is a normative expression of the general public's relationship with the coast. The ability to access and enjoy the coast (in permitted locations) is one of the rationales for coastal zone management. In this book, we therefore discuss the right of public access in greater detail than usual. We also address aspects of accessibility that are rarely discussed in the context of regulatory aspects of coastal land management.

The European ICZM Recommendation (2002) indicates that a strategic approach to ICZM should be based (in part) on:

> *adequate accessible land for the public, both for recreational purposes and aesthetic reasons* (Chapter I(f))

From the wording of this phrase, the reference is probably only to physical access along or to the coast. The ICZM Protocol, too, includes freedom of access in its "criteria for sustainable use of the coastal zone":

> *"providing for freedom of access by the public to the sea and along the shore"* (Article 3(d))

Here, the wording does distinguish between access **to** the sea (vertical accessibility) and **along** the shore (horizontal accessibility). In this book, we take an even broader view of accessibility and in addition to the usually mentioned two, we add three more:

1 Horizontal accessibility – Walking, playing, and swimming along the shoreline
2 Vertical accessibility – Reaching the shoreline
3 Accessibility for people with disabilities
4 Social justice in accessibility – For the poor and special sociocultural groups
5 Visual accessibility – Ability to view the coast from a distance

Questions of accessibility often relate directly to land rights and are therefore likely to be addressed by any ICZM regulatory document. In some of the jurisdictions analysed in this book, the conflicts between the right of public access and land rights have reached the courts.

The questions we ask under this parameter include:

- Is there a legal right to horizontal access? What is the legal source (legislation and regulatory plans)? What are the rules?
- Is there a legal right to vertical access? What is the legal source (legislation and regulatory plans)? What are the rules?
- Do accessibility rules apply to private land as well as public?
- Is accessibility for people with disabilities taken into account in law or practice?
- Are entrance fees charged in all/some beaches? Any other socio-economic barriers?
- Are there rules about visual accessibility?
- Is there significant jurisprudence about accessibility?

One might have thought that accessibly would be a relatively straightforward norm. The accounts from the fifteen countries show how complex and often contentious is this norm in practice. Introducing new rules for public access or implementing existing ones may be difficult. Due to this complexity, we do not attempt to rank the set of jurisdictions on a scale reflecting degree of accessibility.

Now we turn to the **second set of five parameters** – those focused on institutions and governance (as related to land management). Both the ICZM Protocol and the EU Recommendations do address these parameters. However, as noted, these parameters refer to rather broad norms that are difficult to adjudicate and, in our view, are likely to be regarded as "soft law" in both documents.

Parameter F: Land use planning – institutional aspects and dedicated instruments

Every ICZM program gives planning, in its broad sense, a front seat. Planning is seen as a key vehicle for ICZM – as a primary integrative way of making decisions (Portman, 2016). Under the parameters "public coastal land" and "coastal setback zones", the contributing authors discuss the special land use regulation relevant to those zones. Under the present parameter, we address the broader institutional framework for land use planning. We wish to know whether the coastal zone is seen as meriting special planning institutions or instruments for the promotion of better ICZM.

The Mediterranean ICZM Protocol mentions "the process of planning" under the heading of "Land Policy". We thus assume that this refers to land use planning.

> *For the purpose of promoting integrated coastal zone management, reducing economic pressures, maintaining open areas and allowing public access to the sea and along the shore, Parties shall adopt **appropriate land policy instruments** and measures, including the **process of planning**.* (Article 20(1)) (emphasis added)

The wording "appropriate… process of planning" leaves much to local discretion. This is reasonable indeed regarding urban and regional planning in general. But what is "appropriate" under ICZM? What is an appropriate division of responsibility between the local and national echelons? Indeed, as noted, there is no consensus among planners about what is "the process of planning". Planning theorists still contend over this very concept (Allmendinger, 2017). The planning process is not a technical matter of following a sequence of steps; it is a sociopolitical process often characterized by a tug-of-war over its very format. Coastal land, one would expect, would be especially prone to conflicts. Once the international ICZM Protocol becomes an active legal norm in domestic (national) law, one would expect contestation about the meaning of an "appropriate process of planning". However, we do not know of any jurisprudence that has yet confronted the need to decide what planning process comes up to the standard of "appropriate".

Our questions to the authors are:

- Does your country have planning bodies dedicated to coastal planning?
- Is land beyond the setback zone subject to special planning regulations?
- Are there dedicated plans or other instruments for coastal areas?

Our questions within the scope of this book look only at the institutions and instruments and not their outputs. Yet efforts to adjust the legal and institutional frameworks, especially for coastal management, are, in themselves, steps towards ICZM. The comparative overall findings about this parameter are among the more encouraging. Several of the country reports speak about concerted efforts to create dedicated planning institutions and special instruments for the coastal zone. These may be contributing to more sustainable outcomes.

Parameter G: Climate change – awareness and regulatory actions

The effect of climate change on coastal zones, especially sea level rise, should be a crucial consideration in coastal planning and land management (Peterson, 2019; OECD, 2019). The reasons are well known: Coastal areas will be the first affected in the case of sea level rise, which carries with it increased rates of coastal erosion, damage to property, and major public or private expenditures. Coastal areas are also vulnerable to flooding from extreme weather events, which are expected to increase in frequency and magnitude as global temperatures rise. In some cases, retreat from the shoreline may be necessary, either following damage or as a preventative measure.

Adaptation to the effects of climate change on coastal land is likely to lead to clashes with property rights and investments. A preview of these is provided in a few of the country reports.

Both the EU ICZM Recommendation (2002) and the Mediterranean ICZM Protocol (2008) refer to climate change and associated risks. The former indicates that a strategic approach to ICZM should be based (in part) on:

> *recognition of the threat to coastal zones posed by climate change and of the dangers entailed by the rise in sea level and the increasing frequency and violence of storms* (Chapter I(b))

The ICZM Protocol addresses climate change in its Objectives section (Article 5):

> *(e) prevent and/or reduce the effects of natural hazards and in particular of climate change, which can be induced by natural or human activities*

The Protocol goes further and dedicates an entire Article (22) to natural hazards and climate change:

> *Within the framework of national strategies for integrated coastal zone management, the Parties shall develop policies for the prevention of natural hazards. To this end, they shall undertake vulnerability and hazard assessments of coastal zones and take prevention, mitigation and adaptation measures to address the effects of natural disasters, in particular of climate change.*

Not many jurisdictions have already taken on board land-management measures to adapt land and development rights to climate change. Such measures may have to reinvent land rights and rethink the social justice norms regarding who bears responsibility for property damage. A concrete climate adaptation plan would need to reconsider public finance in cases of unplanned or planned retreat – such as compensation for massive damage – and re-evaluate the role of insurance companies.

In our research, we ask whether awareness of climate change in coastal zones has seeped into legislation and formal policy. Under this parameter, we ask:

- Do the relevant laws/regulations address climate change on coastal land (or land that includes the coast)?
- Are there specific legal-regulatory tools, or only general statements about climate change? If specific tools, what are they?
- Specifically: If existing buildings are threatened due to cliff erosion or sea rise, do landowners have compensation rights? Rights to be paid for relocation? Have these situations been encountered in practice?
- Are government bodies authorised to expropriate coastal property under major hazard risk and to what extent do they exercise this in practice?
- Are insurance companies permitted to insure landowners for the full possible damages due to natural hazards? Is this tool used extensively by landowners in practice?

In the comparative analysis in Chapter 20, we develop a rough ordinal scale of degrees of regulatory specificity regarding climate change challenges in coastal zones. On the highest tier are several jurisdictions where climate change is addressed with more targeted legislation or regulations than in the others. On the positive side, the findings show some momentum in acknowledging that climate change should be a policy consideration in coastal zones. However, most jurisdictions – even on the highest tier – probably still fall short of the necessary adaption measures for coastal land. Our comparative findings contribute a new perspective for future discussion and research about policies for climate change in coastal zones.

Parameter H: Public participation and access to justice

Almost every definition of integrated coastal zone management mentions public participation as an essential ingredient (see also Areizaga et al., 2012). The authors of these definitions – whether legislative, academic, or government policy – seem to assume that, on balance, the participation process will be supportive of coastal zone protection. However, participation is a general and rather elusive concept and is itself part of the sociopolitical context in each case, as Arnstein (1969) taught us long ago (see also Alterman, 1982; Fung, 2006; Stringer et al., 2006).

Participation is addressed both by the European ICZM Recommendation (2002) and the Mediterranean ICZM Protocol (2008). The former does not devote much space to participation. However, by referring to promoting "bottom up initiatives", the Recommendation does imply a broader conception of participation than just reaction to government's proposed policy:

> ... *identify measures to promote bottom-up initiatives and public participation in integrated management of the coastal zone and its resources* (Chapter IV(3)(d))

The ICZM Protocol's Article 14 addresses participation in a more detailed way (see Box 2.1). The Article lists stakeholders who should be involved in participation processes and does not

---

Box 2.1

Article 14 of the ICZM Protocol

ICZM Protocol Article 14

1. *With a view to ensuring efficient governance throughout the process of the integrated management of coastal zones, the Parties shall take the necessary measures to ensure the **appropriate involvement** in the phases of the **formulation and implementation** of coastal and marine strategies, plans and programmes or projects, as well as the issuing of the various authorizations, of the **various stakeholders**, including:*
   - *the territorial communities and public entities concerned;*
   - *economic operators;*
   - *non-governmental organizations;*
   - *social actors;*
   - *the public concerned.*
   *Such **participation** shall involve inter alia consultative bodies, inquiries or public hearings, and may extend to partnerships.*
2. *With a view to ensuring such participation, the Parties shall provide **information in an adequate, timely and effective manner**.*
3. ***Mediation or conciliation procedures and a right of administrative or legal recourse** should be available to any stakeholder..."*

leave out economic development interests. It also specifies that participation requires that information be provided in an "adequate, timely and effective manner" and sets out that the public should be able to challenge "decisions, acts or omissions" relating to the coastal zone.

It is noteworthy that EU member countries in this book – eleven out of the fifteen – are signatories to the Aarhus Convention on Access to Information, Public Participation in Decision-Making and Access to Justice in Environmental Matters (UNECE, 1998). This Convention, signed by most European countries in 1998, refers to a set of "rights" of the public with regard to environmental decision-making (which includes land use planning). Topics covered are the right to receive environmental information through open access; the right to participate in decision-making; and the right to review and challenge public decisions.

Our contributing authors report about how participation is expressed in national (sometimes regional) laws and regulations pertaining to land use planning in coastal zones. The questions posed under this parameter are:

- What are the policies/regulations/practice for public participation in planning?
- Are there special policies or practices for coastal zones?
- Do you have critical thoughts about the process or its effectiveness?
- How broadly defined is access to tribunals and courts?
- To what extent are NGOs involved in coastal issues and in action before the courts?
- How publicly accessible is information on coastal issues, planning, and regulation?

The findings concerning this parameter are not amenable to systematic cross-national comparison. Public participation is deeply grounded in local modes of governance. However, the country reports provide important contextualized information on participation. Of special interest are the NGO initiatives that have achieved major impacts and the different degrees of involvement of courts in promoting better ICZM.

Parameter I: Integration and coordination

Integration and coordination are part of the conceptual core of ICZM. A high level of substantive *integration* – or comprehensiveness – would see linked policies across a wide range of subjects and disciplines – environmental, economic, and social. Of special importance is integration across the land–sea divide (Portman, 2016, pp. 61–69). A high level of *coordination* would see institutions working in tandem towards management goals, both horizontally (within a parallel level of government) and vertically (between the national, regional, and local levels).

Both supra-national ICZM documents address integration and coordination, though often without distinguishing between the two. The EU Recommendation on ICZM (2002) indicates that Member States should develop ICZM strategies which:

> *… identify the roles of the different administrative actors within the country or region whose competence includes activities or resources related to the coastal zone, as well as mechanisms for their coordination. This identification of roles should allow an adequate control, and an appropriate strategy and consistency of actions* (Chapter IV(3)(a))

Box 2.2

Article 7 of the ICZM Protocol

ICZM Protocol Article 7 Coordination

1. *For the purposes of integrated coastal zone management, the Parties shall:*
   a. *ensure institutional coordination, where necessary through appropriate bodies or mechanisms, in order to avoid sectoral approaches and facilitate comprehensive approaches;*
   b. *organize appropriate coordination between the various authorities competent for both the marine and the land parts of coastal zones in the different administrative services, at the national, regional and local levels;*
   c. *organize close coordination between national authorities and regional and local bodies in the field of coastal strategies, plans and programmes and in relation to the various authorizations for activities that may be achieved through joint consultative bodies or joint decision-making procedures.*
2. *Competent national, regional and local coastal zone authorities shall, insofar as practicable, work together to strengthen the coherence and effectiveness of the coastal strategies, plans and programmes established.*

The ICZM Protocol places even more attention on integration and coordination. First, under General Principles of Coastal Zone Management, the Protocol states:

> *Cross-sectorally [sic] organized institutional coordination of the various administrative services and regional and local authorities competent*[2] *in coastal zones* **shall be required.** (Article 6(e)) (emphasis added)

The language here already conveys an obligation. In addition, the Protocol dedicates an entire article (Article 7) to promoting coordination (Box 2.2).

A legal obligation to coordinate cannot do much more than to signify a general direction. There are no "recipe books" for achieving good coordination and integration across existing legal-institutional contexts. Instead of attempting to evaluate the degree to which coordination is achieved, our contributing authors report on institutions with special coordinative roles and on visible instruments to improve coordination. The questions we pose are:

- What are the bodies responsible for coastal management and what is the distribution of authority among them?
- What are the mechanisms, if any, for vertical integration and coordination across national, regional, and local scales? Have new ones been added?
- What are the mechanisms, if any, of horizontal (inter-sectoral) integration and coordination? Have new ones been added?

The struggles to reduce institutional fragmentation are apparent in several of the country chapters. We do observe positive momentum in the direction of improved coordination in the spirit of ICZM. New, dedicated institutions for vertical or horizontal coastal coordination are established in some jurisdictions. However, each jurisdiction has its unique institutional structure, and no shared model has emerged.

Parameter J: Compliance and enforcement

The last parameter is, in our view, very important, yet it has been almost neglected to date. It is often mentioned only in passing in conjunction with implementation, but these issues have never, to our knowledge, been addressed comparatively in the context of ICZM.[3] Having wonderful laws, regulations, and plans as part of ICZM is not enough. Even a good record of coordination among agencies will not be sufficient. The "bottom line" of laws and regulations is compliance by the general public. There are usually administrative units dedicated to enforcement, but they are often short of resources and with limited legal powers (Calor & Alterman, 2017).

Compliance and enforcement are not mentioned in either the EU ICZM Recommendation (2002) or the Mediterranean ICZM Protocol (2008). This omission reflects insufficient awareness of the special characteristics of some coastal zones: A unique intersection of very high real estate values with older, established neighbourhoods or settlements that are home to relatively low-income populations. As such, we view this parameter as an important indicator of ICZM implementation.

Under this parameter, we ask each contributing author to address:

- What is the extent of noncompliance in the coastal zone (and its various subzones – public domain and setback zone)?
- How are coastal planning rules enforced?
- How effective are the enforcement measures? To what extent are they used?
- Is demolition an available tool? Is it used in practice?
- Who is in charge of enforcement?

The comparative analysis of the compliance and enforcement parameter turned out to be very interesting. We were able to classify the fifteen countries along a rough scale. The insights gained should help to invigorate this neglected topic.

Fiscal aspects of coastal zone management

There is an additional topic for analysis – fiscal issues, often interlinked with legal issues. This topic is a world in its own and merits a focused comparative research project of its own. We nevertheless went ahead and incorporated some key fiscal policy issues into the relevant parameters.

The fiscal dimension is important because regulation of property rights and development may involve major loss (or indeed, gain) in economic property values. In coastal zones, some of these values may be very high. Each country is likely to have different approaches and instruments regarding the land value and public finance aspects of regulation. Expropriation of real property likely involves compensation, but conceptions and calculations of compensation rights differ across jurisdictions. Different countries may or may not have compensation rights for landowners in case of "regulatory takings" (reducing or abolishing development rights while leaving the land in private hands; Alterman, 2010). There may be public policies regarding insurance schemes for natural hazards; there may be different policies about fees and charges for use or development on coastal land; and there are also fiscal policies related to enforcement against illegal use or development.

Several authors point out the role of fiscal issues regarding capacity to implement land management for ICZM. Where relevant, we incorporated their insights in the relevant parameters.

A preview of the comparative analysis

The picture that emerges from reading the fifteen country reports shows less convergence than one would have expected decades after the notion of integrated coastal zone management was introduced in 1972. The evidence shuns any "explanations" of shared or differing approaches. Our comparative analysis (Chapters 18–20) shows that some countries located in different parts of the world and with different legal traditions nevertheless share some similar laws or regulations, while countries with similar legal or cultural traditions show very different approaches.

The fifteen country reports and the comparative chapters will show that no country is an optimal achiever along all parameters. At the same time, several countries do stand out as better achievers along some of the parameters (among those that have a normative direction). However, it is difficult to say which parameters of ICZM are more important and to determine the trade-offs among them. Methodologically, overall comparative evaluation is untenable because the contexts are very different.

When ICZM meets land, it meets different terrains, both literally and figuratively. Some countries face high density and development pressures along their coasts; others have ample space and not much pressure. Some countries have a long tradition of excellent governance, as indicated by the various international rankings. These contextual factors should be taken into account when reading the fifteen country reports and the three comparative chapters.

Notes

1. A similar classification along the first dimension only is proposed by Kay and Alder (2005, pp. 3–6).
2. "Euro-English" meaning "with authority over".
3. This is true also for environmental regulation in general. See, for example, the UN report by Kumar et al. (2019). While enforcement or compliance are mentioned many times in passing, there is no direct focus on this major issue.

References

Allmendinger, P. (2017). *Planning Theory* (3rd ed.). Palgrave.

Alterman, R. (1982). Planning for public participation: The design of implementable strategies. *Environment and Planning B: Planning and Design* 9(3), 295–313.

Alterman, R. (2010). *Takings International: A Comparative Perspective on Land Use Regulations and Compensation Rights*. American Bar Association.

Areizaga, J., Sanò, M., Medina, R., & Juanes, J. (2012). Improving public engagement in ICZM: A practical approach. *Journal of Environmental Management* 109, 123–135.

Arnstein, S. R. (1969). A ladder of citizen participation. *Journal of the American Institute of planners* 35(4), 216–224.

Calor, I., & Alterman, R. (2017). When enforcement fails: Comparative analysis of the legal and planning responses to non-compliant development in two advanced-economy countries. *International Journal of Law in the Built Environment* 9(3), 207–239.

Davis, R. A., Jr., & Fitzgerald, D. M. (2004). *Beaches and Coasts*. Blackwell Science Ltd.

Fung, A. (2006). Varieties of participation in complex governance. *Public Administration Review* 66, 66–75.

Kay, R., & Alder, J. (2005). *Coastal Planning and Management*. Taylor and Francis.

Kumar, S., Ugirashebuja, E., Carnwath, L., Tamminen, T., & Boyd, D. (2019). *Environmental Rule of Law: First Global Report*. UN Environment Programme.

OECD. (2019). *Responding to Rising Seas: OECD Country Approaches to Tackling Coastal Risks*. OECD Publishing. doi: 10.1787/9789264312487-en

Oertel, G. F. (2005). Coasts, coastlines, shores, and shorelines. In *Encyclopedia of Coastal Science*, pp. 323–327.

Peterson, J. (2019). *A New Coast: Strategies for Responding to Devastating Storms and Rising Seas*. Island Press.

Portman, M. E. (2016). *Environmental Planning for Oceans and Coasts*. Springer.

Rochette, J., & Billé, R. (2010). *Analysis of the Mediterranean ICZM Protocol: At the crossroads between the rationality of provisions and the logic of negotiations*. Institute for Sustainable Development and International Relations (IDDRI), SciencePo. Available at: http://www.cirspe.it/gizc/Pubblicazioni/Pubblicazioni%202/4-%20ICZM_Med_IDDRI.pdf

Ryan, E. (2020). A Short History of the Public Trust Doctrine and its Intersection with Private Water Law. *Virginia Environmental Law Journal* 39.

Sanò, M., Jiménez, J. A., Medina, R., Stanica, A., Sanchez-Arcilla, A., & Trumbic, I. (2011). The role of coastal setbacks in the context of coastal erosion and climate change. *Ocean & Coastal Management* 54(12), 943–950.

Sanò, M., Marchand, M., & Medina, R. (2010). Coastal setbacks for the Mediterranean: A challenge for ICZM. *Journal of Coastal Conservation* 14 (4), 295–301.

Stringer, L. C., Dougill, A. J., Fraser, E., Hubacek, K., Prell, C., & Reed, M. S. (2006). Unpacking "participation" in the adaptive management of social–ecological systems: A critical review. *Ecology and Society* 11(2), Article 39. Available at: http://www.ecologyandsociety.org/vol11/iss2/art39/

Takacs, D. (2008). The public trust doctrine, environmental human rights, and the future of private property. *NYU Environmental Law Journal* 16, 711–765.

International law and policy (listed chronologically)

UNECE (United Nations Economic Commission for Europe) (1998). Convention on Access to Information, Public Participation in Decision-Making and Access to Justice in Environmental Matters, Aarhus, Denmark, 25 June 1998. Available at: https://www.unece.org/fileadmin/DAM/env/pp/documents/cep43e.pdf

European Parliament (2002). Recommendation of the European Parliament and of the Council of 30 May 2002 concerning the implementation of Integrated Coastal Zone Management in Europe. Official Journal L148, 06/06/2002 pp. 0024 – 0027. Available at: https://eur-lex.europa.eu/legal-content/EN/TXT/?uri=CELEX%3A32002H0413

UNEP (United Nations Environment Programme), MAP (Mediterranean Action Plan), PAP (Priority Actions Programme) (2008). Protocol on Integrated Coastal Zone Management in the Mediterranean. Split, Priority Actions Programme. Available at: http://iczmplatform.org//storage/documents/sewmrX-IR9gTwfvBgjJ4SAjhvqsLrBF6qB0B89xK8.pdf

Part II

Country reports

Group 1: European Countries – Non-Mediterranean

3 United Kingdom

Linda McElduff and Heather Ritchie

Overview

As an island nation, the UK has a close relationship to the coast and has made several efforts to secure a more sustainable and holistic approach to the management of the coastal zone, given the inevitability of future change. Yet coastal management approaches continue to be characterised by fragmentation across the devolved administrations and over different spatial scales; short-term planning; insecure funding; and partial policy implementation. At this juncture, we are experiencing an evolving policy landscape of the UK at all levels, including local government reforms, the introduction of the marine planning agenda at the national and regional level, and the UK's exit from the European Union. The convergence of these events means that coastal initiatives and partnerships are competing with other emerging forms of regulation for funding, time, and recognition. This is an opportune time to reflect on current practice, identify potential issues for future practice, and draw lessons from elsewhere.

Introduction to the UK coastal zone

As an island nation, the United Kingdom (UK) has a close affiliation with the coast. According to European Commission statistics in the UK Climate Change Risk Assessment (CCRA) 2017, over one-third of the UK population resides within 5 km of the coast (defined as mean high-water level), which rises to two-third within 15 km. The UK has a long history of responding to coastal issues, and coastal management in the form of coastal defences has existed since Roman times. More concerted efforts relating to coastal management came to the fore in the 1960s and 1970s due to increasing concerns with protecting the 'undeveloped' coast and to growing developmental pressures emerging from certain offshore activities (particularly North Sea oil and gas in Scotland). Traditional governance arrangements for planning and managing the coastal zone were characterised by an extension of land-based policies and controls, a plethora of sector-based policies and initiatives, and a complex mix of ownership, property rights, rules, and regulations (Lloyd and Peel, 2004). The marine-coastal zone remains a complex system of rights and responsibilities, and the effectiveness of established institutional arrangements and policies for coastal governance has become increasingly questioned within the sustainability paradigm.

Governance arrangements across the UK are in a period of flux. First, in terms of the terrestrial land use planning system(s), a range of legislative changes, planning reforms, and a move towards policy consolidation in recent years have affected how social, economic, and environmental issues are addressed. From a coastal management perspective, these changes have the potential to provide for more sustainable, long-term solutions to the challenges facing coastal areas, but their impact largely remains to be seen. Second, the emergence and growth of the marine planning agenda in the UK, as elsewhere, provides, on the one hand, opportunities to reinvigorate attention, debates, and momentum around coastal planning and management. On the other hand, there are challenges in terms of finding an established role for ICZM within the marine governance architecture. Third, the consequences of the UK's impeding exit from the European Union ('Brexit') are unclear. The UK will need to decide how to proceed and how this situation will affect the legislative context and the capacity to sustainably manage the UK's coastal marine environment in a future outside of Europe (Boyes and Elliott, 2018). Such evolving policy landscapes have affected the approach to, attitude to, and momentum towards coastal zone management. Greater levels of collaboration, cooperation, and coherence across spatial scales and across marine and terrestrial planning are required.

This chapter explores the current legislative and administrative frameworks for coastal management across the devolved administrations of the UK. In particular, we highlight instances of policy convergence and divergence across the administrations, and the shifting roles and responsibilities of the various actors involved. In light of the aforementioned changes, this is an opportune time to reflect on current practice, identify potential issues for future practice, and draw lessons from elsewhere to identify how a more holistic approach to coastal zone management in the UK might be secured.

The UK coast in context

Whilst the UK has a relatively small landmass (the furthest place from the coast is approximately 117 km inland; Zsamboky et al., 2011), it has one of Europe's longest coastlines, at 12,429 km (World Factbook, n.d.). This coastline is extremely varied from hard to soft cliffs, sand and shingle beaches, salt marsh, dunes, and machair, as well as approximately 1,000 islands, of which 291 are inhabited. Much of the coastline is of international or national ecological and cultural significance and contains important resources that provide economic, recreational, aesthetic, and conservation benefits for the whole country. Specific coastal uses include agriculture, aquaculture, mariculture, industry, recreation and tourism, commercial harbours, and military ranges, as well as power generation, waste disposal, and aggregate mining and extraction. These various uses and associated users have shaped the socioeconomic makeup of coastal communities, with some being economically reliant on marine and coastal resources. This dependency has consequent implications for their effective planning, management, and regeneration.

Coastal communities across the UK have experienced cycles of growth and decline (McElduff et. al, 2013) variously driven by factors such as economic instability (e.g. decline of traditional coastal industries and reliance on tourism), social change (e.g. transient populations and ageing demographic), shifting environmental parameters (e.g. increased storm intensity and erosion), and evolving governance structures and priorities (e.g. local government reform and the rise of 'Blue Growth'). The last decade witnessed an awakening to the specific challenges and opportunities facing coastal communities in the UK. The UK House of Commons 2006 Select Committee report on Coastal Towns, for example, helped to generate greater political awareness of coastal issues and attract increasing policy and academic interest at the national, regional, and local scales. Nevertheless, there remains a knowledge gap pertaining to effective coastal interventions, resulting in coastal towns being identified as 'the least understood of Britain's "problem areas"' (Beatty & Fothergill, 2003, p. 9), in part to due to

> … government's historic reluctance to recognise the importance of this kind of settlement, (and) the distinctive problems that the coast poses (beyond the obvious technical ones of sea defences). (Walton, 2010, p. 67)

In addition to social and economic challenges, environmental parameters are changing. The winter storms of 2013–2014 brought the fragility of the UK's coastline to the public's attention, and to the forefront of media and political discourse. Throughout the UK, it is increasingly recognised that long-term strategies accounting for the uncertainty facing coastal systems are needed to ensure both the protection of the natural ecosystem and economic sustainability. Yet subsequent action remains reactive, sectoral, and piecemeal. Coastal zone management plans are required to provide adaptive approaches better suited to a dynamic environment, which consider alternative solutions and seek to reduce future risk (Creed et al., 2018).

Administrative overview

To aid understanding of the complex coastal zone management framework in the UK, this section provides a brief introduction to the UK administrative context. The UK is divided into four devolved administrations: England, Wales, Scotland, and Northern Ireland (Figure 3.1). Since the 1990s, the UK government has gradually devolved a range of powers to these administrations through the Scotland Act 1998, the Government of Wales Act 1998, and the Northern Ireland Act 1998. Each country has subsequently developed policies aligned to the priorities and needs of their respective territories, resulting in customised approaches to marine and coastal governance. This has led to a divergence of policy, except in areas where the UK Government maintains control, such as security, policing, and macroeconomic policy.

The use and development of land in the UK is controlled and regulated primarily through statutory processes of devolved decision-making in the four administrations. The UK has a discretionary planning system where the scope of control is defined in the first instance through planning legislation, with subsequent legal interpretation provided by judges in the courts dealing with case law. Case law decisions have helped the operation and application of the planning system to be understood and practised (Sheppard et al., 2017). Land use planning operates through several mechanisms and supporting tools, such as structure plans, local development frameworks, and planning policy statements.

Coastal zone management does not lie within the remit of a single authority or organisation; rather, there are a range of government departments, semi-government bodies, conservation bodies, and (public and private) organisations responsible for varying aspects of coastal management. These sectoral arrangements use different regulatory systems operating for the multitude of different activities and uses, frequently over different geographical areas (Taussik, 2007). This 'patchwork' framework can lead to confused roles and responsibilities and is particularly challenging with respect to recent changes in coastal and marine policy specifically and land use planning reforms in general.

Coastal management in the UK: An historical overview

The UK has an established maritime history, but its coastal zone remained relatively under-developed until the 20th century (Craig-Smith, 1980). During the interwar period, increased

Figure 3.1 Map of the UK and Ireland

Source: Created by Linda McElduff

development associated with port, fishing, trade, and defence-related activities prompted calls for increased regulation. As a result, the Lincolnshire County Council (Sandhills) Act 1932 (formally, Lindsey County Council) pioneered development control legislation at a time when terrestrial planning was in its infancy. Notably, this Act preceded the 1947 Town and Country Planning Act that nationalised development rights in land and initiated the statutory land use planning system.

Unregulated coastal development continued to cause widespread concern over the following decades and led to increased lobbying by environmental groups. The expansion of the caravan industry in coastal locations attracted political attention, prompting the licensing and control of caravan sites through the Caravan Sites and Control of Development Act 1960. In 1963, the Ministry of Housing and Local Government issued Circular *Coastline Preservation and Development 56/63*, which argued for local authorities to identify areas meriting special study and control, and that coastal matters should be incorporated into local development planning frameworks.

In response to unprecedented demands for development on the Scottish coast in the late 1960s and 1970s due to oil and gas exploration and drilling, the *North Sea Oil and Gas Coastal Planning Guidelines* were published in 1974. These guidelines identified 'preferred conservation zones' and 'preferred development zones'.

This early development of coastal policy responded to localised issues and conditions and was both iterative and incremental (Lloyd, 1998). Nevertheless, it demonstrates how statutory land use planning began to respond to acknowledged developmental pressures in the coastal zone. The terrestrial planning system was subsequently identified as inadequate in terms of managing the dynamism and complexity of the coast. In the 1990s, Hansom (1995) high-lighted several weaknesses in the institutional planning regimes for the coast, including a lack of data, limited awareness of scalar contexts, and a tendency to rely on voluntary activities. Additionally, he argued:

> Perhaps at the very nub of the problem is not only the British tradition of planning being a 'control' mechanism rather than a pro-active process but also a preference for regulating and legislating for defined activities rather than for defined environments (Hansom, 1995, p. 191).

The House of Commons Environmental Select Committee Inquiry (1992) on *Coastal Zone Planning and Protection* brought coastal planning and management to the fore in the UK. The resultant report included several recommendations aimed at achieving a closer coordination of coastal policy. Notably, the UK government rejected the Committee's recommendation to introduce a statutory framework for ICZM, arguing that integration could be achieved through existing planning legislation. Instead, it commissioned various reports and produced policy papers which focused on information gathering and management structures. [1]In accordance with the European Recommendation 2002/423/EC on ICZM, in 2004 the UK Government published their stocktake on the management of the national coastal zone (DEFRA, 2004), which was used as the basis for preparing ICZM strategies for each of the devolved administrations discussed later in this chapter.

Contemporary legislative and policy changes, including the Climate Change Act 2008, the Marine and Coastal Access Act 2009, and terrestrial land use planning reforms, collectively represent an apparent paradigm shift in how coastal management is devised, delivered, and governed. This includes a potential move away from land-based fixed assumptions towards a more holistic understanding of the coast as a dynamic social-ecological system.

Definitions of the UK shoreline and coastal zone

Definitions of the UK shoreline and coastal zone are ambiguous and contested. Clear boundaries are not set into the legal framework for the UK; rather, definitions in the relevant legislation are nebulous, normally to allow flexibility in the application of the law. Coastal terminology is determined through guidance documents and clarified by case law, thereby relegating important legislative considerations to matters of administrative discretion.

In the UK, the term 'shoreline' does not refer to a boundary line between land and sea. Rather, it denotes the zone between the water marks (high and low tides), which continually fluctuates depending on the time of the tide and the influence of the waves (Jay, 2010).

One instance in which a boundary between land and sea is defined is in determining the legal jurisdiction of terrestrial planning authorities, which ends at the mean low-water mark (MLWM) (Local Government Act, 1972; Department of Environment and Welsh Office, 1992; Scottish Office, 1997). This is in accordance with the oft-quoted Scottish case of Argyll and Bute District Council v Secretary of State for Scotland [(1976) SC 248], where it was stated that planning control never extends below the low-water mark (the Mean Low Water Mark Ordinary Spring Tides). In Scotland, this jurisdiction has been extended to include marine fish farming (Scottish Government, 2010, p. 20). There is no clear definition of the MLWM, as it fluctuates with the changing of seasons and tides, meaning that the administrative boundary of coastal authorities regularly changes with the different levels of the tide. For example, the average time between high tides is 12 h 25 min (NTSLF, 2019).

Another relevant definition is that of the 'intertidal area', which is the area above water at low tide (MLWM) and underwater at high tide (MHWM). This area is also referred to as the 'foreshore', 'seashore', or 'littoral zone' (also known as the 'nearshore'). The Joint Nature Conservation Committee (JNCC; advisers to UK Government) uses the term 'littoral zone' as containing features such as beaches, sand banks, and intertidal mudflats. McGlashen et al. (2004) explain that the foreshore is part of the zone of physical interaction between land and sea. It is neither dry land nor sea and is constantly being covered and uncovered by water driven by tidal processes. In common law, the foreshore lies between the high-water mark of medium high tides and the low-water mark. However, the foreshore has been defined in different ways under statute. For example, the Limitation (Northern Ireland) Order 1989 (section 2(2)) defines the foreshore as:

> *the bed and shore, below the line of high water of ordinary or medium tides, of the sea and of every tidal river and tidal estuary and of every channel, creek and bay of the sea or any such river or estuary.*

The definition of the 'coastal zone' is equally elusive and, in legal terms, the coastal zone has an extent that often differs according to the statute under consideration. The aforementioned UK House of Commons Environment Select Committee into *Coastal Zone Protection and Planning* (1992) acknowledged that the definition of 'coastal zone' varies depending on the area and issue at hand and recommended that a pragmatic approach be adopted at all levels of governance. It is UK policy that there should be no nationally agreed boundaries of the coastal zone; rather, local planning authorities (LPAs) should consider and define the most appropriate zone in their jurisdiction based on direct physical, environmental, and economic linkages between land and sea. Accordingly, many local coastal authorities have delineated a coastal zone within their Local Development Plans (LDPs). A recent study of planning policies related to the Welsh National Marine Plan found that most LDPs referred to the specific characteristics of coastal areas in supporting text but only 29% of adopted plans (and 18% of draft plans) explicitly defined a coastal zone (Ballinger, 2016). Criteria for determining the width of the coastal zone were outlined in Planning Advice Note 53: *Classifying the Coast for Planning Purposes* (Scotland; Scottish Office, 1998), including the degree of inter-visibility between the coast and the land; the extent of land created by coastal processes; and the degree to which development would impinge on the coast.

The delineation of the coastal zone in the UK is further complicated by the historic legacy of the Crown, which owns approximately half of the foreshore around the UK and the majority of the seabed out to the territorial limit (out to 12 nm). The traditional property rights of the

Crown indirectly defined the jurisdictions of public authorities, which were re-enacted in the Local Government Act of 1972 without taking into account the needs of coastal zone management (Gibson, 1993).

The introduction of specific ICZM policies and strategies in the UK in the early to mid 2000s (based on EU Recommendation 2002/413/EC) sparked a debate on whether boundaries for the coastal zone are fixed or flexible and whether they should be drawn in relation to existing environmental, economic, or administrative regions. As a result, different definitions of the 'coastal zone' emerged.

In defining the extent of the coastal zone at the regional level, the Northern Ireland ICZM strategy outlines a 3 km inland limit. The strategy does not specify the seaward boundary from which this 3 km limit is measured but highlights the need for a flexible definition where factors beyond 3 km have an impact on the coastal zone. One of the key reasons for selecting the 3 km limit was the availability of data at the local level as the boundaries of electoral wards (the smallest administrative unit) can be aligned to the 3 km limit in a 'best fit' approach; if a certain proportion of the ward is within 3 km, it is classified as coastal. A total of 160 out of 582 wards have been identified as coastal wards using this measure. In LDPs, not all of these wards are acknowledged as falling within the coastal zone, emphasising the differing interpretations and articulations of the coastal zone in local planning policies and plans in the region at present.

Overall, the UK experience in ICZM has been based on a weak interpretation of the coastal zone. The traditional focus on the terrestrial environment has meant that coastal management activity has largely been subsumed within the terrestrial spatial planning framework. In this context, the coast has often been defined in relation to specific planning purposes and local concerns, such as for Coastal Change Management Areas (CCMA), Shoreline Management Plans (SMPs), and Heritage Coasts. Otherwise, it has been classified in relation to its development status (e.g. developed, undeveloped, or isolated) as a pragmatic approach to provide a coherent and consistent framework for the promotion and control of development. We return to these aspects later in the chapter.

The lack of a clear definition in legislation and policy has implications when considering the appropriateness of development in the coastal zone and the protection of the coastal ecosystem. In an attempt to address such concerns and facilitate 'blue growth', Scotland, England, and Wales have variously sought to define 'coastal *communities*' to help inform planning and development decisions. Coastal community typologies in England (Marine Management Organisation [MMO], 2011) and Wales have adopted the same definition of 'coastal' as the area extending 10 km inland from the LWM, including around each defined estuary and river limit to include all transitional waters. These typologies provide a more detailed understanding of local coastal areas than has been available previously and are intended as tools for marine planners and other users.

Public ownership

Ownership patterns differ across the coastal zone of the UK. Most of the land bordering the intertidal area is held in private ownership and used for agricultural purposes. Two-thirds of the intertidal area and the full extent of UK territorial waters are vested in the Crown and managed by the Crown Estate. In the intertidal area, Crown land is considered a 'movable freehold' (movable because of the changing tides). Although not a government body, the Crown Estate is a public body that acts as an enabler of government policy and has statutory functions under the Crown Estate Act of 1961. It therefore has a distinct role in the management of the

UK's marine and coastal area. Acting as landlords, the Crown Estate provides for public rights of fishing and navigation and grants general permissive consent for certain uses on the shore, including metal detecting.

The Crown Estate leases much of its foreshore holdings to third parties. As a result, local coastal authorities have significant coastal land holdings, particularly the ownership of popular beaches, holiday and leisure parks, and caravan parks. In an effort to enhance the effective management of these areas, many local coastal authorities have prepared separate guidance and strategies, including beach management plans, Shoreline Management Plans (SMPs), and plans for Coastal Change Management Areas (CCMA), as discussed later in this chapter.

In Scotland, Crown Estate Scotland[2] manages land and property owned by the Monarch in right of the Crown. In relation to the coast, Crown Estate Scotland is responsible for managing a range of rural, coastal, and marine assets, as well as some commercial properties; supports aquaculture, tourism, and offshore renewables through leasing, research, and other activities; and invests in marine leisure facilities to support coastal communities.

Ports and harbours

Much of the governance structure of UK ports was in place before devolution, and subsequently, the role of government has remained similar in all jurisdictions. In general, the UK has a highly privatised port system as a result of the 1979–1997 Conservative Government.[3] There are three main types of port ownership: private ownership (e.g. Bristol Port Company, England); trust ports (independent bodies strategically and financially dependent on statutory corporations, e.g. Belfast, Northern Ireland); and municipal ports (e.g. oil terminals in Orkney and Shetland, Scotland). Ports are responsible for their own planning and development, subject to approval. The role of the UK government is indirect, largely dealing with disputes or complaints in relation to charges and dues.

The National Trust

The National Trust[4] is the UK's largest coastal landowner, having 1,247 km of coastline in their care (9.7% of the total coastline of Northern Ireland, Scotland, and England; National Trust, 2015). The Trust uses the mean high-water mark to define the coastline and normal tidal limits to determine how far into estuaries it extends. The Trust's holdings within the UK coastal zone provide a significant contribution to the protection of landscapes, seascapes, history, archaeology, culture, habitats and wildlife, and the provision of coastal access (albeit at a cost). Many of their sites are of high nature conservation value, with several of international importance designated under international or national legislation. Of particular note in this respect is Strangford Lough, the UK's largest Marine Nature Reserve, having Special Area of Conservation (SAC), Special Protected Area (SPA), Ramsar site, and Area of Special Scientific Interest (ASSI) designations, and where the Trust is the largest single private landowner. Indeed, in Northern Ireland, the National Trust owns and manages almost a third of the length of the coastline, including the Giant's Causeway: the region's only World Heritage Site and its largest tourist attraction.

Setback from the shoreline

Despite increased rates of erosion and flooding and increased storm activity since the early 2000s, coastal setbacks have not been widely adopted in the UK. Neither ICZM strategies nor planning policies of the four administrations define any specific setback rule. Many coastal local authorities develop specific development management policies for their coastal zone, which may or may not include a defined setback zone. For example, Poole Local Plan (England) outlines a 25 m zone from the Sandbanks beachline where development is excluded to protect the undeveloped nature. There are also certain restrictions imposed in relation to development in the coastal zone.

In England, the National Planning Policy Framework (NPPF, s167–169; Ministry for Housing, Communities and Local Government, 2018) specifies that areas likely to be affected by coastal change should be identified as Coastal Change Management Areas (CCMAs) in local development plans. 'Coastal change' is defined as physical change to the shoreline through erosion, landslip, coastal accretion, or permanent inundation. The identification and classification of CCMAs should be undertaken in conjunction with SMPs. SMPs identify coastal risk in three time horizons (up to 20, 50, and 100 years) and include maps of the geographical extent of each risk area. LPAs have discretion to determine how these are interpreted to define and delineate the CCMA.

Development within a CCMA is considered appropriate only where it is demonstrated that it will be safe over its planned lifetime, will provide wider sustainability benefits, and will not have an unacceptable impact on coastal change. In addition, the development may not compromise the character of the coast or hinder public access. Within short-term risk areas (i.e. a 20-year time horizon), only certain types of development directly linked to the coast – such as beach huts, cafés, car parks, and sites used for holiday or short-let caravan and camping may be permitted – subject to time-limited planning permission. Within the medium (20- to 50-year) and long-term (up to 100-year) risk areas, a wider range of time-limited development may be appropriate, including hotels, shops, office, or leisure activities which require a coastal location and provide substantial economic and social benefits to the community. Small-scale development associated with existing buildings, such as extensions to existing properties and some commercial development, may also be acceptable, but permanent new residential development will not usually be permitted within a CCMA. A Coastal Erosion Vulnerability Assessment must accompany development proposals within a CCMA.

In Northern Ireland, the Strategic Planning Policy Statement (SPPS; Department of the Environment, 2015) advocates a precautionary approach towards the identification of coastal land for development through the LDP process and the determination of development proposals. However, whilst planning policy has stated that no development should take place in areas known to be at risk from coastal erosion, authorities have not applied that policy consistently, if at all (Cooper, 2015). The Northern Ireland ICZM Strategy (Department of the Environment, 2006) similarly called for coastal managers to anticipate problems and err on the side of caution in relation to the potential environmental consequences of their decisions. It further suggested the use of 'soft' mitigation measures that work with natural processes, such as 'setback and retreat' options. Yet, at most decision-making levels, Northern Ireland still assumes a 'hold the line' position, meaning it intervenes to prevent any further shoreline retreat.

Right of public access

As a predominant landowner, the Crown Estate provides opportunities for horizontal access and recreation along the UK foreshore on a permissive basis.[5] However, access is not universally guaranteed by law and may not be available where the foreshore is leased to another party. Horizontal access may also be frustrated by the lack of vertical access to the foreshore;

in accessing the foreshore, one may need to cross over private land, where common law of trespass may be used to prevent access. Legislation in relation to vertical public access to the coast varies across the four administrations.

England and Wales

Public access to the countryside in England and Wales is permitted under various laws; notably, the Countryside and Rights of Way Act (CROW) 2000, which created the legal concept of 'Access Land', commonly referred to as the 'right to roam'. The public thus have the 'right to roam' across some land in England and Wales, known as 'open access land' or 'access land' (includes privately owned mountains, moors, heaths, and downs), without having to use paths. Whilst the primary legislation is the same in England and Wales, there are differences in secondary legislation and in implementation.

In England, the Marine and Coastal Access Act (MCAA) 2009 (s.296, Part 9) aims to improve public access to and enjoyment of the English coastline by creating clear and consistent public rights of access. It tasks Natural England [6]and the Secretary of State with creating 'the English Coastal Route', which will enable, for the first time, a secure and legal right of public access around the whole of the English coast (approximately 4345 km), along beaches, sand dunes, and cliff tops. These 'coastal access rights' will apply throughout the coastal margin and replace other access rights. Activities permitted along the coastal route include most types of open-air recreation on foot or by wheelchair, including walking, running, watching wildlife, and climbing. Prohibited activities include horse riding, cycling, camping, and water sports. Such recreational uses may take place by virtue of an existing right, with the landowner's permission, or have traditionally been tolerated in the absence of formal permission, with no effect on public rights of way.

The MCAA 2009 also seeks (at Section 23) to balance the access interests of the public with the interests of owners and occupiers of land, over which coastal access rights would be conferred. Consequently, some coastal land will remain 'excepted land'. Houses and gardens, for example, remain private; major ports and industry will be respected, and appropriate mitigation measures will be implemented to protect sensitive species and habitats. In some locations, these provisions may prevent people reaching the shoreline or cliff edge. Coastal access rights do not prevent coastal land from being developed or redeveloped. If development occurs, the developed land is likely to become excepted land under the Countryside and Rights of Way Act (para. 9 of Schedule 1A) and therefore outside the coastal access rights.

Users of the English Coastal Route are expected to take primary responsibility for their own safety; thus, land subject to coastal access rights benefits from the lowest level of Occupiers' Liability known under English law. Consequently, it is unlikely in normal circumstances that a landowner/occupier will be successfully sued in relation to injury on land with coastal access rights. However, as elsewhere, liability still applies in relation to reckless or deliberate acts or omissions by the occupier and to injury caused by the condition of physical infrastructure installed by the occupier, such as gates or steps.

In Wales, the Welsh Government has invested in enhancing public access to the Welsh coast since 2007 through its Coastal Access Improvement Programme. It developed the Wales Coast Path in partnership with Natural Resources Wales, local coastal authorities, and two National Parks. In comparison to the approach being undertaken in England, the Welsh Coastal Path was created using a voluntary approach, mostly by agreement with landowners. The 1400 km coastal path was completed in May 2012 and is the first continuous route along a national coastline. National Resources Wales is responsible for the management and promotion of the path.

Scotland

In Scotland, there is no inclusive coastal access path as in England or Wales, but there are eight Great Trails that allow access to the Scottish Coast, and in any case, the public have the right to access most land and inland water in Scotland. In order to regulate this access and bring codes of conduct in line with modern patterns of behaviour and ownership, Scottish Natural Heritage (SNH) [7] and the Scottish Executive produced the Land Reform (Scotland) Act 2003, which included the Scottish Outdoor Access Code. This Code reflects many of the principles set out in England and Wales but allows for a wider range of freedoms and established rights for non-motorised access (walking, cycling, horse riding, and canoeing) to land and inland water for passage, recreational, educational, and commercial use. The Land Reform (Scotland) Act 2003 ensures that everyone has statutory 'right to responsible access' to most of Scotland's outdoors if these rights are exercised responsibly with respect for people's privacy, safety, and livelihoods and for Scotland's environment. It requires responsible land and water management in relation to access rights.

Northern Ireland

Traditionally, Northern Ireland's countryside and coastal lands are held in private ownership, and access through private land is not guaranteed by law (Figure 3.2). As such, access is severely restricted in comparison with other parts of the UK. The exceptions include a limited number of public rights of way, Waymarked Ways (e.g. North Down Coastal Path, The Causeway Coast Way, and The Lecale Way), and the parts of the coastal zone that are owned by the

Figure 3.2 Access restrictions on the Northern Ireland Coast – Ministry of Defence property (firing range) at Benone Beach (left); private land at Seacoast Road, Bellarena (right)

Source: Photos by Heather Ritchie

National Trust or local authorities. There are some problematic areas along the coast where the legal land ownership and access arrangements are unclear. In an increasingly litigious society, it is essential that such cases be clarified, particularly in relation to liability and rights of way.

On private land, access often takes the form of de facto or 'permissive access': that is, access is at the discretion of the landowner. Farmers and other landowners have traditionally been reluctant to provide or have outright opposed public access over their land – mainly due to concerns about public liability and a desire to protect private property rights and privacy. In 1999, the Department of the Environment (now the Department of Agriculture, Environment and Rural Affairs, DAERA) undertook a consultation looking at establishing a 'right to roam' in the region but faced strong opposition to the proposal. In a 2007 position paper, the Council for Nature Conservation and the Countryside (CNCC, advisers to Government) recommended that the Northern Ireland Executive develop a coastal path similar to that of England and Wales. However, to date, there has been no commitment from the Northern Ireland Executive to create such a path.

There are certain mechanisms at the local level that help secure public access: The Access to the Countryside (NI) Order 1983 provided local authorities with a duty to protect public rights of way; provided powers to create or extinguish public paths; enabled councils to secure access to open countryside (including cliffs and foreshore) by access agreement, access order, or land acquisition. However, access legislation is cumbersome and most local authorities have not taken full advantage of it to safeguard public rights of way or create new paths or open access opportunities. Local bylaws affecting access to the coast deal with recreational uses, dog-fouling, drinking alcohol in public places, and access to open spaces and local authority beaches.

With over 200 km of coastline in its care, the National Trust provides public access to a significant proportion of Northern Ireland's coastal zone. All of the Trust's coastal properties are open to the public and are thus important for the provision of access to the coast in Northern Ireland. However, access to National Trust properties usually involves a cost, which has proven to be contentious at times. For example, the National Trust has been accused of 'misleading' tourists into paying an entry fee to the Giant's Causeway. The National Trust has a Visitor's Centre at the UNESCO World Heritage Site, but the public can visit for free via a public path to the side of the centre. The local council has vowed to 'assert and protect' the public right of way.

Some beaches permit vehicles onto beaches. At Portstewart Strand, Co. Antrim, for example, the National Trust permits cars onto the beach at a charge of £6.50 (c. €7.40) [8]per car (but free to pedestrians), or 'free' with an annual membership of £120 per year, which goes towards the continual maintenance of the area.

Land use planning

The use and development of land in the UK is controlled and regulated primarily through statutory processes of devolved decision-making in the four administrations. There are, however, similarities across the devolved administrations due to the nature of the British planning tradition. The terrestrial planning system is based on a hierarchy of plans, whereby higher-level plans set the policy context for the plans below. These plans guide the direction of future development on the coast, but importantly, are non-binding: They provide a discretionary framework for decision-making. In addition to the traditional planning framework, recent and emerging legislation and policy in relation to the marine environment is changing the way decisions are made and implemented, in the coastal zone.

In England, Planning Policy Guidance (PPG) 20: The Coast (Ministry for Housing, Communities and Local Government, 1992) provided the first set of policy guidance specifically for development in English coastal areas. In 2010, the Ministry replaced the 1992 policy with Planning Policy Statement (PPS) 25: Development and Flood Risk (incorporating the supplement Development and Coastal Change). PPS25 outlines the policies planning authorities should use in order to prevent inappropriate development on the coast and to protect new (and existing) developments from physical changes to the coastline, such as erosion and accretion. The National Planning Policy Framework (NPPF; MHCLG, 2018) sets out the government's policies for planning and how these are to be applied. The NPPF sought to reduce the complexity of the planning system by replacing sector-specific planning policy statements and guidance. The NPPF (paragraphs 166–169) deals with coastal change and calls for ICZM to be actively pursued to ensure the alignment of marine and terrestrial planning; for inappropriate development in vulnerable areas to be avoided; and for LPAs to define Coastal Change Management Areas (CCMAs) to restrict the type and lifetime of development.

In Wales, the Welsh Government is responsible for the preparation of the Wales Spatial Plan (WSP; Welsh Assembly Government, 2008)[9] and Planning Policy Wales (PPW; Welsh Assembly Government, 2016), which provide the overarching policy for terrestrial planning. PPW is supplemented by Technical Advice Notes (TANs), which provide more detailed subject-specific guidance on topic areas. TAN 14: Coastal Planning (Welsh Office, 1998) provides details of the planning considerations to be taken into account in relation to the coastal zone.

In Scotland, the National Planning Framework (NPF; Scottish Government, 2014a) and Scottish Planning Policy (SPP; Scottish Government, 2014b) provide the overarching policy for terrestrial planning. The SPP states that coastal areas suitable for development should be identified based on a clear understanding of the physical, environmental, economic, and social characteristics and effects of climate change (paragraphs 98–103). In considering such development, planning authorities should take account of the likely impact on the marine environment. The SPP suggests that as a strategic management process, ICZM may be of use in addressing areas and issues of shared interest between regional marine plans and development plans. Previously, Scottish Planning Advice Notes (PANS) played a similar role to that of Welsh TANs. *Planning Advice Note 53: Classifying the Coast for Planning Purposes* (Scottish Office, 1998) recommended the classification of coastal areas (defined by local authorities) as 'developed', 'undeveloped', or 'isolated'. This classification system sought to provide a practical framework to identify where development should be promoted or controlled. In 2010, the consolidation of coastal policy in Scottish Planning Policy revealed a shift, which saw coastal areas as 'an important contributor to sustainable economic growth' (Scottish Government, 2010, p. 20).

In Northern Ireland, the Regional Development Strategy (RDS) 2035 (Department for Regional Development, 2012) provides the statutory spatial framework for Northern Ireland governance and is a material consideration [10]in land use planning, regional planning policy, planning legislation, and performance management. Whilst acknowledging the ecological importance of the coast, the RDS places responsibility on the UK Marine Policy Statement (HM Government, 2011) and subsequent Marine Plans to provide spatial guidance, and detailed policy where appropriate, for the terrestrial/marine interface. Unlike the rest of the UK, there is no coastal-specific policy in Northern Ireland, despite numerous calls for such (e.g. OFMDFM, 2006). The Strategic Planning Policy Statement (SPPS) (DOE, 2015) sets out the regional planning policies for securing the orderly and consistent development of land. It contains a section on Coastal Development and seeks to protect the undeveloped coast from inappropriate development and support the sensitive regeneration of the developed coast. It also requires (para. 6.47) that, in preparing their new local development plans, local authorities promote and protect public access to and along the coast where possible.

Whilst the four administrations have developed their own strategic policy guidance (Table 3.1), similarities can be identified. First, there has been a trend towards a single national policy statement rather than a suite of sector-specific policies. These national statements – the NPPF in England, PPW in Wales, SPP in Scotland, and SPPS in Northern Ireland – seek to promote

Table 3.1 Key strategic planning policy and guidance in relation to the coast across the UK administrations

Jurisdiction	Policy/Guidance	Summary
ENGLAND	National Planning Policy Framework (NPPF) (2018)	Asserts that LPAs to improve public access to, and enjoyment of, the coast.
	Planning Policy Statement 25 (2010)	Outlines the policies planning authorities should use in order to prevent inappropriate development at the coast and to protect new (and existing) developments from physical changes to the coastline, such as erosion and accretion.
	PPS 25 Supplement: Development and Coastal Change (2010)	Sets out a planning framework for the continuing economic and social viability of coastal communities. The policy aims to strike the right balance between economic prosperity and reducing the consequences of coastal change on communities.
	Planning Policy Guidance 20 (1992)	Provided the first set of policy guidance specifically for development in coastal areas. Superseded by PPS25.
WALES	Planning Policy Wales (2016)	Chapter 5: Conserving and Improving Natural Heritage and the Coast advocates the key principles of ICZM be embedded within relevant plans and projects. States that local coastal authorities should acknowledge the interrelationships between physical, biological, and land use characteristics of coastal areas and the impacts of climate change to help identify areas suitable and unsuitable for development. The need to protect the character and landscape of the undeveloped coast and conserve the natural heritage is emphasised.
	Wales Spatial Plan (2008)	Argues the need to link terrestrial and marine planning to ensure the best protection and use of the resources in line with objectives of ICZM strategy for Wales. Coastal erosion identified as presenting a potentially significant economic threat. Need to adapt to climate change is highlighted. Contains ambitions to improve access to the coast. Acknowledges the economic decline of some coastal tourism resorts and the need to diversify local coastal economies. *The Wales Spatial Plan will be replaced by the National Development Framework (NDF).
	Technical Advice Note (TAN) 14: Coastal Planning (1998)	Provides advice and information on recreation development, heritage coasts and non-statutory coastal groupings, and SMPs.

(continued)

Table 3.1 (continued)

Jurisdiction	Policy/Guidance	Summary
SCOTLAND	National Planning Framework (2014)	Importance of the coast and islands as an economic opportunity and a resource to be protected and enjoyed is emphasised. Particular opportunities for renewable energy generation and tourism are highlighted. Advocates the need to work with marine planning to deliver economic and social benefits for island and coastal communities. Specific reference is made to the oil and gas sector and aquaculture as important aspect of the economy across many parts of coastal Scotland.
	Scottish Planning Policy (SPP) (2014)	Advocates an integrated approach to coastal planning to ensure that development plans and regional marine plans are complementary. Specifies that development plans should take account of the likely impacts of climate change and adopt a precautionary approach to development on the coast. LPAs should identify areas at risk of coastal erosion and flooding, and thus where development should not be supported, and areas suitable for further development.
	Planning Advice Note 53: Classifying the Coast for Planning Purposes (Scottish Office 1998).	Provides explanation and guidance in relation to the classification of Scotland's coasts as either 'developed', 'undeveloped', or 'isolated'. Now superseded by SSP.
NORTHERN IRELAND	Regional Development Strategy (2012)	Acknowledges the ecological importance of the coast; places responsibility on the Marine Policy Statement (2011) and subsequent Marine Plans to provide spatial guidance, and detailed policy where appropriate, for the terrestrial/marine interface.
	Strategic Planning Policy Statement (2015)	Contains a specific section on Coastal Development. Seeks to protect the undeveloped coast from inappropriate development, consistent with the objectives of the RDS, and to support the sensitive enhancement and regeneration of the developed coast within coastal settlements.

consistency in the planning application process by guiding the preparation of local development plans and encouraging good quality of design in development, and are a material consideration in the determination of planning applications and appeals. Generally, these national policies share similar ambitions in relation to the coast and seek to (for example) direct the growth of coastal settlements towards their landward boundary rather than along the coastal frontage; identify areas where development should be restricted to take account of amenity or landscape value, nature conservation interest, or historical importance; preserve and enhance public access to the coast; and identify areas of the coast at risk from flooding, coastal erosion, or land instability where new development should not be permitted.

In accordance with the plan-led approach, national plans and policies guide LDPs, which are considered by scholars and others to be at the heart of the British planning system (Sheppard et al., 2017). Specifically, LDPs set out a vision and framework for the future development of an area over the designated plan period, where and when this will occur, and how it will be delivered. Coastal matters are dealt with both explicitly and implicitly within LDPs, with some topics such as nature and ecological conservation and landscape protection deeply embedded in terrestrial planning culture. The approach taken towards coastal policy tends to reflect the geographical remit of the plan area as well as formal planning guidance from Government at the time of plan preparation.

In recent years, second-home ownership has become an increasing policy issue in some areas. Consequently, the development of second homes in some coastal towns has been restricted or outright banned by local coastal authorities, through council tax increases for second-home owners and through the use of Neighbourhood Residential Plans. St Ives, England, is the most high-profile example. In May 2016, the St Ives Area Neighbourhood Development Plan was passed by referendum. Neighbourhood Plans typically cover policies in relation to, for example, land allocation, sustainable transport, and housing supply. In the housing section of the St Ives Area Neighbourhood Plan, clause H2 restricts the sale of new open-market homes to people who can prove that the home will be their principle residency. The clause has become commonly referred to as the 'second home ban' and was the first of its kind in the UK. It was designed in response to a growing number of people from out of town purchasing holiday homes in St Ives and pricing locals out of the housing market. In response, an architectural firm claimed there had been inadequate consideration of reasonable alternatives to the policy, contrary to the Strategic Environment Assessment (SEA) Directive, and questioned whether it was compatible with human rights legislation. They subsequently bought about a legal challenge to the policy (*RLT Built Environment Ltd v Cornwall Council [2016] EWHC 2817*). However, the High Court found the policy to be lawful.

Marine planning in the UK

Across the UK, there has been increasing emphasis on the (potential) role of marine planning and marine plans to facilitate effective coastal management. The terrestrial planning system and the marine planning system are legally and functionally separate but overlap in the intertidal area (Figure 3.3). LDPs and regional marine plans should therefore be complementary, particularly with regard to the intertidal area, but also for the wider coastal zone. The Scottish Government (2010), in particular, identified the potential of ICZM in addressing the areas and issues in which regional marine plans and terrestrial development plans have a shared interest.

The Marine and Coastal Access Act (MCAA) 2009 was the UK's first piece of comprehensive legislation focused on the governance of the marine and coastal environment. It represented an acknowledgement of the need to update the UK marine and coastal governance framework so that it could be better equipped to deal with the challenges of the twenty-first century and enable the sustainable development of the UK seas. The devolved administrations subsequently adopted a set of high-level marine objectives to ensure consistency in approach towards the UK government vision for 'clean, healthy, safe, productive and biologically diverse oceans and seas'. This alignment was furthered by the UK-wide Marine Policy Statement 2011, which placed a statutory obligation to develop marine plans. Whilst each devolved administration will develop its own approach to marine planning and delivery mechanisms to reflect the specificities of their seas and local approaches to marine governance, all marine plans must be consistent with the Marine Policy Statement.

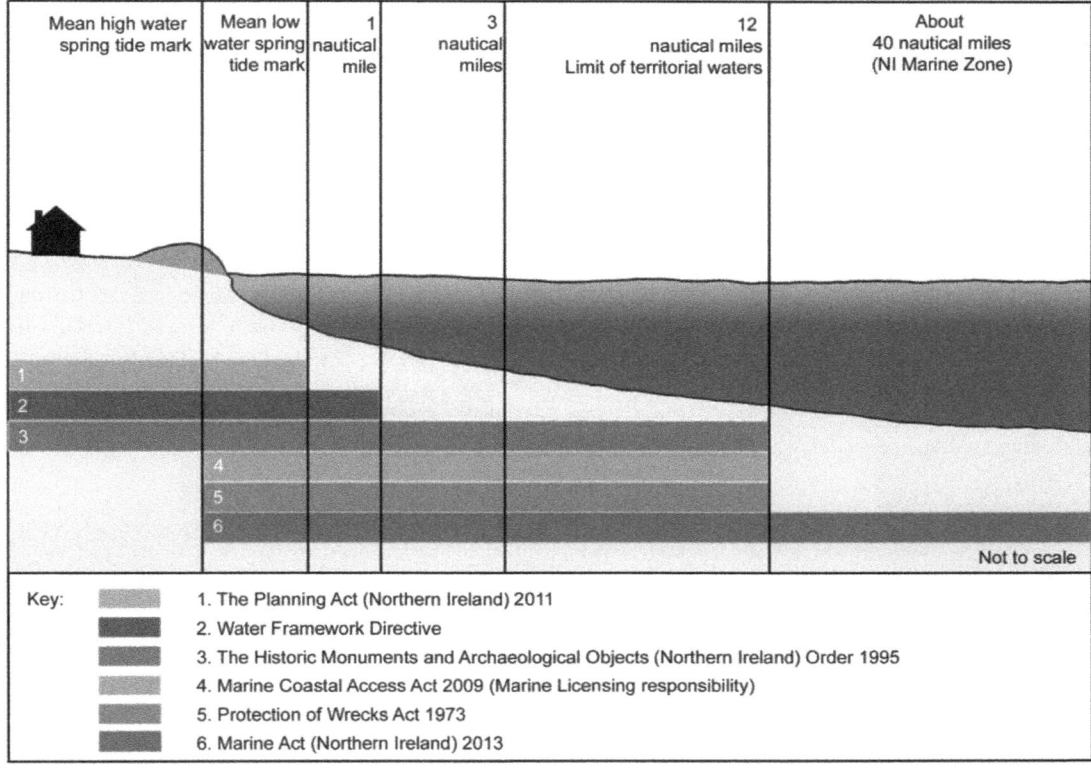

Figure 3.3 The geographical overlap between the marine and terrestrial environment in Northern Ireland (DAERA, 2017)

Source: With kind permission of DAERA Marine and Fisheries Division

Whilst marine spatial planning is not discussed in detail in this chapter, the new governance and legislative architecture introduced as part of the marine planning agenda in recent years has already had important consequences for coastal planning and management. In England, as part of this new governance agenda, the Marine Management Organisation (MMO) was established. In addition to a range of marine functions (e.g. fisheries, offshore renewable energy, Marine Conservation Zones, and marine planning), the MMO has a statutory duty to improve access to the coast. Yet questions are raised as to the specific role and significance given to ICZM within a marine policy arena dominated by an economic growth agenda (Flannery & O'Cinneide, 2012). Crawford (2019, p. 312) argues that 'ICZM has been largely reframed as a mechanism for suturing marine and terrestrial planning systems along a narrow interface'.

There is an identified need across the UK for better coherence between terrestrial and marine planning and between the UK jurisdictions. Several mechanisms have been introduced in an effort to achieve that end. For example, in 2013, the Department of Environment, Food and Rural Affairs (DEFRA) introduced the Coastal Concordat, a voluntary non-statutory agreement between relevant government bodies and a *'framework within which the separate processes for the consenting of coastal developments in England can be better coordinated'*

(DEFRA, 2013). The Concordat seeks to reduce regulatory duplication, provide better sign-posting to relevant agencies, streamline assessments, and increase transparency and consistency of advice. It can be applied to any development in the intertidal area that requires multiple marine licence consents and terrestrial planning permission.

Shoreline management planning

In the context of increased intensity and occurrence of coastal hazards (particularly flooding and erosion) and a growing awareness of the need to move away from the traditional parochial, scheme-by-scheme approach to coastal defence, Shoreline Management Planning emerged in the UK during the 1990s. The rationale was to provide a strategic, regional context for local coastal strategies and coastal engineering schemes. SMPs are non-statutory, high-level planning documents that set out how the coast should be managed for future uncertainty and risk. Based on 49 'management units' across England and Wales, these plans provide data on coastal change and seek to create sustainable management approaches for the future.

The first round of SMPs organised boundaries based on sediment cells that concentrated on the movement of beach material. These sediment cells were enclosed with no input or export of beach sediment (Hansom et al., 2004). The geographical areas that contained the sediment cell boundaries identify the region where shoreline management plan would function. SMPs have been the first attempt within Europe to provide planning based on large-scale assessment of shoreline management processes over long-term timeframes. Second-generation SMPs (SMP2s) define options for each of three designated planning epochs, up to 2025, 2055, and 2100. SMPs assign one of the four generic policy options for each stretch of shoreline, based on physical and human characteristics (Table 3.2). These policy options are intended to inform the development of more detailed and informed coastal defence strategies.

SMPs are non-statutory documents, and the terrestrial land use planning system was slow to engage with them. However, recent studies suggest a growing acknowledgement of SMPs within statutory land use planning policy (Ballinger, 2016), and they may therefore go some way towards shaping the coastline in England and Wales over the next century. The designation of policy options for areas can be contentious, and issues of social justice have arisen. For example, in Wales, the SMP covering the town of Fairbourne (population c. 850) has suggested that the town will be lost to the sea by 2055 and that 'decommissioning' is needed. It is proposed that maintenance work on existing sea defences will stop in 2045. Thus, Fairbourne could become the first town to be relocated due to threat of rising seas and climate change in the UK. Notably, SMPs have been produced for only some sections of the Scottish coast and, despite repeated calls, there are no SMPs in Northern Ireland.

A number of other non-statutory mechanisms and schemes are also in place. The Heritage Coast scheme, for example, was initiated in 1972 to protect stretches of the coastline with special scenic and environmental value from undesirable development. Heritage Coasts now cover around 30% of the coast in England and 40% in Wales. Much of this coastline is owned by the National Trust, through Project Neptune, [11]and is part of larger National Parks or Areas of Outstanding Natural Beauty (AONB). For many of these coasts, their protected areas extend inland for an average of 2.4 km. The management of Heritage Coasts is the remit of the relevant LPAs with help from national (namely Natural England and Natural Resources Wales) and local stakeholders and local communities. Heritage Coast status carries no legal

Table 3.2 The first- and second-generation SMP policy options

SMP 1 (1996–1999)		SMP 2 (2007–)	
Policy option	*Description*	*Policy option*	*Description*
Do nothing	No action taken to affect coastal erosion or flooding within the defined management unit (except for safety reasons).	No active intervention.	A decision not to invest in providing or maintaining coastal defences or operations. The coast can develop naturally.
Hold the line.	Maintain the existing coastline in its present position whether by maintaining the existing defence line or enhancing its role as a coastal defence.	Hold the line.	Maintain or change the standard of protection. This policy includes scenarios where operations are carried out seaward of the existing defences to improve, maintain, or change the standard of protection provided by the existing defence line. It also includes operations landward of the existing defences (e.g. construction of a secondary flood wall) where they form an essential part of maintaining the current coastal defence system.
Advance the line.	New coastal defences are built seaward of the present line of defence.	Advance the line.	Building new defences seaward of the original defences. The advancement of the existing defence line assumes land reclamation and increased level of protection from flooding and erosion.
Retreat the line.	*Coastline backed by floodable low-lying land* – adopt a more landward defence position. *Coastline backed by eroding cliff areas* – alter the natural rate of cliff retreat to a predetermined defence position.	Managed realignment	Allowing the shoreline to move backwards or forwards, with management to control or limit movement. This may include reducing erosion or building new defences on the landward side of the original defences.
Adapted from: Ballinger & Dodds, 2017; DEFRA, 2006			

protection, but LPAs must take the designation into account when making decisions on development. The NPPF (2018, para. 173) states that planning policies and decisions should be consistent with the special character and conservation value of the Heritage Coast. Major development in these areas is unlikely to be permitted.

Compliance and enforcement

First, we deal local government compliance with national-level regulations. Whilst, as previously outlined, planning frameworks and policies generally restrict development in coastal areas, local authorities often find that there is a lack of evidence to inform and support decisions to deny development, particularly in terms of coastal change. This is particularly salient in Northern Ireland in the absence of SMPs. Consequently, in some cases, inappropriate developments have been permitted, many of which will require associated sea defence works to be carried out, thus potentially accentuating environmental hazards.

While there are no recorded figures that describe the extent of illegal development, we note that illegalities on the coast most commonly take the form of works for the protection of private property. On private land, it is the owner's responsibility to manage and prevent erosion, but owners must obtain consent for any coastal protection works from the relevant local authority and other relevant administrations, as outlined in the SMP (if one is in place). Cases of illegal works for coastal protection can be found across the four administrations.

In 2015, approximately 20,000 waste tyres were dumped on agricultural land along the coastline of Lough Foyle, in the northwest of Northern Ireland, in order to protect the land from erosion. The landowners did not have a licence to keep controlled waste or use any materials as sea defences. Two men, including the landowner, received suspended jail sentences under the Waste and Contaminated Land (NI) Order 1997 and one marine charge under the Marine and Coastal Access Act 2009.

A different case related to works to protect property in East Bavents in Southwold (Suffolk, England) from erosion. Since World War II, erosion of the cliffs has claimed 14 of the 28 houses within this small seaside community. A property owner and retired engineer, Boggis, sought to protect his property by placing 250,000 tonnes of building waste along a 1 km embankment at the foot of the cliff. Boggis believed that these works were lawful under waste disposal exemptions. Yet the stretch of cliffs in Suffolk had previously been declared a Site of Special Scientific Interest (SSSI) for their geological value. As such, according to Natural England, the construction constituted an offence under the Coast Protection Act 1949 (Section 16), as it was carried out without the consent of the coastal protection authority. But in fact, due to erosion, the original SSSI marked on the official map applied seaward of the cliffs and Boggis's property. While the local authority supported Boggis, Natural England did not.

In response, Natural England extended the original SSSI to include the strip of land owned by Boggis, with the effect that the former's consent would be required for the erection of sea defences. Such consent would unlikely be granted, as Natural England's policy for the SSSI was to allow nature's acts to take their course, and thus, it was predicted that within 50 years, the sea would naturally erode the land to beyond the property. Boggis launched a Judicial Review to the High Court, claiming that the declaration of SSSI over his property was *ultra vires* (*Boggis and Anor, R (on application of) v Natural England and Anor [2009] JPL 729*). The question was not whether Natural England should have extended the SSSI, on which views will radically differ, but whether it could have done so as a matter of law. The Court found that the SSSI was unlawful insofar as it applied to the area of the seaward side of the cliffs, where the sea defences were situated, and the land behind but that elsewhere it was lawful. In his closing statement, Judge Mr Nicholas Blake QC said:

> *I make it clear that no criticism is intended of Natural England. It has been trying to do its duty to preserve the scientific value of the site. But without some form of defence, the claimants' homes will soon be swept away by the sea, and their very human predicament must be taken account of too.*

These cases highlight the complexities and tensions involved in responding effectively to changing environmental parameters. In the context of global climate change, it is increasingly acknowledged that coasts are vulnerable and are facing uncertain and unpredictable futures.

Increased erosion, in particular, presents a challenge for many coastal communities and governments, including those in the UK. Erosion threatens physical infrastructure (roads, buildings, etc.) and established land-based fixed asset assumptions but is also a vital natural process that sustains a healthy coastal ecosystem.

Climate change awareness – legal aspects

The UK was the first country in the world to adopt a legally binding long-term framework to cut carbon emissions and a framework to adapt to climate change. The Climate Change Act 2008 commits the central government to carry out a UK-wide Climate Change Risk Assessment (CCRA) every five years. The CCRA informs each UK administration about climate change risks and helps them set priorities for adaptation programmes for their respective regions. In the latest CCRA (2017), flooding and coastal change risks to communities, businesses, and infrastructure were identified as a research priority area for all four administrations. According to the Marine Climate Change Impacts Partnership (CCIP), 17.3% of the UK coast is eroding. But rates of coastal erosion vary greatly around the UK: England has the highest rate, with almost 30% of its coastline suffering from erosion, compared to 23.1% in Wales, 19.5% in Northern Ireland, and 11.6% in Scotland. In line with its greater levels of erosion, the English coastline is the most protected, with 45.6% of its length having some form of coastal defence (McKibbin, 2016).

Responsibility for coastal defence is a devolved matter in the UK.[12] Accordingly, the devolved administrations develop strategies and documents independently to deal with current and future risks. Whilst there is no overarching UK-wide plan or coastal defence policy, policy initiatives relating to climate change adaptation of the different jurisdictions are driven by national guidelines and strategies, including the Climate Change Act 2008, and the strategy document *Safeguarding Our Seas* (DEFRA, 2002). The Safeguarding Our Seas strategy (drafted with the support of DEFRA, the Scottish Government and Welsh Assembly Group) advises that climate change adaptation be considered in all coastal and flood defence plans.

In terms of managing coastal change, the Coast Protection Act 1949 is one of the most important pieces of legislation in the UK. The Coast Protection Act applies across the UK, except Northern Ireland. It provides the legal framework for the protection of the coast against erosion and encroachment and provides permissive powers to local coastal authorities to undertake coast protection works. These 'coastal protection authorities' have the power to carry out any necessary or expedient work for the protection of land from erosion or encroachment by the sea. These authorities may enter into agreements with any other person to carry out protection works and may also buy any land required to carry out coast protection works or land that is to be protected by new coast protection works. They also have powers to compulsorily acquire land in accordance with the Acquisition of Land Act 1981. The powers also enable construction, alteration, improvement, repair, maintenance, demolition, or removal if undertaken solely for the purpose of protecting land from erosion and encroachment.

In England and Wales, strategic oversight of flood and coastal erosion management is assigned to one body: The Environment Agency. The Flood and Water Management Act (England and Wales) 2010 is the only legislation in the UK that recognises the inseparable processes of coastal erosion and coastal flooding.

A key difference between Northern Ireland and the rest of the UK is that local authorities do not have direct responsibility for protecting the coast from flooding or erosion. Rather, several Northern Ireland Executive Departments are accountable under the Bateman Formula. The Bateman Formula is an administrative arrangement established in 1967 whereby each government Department takes responsibility for the construction, maintenance, and repair of coastal protection works, as required for their respective infrastructure assets. For example, within the Department for Infrastructure (DfI), the Rivers Agency has powers to maintain 26 km of sea defences and two tidal barriers designed to reduce the risk of flooding (but not coastal erosion) to low-lying coastal land, and Transport NI has responsibility for coastal defences that protect the public road and railway network. Thus, 'at an operational level coastal defence in Northern Ireland is undertaken on an *ad hoc* basis, carried out as and when needed' (Dobbs et al., 2010, p. 782). This reactive approach impedes the implementation of more adaptive forms of coastal erosion management, which has led Cooper (2015) to forewarn that the Northern Irish coast is destined to be rimmed in concrete. A more strategic vision is necessitated, together with the knowledge, information, tools, and resources to achieve such a vision. The most recent CCRA (ASC, 2016) highlighted a need to assess whether current policies to manage coastal flooding are realistic in the context of climate change and national/local value for money and affordability constraints and to identify infrastructure assets at risk if holding current defence lines is economically unrealistic. In response to such challenges, there are calls for the development and implementation of SMPs in Northern Ireland, as in the rest of the UK, to assess and plan for future changes to coastal communities.

There is growing recognition of and support across the UK for embracing alternative adaptive responses to managing coastal change, highlighting an important role for planning in terms of responding to, accommodating, and planning for anticipated and contingent physical change. There are good-practice examples across the UK, not least from the National Trust, which, in line with its policy of a managed coastal retreat, advocates a move away from hard engineering 'solutions' where appropriate. Other National Trust initiatives include the provision of tourism facilities at Portstewart Strand (Northern Ireland) where the building is demountable, allowing it to be moved. Whilst there are examples of innovative adaptive responses at the local level, these remain the exception, not the rule, and what emerges in all these cases is the need for a more collaborative approach so that positive outcomes may be 'scaled up'. The wide-reaching impacts of climate change will necessitate greater cross-border dialogue and coordination.

Coastal management: Coordination and integration

Historically, as previously outlined, disparate pressures on the coastal zone resulted in a reactive, ad hoc approach to policy development, leading to complex and fragmented institutional arrangements across the UK administrations. Coastal management does not lie within the remit of a single authority or organisation, rather there are a range of government departments, semi-government bodies, conservation bodies, and (public and private) organisations responsible for varying aspects of coastal management.

The need to move away from the piecemeal management of the coastal zone and adopt a more strategic and holistic approach has been acknowledged for many years across the UK, perhaps best illustrated by the introduction of ICZM policies and strategies. The UK government adopted the EU's ICZM Recommendation (2002/413/EC), and a separate ICZM strategy was developed for each of the devolved administrations, as outlined in Table 3.3.

Despite the existence of these national ICZM strategies, there is no formal framework for coordination across the UK. Rather, ICZM has been championed at the local level on a relatively ad hoc basis by coastal partnerships (Hewett & Fletcher, 2010). Dedicated coastal partnerships were set up to deliver the coordination aspects of ICZM at the local and/or regional scale through voluntary partnership working between coastal and marine stakeholders.

Table 3.3 ICZM strategies across the UK

Title	Year	Author	Vision / Aims
ENGLAND			
A Strategy for Promoting an Integrated Approach to the Management of Coastal Areas in England	2009	DEFRA	Sustainably managed coastal areas, where competing demands and pressures have been taken into account and the social and economic needs of society have been reconciled with the need for conservation of the natural and historic environment. A clear policy and regulatory framework into which the principles of a holistic and co-ordinated approach are embedded. A new, strategic management approach in the marine environment, which is effectively integrated with the management of the land. More consistent application of the principles of good, holistic and coordinated management around the coast. A management approach that builds on existing structures and responsibilities, whilst encouraging organisations to work better together. A flexible management approach, which supports local initiatives and solutions to address local circumstances, within an overall regulatory framework. Appropriate and effective stakeholder and local community involvement throughout management processes.
WALES			
Making the Most of Wales' Coast	2007	The Welsh Assembly Government	Aims to provide a management framework to facilitate integrated working on the coast by the different interests involved in managing coastal assets, helping to ensure that these assets are maintained and enhanced for the benefit of present and future generations. It also sets out the links that must be made between diverse national and local policies and strategies so that the people involved in managing and using the coast can do so in a way that takes into account the needs of others.
SCOTLAND			
Seas the Opportunity: A Strategy for the Long Term Sustainability of Scotland's Coasts and Aeas	2005	Scottish Executive	Clean, healthy, safe, productive and biologically diverse marine and coastal environments, managed to meet the long term needs of nature and people.

(continued)

Table 3.3 (continued)

Title	Year	Author	Vision / Aims
NORTHERN IRELAND			
An Integrated Coastal zone Management Strategy for Northern Ireland 2006–2026	2006	Department of the Environment (DOE)	A coastal zone which through an ecosystem approach and the sustainable management of natural and built resources supports a vibrant, viable and informed population, and, through sustainable development contributes strongly to the overall economy. Where decisions about development and conservation of the coastline are taken with timely and accurate knowledge of their impacts within the context of the Precautionary Principle, and in an integrated way with all of these people, communities, organisations, and Government Departments with a responsibility or an interest engaged in decisions. Where natural and built resources are protected, maintained, enhanced and promoted through legislation, good practice mechanisms and through the concern and interest of the public, Government, and industry.
Compiled from: DEFRA, 2008; DOE, 2006; Scottish Executive, 2005; Welsh Assembly, 2007			

Indeed, coastal partnerships have been an important component of the informal UK coastal governance framework since the early 1990s and operate at a variety of scales. At the national level, for example, the Scottish Government formed the Scottish Coastal Forum in 1996 to encourage debate on coastal issues. Its members advise Marine Scotland, from an operational perspective, on the development of policy relating to marine planning and licensing and provide a network for circulating information and best practice in coastal management. The Scottish Coastal Forum supports six local coastal partnerships that cover much of the Scottish Coastline.

At the local authority level, the Coastal Communities Alliance was set up by local authorities in England in response to the first Government Response to the House of Common Select Committee Coastal Towns Inquiry. This virtual network consists of over forty local authorities and coastal organisations. It seeks to promote best practice in coastal regeneration and inform policy and funding by providing local evidence and solutions to the challenges facing coastal towns.

In addition, many partnerships have emerged in response to specific localized issues and characteristics, within a defined geographical area by concerned member(s) of the public, illustrating the close connection and concern for coastal matters. The Strangford Lough and Lecale

Partnership (SLLP), for example, coordinates the management of the Strangford and Lecale Area of Outstanding Natural Beauty (AONB) in Northern Ireland. SLLP brings together stakeholders and local interests in an Advisory Committee of 20 organisations and seeks to balance the diverse natural, cultural, and historic heritage of the area with appropriate economic growth and recreational activity. The Strangford Lough Management Scheme was identified as an existing integrated coastal management approach within the NI ICZM strategy (DOE, 2006), which recommended similar schemes for Belfast Lough, as well as Lough Foyle and Carlingford Lough, which share a boundary with the Republic of Ireland. In the context of Brexit, this cooperation becomes even more pertinent.

The extent to which coastal partnerships have delivered integration in coastal governance, and the ability to sustain activities and membership is questionable. Many partnerships have closed in recent years. For example, in 2006, the NI government sets up the Northern Ireland Coastal and Marine Forum (NICMF), a non-statutory body made up of a cross-section of interests, to help monitor the implementation of Northern Ireland's ICZM strategy. This body provided expert advice and support towards the achievement of the strategy's objectives and played an important role in integration by taking a lead in addressing interdepartmental issues for which there is no formal proactive integrative mechanism (Cooper, 2011). However, the Forum has since gone into abeyance. Other partnerships have been able to craft out a specific niche in their local governance context and continue to function. Many are, however, hindered by their voluntary status, limited geographical coverage, and informal role in the overall coastal governance framework. Over-reliance on the local level can cause national governments to evade their responsibilities in supporting such practices. This is evidenced across the UK where central government has acknowledged the successes of local coastal partnerships but has provided limited resources to ensure their longevity or extend their current reach.

Generally, ICZM progress in the UK has been widely criticised (see for example, McKenna et al., 2008) and the extent to which the vision and objectives of the regional strategies (Table 3.3) have been achieved to date is limited. Fletcher et al. (2014) suggest that the momentum surrounding ICZM was hindered by the legislative and policy developments associated with the marine environment and, in particular, the MCAA 2009. The legislation enacted to support the development of MSP in the UK has not fully grasped the opportunity to create a radical restructuring of marine and coastal governance (Boyes & Elliott, 2015). For example, the Coastal Partnerships Working Group (now called the Coastal Partnership Network) was formed during the development of the MCAA 2009 to help provide an umbrella organisation to support coastal partnerships and provide a single voice to lobby government for a formal role for coastal partnerships in the delivery of ICZM and marine planning within England. However, no formal role for coastal partnerships was identified in the MCAA, and the position of coastal partnerships remains ambiguous.

Public participation and access to justice

Engagement in environmental decision-making in the UK is mandated through the EU Directive on public participation in environmental decision-making (European Parliament and the Council of the European Union, 2003), which is based on the Aarhus Convention 1998 on access to information public participation in decision-making, and access to justice in environmental matters. This applies to any plans or programmes relating to the environment.

Within the UK, participation in environmental decision-making is a well-established process, operating mainly through the provisions of the terrestrial planning system in respect to proposed developments and processes such as Sustainability Appraisal and Environmental Impact Assessment. At the time of writing, the future impact of Brexit on environmental legislation is largely unknown. However, it can be assumed that since the UK ratified the Aarhus Convention (which is independent of the EU), the need to provide for public involvement and access will still be recognised.

Public participation in terrestrial land use planning is actively encouraged and facilitated by several policies. In particular, local authorities are required to prepare a Statement of Community Involvement (SCI) outlining how a council proposes to engage the community and stakeholders in exercising its planning functions. Whilst a SCI does not stipulate any special provisions for public participation in the coastal zone, it nevertheless provides an opportunity for the public to shape policies affecting the coast.

The UK has an active environmental and community sector, and there are a number of NGOs with a specific remit relating to coastal management. These organisations provide an important role in identifying issues, gathering evidence, educating local communities, and advocating policy change. Many of these groups focus on the protection and enhancement of the coastal ecosystem, including the work of the Royal Society for the Protection of Birds (RSPB) and Wildlife Trusts. Others have emerged in response to specific coastal management decisions. For example, the second wave of SMPs placed an increased emphasis on adaptive management, provoking a strong reaction from local coastal communities who felt their voice and their concerns were being ignored. Coastal Action Groups (CAGs) subsequently emerged and have become effective pressure groups. CAGs are defined as:

A group of voluntary bodies and stakeholders which seeks as its prime aim to influence actively the decision-making process of management authorities in an attempt to secure social justice in shoreline governance. (Famuditi et al., 2018, p. 271)

Such groups demanded changes in the local policy and called for social justice and compensation. Famuditi et al. (2018) found that CAGs have had limited success in terms of changing the decisions of local SMPs but have effectively challenged the concept of meaningful public engagement in the coastal planning process, leading to more participatory approaches. They have also helped to increase community awareness of coastal issues and generate a collective voice to challenge decision-makers. Some CAGs have also developed links outside their local area to form alliances with other groups and even linkages with the statutory authorities they formerly opposed. In 2008, an umbrella organisation National Voice of Coastal Communities was set up in an effort to improve coordination and cooperation between CAGs and to act as a focus for national campaigningd.

Perhaps one of the largest and most influential NGOs operating in the coastal zone of the UK is the National Trust. Of particular note in this regard is the Neptune Coastline Campaign, which commenced in 1965 and resulted in the National Trust acquiring, to date, land spanning 780 miles along the coastlines of England, Wales, and Northern Ireland. The Trust manages the land to permit public access; for long-term preservation; to provide recreational opportunities; and to respond proactively to coastal change. The Coastal Guardians Scheme encourages primary schools to adopt a stretch of coastline both to learn about the coast and to help the local National Trust warden look after it.

Fiscal aspects: Incentives and disincentives regarding ICZM

The financial arrangements described in this section relate primarily to questions of raising money for coastal management activities and to allow works in response to coastal change (including demolition and land acquisition).

Sustaining coastal partnerships and projects

In the absence of statutory backing, coastal projects and partnerships across the UK proceed via several different bodies, with varying degrees of financial support. The voluntary nature of much of coastal policy, including that relating to ICZM strategies, means there is no obvious economic benefit or disincentive for adopting those policies and strategies. Where specific actions have been taken up by coastal partnerships, funding has traditionally been limited and inconsistent (McGowan, 2011). Coastal Partnerships are generally formed from a mixture of interested stakeholders from local communities, local government, government agencies, the private sector, and academia. They rely on funding from partners, which, in conjunction with their non-statutory position, has been regarded as the key constraint to the delivery of projects (McGowan, 2011).

There are numerous consequences of this precarious financial position and voluntary nature of projects. First, many partnerships have suffered from rapid turnover of project officers and an associated loss of corporate memory, as well as breakdown of relationships with stakeholders and potential funding partners. Second, the situation has led to an uneven geographical spread of relevant active organisations around the UK. For example, a small number of organisations cover geographically large areas in Scotland, whilst a greater number of (smaller) groups have emerged around the English coastline. Furthermore, sources of funding have dictated administrative arrangements. For example, many coastal partnerships in England are funded by LPAs (e.g. the Dorset Coast Forum, the Sefton Coast Partnership, and the East Riding Coastal Forum) and often receive financial support and benefits 'in kind' in the form of office space and support staff. Other partnerships are hosted by university departments due to aligned research interests (e.g. the Colne Estuary Partnership is hosted by Essex University and the East Grampian Coastal Partnership is hosted by the Macaulay Land Use Institute in Aberdeen). Some partnerships have established themselves as charitable organisations (e.g. the Morecambe Bay Partnership and the Solway Firth Partnership). Other sources of funding have included project funding from the European Union and national bodies such as the Environment Agency, DEFRA, MMO, private-sector sponsors, NGOs, and small community grants or charitable funds.

Unlike the stakeholder forum model in the rest of the UK, the Northern Ireland Coastal and Marine Forum (NICMF) was established and resourced by the NI government as a formal part of their response to the ICZM Recommendation. It therefore did not face the problems of sustainability and short-term funding as did other groups at the time, and a direct link between the NICMF and NI government was ensured. Nevertheless, as previously outlined, participation in the NICMF, as for similar groups/forums, was on a voluntary basis and thus reliant on sustained interest and goodwill. The group has since ceased meeting.

The Coastal Communities Fund (CCF) is a UK-wide programme funded by the UK Government that aims to encourage the economic development of coastal communities. The programme is administered and delivered by the Big Lottery Fund. Funding is allocated on a competitive basis for individual projects seeking to create sustainable economic growth and jobs. In 2017, Dumfries and Galloway Council in Scotland was awarded £300,000 from the CCF to establish, amongst other projects, 64 miles of coastal path and to improve public access routes.

Dealing with coastal change

In general, in the UK, there is no compensation scheme for coastal homeowners to allow them to move to a safer location. Similarly, there is no statutory recourse for compensation for property lost or damaged due to coastal changes.

In its 2018 report, the Committee on Climate Change (CCC) argued that current policies on the long-term future of England's coastline are unreliable, as they are non-statutory plans containing unfunded proposals. It calculated that the cost of implementing existing SMPs would be between £18 and £30 billion (depending on rate of climate change) and that it would not be cost beneficial to protect or adapt much of the English coastline. This is alarming as English coastal authorities have proceeded with planning on the basis of protection and adaption, using SMPs as the primary source of evidence in defining Coastal Change Management Areas and informing local land allocation within it.

In recent years, the UK Parliament has increased investment in flood management and protection from coastal erosion, partly in response to an increase in storm surges since 2014. DEFRA states that there are now long-term investment strategies in place for flood defences to protect 15,000 homes by the end of 2020. Most recently, in 2019, the Environment Agency launched a draft National Flood and Coastal Erosion Risk Management Strategy for England for consultation. To manage the costs associated with the loss of homes to erosion, including demolition and removal costs, LPAs may apply for grants from the Environment Agency (acting on behalf of DEFRA). In addition, under the Flood and Water Management Act 2010, Regional Flood Defence Committees (RFDCs) have levy-raising powers, which may be used to fund locally important coastal erosion risk management projects. We present two examples of local solutions in this context.

Example 1: In 2009, DEFRA invited coastal councils in England to apply to an £11 million funded Coastal Change Pathfinder Programme set up to develop and trial ideas for responding to coastal change. North Norfolk District Council was awarded £3 million under the scheme and undertook a number of projects in Happisburgh. Projects included the removal of beach debris; providing beach access; the re-provision of infrastructure, including a car park and public toilets; and the purchase, demolition, and replacement of residential properties predicted to be lost to coastal erosion within a 20-year timeframe. Within the framework of that last project, the council purchased nine residential properties, offering up to 40% of the value of the homes to enable residents to relocate inland. The property owners were thus able to recover value from their properties that were previously considered virtually worthless. Once the owners and occupiers of the properties agreed to the sale, they moved out, leaving the Council in vacant possession. The properties were then demolished, and the area landscaped and made available for informal recreational access. A suitable site for the replacement properties was identified in the town and outline planning consent was granted. The Council's share of the proceeds from the sale of the site have been put into a reserve to be used for future coastal adaptation initiatives.

Example 2: East Riding Council in Yorkshire is taking action in areas where they are unable to build or maintain coastal defences that are at risk of coastal erosion. They offer support to residents who live in 'at risk areas'. The LPA can assist with applying for planning permission for a new dwelling further inland to replace threatened property. They can also replace threatened utility supplies in order to increase the life of properties. Further, the East Riding Coastal Change Fund offers limited financial assistance in the form of relocation packages and adaptation packages. Relocation packages can cover total costs for demolition of property and site restoration and £1,000 towards the cost of moving home. An adaptation package will provide 'rollback', which refunds the cost of planning permission and architect fees if an affected resident decides to move away from a threatened property. There is also a grant for relocating utilities such as septic tanks or property access if the property is not at imminent risk but there is a need for modifications. There is no funding for the cost of buying land or building new property.

The above projects provide just two examples delivered in England to 'test bed' adaptive responses to coastal change and could be considered compensatory. However, in the UK, there is no insurance or compensation for losses from coastal erosion for homeowners to mitigate the risk of losing their properties. The Committee on Climate Change's 2018 report on managing the coast in a changing climate recommended that the Government makes available long-term funding/investment to deliver a wider set of adaptation actions. Funding decisions should also be based on a broader, more inclusive economic case than is current practice to incorporate both environmental and social justice implications and considerations.

Overall assessment

We provide an overview of the key themes discussed throughout this chapter in Table 3.4. Overall, the chapter demonstrates that coastal zone management in the UK is covered by a complex patchwork of legislation and policy guidance across the national, regional, and local spatial scales.

Much of coastal legislation and policy is overseen by the four devolved administrations. England, Wales, Scotland, and Northern Ireland have made progress at different speeds, in response to their respective contextual priorities and issues. In England and Wales, there has been a particular emphasis on securing wider public access to the coastline as a valuable public resource and asset. In contrast, Scotland's coastal management has long been led by concerns regarding the impact of exploitation of marine resources (oil and gas). Northern Ireland lags behind the rest of the UK in terms of moving towards a more integrated approach to coastal management, given its restricted public access to the coast, an absence of long-term coastal plans (e.g. SMPs), and the lack of national climate change legislation. Yet there is hope: The recent reform of public administration and planning means that for the first time in over forty years, local authorities in Northern Ireland have the power to make decisions and introduce appropriate policies for their respective coastlines. We await the first local development plans and local policy plans with anticipation.

Coastal governance across the UK remains complex and is at times fragmented, with inconsistent and ad hoc approaches. Better vertical and horizontal integration across the administrations of the UK, different levels of government, and the various agencies with responsibility for matters affecting coastal areas is required.

Nevertheless, a new era is emerging for coastal zone management in the UK – a result of changing policy priorities and approaches, particularly in the context of marine planning and reforms in terrestrial land use planning. Changes to UK national legislation have the potential to drive positive change within coastal governance, sustainable development, and management.

Table 3.4 Overview of key themes across the UK

Theme	Summary description
Delineation of the coastline and coastal zone	Definitions of the coast are ambiguous and contested across the UK. In line with the discretionary planning system, definitions are unclear in the relevant legislation, normally to allow flexibility in the application of the law. Coastal terminology has been clarified either by case law or within guidance documents, essentially relegating important legislative considerations to matters of administrative discretion. Therefore, there is no agreed definition of the coastline or coastal zone at the national level.
Public ownership	While these is no rule specifically requiring public ownership, two-thirds of the intertidal area and the full extent of UK territorial waters are vested in the Crown and managed by the Crown Estate, which provides for public rights of fishing and navigation and grants general permissive consent for certain uses (e.g. metal detecting). Other activities, such as hand harvesting of seaweed for monetary benefit, require a licence in accordance with the Crown Estate Act 1961. The National Trust (conservation body) is the UK's largest coastal landowner, with around 1,247 km in their care.
Coastal setbacks	There is no defined setback rule in UK legislation or policy, but there are other mechanisms of restricting development on the coast, primarily through terrestrial land use plan instruments; e.g. Coastal Change Management Areas in England and other designations based on heritage and cultural assets (such as Heritage Coasts) and/or environmental importance (e.g. Areas of Outstanding Natural Beauty). SMPs in England, Wales, and, to a lesser extent, Scotland, outline areas at risk of coastal change over 20, 50, and 100 years. There are no SMPs in Northern Ireland. A precautionary approach is advocated in terrestrial planning policy regarding development on the coast. There is generally perceived to be a lack of data and evidence to support decision-making in relation to coastal setbacks.
Accessibility	Provision for public access to the coastal zone is an important element of coastal planning and policy in the UK. Levels of access vary across the jurisdictions. In accordance with the MCAA 2009, the English Coastal Route is being developed around entire coastline (completion due 2022). In accordance with the MCAA 2009, Wales has developed a coastal path around its coastline on a voluntary, partnership approach. Scotland enjoys the most freedoms under 'right to roam'. Public access to the coastal zone is much more restricted in Northern Ireland compared to other UK jurisdictions, with the exception of a limited number of public rights of way.
Urban and regional planning laws and implementation	Terrestrial land use (spatial) planning is a devolved matter in the UK and is implemented by national and LPAs through local development plans. There are varying levels of mandatory versus guiding considerations in planning law. There are similarities across the UK in terms of securing public access, protecting the 'undeveloped' coast, directing new development to the landward side of settlements, and preventing urban ribboning along the coastline.
Illegality and enforcement	It is the responsibility of LPAs to deal with planning enforcement. Illegal development on the coast has tended to be in the form of works for the protection of private property.

(continued)

Table 3.4 (continued)

Theme	Summary description
Climate change awareness	There is a reasonable degree of climate change awareness across public policy agencies and the general public in the UK, as accumulated in the Climate Change Act 2008. There is a gap between policy and practice, however and, in particular, issues with a lack of joined-up working and evidence in relation to coastal change. SMPs in England, Wales, and Scotland provide long-term plans for coastal change but are non-statutory and lack resources. In Northern Ireland, the situation is more fragmented under the antiquated Bateman Formula.
Overall management and coordination	The four administrations of the UK developed their own ICZM strategies following the UK ICZM national stocktake in 2002. There is no overarching strategy. Rather, a diverse range of national, regional, and local bodies have responsibility for certain aspects of coastal governance. Coastal partnerships have traditionally played a key role in advancing coordination. However, inherent problems related to their informal status, limited geographical scope, and inadequate resourcing have restricted their influence.
Public participation	Formal provisions for public participation are set out in terrestrial land use planning systems of the devolved administrations. The UK is a signatory of the Aarhus Convention.
Fiscal aspects	There is no insurance or compensation for losses from coastal erosion for homeowners to mitigate the risk of losing their properties. This has resulted in a reactive approach to coastal change, in particular, the building of hard engineering solutions. LPAs may use compulsory purchase powers, but there is limited government funding to acquire sensitive coastal sites.

The Climate Change Act 2008 and Climate Change (Scotland) Act 2009, for example, represent a growing environmental consciousness and demonstrates an acknowledgement of shifting environmental parameters. Coastal issues, in particular flooding and erosion, have emerged in subsequent Climate Change Assessments as key issues to be addressed in all jurisdictions and there are calls for more up-to-date data and information. Coastal erosion is challenging established fixed land-based assumptions and subsequent planning responses, and there is an established need for local authorities to move beyond time-limited project based initiatives towards more proactive planning approaches to secure the resilience of coastal communities.

Given the historical fragmentation within coastal governance, marine legislation provides an opportunity for improving collaboration, cooperation, and coherence for future coastal management and policy development. However, there is a potential coastal–marine policy squeeze with (predominately economic) marine interests overshadowing coastal management, notably through EU policy and the UK's Marine and Coastal Access Act (2009).

The result of the 2016 European Union referendum ('Brexit') and its implications on the nature of the UKs relationship with the EU will further alter the wider planning and development context. This fluid constitutional context opens up specific concerns at the coastal–marine boundary between Northern Ireland and Ireland. For the most part, basic principles and terminology are similar on the island of Ireland, but there are subtle territorial differences that reflect different sociocultural and development priorities.

As the UK enters this new era of marine and coastal governance, it is perhaps better prepared than ever before. But there is still a way to go.

Notes

1. In Northern Ireland, a number of papers in the mid-1990s – *Coastal Zone Management Policy* (Council for Nature Conservation and the Countryside, 1994) and *Delivering Coastal Zone Management in Northern Ireland* (DOENI, 1995) – called for the gathering of more information on the coastal zone and the setting up of additional area-based management structures in the region.
2. Crown Estate Scotland is a public corporation which manages the assets on an interim basis until new legislation sets out permanent arrangements.
3. Privatisation was a flagship policy of the 'Thatcher years'.
4. The National Trust is Europe's largest conservation organisation. It was set up in 1895 as a charity to protect places of historic or natural beauty in England, Wales, and Northern Ireland.
5. A permissive path is not a public right of way, can operate under limitations, and can endure for as long as the council and landowner are willing to agree.
6. Natural England is an executive non-departmental public body, sponsored by the Department for Environment, Food & Rural Affairs (DEFRA). It is government's adviser for the natural environment in England.
7. Scottish Natural Heritage is a non-departmental public body established in 1992 under the Natural Heritage (Scotland) Act 1991. SNH seeks to promote, care for, and improve Scotland's natural heritage and is the Scottish Government's adviser on all aspects on nature and landscape across the region.
8. Prices are from summer 2018.
9. The Planning Directorate is working on the production of a National Development Framework (NDF). The NDF will set out a 20-year land use framework for Wales and will replace the current Wales Spatial Plan.
10. A material consideration is a matter that should be taken into account in deciding a planning application or on an appeal against a planning decision.
11. Project Neptune is a long-term project of the National Trust to acquire or put under covenant a substantial part of the Welsh, English, and Northern Irish coastline. The Project currently looks after 1,140 km of coastline.
12. 'Devolved matter' – meaning, delegated to devolved administrations.

References

ASC. (2016). *UK Climate Change Risk Assessment 2017 Evidence Report – Summary for Northern Ireland*. Adaptation Sub-Committee of the Committee on Climate Change, London.

Ballinger, R. C. (2016). *A review of terrestrial planning policies relevant to the Welsh National Marine Plan*. A report by the Severn Estuary Partnership/Cardiff University, Cardiff, Available at: http://www.severnestuarypartnership.org.uk/files/2015/10/Full-Project-Summary-FINAL-2016.pdf

Ballinger, R. C., & Dodds, W. (2017). Shoreline management plans in England and Wales: A scientific and transparent process? *Marine Policy* 84

Beatty, C. & Fothergill, S. (2003). The Seaside Economy: the final report of the seaside towns research project, Centre for Regional Economic and Social Research, Sheffield Hallam University.

Cooper, J. A. G. (2011). Progress in integrated coastal zone management (ICZM) in Northern Ireland. *Marine Policy* 35, pp.794–799.

— (2015). *Shoreline management planning in Northern Ireland*. Northern Ireland Assembly. Available at: http://www.niassembly.gov.uk/globalassets/documents/raise/knowledge_exchange/briefing_papers/series4/2015-04-15-kess-shoreline-management-planning-in-northern-ireland1.pdf

CNCC (Council for Nature Conservation and the Countryside). (1994). *Coastal zone management policy*. Belfast, DOENI.

Creed, R., Baily, B., Potts, J., Bray, M., & Austin, R. (2018). Moving towards sustainable coasts: a critical evaluation of a stakeholder engagement group in successfully delivering the mechanism of adaptive management. *Marine Policy* 90, 184–193.

Crawford, J. (2019). The construction of 'coast' in national planning policy. *Town Planning Review* 90(3), 299–320.

Department for Regional Development. (2012). *Shaping Our Future: Regional Development Strategy for Northern Ireland 2035*. Corporate Document Services.

Department of Environment and Welsh Office. (1992). *Planning Policy Guidance: Coastal Planning (PPG 20)*. DoE and Welsh Office.

DEFRA (Department for Environment, Food and Rural Affairs). (2002). *Safeguarding Our Seas: A Strategy for the Conservation and Sustainable Development of Our Marine Environment*. London, Defra. Available at: http://www.defra.gov.uk/marine/pdf/environment/marine_stewardship.pdf

— (2004). *ICZM in the UK: A Stocktake*. Report by WS Atkins for DEFRA. London, Available at: http://archive.defra.gov.uk/environment/marine/documents/protected/iczm/st-full-report.pdf.

— (2006). *Shoreline Management Plan Guidance: Vol 1: Aims and Requirements*. London, Defra. Available at: https://assets.publishing.service.gov.uk/government/uploads/system/uploads/attachment_data/file/69206/pb11726-smpg-vol1-060308.pdf

— (2009). *A Strategy for Promoting and Integrated Approach to the Management of Coastal Areas in England*. DEFRA.

— (2013). *A Coastal Concordat for England*. Available at: https://www.gov.uk/government/publications/a-coastal-concordat-for-england.

DOE (Department of the Environment). (1992). *Planning Policy Guidance (PPG) 20: The Coast*. DEFRA.

DOE (NI). (1995) Delivering Coastal Zone Management in Northern Ireland. A consultation paper published by Environment Service on behalf of Government in Northern Ireland.

DOE (Department of the Environment Northern Ireland). (2006). *Towards an Integrated Coastal Zone Management Strategy for Northern Ireland*. Department of the Environment.

— (2015). *Strategic Planning Policy Statement for Northern Ireland*. Department of the Environment. Available at: http://www.planningni.gov.uk/spps

Environment Agency. (2019). Draft National Flood and Coastal Erosion Risk Management Strategy for England. Available at: https://www.gov.uk/government/consultations/draft-national-flood-and-coastal-erosion-risk-management-strategy-for-england

Famuditi, T., Bray, M., Potts, J., Baily B. and Inkpen, K. (2018). Adaptive management and community reactions: the activities of Coastal Action Groups (CAGs) within the shoreline management process in England, *Marine Policy*, 97, 270–277.

Fletcher, S., Jefferson, R., Glegg, G., Rodwell, L., & Dodds, W. (2014). England's evolving marine and coastal governance framework. *Marine Policy* 45, 261–268.

Gibson, J. (1993). Coastal zone planning law: Role of law in management of the coastal zone in England and Wales. *Marine Policy* 17(2), 118–129.

Gubbay, S. (2002). *Just Coasting: An Assessment of the Commitment of the Devolved Administrations and the English Regions to Integrated Coastal Management*. A report to the Wildlife Trusts and WWF. Godalming, WWF-UK Available at: http://assets.wwf.org.uk/downloads/just_coasting.pdf

Hansard. (1963). Seaward Boundary of River Authority Areas. House of Lords, UK Parliament.

Hansom, J.D., Lees, G., McGlashan, D.J., & John, S. (2004). Shoreline management plans and coastal cells in Scotland. *Coastal Management* 32, 227–242.

Hewett, T., & Fletcher, S. (2010). The emergence of service-based integrated coastal management in the UK. *Area* 42(3), 313–327.

HM Government. (2011). UK Marine Policy Statement. The Stationary Office.

House of Commons Communities and Local Government Committee. (2006). *Coastal Towns: Second Report of Session 2006–07 HC351*. TSO.

House of Commons Environment Select Committee. (1992). *Coastal Zone Protection and Planning*. HMSO.

Jay, S. (2010). Marine management and the construction of marine spatial planning. *Town Planning Review* 81(2), 173–191.

MMO (Marine Management Organisation). (2011). *Maximising the Socio-economic Benefits of Marine Planning for English Coastal Communities*. Tym & Partners.

McElduff, L., Peel, D., & Lloyd, M. G. (2013). Informing a collaborative framework for coastal planning on the island of Ireland. *Town Planning Review* 84(4): 397–418.

McGlashen, D. J., Duck, R. W., & Reid, C. T. (2004). The Foreshore: geographical implications of the 3 legal systems in Great Britain. *Area* 36(4), 338–347.

McGowan, L. (2011). *Practice and prospects for integrated coastal zone management in the UK* (unpublished PhD thesis). University of Liverpool.

McKenna, J., Cooper, A., & O'Hagan, A. M. (2008). Managing by principle: A critical analysis of the European Principles of Integrated Coastal Zone Management (ICZM). *Marine Policy* 32, 941–955.

Ministry for Housing, Communities and Local Government (MHCLG). (2018). (Revised) National Planning Policy Framework (NPPF). Available at: https://www.gov.uk/government/collections/revised-national-planning-policy-framework.

National Trust. (2015). Mapping our shore: 50 years of land use change at the coast. Available at: https://nt.global.ssl.fastly.net/documents/mapping-our-shores-fifty-years-of-land use-change-at-the-coast.pdf

National Tidal and Sea Level Facility. (2019). All about Tides. Available at: https://www.ntslf.org/about-tides/tides

Scottish Executive. (2005). *Seas the Opportunity: A Strategy for the Long Term Sustainability of Scotland's Coasts and Seas*. The Scottish Executive.

Scottish Government. (2010). *Scottish Planning Policy: A Statement of the Scottish Government's Policy on Nationally Important Land Use Planning Matters*. The Scottish Government.

— (2014a). *National Planning Framework (NPF)*. The Scottish Government.

— (2014b). *Scottish Planning Policy*. The Scottish Government.

Scottish Office. (1997). *National Planning Policy Guidance: Coastal Planning (NPPG 13)*. Scottish Office.

— (1998). *Planning Advice Note 53 – Classifying the Coast for Planning Purposes*. HMSO.

Sheppard, A., Peel, D., Ritchie, H., & Berry, S. (2017). *The Essential Guide to Planning Law: Decision-Making and Practice in the UK*. Policy Press.

Taussik, J. 2007. The opportunities of spatial planning for integrated coastal management. *Marine Policy* 31, 611–618.

Walton, J.K. (2010). Regeneration policies and their impact on coastal areas, in: J.K. Walton & P. Brown (Eds) *Coastal Regeneration in English Resorts - 2010*, Lincoln: Coastal Communities Alliance.

Welsh Assembly Government. (2007). *Making the Most of Wales Coast*. Welsh Government.

— (2008). *Wales Spatial Plan (WSP): People, Places, Futures*. Welsh Government.

— (2016). *Planning Policy Wales*. Welsh Government.

Welsh Office. (1998). *Planning Guidance (Wales), Technical Advice Note (Wales) 14, Coastal Planning*. Welsh Government.

World Factbook. (n.d.). United Kingdom. Available at: https://www.cia.gov/library/publications/the-world-factbook/geos/uk.html [Accessed September 2019].

Zsamboky, M., Fernandez-Bilbao, A., Smith, D., Knight, J., & Allen, J. (2011). *Impacts of Climate Change on Disadvantaged UK Coastal Communities*. York: Joseph Rowntree Foundation.

Legislation (listed chronologically)

Lincolnshire County Council (Sandhills) Act 1932
Town and Country Planning Act 1947
Coast Protection Act 1949
Caravan Sites and Control of Development Act 1960
Crown Estate Act 1961
Local Government Act 1972
Acquisition of Land Act 1981
Government of Wales Act 1998

Northern Ireland Act 1998
Scotland Act 1998
Countryside and Rights of Way Act 2000
Land Reform (Scotland) Act 2003
Climate Change Act 2008
Climate Change (Scotland) Act 2009
Marine and Coastal Access Act 2009
Flood and Water Management Act (England and Wales) 2010

English High Court cases

Argyll and Bute District Council *v* Secretary of State for Scotland [(1976) SC 248
Boggis and Anor, R (on the application of) *v* Natural England and Anor [2009] JPL 729
RLT Built Environment Ltd *v* Cornwall Council [2016] EWHC 2817

4   The Netherlands

Pieter Jong and Hendrik van Sandick

Overview

More than half of the Dutch territory is flood prone, being below sea level and vulnerable to flooding from the major rivers. Thus, protection against flooding is a key defining issue in the Netherlands, significantly affecting its approach to coastal zone management. In the wake of a catastrophic storm surge disaster in 1953, the Dutch developed legislation and strategies for the management of the Delta and constructed substantial flood defences. That 1953 event, together with smaller-scale events in 1993 and 1995 around the major rivers, has led to strong public awareness and political pressure concerning the necessity of planning for coastal areas.

Nevertheless, current spatial planning legislation in the Netherlands provides local authorities with significant leeway to approve some types of development on the coast. The key precondition is that developments do not hinder the primary function of the flood defence structures. Recently proposed changes to the spatial planning regulations will expand the range of permitted development in coastal areas. The relative freedom granted to local authorities in approving developments has been the subject of significant public debate in recent years, as members of civil society seek a more consistent and wide-reaching approach to the protection of coastal areas.

Introduction to Dutch coastal issues: Struggle against the forces of nature

The Dutch have a saying: '*God created the Earth, but the Dutch created Holland*'. Centuries ago, the Dutch began to build dikes and polders to protect their low-lying land. They used windmills to pump water from low polders to the rivers and canals, from which it flows to the sea. Another Dutch saying – '*I struggle and I will overcome*' (in Latin: *Luctor et emergo*) – refers both to the historic struggle of the Dutch against Spain and to the struggle of the Dutch against the threatening waves of the sea. The Dutch have built flood defences and have succeeded in their struggle to this point. But the struggle is an ongoing process and climate change increasingly presents new challenges.

Flooding from sea and rivers

More than half of the Dutch territory and population, including 60% of economic activities, is flood prone, as the land is below sea level and vulnerable to flooding from the major rivers (OECD, 2014, p. 35). As such, protection against flooding is imperative. The country has been impacted by numerous serious floods. The disastrous sea flood caused by storm surges in 1953 saw 200,000 hectares of land inundated, 2,000 human casualties, and the loss of approximately 100,000 animals. The most recent serious flood occurred in 1995 and originated from river waters. But the risk is ever-present. A worse-case scenario for flooding from the sea bordering the province of South Holland forecasts more than 30,000 casualties and damage totalling over 30 billion euros (Rijkswaterstaat Waterdienst, 2010). On a national scale, the worst case is that one-third of the country could be flooded.

The 1953 storm surge disaster very much shaped current Dutch flood management system (Aerts et al., 2011). This flooding disaster created a sense of urgency which resulted in the government establishing a Delta Advisory Commission (1953–1960) that prepared an action plan to protect the country against flooding (Delta Plan, 1955). The core of this Delta Plan was a list of so-called 'Delta Works', i.e. the building of new dams and dikes to strengthen the southwestern coastline (Watersnoodmuseum, n.d.). The building of the Delta Works listed in the action plan began in 1958 and was completed in 1997; structural faults in coastal dikes were repaired by 2010 and in the dunes by 2016.

The storm surge events of 1993 and 1995 originated from river waters and stimulated the establishment of a second Delta Advisory Commission (2008). The second Delta Commission had a much broader focus than the first. Whereas the first Delta Commission focused on the dikes (flood defence structures), the second Delta Commission looked at the broad question of how to maintain the Netherlands as a climate-proof and attractive country to live in safely protected against flooding (Van der Most, 2010, p. 15).

The flooding in the area of the major rivers resulted in new legislation (Delta Act Major Rivers, 1995). In addition, a budget of two billion euros was dedicated to a 'river-widening' plan to raise the discharge capacity of the main Dutch rivers (Van den Brink, 2009, p. 135). These flooding events also raised awareness among politicians and the general public about the necessity of water and climate-proof spatial planning (Hendriks and Buntsma, 2009, p. 146–147).

The Netherlands has a long history with regulation regarding flood protection and other water-related issues. In 2009, the Water Act was drafted as an amalgamation of eight previous laws related to water management, water quality, and groundwater. The Water Act sets objectives and standards for flood defence structures. It also introduced the National Water Plan, which includes the national Flood Risk Management Plan based on the EU Floods Directive.

In 2012, the old Delta Act (1958) and the Delta Act Major Rivers (1995) were superseded by a new Delta Act. The accompanying Delta Programme sets out how the Netherlands will adapt to climate change (Dutch government, 2015, p. 9). Central government, provinces, water authorities, and municipalities have drawn up a joint plan in an effort to ensure that robust and climate-proof design is incorporated into flood management policy and implementation.

Challenges and competing interests on coastal land

Dutch coastal land is under threat – not only from future flood events but also from sea level rise caused by climate change. These threats are compounded by high residential density: The Netherlands has a population of about 17 million inhabitants and a land area of approximately 34,000 km^2 (World Factbook, n.d.) – a population density of 500 people per square kilometre. The country's coastline, which is along the North Sea, is 451 km long (World Factbook, n.d.). It is characterized by broad dune areas, dams, and dikes in the Southern Delta and in the bio-diverse Wadden Sea area in the North. The Dutch coast draws tourists from the Netherlands,

Germany, and across Europe. It is also a magnet for property developers seeking to develop recreational homes and parks in the coastal zone.

Apart from flood defences, tourism, and development, the Dutch coast is also home to several additional economic activities. These include, for example, the port of Rotterdam (Europe's largest port), industry (e.g. Tata Steel Industries), fisheries, hotels, and recreational bathing beaches. Dutch spatial planning law works to balance these interests, but for decades, planning law did not explicitly take specific water interests into account. Spatial planning was generally regarded as the process to balance all kinds of interests: Why should 'water-related interests' be given special attention or considered as more important compared with other specific interests? This changed in 2003, with the introduction of the Water Assessment policy, which required that water interests be explicitly considered in the preparation of spatial plans. Later, in 2011, flood defence functions were regulated in the General Spatial Planning Rules as the primary functions which other uses (secondary functions) had to consider. Multifunctional use of flood defences is only allowed insofar as it does not hinder the primary function (Jong & Van den Brink, 2013).

Dutch coastal policy and regulation

The Dutch struggle against the threats of the waters (sea and main rivers) has long acted as a stimulant for cooperation. In the Middle Ages, the farmers and lords united to build dikes to protect their low-lying farmland (polders). The tendency to resolve conflicts through broad agreements is known as the Dutch polder model. The polder model is also evident in the way that policies and plans are made.

Dutch coastal policy and regulation has a long history, which is summarized at Table 4.1 at the end of this chapter. It has four key dimensions: (i) water governance; (ii) spatial planning; (iii) nature conservation; and (iv) delta management.

Water governance

The oldest government organisation in the Netherlands is the Water Authority. Long before the State of the Netherlands existed, farmers developed local organisations to protect their farmland (dikes, mills, polders, etc.). Dutch water management started 'bottom up': First the farmers, later the regional water authorities (water boards), and later the national water authority.

The national government manages the 'main water systems' (the territorial part of the North Sea, the main rivers, and the Wadden Sea). As such, the water management unit of the Ministry of Infrastructure and Water Management (known as *Rijkswaterstaat*) is responsible for preserving the basic coastline and manages the major flood defence structures along the coast.

All other water systems (regional and local waters) and the non-primary flood defences are managed by the regional water authorities. The regional water authorities, also called 'water boards', are known as the oldest form of democratic government in the Netherlands. They existed centuries before the creation of the State. The regional water authority of Rhine Land, established in 1232, is the oldest regional water authority which still functions to this day (Dutch Water Authorities, 2017).

The total management cost for the water system in the Netherlands amounts to around €3 billion per year. Since 2014, the regional water authorities and the national government have jointly funded the primary flood defences managed by the regional water authorities, in a 50/50 ratio. The joint funding is regulated by the Water Act.[1]

Spatial planning

The Netherlands is a strongly decentralized country. Although central (State) government has established some spatial planning frameworks, the State leaves a lot of room for development to municipalities and provinces, particularly since the Spatial Planning Act was adopted in 2008. The most important and legally binding spatial plan is the municipal land use plan.

Nature conservation

Sensitive natural areas along the Dutch coast are protected by the Nature Conservation Act 2017, but most nature protection policy has been decentralized to the provinces. Provincial authorities set rules and regulations for their respective jurisdictions. They are also responsible for environmental permits in protected areas. Central government remains responsible for policy on major water bodies (including the North Sea) and international nature conservation policy.

Delta management

As outlined above, delta management began in the 1950s. A new wave of delta management in the Netherlands began about 10 years ago. The introduction of climate change scenarios played an important role in this context. Today, the Delta Plan, Delta Fund, and Delta Commissioner are strong institutions which protect safe spatial development of the Dutch coast in the context of flooding and climate change risks.

The Dutch coastal (foundation) zone: Definition and regulation

The national Coastal Policy (2007) defines the Coastal (Foundation) Zone as follows:

> The Coastal (Foundation) Zone consists of the whole of coastal sea, beaches, sea dikes, dunes and sea dikes and the landward strip with a functional or cultural relationship with the coast. In the Coastal Foundation Zone are also situated: coastal towns, harbours, industrial areas, nature reserves and valuable landscapes.

The National Spatial Policy Document (VROM, 2006) and the national Coastal Policy (Dutch government, 2007) describe the borders of the Coastal Foundation Zone as follows:

The seaward boundary is at the –20 m NAL line (20 m under Normal Amsterdam Level; in Dutch: NAP). Landwards, the Coastal Foundation Zone includes all dunes and sea flood defences (both 'soft' and 'hard' defences) and land to be required for flood defence works in anticipation of a 200-year sea level rise. These measures are determined by data and estimates from the Royal Netherlands Meteorological Institute (KNMI) – the Dutch national weather service. Whenever there are Nature Conservation Act areas or Natura 2000 sites that are part of the Ecological Network and these adjoin the edge of the dunes or defence structures, the boundaries of the Coastal Foundation Zone follow the boundaries of the relevant conservation areas.

The sandy part of the Dutch coastal zone has a dynamic character in that the dynamics of the interaction between sea, sand, and wind may cause a 'moving' coastline (De Ruig, 1998).

To prevent loss of land, sand is replenished on a regular basis. Sand replenishment aims at preserving the sand balance along the Dutch coast (Dutch government, 2016, p. 54). Protection of the coastline and sand replenishment falls under the responsibility of the Ministry of

Infrastructure and Water Management. The State is obliged to prevent recession of the coastline, insofar as is necessary for the sake of flood defence (Water Act, Section 2.7).

The General Spatial Planning Rules (2011) include a map in GML (Geography Markup Language) format which sets out the boundaries of the Coastal Foundation Zone.

Public ownership of the Coastal Foundation zone

According to the Dutch Civil Code,[2] the State owns the seabed (Book 5, Section 25). The State is also presumed to be the owner of beaches, up to the foot (seaward side) of the sand dunes (Book 5, Section 26), unless other claimants brings proof of ownership of any part of that land. The extent of publicly owned land is delineated on the Dutch cadastre. There are no legal restrictions on ownership of the dunes and beyond. Significantly, most policies and regulations pertaining to the coastal zone apply regardless of ownership patterns.

The State, nature conservation organizations, and drinking water companies (which are all publicly owned in the Netherlands) own a significant proportion of the dunes. In urban areas, parts of flood defence structures, including dunes and dikes, are often privately-owned.

Definition of the beach

We refer to the 'beach' throughout this chapter. The beach is not defined in national law or policy, but rather in municipal bylaw of coastal towns. Municipal descriptions of the beach include the shoreline, the sand dunes, and parts of the surrounding roads and paths which provide access to the shore.

Is the coastal zone accessible?

In the Netherlands every beach is publicly accessible. The Pact on the Coast (February 2017) mentions the Dutch coast as the largest freely accessible area of the Netherlands. But the mode of access is restricted: Most municipal ordinances forbid the use of vehicles on the beach without a permit.

Beyond the beach, there is no guarantee of accessibility. Owners who are public bodies, such as drinking water companies and nature conservation organizations, generally grant limited access to pedestrians. The dunes accommodate an elaborate system of public footpaths and cycle paths for recreational purposes.

Another aspect of accessibility is access to views. The General Spatial Planning Rules (2011) contain a specific rule to protect the view of the horizon when looking towards the sea. A land use plan may not permit activities which obstruct the view of the horizon from the mean high-water mark (Section 2.3.2). According to the explanatory notes to the General Spatial Planning Rules (2011), the exact location of the mean high-water mark is to be determined according to the most recent topographical maps published by the Cadastre (the Dutch Land Registry and Mapping Agency).

Regulating flood defence structures

As mentioned above, flood defence is a key aspect of Dutch law and policy for the coastal area. In this section, we expand on the key regulations relating to flood defence structures.

According to the Water Act, flood defence structures must be stable and tall enough to withstand a flood. In 2017, new standards for flood protection were laid down in the Water Act.

The Dutch flood standards from before 2017 were based on the probability of a flood given a certain water level that can be expected during an extreme storm event. The new flood standards are risk-based, requiring protection from 1:100,000-year probability floods for every citizen living behind levees or dunes. By 2050, all flood defence structures involved must meet the failure probability standard that has been derived from the maximum allowable flood risk. The national flood defence system is divided into 200 levee sections. For every levee section, a certain failure standard is specified in the Water Act, ranging from 1:300 to 1:1000,000. The flood protection standards are specified in Annexes to the Water Act (Section 2.2).

The Water Act provides special procedures for the construction or modification of any water management structure. The relevant water management authority must adopt a project plan for construction. If that project plan does not comply with the existing binding land use plan, and the municipality refuses to grant an exemption from the land use plan, the Provincial Executive can overrule the municipality. In practice, the Water Authority and municipality tend to agree on flood structures so, as far as we know, this power has not been used.

Regulating use of the Coastal Foundation Zone

The General Spatial Planning Rules (2011) contain provisions to ensure that flood defence structures are taken into consideration whenever a binding land use plan or an exemption from that plan is prepared. Land can have multiple functions simultaneously, but the legislator defines the 'flood defence function' as the primary function. Any land area that functions as a primary flood defence structure should be designated in any new land use plans as 'flood defence structure' (Section 2.3.3). Nevertheless, land use plans may allow new development on land use used for flood defence, but only on the condition that the development does not hinder

Figure 4.1 Beach near Zoutelande: Free public access, recreational beach cabins, and dunes for flood defence

Source: Anna & Michal. CC BY-SA 2.0 license. Available at: https://www.flickr.com/photos/michalo/5947043608/

the maintenance and upgrading of the sandy part of the coast foundation of the primary flood defence structure (Section 2.3.4).[3]

The General Spatial Planning Rules forbid new land use plans which allow development in the Coastal Foundation Zone outside urban areas (Section 2.3.5, subsection 1). However, subsections 2 and 3 contain significant exceptions to this prohibition. Importantly, the prohibition does not apply to (a) buildings for temporary or seasonal activities and (b) reconstruction or renovation of an existing building through a one-time extension of the ground surface by up to 10%. In addition, works for telecommunications and works to improve the Coastal Foundation (flood defence works) are exempted (and thus permitted). Ultimately, all land uses in the coastal zone are regulated through municipal land use plans or municipal ordinances.

Spatial planning

Spatial planning in the Netherlands is very elaborate (you could call it a national hobby) and influential. One of the characteristics of planning in the Netherlands is that it operates in a decentralized manner: The State provides a national framework, but municipalities have significant decision-making powers. Although spatial planning and water management are interconnected through policy and legislation at the national level, tensions do arise between the need for flood defence and competing land uses.

At the national level, the Spatial Planning Act (SPA, 2008) prescribes that the government (national or provincial) must adopt 'Structure Visions', which are broad policy documents which guide development but are not binding on lower levels of government (Section 2.3). Both National Water Policy plans and National Spatial Policy plans are Structure Visions. But given the strategic and non-binding nature of these documents, they do not restrict specific development outcomes.

At the province level, all provincial councils have adopted Structure Visions based on the Spatial Planning Act, often not only for spatial planning but also for the environment, including water (Section 2.2). In addition, all provinces have adopted provincial orders which contain binding rules regarding the content of local land use plans.

At the municipal level, each municipality must adopt land use plans for the whole of the municipality (which includes the beach). These plans can designate land and water use and limit development outcomes. Before adopting a land use plan, each municipality must carry out a water assessment and consult with the regional water authority, the province, and the relevant ministries. A land use plan must comply with the national General Spatial Planning Rules and provincial planning rules, unless an exemption is granted. A local land use plan is binding, but developers may seek exemptions on a case-by-case basis.

As outlined in the previous section, there are General Spatial Planning Rules which apply explicitly to the coastal zone. But provinces and municipalities may provide exemptions from those Rules if their policy interests are unreasonably impacted. Nevertheless, official exemptions are quite rare. An example is an exemption granted to the Harlingen municipality on the Wadden Sea in 2016 for redevelopment of the local harbour (IenM, 2016).

Over the years, State control over new development along the coast has become less stringent, giving more scope for municipalities to develop the coastal area, under certain conditions. To illustrate this point, we bring the example of the land use plan for Scheveningen Harbour (city of The Hague), adopted in 2013. The land use plan allows development of a five-star hotel with a maximum height of 90 m at the intersection of the sea, dunes, and Scheveningen Harbour. The building may be constructed with its foundations reaching the bottom of the sea and be accessible from the promenade. This kind of permission is quite rare. The explanatory notes to the land use plan indicate that the special permission to develop came only after an extensive assessment and consultation with the provincial council, the regional water authority (Water Assessment), and the Ministry of Infrastructure and Water Management. The effects of the plan on nature conservation goals, wind disturbance, and nautical activities were also assessed. The outcomes of these consultations and assessments were then incorporated into the plan. For example, it was explicitly regulated that the floor level of the first storey of the hotel had to be at least 8 m above sea level. Despite the allowance for the hotel, the plan makes sure to designate the Coastal Foundation Zone as 'Water – Flood Defences' to ensure preservation. This example shows that the Coastal Foundation Zone may be developed for additional functions that fully respect the primary function of the site (i.e. flood defence).

Public participation, awareness, and debate

Dutch law requires that the public be afforded the opportunity to participate in the making of land use plans (Spatial Planning Act, Section 3.9) and in decisions regarding exemptions from land use plans (Environmental Licencing (General Provisions) Act 2010, Section 3.10). The public must also be allowed to participate in the preparation of Structure Visions (Spatial Planning Decree, Section 2.1.1).

There are no special participation provisions for planning or policymaking for the coastal zone. However, Dutch environmental NGOs have a special and significant influence on the public discourse relating to coastal issues. This was demonstrated in a case known as the Dutch Baywatchers case. The story is as follows:

In December 2015, the Minister of Infrastructure and the Environment released a draft revision to the General Spatial Planning Rules (Dutch parliament, 2016a). As outlined in the explanatory notes to the draft Rules, the Minister's intention was that a new National Vision on the Coast would provide more scope for provincial and local governments to consider development in the Coastal Foundation Zone. As such, the draft amendment proposed that the general prohibition on development should be removed from the General Spatial Planning Rules. Yet to guarantee flood defence, the rules would still only allow development in the Coastal Foundation Zone if the proposal met flood defence requirements.

The authors of the draft Rules also justified the amendment by citing the principle of decentralization laid down in the Structure Vision Infrastructure and Spatial Planning (IenM, 2012). They noted that 'spatial quality' (which denotes a combination of physical, social, and environmental values protected by planning regulations)[4] is no longer a State responsibility, but rather the responsibility of municipalities and provinces (IenM, 2015, p. 7). Thus, the proposal was to transfer all responsibilities for spatial quality of the coast to the provinces and municipalities.

In response to the draft Rules, several environmental NGOs[5] promptly came together to start what was known as the Baywatch Action. Their main concern was that the extreme decentralization proposals would jeopardize the overall vision for protection of the coastal zone, leading to accelerated development. The Baywatch Action included a petition: 'Protect the Coast'. Within one week after the petition went online,[6] it garnered over 100,000 signatures.

The draft Rules were debated in the Dutch parliament on 21 January 2016. Representatives of parties from across the political spectrum argued against the proposal. The Labor and Liberal-Democratic parties argued for protection of the coast as a resource of national importance; the Liberal Party advocated for provisions which would limit development along the coast; and the Party for the Protection of Animals sought to introduce a new legislative paradigm which would protect not only environmental and recreational values of the coast but also values such as 'silence', 'darkness', and landscape quality (Dutch parliament, 2016b).

These opponents of the draft Rules brought several examples of existing developments to support their claim that greater, not lesser, protection of the coast was needed at the national level. Examples cited include building in the dunes of Cadzand; a huge recreational park in the Nolle Forest in Vlissingen; a 150 m high tower at Veerse Dam; and permanent beach houses in Kamperland. In response, the Minister for Infrastructure and the Environment claimed that the new Rules would facilitate economic development without compromising on flood defence and spatial quality. She noted that in the development process for the National Coastal Strategy (IenW, 2013), several stakeholders had sought further opportunities for development which would serve tourism, recreational, and economic purposes. Yet ultimately, the Minister concluded that there was not enough political support for the draft Rules. She thus initiated a consultation process with environmental NGOs, municipalities, and provinces.

In parallel with the ongoing consultation process, in June 2016, one of the largest environmental NGOs in the Netherlands, Nature Monuments, conducted a research project about buildings and building projects on parts of the Dutch coast.[7] The study focused on the area within a 1.5 km strip inland from the beach.[8] The research findings were dramatic: In the previous three years, 1,866 villas, apartments, beach houses, hotel rooms, and marinas had been built between Cadzand (a southern village on the Dutch coast) and Den Helder (a northern town on the Dutch coast). An additional 6,277 new developments were permitted by land use plans. Within 6 years from the publication of the study, 8,143 new developments were expected within the Dutch coastal area. The conclusion reached by Nature Monuments was that it would not be wise to leave regulation of the coastal zone to provinces and municipalities, as this could lead to overdevelopment of the coast. They sought a stronger commitment from all levels of government to ensure protection of the natural and recreational values of the Dutch coast.

The Minister's consultation process, perhaps assisted by the Nature Monuments report, has yielded results. In February 2017, a Pact on the Coast (henceforth, the Coastal Pact), which had been developed in consultation with over 60 stakeholders (NGOs, provinces, and municipalities), was adopted. The result of this Coastal Pact was an explicit description of collective core values regarding the spatial quality of the coast of the provinces of Zeeland, South Holland, and North Holland. At its core is a recognition that the national interests of water safety (flood defence), nature conservation, and fresh water supply must be met as a precondition for allowing development in the coastal zone. In other words, if the interests of flood defence, nature conservation, and fresh water supply are accounted for, further development in the coastal zone may be permitted.

The province of Friesland, with its unique wetlands on the Wadden Sea, has opted to continue its restricted policy regarding recreational buildings in the coastal zone. But the other three provinces aim to allow for 'recreational buildings' in their coastal areas if the above precondition is met. In the context of the Pact, recreational buildings include those used for tourist accommodation or for serving or preparing food and drink.

These outcomes demonstrate that the Baywatch Action was successful and that environmental NGOs have significant political influence. Before the Baywatch Action began, the minister of Infrastructure and the Environment intended to shift the responsibility for 'spatial quality' completely to provinces and municipalities. A remarkable outcome of the lengthy and intense debate that followed in the Dutch Baywatchers case was that the Minister proposed to regulate a definition of spatial quality in the next revision of the General Spatial Planning Rules, which took place in May 2020. Thus, the core qualities and collective values of the Coastal Foundation Zone are now included in the General Spatial Planning Rules. These values include an unobstructed view; the natural dynamics of the coastal system; robust water management; contrast between compact built-up areas and expanses of undeveloped areas; contrast between Coastal Foundation and hinterland; the unique characteristics of coastal towns; and specific usage qualities (Dutch government, 2020). In addition, provinces will be obliged to further regulate to preserve these core qualities and collective values of the Coastal Foundation by ordinance. Provincial ordinances must contain rules regarding the content of land use plans and decisions to deviate from a land use plan concerning recreational building.

Parties of the Coastal Pact have sought to find a balance between preservation of the unspoilt coast and allowing some development on the coast. All authorities involved express the intention to prohibit new recreational buildings on the dunes and the beach. An exception is made for building plans for which agreements have already been made in conjunction with a land use plan, permit, or other agreement; building plans where such agreements apply are still possible. In line with the Coastal Pact, all buildings along the coast must be located strictly in designated zones. There is no room for new recreational buildings outside these designated zones. The zones are laid down in maps attached to the provincial ordinances.

Compliance and enforcement

Illegal development is not common in the Netherlands. Particularly in the coastal zone, the public and NGOs are very active in monitoring development. If a developer dares to lay the foundations for any new development which has not been approved, chances are very high that a concerned citizen – a 'Baywatcher' – will quickly discover the illegal activity and report it to the authorities.

In the case of illegal development, the Dutch authorities may start a procedure to have it removed, by issuing a directive to the owner (General Administrative Law Act, Sections 5:21 and 5:32). If the owner does not comply within a given timeframe, the authorities may carry out demolition at the former's expense. To end illegal uses, municipalities often choose to impose a penalty payment.

The problem of illegal use of vacation homes

Though illegal development is rare, this is certainly not the case with the illegal use of legally constructed buildings. On the coast, there has historically been a prevailing problem of illegal permanent occupation of vacation homes.

The attraction of vacation homes is understandable: On average, vacation homes are much cheaper to build than regular homes. In addition, they are usually located in attractive areas with natural values, including the coast. Thus, although most land use plans prohibit permanent living in vacation homes, this rule is often broken. Historically, local enforcement agencies have not prioritized this issue, allowing the inhabitants of coastal vacation homes to enjoy living there permanently. In addition, given that it can be difficult to prove the permanent use of these homes, municipalities would usually wait until informants from the general public reported the illegality.

The matter reached the Dutch parliament in 2003, where it engendered intense debate. The outcome of those debates was that the government decided that municipalities can allow for the permanent use of vacation homes, under certain conditions (Dutch parliament, 2002a; 2002b). If permanent use is not allowed under that arrangement, owners can sometimes obtain an environmental permit.[8] The conditions of such permits include full accordance with all relevant housing and environmental legislation, as well as a requirement that the occupant has lived in the vacation home uninterruptedly since 31 October 2003. The permit must specify that it is only valid for the duration that the occupant lives in that home uninterruptedly. Such a permit is strictly granted to individuals and cannot be sold or inherited.

Climate change action and awareness

Climate change adaptation in the Netherlands is coordinated primarily in conjunction with the Delta Programme. On 1 January 2012, the Dutch Delta Act entered into force. This Act forms the legal basis of the Delta Programme, the Delta Fund, and the Delta Commissioner.[9] The Delta Programme sets out how the Netherlands will adapt to climate change with respect to the water issues (Dutch government, 2015). Central government, provinces, water authorities, and municipalities have drawn up a joint plan to monitor how water-robust and climate-proof design is incorporated into their policy and implementation.

The Delta Commissioner oversees the Delta Programme. They act under the direct responsibility of the coordinating cabinet minister, the Minister of Infrastructure and Water Management. The Commissioner provides advice to all relevant cabinet ministers and may participate in the advisory council of the Council of Ministers. Every year, the Delta Commissioner presents an updated version of the Delta Programme to Parliament (Jong & Van den Brink, 2013, pp. 7–8). The Delta Fund consists of a budget earmarked for the projects in the Delta Programme.

The Delta Decision on Spatial Adaptation (2014) sets the ambitious goal of ensuring that the Netherlands is 'water-robust' and 'climate-proof' by 2050. That ambition is regarded as one of the most significant challenges to come out of the Delta Programme. It requires input not only from government at all levels but also from economic partners, civic society organizations, and citizens. 'Water-robust and climate-proof' spatial development is not precisely defined by the central government. However, the Delta Programme makes clear that in any case, 'vital and vulnerable' functions (functions of land which are crucial for crisis management in case of flooding, e.g. drinking water) must be protected (Dutch government, 2017, p. 6).

To have the Netherlands as water-robust and climate-proof as possible by 2050, flood risk management and climate-proofing must be integrated into planning for new development, redevelopment, and investments in management and maintenance (Dutch government, 2015, p. 22). The long-term goal (to 2050) is clear and ambitious. The short-term ambition was that by 2020 climate-proof action and water-robust design would constitute an integrated component of the policies and actions. Several supporting instruments are available to this end, including an incentive programme with an associated digital knowledge portal, guidelines for spatial adaptation, and Water Assessment (Dutch government, 2015, p. 56).

Fiscal aspects

Compensation and expropriation measures used in Dutch coastal land policy concentrate on flood risk and flood defence works, as follows:

Compensation for flood risk

Owners of buildings and land built seaward of the dikes may be compensated for their lack of protection against flooding, through an offset to the Water System Tax. The regional water authorities may apply a discount of up to 75% on the tax (Water Board Act, Section 122, para. 1). In the case of other flood damages, there is no compensation scheme in place.

Expropriation for flood defence works

If necessary, the State can expropriate land and buildings for flood defence works. The Expropriation Act (1851) specifically states that expropriation may be used for water defence structures (Section 62). The formal decision to expropriate is taken by the Crown, after public participation and advice from the Council of State, but the operational decision is made by the Minister of Infrastructure and Water Management. The amount to be paid is decided through the Civil Court, but is based on the full value of expropriated land, including the costs of moving or transferring any business on the land.

Because the coastal defence structures are generally already owned by the State or water authorities, expropriation is rare. Yet the government has frequently used expropriation to allow improvement of flood defence structures (dikes) along the major rivers.

Permission for flood defence works

In addition to expropriation measures, the Water Act (2009) contains provisions which can compel private landowners in the coastal zone to allow access to their land for maintenance of flood defence structures (Section 5.23) or even the construction or alteration of a flood defence work, in case expropriation is not in order (Section 5.24). Thus, the government can operate its water management programme without taking ownership of the land. In such cases, any damage must be compensated but landowners are not entitled to recompense for use of their land for defence works.

Managed retreat or abolition of unused development rights

To our knowledge, there are no unused development rights in approved land use plans regarding flood defence structures for the coastal zone. They did exist along major rivers. Where they exist, such rights are fully compensated in an expropriation procedure. If the land use plan is changed and the development rights are taken away but expropriation is not deemed necessary, the owner can request compensation (Spatial Planning Act, Section 6.1). In such cases, compensation will be granted depending on the period for which the development right existed.

Coordination and integration

As in coastal management in any country, in the Netherlands too, there are coordination challenges due to institutional fragmentation. Over the years – indeed, the centuries – Dutch policymakers have achieved a relatively good level of coordination. Yet, being aware that there is room for further improvement, they have initiated further coordination initiatives.

As we have indicated throughout this chapter, the management of the Dutch coastal zone has four dimensions: Water management (flood defence); spatial management (planning); nature conservation (environmental) management; and delta management (Table 4.1). The last, delta management, is the secret to the success of Dutch coastal policy, given its unique broad-ranging approach. The Dutch Delta Commissioner has access to all cabinet ministers involved and thus holds a lot of 'coordination power'.

Water management authorities and spatial planning authorities operate at the national, provincial, and municipal levels (Jong & Van den Brink, 2013), while nature conservation management has been delegated to provinces since 2013.[10] Overall, coastal zone management in the Netherlands is clearly a matter involving multi-level and multi-sectoral governance. Coordination and collaboration between administrative bodies is prescribed by law. The Dutch General Administrative Law Act (1994) requires that administrative authorities collect the necessary information concerning the relevant facts and interest to be weighed, including when spatial decisions are being prepared (Section 3:2). There also is a duty to weigh the interests directly involved (Section 3:4, para. 1).

Several 'pearls of the Dutch coast' – locations with high development potential and with governance capabilities to realise ambitious goals – are currently under development. Governance of these 'coastal pearls' aims at an integrated approach. In some areas, relevant authorities work together to connect the flood defence task with economic and ecological development ambitions (Dutch government, 2018, p. 102). Examples of the 'coastal pearls' are: The Hague: plans for revitalisation of the coastal zone north of the Kurhaus; National Park Dutch Dunes; and the exploration of the development of water-safe and climate-proof housing in the harbour area of Velsen.

New initiatives promoting coordination

The Dutch government is working on integrating the Water Act (2009), the Spatial Planning Act (2008), the Environmental Management Act (1992), and twenty more Acts into a single Environment and Planning Law.

The new Environment and Planning Law will come into effect in 2022. Under the new law, national, provincial, and local governments must adopt an environmental strategy which encompasses all elements of land use and protection of the environment. Programmes may be developed for specific objectives for use, management, protection, or preservation of the physical environment. Such programmes can involve all relevant government bodies, in an integrated manner. On the municipal level, the land use plan will be replaced by the environmental plan, which has a much broader scope.

According to the new Environment and Planning Act (2021), administrative bodies shall consider each other's duties and powers, while performing their own (Section 2.2, para. 1). The administrative bodies involved shall take into account the relationship between the relevant components and aspects of the physical environment and the interests directly involved (Section 2.1, para. 2). In this context, several considerations might be relevant in any given case, including safety, climate change, and access to public outdoor space (Section 2.1, para. 3). The Dutch beach is public outdoor space *par excellence*.

Overall assessment

Long before the EU released directives regarding marine strategy and marine spatial planning, the Dutch were already aware of the necessity for effective management of the coastal zone. This awareness is largely due to the fact that the western part of the Netherlands is below sea level (and therefore dependent on strong flood defences) and that major and disastrous flood events have occurred twice in modern history (1953 and 1995).

Flood defence is *Priority Number One* in the Netherlands. The State provides for a stable basic coastline by sand replenishment. The Dutch Delta Commissioner is empowered to remind governments of their joint responsibility for flood protection measures. Administrative agreements between the State, provinces, regional water authorities, and municipalities show broad support for these measures.

The laws governing the physical environment (including planning law and water law) facilitate integrated planning. Multifunctional use of flood defences offers economic, recreational, and other opportunities. Flood defence in the Netherlands is pre-conditional for spatial planning in the coastal zone. First, flood defence must be established to a minimal required level. 'Weak links' (locations along the coast where defences are not strong enough) must be strengthened. Flood defence standards are set in the Water Act. After the improvement of the flood defence system near Cadzand-Bad in Zeeland was completed in 2016, the Delta Commissioner noted the following in his Delta Programme 2017: 'The current flood defence system meets the standard' (Dutch government, 2016, p. 53). By safeguarding the coast from flooding, the State facilitates further development along the Dutch coast where it is deemed appropriate, including the 'pearls of the Dutch coast'.

Centuries of struggling with the threats of the water give hope that the Netherlands will succeed in strengthening the dikes, introducing strong coastal covenants and further innovation in its legislation. Will all these arrangements be sufficient to overcome the powers of nature and climate change? Only our great-great-grandchildren will know.

Table 4.1 History, policy, and legislation regarding the Dutch coastal zone (a brief summary)

Years	Trigger	Policy or legislation introduced	Purpose/key points	DIM
1904		Polders and Land Reclamation Act (14 July 1904)	Flood protection	WG
1916	Storm surge disaster Zuiderzee	Zuiderzee (bay of the North Sea in the northwest of the country) was closed off from the North Sea by the construction of the Afsluitdijk, (32 km) turning it into Lake IJssel (1927–1932)*	Flood protection	DM
1953 to 1958	Storm surge disaster in southwestern Netherlands	Delta Advisory Commission (1953–1960)	Flood protection on the coast	DM
		First Delta Plan (1955)		DM
		Delta Act 1958		DM
		Delta Works (1958–1997)*	Building of new dams and dikes to strengthen the southwestern coastline	DM
1990		First national Policy Document on the Coast: Flood Defence after 1990 (1990)	Coastal defence/flood protection	DM
1993 to 1995	Floods around the major rivers	Second national Policy Document on the Coast; *Coastal Balance* (1995)	Coastal defence/flood protection	DM
		Delta Plan and Delta Act Major Rivers 1995	Flood protection around rivers	DM

(continued)

Table 4.1 (continued)

Years	Trigger	Policy or legislation introduced	Purpose/key points	DIM
1996		Flood Protection Act 1996	Flood protection	DM
1997		Fourth Water Management Policy 1997	Policy for water management	WG
2000		Third Policy Document on the Coast: *Traditions, Trends, and Future* (2000)	Flood protection and spatial planning (coastal zoning)	DM/SP
2006		The National Spatial Policy Document (2006)	Defines Coastal Foundation Zone, spatial planning	SP
2007		Policy Document on the Coast (2007)	Defines Coastal Foundation Zone, policy rules for development	SP
2008		Spatial Planning Act (2008)	Constitutes procedures and instruments for spatial planning, like General Spatial Planning Rules and Structure Visions, Delegates most responsibilities regarding development approvals to municipalities and provinces.	SP
2009		National Water Plan (2009–2015)	A.o. flood defence standards and policy for the coast	WG
		Policy Document on Water Safety (2009)	Key concept: multi-layered safety	WG
		Water Act (2009)	Integrated eight existing water-related Acts, including the Flood Protection Act. Rules on flood defence, water quality, water quantity, water shortage, and water excess Key concept: water system	WG
2010		Environmental Licencing (General Provisions) Act 2010	Environmental permits for development	SP
2011		Second Delta Plan (after the first Delta Plan 1955)	Flood protection and climate-proofing	DM
		General Spatial Planning Rules (2011)	Including coastal foundation, rules regarding flood defence structures, and a general prohibition on development in the Coastal Foundation Zone	SP

(continued)

Table 4.1 (continued)

Years	Trigger	Policy or legislation introduced	Purpose/key points	DIM
2012		Delta Programme 2013 (yearly update)	Flood protection and climate-proofing	DM
		Structure Vision Infrastructure and Spatial Planning (2012)	Spatial planning (contains no decisions on the coast)	SP
		Delta Act (2012)	Flood protection and climate-proofing	DM
2013		National Vision on the Coast (September 2013)	Part of Delta Programme 2013: flood defence measures and spatial planning	SP/DM
		Delta Programme 2014 (yearly update)	Flood protection and climate-proofing	DM
2014		Delta Decision on Spatial Adaptation (2014)	Spatial adaptation and adaptations of buildings with respect to climate change and consequences of flooding	SP/DM
		Delta Programme 2015 (yearly update)	Flood protection and climate-proofing	DM
		Preferential Strategy Coast	Part of Delta Programme 2015	DM
		Decision on Sand Replenishment	Part of Delta Programme 2015	DM
		Delta Decision Water Safety (2014)	Part of Delta Programme 2015	DM
2015		Revised Policy Document on the Coast (2015)	Subtitle: 'Preconditions for initiatives' (water safety perspective)	DM
		Draft Revision of the General Spatial Planning Rules regarding the Coast (2015)	Proposed that the general prohibition on development should be removed from the General Spatial Planning Rules.	SP
		Delta Programme 2016 (yearly update)	Flood protection and climate-proofing.	DM
2016		Delta Programme 2017 (yearly update)	Flood protection and climate-proofing.	DM
		National Water Plan 2016–2021	A.o. flood defence standards and policy for the coast	WG/SP
2017	Baywatchers Case (refer to the section on public participation)	Coastal Pact 2017–2019 (21 February 2017)	Defines preconditions for further development of the coastal zone: Water safety (flood defence), nature conservation, and fresh water supply.	SP
		Delta Programme 2018 (yearly update)	Flood protection and climate-proofing.	DM
		New Nature Conservation Act (1 January 2017)	Protects natural features of the coastal zone.	NC

(continued)

Table 4.1 (continued)

Years	Trigger	Policy or legislation introduced	Purpose/key points	DIM
2018		Delta Programme 2019 (yearly update)	Flood protection and climate-proofing.	DM
2019		New Draft Revision of the General Spatial Planning Rules regarding the Coast (2019)	Define the core qualities and collective values of the Coastal Foundation Zone.	SP
		National Environmental and Spatial Vision (Draft June 2019)	Spatial Planning	SP

DIM = Dimension. WG = Water Governance; SP = Spatial Planning; NC = Nature Conservation; DM = Delta Management

* The American Society of Civil Engineers declared the Zuiderzee Works (which also included other dikes, water drainage works, and the reclamation of land in new polders), together with the Delta Works in the South West of the Netherlands, as among the Seven Wonders of the Modern World

Notes

1. Both parties contribute 181 million euros a year. The financial contribution of the water authorities is divided into a solidarity component of 40% and a project-related share of 10%.
2. The Dutch Civil Code regulates property. It states that the right to property ownership is the most comprehensive right but that property rights may be limited if necessary (Book 5, Section 1).
3. An explanatory note to the General Spatial Planning Rules explains that Section 2.3.4 refers to the protection zone of the flood defence structure that has been laid down by the Water Board in the Ledger of Flood Defences (Dutch: *legger*), on the principle of the space needed for adjustment of the flood defence structure to two hundred years of sea level rise.
4. 'Spatial quality' refers to the values related to land use planning: 'Use' value, for example: water, clean environment, mixed use; 'experiencing' value, for example: beauty of nature, attractiveness; and 'future' value, for example: cultural heritage, social support (Town-Net, n.d.).
5. Nature and Environmental Federation South Holland, the Environmental Federation Zeeland, Landscape organizations of the provinces of Zeeland and South Holland, the Foundation Dune Protection, and Nature Monuments.
6. Dutch: www.beschermdekust.nl. English: www.protectthecoast.nl
7. The research did not cover the coast of the isles in the Wadden Sea area or the sea arms of the provinces Zeeland and South Holland. The research focused on the building projects that were started or finished over the previous three years and upcoming building projects 'in procedure' (revision of land use plan and/or permit procedure).
8. Environmental permits are regulated by the Environmental Licensing (General Provisions) Act; see especially Section 2.1 of this Act.
9. The provisions of the Delta Act are laid down in a chapter of the Water Act.
10. In September 2013 the State and the Provinces established a Nature Pact regarding the decentralization of nature policy. Source: http://www.ipo.nl/publicaties/provincies-ruim-op-schema-bij-inrichting-natuurnetwerk-nederland.

References

Aerts, J., Botzen, W., Bowman, M., Ward, P., & Dircke., P. (2011). *Climate Adaptation and Flood Risk in Coastal Cities*. Routledge.

De Ruig, J. H. (1998). Coastline management in the Netherlands: Human use versus natural dynamics. *Journal of Coastal Conservation* 4(2), 127–134.

Dutch government. (2007). Beleidslijn Kust [Coastal Policy]. Official Publications of the House of Representatives, 2006–2007, 30 195, no. 22.

— (2014). *Delta Programme 2015: Working on the Delta: The Decisions to Keep the Netherlands Safe and Liveable.* Available at: https://english.deltacommissaris.nl/delta-programme/documents/publications/2014/09/16/delta-programme-2015

— (2015). *Delta Programme 2016: Work on the Delta: And Now We're Starting for Real.* Available at: https://deltaprogramma2016.deltacommissaris.nl/viewer/publication/1/delta-programme-.html

— (2016). *Delta Programme 2017: Work on the Delta: Linking Taskings, on Track Together.* Available at: https://english.deltacommissaris.nl/binaries/delta-commissioner/documents/publications/2016/09/20/dp2017-en-printversie/DP2017+EN+printversie.pdf

— (2017). *Deltaprogramma: Ruimtelijke adaptatie: Aanpak nationale Vitale en Kwetsbare functies Derde voortgangsrapportage* [Delta Programme: Spatial Adaptation: Approach to National Vital and Vulnerable Functions (third progress report)]. Available at: https://ruimtelijkeadaptatie.nl/publish/pages/118833/derde_voortgangsrapportage_aanpak_nationale_vitale_en_kwetsbare_functies.pdf

— (2018). *Delta Programme 2019: Continuing the Work on the Delta: Adapting the Netherlands to Climate Change in Time.* Available at: https://english.deltacommissaris.nl/binaries/delta-commissioner/documents/publications/2018/09/18/dp2019-en-printversie/DP2019+EN+printversie.pdf

— (2020). Decision of the 27th of May 2020 regarding revision of the General Spatial Planning Rules. Staatsblad [Government Gazette] 2020, 204. Available at: https://zoek.officielebekendmakingen.nl/stb-2020-204.pdf

Dutch parliament. (2002a). *Official Publications of the House of Representatives*, 2002–2003, 27 867, no. 4 (policy letter).

— (2002b). *Official Publications of the House of Representatives*, 2002–2003, 28600-XI, no. 72 (debate).

— (2010–2014). *Official Publications of the House of Representatives*, 32 366 (Regels voor het verlenen van vergunning voor de onrechtmatige bewoning van recreatiewoningen; Wet vergunning onrechtmatige bewoning recreatiewoningen).

— (2016a). Official Publications of the House of Representatives, 2015–2016, 29 383, no. 252 (Draft decision to revise the General Spatial Planning Rules). Available at: https://zoek.officielebekendmakingen.nl/blg-665034.pdf

— (2016b). *Official Publications of the House of Representatives*, 2015–2016, 33 118, no. 21 (debate).

Dutch Water Authorities. (2017). *Water Governance: The Dutch Water Authority Model.* The Hague, June 2017.

Hendriks & Buntsma (2009). Water and spatial planning in the Netherlands: Living with water in the context of climate change. In F. Ludwig, P. Kabat, H.V. Schaik, & M.V.D. Valk (Eds.). *Climate Change Adaptation in the Water Sector.* London: Routledge.

IenM [Ministry of Infrastructure and the Environment]. (2012). Structure Vision Infrastructure and Spatial Planning. Available at: https://www.rijksoverheid.nl/documenten/rapporten/2012/03/13/structuurvisie-infrastructuur-en-ruimte

— (2013). National Coastal Strategy: Compass for the Coast. Available at: http://rijksoverheid.minienm.nl/nvk/NationalCoastalStrategy.pdf

— (2016). Exemption from the Spatial Planning Act and General Spatial Planning Rules for the redevelopment of Willemshaven in Harlingen. 9 June 2016. Available at: https://www.planviewer.nl/imro/files/NL.IMRO.0072.Willemshaven-VG02/b_NL.IMRO.0072.Willemshaven-VG02_tb7.pdf

Jong, P., & Van den Brink, M. (2013). Between tradition and innovation: Developing flood risk management plans in the Netherlands. *Journal of Flood Risk Management* 10 (2), 155–163. doi:10.1111/jfr3.12070

OECD. (2014). Water Governance in the Netherlands – Fit for the future? Available at: https://www.oecd.org/governance/water-governance-in-the-netherlands-9789264102637-en.htm

Rijkswaterstaat Waterdienst [Ministry of Infrastructure and Water Management]. (2010). *Veiligheid Nederland in kaart*, dijkringrapport 14, overstromingsrisico dijkring 14 Zuid-Holland [Mapping the Safety of the Netherlands, Dyke Ring Report 14, flood risk dyke ring 14 South Holland].

Town-Net. (n.d.). *Methodology for Spatial Quality* (Interreg IIIB programme, North Sea region). Available at: www.werkpartners.net/uploads/Gorecht.pdf

Van den Brink, M. (2009). *Rijkswaterstaat: On the Horns of a Dilemma.* Uitgeverij Eburon, Delft.

Van der Most, H. (2010). *Kijk op waterveiligheid* [A View of Water Safety]. Uitgeverij Eburon, Delft.

VenW [Ministry of Transport, Public Works and Water Management]. (1990). *Coastal Defence after 1990: A Policy Choice for Coastal Protection*. First Coastal Policy Document (1e Kustnota). The Hague.

— (1995). *Coastal Balance 1995*. Second Coastal Policy Document (2e Kustnota). The Hague.

— (1997). Fourth Water Management Policy (NW4). The Hague.

— (2000). *Tradition, Trends and Tomorrow*. Third Coastal Policy Document (3e Kustnota). The Hague.

VROM [Ministry of Housing, Spatial Planning and the Environment]. (2006). *Nota Ruimte* [National Spatial Policy Document]. The Hague.

Watersnoodmuseum [Flood Museum]. (n.d.). Delta Works. Available at: https://watersnoodmuseum.nl/en/knowledgecentre/delta-works/

World Factbook (n.d.). Netherlands. Available at: https://www.cia.gov/library/publications/the-world-factbook/geos/nl.html [Accessed September 2019]

Legislation (www.wetten.nl) (listed chronologically)

Civil Code (1838, revised 1970–1992)

Expropriation Act (1851)

Delta Act (1958) – Staatsblad [Government Gazette] 1958, 246

Environmental Management Act (1992)

Water Board Act (1992)

General Administrative Law Act (1994) (Wet algemene bepalingen omgevingsrecht).

Delta Act Major Rivers (1995) – Staatsblad [Government Gazette] 1995, 210

Spatial Planning Act (2008)

Spatial Planning Decree (2008)

Water Act (2009)

Environmental Licencing (General Provisions) Act (2010)

General Spatial Planning Rules (2011) – Original version published in: Staatsblad [Government Gazette] 2011, 391. Available at: https://zoek.officielebekendmakingen.nl/stb-2011-391.pdf. Revised 2018 version available at: https://wetten.overheid.nl/BWBR0030378/2018-01-01.

Delta Act (2012) – Staatsblad [Government Gazette] 2011, 604

Nature Conservation Act (2017)

5 Denmark

Helle Tegner Anker

Overview

Denmark is a small country with a relatively high proportion of coastal land. The country relies on its coastal resources for their significant contribution to its environment and economy and has traditionally implemented strong measures to ensure their protection. These measures include not only a minimum 100 m wide coastal setback zone, but also a 3 km wide Coastal Planning Zone – the widest protection zone identified across the countries in this book. Nevertheless, since 2015, following the election of a liberal-conservative government, the country has seen a pushback against some of its most stringent coastal regulations, particularly affecting the Coastal Planning Zone, in favour of landowner interests, and a decentralisation of the coastal protection administration. This chapter provides a snapshot of Danish coastal zone regulation at this juncture.

Introduction: The Danish coast in context

The Danish coastline is approximately 7,300 km long (World Factbook, n.d.). Given Denmark's relatively small land area of 43,000 km², the longest distance to the coast from any point on land is 50 km. Denmark has 5.6 million inhabitants (about 130 people per square kilometre), and many cities are located on the coast. The country's urban area occupies only about 10% of the land area, whereas more than 60% is agricultural land.

There are a number of strong interests related to the use of the coastal zone in Denmark. These include harbours, maritime transport, raw material extraction, oil and gas extraction, renewable energy (wind energy), fishery, aquaculture, military installations, infrastructure, flood defence, recreational use, and urban development. Furthermore, several aspects of the coastal zone environment, including water quality, landscape, and cultural heritage, require protection to maintain the integrity of these resources.[1]

Legislative framework for coastal protection and management

The protection of coastal landscapes has been a major concern in Danish environmental legislation for decades, as reflected in both the Nature Protection Act (2019), which first instituted a coastal setback zone in 1937, and in the Planning Act (2018), which since 1994 identifies land within a 3 km strip of the coast as a Coastal Planning Zone. The Planning Act emphasises the significance of the coastal landscape in its introductory section and requires that national priorities relating to the coastal landscape be considered in Municipal and Local Plans prepared by the municipalities.

Figure 5.1 Wind energy facilities off the coast of Østerbro, Copenhagen

Source: CGP Grey. CC BY 2.0 license. Available at: https://www.flickr.com/photos/cgpgrey/4890894762/

In addition, Danish legislation is heavily influenced by EU legislation, including the ecosystem-based approach as reflected in the EU Water Framework Directive, the Marine Strategy Framework Directive, and the Maritime Spatial Planning Directive.

Nevertheless, there are no specific ICZM (Integrated Coastal Zone Management) initiatives embedded in Danish legislation and policy[2] and there appears to be no evidence of explicit ICZM language seeping into the legislation. On the contrary, a regulatory split between onshore (landward of the shoreline) and offshore (seaward of the shoreline) issues characterises the Danish legislation (Anker, 2004). The Planning Act applies only to onshore areas and activities, whereas sectoral legislation governs offshore areas and activities (e.g. the Harbours Act 2012 and the Fisheries Act 2017). To some extent, the Coastal Protection Act (2019) transcends the shoreline with its particular focus on coastal defence works. Since 2006, this legislation has also stipulated the general permit procedure for offshore installations and activities, unless the relevant activities are regulated under separate sectoral legislation. Due to the crosscutting nature of some EU legislation – including the Environmental Impact Assessment (EIA) and Strategic Environmental Assessment (SEA) Directives, as well as the Birds and Habitats Directives – requirements relating to, for example, environmental assessment, public participation, and access to justice have also seeped into sectoral legislation governing offshore activities, including the Coastal Protection Act.

Administrative responsibilities

Within the Danish national government, the main responsibility for coastal zone management at ministerial level rests with the Ministry for Environment and Food (formerly Ministry for the Environment).[3] Until June 2015, the Danish Nature Agency (Naturstyrelsen) held the main responsibilities relating to planning and environment. In June 2015, however, the new Government transferred the responsibilities for the Planning Act to the Ministry for Business (Erhvervsministeriet), while responsibilities regarding nature protection and water legislation remained with the Nature Agency (now the Environmental Protection Agency). However, the administration of the setback zone has been transferred to the Coastal Authority (Kystdirektoratet). Administrative appeals boards play an important role in coastal zone management; since February 2017, the relevant bodies are the Planning Appeals Board and the Environment and Food Appeals Board.

As mentioned above, the Danish governance structure is characterised by a regulatory split between land and sea, with the shoreline as the dividing line. Sectoral state authorities hold the primary powers for offshore activities, whereas the 98 municipalities hold the primary powers for onshore activities. For offshore activities, the relevant state authorities include the Environmental Protection Agency (raw material extraction, nature protection, water quality, and pollution), the Energy Agency (oil and gas extraction, wind energy, etc), the Fisheries Agency (aquaculture), the Danish Transport and Construction Agency (harbours), the Danish Maritime Agency (maritime transport and maritime spatial planning), and the Coastal Authority (other offshore installations, flood defence, and setback zone). Since September 2018, however, many of the responsibilities regarding local flood defence works have been transferred from the Coastal Authority to the municipalities.

Current issues

Climate change is a major concern in Denmark, particularly given the risk of flooding, due not only to rising sea levels but also to storms. Recent storms (most recently in December 2016) have resulted in flooding of property, including housing. As part of the implementation of the EU Floods Directive, fourteen flood risk areas have been designated and Flood Risk Plans have been prepared by the relevant municipalities. In addition, following an agreement in 2013, municipalities have drawn up Climate Adaptation Plans as part of municipal planning. The municipalities are, as of 2018, obliged to designate flood- and erosion-prone areas in the Municipal Plans. In recent years, there has been increasing political pressure to allow more flood defence works, as well as to streamline the decision-making processes, resulting in several amendments to the Coastal Protection Act in 2016 and 2018, as discussed further below.

Another issue which has received attention in Denmark in recent years is wind energy development in coastal areas; particularly the current plans for so-called "nearshore" wind farms, to be located 4–8 km offshore, which have been heavily debated. After a highly controversial process, concessions for two of six designated sites were finally granted in October 2016 Energistyrelsen, 2016). But in December 2018, the concessions were halted by the Energy Appeals Board due to environmental impact assessment procedures (Anker & Olsen, 2019). The debates on this matter clearly highlights the regulatory split and the differences in governance structure and legislation for offshore and onshore wind energy projects (Ram et al., 2017).

Finally, the relatively strict protection of coastal landscapes – through the setback zone and the Coastal Planning Zone – has also been the subject of significant public debate. This debate has led to changes to the relevant legislation, including amendments to the Planning Act and the Nature Protection Act in June 2017, as discussed below.

Delineation of the shoreline and the beach

In Denmark, the shoreline signifies the regulatory split in governance structure – specifically, between the municipalities' responsibilities onshore (through the Planning Act) and the state authorities' responsibilities offshore. There are, however, no formal rules on defining or demarcating the shoreline. Thus, the demarcation of the shoreline relies on the actual circumstances in each case and on geomorphological changes. Traditionally, the daily high-water mark (reach of the highest tide) has been used to demarcate the line between land and sea, for the purpose of identifying both the setback zone and fishing territory. Some coast-related lines or demarcations have been marked on legally binding maps. Offshore, this includes the "baseline", which is demarcated on maps in accordance with the Delineation of the Territorial Sea Act 1999. The baseline is used as a marker for the outer territorial sea and the inner territorial sea, which includes harbours, bays, fiords, and any other features between the baseline and the shoreline. Onshore, a coastal setback zone, ranging between 100 m and 300 m in width, has been demarcated since 2004, in accordance with the Nature Protection Act and following a detailed examination of the entire coast over the period 1994–2004.[4] In addition, a Coastal Planning Zone, which has a width of 3 km inland from the shoreline (and applies outside urban areas), is demarcated in an appendix to the Planning Act.[5]

The delineation of the territorial sea (and the EEZ) has jurisdictional implications in accordance with international law. The shoreline sets the seaward boundary for ownership of land property. While the shoreline may evolve on a day-to-day basis, the demarcations that are fixed by binding maps remain the same until they are officially adjusted and new binding maps are issued.

Beside the shoreline, another definition that is important in the context of coastal regulation is that of the beach. The beach is defined in the Nature Protection Act as the area between the daily low-water mark (low tide; seaward) and land vegetation (not "salt tolerant" plants or beach vegetation; landward).

Public domain

The outer seaward limit of land ownership is the shoreline, i.e. the daily high-water mark, as there is no ownership for offshore areas. Offshore areas can thus be regarded as public domain. The implication is that offshore construction, including for piers, boat ramps, and the like, requires a permit according to the Coastal Protection Act, or relevant sector legislation.

Landwards of the shoreline, there is no imperative that Danish coastal land be defined as public domain. Ownership of coastal land areas can be public or private. In situations where the coastal land area expands into the sea (as in the case of reclaimed land), new coastal land will follow the ownership pattern (public/private) of the immediately adjacent land.

Setback from the shoreline

The Nature Protection Act stipulates a setback zone along the entire coast – in general, the setback zone is 300 m from the landward boundary of the beach, as defined above. The Nature Protection Act distinguishes between the Dune Protection Zone, applying along the west coast of Jutland, and the Beach Protection Zone along the remaining coastline – collectively, these form the Danish coastal setback zone. The setback zone includes the beach, as well as a demarcated zone inland from the landward boundary of beach.

While the Dune Protection Zone dates back to laws which sought to protect the coast from sand erosion since 1792, the Beach Protection Zone was introduced in 1937 as a 100 m wide zone in which new construction was prohibited. In 1969, the prohibitions applying to the Beach Protection Zone were expanded to include other development activities, such as fencing and subdivision.

In 1994, an amendment to the Nature Protection Act extended the width of the Beach and Dune Protection Zones from 100 m to 300 m. The location of the new boundary was identified through site inspections (property by property) along the entire applicable parts of the coast and finally, in 2004, was delineated on maps in statutory orders, as well as in the land registry for each property. In designated Holiday Home Zones, the 100 m wide zone was maintained, whereas in other areas, the 300 m zone was applied, even if it incorporated existing development. The Dune Protection Zone along the west coast may extend up to 500 m in width in some areas. In urban areas, the setback zone can either be reduced or eliminated entirely. The Minister for the Environment and Food can exempt specific areas from the setback zone and adjust the zones according to geomorphological changes. Such changes will be noted in the land registry.

Within the setback zone, any works which disturb the natural or current state of the ground are prohibited. Fencing, subdivision, and land transfer are also prohibited. Within the Dune Protection Zone, there is an additional prohibition against animal grazing. In general, these restrictions have been interpreted in a broad sense by the Appeals Board and the courts. As a result, even changes in the use of existing buildings or construction of minor structures (e.g. benches) have been regarded as prohibited. Nevertheless, certain activities, such as planting in existing gardens, or minor renovations (e.g. replacing windows or roofs) are exempt. Furthermore, it is possible to apply to the Coastal Authority for additional exemptions.[6]

Historically, the administrative practice for granting exemptions for works or development in the Beach Protection Zone or Dune Protection Zone was quite restrictive. In 2017, however, following a public and political debate on the (very) stringent setback rules, an amendment to the Nature Protection Act introduced some more moderate criteria relating to certain "low impact" activities, boardwalks, and other recreational facilities, as well as certain minor modifications of existing housing. Furthermore, some minor construction works, including patios in gardens, playgrounds, and other recreational facilities in harbour areas, were exempted from the prohibition on development and thus no longer require an exemption.

The level of compliance with the restrictions on construction in the setback zone is estimated to be relatively high. It is conceivable, however, that some (private) landowners were not fully aware of the scope of the prohibition, including, for example, minor construction works or planting beyond existing gardens.

The setback zone has increasingly been seen as an obstacle to growth and development, particularly in rural areas. There are, however, no clear indications that it has negative socio-economic implications at the macro level. Nevertheless, there has been ongoing and strong political pressure to amend the legislation and allow for more activities within the setback zone, as expressed in the 2017 amendment. Earlier, in 2014, this pressure resulted in an amendment to the Nature Protection Act (and the Planning Act), which allows the Minister for the Environment (now Environment and Food) to grant exemption to ten tourism projects within the Beach Protection Zone. This exemption was then expanded in 2017 to another fifteen tourism projects, in addition to the general amendments to the setback zone provisions discussed above.

Right of public access

Danish regulations seek to ensure both vertical (to the coast) and horizontal (along the coast) accessibility.

Vertical accessibility

Access to (and along) the coast is regulated by the Nature Protection Act. In addition, the Planning Act includes a provision that public access to the coast shall be ensured and, if relevant, improved (for example, by providing footpaths or other facilities) when planning for new development in the Coastal Planning Zone (3 km from the shoreline). The specific provision on access to the coast in the Nature Protection Act stipulates that the public has the right to access beaches (as defined above) and other coastal stretches. Furthermore, signs or other measures (fences and structures) which signal restricted access, are also prohibited under the Nature Protection Act.

The requirements relating to public access apply to both public and private land. The right of access includes access on foot, short stays, and bathing. On privately owned beaches, short stays and bathing are, however, not permitted within 50 m of dwellings.

Areas which were private gardens or part of an industrial or commercial property prior to 1 January 1916 are exempt from these access requirements, in order to avoid retroactive implications of the first Nature Protection Act adopted in 1917. In addition, military areas and harbour installations are exempt from public access requirements.

Horizontal accessibility

The provisions of the Nature Protection Act mentioned above also provide protection for horizontal access along the coast, as access to beaches and other coastal stretches should not be restricted. Furthermore, there is a general provision applying to rural areas, which allows for public access to uncultivated areas. Nevertheless, private land may be properly fenced if fencing is necessary for the agricultural or commercial use of the area or for specific privacy needs. The public also has access to footpaths in the countryside, and footpaths that lead to beaches may not be removed without prior notice to the local authorities. The local authorities may refuse the removal or closure of a footpath if it has significant recreational value and if there are no suitable alternatives.

Compliance in accessibility matters

There are no official figures on non-compliance relating to accessibility in the coastal zone and only a limited number of criminal cases have been heard. There are some appeal cases regarding non-compliance where the authorities have issued orders to remove obstacles to public access, for example, fences or signs, or have ordered reopening of footpaths. Non-compliance is, however, not known as a general problem, although it is likely that in densely populated urban areas with private properties located along the coast, fences, walls, and other barriers restricting vertical and horizontal access have been erected.

Creation of public access – permission and fiscal aspects

Public access in the coastal zone can be promoted on public as well as private land through, for example, the development of recreation facilities, or possibly as part of nature restoration or conservation projects. The latter may require compensation to private landowners, public purchase, or even expropriation. Public access may, however, also be restricted in order to protect sensitive natural areas, habitats, or species. Establishment of footpaths, boardwalks, and other recreational facilities may require an exemption from other rules, such as setback zone restrictions. Levelling out of sand dunes is unlikely to be permitted.

Urban and regional/land use planning – laws and implementation

Coastline preservation is a key concern in the Danish Planning Act. The introductory provision of the Planning Act states that the open coasts shall be maintained as a significant natural and landscape resource. This is an indication that the coasts are a national priority. Furthermore, since 1994, specific planning provisions apply in coastal areas in the form of "national planning provisions", which steer local-level planning.[7] Planning at local level (Municipal Plans and Local Plans) may not contradict national planning provisions. The Ministry for Business has national planning powers to veto proposals for Municipal or Local Plans that contradict the national planning priorities. Conflicts may, however, be resolved through negotiations between the Ministry and the municipalities.

According to the Planning Act (Section 5a), coastal areas shall be kept free of development that does not rely on proximity to the coast, and the Minister is obliged to use the national planning powers (national planning provisions and veto powers) to safeguard national planning interests in coastal areas. The same section of the Act also defines the Coastal Planning Zone (3 km inland from the shoreline and delineated on a map), which applies special rules in rural zones and Holiday Home Zones (outside urban areas). In urban areas, there are also a few specific provisions for the "coastal-adjacent" parts of the cities: For example, authorities must assess potential visual effects on the coast and justify any significant changes in the height or volume of buildings when drawing up Local Plans for new development.

The Planning Act (Sec. 5b) also stipulates specific requirements for planning at local level (Municipal Plans and Local Plans) within the Coastal Planning Zone (CPZ). Municipalities may only plan for new urban zones and development in rural areas within the CPZ if there are specific planning or functional arguments for locating the proposed development near the coast. New Holiday Home Zones may not be established, and existing holiday homes in these zones may not be converted into permanent dwellings (Figure 5.2). However, under specific circumstances and as specified by the Minister, it may be possible to establish a limited number of new Holiday Home Zones. The same section of the Act (5b) also dictates that holiday resorts and similar shall be located adjacent to existing urban development or larger recreational facilities. When planning for new development within the Coastal Planning Zone, a Local Plan must include information on the visual effects and other important aspects regarding nature and recreational interests. In addition, a Municipal Plan which includes land in the CPZ must, in the accompanying regulations, include information on future development in the CPZ and nearby coastal areas.

In line with the trends highlighted above, the Coastal Planning Zone has been under political pressure. In 2017, the Parliament adopted what was called a "liberalization" or "modernization" of the Planning Act – with a particular focus on coastal development. This included adding the option for the municipalities to apply for the Ministry to designate "development areas" in the CPZ, where the planning restrictions will not apply. Local politicians in rural areas argued that the Planning Act prevents economic development, although there are no official reports which support this assertion.

Figure 5.2 Holiday homes at Lien, Skallerup

Source: Tomasz Sienicki. CC BY 3.0 license. Available at: https://da.wikipedia.org/wiki/Sommerhusomr%C3%A5de#/media/Fil:Sommerhusene_ved_Lien_(2012,_ubt).JPG

The restrictions in the Coastal Planning Zone, however, are planning restrictions and not prohibitions, as opposed to the restrictions related to the setback zone, outlined above. If a plan proposal for development within the CPZ is well supported, it may be accepted. An example is the 2015 decision on the development of 70 holiday apartments only 350–400 m from the coast in Northern Jutland, where the Appeals Board accepted arguments that a coastal location was important in order to attract tourism (Natur- og Miljøklagenævnet, 15 February 2015).

Compliance and enforcement

The extent of illegal development within the setback zone defined above (Dune Protection Zone and Beach Protection Zone) is difficult to ascertain, as Denmark does not keep official records of all illegalities. There are only few reported criminal cases. There are, however, a number of cases in which the relevant authority (previously the Nature Agency, now the Coastal Authority) has refused to grant an exemption to retroactively provide permission for illegal development in the setback zone. Such decisions are often brought to the Environment and Food Appeals Board and may also reach the courts. Yet both the Appeals Board and the courts have maintained a fairly restrictive stance on the setback zone. If an exemption is not granted, any illegal development must cease, and the land must be restored to its previous state. Illegal construction must be removed or demolished. This has been confirmed by the courts, including in a case in which four holiday homes were removed (Vestre Landsret, ref. MAD2015.7) and another in which unauthorised private coastal defence works were removed (Østre Landsret, ref. MAD2013.891).

Many court cases on illegal development within the setback zone have been related to minor issues, such as renovations, patios, benches, and planting beyond garden boundaries. Relatively few cases relate to entirely new buildings.

The coastal planning rules are mainly enforced through the veto powers of the Ministry for Business, as well as through appeals to the Planning Appeals Board by neighbours, citizen groups, or other third parties who object to new plans in coastal areas.

Climate change awareness – legal aspects

Climate change awareness is regulated by several pieces of Danish legislation. The Coastal Protection Act lays down the framework for flood control on the coast. The EU Flood Risk Directive has been implemented through a separate Flood Risk Act (2017). However, due to the regulatory split between onshore and offshore issues (and a lack of ICZM), the Flood Risk Act addresses flood risks only from inland surface waters (i.e. rivers and lakes). Flood risks from the sea are regulated through a Statutory Order on Flood Risk Assessment and Management (2016) issued in accordance with the Coastal Protection Act and administered by the Coastal Authority. Nevertheless, in practice, it appears that implementation of these separate acts is pursued in a coordinated manner, given that fourteen potential flood risk areas have now been designated jointly by the Nature Agency (now the Environmental Protection Agency) and the Coastal Authority. Yet it should be noted that the designation of these flood risk areas is considered a minimal response to the Flood Risk Directive, particularly as these areas generally exclude flooding due to stormwater runoff.

In 2016, the administration of the Flood Risk Act was transferred to the Coastal Authority. The relevant municipalities are charged with the task of drawing up Flood Risk Plans for their part of the designated potential flood risk areas. These Flood Risk Plans are binding and must be taken into account in the drawing up of Municipal Plans or Local Plans under the Planning Act. Since March 2018, the Planning Act also obliges municipalities to mark (additional) areas prone to flooding or erosion in their Municipal Plans. When planning for urban development in such areas, appropriate mitigation measures must be included in Local Plans.

In 2013, a guidance note was issued under the Planning Act, on the preparation of Climate Adaptation Plans for each municipality, to form part of their Municipal Plans (Naturstyrelsen, 2013). Such Climate Adaptation Plans may address flood risks from the sea, rivers, or lakes, as well as from storm runoff or sewage water. According to the guidance note, a Climate Adaptation Plan shall include a flood risk map, a prioritization, and an action plan for climate adaptation. The Climate Adaptation Plans primarily address new urban development but also, to some extent, new initiatives (e.g. dams, wetlands, and reconstruction of roads) to protect existing urban areas. Yet it is important to note that Climate Adaptation Plans, being a component of Municipal Plans, are not directly legally binding. Each municipality is obliged to strive for the implementation of its Municipal Plan and may not adopt a Local Plan that is not in accordance with the former. Local Plans may include binding provisions related to climate adaptation but cannot impose requirements for adaptation works by private parties, unless such works are in conjunction with permission for new development.

A crucial question is whether or not the authorities have any obligations to protect individual properties against flood risks. In general, property owners cannot claim rights of protection against nature. The overarching principle is that property owners must themselves bear the consequences of flooding, including the full loss of property. However, according to the Flood and Storm Act (2018), a public insurance scheme may address losses due to stormwater floods or extreme rises in the water levels in sea, rivers, and lakes. Such a scheme would not cover losses due to other potential effects of climate change, including coastal erosion.

In coastal areas, landowners may apply for a permit to establish private coastal defence projects, but such permits have often been rejected, as the Coastal Protection Act has safeguarded not only economic interests but also the coastal landscape and the natural development of the coast. Nevertheless, following several severe storm events in recent years and the resulting political pressure, the legislation was amended in 2018 to pave the way for greater consideration of landowner interests.

In January 2018, the introduction to the Coastal Protection Act was amended to remove the explicit references to the protection of the coastal landscape and the natural dynamics of the coast and to replace those references with a general commentary on the natural and environmental benefits of flood defence measures. In addition, in September 2018, the responsibility for permits for coastal defence projects was transferred from the Coastal Authority to the municipalities, with the exception of state-funded projects. Furthermore, a permit granted by the municipalities under the Coastal Protection Act will replace most other permit requirements under other acts (e.g. the Nature Protection Act), to some extent restricting the options for appeals of such decisions. Similarly, a 2018 amendment to the Planning Act has made it possible for municipalities to avoid adopting a Local Plan which includes (onshore) coastal defence works if the planning process will likely cause significant delays leading to significant adverse effects, for example, financial losses or environmental damage.

These legislative changes clearly indicate that those who initiated them sought to make it easier for applicants, including public and private landowners, to obtain permits for coastal defence projects. Prior to the amendments, the Coastal Authority had been particularly reluctant to give permits for "hard" coastal defence projects to protect individual properties, preferring "soft" options such as beach renourishment (Kystdirektoratet, 2011). This reluctance has primarily pertained not only in rural areas but also in less densely populated urban areas. Apparently, a December 2016 amendment to Coastal Protection Act which addressed a perceived need to ensure a more effective decision-making process regarding coastal defence projects in order to avoid long delays was considered insufficient to counter the political pressure in this realm and led to the 2018 amendments. It now remains to be seen how the 98 municipalities will administer their extended powers regarding coastal defence projects. In most cases, however, the municipalities will be obliged to consult with the Coastal Authority, which has the expertise on coastal defence. This does not apply to individual projects, but only to projects that are promoted as joint projects covering more than one property. Furthermore, joint projects can be appealed in full, whereas individual projects can be appealed only on the basis of legality.

In urban areas, the extent to which climate change may lead to initiatives to protect existing urban development against flooding and other risks is mainly a question of political priorities within the municipalities. As mentioned above, there are now some initiatives with respect to the drawing up of local Flood Risk Plans and Climate Adaptation Plans. So far, there are no examples of municipalities being held liable for "bad" planning for development in flood- or erosion-prone areas.

Integration and coordination

As indicated throughout this chapter, responsibilities for coastal zone management are spread across several government ministries and the local municipalities. As mentioned earlier, there is a regulatory split in Danish legislation, which attributes responsibilities for offshore issues to state authorities under sectoral legislation and responsibilities for onshore issues primarily to local authorities under the Planning Act. There are only few examples of legislation and administration transcending the shoreline.

At national level, the main coastal responsibilities rest with the Ministry for Environment and Food, particularly since the Coastal Authority has been part of that Ministry as of February 2014. This Authority administers the general permit requirement for offshore construction. Since 2016, the Coastal Authority has also been responsible for the administration of the setback zone and the Flood Risk Act, which were previously the responsibility of the Environment Protection Agency.

The Environmental Protection Agency (formerly the Nature Agency) administers the Nature Protection Act. Despite having lost responsibility for the setback zone and the Flood Risk Act, it is still responsible for the implementation of the EU Water Framework Directive and the Marine Strategy Framework Directive. Until June 2015, the Nature Agency also had the overall responsibility for the Planning Act, but this was then transferred to the Ministry of Business. With this transfer, the Ministry of Business (and the Business Authority) also took over responsibility for the implementation of the EU Maritime Spatial Planning Directive and the adoption of a new Act on Maritime Spatial Planning (2016) – thus, responsibility for both terrestrial and marine spatial planning rest with the same Ministry but under different agencies (the latter being administered by the Danish Maritime Authority).

The Ministry for Transport has the main responsibility for harbours, whereas the Ministry for Climate, Energy and Utilities holds responsibility for issues associated with offshore oil and gas extraction, as well as offshore wind energy development.

The local authorities hold the main responsibilities onshore, although the setback zone is administered by the Coastal Authority. The responsibilities of the local authorities include Municipal and Local Planning, as well as granting permits for new activities in the rural zones. As mentioned earlier, the municipalities also draw up Flood Risk Plans and Climate Adaptation Plans. In addition, as of September 2018, the local authorities have assumed primary responsibilities in relation to flood defence. This includes both coastal defence projects for more than one property (joint projects) as well as projects initiated by individual landowners.

Prior to the 2007 local government reform, the then 14 county councils had important coastal responsibilities related to drawing up regional plans and administration of the Beach Protection Zone. The regional plans have, however, been abolished and replaced by much more strategic regional growth and development strategies which are not part of the land use planning system. Thus, the regional authorities – five regional councils – have very limited responsibilities relating to coastal issues.

For onshore areas, the Planning Act ensures both vertical and horizontal coordination between relevant authorities in planning matters, but there are a few exceptions in relation to offshore areas. For example, it is possible to plan for houseboats, as well as for land reclamation in coastal areas for development purposes, but a permit from the Coastal Authority is also required for such a proposal. Vertical coordination is clearly expressed in the Planning Act through the planning hierarchy, where Municipal and Local Plans may not strive against national planning provisions, including Flood Risk Plans. Furthermore, the Planning Act provides for fairly extensive public participation, as discussed below. Horizontal coordination is also ensured under the Planning Act, providing for coordinated planning. The Municipal Plans establish guidelines not only for (urban) development but also for the safeguarding of recreational, landscape, natural, and cultural heritage interests. Thus, the Danish planning system provides an appropriate framework for the coordination of different sectoral land use interests onshore.

For offshore areas, there are few formal requirements for coordination, and until recently there was no overarching marine or maritime planning system in place. However, due to the implementation of the EU Maritime Spatial Planning Directive (2014/89/EU), Denmark adopted a new Act on Maritime Spatial Planning in June 2016. In 2015, the Coastal Authority issued a publication laying out general principles and criteria for the administration of the permit scheme for offshore activities (Kystdirektoratet, 2015). This could be regarded as a first step towards a more strategic planning document, although it applies only to the administration by the Coastal Authority. Horizontal coordination is traditionally ensured through consultation at state level, involving the relevant sectoral ministries.

Within sectors, vertical coordination, between different levels of authority, takes place on an ad hoc basis. Whereas consultation by some state authorities is sporadic, it is notable that the Coastal Authority regularly consults with relevant local authorities. The requirements for SEAs for plans and programmes and for EIAs for projects should ensure that broad consultation with relevant authorities and the public does take place.

As discussed in the introduction to this chapter, the lack of vertical coordination in relation to offshore activities has recently been demonstrated in heated debates regarding "nearshore" wind farms, which will be situated 4–8 km offshore. The legislation does not specify how and when local authorities or the public should be involved in decision-making, apart from the requirements set out for environmental assessment procedures. It is likely that new decision-making procedures may specify involvement of local authorities in such decisions.

Public participation and access to justice – legal anchoring

Public participation is a key element in the planning procedures defined in the Danish Planning Act for onshore areas. A minimum consultation period of 8 weeks is required in the preparation of Municipal Plans and was previously also required for Local Plans. In 2017, however, the minimum consultation period for Local Plans was reduced to 4 weeks, or even as little as 2 weeks for plans of minor importance. Municipal Planning also includes public participation prior to the drawing up of a proposal for a Municipal Plan, either as part of a strategic Municipal Plan document or on an ad hoc basis. As mentioned above, there are specific requirements for plan proposals in the coastal zone – the purpose being to explain or illustrate the potential visual effects of new development. These rules aim to ensure meaningful public participation.

Overall, it is difficult to evaluate the effectiveness of the public participation procedures. In general, the local authorities adhere to the public participation requirements of the Planning Act. Nevertheless, there have been examples of process issues, such as inadequate visualization in plan proposals, which led to rejection of plans by the Appeals Board, for example, a local plan for twelve new houses (Naturklagenævnet, ref. MAD2007.2270)

For offshore areas, there are few formal requirements relating to public participation in decision-making. According to the Coastal Protection Act, applications must be made publicly available if they are of general interest. In most cases, neighbours must be informed, and the responsible authority will often consult relevant organizations and other parties who will potentially be affected by the project.

Public participation is mandatory both offshore and onshore if a plan or project is subject to an environmental assessment procedure – either SEA or EIA. The degree of participation may vary from minor participation in strategic planning or assessment to intense participation in detailed project planning or assessment. Either way, the participation may not affect the actual outcome, despite objections from the public.

The Aarhus Convention is specifically incorporated into Danish law in that the law grants wide access to administrative appeals for environmental NGOs (ENGOs). With effect from February 2017, the former Nature and Environment Appeals Board was split into a Planning Appeals Board and an Environment and Food Appeals Board. Since the transfer of the Coastal Authority to the Ministry for the Environment in February 2014, some decisions made under the Coastal Protection Act can also be appealed to the Environment and Food Appeals Board. Regarding offshore renewable energy installations such as wind turbines, appeals can be made to the Energy Appeals Board. However, according to the Act on Renewable Energy, wide access for ENGOs is granted only for EIA procedures and nature protection issues (Promotion of Renewable Energy Act, 2019).

Administrative appeals under the Coastal Protection Act and the Planning Act are generally restricted to legality issues, as opposed to a full review of proposals under the relevant legislation. However, joint coastal defence projects can be appealed in full under the Coastal Protection Act. Following, an amendment in 2020 the Minister may, however, in particular circumstances deny access to administrative appeals for such projects. Access to courts is normally subject to traditional legal standing requirements, granted to those significantly and individually affected. However, cases brought by ENGOs are generally accepted by the courts.

There is no specific information service available relating to coastal planning and regulation. Information is normally provided by each of the relevant authorities on the issues for which they have responsibility.

Fiscal aspects: Incentives and disincentives regarding coastal zone management

The municipalities, in general, have very wide powers to repeal existing plans (Municipal Plans and Local Plans) through the adoption of new plans without compensating landowners. The local authority may also issue a preliminary prohibition against new projects that are in accordance with existing plans if they intend to prepare a new Local Plan within one year. Due to the coordinated nature of land use planning in Denmark, plans can be made for a broad range of purposes, including development, landscape protection, and recreational purposes. If, however, a (new) Local Plan reserves a property for public purposes, including parks, roads, or public infrastructure, the landowner may compel the authority to purchase the whole or part of the property.

As noted at Section 4, within the setback zone defined under the Nature Protection Act, only minor renovations to existing buildings (such as replacing windows or the roof) are permitted. Extensions require an exemption under a relatively strict procedure. A change in the use of a building may also require an exemption if it can lead to alterations in the state of the protected area. Given that the authorities and Appeals Board tend to stringency in these matters, landowners cannot take for granted that they will receive any exemption they seek for the purposes of constructing an extension, upgrade, or change in the use of a building.

Landowners can, in general, not claim compensation rights for properties that are threatened by coastal erosion or sea rise. There is also no compensation for such landowners to be relocated. Unwritten rules would normally prevent local authorities from spending money on the relocation of individual landowners, even if this would be less expensive than flood prevention measures. The municipalities may, however, decide to buy properties to carry out coastal protection measures, such as establishing reservoirs or similar flood prevention facilities. The local authorities (municipalities) may also expropriate properties for the purpose of coastal defence projects (Coastal Protection Act) or for the purpose of implementing Local Plans (under the Planning Act). In general, expropriation is only used in few cases (Erhvervsministeriet, 2018).

In most cases, private property insurance will not cover damage due to rising sea levels (or rising rivers or lakes). There is a public insurance scheme for damage to property that has been flooded by extreme flood events (those which statistically do not occur more frequently than every 20 years), as set out in the Flood and Storm Act (2018). If that scheme is triggered, the Danish Storm Council determines landowners' rights to compensation on a case-by-case basis.[8]

Taxation or other fiscal measures are not used in relation to flood-prone areas or protected zones. The property value on which property taxes is based may, however, depend upon the character of the area, including relevant restrictions on development.

Overall assessment

Danish legislation identifies the coast as having national priority status and provides several strong measures to protect the coastal zone, including its generally 300 m wide coastal setback zone and 3 km wide Coastal Planning Zone. However, the country's traditionally stringent protection of the coast has been recently challenged in public debate, resulting in amendments to both the Nature Protection Act and the Planning Act, most recently in 2017, and to the Coastal Protection Act in 2018.

Despite strong protection of the coasts, Integrated Coastal Zone Management has received only limited attention in Danish legislation and policies. Denmark has not produced an ICZM strategy, and this is perhaps most evident in the lack of legislative and administrative integration across the shoreline. Onshore areas are primarily governed by the local authorities and subject to a coordinated land use planning system within which there is horizontal and vertical coordination. Offshore areas, on the contrary, are primarily governed by state authorities and have previously not been subject to coordinated maritime planning. Yet this will change with the adoption of the 2021 Maritime Spatial Plan in accordance with the 2016 Maritime Spatial Planning Act. Furthermore, processes for state consultation with local authorities and the public are not clearly defined for offshore projects.

Climate change and adaptation is receiving increasing attention in Denmark – particularly following recent storms which resulted in urban areas being flooded, as well as flooding due to heavy rainfall. State and local authorities have begun to implement the EU Flood Risk Directive and the initial designation of flood risk areas has been revised, resulting in designation of fourteen instead of ten areas. Notably, the implementation of the Floods Directive has been hampered by Denmark's regulatory split, resulting in two parallel sets of legislation – one for flood risks from the sea and one for rivers and lakes. In addition, separate measures of municipal Climate Adaptation Plans and designation of flood- or erosion-prone areas have been introduced as part of Municipal Planning under the Planning Act. The result is a somewhat fragmented legal framework, although some attempts have been made to coordinate the administration.

Finally, the balance of interests under the Coastal Protection Act has recently shifted in favour of landowners, who may now find it easier to obtain permits for coastal defence works. On the other hand, the legislation still offers limited protection to owners of property in flood-prone areas. Such landowners must rely on the public storm flood insurance scheme for flooding due to extreme weather conditions. As such, it appears that the recent changes to the Coastal Protection Act reflect attempts to address only very specific concerns of individual landowners, rather than being based on a coherent and integrated strategy.

Notes

1. For an overview of different coastal interests see Kaa (2014).
2. Yet the former Danish Nature Agency initiated (mainly in the run-up to EU initiatives) ICZM studies in 1998 and 2013. In 2006, a report was published as a follow-up to the 2002 Recommendation of the EU on the basis of twelve Danish cases, as well as a survey (see NIRAS, 2006).
3. After the 2015 Parliamentary election, a new liberal-conservative Government merged the Ministry for the Environment and the Ministry for Food and Agriculture to form a new Ministry for Environment and Food with effect from July 2015.
4. Prior to the demarcation of the setback zone, the zone in principle had to be determined in each case considering the actual shoreline, including the daily high-water mark.
5. The Coastal Planning Zone demarcation is based on (slightly) more detailed maps (1:100,000), issued in accordance with a guidance note from 1983. In practice, the zone is shown in a web portal: http://arealinformation.miljoeportal.dk/distribution/
6. The granting of exemptions was in 2016 transferred from the Nature Agency to the Coastal Authority as part of a major relocation of State jobs. The Coastal Directorate is located in West Jutland, whereas the Nature Agency was located in Copenhagen.
7. Prior to the inclusion of the coastal planning provisions in the Planning Act in 1994, similar provisions existed in a national planning circular issued by the Ministry in 1981.
8. The Storm Council also provides information and reports on storm events. See http://www.storm-raadet.dk/.

References

Anker, H. T., Nellemann, V., & Sverdrup-Jensen, S. (2004). Coastal zone management in Denmark: Ways and means for further integration. *Ocean & Coastal Management* 47(9–10), 429–535.

Anker, H. T., Kaa, B., & Nellemann, V. (2014). *Forvaltning af kystzonen. Rammer, udfordringer og scenarier.* IGN Rapport, Institut for Geovidenskab og Naturforvaltning. Available at: http://research.ku.dk/search/?pure=en/publications/forvaltning-af-kystzonen(3dd5955b-1b2f-42bb-85a3-99ea43dbfb6b).html

Anker, H. T., & Olsen, B. E. (2019). Blæst på havet – om beslutningsprocesser for vindmøller i Danmark [Wind at sea – on decision-making processes for wind turbines in Denmark]. In Darpö, J., Forsberg, M., Pettersson, M. & Zetterberg, C. (Eds.) *Miljörätten och den föhandlingsovillaga naturen.* Iustus Förlag, Uppsala, pp. 13–31.

Energistyrelsen [Energy Agency]. (2016). Nearshore Wind Tender. Available at: https://ens.dk/en/our-responsibilities/wind-power/ongoing-offshore-projects/nearshore-wind-tender

Erhvervsministeriet [Ministry of Business]. (2018). *Betænkning No. 1569 om ekspropriation efter plan-loven* [Report No. 1569 on Expropriation under the Planning Act].

Kaa, B. (2014). Aktuelle udfordringer for ICM og MSP: Ressourcer og aktiviteter i kystzonen og på havet. In Anker, H.T., Kaa, B., & Nellemann, V. *Forvaltning af kystzonen. Rammer, udfordringer og scenarier.* IGN Rapport, Institut for Geovidenskab og Naturforvaltning. Available at: http://research.ku.dk/search/?pure=en/publications/forvaltning-af-kystzonen(3dd5955b-1b2f-42bb-85a3-99ea43dbfb6b).html

Kystdirektoratet [Coastal Authority]. (2011). *Kystbeskyttelsesstrategi, Kystdirektoratet* [*Coastal Protection Strategy*].

—(2015). Kystdirektoratets administrationsgrundlag for søterritoriet [The Coastal Authority's administrative guidance for offshore activities].

Naturstyrelsen [Environment Agency]. (2013). Vejledning om klimatilpasningsplaner og klimalokalplaner [Guidance Note on Climate Adaptation Plans]. Miljøministeriet.

NIRAS. (2006). Analyse af kystzoneadministration i Danmark [Analysis of coastal zone administration in Denmark]. Available at: http://naturstyrelsen.dk/media/nst/65510/analyse_kystzoneadministrationen.pdf

Ram, B., Anker, H. T., Clausen, N.-E., & Nielsen, T. R. L. (2017). *Public Engagement in Danish Nearshore Wind Projects in Law and Practice.* DTU Wind Energy Report-E-0142. Available at: http://www.wind2050.dk/publications

World Factbook (n.d.). Denmark. Available at: https://www.cia.gov/Library/publications/the-world-factbook/geos/da.html [Accessed September 2019]

European Legislation (listed chronologically)

Council Directive 92/43/EEC of 21 May 1992 on the conservation of natural habitats and of wild fauna and flora OJ L 206, 22.7.1992, pp. 7–50

Directive 2000/60/EC of the European Parliament and of the Council of 23 October 2000 establishing a framework for Community action in the field of water policy, OJ L 327, 22.12.2000, pp. 1–73

Directive 2008/56/EC of the European Parliament and of the Council of 17 June 2008 establishing a framework for community action in the field of marine environmental policy (Marine Strategy Framework Directive), OJ L 164, 25.6.2008, pp. 19–40

Directive 2014/89/EU of the European Parliament and of the Council of 23 July 2014 establishing a framework for maritime spatial planning, OJ L 257, 28.8.2014, pp. 135–145

National Legislation (available at www.retsinformation.dk) (listed chronologically)

Delineation of the Territorial Sea Act (1999) Act no. 200/1999 (lov om afgrænsning af søterritoriet)

Harbours Act (2012, as amended) Consolidated Act 457/2012 (bekendtgørelse af lov om havne)

Amendment to the Planning Act and the Nature Conservation Act (2014) Act no. 1529/2014 (lov om ændring af lov om planlægning og lov om naturbeskyttelse)

Maritime Spatial Planning Act (2016) no. 615/2016 (lov om havplanlægning)

Flood Risk Assessment and Management Statutory Order (2016) no. 894/2016 (bekendtgørelse om vurdering og risikostyring for oversvømmelser fra havet, fjorde eller andre dele af søterritoriet)

Flood Risk Act (2017, as amended) Consolidated Act no. 1085/2017 (bekendtgørelse af lov om vurdering og styring af oversvømmelsesrisikoen fra vandløb og søer)

Flood and Storm Act (2018, as amended) Consolidated Act no. 281/2018 (bekendtgørelse af lov om stormflod og stormfald)

Planning Act (2018, as amended) Consolidated Act no. 287/2018 (bekendtgørelse af lov om planlægning)

Coastal Protection Act (2019, as amended) Consolidated Act no. 57/2019 (bekendtgørelse af lov om kystbeskyttelse)

Nature Protection Act (2019, as amended) Consolidated Act no. 240/2019 (bekendtgørelse af lov om naturbeskyttelse)

Fisheries Act (2019, as amended) Consolidated Act 261/2019 (bekendtgørelse af lov om fiskeri og fiskeopdræt)

Promotion of Renewable Energy Act (2019, as amended) Consolidated Act no. 356/2019 (bekendtgørelse af lov om fremme af vedvarende energi)

Court and Appeal Board cases

Natur- og Miljøklagenævnet [Nature and Environment Appeals Board] 15 February 2015, NMK-33-02860 and NMK-41-00198

Naturklagenævnet [Nature Appeals Board] 13 November 2007, NKN-33-01617, MAD2007.2270

Østre Landsret [Eastern High Court] MAD2013.891

Vestre Landsret [Western High Court] MAD2015.7

6 Germany

Eva Schachtner

Overview

Germany has two different coastlines, given that it borders two seas; the North Sea and the Baltic Sea. The environmental characteristics of these seas are vastly different and thus pose different management challenges. Although Germany's coastline length does not make up a high proportion of its borders, as in other countries in this book, it is a significant resource for the country: It is highly varied, home to several major cities, and a popular tourist destination in the summer months.

Germany has adopted comprehensive climate change policies on both national and state levels, and its environmental legislation includes strong protection of the coastal zone from inappropriate development. Only the basic protection of coastal land is safeguarded through federal regulations. More detailed coastal protection measures are administered through state-level land use regulations. Those regulations vary considerably across the states and even across neighbouring municipalities. Nevertheless, Germany demonstrates good, sound practice in coastal zone management. In addition, Germany was an early adopter of the Integrated Coastal Zone Management (ICZM) strategy format recommended by the European Parliament and the Council in 2002.

The context: Introduction to the coastal issues in Germany

The German coastline is about 2,400 km long (World Factbook, n.d.), which is split between the Baltic Sea (northeast) and the North Sea (northwest). Both coasts lie within a temperate climate zone. However, there are significant morphological and biological differences between the two seas.

For example, tidal movement is significant on the North Sea coast, whereas this phenomenon is barely noticeable in the brackish Baltic Sea (Schernewski, 2002, p. 3). The North Sea is one of the most productive and biologically diverse seas in the world and encompasses the Wadden Sea, which is the world's largest ecosystem of its kind (see Figure 6.1). The Baltic Sea, in contrast, is largely isolated from other seas and has low water exchange. As a consequence, it has low oxygen content and salinity, high pollution levels, and low species diversity. Germany's coastal areas include lagoons, estuaries, bays, mudflats, peninsulas, islands, cliffs, and flat coastal plains, that together form a beautiful and diverse coastal landscape.

Several of Germany's big cities are located along the coast, including Hamburg, Kiel, and Rostock. Hamburg is also home to Germany's largest seaport (Statista, 2018c). Outside these cities, the coastal regions have a relatively low population density (Federal Institute for

Figure 6.1 Borkum island coast on the Wadden Sea, Germany

Source: Detmold. Available at: https://pixabay.com/photos/borkum-island-gulls-wadden-sea-4428395/

Population Research, 2018); for example, the population density of Hamburg was 2.334 inhabitants per square kilometre in 2015, while in Lower Saxony, it was 164; in Schleswig-Holstein, 179; and in Mecklenburg-Western Pomerania, 69 (Office of Statistics of Lower Saxony, 2016). The coast is a popular tourist destination, particularly in the summer months. More than 5 million tourists spent their holidays at the North Sea coast in 2018 (Statista, 2018a) and almost 7 million at the Baltic Sea coast (Statista, 2018b). Germany's coastal zone and marine environment host a wide range of activities, including mineral extraction, aquaculture, and fisheries (Schernewski, 2002, p. 4). As part of Germany's efforts to transition to renewable energy sources, 1,196 wind turbines had been installed offshore by the end of 2017, and more are expected (Bundesverband WindEnergie, 2018).

German administrative structure

In any discussion of coastal zone management in Germany, it is important to understand the decentralized structure of governance in the country. Germany is a federation, with a central government ('Bund') and sixteen states ('Länder'). According to the German Constitution (Article 30), state functions are the responsibility of the states, unless the constitution expressly provides for federal law. Where it applies, federal law takes precedence over Länder law (German Constitution, Article 31). Each state consists of several regions, districts, and municipalities. A total of five states are located along the German coast: Lower Saxony, Schleswig-Holstein, Mecklenburg-Western Pomerania, and the city-states Hamburg and Bremen.

Introduction to the legal framework for coastal zone management in Germany

Unlike countries which have a law specifically designed to deal with coastal zone protection and management, in Germany this is not the case. Yet the absence of a dedicated law does not mean that the relevant issues are not addressed in German law: More than 30 sectoral laws, regulations, and directives have relevance for the coastal zone, and various federal, state, and regional authorities are responsible for their implementation (Federal Ministry for the Environment, 2006b, pp. 19–20). Indeed, taken together, the relevant laws are meticulous in their approach to coastal zone management issues.

A key piece of legislation relevant to the German coastal zone is the Federal Nature Conservation Act, which, as discussed below, defines a set of restrictions on development in coastal zones. This law is the primary source of nature conservation law in Germany and contains provisions pertaining to various EU directives for species protection and protected areas; provisions on landscape planning; provisions for access to nature and landscape for recreational purposes; and provisions for the participation of recognized nature conservation associations in certain decision-making processes. Valuable coastal biotopes such as cliffs, beach embankments, salt marshes, and tidal flats are generally protected from development by that law (Federal Nature Conservation Act, Section 30). This federal legislation is supplemented in each of the 16 German states by state conservation acts, which may include detailed provisions relating to coastal zone management.

As a general rule, nature conservation laws in Germany are stringent and work on the principle that any significant adverse effect on nature and landscape should be avoided. Adverse effects which are significant and unavoidable are to be offset – either through compensation or substitution measures or, but only in cases where such offset is not possible, via monetary substitution (Federal Nature Conservation Act, Section 13).

Additional laws relating to the protection and management of the coastal zone include planning legislation and building laws. Federal spatial planning is limited to the development of guiding targets and principles. State spatial planning gives more concrete form to those principles, but the most detailed planning decisions are taken at the local level. It is thus the responsibility of local authorities to comprehensively regulate the use of land for building and other purposes (Pahl-Weber & Henckel, 2008, p. 40). Sectoral planning complements the cross-sectoral and comprehensive local land use planning, regional planning, and state spatial planning. It can be roughly divided into the sectors transport and communications, utilities, defence, agriculture, and environmental protection and nature conservation (Pahl-Weber & Henckel, 2008, p. 50).

Key definitions for Germany's coastal areas

In German law and practice for coastal zone management, the following geographical concepts apply: The shoreline, the coastal zone, and the beach.

The concept of the shoreline

In order to prevent construction close to the water, German law (specifically, the Federal Nature Conservation Act) contains two different definitions of the shoreline – one for each of the country's seas. At the North Sea, the shoreline is identified as the 'average high water line', whereas at the Baltic Sea, the definition is the 'average water line'. The reason for the difference is that in the North Sea tidelands, the water drains away at low tide, to a width of up to 40 km (Nordsee24, n.d.).

For the determination of property boundaries at the coast, the respective Water Acts of the coastal states contain more detailed rules. For example, the Lower Saxony Water Act (Section 41) refers to the medium tide height.[1] The Schleswig-Holstein Water Act (Section 95) states that the boundary between the sea and the waterside properties is determined by the average water level and, within the tidal area, by the average high water level. According to the Mecklenburg-Western Pomerania Water Act (Section 53), the average water level is the arithmetic average of all annual average water levels of the past 20 years.[2]

Germany's coastal zone

The term 'coastal zone' is not clearly defined in Germany. The German ICZM Strategy applies to the coastal zone in a broad sense – taking into account the interactions between the marine Exclusive Economic Zone (EEZ), the coastal sea (the 12 nautical mile zone), the transitional waters (as per the European Water Framework Directive 2000/60/EC), areas adjoining the estuaries and influenced by the tides, and the adjoining rural districts[3] and respective administrative units on shore (Federal Ministry for the Environment, 2006a, p. 7).

According to a rather 'functional' definition in a Schleswig-Holstein guidance document on ICZM, '… the coastal zone marks the border between sea and dry land. In every single case, its relevant extent is defined by the area in which terrestrial and maritime processes (economic, ecological, and socio-cultural) depend on – or influence – each other (zone of problems and potentials)' (Schleswig-Holstein Ministry of the Interior, 2003, p. 5).

The definition of the 'coastal zone' is therefore flexible and may, depending on the problem being addressed, extend far into the hinterland. The Schleswig-Holstein Land Development Plan from 2010, for example, recommends including, at least for orientation purposes, an area extending 3 km landwards. In some cases, the coastal zone may extend up to 100 km inland, for example, in the context of determining the necessary extent of coastal protection measures for residential and economic areas (Ministerial Conference for Spatial Planning, 2013, p. 17). Seawards, the territorial sea, but often also the EEZ, is considered to belong to the coastal zone (Gläser, 2005, p. 13). In reality, however, administrative boundaries mainly influence the delimitation of coastal management units. Rather than presenting itself as a single administrative unit, the coastal zone is therefore mostly managed on the level of the coastal states, regions, municipalities, and sectoral administrative areas (Gee, Kannen, & Licht-Eggert, 2006, p. 5).

The beach

The term 'beach' is used across coastal legislation and regulations in Germany. In common usage, the term 'beach' designates the shallow, sandy, or gravelly edge of the sea (Bibliographisches Institut GmbH, 2018). The Water Act of Schleswig-Holstein defines the beach in Section 64 as the coastal strip that consists of sand, gravel, scree, boulder clay, or similar materials and that lies within the range of influence of the waves. The seaward boundary of the beach is considered to be the shoreline; the landward boundary is marked by the beginning of dense vegetation, the foot of steep banks, dunes, dikes, or building developments. Section 85 of the Water Act of Mecklenburg-Western Pomerania contains a similar definition. Thus, even though there is no consistent definition of the term 'beach', the meaning of the term in common usage, as well as the corresponding definitions in the state laws, provides an indication. In any case, a sharp delineation of the beach has been considered difficult because of the varying natural conditions (NdsOVG, 2016, recital 88).

According to a recent judgement of the Federal Administrative Court, the beach includes the dry sand areas between the foot of the dike and the shoreline, determined by the average high water line, as well as the wet sand areas seawards of the shoreline that extend to the average low water line, thus, the areas suitable for bathing or mudflat walking (BVerwG, 2017, recital 38). This definition, however, seems to be influenced by the context of the specific case, in which the court had to decide on the extent of the right to free access to the beach at the North Sea coast. It therefore includes the area needed for the activities covered by the right to free access and might not be conclusive for other cases.

Coastal public land

The term 'public property', which stems from the French concept of 'domaine public', is unknown in German federal law. The Länder legislatures are allowed to create public property but have rarely made use of this possibility (Althammer, 2016, recital 48). To determine the owner of beachfront properties (which may include land up to the shoreline), it is often necessary to consult very old laws and to trace back the ownership structure. In most cases, the research shows that those properties have been assigned to the respective coastal state (BGH, 1989; Bosecke, 2005a, p. 462).

Only one coastal state has decided to explicitly regulate the ownership of the beach: Mecklenburg-Western Pomerania. That state's Water Act (Section 85, 1992) states that, without prejudice to properly acquired rights of third parties, the state owns the beach. Nevertheless, plots on the beach can become the property of individuals in line with the general provisions for the transfer of property (SchlHOLG, 2000). If a plot of land (or parts of it) which is privately owned becomes part of the beach, for example, through a natural disaster, it remains private property. The exercise of property rights on the beach, however, is made subject to certain restrictions (referred to as 'modified' private ownership; Althammer, 2016, recital 49). Those restrictions mainly result from the stipulations of the respective Nature Conservation Acts concerning, for example, free public access (SchlHOLG, 2003).

Permitted uses and development on the beach

The permitted uses and development on the beach are regulated on the state and municipal levels. In Mecklenburg-Western Pomerania, the Implementing Law to the Nature Conservation Act of 2010 (Section 27) regulates uses of the beach. It forbids inter alia campfires on the dunes as well as driving and camping outside of marked areas. Municipalities may reserve a part of the beach for special use, such as for landing boats and bathing. The Schleswig-Holstein State Conservation Act allows beach visitors to use roofed wicker beach chairs, which are very popular on the windy German beaches, but does not allow camping (Sections 32, 33).

Municipal beach ordinances further specify permitted and prohibited uses for many beaches. For example, they forbid the building of huts with flotsam and jetsam or other materials (Municipal Beach Ordinance of Heringsdorf, 2015, Section 4). For permanent kiosks, for which a building permit is required, an additional permit of the municipality is often required (cf. Municipal Beach Ordinance of Lubmin, 2011). Further use restrictions may result from the provisions for coastal protection (cf. for example, Water Act of Schleswig-Holstein, Section 78).

Figure 6.2 The Beach in Binz, Germany

Source: dicau58 on Flickr. CC BY-SA 2.0 license. Available at: https://www.flickr.com/photos/dicau58/14156098633

Permitted development on the beach is defined by individual binding land use plans, developed at the local level. For example, the binding land use plan for the coastal resort of Binz on the island of Rügen (Figure 6.2) permits only development which is compatible with the intended use of the area as a bathing and sports beach (e.g. snack bars). Since the plan concerns an area located completely within the coastal setback zone (see the next section), the uses permitted, such as kiosks, represent exceptions to the general ban on development. To ensure that these facilities are constructed in keeping with nature conservation and coastal protection goals, the binding land use plan restricts their floorspace to 15 m². After the bathing season, all construction must be removed to allow the dunes and beach to regenerate. These regulations are intended to reinforce the temporary nature of kiosks and to prevent unacceptable building densities on the beach (Binding Land Use Plan No. 29 for Binz, 2012, pp. 11–12).

Coastal setback zone and permitted uses

According to the Federal Nature Conservation Act of 2009 (Section 61), development must not be permitted within a distance of at least 150 m from the shoreline (with its varying definitions at the North Sea and Baltic Sea, as described above). This setback requirement does not apply to structures that were legally constructed or approved at the time the Federal Nature Conservation Act entered into force. Exceptions also include structures needed for infrastructure, emergency response, or coastal protection. Additional exceptions may be granted on a case-by-case basis, with consideration of the effect of the proposal on the environment, as well as the public interest. The individual states may extend the setback zone or provide for further exceptions. As will be shown below, two states have made use of this possibility. They actually permit exceptions to such an extent that they risk undermining the objective of the setback zone.

Mecklenburg-Western Pomerania setback rules

Mecklenburg-Western Pomerania instituted a 200 m setback zone in the state's Nature Conservation Act of 2002. In a 2009 draft revision of that law, the maintenance of that setback zone was recommended (Mecklenburg-Western Pomerania Parliament, 2009, p. 81). Yet the Implementing Law to the Nature Conservation Act finally adopted in 2010 reaffirms in Section 29 the regulation of the Federal Nature Conservation Act by prohibiting development only within 150 m of the shoreline, with the added proviso that the prohibition extends both landwards and seawards from the shoreline. And even within that 150 m zone, the Act allows development that is in accordance with a legally binding land use plan or that blends in well with an already existing built-up area.[4] The adoption of a binding land use plan which allows development within the setback zone requires prior permission via granting of an exception by the responsible nature protection authority. Section 29 of the same Act, moreover, provides a detailed list of infrastructure facilities that are excluded from the prohibition on development. This takes account of the fact that the coast provides a significant locational advantage for certain facilities such as wind farms. Further exceptions, including for water sports installations or installation for fishing or hunting, may be granted on a case-by-case basis.

Schleswig-Holstein setback rules

The Schleswig-Holstein State Conservation Act of 2010 (Section 35, as amended in 2016) states that construction is not permitted within 150 m landwards of the shoreline. Where the coast is at a cliff-face, the shoreline is defined as the peak of the cliff for this purpose. The setback rules do not apply to building projects within the scope of application of a legally binding land use plan or for the structural extension of agricultural and commercial enterprises. Prior to 2016, the setback zone was only 100 m (narrower than specified in Federal law). The extension of the setback zone was considered necessary by the Ministry for the Environment due to the common practice of coastal municipalities of adopting land use plans that allow touristic developments close to the sea for purely economic reasons. The adoption of binding land use plans remains possible with the consent of the responsible nature protection authority and, consequently, building projects within the setback zone, yet the 2016 change triggered protests by the tourist industry (Jung, 2016).

Right of public access

The Federal Nature Conservation Act states, as a general principle (Section 59), that the general public are permitted to enter the open landscape on roads and pathways and on unused land areas for purposes of recreation. The right to 'enter' the open landscape within the meaning of the law includes the right to stay for some time, to relax, and to enjoy nature (Fischer-Hüftle, 2010, § 59, recital 12). Open landscapes are the areas outside of settlements (OVG NRW, 2013). Beaches, including artificial beaches (BVerwG, 2017, recital 54), usually form part of the open landscape, even if there are individual buildings in the area (BVerwG, 2017, recital 51). Roads and pathways include pathways on private property, such as field margins and beaten paths (OVG Bbg, 2004). Nevertheless, state laws can specify the conditions under which the right to enter the open landscape can be exercised. Thus, in Schleswig-Holstein, apart from beaches, the public does not have the right to enter unused areas not dedicated to public use (Schleswig-Holstein State Conservation Act, Section 30).[5]

Specific provisions relating to accessibility of the beach can be found at the state level, as follows:

Access to the coastal zone in Mecklenburg-Western Pomerania

In Mecklenburg-Western Pomerania, everybody is allowed to enter and stay on the beach at any time, unless there are legal provisions stipulating otherwise. Hiking along the beach must not be obstructed and must be free of charge (Implementing Law to the Nature Conservation Act 2010, Section 27).

Regarding usage fees, the Implementing Law requires that a reasonable balance[6] be maintained between the part of the beach whose use is subject to a charge and the part of the beach that may be used free of charge. In addition, the State Water Act allows the use of coastal waters for bathing and for water and ice sports free of charge and the entry to the beach for that purpose (Section 22).

There are generally no fences around beaches in Mecklenburg-Western Pomerania, and there are still many beaches that are free of charge. If there are fees and charges, they are set at the municipal level. For example, the municipality Bad Doberan manages a spa resort on the Baltic Sea coast. To cover maintenance costs incurred by the municipality, a local statute from 2013 required that visitors pay a spa tax (1–2 euros per day, depending on the season). Yet this provision was struck down by the higher administrative authority, which confirmed that entry to the beach, as well as for bathing and hiking, must be free of charge. Only patrons who settle on the beach and are, for example, caught sitting on a bath towel or a beach chair, can be required to pay the tax. It is unclear, however, if actions such as taking a little break to drink some water while hiking on the beach require payment of the spa tax (Oehlers, 2013). The instruction of the higher administrative authority is thus very difficult to implement and enforce, and conflicts are likely to arise (Werner, 2014). Day-trippers in particular often completely ignore the automatic pay stations (Sass, 2016). Despite the difficulties, several municipalities already plan additional taxes (e.g. for dogs on the beach), or the elimination of winter discounts to cover their expenses (Rathke, 2017).

Access to the coastal zone in Schleswig-Holstein

Schleswig-Holstein has similar regulations on the access to the beach as Mecklenburg-Western Pomerania (Sections 32, 33, and 34 of the State Conservation Act 2010 and in Section 17 of the Water Act 2008). An ordinance specifies the conditions for restrictions on the free entry to areas designated for special use. According to that ordinance, hiking along the waterline must always be free of charge. Hikers can only be required to walk around a beach (rather than through it) if the municipality provides a special path for them, preferably within sight of the shore (Section 1 Schleswig-Holstein Ordinance on Special Use of the Beach). However, it is not clear whether (and if so, where) access to the water must be free of charge (Schleswig-Holstein Parliament, 2017).

Access to the coastal zone in Lower Saxony

In Lower Saxony, neither the Implementing Law to the Nature Conservation Act nor the Water Act regulates access to the beach, despite the fact that a proposal for a respective amendment was made in 2012 (Lower Saxony Parliament, 2012).

In this state, decisions regarding fees for the use of the beach are at the discretion of municipalities. The result is that the use of almost three-quarters of the beaches is subject to a charge (about 3 euros) during the bathing season. Beaches in Lower Saxony are often surrounded by fences to ensure payment. Hikers are thus required to walk around those fences, which is a further cause of controversy going back decades in some municipalities (Kreutzträger, 2014). For example, the initiative 'Free Beaches for Free Citizens' generated a lot of public support (cf. almost 50,000 signatures for a petition/Initiative 'Freie Bürger für freie Strände', 2014).

In Wangerland, 90% of the beach has been fenced and a fee imposed on those wishing to enter the beach. In a claim by residents against those fees, the administrative court and appeal court upheld the legitimacy of the imposition of fees (VG Oldenburg, 2014; NdsOVG, 2016). The reasoning of the courts was that the beach in Wangerland more closely resembles a commercial recreational facility than an 'unused land area' and that it requires extensive maintenance. The case was then brought before the Federal Administrative Court, which ultimately decided that it is not legal to commercialize the beach on such a large scale. The court further decided that neither maintenance and cleaning measures nor the provision of individual waste containers and sanitary buildings turns the beach into a 'used area' within the meaning of Section 59 of the Federal Nature Conservation Act. According to the court, access can be made subject to a fee only for areas containing comprehensive infrastructure facilities, such as ambulance stations, sanitary buildings, kiosks, and playgrounds. A further prerequisite for charging fees is that they do not only serve to commercialize taking walks and bathing – activities that are to be free of charge according to Section 59 (BVerwG, 2017). Since the decision, the municipality of Wangerland has given in and now provides free access to two-thirds of its beaches (Wolf, 2018).

Given the decision of the above Federal Administrative Court, particularly on beaches that do not have any service infrastructure or on which that infrastructure is only available in a small part of a beach, the decision to charge fees is likely to be challenged and even overturned. Nevertheless, not all coastal municipalities plan on relinquishing their fees. For example, some are arguing that the fee they charge is not an entrance fee but a spa tax (Fründt, 2018). As such, the result of the decision is that coastal municipalities are finding creative alternative sources of financing which are not resolving the limit to accessibility created by instituting fees on the beach. It makes no difference to most of those entering the beach what the charge is for, given they are interested only in enjoying the beach and not in additional municipal/spa services. Generally, the fees are not well received by the German public, since entry to mountains, lakes, and rivers usually does not incur fees even though similar maintenance is required to keep those areas clean and safe.

Planning for the coastal zone

In discussing the planning aspects for coastal zones, one should distinguish between the various levels of government.

Supra-local spatial planning

According to the Federal Spatial Planning Act, spatial planning aims to ensure sustainable development and that social and economic demands made on any area are balanced with its ecological functions. In plans that relate to coastal waters, land–sea interactions must be taken into account (Section 13). The Federal Spatial Planning Act also includes (since a 2004 amendment) provisions relating to marine spatial planning, which specifically apply to the EEZ. Providing for a comprehensive and coherent spatial planning concept that spans the marine area is consistent with the ICZM principle of integration of terrestrial and marine components of the coastal zone (German Federal Government, 2011b). Notably, since there is no additional and separate planning and decision-making instrument for ICZM in Germany, spatial planning is considered the most suitable platform for its implementation (Lower Saxony Ministry of Agriculture, n.d.b).

Responsibility for spatial planning in the EEZ has been assigned to the Federal Ministry of Transport and Digital Infrastructure (Section 17, as revised in 2017). The Federal Spatial Planning Act stipulates that spatial plans for the EEZ should consider land–sea interactions and contain provisions concerning the safety and efficiency of maritime traffic, economic and scientific uses, and the protection and improvement of the marine environment. The sustainable development of the marine areas furthermore has to be supported through the application of an ecosystem approach in accordance with the European Maritime Spatial Planning Directive (2014/89/EU) of 2014 (Section 2). With regard to planning at sea, Germany can be considered a forerunner, at least within the European Union. The spatial plans for the German EEZ in the North Sea and Baltic Sea were drawn up in 2009, thus, long before the Maritime Spatial Planning Directive was adopted. Now the second generation of plans is already in preparation, building on the experience gained within the last decade (Federal Maritime and Hydrographic Agency, n.d.a).

Local land use planning

According to the Federal Building Code, the main planning instruments at the local level are (a) the preparatory land use plan (Flächennutzungsplan) and (b) the binding land use plan (Bebauungsplan). The preparatory land use plan provides strategic direction. The binding land use plan is based on the preparatory plan and details the type and degree of building and land use permitted. An important objective of the German land use planning system is to prevent urban sprawl by allowing only certain types of construction projects ('privileged projects') outside of settlements. A binding land use plan may apply to a specific coastal area and define specific permitted land uses and conditions for development, as in the example of the Binz coastal resort, discussed earlier in this chapter. The binding land use plan for the Binz beach covers an area stretching from the seafront promenade to the shoreline (as defined above for Mecklenburg-Western Pomerania on the Baltic Sea). The objective of the plan is to meet the needs of tourists, so the area is designated as 'green area' (bathing and sports beach). To take account of the specific sensitivity of the beach, the plan describes, in great detail, the conditions for the permissibility of kiosks and other service facilities.

National ICZM strategy and related regulations

In response to the European Council recommendation concerning the implementation of Integrated Coastal Zone Management (2002/413/EC), the German Federal Ministry for the Environment published an ICZM Strategy in March 2006. According to the strategy,

> *ICZM is an informal approach to supporting sustainable development of coastal zones through good integration, coordination, communication and participation. On one hand, ICZM is a process that should permeate all planning and decision-planning levels as a guiding principle and, on the other hand, is a tool applied for the purpose of integrated identification of potential development and conflicts, as well as for resolving conflicts in an unbureaucratic manner* (Federal Ministry for the Environment, 2006a, p. 3).

This strategy was the first management approach in Germany which applied to a zone defined on the basis of its functional character – the coastal zone – in its entirety (Federal Ministry for the Environment, 2006a, p. 7).

In the run-up to the development of the ICZM Strategy in Germany, there were discussions on how to achieve added value compared to existing spatial planning regulations. For example, the creation of a special planning zone for the coast was proposed, in order to overcome administrative boundaries and to ensure a comprehensive and coherent management of the coastal zone. In addition, an ecologically sound environment was considered a prerequisite for an equitable and sustainable economic and social development of the coastal zone. Therefore, it was considered necessary to ensure a relative prioritization of ecological concerns and, at the very least, a respect for the carrying capacity of the coastal zone (Bosecke, 2005b, pp. 63-65). However, ultimately, only a strategic document was adopted on ICZM. The document has not been instituted as a formal planning instrument (4.4 ICZM Strategy) but is used only as a means of public information (cf. Land Development Plan of Schleswig-Holstein).

The authors of the Report on the Implementation of ICZM in Germany for the period 2006–2010 noted that there has been good progress and that ICZM principles are already being applied to some extent. Nevertheless, they identified a need for further action in order to safeguard Germany's coastal zone in the long term. Such action might include optimization of instruments and procedures or adaptation of existing instruments to new challenges, including the challenge of climate change (German Federal Government, 2011b, p. 18). Nandelstädt adds that the application of ICZM principles in Germany is particularly hindered by a difficulty in translating the concept and principles into concrete measures; by a lack of knowledge, awareness, and participation; by a lack of communication between the public, the administration, relevant stakeholders, and scientists; and by a lack of coordination between the federation and the states and between national and international bodies promoting ICZM (Nandelstädt, 2008, p. 22).

At the state level, the three coastal states have instituted specific initiatives and provisions relating to ICZM, mostly within their spatial development concepts. The two city-states (Hamburg and Bremen), which have a significant maritime infrastructure, also participate in ICZM projects.

The provisions of the states are as follows:

Mecklenburg-Western Pomerania

The Mecklenburg-Western Pomerania Act on Spatial Planning and State-Level Planning of the Land (LPlG), 1998, states in Section 6 that the State Spatial Development Programme[7] shall set out the targets and principles of spatial planning and state-level planning that relate to the whole state, including its coastal waters.

The State Spatial Development Programme of 2016 contains, as did its previous version from 2005, a separate chapter on ICZM which aims at reducing conflicts within the coastal zone. It includes specific provisions concerning wind farms, cables, shipping, fisheries, tourism, coastal protection, raw material extraction, and nature conservation. Several international and national projects have further contributed to the improvement of ICZM processes within Mecklenburg-Western Pomerania, including the EU-funded projects BaltCoast and BaltSeaPlan.

Lower Saxony

In 2005, an amendment to the Lower Saxony Spatial Planning Programme was prepared to designate special areas for offshore wind energy projects. Thereby, the need for a cross-sectoral instrument to regulate uses in the coastal waters was recognized (Lower Saxony Ministry of Agriculture, 2005, p. 5). The first step towards a Lower Saxon ICZM Strategy was the non-binding Spatial Planning Concept for the Lower Saxon Coastal Waters (Lower Saxony Ministry of Agriculture, 2005). The current Lower Saxony Act on Spatial Planning and Land-Level Planning (2017) now institutes ICZM as basic principle of spatial planning (Section 2). The Lower Saxony Land Spatial Planning Programme (2017) further cements the requirements of ICZM. Notably, the Programme requires a thematically and geographically comprehensive consideration of all relevant concerns in the coastal zone and a broad involvement of stakeholders. Land use conflicts are to be avoided at an early stage and interests balanced within the planning process. In accordance with the Act on Spatial Planning, which encourages the promotion of participation in the ICZM process, the Lower Saxony Government has, in addition, established an ICZM information platform. The platform aims to enhance the transparency of the ICZM process and to support the actors in coastal areas in their planning activities. It provides information about major projects, plans, and processes relevant to ICZM (Lower Saxony Ministry of Agriculture, n.d.a).

Schleswig-Holstein

The sea is perhaps most significant to Schleswig-Holstein, as its coastlines are relatively long compared to the state's size, spanning both the North Sea and the Baltic Sea (Nandelstädt, 2008, p. 4). Perhaps it is for this reason that the state developed an initial conceptual framework for ICZM as early as 2003. The Schleswig-Holstein Land Development Plan (2010) now contains special provisions relating to both coastal waters and development in the coastal zone. These provisions are based on the findings of the state's Spatial Planning Report Coast and Sea (Schleswig-Holstein Ministry of the Interior, 2006), which identified all relevant uses in the coastal area. The Schleswig-Holstein Land Development Plan states that, as a basic tenet of ICZM, the different spatial demands are to be coordinated in the coastal zone to avoid conflicts. An update of the plan is in preparation (Schleswig-Holstein Ministry of the Interior, n.d.). For the marine area, in 2004, the Schleswig-Holstein government developed an initiative named 'Sea – Our Future' to raise awareness for the protection of the sea and to foster interdepartmental cooperation. Subsequently, a 'Maritime Action Plan' was drawn up in 2008 and updated in 2013 (Ministry for Economic Affairs, 2013). The 'Maritime Action Plan' sets out the key guidelines for the implementation of an integrative maritime policy.

The recently updated spatial development plans and programmes of the coastal states thus still clearly reflect the ideas of ICZM. Their very general requirements, however, do not differ much from the requirements of the Federal Spatial Planning Act and the Federal Building Code with regard to planning within the whole territory of Germany. According to Section 1 of the Federal Spatial Planning Act, different spatial demands on an area shall be coordinated and conflicts resolved and, according to Section 7, all relevant public and private concerns must be balanced in the planning process.

Integration and coordination

Responsibilities for coastal zone management are somewhat fragmented in Germany. The general administrative structure already entails a certain degree of complexity, since each state consists of several regions, districts, and municipalities, to which different responsibilities are assigned by law. Moreover, different states may have a different administration structure.

Sectoral responsibilities are also split between different authorities with different organisational structures. The spatial distribution of responsibilities in German waters makes a coherent implementation of ICZM particularly difficult (Schernewski, 2002, pp. 4–5). For example, the Federal Maritime and Hydrographic Agency carries out the application procedure for wind farms in the EEZ (Federal Maritime and Hydrographic Agency, n.d.b). Within the 12 nautical mile limit, however, in the area of the territorial sea, responsibility for the approval of wind farms rests with the German coastal states.

ICZM, specifically, is considered to be ideally implemented both using a top-down approach – federal and state authorities are responsible for setting the direction – and a bottom-up approach whereby regions and municipalities may develop their own ICZM projects (Nandelstädt, 2008, p. 24). In practice in Germany, ICZM is mainly implemented through spatial planning. The planning system is, in line with the administrative structure, decentralized and consists of legally, organizationally, and substantively differentiated planning levels. Those planning levels are nevertheless interlinked to form a coherent system by the mutual feedback principle, as well as by comprehensive requirements of notification, participation, and coordination (Turowski, 2005, p. 895).

Since cooperation is a crucial tenet for the implementation of ICZM, the Federal Ministry for the Environment, Nature Conservation, and Nuclear Safety proposed, in 2006, to introduce an ICZM Secretariat in order to coordinate the German ICZM process over all levels of government. The Secretariat was planned to be responsible for functions such as knowledge transfer, creation of international contacts, networking, political consulting, and the analysis of long-term changes in the coastal area. The Ministry further proposed the establishment of a coastal forum spanning both the North and Baltic seas (Federal Ministry for the Environment, 2006b, pp. 82–83).

To start putting those ideas into action, in 2008, the Government initiated the Küsten-Kontor pilot project. The project involved important stakeholders from politics, governmental organizations, the business sector, the academic community, and civil society. The cooperation process was supervised by an advisory council with representatives from the relevant federal ministries, the five coastal states, and three local authority associations. The Küsten-Kontor pilot project ended in 2010 (German Federal Government, 2011b, p. 5). Even though the benefits of the networking have been demonstrated, financing issues have hindered the perpetuation of the project (German Environment Agency, n.d.b). The advisory council held meetings until 2013. Its role was to act as a source of ideas, without interfering with the responsibilities of the federation or the coastal states (German Environment Agency, n.d.a).

Participation

In Germany, general procedural law contains requirements for involvement of the public in administrative decisions. Since 2013, the Administrative Procedure Act has even required that the responsible authority encourages project developers to inform the public about the impacts of a project before they apply for a permit, in order to increase public acceptance for major projects (Section 25). The relevant sectoral regulations (e.g. the Emission Control Act) offer further possibilities for the public to participate in approval procedures. In particular, the laws on environmental protection (e.g. the Environmental Impact Assessment Act) provide extensive opportunities for the public to take part in decision-making processes.

The Federal Spatial Planning Act requires that the public and relevant authorities be notified about the preparation of spatial plans at an early stage and have the opportunity to comment (Section 9).

This process can have a real impact on decisions. For example, in Mecklenburg-Western Pomerania, public participation led to an increase in the required seaward distance from the shoreline for offshore wind farm development in the regional development program, from 6 km to 10 km (Mecklenburg-Western Pomerania Ministry of Energy, n.d.).

Under the Federal Building Code, members of the public and public authorities are involved in land use planning procedures in two stages – early and formal participation. Early public participation serves to inform the public about the general aims and purposes of planning and helps the authorities to understand the positions of the public while planning possibilities are open. Formal participation comes after a draft plan has been developed (Sections 3 and 4; Pahl-Weber & Henckel, 2008, pp. 81–82). However, while those procedures aim to ensure that all relevant interests are taken into consideration, there is no obligation to comply with public opinion.

The municipality of Binz, a popular holiday destination discussed earlier in this chapter, offers examples for three forms of public participation. In Binz, there is a plan for a huge old holiday complex (originally built by the Nazis) to be rebuilt as a modern resort. The respective binding land use plan has been changed after the public participation process, particularly to reduce impacts on surrounding valuable landscapes (Binding Land Use Plan No. 14 for Binz, 2015, p. 5). In addition, a referendum put a stop to the plans to sell a property belonging to the municipality to an investor (dpa, 2016). The investor planned to build a high-rise building close to the beach, which many feared would affect the beautiful natural setting (Rathke, 2016).[8] For another area on the coast, the municipality decided to invite citizens and guests to provide ideas for its future use. Through the informal use of an internet platform, the public not only were able to react to municipal planning intentions but had the opportunity to shape municipal land use decisions (Ziebarth, 2018).

Compliance and enforcement

Under German law, most forms of new development or alterations are subject to a permit process. Enforcement provisions against illegal development are found in state laws (e.g. Mecklenburg-Western Pomerania Regional Building Regulation, Sections 79–80). All states provide for stop-work orders, fines, and demolition. Illegal development is, however, not a big issue on the German coast. Especially in areas of special interest to tourists and close to the beach, authorities try to avoid setting a precedent by strictly requiring the demolition of illegal construction (Appunn, 2011). Small infringements – for example, the use of a garage as a holiday apartment – are, however, frequent in coastal areas. In 2013, through an anonymous complaint, more than 700 such infringements were identified just on the small island of Langeoog (Norderney Nordsee-Magazin, 2013).

Climate change action and awareness

In view of its relatively temperate coastal climate, regional climate models for Germany project a comparatively small temperature rise for its coastal regions by the end of the twenty-first century. However, summers are expected to become drier and, in the second half of this century, the coastal regions could increasingly be at risk of rising sea levels and a change in storm climate. This could, in the long term, lead to accelerated coastal erosion. Wetlands and low-lying areas (amounting to about 13,900 km²; Knieling, Kretschmann, & Zimmermann, 2016, p. 56) and regions with a high damage potential, such as the Port of Hamburg, are in the greatest danger. Coastal protection measures which have already been adopted throughout the coastal region will therefore likely be extended in the future (German Federal Government, 2008, p. 22).

In seeking to mitigate the consequences of climate change, federal, state, regional, and local governments have developed a plethora of strategies, guidance documents, roadmaps, and laws. The German Strategy for Adaptation to Climate Change was adopted by the Federal Government in 2008 (German Federal Government, 2008). The Strategy lays the foundations for the implementation of adaptation measures according to identified goals and needs. In addition to giving a concrete description of possible consequences of climate change and outlining action options for fifteen fields of action, including the building sector, biological diversity, and the tourism industry, the Strategy provides an overview of the international context and Germany's contribution to adaptation in other parts of the world. In 2011, the German Federal Government adopted an Adaptation Action Plan to accompany the Strategy (German Federal Government, 2011a). This Action Plan specifies objectives and options for action and determines the activities that are planned to be carried out by the German Federal Government in the years to come. Key principles of the Action Plan are an integrated approach and the consideration of climate change impacts in all plans and decisions. In November 2015, a progress report was compiled which indicated the state of implementation of the Strategy and the Action Plan and updated the framework for adaptation to climate change. For example, more flexible spatial planning targets (point 6.1) and a 'climate proofing' of projects, plans, and programmes were recommended (point 7.13) (German Federal Government, 2015).

Climate change and ICZM

Climate change is also taken into account in the German ICZM Strategy 2006. The ICZM Strategy recommends, in that regard, the designation of flood risk areas and the establishment of buffer zones on the coast to facilitate further coastal protection measures and to prepare for coastal retreat due to rising sea levels. Integrated conflict management, embedded in the ICZM concept, was suggested to assist in coping with the resulting restrictions and the effects of climate change (Federal Ministry for the Environment, 2006b, p. 56). However, an implementing structure for such conflict management has not yet been established.

Climate change in planning and building

Spatial planning, regional planning, and urban land use planning are at the first line of risk avoidance in Germany (German Federal Government, 2008, p. 40). According to the Federal Spatial Planning Act, the principles of spatial planning include the promotion of preventative flood protection, as well as adaptation to climate change (Section 2). In view of the limited predictability of the effects of climate change, however, the adoption of binding spatial planning targets, which must be based on reliable findings, is a challenging task (Born, 2016, p. 46). In 2013, the Ministerial Conference for Spatial Planning highlighted the importance of foresight in the allocation of uses (Ministerial Conference for Spatial Planning, 2013, p. 20). It has furthermore proposed inclusion of a 'climate check' in the environmental assessment procedure for spatial plans, to ensure that future spatial structures are resilient to the effects of climate change. The focus of this assessment would be not on the impacts of the plan on the environment, as is the case within the framework of the 'traditional' environmental assessment, but on the consequences of climate change for spatial development (Ministerial Conference for Spatial Planning, 2013, p. 34). In follow-up to the conference, a research project developed a guidance document for appropriate regional planning in the face of climate change. The suggestions include the establishment of safety zones around eroding shorelines and even the preparation of a future retreat of settlements, infrastructure, and productive activities from high-risk areas (Knieling, Kretschmann, & Zimmermann, 2016, pp. 56–57).

The Federal Building Code also includes provisions relating to a better adaptation to climate change, which are relevant to the coastal zone. Generally, within binding land use plans, the type and degree of building and land use can be regulated to avoid damages from the effects of climate change. Coastal protection needs (e.g. dike construction; Gierke, 2018, recitals 516–523) must be considered (Section 1), and plans should depict areas in which structural or technical measures must be taken to prevent damages from flooding or other natural forces (Section 9). A 2011 amendment to the Federal Building Code was specifically aimed at strengthening the resilience of towns and municipalities against the effects of climate change (German Parliament, 2011). However, many land use plans were adopted at times where knowledge on climate change was not available and urgently need to be amended to be able to fulfil their damage prevention function (Die Deutschen Versicherer, 2018). The Federal Water Resources Act contains even more comprehensive provisions for flood protection, including the development of risk maps and restrictions for the designation of building areas in land use plans, especially within flood plains. Many of those provisions preclude contrary planning decisions (Reese, 2015, p. 76). In 2017, an amendment to the Water Resources Act and other laws was approved for a more effective flood protection and damage avoidance (German Parliament, 2017b). Water Acts of the coastal states further restrict buildings on the coast and, for example, require the prohibition of new buildings if they would be threatened by coastal erosion (cf. Mecklenburg-Western Pomerania Water Act, Section 89).

A significant problem in the building sector in Germany, especially given the longevity of most buildings and structures, is that building standards are largely based on data from past observations. Data on future climate trends are rarely taken into account (German Federal Government, 2008, p. 19). Consequently, buildings are often not sufficiently protected against extreme weather conditions, such as storms, hail, and heavy rainfall (Küsel, 2018, p. 20). There are, however, extensive guidance documents issued by public authorities on how to protect buildings, such as a Federal Government flood protection guide (Federal Ministry for the Environment, 2016). In the progress report of 2015 on the Strategy for Adaptation to Climate Change, it has been suggested that building regulations are changed to encourage, for example, roof greenings and percolation measures (point 2.36). The city of Hamburg is following those recommendations and inter alia extensively supports the greening of roofs (Hamburg.de, n.d.). Furthermore, following a 2017 amendment to the Federal Environmental Impact Assessment Act, the vulnerability of major projects given the consequences of climate change, such as potential catastrophic effects due to an increased risk of flooding, must now be considered in the Environmental Impact Assessment procedure (German Parliament, 2017a, p. 113).

Climate change action at the state level

Each of the three coastal states has adopted comprehensive climate change policies. For example, the State Parliament of Schleswig-Holstein adopted a Report on Climate Protection and Adaptation to Climate Change with corresponding adaptation measures in 2009 and a roadmap for the adaptation to climate change in 2017 (Schleswig-Holstein Government, 2018b). Moreover, the state has prepared reports on climate protection every year since 2013 (Schleswig-Holstein

Government, 2018a). A law concerning energy transition and climate protection was, further-more, adopted in 2017, requiring the State Government to develop and implement an adap-tation strategy (Schleswig-Holstein Climate Protection Law, Section 10). With regard to the protection of the coast, the General Coastal Protection Plan of 2012 requires that dikes be constructed 50 cm higher than storm-tide water levels observed to date and that their top must be flat to enable future extension (Schleswig-Holstein Ministry for the Environment, 2013, pp. 44–46). However, according to recent calculations, an extension to the height of projected sea level rise is not sufficient to cope with the effects of climate change (Rahmstorf, 2017). Specifically, it is feared that the Wadden Sea, which constitutes an important component of coastal protection in Schleswig-Holstein since it helps to weaken storm surges, will 'drown' due to the expected sea level rise. The Wadden Sea Strategy 2100 of 2015 therefore includes a plan to bring massive amounts of sand from the North Sea to the Wadden Sea ('sediment management') (Schleswig-Holstein Ministry for the Environment, 2015, p. 66). In addition to those state-specific initiatives, representatives from all of Germany's coastal states come together regularly for a conference on adaptation to climate change, with special focus on the coastal zone. The fifth conference took place in Schwerin (Mecklenburg-Western Pomerania) in September 2018 and focused on the challenges of climate change with regard to infrastruc-ture (Mecklenburg-Western Pomerania Ministry of Energy, 2018).

In summary, the public sector has to take various measures to prevent damage from climate change and is very committed to this task. Nevertheless, landowners must take some respon-sibility to prevent damages and to appropriately insure their properties. Coastal protection is considered a task of general public interest and primarily serves to protect settlements. Notably, the provisions on coastal protection confer no rights on individuals for specific protection for their building projects (Mohaupt, 2013; cf. also Section 83 Mecklenburg-Western Pomerania Water Act; Schleswig-Holstein Water Act, Section 63).[9]

Fiscal measures

Fiscal measures relevant to coastal zone management in Germany include pre-emption and expropriation of properties in the coastal zone and insurance against damages related to cli-mate and natural hazards.

Pre-emption and expropriation

German municipalities are, inter alia, entitled to exercise a pre-emption right in respect to the purchase of property located in flood areas that are to be kept free of development. Any pre-emption right may only be used for purposes in the public interest (Federal Building Code, Section 24). A special pre-emption right is also provided through the Federal Nature Conservation Act (Section 66). Under that Act, the states have pre-emption rights for land located in national parks, national nature monuments, and nature conservation areas, as well as for land containing water bodies. The states may exercise these rights if so required to ensure protection of the environment, to manage the environment and landscape, or for recre-ational purposes. In 2017, new provisions were included in the Water Resources Act through the Flood Control Act II: If required to implement flood or coastal protection measures, states now have the pre-emptive right to purchase properties (Section 99a).

The Federal Building Code also permits the expropriation of private property if it serves the common good (Section 87), with compensation. According to the 2017 amendment to the Water Resources Law, expropriation serves the common good if it is necessary to implement a plan for coastal or flood protection (Section 71).

Insurance against climate-related damages and natural hazards

In Germany, natural hazard insurance that complements building insurance and household insurance is usually offered by insurance companies. This insurance covers extreme damages caused, for example, by flooding, earthquakes, or avalanches. The insurance fee depends on the location of the building and the corresponding risk category. In some cases, however, insurers are not able to insure property in high-risk regions, given that existing instruments and business models are not equipped to cater to major climate change events. The German Government has therefore anticipated the need for prospective (instead of retrospective) under-writing and has recommended that insurance companies consider expected future damage trends when calculating premiums, rather than basing premiums on past experience alone (German Federal Government, 2008, p. 34).

To identify the risks of climate change, insurance companies nowadays calculate the like-lihood of future natural disasters based on meteorological parameters. Moreover, innovative solutions for fields of business particularly affected by climate change are currently being explored (Münchener Rückversicherungs-Gesellschaft, n.d.). However, a precise forecast of climate-related damages is difficult to undertake and, most notably, the awareness of home-owners and business owners of increased insurance needs is still lacking (Welp et al., 2011, pp. 3–4). To keep insurance rates affordable in the face of climate change, an efficient interplay of planning stipulations, building regulations, and the assumption of individual responsibility is, in any case, considered necessary by the insurance industry (Küsel, 2018, p. 21).

Overall assessment

Germany's tiered approach to spatial planning, with many possibilities for public participation and integrated environmental assessments, helps to ensure a comprehensive consideration of coastal issues at the appropriate levels. The extensive responsibilities of municipalities enable them to find the best local management solutions, for citizens, tourists, and the environment alike. Since regulations are, in general, also strictly enforced, the coastal zone is effectively man-aged in Germany. Nevertheless, there are still some challenges. Notably, because of the many different legal bases and the diverging responsibilities for the management and protection of the coastal zone, efficient integration of process steps and the implementation of a coherent manage-ment concept often proves difficult. The fact that the provisions for the protection of the coast are allowed to greatly differ from one municipality to another drives competition for the creation of economically favourable conditions, to the detriment of the coastal environment. Moreover, even though there is a growing awareness of the effects of climate change, their inherent uncertainties are difficult to take into account within the rather static German planning and approval system.

To alleviate some of the weaknesses of the German coastal management system, ICZM was introduced more than a decade ago. In particular, the 2002 EU Recommendation on ICZM has triggered more than thirty ICZM initiatives on federal, regional, and local level (Gellermann et al., 2012, pp. 377–378). These include the promotion of research projects, the development of strategies and the adoption of legal amendments. However, Germany has not yet managed to fully exploit the potential of ICZM. Rather, the ICZM concept lately seems to have lost its momentum and many of the promising ICZM initiatives have slowly petered out. The Federal Government has pushed forward the establishment of a networking platform on the coast through temporary projects, but the coastal states that are responsible for the implementation of ICZM have not yet effectively taken up the starting aid. Even though ICZM has been considered to be an effective means to manage the coast, it is not a mandatory task and its financing is therefore a challenge for the coastal states (German Environment Agency, personal communication, 5 November 2018). Without a revival of the advisory council on ICZM, the Küstenkontor, or the creation of other easily accessible offers of participation, it is questionable what remains of the added value of the ICZM idea today.

The new requirement to apply an ecosystem approach within spatial planning in the marine area now seems to be the impetus that was required to move forward to ensure a better balance between the diverging priorities in protecting and using the coastal zone. The ecosystem approach is a comprehensive, integrative, and participatory approach for the management of human activities and is focused on the objective to preserve ecological functions (Täufer, 2018, p. 98). In particular, strengthening the participatory opportunities within ICZM can contribute to its implementation (Czybulka, 2015, p. 31). To prevent further degradation of the coastal environment, it is thus important to seize the opportunity to develop ICZM and the ecosystem approach as mutually reinforcing sets of ideas (Haines-Young & Potschin, 2011, p. 12).

Notes

1. The Lower Saxony Water Act specifies (at para. 2) that the medium tide height corresponds to the average height of all water levels observed over the 20 years (from 1 November to 31 October) that precede the procedure of establishing the boundaries and whose last digit is divisible by five. If there are no observations for 20 years, the average height of the water levels of the five previous discharge years is used. If there are no adequate observations at all, the property boundaries are determined based on natural features, usually the beginning of the grassland.
2. If there are no complete measurements, the responsible water authorities determine the observations on which the determination of the boundary has to be based.
3. Rural districts differ from urban areas in having lower population and settlement densities. In addition, they are primarily typified by agricultural uses.
4. The type and degree of building and land use, the design of the planned building, and the size of the area planned to be covered are decisive factors for the permissibility of a construction project (Federal Building Code, Section 34, para. 1). According to the Federal Administrative Court, the size of the floor area and the height of the planned building are the most visible characteristics of a building and therefore must be similar within a built-up area (BVerwG, 2013; recital 5).
5. Within the open landscape, there is no liability for the property owners for typical risks resulting from staying in nature (Federal Nature Conservation Act, Section 60). Property owners are obliged by law to allow the public to enter their properties. Making them, in addition, liable for all risks is considered to place an excessive burden on them. It may be a different situation, however, if a property owner 'invites' people to stay on the property, for example, by providing a certain service infrastructure or requiring the payment of an entrance fee (Fischer-Hüftle, 2010; § 60, recital 5).
6. There is some discretion with regard to the meaning of 'reasonable': cf. for Section 62, Federal Nature Conservation Act: VG Oldenburg, 2014 (Fischer-Hüftle, 2010, § 62, recital 3).
7. The legal nature of spatial plans is a controversial issue. In 2003, the Federal Administrative Court decided that at a minimum, the binding targets set in spatial plans are considered statutory provisions (BVerwG, 2003).
8. According to Section 20 of the Municipal Constitution, decisions on building projects cannot be taken by referendum. In this case, however, the decision concerned the sale of a municipal property.
9. For example, municipalities still consider allowing restaurants close to the beach on the endangered west coast of the island of Sylt; cf. Binding Land Use Plan No. 48 for Sylt, draft of 2018.

References

Althammer, C. (2016). Einleitung zu §§ 903 ff [Introduction to §§ 903 ff]. In *Staudinger BGB*. Sellier – de Gruyter.

Appunn, K. (2011). Abrissbirne statt Alterssitz [Wrecking ball instead of retirement plan]. *SHZ*, 8 March. Available at: www.shz.de/regionales/schleswig-holstein/panorama/abrissbirne-statt-alters-sitz-id1221091.html

Bibliographisches Institut GmbH. (2018). Strand, der [Beach, the]. Available at: www.duden.de/rechtschreibung/Strand

Born, M. (2016). *Anpassung an den Klimawandel in Stadt und region [Adaptation to Climate Change in City and Region]*. Edited by Bundesamt für Bauwesen und Raumordnung (BBR). Bundesamt für Bauwesen und Raumordnung (BBR). Available at: www.bbsr.bund.de/BBSR/DE/Veroeffentlichungen/Sonderveroeffentlichungen/2016/anpassung-klimawandel-dl.pdf?__blob=publicationFile&v=2

Bosecke, T. (2005a). *Vorsorgender Küstenschutz und Integriertes Küstenzonenmanagement (IKZM) an Der Deutschen Ostseeküste [Preventive Coastal Protection and Integrated Coastal Zone Management (ICZM) on the German Baltic Sea Coast]*. Edited by C. Carlsen. Springer-Verlag.

— (2005b) Schutz der Biodiversität durch IK(M)ZM – inhaltliche und konzeptionelle Überlegungen für eine nationale Strategie [Protection of biodiversity through ICZM – content and conceptual considerations for a national strategy]. In: Nationale IKZM-Strategien – Europäische Perspektiven und Entwicklungstrends. Edited by Bundesministerium für Verkehr, Bau- und Wohnungswesen (BMVBW) and Bundesamt für Bauwesen und Raumordnung (BBR). Available at: https://d-nb.info/985564628/34

Bundesverband WindEnergie. (2018). *Offshore: Windenergiegewinnung auf See [Offshore: Wind Energy Production at Sea]*. Available at: www.wind-energie.de/themen/anlagentechnik/offshore/

Czybulka, D. (2015). *Sind 'marine governance' und Ökosystemansatz miteinander vereinbar? [Are marine governance and ecosystem approaches compatible?]*. KDM Symposium Küste.

Die Deutschen Versicherer. (2018). *Sieben Positionen deutscher Versicherer zu den Folgen des Klimawandels [Seven Positions of German Insurers on the Consequences of Climate Change]*. Available at: www.gdv.de/de/themen/news/klimawandel-versicherung-29086

dpa. (2016). Nein zu Hochhaus in Prora [No to high-rise in Prora]. *Spiegel*, 5 September. Available at: www.spiegel.de/panorama/kein-hochhaus-in-prora-bauprojekt-auf-ruegen-gescheitert-a-1110875.html

Federal Institute for Population Research. (2018). Höchste Bevölkerungsdichte entlang des Rheintals [Highest population density along the Rhine Valley]. Demografie Portal des Bundes und der Länder. Available at: www.demografie-portal.de/SharedDocs/Informieren/DE/ZahlenFakten/Bevoelkerungsdichte_Gemeinden.html

Federal Maritime and Hydrographic Agency. (n.d.a). *Nationale Raumplanung [National Spatial Planning]*. Available at: www.bsh.de/DE/THEMEN/Offshore/Meeresraumplanung/Nationale_Raumplanung/nationale-raumplanung_node.html [Accessed 15 December 2018]

— (n.d.b). *Windparks*. Available at: www.bsh.de/DE/THEMEN/Offshore/Offshore-Vorhaben/Windparks/windparks_node.html [Accessed 15 December 2018]

Federal Ministry for the Environment. (2006a). *Integrated Coastal Zone Management in Germany*. Bonn. Available at: www.ikzm-strategie.de/dokumente/ikzm_englisch_final.pdf

— (2006b). *Integriertes Küstenzonenmanagement in Deutschland [ICZM in Germany]*. Bonn. Available at: www.bmu.de/fileadmin/bmu-import/files/pdfs/allgemein/application/pdf/kuestenzonenmanagement.pdf

— (2016). *Hochwasserschutzfibel [Flood Protection Primer]*. Berlin. Available at: www.fib-bund.de/Inhalt/Themen/Hochwasser/2016-08_Hochwasserschutzfibel_7.Aufl.pdf

Fischer-Hüftle, P. (2010). Erholung in Natur und Landschaft [Relaxation in Nature and landscape]. In J. Schumacher and P. Fischer-Hüftle (Eds.), *Bundesnaturschutzgesetz* (2nd edn.). Verlag W. Kohlhammer.

Fründt, S. (2018). Die große Abzocke an deutschen Stränden [The big rip-off German beaches]. *Welt*, February 5. Available at: www.welt.de/wirtschaft/article173201979/Kurtaxe-Badeorte-erheben-trotz-Urteil-weiterhin-Gebuehren.html

Gee, K., Kannen, A., & Licht-Eggert, K. (2006). *Raumordnerische Bestandsaufnahme für die deutschen Küsten- und Meeresbereiche* [*Spatial Inventory for the German Coastal and Marine Areas*]. Report of the Forschungs- und Technologiezentrum Westküste der Universität Kiel Nr. 38. Büsum. ISSN 0940-9475.

Gellermann, M., Stoll, P.-T., & Czybulka, D. (2012). *Handbuch des Meeresnaturschutzes in der Nord- und Ostsee* [*Handbook of Marine Conservation in the North and Baltic Seas*]. Edited by H. W. Louis & J. Schumacher. Springer-Verlag.

German Environment Agency. (n.d.a). *IKZM-Beirat* [*ICZM Advisory Board*]. Available at: www.ikzm-strategie.de/ikzm-stelle-projektbeirat-rolle.php [Accessed 15 December 2018]

— (n.d.b). *IKZM auf Bundesebene* [*ICZM at the Federal Level*]. Available at: www.ikzm-strategie.de/bmu.php [Accessed 15 December 2018]

German Federal Government. (2008). *German Strategy for Adaptation to Climate Change*. Available at: www.bmu.de/fileadmin/bmu-import/files/english/pdf/application/pdf/das_gesamt_en_bf.pdf

— (2011a). *Aktionsplan Anpassung* [*Action Plan Adjustment*]. Available at: www.bmu.de/fileadmin/bmu-import/files/pdfs/allgemein/application/pdf/aktionsplan_anpassung_klimawandel_bf.pdf

— (2011b). *Report on the Implementation of Integrated Coastal Zone Management in Germany (National ICZM Report)*. Available at: www.ikzm-strategie.de/dokumente/national_report_iczm_in_germany.pdf

— (2015). *Fortschrittsbericht zur Deutschen Anpassungsstrategie an den Klimawandel* [*Progress Report on the German Adaptation Strategy to Climate Change*]. Available at: www.bmu.de/fileadmin/Daten_BMU/Download_PDF/Klimaschutz/klimawandel_das_fortschrittsbericht_bf.pdf

German Parliament. (2011). *Entwurf eines Gesetzes zur Stärkung der klimagerechten Entwicklung in den Städten und Gemeinden* [*Draft Law to Strengthen Climate-Friendly Development in Cities and Towns*]. 17/6076. Available at: http://dip21.bundestag.de/dip21/btd/17/060/1706076.pdf

— (2017a). *Entwurf eines Gesetzes zur Modernisierung des Rechts der Umweltverträglichkeitsprüfung* [*Draft Law Modernizing the Law of Environmental Impact Assessment*]. 18/11499. Available at: http://dip21.bundestag.de/dip21/btd/18/114/1811499.pdf

— (2017b). *Entwurf eines Gesetzes zur weiteren Verbesserung des Hochwasserschutzes und zur Vereinfachung von Verfahren des Hochwasserschutzes* [*Draft Law to Further Improve Flood Protection and Simplify Flood Protection Procedures*]. 18/10879. Available at: http://dip21.bundestag.de/dip21/btd/18/108/1810879.pdf

Gierke, H.-G. (2018). § 1. In H. Brügelmann (Ed.), *Baugesetzbuch* [*Building Code*]. 105th ed. Kohlhammer.

Gläser, B. (2005). Die Küstenproblematik zwischen Ethos und Management – zur Nachhaltigkeitsperspektive im IKZM [The coastal problem between ethos and management – for the sustainability perspective in the ICZM]. In B. Gläser (Ed.), *Küste, Ökologie und Mensch*. oekom verlag.

Haines-Young, R., & Potschin, M. (2011). *Integrated Coastal Zone Management and the Ecosystem Approach*. Available at: www.nottingham.ac.uk/cem/pdf/CEM_Working Paper 7(1).pdf

Hamburg.de (n.d.). *Gründachstrategie Hamburg* [*Green Roof Strategy Hamburg*]. Available at: www.hamburg.de/gruendach/4364586/gruendachstrategie-hamburg/ [Accessed 16 December 2018]

Initiative 'Freie Bürger für freie Strände'. (2014). Freie Strände für freie Bürger 40 Jahre Zäune und Strandgebühr sind genug! [Free beaches for free citizens 40 years of fences and beach fees are enough!] (petition). Available at: www.change.org/p/niedersächsische-landesregierung-freie-strände-für-freie-bürger-40-jahre-zäune-und-strandgebühr-sind-genug

Jung, F. (2016). 150 Meter Puffer: Küsten-Koalition will Bauverbot an Stränden [150-metre buffer: Coastal coalition wants to ban construction on beaches]. *SHZ*, 26 April. Available at: www.shz.de/regionales/schleswig-holstein/150-meter-puffer-kuesten-koalition-will-bauverbot-an-straenden-id13370516.html

Knieling, J., Kretschmann, N., & Zimmermann, T. (2016). *Handlungshilfe Klimawandelgerechter Regionalplan* [*Action Aid Climate Change–Compatible Regional Plan*]. Edited by Federal Ministry of Transport. Berlin: Bundesinstitut für Bau-, Stadt- und Raumforschung (BBSR). Available at: www.klimamoro.de/fileadmin/Dateien/Veröffentlichungen/KlimREG/BMVI_2017_KlimREG_Handlungshilfe_Klimawandelgerechter_Regionalplan.pdf

Kreutzträger, I. (2014). Baden gehen. [Go swimming]. die tageszeitung (taz), 20 June. Available at: https://taz.de/SchwimmerInnen-auf-dem-Trockenen/!5039513/

Küsel, A. (2018). *Schutz vor Extremwetter – Wie können sich Hausbesitzer vor Folgen des Klimawandels wappnen?* [*Protection against Extreme Weather – How Can Homeowners Arm Themselves against the Consequences of Climate Change?*] Berlin: Gesamtverband der Deutschen Versicherungswirtschaft. Available at: www.klimaschutzaktionen-mv.de/static/KSA/Dateien/2018/RK 2018/KUESEL_180926_Schutz_vor_Extremwetter_Veroeffentlichung.pdf

Lower Saxony Ministry of Agriculture. (2005). *Raumordnungskonzept für das niedersächsische Küstenmeer* [*Spatial Planning Concept for the Niedersächsische Küstenmeer*]. Oldenburg.

— (n.d.a). *IKZM-Plattform Niedersachsen* [*ICZM Platform Lower Saxony*]. Available at: www.ml.niedersachsen.de/themen/raumordnung_landesplanung/maritime_raumordnung/ikzm-plattform-niedersachsen-5223.html [Accessed 15 December 2018]

— (n.d.b). *Integriertes Küstenzonenmanagement – IKZM* [*ICZM*]. Available at: www.ml.niedersachsen.de/themen/raumordnung_landesplanung/maritime_raumordnung/integriertes-kuestenzonenmanagement–ikzm-5190.html [Accessed 15 December 2018]

Lower Saxony Parliament. (2012). *Gesetzentwurf*. 16/5050.

Mecklenburg-Western Pomerania Ministry of Energy. (2018). Regionalkonferenz beschäftigt sich mit Anpassung an Klimawandel [Regional conference deals with adaptation to climate change] (press release). Available at: www.regierung-mv.de/Aktuell/?id=143050&processor=processor.sa.pressemitteilung

— (n.d.). *Landesraumentwicklungsprogramm Mecklenburg-Vorpommern (LEP M-V) 2016 Abwägungsdokumentation zur zweiten Stufe des Beteiligungsverfahrens* [*State Regional Development Program 2016 Documentation for the Second Stage of the Participation Procedure*]. Available at: http://awd.mv-regierung.de/lep_2016_01/anz_kuerzel.php [Accessed 15 December 2018]

Mecklenburg-Western Pomerania Parliament. (2009). *Entwurf eines Gesetzes zur Bereinigung des Landesnaturschutzrechts* [*Draft revision to the Nature Conservation Law*]. 5/3026. Available at: www.landtag.nrw.de/portal/WWW/dokumentenarchiv/Dokument/KVD05-3026.pdf?von=00001&bis=00089

Ministerial Conference for Spatial Planning. (2013). *Raumordnung und Klimawandel* [*Spatial Planning and Climate Change*]. Available at: www.klimamoro.de/fileadmin/Dateien/Transfer_KlimaMORO/Beratungsmodul/Leitfäden/Leitfäden mit Maßnahmenvorschlägen in relevanten Handlungsfeldern/MKRO-Handlungskonzept der Raumordnung.pdf

Ministry for Economic Affairs. (2013). *Maritimer Aktionsplan Schleswig-Holstein* [*Maritime Action Plan Schleswig-Holstein*]. Kiel. Available at: www.schleswig-holstein.de/DE/Fachinhalte/M/meerespolitik/Downloads/maritimer_Aktionsplan_Brosch.pdf?__blob=publicationFile&v=1

Mohaupt, D. (2013). Sicherheit auf Zeit [Temporary security]. *Deutschlandfunk*, 4 August. Available at: www.deutschlandfunk.de/sicherheit-auf-zeit.724.de.html?dram:article_id=256476

Münchener Rückversicherungs-Gesellschaft (n.d.). Mission. Available at: www.munichre.com/de/service/imprint/index.html

Nandelstädt, T. (2008). *Guiding the Coast – Development of Guidelines for Integrated Coastal Zone Management in Germany*. Technical University of Berlin. Available at: www.ikzm-oder.de/download.php?fileid=3359

Norderney Nordsee-Magazin. (2013). Bauen mit Genehmigung [Build with permission]. *Norderney Nordsee-Magazin*, 2 December. Available at: https://magazin.norderney-zs.de/news/politik/baurecht/

Nordsee24. (n.d.) *Der Nationalpark Schleswig-Holsteinisches Wattenmeer* [*The National Park Schleswig-Holstein Wadden Sea*]. Available at: www.nordsee24.de/nordsee-urlaub/umwelt/flora-und-fauna/nationalpark-schleswig-holsteinisches-wattenmeer [Accessed 8 December 2018]

Oehlers, U. (2013). Gebühren für Strandwanderer unzulässig [Fees for beach walkers inadmissible]. *Ostsee Zeitung*. 19 July. Available at: https://www.ostsee-zeitung.de/Mecklenburg/Wismar/Gebuehren-fuer-Strandwanderer-unzulaessig

Office of Statistics of Lower Saxony. (2016). Statistische Informationen über die Bevölkerung des Landes Niedersachsen [Statistical information about the population of Lower Saxony]. Available at: https://niedersachsen.de/land_leute/land/zahlen_fakten/bevoelkerung/statistische-informationen-ueber-die-bevoelkerung-des-landes-niedersachsen-19947.html

Pahl-Weber, E., & Henckel, D. (Eds.). (2008). *The Planning System and Planning Terms in Germany: A Glossary.* Academy for Spatial Research and Planning. Available at: https://shop.arl-net.de/media/direct/pdf/ssd_7.pdf

Rahmstorf, S. (2017). Um wie viel müssen wir die Deiche an der Nordsee erhöhen? [How much do we have to increase the dikes on the North Sea?]. *Spektrum.de*, 24 May. Available at: https://scilogs.spektrum.de/klimalounge/um-wie-viel-muessen-wir-die-deiche-der-nordsee-erhoehen/

Rathke, M. (2016). Bauunternehmer plant 100 Meter Wohnturm auf Rügen [Contractor plans 100-metre residential tower on Rügen]. *Nordkurier*, 13 January. Available at: www.nordkurier.de/mecklenburg-vorpommern/bauunternehmer-plant-100-meter-wohnturm-auf-ruegen-1319940701.html

— (2017). Touristen müssen mehr Kurtaxe zahlen [Tourists have to pay more tourist tax. *Nordkurier*, 24 March. Available at: www.nordkurier.de/mecklenburg-vorpommern/touristen-muessen-mehr-kurtaxe-zahlen-2427403303.html

Reese, M. (2015). Klimaanpassung im Raumplanungsrecht [Climate adaptation in spatial planning law]. *Zeitschrift für Umweltrecht* 26(1), 16–26.

Sass, K. (2016). Viele Tagesgäste ignorieren Kurtaxe [Many day visitors ignore tourist tax]. *Ostsee Zeitung*, 30 June. Available at: www.ostsee-zeitung.de/Mecklenburg/Bad-Doberan/Viele-Tagesgaeste-ignorieren-Kurtaxe2

Schernewski, G. (2002). *Integrated Coastal Zone Managament (IKZM): From European Strategy to Practice in Germany.* European Union for Coastal Conservation (EUCC).

Schleswig-Holstein Government. (2018a). Energie- und Klimaschutzberichte [Energy and climate protection reports]. Available at: www.schleswig-holstein.de/DE/Fachinhalte/K/klimaschutz/energiewendeKlimaschutzberichte.html

— (2018b). Klimawandel [Climate change]. Available at: www.schleswig-holstein.de/DE/Fachinhalte/K/klimaschutz/klimawandel.html

Schleswig-Holstein Ministry for the Environment. (2013). *Generalplan Küstenschutz des Landes Schleswig-Holstein [General Coastal Protection Plan of Schleswig-Holstein].* Kiel. Available at: https://www.schleswig-holstein.de/DE/Fachinhalte/K/kuestenschutz/Downloads/Generalplan.pdf;jsessionid=08C423B1FFC87A0C9303E20A9A5C64D0.delivery2-master?__blob=publicationFile&v=1

— (2015). *Strategie für das Wattenmeer 2100 [Strategy for the Wadden Sea 2100].* Kiel. Available at: www.nationalpark-wattenmeer.de/sites/default/files/media/pdf/strategie-wattenmeer-2100-web.pdf

Schleswig-Holstein Ministry of the Interior. (2003). *Integrated Coastal Zone Management in Schleswig-Holstein.* Kiel. Available at: www.zeeland.nl/digitaalarchief/zee0701277

— (2006). *Raumordnungsbericht Küste und Meer 2005 [Regional Planning Report Coast and Sea 2005].* Kiel. Available at: www.schleswig-holstein.de/DE/Fachinhalte/L/landesplanung_raumordnung/Downloads/rob_kueste_meer_neu.pdf?__blob=publicationFile&v=3

— (n.d.). *Landesplanung – Neuaufstellung der Regionalpläne [State Planning – Reorganization of Regional Plans].* Available at: www.schleswig-holstein.de/DE/Fachinhalte/L/landesplanung_raumordnung/raumordnungsplaene/regionalplaene/regionalplaene_neuaufstellung.html [Accessed 15 December 2018]

Schleswig-Holstein Parliament. (2017). *Freier Zugang zu Schleswig-Holsteins Meeresstränden [Free Aaccess to Schleswig-Holstein's Sea Beaches].* 18/5418. Available at: www.landtag.ltsh.de/infothek/wahl18/drucks/5400/drucksache-18-5418.pdf

Statista. (2018a). Statistiken zur Urlaubsregion Nordsee [Statistics for the North Sea holiday region]. Available at: https://de.statista.com/themen/3057/urlaubsregion-nordsee/

— (2018b). Statistiken zur Urlaubsregion Ostsee [Statistics for the Baltic Sea holiday region]. Available at: https://de.statista.com/themen/3015/urlaubsregion-ostsee/

— (2018c). Top 10 Seehäfen in Deutschland in den Jahren von 2015 bis 2017 nach gesamten Güterumschlag (in 1.000 Tonnen) [Top 10 seaports in Germany from 2015 to 2017 after total cargo turnover (in 1,000 tons)]. Available at: https://de.statista.com/statistik/daten/studie/239221/umfrage/groesste-haefen-in-deutschland-nach-gueterumschlag/

Täufer, K. (2018). *Die Entwicklung des Ökosystemansatzes im Völkerrecht und im Recht der Europäischen Union [The Development of the Ecosystem Approach in International Law and European Union Law].* Edited by D. Czybulka. Nomos Verlagsgesellschaft.

Turowski, G. (2005). Raumplanung (Gesamtplanung) [Spatial planning]. In *Handwörterbuch der Raumordnung*. Akademie für Raumforschung und Landesplanung (ARL). Available at: www.arl-net. de/system/files/r_s0831-0996.pdf

Welp, M., Gebauer, J., Wurbs, S., Lotz, W., & Partzsch, K. (2011). *Themenblatt: Anpassung an den Klimawandel/Versicherungen [Topic: Adapting to Climate Change/Insurance]*. Dessau-Roßlau. Available at: www.umweltbundesamt.de/sites/default/files/medien/364/publikationen/kompass_themenblatt_versicherung_2015_net.pdf

Werner, L. (2014). Wer nur badet, muss keine Kurtaxe zahlen [Those who only bathe are exempt from tourist tax]. *Ostsee Zeitung*, 30 April. Available at: www.ostsee-zeitung.de/Mecklenburg/Bad-Doberan/Wirtschaft/Wer-nur-badet-muss-keine-Kurtaxe-zahlen

Wolf, R. (2018). Wangerland will wieder Strandgebühren erheben [Wangerland wants to raise beach fees again]. *NWZ*, 27 July. Available at: www.nwzonline.de/wangerland/wangerland-umstrittener-eintritt-wangerland-will-wieder-strandgebuehren-erheben_a_50,2,366018618.html

World Factbook. (n.d.). *Germany*. Available at: www.cia.gov/Library/publications/the-world-factbook/geos/gm.html [Accessed 20 November 2018]

Ziebarth, A. F. (2018). Bürgerbeteiligung in Binz digital möglich [Citizen participation in Binz online]. *Ostsee Zeitung*, 3 February. Available at: www.ostsee-zeitung.de/Vorpommern/Ruegen/Buergerbeteiligung-in-Binz-digital-moeglich

Legislation

Binding Land Use Plan for Binz: Bebauungsplan No. 29 'Strandversorgung' Gemeinde Ostseebad Binz of 02.07.2012, www.gemeinde-binz.de/bauplan/bp29_begruendung.pdf

Binding Land Use Plan for Binz: Bebauungsplan No. 14 'Kultur in Prora' Gemeinde Ostseebad Binz of 10.09.2015, www.gemeinde-binz.de/bauplan/bp14_begruendung.pdf

Binding Land Use Plan for Sylt (draft): Bebauungsplan No. 48 'Austernperle' Gemeinde List auf Sylt of 18.07.2018, www.grips-sylt.info/grips_daten/b_li48/im_verfahren/Li.B.48.00.Auslegungsunterl.Plan.Text.Begruendung.pdf

European Maritime Spatial Planning-Directive: Directive 2014/89/EU of the European Parliament and of the Council of 23 July 2014 establishing a framework for maritime spatial planning (OJ L 257, 28.8.2014, pp. 135–145).

European Water Framework Directive: Directive 2000/60/EC of the European Parliament and of the Council of 23 October 2000 establishing a framework for Community action in the field of water policy (OJ L 327, 22.12.2000, pp. 1–73).

Federal Administrative Procedure Act (Verwaltungsverfahrensgesetz) as amended by the announcement of 23.01.2003 (Federal Law Gazette, Part I, p. 102), last amended by Art. 11 of the Act of 18.07.2017 (Federal Law Gazette, Part I, p. 2745).

Federal Building Code (Baugesetzbuch) as amended by the announcement of 3.11.2017 (Federal Law Gazette, Part I, p. 3634).

Federal Emission Control Act (Bundes-Immissionsschutzgesetz) as amended by the announcement of 17.05.2013 (Federal Law Gazette, Part I, p. 1274), last amended by Art. 3 of the Act of 18.07.2017 (Federal Law Gazette, Part I, p. 2771).

Federal Environmental Impact Assessment Act (Gesetz über die Umweltverträglichkeitsprüfung) as amended by the announcement of 24.02.2010 (Federal Law Gazette, Part I, p. 94), last amended by Art. 2 of the Act of 8.09.2017 (Federal Law Gazette, Part I, p. 3370).

Federal Flood Control Act II (Hochwasserschutzgesetz II) of 30.06.2017 (Federal Law Gazette, Part I, p. 2193).

Federal Nature Conservation Act (Bundesnaturschutzgesetz) of 29.07.2009 (Federal Law Gazette, Part I, p. 2542), last amended by Art. 1 of the Act of 15.09.2017 (Federal Law Gazette, Part I, p. 3434).

Federal Spatial Planning Act (Raumordnungsgesetz) of 22.12. 2008 (Federal Law Gazette, Part I, p. 2986), last amended by Art. 2 of the Act of 20.07.2017 (Federal Law Gazette, Part I, p. 2808).

Federal Water Resources Act (Wasserhaushaltsgesetz) of 31.07.2009 (Federal Law Gazette, Part I, p. 2585), last amended by Art. 2 of the Act of 4.12.2018 (Federal Law Gazette, Part I, p. 2254).

German Constitution (Grundgesetz für die Bundesrepublik Deutschland) of 23.05.1949 (Federal Law Gazette, Part III, Nr. 100-1) last amended by Art. 1 of the Act of 13.07.2017 (Federal Law Gazette, Part I, p. 2347).

Lower Saxony Act on Spatial Planning and Land-Level Planning (Niedersächsisches Raumordnungsgesetz) of 06.12.2017 (Official Gazette 2017, p. 456).

Lower Saxony Implementing Law to the Nature Conservation Act (Niedersächsisches Ausführungsgesetz zum Bundesnaturschutzgesetz) of 19.02.2010 (Official Gazette 2010, p. 104).

Lower Saxony Land Spatial Planning Programme (Landes-Raumordnungsprogramm Niedersachsen) of 17.02.2017, approved by the Regional Decree of 16.02.2017.

Lower Saxony Water Act (Niedersächsisches Wassergesetz) of 19.02.2010 (Official Gazette 2010, p. 64), last amended by Art. 2 of the Act of 12.11.2015 (Official Gazette, p. 307).

Mecklenburg-Western Pomerania Act on Spatial Planning and State-Level Planning of the Land (Gesetz über die Raumordnung und Landesplanung des Landes Mecklenburg-Vorpommern) of 05.05.1998 (Official Gazette 1998, pp. 503, 613), last amended by Art. 5 of the Act of 05.07.2018 (Official Gazette 2018, pp. 221, 228).

Mecklenburg-Western Pomerania Implementing Law to the Nature Conservation Act (Naturschutzausführungsgesetz) of 23.02.2010 (Official Gazette 2010, p. 66), last amended by Art. 3 of the Act of 05.07.2018 (Official Gazette 2018, pp. 221, 228).

Mecklenburg-Western Pomerania Regional Building Regulation (Landesbauordnung Mecklenburg-Vorpommern) of 15.10.2015 (Official Gazette 2015, p. 344), last amended by Art. 4 of the Act of 05.07.2018 (Official Gazette 2018, pp. 221, 228).

Mecklenburg-Western Pomerania State Spatial Development Programme (Landesraumentwicklungsprogramm Mecklenburg-Vorpommern) of 09.06.2016, approved by the Regional Decree of 27.05.2016.

Mecklenburg-Western Pomerania Water Act (Wassergesetz des Landes Mecklenburg-Vorpommern) of 30.11.1992 (Official Gazette 1992, p. 669), last amended by Art. 2 of the Act of 05.07.2018 (Official Gazette 2018, pp. 221, 228).

Municipal Beach Ordinance of Heringsdorf: Satzung über die Einschränkungen des Gemeingebrauchs an dem der Sondernutzung unterliegenden Ostseestrand im Gebiet der Gemeinde Ostseebad Heringsdorf of 30.04.2015.

Municipal Beach Ordinance of Lubmin: Strandordnung und Satzung für die Sondernutzung am Strand der Gemeinde Seebad Lubmin of 24.06.2011.

Schleswig-Holstein Climate Protection Law (Gesetz zur Energiewende und zum Klimaschutz in Schleswig-Holstein) of 07.03.2017 (Official Gazette 2017, p. 124).

Schleswig-Holstein Land Development Plan (Landesentwicklungsplan Schleswig-Holstein) of 04.10.2010 (Official Gazette 2010, p. 1262).

Schleswig-Holstein Ordinance on Special Use of the Beach (Landesverordnung zur Sondernutzung am Meeresstrand und über Schutzstreifen an Gewässern II. Ordnung) of 08.12.2008, valid until 17.12.2018.

Schleswig-Holstein State Conservation Act (Landesnaturschutzgesetz) of 24.02.2010 (Official Gazette 2010, p. 301), last amended by Art. 2 of the Act of 22.10.2018 (Official Gazette 2018, p. 690).

Schleswig-Holstein Water Act (Wassergesetz des Landes Schleswig-Holstein) of 11.02.2008 (Official Gazette 2008, p. 91), last amended by Art. 17 of the Act of 02.05.2018 (Official Gazette, p. 162).

Court cases

BGH – Bundesgerichtshof [Federal Court of Justice] (1989) Judgement of 22.06.1989, III ZR 266/87.

BVerwG – Bundesverwaltungsgericht [Federal Administrative Court] (2003) Judgement of 20.11.2003, 4 CN 6.03.

—— (2013) Order of 14.03.2013, 4 B 49.12.

— (2017) Judgment of 13.09.2017, Freier Zugang zum Meeresstrand, 10 C 7.16.

NdsOVG – Oberverwaltungsgericht [Higher Administrative Court] Lüneburg (2016). Judgment of 19.01.2016, 10 LC 87/14.

OVG Bbg – Oberverwaltungsgericht [Higher Administrative Court] Brandenburg (2004). Order of 14.10.2004, 3a B 255/03.

OVG NRW – Oberverwaltungsgericht [Higher Administrative Court] Nordrhein-Westfalen (2013). Order of 08.10.2013, 16 A 2083/10.

SchlHOLG – Oberlandesgericht [Higher Regional Court] Schleswig (1992) Judgement of 10.12.1992, 11 U 39/92.

— (2000) Judgment of 14.12.2000, 11 U 89/99.

— (2003) Order of 09.04.2003, 2 W 164/02.

VG – Verwaltungsgericht [Administrative Court] Oldenburg (2014). Judgement of 23.09.2014, 1 A 1314/14.

7 Portugal

Paulo V.D. Correia and Inês Calor

Overview

Having a significant portion of its borders on the coast, one of the largest Exclusive Economic Zones in Europe and a strong tradition of sailing, the Portuguese government and population are distinctly aware of coastal management issues. Though its coast is on the Atlantic Ocean, Portugal shares many key characteristics – climatic, geographical, and cultural – with its Mediterranean neighbours. The similarities extend to the realm of coastal zone management: The country has adopted ambitious legislation for the protection of its coastal zone but has not always been successful in its implementation.

Despite major development pressures, recent legislation has effectively defined the limits and status of the Maritime Public Domain. Yet in some areas, particularly the Algarve region on the country's sunny south coast, widespread illegal development has occurred on coastal public land and even in high-protection environmental zones. Such development includes many scattered private homes – many of them summer homes – and even entire settlements. These harm the natural landscape, ignore environmental risks, and constrain the rights of other citizens to access the coast. The issue has been subjected to several court challenges, and some demolitions have been undertaken.

This chapter addresses the general features of the management of the coast in Portugal, with a closer analysis of the Algarve Region.

The context: Introduction to the country's coastal issues

Portugal faces the Atlantic Ocean on its west and south coasts (Figure 7.1) and has an old and important connection with the ocean. Its coastline is 1,793 km long (World Factbook, n.d.) – a figure which includes the coastlines of the Azores islands and Madeira. Portugal has the third largest Exclusive Economic Zone (EEZ) in Europe, with an area of 3,877,408 km² (United Nations Convention on the Law of the Sea of 1982, with amendment from May 2009).

Despite not bordering the Mediterranean Sea, Portugal's climate, natural environment, agriculture, culture, and social features closely resemble those of Mediterranean countries. The southeastern part of the country, in the region of the Algarve, has even stronger ties to Mediterranean countries than the rest of Portugal, especially in the stretch of coast along the Gulf of Cadiz, situated between the Cape of Saint Mary (the southernmost point of mainland Portugal) and the Strait of Gibraltar (Figure 7.1).

Over the past 50 years, the Portuguese population and its economic activities have moved towards the coast. Today, about 75% of the population resides in coastal areas, which provide

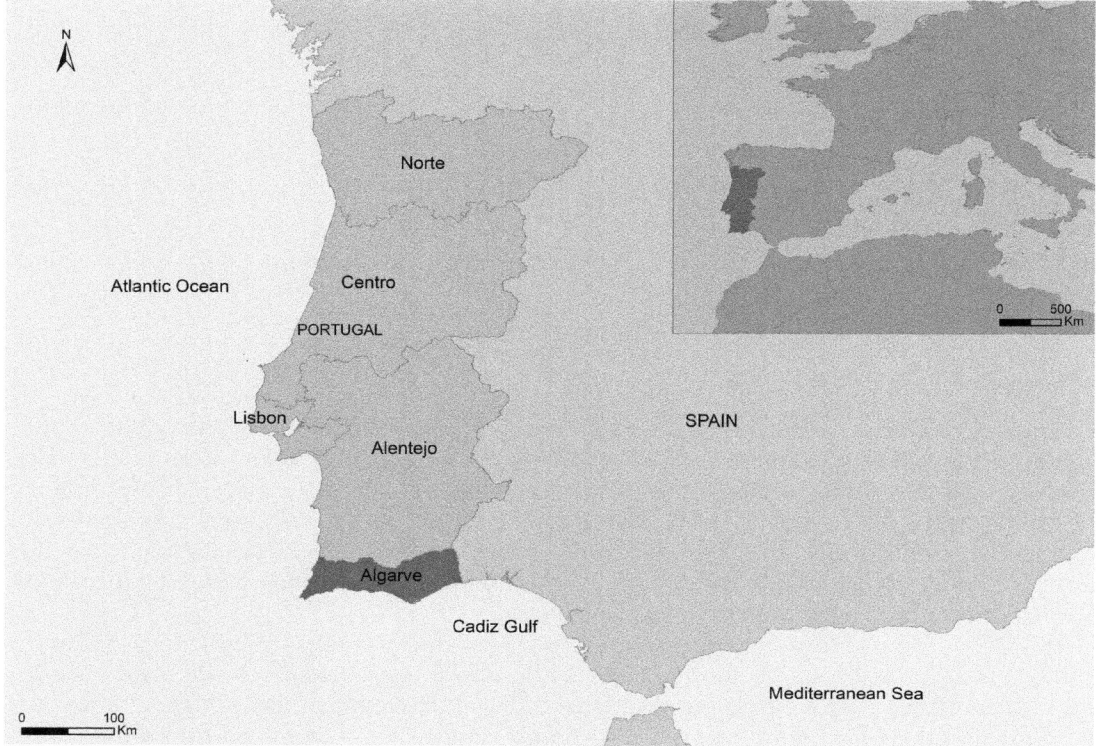

Figure 7.1 Location of Portugal and of Algarve region in Europe

Source: Authors

a relatively high quality of life and improved economic conditions (Schmidt et al, 2013). Yet the diversity of the activities supported by coastal areas frequently result in land use conflicts and threaten the integrity of the coastal area (GTL, 2014).

The growing natural hazards that affect the coast have encouraged the implementation of integrated coastal and maritime policies in Portuguese law, although it has had a limited effect on the ground (Carneiro, 2007; Ferreira et al., 2013).

Administrative structure and responsibilities

To aid the reader's understanding of coastal zone management in Portugal, we note that the governance system has three tiers: national, regional, and municipal. There are eight planning regions: Lisbon Metropolitan Area, West, North, Centre, Alentejo, Algarve, and the archipelagos of Azores and Madeira. The Maritime Public Domain (MPD) is managed at the national level, by the Ministry of the Environment. Also at the national level, the Central Administration is responsible for preparing Regional Spatial Plans and Coastal Zone Plans (POOCs) for each of the eight regions. At the regional level, regional Coordination and Development Commissions (mainland Portugal) and regional governments (autonomous regions of Azores and Madeira) are responsible for preparing Regional Spatial Plans. At the local level, municipalities administer 308 municipal master plans (40 of which in the Azores and Madeira).

Through the POOCs, the Central Administration has committed itself to promoting conservation and enhancement of the coastal zone in the public interest, through measures such as artificial nourishment of beaches and dune systems. Additional coastal programmes, such as a plan for a network of coastal cycle paths, are to be implemented in conjunction with the municipalities.

Legal and regulatory context

The legal regime for Portuguese coastal zone management is complex and is split across five key themes: (i) Protection of coastal land for public use; (ii) urban planning; (iii) planning for coastal zone management and integrated coastal zone management (ICZM); (iv) environmental protection; and (v) water management.

Protection of coastal land for public use

A decree adopted in 1926 (Decree 12445) introduced and defined the Maritime Public Domain (MPD), recognizing the coast as a public resource which should be open for use by the public. That decree has since been repealed and replaced with a new law (Decree-Law 468/71) which updated the legal regime for land in the MPD but maintained the spirit of the initial law. The 1971 law has been amended three times: In 1974, 1987, and 2005. These amendments refined the definition of the MPD, which now includes the Exclusive Economic Zone, and modified the management arrangements by public entities, the exceptions which allow private ownership (for historical legal reasons), the public rights over private coastal land ownership, risk assessment, and control.

The National Strategy for the Portuguese Coast was approved in 1998 and sets a range of guidelines towards sustainable use and protection of people, property, the natural values, and heritage of the coast. It sets out strategies for integrated and coordinated coastal management, clarifies administrative responsibilities, and defines land use rules (Portuguese government, 1998).

Urban planning

Urban planning in Portugal is regulated by the Land and Planning Act (LBPSOTU). This Act was first introduced in 1998 (Law 48/1998) but was thoroughly revised in 2014 (Law 31/2014) and again amended in 2017; an amendment which was particularly relevant to coastal plans. The Land and Planning Act contains general guidelines, which are further elaborated by the Territorial Management Instruments Legal Framework (Decree Law 80/2015). The current version encompasses all the provisions relating to the preparation of Regional Spatial Plans, coastal plans, and Municipal Master Plans, including responsibilities and requirements for public participation.

Planning for coastal zone management

The primary law regulating planning for the coastal zone pertains to specialized Coastal Zone Plans (POOCs). The initial law regulating POOCs (Decree-Law 309/93) focused on their development and approval and its successor (Decree-Law 159/2012) focuses on their implementation, as well as enforcement against illegal development. POOCs are legally binding and must be compatible with all other relevant plans at the national and regional levels, including Regional Spatial Plans (PROTs) and Estuaries Zoning Plans (POEs).

By 2005, nine Coastal Zone Plans (POOCs) had been approved, each applying to a group of several coastal municipalities. Today, the entirety of the Portuguese mainland coast is covered by six coastal plans. In the region of the Azores, each of the nine islands has its own Coastal Zone Plan (except São Miguel and the main island, which has one for the north coast and one for the south coast). The Region of Madeira has no approved Coastal Zone Plan to date.

Meanwhile, in 2002, Portugal adopted the European Parliament and the Council Recommendation concerning the implementation of Integrated Coastal Zone Management (ICZM; 30 May 2002). National plans and strategies followed in succession: The National Ocean Strategy (DQUEM; Portuguese government, 2006) and the National Strategy for Integrated Coastal Zone Management (ENGIZC; Portuguese government, 2009). The latter is a policy document which envisages an integrated approach to the management of the coastal zone to 2029.

The Spatial Plan for the Maritime Zone, POEM, was completed in 2012 (Portuguese government, 2012) for the sea adjacent to the Portuguese mainland, but is yet to be approved.

POOCs must be amended to be compatible with all the above plans and strategies and to set ICZM principles. Furthermore, since the publication of the present POOCs, an extensive reform of the legal framework for general spatial planning and regulation of water resources has taken place; a new Land and Planning Act, a new Water Act, and a new National Ecological Reserve legal framework have all been adopted. Thus, the plans must be reviewed for compatibility with those new laws.

To date, only one POOC, Alentejo, has been amended, in 2010, to implement the National Strategy for ICZM. Other POOCs have been under review, but none of these reviews has been concluded (Ferreira et al., 2013). Once reviewed and updated, the nine existing POOCs will be replaced by five Coastal Zone Programs (POC), corresponding to coastal management units defined by the National Environmental Agency (APA).

Environmental protection and water management law

The key environmental protection and water management laws pertaining to coastal zone management include the *Water Act* (58/2005), which sets the framework for the management of surface waters, such as interior transitional, coastal, and underground waters; the *Regulation for the Use of Hydrological Domain* (226-A/2007), which establishes procedures for authorization, licensing, or concession for operations on the public and private hydrological domain; the *Public Water Domain Definition Law* (54/2005), which defines procedures related to the public water domain; and the *Strategic Environmental Assessment Decree-Law* (232/2007), which requires an Environment Impact Assessment on plans and programmes.

The National Strategy for Environmental and Biodiversity Conservation 2030 (Portuguese government, 2018) is a reference document towards reduction of biodiversity loss, underpinned by the international and national commitments under the EU's 2030 Agenda for Sustainable Development.

Overall, the compendium of laws regarding the coast does not encourage simplicity. On the contrary, in many cases it impedes or prevents integrated and sustainable management (GTL, 2014).

POLIS SOCIETIES AND PROGRAMMES

POLIS societies are public companies with commercial status. Three societies are responsible for managing POLIS Littoral programmes, which are designed for specific stretches of the coast which are regarded as 'priority intervention areas', namely Ria Formosa, in the Algarve region; Litoral Norte, in northern Portugal; and Ria de Aveiro, in central Portugal.

These societies are financed by the State, the relevant municipalities, and private companies, and are underpinned by EU funding and assigned through the National Strategic Reference Framework, which sets priorities for the available funds. As we will discuss below, POLIS societies have sometimes been effective in ensuring coastal preservation and enforcement against illegal structures in the public domain, in the form of demolitions.

Definition of the Portuguese coastal zone and shoreline

The National Strategy for ICZM (ENGIZC) defined the coastal zone as:

> the buffer zone which protects land from sea advance and climate change, and which should be considered as legally superior to spatial land use planning instruments, and abide by the principle of a non aedificandi zone. (Portuguese government, 2009)

The POOCs (plans for the coastal zone made by the central administration) include several subzones of the coastal zone. Notably, the relevant definitions, though legally binding, do not have direct implications on land ownership or the land registry – only to land use planning, as the planning and registry systems are not coordinated.[1] The sub-zones, initially established by the Regional Plan of the Algarve, are illustrated in Figure 7.2.

The **Maritime Protection Zone** includes all coastal waters. The **Shore Coastal Strip** includes all land in the coastal zone, from the highest equinoctial high tide to up to 2 km inland (measured perpendicular to the shoreline; Decree-Law 309/93). This width may be adjusted

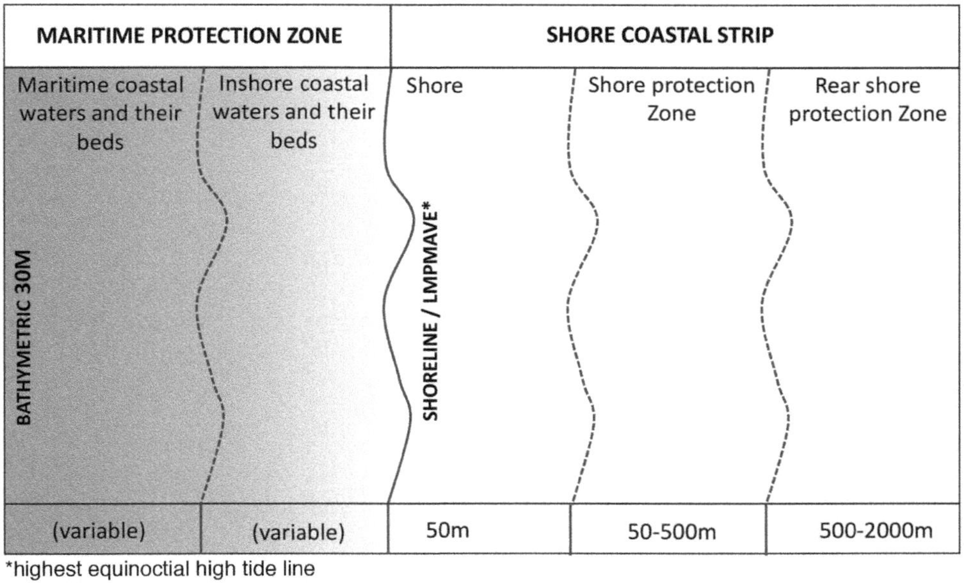

MARITIME PROTECTION ZONE		SHORE COASTAL STRIP		
Maritime coastal waters and their beds	Inshore coastal waters and their beds	Shore	Shore protection Zone	Rear shore protection Zone
(variable)	(variable)	50m	50-500m	500-2000m

(left vertical label: BATHYMETRIC 30M)

(vertical label between Maritime Protection Zone and Shore Coastal Strip: SHORELINE / LMPMAVE*)

*highest equinoctial high tide line

Figure 7.2 Coastal system

Source: Authors, based on Algarve Regional Spatial Plan (Vol. I, p. 89)

according to detailed biophysical, functional, and land use features related to the sea. The Shore Coastal Strip comprises:

- **Shore:** A strip of land with a width of 50 m measured inland from the level of the highest equinoctial high tide. Where the shore is composed of cliffs, the 50 m strip is measured inland from the cliff edge. When the beach features extend further inland than 50 m, the shore width is extended accordingly. The actual extent is defined within the relevant POOC.
- **Shore Protection Zone:** A strip of land between the landward boundary of the Shore and 450 m from the shoreline. In this zone, specific planning and environment provisions relating to the protection of the coastal zone may apply (outside urban areas).
- **Rear Shore Protection Zone:** A strip of land between the outer boundary of the Shore Protection Zone (500 m from the shoreline) and 2,000 m from the shoreline.

Using these definitions, the POOCs can 'stretch' the coastal zone to a width of up to 2 km from the shoreline, where justified by the need to protect coastal biophysical systems.

Shoreline definition

The Portuguese shoreline corresponds to the limit of the highest equinoctial high tide line (LMPMAVE), under normal atmospheric conditions. LMPMAVE is broadly defined in the Public Water Domain Definition Law (54/2005):

> *The bed of the waters of the sea, as well as of the other waters subject to the influence of the tides, is limited by the line of the maximum high water of equinoctial waters. This line is defined, for each location, accordingly to the agitation of the sea, in the first case, and in medium flood conditions, in the second.*

Regarding sheltered areas not significantly influenced by tidal movement, the Minister of Environment, Planning and Territory and Regional Development issued Normative Dispatch 32/2008, which clarified the shoreline position: LMPMAVE is *'set by the level curve corresponding to the 2.00m height (above mean sea level) in sheltered areas that do not suffer significant influence of the agitation particularly in rivers, estuaries and ports'*.

The Central Administration has progressively defined the shoreline in short stretches whenever land ownership and land registry issues have arisen. As such, some stretches of the shoreline are not yet officially defined. The process for defining the line was originally carried out by a National Commission for the Maritime Public Domain, but since 2007, this has been the responsibility of the National Environmental Agency (APA). Significantly, Portugal does not have a complete national landed property cadastre.

As outlined above, Portuguese coastal policies and laws also reference the line indicating the lowest equinoctial low tide (LMBMAVE), defined as the line *'... corresponding to the maximum spread of the waves in medium conditions of sea agitation in the low tide equinoxes sea water level'* (Dispatch 12/2010 from the president of the Water Institute, INAG today – Portuguese Environment Agency). This line was first drawn in Portugal for the coast in Algarve, based on criteria established by Teixeira (2009), which include oceanographic, sediments, and morphological parameters. These standards have since been applied to other stretches of the west coast.

Shoreline erosion

The shoreline evolves due to both natural and artificial causes. At the end of the nineteenth century, the Portuguese shoreline started showing signs of regression which were related to the reduction of sediment resulting from the construction of dams, sand extraction in rivers, agricultural practices for soil retention, and port construction (Teixeira, 2014). The sand budgets have been considerably reduced along the west coast due to dams built along the main rivers. This, together with the artificial structures built at the mouth of the several estuaries and ports, cause significant erosion in the stretches of coast next to those structures, especially in sandy beaches and soft rocky sea cliffs (Teixeira et al., 2000). To avoid these effects, artificial structures have been built, and in some cases beach nourishment has been undertaken in order to prevent further coastal recession and to maintain the beaches. The most severe cases are now subject to POLIS programme interventions.

On the south coast of the Algarve, there is serious coastal recession between the Marina of Vilamoura and cape Saint Mary, caused by the artificial headlands that protect the entrance to the Marina. At Vale do Lobo, a luxury tourist development, the shoreline has receded about 50 m since the development's construction in 1970, and three villas have been lost to the sea. This coastal recession has been halted only by the creation of two artificial beaches over the last fifteen years. These beaches will have to be replenished approximately every three to seven years. The Ofir Towers, next to Ofir beach in Northern Portugal, provide another illustration of the severity of the threat of beach erosion (Figure 7.3). The three towers were built in the

Figure 7.3 Ofir Towers, Esposende, January 2019
Source: Photograph by Inês Calor

1970s and contain approximately 200 apartments overall, primarily for tourist accommodation. Despite being assigned for demolition in 2002 (Fonseca, 2002), these towers are still standing and today are protected by a sea wall and repeated beach nourishing which, nevertheless, have proven insufficient to avoid periodical exposure of the structures.

Coastal public domain

As outlined in the introduction to this chapter, Portuguese law establishes a Maritime Public Domain (MPD) which includes all coastal and territorial waters and all land subject to tidal influence (Public Water Domain Definition Law, 54/2005). This includes all the Maritime Protection Zone (Figure 7.2 – both seawards and landwards). In addition, the law (Decree 12445, 1926) defines a Coastal Public Domain, which corresponds to the 'Shore' portion of the Shore Coastal Strip, as defined above and illustrated at Figure 7.2 (the 50 m strip).

In cases of shoreline recession, the boundaries of the shoreline and the Maritime Public Domain are adjusted. In cases of shoreline advance, the shoreline is adjusted, and the MPD is enlarged in order to encompass the additional land area, which becomes public property.

The definition of the Maritime Public Domain applies in both urban and non-urban areas. However, within older urban areas and urban areas where there has been a coastal recession, the Maritime Public Domain strip may include built-up private land, where land use limitations apply.

The Maritime Public Domain is primarily owned by the State but may also be owned by the autonomous regions (Azores and Madeira), municipalities and civil parishes (*Public Water Domain Definition Law*, Article 2). It is subject to a special regime of protection that makes it inalienable (cannot be sold) and 'non-prescriptible' (GTL, 2014). Yet under the *Public Water Domain Definition Law* (Law 54/2005), plots within the Maritime Public Domain may be recognized as privately owned. When recognized as private, these plots are not subject to the same restrictions as the rest of the land in the public domain and may be sold. In order to gain such recognition, property owners must prove that their land was privately owned before 1864 (or before 1868, when next to cliffs). Those who fail to do so lose their land without compensation.

The deadline for making claims of ownership within the Maritime Public Domain, which involves a court procedure, was initially set as 1 January 2014. But the law was amended in 2014 (Laws 78/2013 and 34/2014) to remove the deadline. At present, only landowners seeking planning approval or a building permit on private land within the Maritime Public Domain outside existing urban areas must request private ownership recognition. Along the mainland Coastal Strip (excluding estuaries, lagoons, and lagoon systems), 500 private properties have been recognized and published in the State Official Bulletin. This equates to approximately 280 km, or about 30% of the mainland Portugal coastline (GTL, 2014).

Permitted uses and development in the public domain

By law (Decree 12445, 1926) the 'Shore' is a *non aedificandi* (construction-free) zone, with some exceptions. Exceptions commonly include buildings used for sea or beach-related uses (under 'concession' – ground leases on public land). The limitations to land use and construction within this zone apply to any future development and/or changes in existing buildings.

Within the Maritime Public Domain, permits for use and development may only be granted to private enterprises for construction related to the sea and to beach uses, such as restaurants, bars, sports facilities, boathouses, and emergency services. These buildings may consist of only light structures and must be of a temporary nature. In general, permits for use of the public domain are granted on a yearly basis, though longer periods are legally possible.

It should be noted that according to the Legal Framework on Urban Development and Building (Law 555/99, Article 60), unchanged buildings have imprescriptible vested rights, which means that limits on construction can only be imposed when owners require a building permit for additional floorspace or for major changes.

Setback from the shoreline

Of the subzones defined above, the 'Shore', within 50 m of the shoreline, is the setback zone; it is protected from construction by national law. For the other zones, 'Shore Protection Zone' and 'Rear Shore Protection Zone', specific provisions are listed in each POOC.

Owners of land in areas of the coastal zone subject to development restrictions may repair existing buildings, but only if they were legally built before the limitations were introduced. The enlargement or rebuilding of existing buildings is not permitted. Relocation of existing buildings to a more convenient location or setback is hardly achievable (even on full reconstructions), either because the National Environmental Reserve (REN) framework forbids the enlargement or changes in the building footprint within coastal areas included in REN (Decree-Law 73/2009, with amendments) or because, in urban areas, no alternative coastal locations are available. The lack of a tool that allows negotiation with owners to relocate buildings to a more convenient location is understood as an impediment for efficient management of coastal areas (GTL, 2014).

Right of public access

Accessibility, both horizontal (along the coast) and vertical (perpendicular to the coast), is a public right under the law. The Public Water Domain Definition Law required that the Shore was made public and accessible by 1 January 2016 (Law 54/2005, Article 9(3)). Thus, along stretches of coast characterized by sandy beaches, vertical access is now fully ensured. However, access is not always guaranteed for cliffy beaches, especially when horizontal access along the Maritime Public Domain is not physically possible. The same law also requires that all private plots on the public Shore are subject to access easements (Article 21(1)). Specifically, private owners of land between the closest public road and the beach are required to provide a public right of way. However, this does not always happen, particularly in some tourist developments, which operate as closed condominiums. Others grant access but build psychological barriers, such as open gates or porches, to dissuade the uninformed public from entering. Access by sea to the beaches is always public and free.

Up until the 1950s, several promenades and parkways were built at the landward edge of the public domain, close to sandy beaches or near cliff edges. These both ensure horizontal accessibility and provide views of the sea. In addition, since that time, vertical accessibility (especially for vehicles) has increasingly been prioritized in policies and plans. There are no quantitative standards set in the law, as this level of detail is reserved for plans, namely the POOCs and municipal plans.

Since access to beaches is ensured, no charges may be imposed on users. In beaches that provide facilities such as umbrellas and chairs, users may be charged only for the use of these facilities, in designated areas. In addition, car parking may incur a charge.

The topography of the beach or coast, especially outside urban areas, may not be modified, as the coast is part of the National Ecological Reserve. In an increasing number of cases, particularly within national parks (known in Portugal as natural parks) along the coast, sand dunes are protected by fences. Access is often by elevated boardwalks built on wooden supports in order to minimize effects on sand movement.

Land use planning

As indicated in the introductory section of this chapter, planning is a significant tool for coastal zone management in Portugal. The planning system incorporates Regional Spatial Plans (PROTs) which are prepared at the national level and Municipal Master Plans prepared at the local level. Only the latter are legally binding, thus the rules and guidelines contained in Regional Spatial Plans must be transposed to Municipal Master Plans. Both these types of plans can include norms and guidelines on coastal protection and management, but an additional plan type – the Coastal Zone Spatial Plans (POOCs) – was specifically designed to address coastal zone management. POOCs are binding land use plans for the coastal zone, which have the following objectives:

- Land use planning specific to the coastal zone
- Classification of beaches and regulations for their use
- Enhancement and improvement of beaches considered to be strategic for environmental and/or touristic reasons
- Environmental protection
- Protection and enhancement of natural resources and of historic and cultural heritage

POOCs include a layout plan for each beach and define what infrastructure and facilities are required. These plans are founded on a classification of beaches according to five typologies, based on whether they are urban or non-urban, as well as on the intensity of use and/or volume of demand. We note that, unlike POOCs and in the context of the Land and Planning Act (LBPSOTU – Law 31/2014), the new Programs for the Coastal Zone (POCs) will be binding only on public entities. For their provisions to be binding on all parties, POCs will need to be integrated into Municipal Master Plans.

Case study of planning in the Algarve region

In Algarve, the coastline is the most striking element, combining a high ecological sensitivity with significant urban development and a concentration of economic activities driven by regional development. According to the Algarve Regional Spatial Plan (PROT), the coast is a dynamic, interactive, and continuous natural resource with heritage value, which calls for the coordination of environmental and socio-economic values (Portuguese government, 2007).

The current Algarve Regional Spatial Plan (PROT; Portuguese government, 2007) was the first to specifically address ICZM (others have since followed). The PROT identifies the following:

- In the Shore Protection Zone (first 500 m inland from the shoreline), built-up areas represent more than a quarter of the total area. Excluding undevelopable areas, only 1.3% of the total area was still eligible for development in 2007
- In the rear shore protection zone (between 500 m and 2 km inland from the shoreline), only approximately 45% and 10% respectively in the western and eastern Algarve

This data indicates the intense pressures on the coast and the present state of near depletion of remaining land available for coastal development. In consideration of these issues, the Regional Plan sets the following guidelines for this area. Note that in all cases, tourism facilities may not be constructed within existing urban areas.

i   New construction within the Shore zone is forbidden outside existing urban areas, with the exception of infrastructure and social facilities which support sea and beach-related activities, as defined in the POOC (see the section on the public domain).

ii   New construction is not permitted in the Shore Protection Zone outside existing urban areas, with the exception of infrastructure and social facilities with a distinct public value or which support sea and beach-related activities or relocation of existing tourist developments further away from the shoreline.

iii New construction or development in the Rear Shore Protection Zone outside urban areas is conditional on the guidelines applicable to the different types of tourist developments. This does not apply to infrastructure and social facilities with clear public value. In the areas adjacent to the Ria Formosa Natural Park (which includes a large lagoon), the rehabilitation of downgraded areas is allowed, particularly for infrastructure, social facilities, urban parks, business facilities, and housing, if there is a local interest.

iv   In reviewing municipal master plans, local authorities should assess all built-up coastal areas to assess potential restructuring. Goals for coastal areas include eliminating land use conflicts; redefining tourist activities, accommodation, and facilities; promoting decongestion of overused areas; identifying and overcoming shortfalls in the provision of infrastructure, social facilities, and open spaces; and identifying built-up parts of the Coastal Strip to be preserved.

v   The region's ecological corridors, both along the southern coast and linking the coast to the inland mountains, must be respected, in accordance with the standards set by the regional environmental guidelines.

In addition to these guidelines, municipal land use plans must: (i) detail planning proposals and rules for natural values and resources of strategic importance; (ii) set standards for the protection of natural and heritage values; (iii) prevent continuous urban land use and built-up areas along the coastline, and new roads on the coast; (iv) promote urban redevelopment of downgraded, overused, and, with inappropriate uses, their open spaces and public spaces; and (v) promote integrated coastal management, including the establishment of public–private partnerships, in view of financial viability and respecting deadlines for implementation.

All Municipal Master Plans within Algarve have been adapted to accord with the provisions of the Regional Plan which are considered priorities. The remaining provisions of the Regional Plan, as well as from the POOCs or the POC if completed and approved in the meantime, will be transposed to the Municipal Master Plans as part of the still ongoing municipal review processes.

Compliance and enforcement

As is the case in many countries even in the Global North, enforcement of illegal development is a major challenge to planning bodies in Portugal. This is especially true for the coastal area. In the private domain, municipalities are the primary body responsible for enforcement. As a rule, these bodies are headed by politicians chosen through local elections, and as such, enforcement is closely linked with local politics. Regional Coordination and Development Commissions (CCDRs) have the power to take enforcement measures against illegal development in any case where the relevant municipality does not initiate procedures. In practice, their actions focus mostly on National Environmental Reserve areas. In addition, other government bodies may take enforcement actions within areas under their jurisdiction; these are the National Environmental Agency (APA) in coastal areas (including public and private domains) and the Institute for Nature Conservation and Forestry (ICNF) in coastal natural parks.

Enforcement tools are defined by the Legal Framework on Development and Building and include inspection events, fines, stop orders, and demolition orders. Under Portuguese law, building without a permit (illegal building) is simply an offence (not a crime). There are no additional enforcement tools at the regional and local levels.

There is no official data on the extent of illegal development. However, for environmental protected areas, on the coast (natural parks), some numbers have been published. In 2005, a report from the (then named) Institute for Nature Conservation (ICN) identified 3,241 illegal structures in these areas, most of which are in natural parks within coastal areas: 1,815 cases in the Ria Formosa Natural Park and 880 in the Alentejo Natural Park and the Vicentine Coast (Carvalho, 2005). In 2006, the director of the North Littoral Natural Park announced the demolition of more than 200 illegal structures (Julião, 2006). These numbers do not make a distinction between Maritime Public Domain and setback zones and are probably far from the real numbers of illegal structures. As such, they provide only a partial picture of illegal development along the coast.

The ICN report indicates that the Algarve region has a significant number of squatter settlements, concentrated in the islands and islets of Ria Formosa (other regions have very few or no squatter settlements). These settlements were first started by fishers or local residents, and many became second homes for weekends and holidays. Because of the geomorphologic conditions (mostly sand dunes), this area, together with the lagoon, is entirely within the public domain. As detailed above, when the beach features extend inland more than 50 m from the shoreline, the shore width is extended accordingly. As such, private structures are not permitted. However, a survey by the Ria Formosa POLIS society revealed that in 2009 there were 2,366 structures in the barrier islands and islets between the Ria Formosa lagoon and the sea (Sociedade POLIS Litoral Ria Formosa, 2009). This number represents an increase of 18.8% in structures since a similar survey was undertaken in 1994. Significantly, however, the 2009 survey includes structures constructed by public bodies that were not included in the first. In Portugal, works undertaken by public authorities are exempt from any requirement for a building permit and, despite the need to comply with spatial plans, several exceptions for public buildings and infrastructure apply in environmental sensitive areas.

Due to political and financial constraints, demolitions of illegal developments or structures are rare. To the best of our knowledge, in the past 30 years there have been only two systematic enforcement actions that led to large-scale demolitions. The demolitions were mostly of squatter housing within the Maritime Public Domain, and the majority were also located in environmentally protected areas. During a period of strong political will and effective governance, between 1986 and 1988, a total of 3,549 buildings were demolished by the Institute for Nature Conservation in nine different locations (Pires, 1996).[2] A second period began in 2010 with the POLIS Programme in Ria Formosa (Algarve). The Vilamoura – Vila Real de Santo António Coastal Plan (POOC) – was enacted in 2005 and empowered the POLIS society with financial, technical, and political means to undertake enforcement actions. Initially, demolition of 800 dwellings was expected and the budget was 14.6 M euros. Of the 800 buildings, 300 have been

Figure 7.4 Vacant plot after demolition, Faro Island, June 2015

Source: Photograph by Inês Calor

demolished since December 2014 – primarily on the fringes of Faro island beach (Figure 7.4). Permanent housing has been spared to date, as demolition is dependent on the construction of alternative housing, according to the POLIS Society policy.

On Fuseta Island, demolition was anticipated by 2010–2011 winter storms which washed away about half of the 77 illegal structures. The remaining structures were then removed by the relevant POLIS Society (Sociedade POLIS Litoral Ria Formosa, 2010). Other structures on islets were also demolished.

The demolition of 400 illegal houses on Faro Island has proved more litigious than other cases. In 2014, an injunction submitted by Olhão Municipality argued that the demolition plan would damage the habitat of a protected chameleon, a species that inhabits the backyards of existing dwellings. Significantly, the mayor of Olhão (one of the municipalities that participates in the POLIS society) is the owner of a house on the island and an active opponent of the demolitions (Revez, 2015). Other residents and local associations have also made known that they oppose the demolitions (Figure 7.5). In April 2015, a court decision from the Administrative and Fiscal Court of Loulé suspended the demolition order for 134 houses on the island. As there is a strict deadline on the use of European Funds for demolition, delays due to court procedures may mean that funds are no longer available when demolition is permitted.

It is difficult to assess public opinion on this matter: Residents' associations and owners opposed to the demolitions are more visible in the media. NGOs such as Quercus and GEOTA have shown their support to enforcement actions on their webpages (Quercus, 2015; GEOTA, 2015). To the best of our knowledge, no survey of the general population has been undertaken; however, we encountered opinions from local citizens that recognize the improvement of the

Figure 7.5 Car sticker saying 'No to demolitions in Ria Formosa', Faro Island, June 2015

Source: Photograph by Inês Calor

quality of Fuseta Island's beach since demolition (and the addition of beach facilities) and the need to prevent private developments inching closer to the shoreline and thus further reducing the beach area in Praia de Faro.

A lesson from the Portuguese attempts at systematic enforcement actions might be that it is difficult to find the balance between political power, proactive approaches, and economic means for enforcement actions.

Climate change awareness – legal aspects

The most significant anticipated consequences of climate change on the coast of mainland Portugal are the rise of the mean sea level, changes in the wave system, and increased meteorological swell, temperatures, and rainfall. These changes will generate impacts on the sediments budget and may have consequences on the intensity of erosion, as well as on the frequency and intensity of coastal flooding and changes in water quality of estuaries, lagoons, and coastal aquifers (APA, 2015).

In the medium and long term (time horizons up to 2050 and 2100, respectively), the rise of the global mean sea level will become an important factor in aggravating storm surges, increased coastal flooding, and coastal erosion. Although the rise of the mean global and local sea levels by the end of the twenty-first century is still uncertain, it is likely to be more than half a metre, possibly 1 m. Such changes will be significant and serious. There is still a considerable deficit of knowledge about these impacts and in terms of the estimates of the associated costs (GTL, 2014).

The impact of climate change is most evident in already vulnerable coastal areas which are prone to erosion and affected by storm surges and flood phenomena. Therefore, there is an increasing concern about coastal areas where the population density is high, both where the coast is not protected or protected by coastal structures, with particular relevance to coastal areas whose geology is soft rock or sand (beaches, dunes, barrier islands, sand barriers, and wetlands).

There are no specific Portuguese laws addressing climate change, but a National Strategy for Adaptation to Climate Change for the 2020 horizon (2020 ENAAC) was approved in 2010. The National Strategy for the Integrated Management of the Coastal Zone (ENGIZC) is consistent with this Climate Change strategy, where relevant. Furthermore, the legal and regulatory context addressed throughout this chapter demonstrates a clear awareness about the need to promote the integration and monitoring of adaptation to climate change in public policies. Yet there is much work to be done to integrate climate change risk and adaptation.

The Sectoral Plan for Risk Prevention and Mitigation, adopted in 2013, covers all natural and artificial hazards and considers the effects of climate change on natural hazards. It provides standards and guidelines for spatial planning for the coastal area.

The Land and Planning Act and the PNPOT (National Programme of Spatial Development Policies, latest review, 2019) clearly state that all instruments related to land use planning and management should promote adaptation policies and be consistent with the 2020 ENAAC.

In order to ensure compatibility with the different adaptation measures proposed and their integration into spatial planning, the PNPOT states the need to promote several activities:

i   Dissemination of data and of other resources which provide guidance to those responsible for the active management of adaptation to climate change on the local and regional levels
ii Analysis and mapping of climate-related hazards and integration into relevant policy and management instruments
iii Development of technical guidelines for integrating climate change adaptation measures into territorial management instruments
iv Integration of adaptation to climate change in the PNPOT programme of action
v   Integration of adaptation to climate change into the PNPOT roadmap and into the Sustainable Urban Development Agendas

Coordination and integration

The main bodies responsible for implementing coastal zone plans are the Ministry of the Environment (through the National Environmental Agency – APA), the Regional Coordination and Development Commissions[3] (CCDR), and Municipalities. The APA is responsible for both coastal zone planning and the management of Maritime Public Domain. CCDRs are responsible for regional plans and for giving external opinions on actions in high-risk areas included in the National Ecological Reserve (e.g. coastal erosion zones). In the autonomous regions of Azores and Madeira, regional governments are responsible for implementing planning instruments.

Portugal's Ministry of the Environment, the National Environmental Agency (APA), is responsible both for coastal zone planning and for the management of the MPD. Municipalities and the Regional Coordination and Development Commissions (CCDR) are jointly responsible for implementing coastal zone plans (POOCs), and several other institutions are involved in planning and management. Other institutions involved in coastal planning and management are the Institute for the Conservation of Nature and Forests (for Protected Areas, i.e. natural parks and nature conservation areas); the Port Administrations or the National Maritime Administration (for Port Areas); and military institutions (on military land).

A major step was accomplished in overcoming institutional coordination needs by the creation of public companies. The POLIS societies described above were introduced to overcome coordination problems in selected areas. It should also be noted that the *Corporation POLIS Litoral* constitutes a management model with several positive aspects, such as the involvement of local authorities in solving problems, openness to financial contributions from various institutions, and the possibility of implementing more effective solutions at both administrative and financial levels. We believe that the model of *Corporate POLIS Litoral* should be revisited in order to find optimum solutions in the same vein, that cover the entire Portuguese coast. Under proactive leadership, the POLIS programmes have shown to be effective in improving coastal preservation and upgrading the quality of coastal areas.

Geographic information systems (GIS) have great potential as a platform for sharing information and coordinating shoreline actions. A good example is the SIARL project: Coastal Resources Management System, launched online in 2011. The initial aim of the project was to restore compliance, but it has since evolved to address other issues and is now an important repository of coastal data and a collaborative platform for administrative bodies, thus helping to implement truly integrated coastal zone management.

Public participation and access to justice – legal anchoring

Public participation in planning follows the framework established by the Land and Planning Act of 2014 and the complementary regulations approved in 2015. This legislative framework establishes the right of the public to access information and to participate in planning decision-making. This applies to all spatial plans, which generally include an environmental assessment, and the public may participate at various points in the plan-making and review process. In addition, the present legal framework incorporates the principles of the Aarhus Convention.

Until now, the Portuguese implementation of ICZM has adopted a top-down, government-led approach. Public participation has usually consisted of public consultation on the final version of plans, just prior to their approval. Limited public participation regarding coastal zone management seems to derive from the technical nature of the plans (Schmidt et al., 2013). Additional research reveals that individual responses to planning proposals tend to be self-interested rather than considering the broader public good (Soares, 2008, in Ferreira et al., 2013).

Information on environmental issues and approved plans, including the coastal area, is becoming increasingly available on the sites of APA, the national environment authority, and the DGT – the Director-General for Spatial Planning, where all current spatial plans and related regulations and guidelines are available to the public.

Since there is no true public planning culture in Portugal (though there is a growing environmental awareness), public participation processes in planning and ICZM generally do not have a strong impact. On the other hand, environmental NGOs such as Quercus and GEOTA have influenced coastal planning. These organizations have, for example, taken legal action against the Portuguese Government to prevent new development in environmentally sensitive coastal areas, such as Costa Terra Resort[4] and Herdade do Pinheirinho Resort[5] on the southwest coast (Alentejo Region) in 2006. In these two cases, the main issue was related to the setback zone (Shore Protection Zone), which includes land within 500 m from the shoreline. The NGOs claimed that this setback had not been observed when the two resorts were initially approved for development, resulting in effects that were contrary to the Alentejo Regional Plan and inappropriate given the environmental sensitivity of the coastal zone. Due to the major setbacks resulting from this legal action, as well as the global economic crisis, the two resorts have not been developed to date.

The organizations also supported civil movements against projects such as the Sintra tourist megaproject, close to Lisbon, in 2008. This large project, though located well within the Lisbon Metropolitan Area, is adjacent to Sintra-Cascais Natural Park, a key nature conservation area on the coast which serves the metropolitan area. The proposed tourist resort megaproject development posed a significant threat to this sensitive area and has not been developed to date.

Any plan that does not respect the legal framework, including the public participation process, can be subject to an injunction by any citizen in an administrative court of law. Though this seldom happens, some such cases have occurred. For example, the Master Plan for Lagos in eastern Algarve, developed in the 1980s, was suspended by court ruling because the time period of public participation in the lead-up to plan approval was shorter than that required by law.

Fiscal aspects of coastal zone management

Although the current legal framework applies deadlines to building permits, this has not always been the case. Development and building rights issued before the more recent laws may still be valid, and compensation is due if the administration chooses to revoke those rights. Thus, along the coast, conflicts arise where environmental restrictions preventing further development are enacted after planning approval or issue of a building permit but prior to the start of development. In these cases, rights still exist but cannot be materialized on site. There are several such situations along the Portuguese coast, especially in the Algarve region. The Administration has often been ordered to pay compensation in these circumstances. As an alternative solution to this issue, the Algarve Regional Plan foresees the possibility of transfer of development rights to other locations, away from sensitive areas, subject to consent by the landowner.

In cases in which land is lost to the sea as a result of coastal erosion – even if this land is in private ownership – there is no right for compensation by the public sector. If no land is lost to sea but the sea level rises so that additional land is subject to tidal influence or flooding, there are no consequences other than an enlargement of the Maritime Public Domain (Bargado, 2013). In these cases, the State may expropriate affected areas.

In legally built-up areas, the State has a so-called extra-contractual responsibility to ensure the protection of all citizens and their legitimate goods against all hazards. This means that if an existing building, legally built, falls into the sea due to cliff erosion or sea level rise, the landowner is entitled to receive compensation for their loss. To safeguard landed properties at risk due to significant erosion, authorities have occasionally opted to build sea groynes (hydraulic structures to interrupt water flow and stop sediment transport). Historically, such structures have been problematic, as they could accelerate erosion of other beaches by limiting the sand they receive. More recently, groynes have been designed in such a way as to restrict the amount of sand that they can hold and thus allow excess sediment to move freely on through the system.

Ironically, the State's attempt to prevent erosion by building groynes at Vilamoura Marina and Quarteira beach likely contributed to erosion at Vale do Lobo luxury tourist development, resulting in three villas being destroyed by the sea. As such, the government was required to compensate the owners for their loss due to damage to which it has contributed.

To avoid the need to eventually pay compensation, the State may expropriate at-risk properties, though this has not occurred to date. In addition, at-risk developments may be relocated. Since the abovementioned villas were destroyed, a specific Vale do Lobo coastal area detailed plan (2010) proposed the relocation of all buildings that are located too close to the soft rock cliffs to a location further inland, in order to avoid the need to build additional coastal structures. Sand nourishment of the beach, undertaken twice since the loss of the three villas mentioned earlier, has delayed the urgency of such a measure, and the local plan, though completed, has not been officially approved.

Insurance companies may insure landowners for full damages in risk areas. However, these companies now have increasingly detailed and accurate data and, as such, may refuse to insure specific at-risk sites. There is no law preventing them from doing so.

Other topics and overall assessment

Portugal has an advanced legal framework with respect to the Maritime Public Domain, coastal planning, and ICZM. In addition, the concept of the public domain and its consequences is strongly rooted in Portuguese culture. Unfortunately, however, implementation of the law is lacking, particularly when it comes to demolition of illegal development and the prevention of additional illegalities. The processes are lacking in several areas, including coordination among relevant institutions; political will, especially at the local (municipal) level; and the public participation process, which does not adequately focus on defending public interests.

The public costs of coastal management in Portugal are very high. For example, the total cost of coastal works undertaken by APA to repair damage sustained over the winter of 2013–2014 was 23 million euros. Given the high costs and its relatively small economy, Portugal is one of the countries that has most benefited from EU funding for coastal protection, together with Romania, Lithuania, and Malta (GTL, 2014). Unfortunately, there is no guarantee that such large-scale funding will continue. And significantly, future access to EU funding will likely depend on demonstrating effective and systematic monitoring of the coastal zone.

Given the above, respect of the Maritime Public Domain and setback zones is of great importance to avoid further burdening the cost of coastal protection works and the rehabilitation of infrastructure damaged over time. Despite its complexity, the Portuguese framework lacks a legal tool that allows the relocation of building rights away from the coast. This or other tools are needed in order to strike the important balance between the public and private interest in high-risk areas, taking into account the rising costs of coastal protection (GTL, 2014).

Notes

1. In Portugal, land use planning, land registry for land tax, and land registry for landed property ownership each follow different rules and are not coordinated.
2. (a) Parque Nacional da Arrábida, (b) Paisagem Protegida da Arriba Fóssil da Costa da Caparica, (c) Parque Natural da Ria Formosa, (d) Lagoa de Albufeira, (e) Parque Natural de Sintra/Cascais, (f) Alcobaça, (g) Baleal – Peniche, (h) São Pedro de Moel, and (i) Parque Natural do Sudoeste Alentejano e Costa Vicentina.
3. Regional Coordination and Development Commissions are decentralized bodies of the Central Administration, corresponding geographically with the EU's nomenclature of territorial units NUT II.
4. Regarding the Costa Terra Resort, there was a Joint Decision of South Central Court (09/07/2009, process n. 03804/08, available at: http://www.dgsi.pt/jtca.nsf/170589492546a7fb802575c-3004c6d7d/48258d6c3dd4ba66802575f200673383?OpenDocument).
5. Regarding Herdade do Pinheirinho, the stop order from the Administrative Court of Lisbon is not available online but is mentioned in the press (Carvalho, 2008).

References

Agência Portuguesa do Ambiente (APA). (2015). *Estratégia Nacional para Adaptação às Alterações Climáticas* [National Strategy for Adaptation to Climate Change] (2020 ENAAC).

Bargado, M. A. C. (2013). O reconhecimento da propriedade privada sobre terrenos do domínio público hídrico [Recognition of private property on MPD land]. Instituto de Ciências Jurídico-Políticas, Faculdade de Direito de Lisboa.

Carneiro, G. (2007). The parallel evolution of ocean and coastal management policies in Portugal. *Marine Policy* 31, 421–433.

Carvalho, M. (2008). Tribunal suspende projeto PIN na Costa Alentejana [Court suspends Project of National Interest in Alentejo's coast]. *Expresso*, 20 February. Available at: https://expresso.pt/actualidade/tribunal-suspende-projecto-pin-na-costa-alentejana=f246899

Carvalho, R. (2005). Três mil casas ilegais nos parques [Three thousand illegal houses in the parks]. *Diário de Notícias*, 23 February. Available at: https://www.dn.pt/arquivo/2005/tres-mil-casas-ilegais-nos-parques-610497.html

Ferreira, M. A., Williams, A. T., & Silva, C. P. (2013). Portuguese shoreline spatial plans: Integrating lessons from the past into second generation plans. *Coastal Management* 41(1), 1–18.

Fonseca, F. (2002). Torres de Ofir vão abaixo no final do ano [Ofir Towers coming down at end of year]. *Público*, 22 February. Available at: https://www.publico.pt/2002/02/22/jornal/torres-de-ofir-vao-abaixo-no-final-do-ano-167677

GEOTA. (2015). A Ria Formosa e mal segura [Ria Formosa and not secure]. 3 September. Available at: http://www.geota.pt/scid/geotaWebPage/printArticleViewOne.asp?categoryID=720&articleID=2567

GTL – Grupo de Trabalho do Litoral. (2014). *Gestão da Zona Costeira, O Desafio da Mudança* [Coastal Zone Management, the Challenge of Change]. Report. December. Available at: http://www.apambiente.pt/_zdata/DESTAQUES/2015/GTL_Relatorio%20Final_20150416.pdf

Julião, P. (2006). Duzentas construções ilegais serão demolidas em Esposende [Two hundred illegal buildings will be demolished in Esposende]. *Diário de Notícias*, 22 June. Available at: https://www.dn.pt/arquivo/2006/interior/duzentas-construcoes-ilegais-serao-demolidas-em-esposende-643695.html

Pires, I. (1996). Demolitions undertaken by ICN (and SNPRCN), 1986–1995. (Unpublished).

Portuguese government. (1998). *National Strategy for the Portuguese Coast*. Available at: https://dre.pt/application/file/484966

— (2006). *National Ocean Strategy* for 2006-2016 (DQUEM). Available at: https://dre.pt/application/file/a/545528

— (2007). *Algarve Regional Spatial Plan* (PROT Algarve). Available at: https://dre.pt/application/file/a/636351

— (2009). *National Strategy for Integrated Coastal Zone Management* (ENGIZC). Available at: https://dre.pt/application/conteudo/489264

— (2012). *Spatial Plan for the Maritime Zone* (POEM). Available at: https://www.dgpm.mm.gov.pt/ordenamento-e-maritimo

— (2018). *National Strategy for Environmental and Biodiversity Conservation 2030*. Available at: https://dre.pt/application/file/a/115227157

Quercus. (2015). Demolições no Parque Natural da Ria Formosa: processo não pode parar! [Demolitions in Ria Formosa should not stop!]. 11 March. Available at: http://www.quercus.pt/comunicados/2015/marco/4208-demolicoes-no-parque-natural-da-ria-formosa-processo-nao-pode-parar

Revez, I. (2015). Em nome do camaleão, estão suspensas as demolições na Ria Formosa [For the sake of the chameleon, the demolitions in Ria Formosa are suspended]. *Público*. 27 April. Available at https://www.publico.pt/2015/04/27/local/noticia/em-nome-do-camaleao-que-tem-casa-ilegal-na-ria-formosa-estao-suspensas-as-demolicoes-1693808

Schmidt, L., Prista, P., Saraiva, T., O'Riordan, T., & Gomes, C. (2013). Adapting governance for coastal change in Portugal. *Land Use Policy* 31, 314–325.

Soares, L. (2008). Gestão do litoral e cidadania ambiental [Coastal management and environmental citizenship]. GEOTA, IPJ, APL. Lisboa.

Sociedade POLIS Litoral Ria Formosa. (2009). *Viver A Ria Formosa* [Living Ria Formosa, Newsletter], 1 August. Available at: http://www.polislitoralriaformosa.pt/publicacoes.php#_1

— (2010). *Viver A Ria Formosa* [Living Ria Formosa, Newsletter], 2 March. Available at http://www.polislitoralriaformosa.pt/publicacoes.php#_1

Teixeira, S. B. (2009). Demarcação leito da margem das águas do mar no litoral sul do algarve [Demarcation of the shoreline on the south coast of the Algarve]. Administração Da Região Hidrográfica Do Algarve, Faro.

— (2014). Gestão da erosão costeira no troço Quarteira-Garrão [Coastal erosion management in Quarteira-Garrão]. In Grupo de Trabalho do Litoral (GTL), *Gestão da Zona Costeira, O Desafio da Mudança* (Report), December. Algarve, Portugal.

Teixeira, A. T., Matos, J., Pimentel, C., & Pinheiro, J. (2000). A map of land at risk on the Portuguese coast. *Periodicum Biologorum* 102 (Suppl. 1), 605–612.

World Factbook. (n.d.). Portugal. Available at: https://www.cia.gov/library/publications/the-world-factbook/geos/po.html [Accessed July 2019]

Legislation (listed chronologically, by earliest date prior to amendments)

Decree 12445, 1926 – Established permitting fees for uses in the public domain and penalties for misuses

Decree-Law 468/71, 1971 (Amended 1974, 1987 and 2005) – Legal framework for land included in the water public domain, which includes the MPD, rivers and streams, lakes and lagoons

Decree-Law 309/93, 1993 (amended in 2012 – Decree-Law 159/2012) – Regulates the drafting and approval of Coastal Zone Plans (POOC) and sets specific provisions regarding use and development in the MPD

Land and Planning Act (LBPSOTU) (Law 48/1998; later Law 31/2014)

Territorial Management Instruments Legal Framework (Decree Law 380/99; later Decree Law 80/2015)

Legal Framework on Urban Development and Building (Decree-Law law 555/1999; with 20 amendments as at 2019)

Public Water Domain Definition Law, 2005 (Law 54/2005, amended by Law 34/2014)

Water Act, 2005 (Law 58/2005, amended by Law 78/2013)

Regulation for the Use of Water Domain, 2007 (Decree-Law 226-A/2007)

Strategic Environmental Assessment, 2007 (Decree-Law 232/2007)

Normative Dispatch 32/2008, 2008 – Rules for delineation of the MPD

Legal Framework of the National Agricultural Reserve (Decree-Law 73/2009; amended 2015)

Country reports

Group II: Countries subject to the Mediterranean ICZM Protocol

8 Spain

Marta Lora-Tamayo Vallvé, Pablo Molina Alegre, and Cygal Pellach

Overview

Spain has an extensive and varied coastline, bordering both the Atlantic Ocean and the Mediterranean Sea. The Spanish coastal area has played an increasing role as a strategic economic asset given its attractiveness to tourists, foreign investors, maritime trade (ports), and the energy industry. So long as it remained unchecked, development of coastal land was extensive and harmful to the coastal environment.

Since the Spanish economic boom of the late 1960s, the country's coastal zone laws and regulations have been highly ambitious and, at the same time, highly controversial. In 1988, the Spanish government adopted a set of environmentally sensitive rules about public land ownership and setback of development – so ambitious that thousands of homes and hotel rooms located on previously privately owned and unencumbered land found themselves on public land or in the setback zone. This chapter recounts the national and international legal and political battles surrounding this and related issues of coastal law and policy. We will see the recent outcomes in a revised, somewhat less ambitious legislation. The story of this chapter is thus of a balancing act which the Spanish authorities and the courts play between strict regulation of future development and the need to manage existing (legal or illegal) development in the coastal zone.

The context: Introduction to the coastal issues in Spain

"*Spain – Everything Under the Sun*" was the slogan of one of Spain's most famed coastal tourism adverts from the 1990s. But... what does *everything* include?

The Spanish coastline is around 4,964 km long (World Factbook, n.d.), with approximately one-quarter of that length classified as sandy beaches. More than half of the country's coastline borders the Atlantic Ocean, where tides can extend well inland, creating wetlands and riverbed deltas. The remaining coast is on the Mediterranean Sea, and that is where much of the development pressure occurs.

Spain's nearly 500 coastal municipalities account for 7% of the country's territory but are home to 45% of its 48.6 million inhabitants (World Factbook, n.d.). It is therefore not surprising that population density in the coastal zone is much higher than it is inland (about four times higher – Ministry of Environment, 2007).[1] Furthermore, as five of the six most popular tourist destinations in Spain are coastal regions (EpData, 2020), the population pressure on the coast increases greatly in peak tourist periods.

The Spanish coastline has developed into an important strategic economic asset. Coastal tourism generates nearly 10% of GDP and 12% of employment in the country (Exceltur, 2015).

In addition, maritime trade plays a growing role; Spain has 46 State-owned ports whose combined activity accounts for about one fifth of the transport sector's GDP (Puertos del Estado, n.d.). The coast and offshore oil deposits are increasingly important resources for the energy industry. These economic functions have replaced traditional coastal activities such as fishing and agriculture, particularly in areas where conditions are most favourable to tourism – the Mediterranean, South Atlantic, and Canary Islands coasts.

The fraught legal framework for coastal zone management in Spain

The first comprehensive Spanish coastal law was introduced in 1969, during the economic boom period known as the "Spanish miracle". The 1969 law promoted development of the coast for tourism purposes, resulting in widespread development (Negro et al., 2014). For decades, the social and environmental values of the Spanish coastline were also threatened by gradual privatization of the coast and the destruction of natural areas.

The paradigm shifted in 1978, with the development of the new Spanish Constitution in the country's transition to democracy. The Constitution defines the State-owned public domain, specifically identifying "... the maritime zone, beaches, territorial waters and natural resources of the economic zone and the continental shelf" (Article 132.2). It also stipulates that public authorities should "... defend and restore the environment" (Article 45.2). Thus, the adoption of the new Constitution required the Spanish authorities to rethink their approach to the environment in general and to the coastal zone in particular. As a result, in 1988, the government adopted a new Coastal Law. This law established the framework for Spain's coastal management as it is practised to this day.

The 1988 Coastal Law expands the principles for environmental protection set out in Article 45 of the Constitution. The enactment of the law was influenced by a series of environmental criteria which emerged from the pathbreaking European documents in the 1970s and 1980s (Council of Europe Committee of Ministers Resolution 29/1973 on the Protection of Coastal Areas; European Coastal Charter, 1981). The Coastal Law focuses on the identification, protection, use, and monitoring of the part of the coastal zone which the law labelled the Marine Terrestrial Public Domain (MTPD). The definition of the MTPD and its importance are discussed in detail below. In summary, that zone's function is to protect the social and environmental qualities of the shore by bringing the land under public ownership and declaring it as public domain. Thus, the 1988 law's focus was on **protection** and **nationalization** of coastal land.

Overall, the 1988 Coastal Law was very progressive: On its adoption, for the first time in the history of Spanish legislation, the law clearly prioritized protection of the coastal environment over tourism and economic development. The law's ambitious goal was to halt the trend of massive development along the coast which had been taking place over several decades. Thus, the Law defined the MTPD very broadly, totally denying private ownership and restricting land uses within it but allowed existing private uses to continue, as long-term "concessions" (ground leases), for a period of 30 years. In addition, the law introduced a 100 m "Protection Zone" (or setback zone), in which construction is prohibited even if the land is privately owned.

But the 1988 Coastal Law was overly restrictive and inflexible, detached from the reality on the ground. Its approach to both the definition of the MTPD and to private property rights generated significant controversy. In response to the law's adoption, a number of autonomous communities (the jurisdictional subdivisions of Spain) appealed to the Constitutional Court, arguing that the law usurped their powers. Several other parties argued that the law would slow economic growth, particularly in tourism and construction; others argued that the Coastal Law did not respect previously existing property rights. In a landmark ruling, the Constitutional Court (STC 149/1991) held that the replacement of property rights with long-term ground leases did not infringe the constitutional definition of the right to property. Accordingly, the law prevailed.

Several aspects of the 1988 Coastal Law were indeed implemented during 1988–2013. The boundaries of the MTPD were delineated and the identified land was brought into public ownership. Many degraded sections of the coastline were gradually recovered and restored. And land use within both the MTPD and the setback zone was regulated in accordance with the Law's framework (outlined below). Yet for many years, enforcement against illegal development on the coast – particularly within the setback zone – was lax and many illegal structures were built (Alterman et al., 2016). Only from the mid-2000s, possibly as an initiative of the socialist government, which sought to distance itself from the previous populist regime, did the Spanish government focus on coastal policy and enforcement. The heightened enforcement actions engendered intense protests among various interest groups, which led to scrutiny by the European Parliament and, eventually, a reconsideration of the application of the law (refer to the section on public participation below).

Spain ratified the ICZM (Integrated Coastal Zone Management) Protocol in 2010 and it came into force in the country in 2011. But as the 1988 Coastal Law was, in some respects, even more ambitious than the Protocol, the ratification may have had only minor effects on the law and its implementation.

By 2012, the Spanish government had become aware that the Coastal Law may have needed some adjustments. The decision to revise the Coastal Law was driven by two key factors: The first was that the 1988 law provided concessions within the MTPD only until 2018, and that deadline was approaching. The second was that the economic collapse of many businesses, which had been required to cease operation in the MTPD, may have exacerbated the Spanish financial crisis which began in 2008. An extensive amendment to the law – *Protection and Sustainable Use of the Coastline and Amendment of the Coastal Law* – was approved in May 2013 (henceforth the 2013 Coastal Law, or 2013 Amendment). The new law's objectives include providing greater legal certainty for property holders and long-term applicability. At the same time, the Law as a whole maintains the key objectives of the original law, to safeguard the integrity of the MTPD, while preventing urban development that is at odds with the coastal goals.

The new law significantly changed the orientation of Spain's coastal regulation, to a focus on **certainty, efficiency,** and **compatibility of uses**. It redefined the MTPD and the procedure for its demarcation, changed the rules governing concessions in that zone, and relaxed some of the rules relating to development within the coastal setback zone beyond the public domain (the Protection Zone). These changes were hotly debated and opposed by some NGOs, particularly environmental ones. Yet the Spanish authorities argued that the changes were necessary to ensure the law's implementation.

Spain's administrative structure and division of powers

To understand Spain's coastal law and practice, we must comprehend the country's government structure. Spain is a highly decentralized state, comprised of seventeen autonomous communities and two autonomous cities. These autonomies have varying levels of devolved power from the State. Some communities, such as Catalonia, have devolved powers relating to coastal law, policy, and enforcement, as well as to planning law, policy, and enforcement, as discussed below. Many of the autonomous communities are divided into provinces, and all are divided into municipalities.

In addition to the protection offered by the State Constitution and the national Coastal Law, several other legislative powers are important for the management of coastal land. The most significant are the planning laws under the authority of the autonomous communities. Provinces also have some administrative functions, but these pertain only indirectly to coastal zone management. Municipalities along the coasts are important players because they are delegated planning powers from the autonomous communities.

The division of powers in coastal zone management has been a source of perennial conflict, particularly between the State and various autonomous communities. In a key decision on this matter in the context of planning law, Spain's Constitutional Court (STC 61/1997) ruled that although spatial and strategic planning powers belong to the autonomous communities, specific State powers do limit those regional powers. Such limits arise where there is a need to ensure an equal exercise of constitutional rights for all Spanish citizens, including the right of property, economic activities, and protection of the environment (Section 149, Spanish Constitution). Furthermore, State powers supersede those of autonomous communities in anything related to procedures set by State laws.

Through several rulings, such as the 1991 Constitutional Court case mentioned above (STC 149/1991), the court has recognized that the coastal area is complex and that its protection depends on the coordination of all relevant levels of government. The specific conflicts which arise in relation to planning and land management in the coastal zone do not have a clear resolution, but devolving powers to the autonomous communities has been the solution in some cases. In other cases, the Spanish State has retained control in its application of the Coastal Law and related regulations.

Definition and demarcation of the Spanish coastal zone – the MTPD

The 1988 Spanish Coastal Law provides a clear definition of the Maritime Terrestrial Public Domain (MTPD) according to natural conditions which are characteristic of coastal land (in geomorphological terms). This definition is very strict, encompassing the *"highest reach of the waves during the strongest known storms"*, all sand dunes, and artificially flooded areas.

The boundary of the MTPD essentially indicates the shoreline – the line between land and sea. However, the original law did not include technical criteria for identifying this line. The result was that the most stringent view was taken: That in theory, even a single uncharacteristic storm episode could shift the definition of the shoreline further inland. Thousands of homes that had been built on what was private land (whether with a legal permit or without) were reclassified overnight as located within the public domain. The land they were living on became public, and the structures were rendered, one might say, "on probation", with onerous restrictions for the future.

Furthermore, the 1988 law did not set a deadline by which the demarcation procedure should be completed. The Spanish authorities did not prioritize the process and there may have been some technological constraints in determining the "highest reach". Thus, the demarcation was (mostly) complete only approximately twenty years after the law was adopted. By early 2006, during the peak of the investment and development boom along the Spanish coasts, only about 60% of the shoreline had been demarcated. After 2006, the process gained speed, possibly due to Greenpeace's annual reports on the environmental destruction of the Spain's coasts (e.g. Greenpeace, 2006). By 2013, an impressive 97% of the Spanish shoreline had been demarcated. The balance pertains to some settlements built prior to 1988. It should be emphasized, however, that the completed demarcation did not resolve the legal ambiguities surrounding the fact that a single storm could, in theory, dramatically extinguish or alter ownership patterns.

Critically, the 2013 Coastal Law Amendment clarifies and narrows the definition of the MTPD. It includes technical criteria for defining the shoreline *"reached by the waves during the strongest known storms"*. The important improvement over the 1988 Law is that there is now a time-based definition of "the strongest known storm". It is now the highest tide reached *"at least five times over a period of five years"*. This rule provides some more certainty for landowners, investors, and governments. In addition, sand dunes, which in the 1988 law were included in their entirety within the MTPD, are now included only to the extent that is necessary to ensure "stability of the beach". Another relaxation pertains to promenades. Under the former law, the MTPD would disregard built-up promenades (and could include them). Now, if there is a promenade, the MTPD would terminate there. Artificially flooded areas are now also excluded from the MTPD, unless they were already publicly owned before being flooded. Finally – and importantly for some landowners – residential areas built prior to 1988 for which construction caused the loss of the coast's natural characteristics are excluded.

In addition to the definitional changes, the 2013 law requires the government to register the MTPD with the Spanish Land Registry and display the demarcation on the government's website. The government has carried this out, but to date only with the line determined according to the 1988 criteria. By 2020, the task of redrawing the MTPD line has been carried out only in selected parts of the coast, in areas that the legislation prioritizes as high-conflict areas. Thus, at this time, the picture is mixed: On the one hand, the official accurate demarcation of the MTPD as it stands before updating is available to all citizens. On the other hand, due to the revised criteria, there are new uncertainties about where the line will be drawn. In addition to the revised legal criteria, there are also technological improvements that might revise some of the detailed demarcation. At the same time, the 2013 law permits any stakeholder to ask the authorities to consider revision of the line.

Ownership and management of the MTPD

In the Spanish system, the public domain is owned by national government and must be intended for a public use. According to the Constitution, the public domain is inalienable (cannot be sold) and "non-prescriptible" (private acquisition through long-term possession of the land is not possible, however long the possession; the State can always repossess public domain land, even without a Court order). In addition, in the public domain, illegal development may be removed at any time – there is no time limit for removal, whereas in other areas, the administration may not remove illegal development after a set number of years from its construction (varies by region). Furthermore, as noted earlier, the Constitution specifically recognizes the maritime zone, beaches, territorial waters, and the natural resources of the economic zone and the continental shelf as public domain. These are the only elements of the public domain which the Constitution *specifically* identifies, indicating the importance that the legal system places on coastal public land.

The management of the MTPD has been the subject of political conflict between the national government and autonomous communities (Carlón, 2013). The autonomous communities claim that although, according to the Constitution, the MTPD is owned by the State, this does not imply that the State has jurisdiction over planning and development within that zone (which are powers of the autonomous communities). The Spanish Constitutional Court (STC) has ruled on this matter on two occasions (STC 149/1991 and STC 31/2010). On the first (STC 149/1991), the Court sought to find a balance between national and autonomous community interests. The Court linked the State's ownership of the MTPD to its constitutional responsibility (under Article 149) to protect the environment and, by extension, the public character of the MTPD. Thus, the Court recognized the State's right, as the public land owner, to decide which land is included within the definition of the MTPD and to apply protective measures in line with the purpose of that zone. In addition, the Court noted the need for uniform legislation to guarantee the same level of access for all Spanish citizens to their constitutional right to a protected environment. Nevertheless, the Court found that the mere fact of ownership by the State does not give the State absolute power to regulate or manage land in the coastal zone, as powers among the different levels of administration need to be coordinated.

In accordance with that ruling, some autonomous communities (Catalonia, Andalusia, and the Balearic Islands) have been granted additional powers over the management of the MTPD by transfer of powers from the State. In these regions, the regional government is empowered to manage the MTPD (e.g. to grant authorizations for seasonal services and facilities), while the State retains the power to demarcate and protect the MTPD. The Catalonian government has the broadest powers in this regard, following the development of its Statute of Autonomy (Estatuto de Autonomía, 2006) and further agreements with the State in 2008 (discussed below). It now holds all powers regarding temporary uses and concessions in the MTPD. The Constitutional Court (STC 31/2010) found this interpretation of the autonomous communities' powers to be reasonable but reiterated that the autonomous communities cannot enact laws which supersede State powers.

Rules for use and limited construction on the MTPD

To ensure that the MTPD is protected and remains open for the public, in general, only light and removable structures are permitted within this zone. These structures are predominantly used for seasonal beach uses (for the summer season, May–October). In order to erect such structures, business owners must obtain a licence from the Ministry of Ecological Transition or from the municipalities where the power to grant such licences has been delegated to local authorities by the Ministry.[2] The 1988 Coastal Law allowed for licences for one-year periods, but the 2013 Coastal Law increased the licensing period to four years. According to the preamble to the new law, this change is intended to give businesses more certainty over time. It also appears that it was intended to reduce the pressure on the bureaucratic system, as it will result in fewer applications over time. Yet some critics are concerned that extending the timeframe for licences will be harmful to the beach environment, as private operators will not dismantle their facilities. This issue has been addressed in the Valencia region by issuing licences that include the dismantling of seasonal facilities at the end of each summer (FEPORTS, 2016).

The licensing of seasonal beach uses is accompanied by strict regulations guiding their establishment. These include maximum occupancy rates, minimum distances between the establishments, and maximum floor areas, depending on the type of business. For example, the 1988 Coastal Law permitted facilities with a maximum floor area of 20 m^2 and specified that they must be located at a minimum distance of 100 m from any other seasonal use facility located within the MTPD. But these provisions were not strictly enforced until the mid-2000s, which in turn generated conflicts between the authorities and many owners of existing seasonal establishments with larger floor spaces than those allowed. The conflicts were then exacerbated by the 2008 economic crisis.

The 2013 Coastal Law introduced a classification of beaches – distinguishing between urban and rural localities. The law then applies differing regulations for seasonal beach uses, based on the classification of the beach. In general, structures for seasonal uses in urban areas may have greater floorspace and be located closer to each other than similar structures in rural areas. In some rural areas, seasonal beach uses are not permitted at all.

Existing construction in the MTPD – System of "concessions"

The 1988 Coastal Law instituted a system of "concessions", granting rights of use for pre-existing development which became incorporated within the MTPD as a result of the law. In essence, landowners whose existing properties became incorporated into the MTPD were granted right of occupancy and use for 30 years, with an option to renew that lease for another 30 years. There is no doubt that this provision prioritized the landowners over protection of the environment, as it did not require the total demolition of buildings on land which was deemed to be sensitive coastal land. Yet the relevant landowners now had limited right of use, uncertainty, and no compensation rights associated with the restrictions. Much to their angst, they could not renovate their properties or transfer (sell, grant or allocate) the concessions, except through inheritance.

In response to the landowners' concerns, the 2013 Coastal Law introduced major changes to the rights of use. The maximum duration of the rights was extended from 60 years (30 plus 30) to 75 years, calculated from the date of the application. Such extensions are not granted automatically; the law states that *the concession holder may request the extension of the concession since the entry into force of this Law*" (i.e. from June 2013) and "*... before the expiry of the period for which it was granted*" (which in most cases was July 2018).

The law includes several qualifications which provide the State with the flexibility to evaluate applications on the basis of the specific environmental conditions of the property in question. For example, some concessions may be granted for shorter periods than provided for in the law. In addition, the law specifically refers to the need to evaluate the grant of concessions on land where the shoreline is receding or where the land is used for industrial purposes. The new law also explicitly introduces the possibility of termination of the concession if the works and installations on a relevant property run a real risk of being reached by the sea.

But there are also added benefits for concession holders under the 2013 law. They may now undertake coastal defence works, on the condition that they do not negatively affect the coastal environment, even if they occupy the beach. The law also extends the works that individuals can carry out on their properties, so long as they do not increase the volume, height, or land surface coverage of the building. Finally, in addition to inheritance, the new law allows for the transfer (selling, granting, etc.) of concessions. Despite all of these changes, the new law still does not really solve the complex property rights issues experienced by concession holders (previously landowners) for properties in the MTPD.

Spain's coastal setback – the "Protection Zone"

The 1988 Coastal Law restricted development within a "Protection Zone" of 100 m from the edge of the MTPD. The Protection Zone derives its name from the idea that its purpose is to protect the values of the public domain (TSJ Galicia, 25 September 2005). Although the general setback width is 100 m, even this early version of the Coastal Law recognized that the setback zone should reflect the reality on the ground, so in urban areas the setback width was set at only 20 m. This reduced setback width was also applied in areas with urban plans approved prior to 1988.

The 2013 law added two additional categories of land where the 100 m setback may be reduced to 20 m:

- Population centres which, despite not being classified as urban in 1988, had urban characteristics at the time (i.e. road access, water supply, waste-water disposal, and electricity supply)
- Around rivers, where the setback distance also takes account of geomorphologic characteristics, vegetation and distance from the river mouth

These changes were ostensibly initiated for practical reasons: To ensure that the law can be implemented more easily, without generating land use conflicts. Yet they make it possible to rezone additional land in proximity to the coast for development purposes. As such, environment conservation organizations were against the change and are justifiably concerned about its outcomes.

Beyond the required setback zone, the Coastal Law notes that State (Autonomous Region) and municipalities may identify areas requiring additional protection due to their environmental characteristics. In those areas, the setback zone may be increased in width by 100 m (total 200 m from the shoreline).

Restrictions on development within the Protection Zone

No permanent residential development is permitted within the 100 m setback zone (limited other types of development are permitted, with conditions). The 1988 Coastal Law prohibited even alterations to previously existing buildings within this zone, but allowed limited repair and "improvement" (refurbishment, renovation, or restoration) works. These restrictions were highly problematic for owners of properties which were built legally prior to 1988 and who after 1988 found themselves in the setback zone. Suddenly these landowners lost the ability to renovate their houses according to their needs.

The 2013 law did relax the rules regarding renovation of buildings which existed within the zone prior to 1988. Landowners may now undertake improvement work, on condition that these do not involve an increase in the height, volume, or surface area of the buildings. The 2013 law also changed the procedure for managing any construction works within the setback zone. Instead of applying for administrative authorization for work, building owners are now required to submit a "statement of responsibility", which applies to all future work as well. That document is to include statements to the effect that any work undertaken will not result in an increase in the volume, height, or surface area of the existing buildings, and that they will comply with standards relating to energy efficiency and water saving, when applicable. This change simplifies the process for landowners in the setback zone and reduces the administrative burden on responsible authorities.

Despite these changes, owners of property within the setback zone still feel that they are unfairly disadvantaged by the law. There is a sense that restrictions on construction on private property within the setback zone amount to an unreasonable regulatory taking and that they should receive compensation. Yet the court has found otherwise.

In describing the nature of the prohibitions in the setback zone, the Galician High Court of Justice (TSJ Galicia, 25 September 2005) noted that the prohibition against construction applies to housing, new roads, intercity transports services, and power lines (with the option to approve these uses on a case-by-case basis). On the other hand, agriculture, open sports facilities, and those facilities which, by their nature, require proximity to the coast, are permitted as-of-right. Other uses may also be allowed with permission. The court implied that the limits placed on property within the setback zone were reasonable.

The Constitutional Court ruled (in STC 149/1991) that the prohibition of development in the setback zone does not deprive landowners of their fundamental property rights: The uses permitted as-of-right are the same as those permitted for any other privately owned land (Carlón, 2013, p. 350). Furthermore, on the matter of compensation on the basis of prohibition, the National Court ruled (on 29 May 2009, in AN) that *"this is a limitation to the property established for lands adjacent to the MTPD and the law does not call for any compensation"*. That ruling was confirmed by the Supreme Court (STS 6613/2012), citing an earlier ruling (Rec. 643/2001; 17 February 2004).

The "Zone of Influence"

The Spanish Coastal Law (1988, Article 30) recognizes one additional category of coastal land: Land within 500 m of the edge of the MTPD, known as the "Zone of Influence". (This zone overlaps with the 100 m setback zone and adds 400 m beyond.) The law outlines three criteria for land within this zone: (a) In areas with road traffic to the beach, land reserves "shall be made" for car parking; (b) development should be in accordance with urban planning legislation, and, specifically, development that is inappropriate for the coastal area in terms of form or density *"should be avoided"*; and (c) for development which involves discharges to the MTPD, the appropriate authorization for those discharges will be required.

These criteria should be read in conjunction with an additional article in the same law (Article 117), according to which municipalities and autonomous communities must gain approval from the State for spatial planning and development decisions in the coastal zone (interpreted as all land within the Zone of Influence). Thus, the criteria provide a guide for preparation of plans for coastal areas, as well as for assessment of those plans by the State. In relation to the third criterion, discharge authorizations are subject to separate environmental legislation, but this is an added layer of protection to ensure that the correct authorizations are in place before coastal development takes place.

Collectively, these provisions of the law signal the importance of considering the effects on the coast of land use and development of land beyond the 100 m Protection Zone. They rely on the State's limited powers in planning and urban development matters (STC 61/1997).

Right of public access

The constitutional protection and status of the MTPD as public land implies that this zone should be freely accessible by the public. The Coastal Law (1988) includes specific provisions to ensure that this right of access is protected – primarily, as discussed above, by restricting use and development. Of course, in practice, parts of the MTPD are not accessible. Past projects and current "concessions" create barriers to accessibility.

The Coastal Law contains several additional provisions relating to accessibility of, and to, the MTPD. First, recognizing that physical structures and uses may not be the only barriers to access, the Law stipulates that any person seeking to use the MTPD for recreational purposes may do so free of charge. Of course, there is nothing to stop the authorities managing the beaches (usually municipalities) from charging parking fees, which are common.

Another accessibility requirement of the Coastal Law is that in urban areas, public vertical access roads to the MTPD are provided at a minimum interval of 500 m. Pedestrian access paths must also be provided, on private or public land, at a minimum interval of 200 m. These roads and paths may be expropriated following their demarcation in land use plans. Yet the practice of identifying and expropriating requires significant political will, as well as funds. Thus, it is perhaps not surprising that there were **no** expropriations of land for this purpose to the year 2008. Since 2008, following a change to the Land Law[3] which saw a general reduction in the level of compensation rates for non-urban land, the incidence of expropriation for the purposes of providing access to the shoreline has increased.

Finally, an easement at least 6 m wide must be provided along the outer (landward) edge of the MTPD (Coastal Law, 1988). Anyone can pass through that easement, regardless of ownership. Where the relevant authority has found fitting and practicable, a road has been constructed in the path of the easement. If required for traffic purposes, the road may be widened to up to 20 m, but to our knowledge, this is not common practice.

Related to accessibility to the coast is access to views of the coast. The Coastal Law (1988, Article 30) stipulates that the widest facades of buildings can form "architectural screens" which block views to the sea, if developed parallel to the shoreline. Therefore, this form of development should be avoided within the Zone of Influence (500 m from the MTPD). This provision has been generally interpreted by responsible authorities to mean that within this zone, the widest part of the building should be perpendicular to the shoreline. To the best of our knowledge, that interpretation has not been tested by the courts.

Compliance and enforcement

Prior to 2008, illegal development of buildings and structures was common in the MTPD and setback zone. Since the (almost complete) demarcation of the shoreline, illegal development within the MTPD has been almost eliminated, assisted by the provision of "concessions", as outlined above. The demarcation process has also helped to raise awareness of the importance of the coast. Illegal development within the setback zone has also been in decline since 2008.

Where illegal development does occur, local authorities may apply fines and issue demolition orders. The issue of demolition was discussed in Supreme Court ruling (2972/2018), in relation to illegal works which enlarged an existing structure in the MTPD, in the region of Galicia. The main issue discussed by the Court was whether demolition orders are time limited (may only be issued within a specified time after the completion of construction); and if so, if that time limit should be the same as the time limit for imposing fines for illegal works. In its ruling, the Court concluded that a time limit on demolition orders would not be logical, as the priority in such cases is to save the coast. Fines, on the other hand, cannot save the coast; they serve only as retrospective punishment for those who carry out illegal works.

The problem of illegal local decision-making

Significantly, some illegal developments – particularly in the setback zone – were approved by local municipalities, in defiance of the Coastal Law. A notorious example is the Algarrobico hotel, which stands 47 m from the shoreline (Figure 8.1). The hotel was initially approved by Carboneras City Council (Almeria province, Andalusia region) in 1988 and was eventually constructed in 2003. The Andalusian government then stepped in, petitioning the Superior Court of Andalusia and the Supreme Court (STS 1739/2012) to require that the hotel be demolished. The Court ordered the demolition in exchange for compensation to the developer, but the demolition has not taken place due to disputes about the sum of compensation. In parallel

Figure 8.1 Algarrobico hotel, Carboneras, Andalusia, Spain

Source: Untipografico. CC BY 2.0 license. Available at: https://commons.wikimedia.org/wiki/File:Hotel_Algarrobico_Gata_Nijar.jpg

to the court proceedings, environmental NGOs (including Greenpeace) protested and successfully stalled the hotel's operation. Thus, while the hotel has not been demolished, it stands empty and unused (Environmental Justice Atlas, 2017).

In response to this and similar cases, the 2013 Amendment to the Coastal Law introduced a provision (at Article 119) which allows the State to suspend local authorities for infringement of the Coastal Law, without recourse to the courts:

> … *the Government Delegate, at the request of the Minister of Agriculture, Food and Environment, may suspend the actions and agreements adopted by local authorities if they affect the integrity of the maritime terrestrial public domain or of the protection (setback) zone, or if they infringe on the provisions of Article 25 of this law [prohibited activities in the Protection Zone]*

Although "actions and provisions" might be defined in several ways, it is clear that planning permission is intended to be included in the definition, given that Spain's Vice President at the time referred to the amendment to Article 119 as "the anti Algarrobicos clause" (Carlón, 2013, p. 416).

Despite the good intentions of the State to protect the public domain, some might question whether the new clause is acceptable in the context of the State's limited powers in urban planning (STC 61/1997). The State does have some scope to challenge local government decision-making, but only if it considers that a municipality's decision undermines the Spanish national interest (Law on Local Government, Article 67).[4] The Constitutional Court has ruled that such State intervention would be of an *"extraordinary and exceptional nature"* and would require justification based on some sense of urgency (STC 214/1989). When later considering the 1988 Coastal Law, the same court annulled an article (118) which gave the State the power to intervene in local authority decision-making, finding that that provision, which was not limited by any conditions, could undermine municipal autonomy (STC 149/1991). These rulings of the Constitutional Court are consistent with the European Charter of Local Self-Government (Article 8.3), which requires that the responsible authority **maintain proportionality between intervention and the interest that it is intended to protect.**

Furthermore, there are existing mechanisms in the Coastal Law (1988) for the State to intervene in local decision-making: Article 117 requires that municipal land use plans for the coastal zone (interpreted as the 500 m Zone of Influence) be approved by the State. Yet, as noted by the Supreme Court, the problem of the Algarrobico hotel arose (at least in part) from the fact that the State did not exercise its powers under Article 117 and could not cancel the plan after it was approved (STS 1739/2012). The 1988 Law does authorize (at Article 119.1) any State or autonomous authority to contest any agreements or decisions which violate the Law's provisions, or to petition the relevant Contentious-Administrative court for their suspension (which was the route followed in the case of the Algarribico hotel – but too late to halt construction).

We also note that urban planning legislation (at the autonomous community level) generally provides mechanisms for autonomous governments to suspend a plan made by municipalities. These powers would allow the autonomous communities to intervene in the case of municipal actions or agreements which put the MTPD or Protection Zone at risk.

Considering all of the above, some scholars (including some of the authors of this chapter) believe that the new clause (119.2) not only does not conform to the appropriate course for State control of local authority decision-making but trespasses on the authority of the autonomous communities in coastal areas. Others see the Clause as a reasonable and potentially positive tool which provides a path for State control of the MTPD to achieve the goals of the Coastal Law.

Fragmentation of responsibilities in coastal zone management

As noted earlier, the Spanish State holds the power to pass basic legislation on environmental protection, while the autonomous communities and municipalities are empowered to establish ancillary law and regulation. Spain's Coastal Law is part of the national suite of environmental legislation and defines the roles and responsibilities of the State, autonomous communities, and municipalities in coastal zone management and planning. We have already discussed the key responsibilities and some of the conflicts which have arisen between the various levels of government. In Table 8.1, we provide a summary of the key responsibilities of each level of government.

Public participation and access to justice

Spain ratified the Aarhus Convention in December 2004, and this ratification came into force on 31 March 2005. Spanish law does not incorporate any requirements specifically related to public participation and information on coastal matters, but the law (Law 27/2006) guarantees a set of rights to citizens about access to environmental information, including the right to receive information, the right to hear the reasons for refusal of access to information, and the right to be informed at an early stage of the decision-making process on environmental matters.

Table 8.1 Responsibilities in coastal zone management

	State	Autonomous communities	Municipalities
Demarcation of MTPD	X		
Access along and to the coast	Within MTPD, road along MTPD and Protection Zone	Within Zone of Influence	Within Zone of Influence
Coastal protection and restoration	X		
Water resource management	X		
Infrastructure, ports, exclusive economic zone	X		
Approval of plans for Zone of Influence (500 m)	X	X	
Strategic planning		X	X
Spatial planning		X	X
Beach services (e.g. cleanliness and lifeguard services)			X

Activism through NGOs

Since the early 2000s, there has been an awakening amongst Spaniards and they have begun to participate more widely in public affairs than they did previously. This rising participation has been noteworthy specifically in matters relating to coastal zone management. One example is the environmental activism against the Algarobicco Hotel, as described above. But it is the impact of the Coastal Law on private property owners which has sparked the emergence of one of the most significant nationwide civil movements in recent Spanish history:

We have detailed above the difficulties faced by property owners whose properties became partially or wholly illegal on the adoption of the 1988 Coastal Law. Those owners founded and manage the AEPLC (Asociación Española de Perjudicados por la Ley de Costas): A nonprofit, politically neutral movement advocating for the rights of those affected by the Coastal Law and related legislation. The AEPLC actively seeks to partner with similar organizations, both within Spain and internationally. It coordinates its actions and advocacy with various Spanish and European administrations.

By petitioning the European Parliament, the AEPLC influenced a 2009 resolution of that body (informed by a report by Danish member Margrete Auken) on *"the impact of extensive urbanisation in Spain on individual rights of European citizens, on the environment and on the application of EU law"* (Auken, 2009). In the explanatory report accompanying that decision, the Parliament was scathing:

> *The Committee understands and supports the Spanish authorities in their attempts to preserve and where possible restore the coastal environment. What it fails to understand is why the 1988 Coastal Law has been resurrected at this stage, in this time, when it has been in practical abeyance for thirty years when so much devastation took place. Why is its application such a shambles [sic] and so arbitrary when traditional coastal housing is*

being demolished and newly developed modern apartments being tolerated? Why were people allowed to buy such property during the last thirty years, respecting all the legal requirements with which they were faced, only to be confronted today with a law with retro-active [sic] effect which denies them the rights associated with legitimate ownership? That speculators and property developers who had the legal resources to know better should be penalised is reasonable; what is not is that people who have bought their property in good faith respecting all the demands made upon them should lose their rights, and that of their families and descendants to their homes (Auken, 2009, pp. 17–18).

The resolution called on the Spanish government to find a solution to the property rights issues ("abuse of rights") provoked by the Coastal Law. It was thus a key driver behind the 2013 Amendment to the Coastal Law.

Finally, we note that several associations (particularly SOS Costa Brava, in Catalonia) continue to lobby autonomous and central governments to adopt more restrictive coastal regulations. This lobbying has so far led the Catalonian government to create a new plan which might change the status of land subject to development along the coast to environmentally protected rural land, thereby extinguishing all development rights.

Climate change issues

In the Coastal Law, climate change is an ancillary subject which is not dealt as a main topic of the Law. The most notable reference in this Law is a provision which sets out that if, due to sea-level rise, the water reaches concession (ground lease) areas within the MTPD, all concessions will be cancelled and the structures built on that land must be demolished.

In addition, the Coastal Law specifies that applications for concessions for uses or development in the coastal zone must assess the effects of the proposed project or activity, taking into account the impact of climate change in the subject area. The concession title or permit will then set out the obligations of the beneficiary to adopt the measures for adaptation to sea level rise, changes in wave patterns, and other effects of climate change. Additionally, in cases where the beneficiary carries out voluntarily measures that increase the resilience of the coastline or mitigate the effects of climate change, the duration of the concession or rights may be increased up to one-fifth of the period initially granted.

In general, Spain's legislation and policy on climate change is lagging behind that of many other countries. In 2007, the government published a national Climate Change and Clean Energy Strategy (EECCEL), which forms part of the Spanish Sustainable Development Strategy (EEDS). The EECCEL promotes several measures which are intended to move the country towards climate change mitigation and adaptation measures. One measure specifically applies to coastal areas as follows:

Impact evaluation of climate change in coastal areas:
    To identify the areas and most vulnerable elements of the Spanish coastal area due to the effects of climate change throughout the 21st century, and to evaluate its environmental value (Spanish government, 2007, p. 36).

In 2018, the Spanish Parliament debated two initiatives[5] which would introduce a general Law on Climate Change, but those initiatives did not pass.

Amongst the autonomous communities, only Catalonia has a Climate Change Act (16/2017). The purpose of this Act is to enable the establishment of general rules, affecting all areas of the economic activity, in order to adjust all public policies and private activities to the aim of mitigating climate change and its impacts. While it does not contain specific regulations relating to coastal areas, several of its mandates (particularly those dealing with water, biodiversity, mobility, and planning) will have an impact on the development of projects along the coast.

Nevertheless, the Catalonian Climate Change Act has had a bumpy start. Upon enactment in 2017, it was challenged by the Spanish Government in the Constitutional Court. That challenge entailed an immediate injunction; the application of the Act was suspended from 3 November 2017 until 21 March 2018, when the suspension was partially lifted. The Suspension was then lifted entirely on 20 June 2019, when the Court handed down its ruling (STC 87/2019), which declared some articles of the law unconstitutional but upheld its core provisions.

The Law obliges the Catalan Government to set a threshold for carbon emissions and assess all projects, public or private, against that threshold. This threshold will be progressively lowered, so as to enable Catalonia to meet targets set by international agreements to which Spain has committed itself, including the Paris Agreement, which Spain ratified early in 2017. Now that it is in force, the Catalan Climate Act will have an enduring effect on land use projects and activities.

Planning for the coastal zone in Catalonia – a case study

Given that planning in Spain takes place at the regional level, there are no State-wide planning policies or regulations. Catalonia not only has the planning powers attributed to all autonomous communities but, by agreement with the State, has wider powers than other regions in the management of the MTPD. In this section, we describe and evaluate planning and management of the coastal zone in Catalonia.

Catalonia's powers

The Catalan and Spanish governments have made several agreements which transferred powers to the autonomous community. The earliest was Royal Decree 3301/1981, which allowed the Catalonian government to draft and approve plans to regulate the coastal zone (but not maritime plans). Much later, in 2006, after a substantial amendment to the Catalonian Statute of Autonomy, the parties reached two new agreements by which several new powers were transferred to Catalonia. The new powers included licensing for seasonal beach uses in the Beaches and on the territorial sea; management of some of the concessions and authorizations granted by the State for the MTPD; and enforcement powers in order to control those matters. Finally, in 2008, the parties agreed that the Catalan government would assume all powers regarding temporary uses and concessions in the MTPD.

Catalonia's Urban Director Plans (PDUs)

In 2002, the Catalan Parliament approved a new Planning Law which allowed the government to approve supra-municipal planning instruments which could directly determine which land would be preserved from urban development. These plans, called "Urban Director Plans" (Plans Directors Urbanístics, hereafter PDUs), are powerful instruments, as they are binding and override all municipal planning instruments already in force.

PDU for Catalonia's Zone of Influence

Within a few years of the introduction of PDUs, the Catalan Government elected to use this instrument to formalize the protection of the Zone of Influence (500 m from the MTPD). The idea was to supress a trend of rapid growth in coastal development, particularly between 1996 and 2001. The resulting plan, approved in 2005, is known as the Urban Director Plan for the Coastal System (PDUSC).

The PDUSC classifies all land within the Zone of Influence according to whether it may be developed or not. In preparing the PDUSC, the Catalan Government considered the land in two stages and accordingly, prepared two separate plans: (a) A plan for land where development was not permitted under planning regulations or where development had not been considered (PDUSC-1) and (b) a plan for land where development was permitted but where preservation was considered essential (PDUSC-2). This division of the PDUSC into two separate plans was deliberate: The government expected that the second plan would be subject to significantly more legal challenges than the first and thus sought to isolate the first plan to ensure a clear passage to its adoption.

In preparing the first plan (PDUSC-1), the government found that the land where development was previously not permitted, or not considered, comprised 38,076.91 hectares. Of that land, the PDUSC protects 23,551.92 hectares from future development. That land was rezoned for preservation, into one of four subcategories: Special Plan for Nature Conservation (PEIN, 7,053 hectares) and three other protection zones with varying levels of protection.

For the remaining land in PDUSC-1, the government applied a set of conditions for planning and development. Interestingly, these include a requirement that the Zone of Influence be extended, where necessary, to consider the effects of development on the coast. The plan also specifically notes that the Protection Zone (setback) may not be reduced from the 100 m standard.

In preparing the second plan (PDUSC-2), the government targeted land available for immediate development. More than two hundred land parcels were considered, but eventually forty-four were retained and included in the PDUSC. A detailed analysis of those forty-four parcels followed, including consideration of the environs and the stage of planning permissions – i.e. was there a particularized plan in place? The process led to a rezoning of twenty-four of the forty-four parcels for preservation. That is, the development rights granted to those parcels by previously approved municipal plans were cancelled by the PDUSC. On an additional three parcels, the development rights were reduced. The rights of the remaining seventeen parcels were not modified.

PDUSC reactions and outcomes

As had been anticipated, the approval of the PDUSC was a controversial issue – particularly PDUSC-2. The key objectors were the municipalities and individual property owners of parcels where development rights had been reduced. The matter, in separate appeals, reached both the Superior Court of Justice of Catalonia (among others, ruling STSJCat 2321/2009) and the Supreme Court (STS 6119/2009). The courts examined two main issues:

- Does the rezoning of land by the Catalan Government constitute an infringement on municipal planning powers?
- Should owners whose land was stripped of building rights be entitled to compensation?

We address each of these question in turn.

Does the rezoning of land by the Catalan Government constitute an infringement on municipal planning powers?

In relation to this issue, the courts determined that, as long as the provisions of the PDUSC were based on supra-municipal values (in this case, protection of the coast), they were acceptable to be applied by the autonomous community.

Should owners whose land was stripped of building rights be entitled to compensation?

On this matter, where there were no extenuating circumstances, the courts ruled consistently with the jurisprudence established by the Supreme Court and the Planning Law: A change of plan (or, regulatory takings) does not entail a right to compensation (Article 11.2, Spanish Law on Land).

There are some exceptions where compensation may be granted for regulatory takings, including where a more detailed "particularized plan" or subdivision plan has been approved (Catalan Planning Law, Article 115.3). Yet, as noted above, the planning stage of the parcels included in the PDUSC was considered as part of the process. Thus, it is not surprising that the Courts upheld the PDUSC in most cases.

PDUSC overall assessment

Overall, the PDUSC is an example of an integrated approach to management of the coast. It is an instrument which supersedes the usual order of planning and preservation processes to apply specific and concrete measures to protect the coastal zone. It is a general planning instrument which establishes general rules for the whole of the coastal zone, but is also particularized; each of the land parcels affected by the plan are identified.

In our opinion, the drawback of the PDUSC as a planning instrument is that its scope is limited to the Zone of Influence, without taking into account the land and activities within the MTPD area. Given that the Catalan Government does indeed have the authority to grant concessions and enforce the regulations within the MTPD, it could have considered that land as part of the plan. Another limitation of the PDUSC is that it could not rezone parcels in advanced planning stages, given the need to pay compensation to landowners. A planning process which is backed by a compensation fund would perhaps give way to a bolder plan of protection of the coastal zone.

Lastly, during the first half of 2019, the planning department of the Catalan Government initiated a new planning process that, if it is approved, might have lasting effects on the integrated management of the coastal zone. This process involves a comprehensive examination of every plot of land and area subject to development in the Coastal areas. The objective of this process is to determine if the development of those areas is environmentally sound or if it might have significant effects on the landscape and environmental conditions of the coastal zone (for instance, it is assumed that properties in the coastal zone with a slope of more than 30% cannot be developed sustainably).

If this new plan is eventually approved, the result will likely be a "declassification" of land formerly earmarked as suitable for development. The land would be reclassified as environmentally sensitive rural land and property owners would be deprived of development rights. Given the context of the Spanish planning system outlined above, the relevant property owners are unlikely to be fully compensated for such a loss.

Catalonia's new Law for the Protection and Management of the Coast

In August 2020, a new Law enacted by the Catalan Government came into force – Act for the Protection and Management of the Coast (Law 8/2020). For the first time, a Catalan Special Commission for Coastal Protection will be empowered to approve a new type of plan dedicated to the coast. The plan will regulate urban and rural land uses and building rights within a 1 km zone inland from the edge of the MTPD. The law also delegates additional powers to municipalities, allowing them to regulate certain concessions in the MTPD. It will be interesting to evaluate the law's implementation in the coming years.

Overall assessment

The Spanish story of coastal zone management, as told in this chapter, has two main elements: The first, a highly ambitious legal regime which has been tempered over time to address practical obstacles to implementation and private property rights; the second, tensions and dilemmas in finding the appropriate balance of powers between the State, autonomous communities, and municipalities.

From the environmental awareness perspective, the 1988 Coastal Law was ahead of its time: It introduced comprehensive public ownership and management of land seaward of the shoreline (MTPD), as well as a 100 m setback zone, a full 20 years before these protective measures were encoded into European law through the ICZM Protocol to the Barcelona Convention. Perhaps it was precisely because Spain was a pioneer in this area that implementation was stilted and eventually necessitated a change in the law. The 2013 Amendment enabled a more practical and stable demarcation process and lightened the burden on property owners in both the MTPD and setback zone. By extending rights of use, however, it did not by any means resolve questions about the long-term future of the affected properties.

The rights of property owners, in the MTPD particularly, remain in limbo. The current system of "concessions" only disguises the effective "taking" of the land and is not sustainable. Ideally, the land would be expropriated in the full sense of the term, with property owners compensated accordingly. But this would be a vast undertaking and will not occur unless there is a change either in Spanish law or in applicable European case law.

Regarding the tensions between the State and autonomous communities, the courts have made determinations addressing the key questions of who holds the power across various aspects of coastal land management and planning. Yet there remains a grey area in relation to the management of the MTPD. The struggle in that area has to some extent been resolved through agreements between the authorities, such as those we have described in relation to Catalonia. There is certainly an argument to be made that the authority which is responsible for planning should concurrently manage the MTPD, to ensure a holistic approach to coastal zone management. Yet to date, even in Catalonia, the MTPD and adjoining land have been managed through separate processes. It will be interesting to see whether additional autonomous communities seek to take over management of the MTPD and how that will affect future planning.

Notes

1. The figure is from an assessment by FEPORTS, based on the Ministry of Environment's Strategy for Coastal Sustainability. FEPORTS also found that in Valencia, the density for coastal areas is 782 inhabitants per square kilometre, compared with 207 inland (based on data from Instituto Valenciano de Estadística, 2013, available at http://www.pegv.gva.es/va/).

2. Seasonal Beach Use Plans are drafted by Municipalities and approved by the Ministry's Provincial branches. Once approved, the Municipalities, under public procedure rules, tender and grant the particular services in the Seasonal Plan.
3. The 2007 amendment to the Spanish Land Law changed the valuation criteria for determining the level of compensation for expropriation of non-urban land. Prior to the amendment, land with the potential for urban development was valued on the basis of prospective building rights. Following the amendment, this land was valued according to its agricultural use. This change significantly reduced the cost incurred by the authorities in expropriation processes and had a flow-on effect for the market.
4. We recently saw an example of the type of matter which may trigger a legal challenge by the State, in accordance with Article 67 of the Law on Local Government: Several municipalities in Catalonia, supporting Catalonia's bid for independence, chose not to fly the Spanish flag on municipal buildings. The State considered this act a threat to the national interest and challenged those municipalities in the courts.
5. Official Journal of the Spanish Parliament no. B-302-1, 7 September 2018, and n° B-283-1, 29 June 2018.

References

Alterman, R., Pellach, C., & Carmon, D. (2016). *Mare Nostrum Project Final Report: Legal-Institutional Instruments for Integrated Coastal Zone Management (ICZM) in the Mediterranean.* Available at: https://alterman.web3.technion.ac.il/files/mare-nostrum/Mare_Nostrum_Final_Report_2016.pdf

Auken, M. (2009). *Report on the Impact of Extensive Urbanisation in Spain on Individual Rights of European Citizens, on the Environment and on the Application of EU Law, Based upon Petitions Received* (2008/2248(INI)). 20 February. European Parliament. Available at: http://www.europarl.europa.eu/sides/getDoc.do?pubRef=-//EP//NONSGML+REPORT+A6-2009-0082+0+DOC+PDF+V0//EN

Carlón, M. (2013). *Disciplina Urbanística de las Costas.* Thomas Reuters Civitas.

Environmental Justice Atlas. (2017). Hotel Algarrobico, Almeria, Spain. Available at: https://ejatlas.org/conflict/algarrobico-hotel

EpData. (2020). El turismo en España y en el mundo, en datos y gráficos. [Tourism in Spain and in the world, in data and graphics]. Available at: https://www.epdata.es/datos/turismo-espana-mundo-datos-graficos/272

Exceltur. (2015). *Perspectivas turísticas: Valoración Empresarial del año 2014 y perspectivas para 2015* [*Tourism Perspectives: 2014 Business Valuation and 2015 Prospects*]. Available at: https://www.exceltur.org/wp-content/uploads/2015/01/Informe-Perspectivas-N51-Balance-2014-y-perspectivas-2015-Definitivo-Web.pdf

FEPORTS (Institute of Port Studies and Cooperation, Valencia). (2016). Interviews with officials for EU Mare Nostrum project.

Greenpeace. (2006). *Destruction at All Co[a]sts 2006: Greenpeace Report about the Spanish Coast Situation.* July. Madrid. Available at: http://archivo-es.greenpeace.org/espana/Global/espana/report/other/destruction-at-all-co-a-sts-20.pdf

Ministry of Environment. (2007). *Estrategia para la Sostenibilidad de la Costa: Documento de inicio* [*Strategy for Coastal Sustainability: Preliminary Report*]. Available at: http://www.upv.es/contenidos/CAMUNISO/info/U0721771.pdf

Negro, V., López-Gutiérrez, J. S., Esteban, M. D., & Matutano, C. (2014). An analysis of recent changes in Spanish coastal law. *Journal of Coastal Research* 70 (sp1), 448–454.

Puertos del Estado [State Ports] (n.d.) About Us. Available at: http://www.puertos.es/en-us/nosotrospuertos/Pages/Nosotros.aspx [Accessed July 2020].

Spanish Government. (2007). *Spanish Climate Change and Clean Energy Strategy Horizon 2007–2012–2020*. Official English version. Available at: http://www.lse.ac.uk/GranthamInstitute/wp-content/uploads/laws/1674%20English.pdf

World Factbook. (n.d.). Spain. Available at: https://www.cia.gov/Library/publications/the-world-factbook/geos/sp.html [Accessed September 2019]

Supra-national Legislation and Agreements

Council of Europe Committee of Ministers Resolution 29/1973 on the Protection of Coastal Areas

European Coastal Charter. Available at: https://ec.europa.eu/environment/iczm/pdf/Charte_Europeenne_du_Littoral.pdf

National Legislation (listed chronologically)

Royal Decree 3301/1981, of 18 December 1981, on the transfer of services regarding the coast to the Catalan Government

Coastal Law 22/1988, of 18 July 1988, amended by the Protection and Sustainable Use of the Coast and Amendment of the Coastal Law (Coastal Law Amendment) 2/2013

Law 27/2006, of 18 July 2006, on Public participation, transparency, and access to information

Land Law 2007 (amended 2008, 2011, 2013) – Now synthesized into Royal Legislative Decree 7/2015, of 30 October 2015 on Land

Catalonia Legislation

Statute of Autonomy of Catalonia, 2006 (Estatuto de autonomía de Cataluña)

Catalan Planning Law 2002, currently Legislative decree 1/2010, of 3 August 2010

Catalonia Climate Change Act (16/2017), dated 1 August 2017

Law for the Protection and Management of the Coast (8/2020), dated 4 August 2020

Court cases[*]

Constitutional Court – STC 214/1989
— STC 149/1991 (4 July 1991)
— STC 61/1997
— STC 31/2010
— STC 87/2019 (25 July 2019)
Galician High Court of Justice – TSJ Galicia (25 September 2005)
Superior Court of Justice of Catalonia – STSJCat 2321/2009
— STSJCat 662/2006
Supreme Court – STS 6613/2012 (17 October 2012)
— STS 1739/2012
— STS 2972/2018 (11 July 2018)
— STS 6119/2009

[*]   There is no official database or format for court case citations in Spain; thus the format of citation differs from case to case.

9 France

Loïc Prieur

Overview

Although residential population pressures in southern France are not as high as in some other Mediterranean coastal regions, the area is famous for its attractiveness as the Riviera for vacations, and thus vacation-related development. Coastal legislation in France differs considerably from that in the other countries in this book in the concepts and criteria it proposes for preventing and regulating development directly along the coast. In France, like in Spain (but in a different legal and policy mode), overly ambitious national regulation has not been implemented to enable realistic decision constraints on the municipal levels. Even French coastal management – which we regard as one of the "better good practices" in the Mediterranean – exhibits difficulties in enforcement against some illegal development.

The context: Introduction to the coastal issues in France

France has an extensive and varied coastline. Its length is approximately 3,400 km (mainland; World Factbook, n.d.)[1] – 1,500 km of which are on the Mediterranean Sea and the remainder on the North Atlantic/Celtic Sea. There are about 950 coastal municipalities (communes, out of a total of 34,968), with a total population of 6.16 million in 2010 (ONML, n.d.). This is only 10% of the total French population of 62.8 million, but in fact the coastal areas play an important role in French culture, economy (tourism and shipping), and environment. The French coastal landscapes ranges from high cliffs in the north to low-lying wetlands in the southwest and mountainous regions in the southeast. These landscapes face many threats, including urban sprawl, flooding, and shoreline recession. The latter affects a significant proportion of the coastline, especially in the southwest of the country.

One indicator of the greater importance of the coastal zones than their share of area is their population density, which is 285 inhabitants per square metre (2.5 times the national average)[2] (ONML n.d.). The proportion of built-up areas in coastal municipalities is two or three times higher than the proportion of built-up areas inland (Ministry of Ecology, Sustainable Development and Energy, 2014, p. 26). In addition, apart from the Paris area, much of France's tourist industry depends on its coastal areas. In 2011, it was estimated that the country's maritime and coastal economy supported 460,000 jobs and provided an added value of 30 billion euros, or about 1.5% of France's GDP (Ministry for the Ecological and Solidary Transition, 2017). Jobs generated by the maritime economy are mainly related to tourism (215,000), while seafood production comes in second, with about 50,000 jobs (Colas, 2015).

Administrative structure

To aid in the understanding of the framework for planning and coastal zone management in France, we provide a brief introduction to the mode of governance. Administrative powers are both dispersed and decentralized: Central government powers are dispersed in that the national government has significant representation – by "prefects" in the regions and by "departments" in sub-regions. These powers are also decentralized in that the regions and departments are independent authorities. Communes (municipalities) hold a double legal function – they are both local authorities and arms of the State. Thus, at times, a mayor acts by authority of the State, and at other times, in the name of the municipality. Under urban planning law, communes that have adopted a statutory land use plan gain the power to issue building permits. In such cases, prefects do not have any power to influence municipal decision-making. If a prefect believes that the mayor has issued an illegal decision, the prefect can appeal the municipality's decision to the administrative court. If there is no such approved plan (as is often the case in smaller communes), the mayor issues the permit in the name of the State.

In addition to regional prefects, another type of prefect is relevant to coastal matters: Maritime prefects (who are Navy admirals) are a military and a civil authority for maritime-related issues, such as regulation of traffic and prevention of marine pollution. The coastal zone is divided into three areas (Channel and North Sea, Atlantic, and Mediterranean Sea).

Overview of the French legal framework for coastal zone management

France began a programme for protecting coastal areas back in the 1960s (Prieur, 2014): In order to preserve the natural character of the Provence and the Côte d'Azur coasts in the southeast, in 1959, a decree (No. 59-768) was issued giving the departments (sub-regions) in the region the authority to declare sensitive areas, over which they received pre-emption rights the following year.[3] That is, a landowner who wished to sell a property located within a sensitive area was first required to inform the relevant department, which had a priority right to buy the land. In time, the order was extended to all coastal departments, and later, to all other departments, becoming one of the trademarks of French land policy. To this day, the demarcation of sensitive areas for protection is a major tool in French land policy in general, and particularly in coastal areas (Le Louarn, 1995, p. 11). But soon, this tool was regarded as still inadequate to provide good coastal management.

The foundations of France's current coastal legislation date back to 1973, with the publication of the well-known Michel Piquard Report. It was based on the work of a state-commissioned team convened in 1972 due to concern about increasing pressures on the coastal zones. This report – quite innovative for its time – proposed a shift in the conception of the coastal zone from only a demarcated area towards a more holistic view, incorporating both terrestrial and maritime zones. The Report also proposed that government policy and regulation no longer be limited to the maritime public domain, which is a narrow strip at the intersection of land and sea, but target a wider area, inland and seaward, in order to take into account the impact of any development in the marine environment.

The Piquard Report recommended that the national government prepare special plans for the coastal zone. These plans would complement existing laws by defining acceptable uses based on the capacity of the environment to accommodate each type of uses. The recommendation was accepted on principle, and the Prime Minister sent several circulars to the prefects (representatives of the State in the regions and departments) in support of such plans. At the time, there was no legal basis for such plans. In 1983, the law did introduce legally binding Sea Development Schemes, but to date, only four have been approved. In addition, some strategic plans can have a coastal chapter with the same legal effect (strategic plan of Corsica, strategic plans for overseas territory and SCOT) (see the section on planning below).

In the meantime, between 1974 and 1983, there were several other developments in French coastal act. In 1975, the State established the Conservatory of Coastal Areas and Lakeshores, which is responsible for acquiring the coastal area and safeguarding its natural character. By 2020, the Conservatory had acquired (through exercise of pre-emption powers and other means) 750 sites spanning over 200,000 hectares of endangered coastal areas (Conservatoire du littoral, n.d.). Over the period 1976–1979, the government introduced the first urban planning policies specifically for the coast. The proposed principles were very innovative for the time, probably on a global scale. They included consolidation of urban development (today's "compact city") and a protected setback zone of 100 m from the shoreline (the latter was later to be incorporated into the Barcelona ICZM Protocol). However, at the time, there were no legally binding rules to ensure that the proposed principles would be followed.

In the early 1980s, the entire French planning system (and other aspects of administration) underwent a dramatic legal and institutional change. From being one of Western Europe's most centralized states (Alterman, 2001), France began a process of major decentralization, which eventually empowered communes to prepare urban plans and issue building permits, so long as they fulfilled some preconditions. In order to avoid the negatives of excessive decentralization, the State began to formulate rules that would allow it to protect environmentally sensitive areas. To this end, a Mountain Law was approved in 1985. The following year, in 1986, the French Coastal Act was introduced. The provisions of the Coastal Act are codified through several codes, as relevant (the Urban Planning Code, the Environment Code, and the General Code of Public Property).

The main purpose of the Coastal Act was to protect the coastal zone from development. The key principles of the Coastal Act must be taken into account in the drafting of urban plans and strategic plans. These principles have remained in force ever since the Coastal Act was initially adopted, and it has been regularly updated to address new land uses and conflicts.

The French Coastal Act predates the Integrated Coastal Zone Management (ICZM) Protocol to the Barcelona Convention adopted in 2008, and in fact served as a model in some respects and exceeded the Protocol in many other respects (Calderaro, 2008, p. 158). But the Protocol did have an important effect in France in bringing the ICZM concept to the forefront of the public agenda (Braud, 2013).

French coastal act and policy have developed well beyond the scope of the ICZM Protocol. The "Grenelle 2" Law[4] on the State's commitment to the environment was adopted in 2010. This law introduced a new system of governance, with the establishment of the National Council for the Sea and Coastal Areas, as well as coastal councils. Four coastal councils were created in 2011, covering France's mainland coastline (North Sea and east channel; west channel and north Atlantic; south Atlantic; and Mediterranean Sea). They are directed by the State (through regional prefects and maritime prefects). The 2012 national government Directive on Sustainable and Integrated Management of the Natural Maritime Public Domain guides the management of the maritime public domain, considering the principles of ICZM. In addition, the Grenelle 2 law requires that the government develop a national strategy for the coast and the preparation of strategic documents for coastal councils. The State (through the Ministry for the Ecological and Solidary Transition) approved a National Strategy for the Sea and Coast in 2017, and under its supervision, Coastal Zone Plans are now under development for all four coastal councils (see the section on planning).

The laws governing the French coastal zone are relatively stringent. The public highly value their coasts and thus generally accept this stringency. A 2014 survey by the IFOP (Institute of Opinion and Marketing Studies in France and Abroad) indicated that 91% of the population agreed that the laws protecting the coastal environment should not be relaxed (IFOP, 2014).

Definition and demarcation of the French coastal zone

The achievements outlined above were made even though to this date there is no official uniform definition of the French coastal zone. There is, however, an all-important definition in the Coastal act, which is based on the Environment Code (C. envir., art. L 321-2). The long discussion about this definition started as early as 1973 with Michel Piquard's report.

The definition states that in the context of implementation of the 1986 Coastal Act, the coastal zone applies to *the entire jurisdiction of every commune that abuts the seashore* (as well as those abutting lakes larger than 1,000 hectares). This means that the Coastal Act applies even to remote mountainous areas where the coast may not be visible. On the other hand, the definition would exclude communities that are close to the seashore but do not abut it.[5] The motivation for this seemingly excessive boundary definition was the concern with the rampant sprawl that had characterized French coastal communes. The major rule that applies to the coastal communes is that they must exercise special control over sprawl in their entire municipality. This definition of the coastal zone resonates with the language of Article 3 of the ICZM Protocol (which refers to the landward limit of "competent coastal units"). As will be noted below, there are gradations within this broad definition, rendering it more logical than may seem at first sight.

The definition in the coastal zone also encompasses the area seaward up to the limit of the territorial waters. The territory of the coastal municipalities extends from the land up all the way up to the seaward boundary of the territorial waters (CE, 20 févr. 1981, n° 16449, Rec. Conseil d'Etat 1981, p. 96). As such, their planning regulations apply equally to all land, including coastal land (CAA Nantes, 10 octobre 2014, req. n° 13NT00220). Within the maritime public domain (MPD), specific zones are created, mainly for marine farming or for mooring or harbour areas. In practice, even if urban plans apply to the MPD up to the limit of the territorial sea, municipalities never use this tool to define land use zones so far seaward. However, the courts have found that the Coastal Act does not apply offshore (CE, 5 juill. 1999, req. n° 197287). As such, it does not apply to offshore projects such as mineral extraction and offshore wind turbines.

Definition of the shoreline and the MPD

The definition of the coastal zone differs from the shoreline. The French shoreline is defined as the landward boundary of the MPD (maritime public domain). The General Code of Public Property (CGPPP) distinguishes the MPD as a special category of public land, with two sub-categories: natural and human-made (artificial).

The natural MPD was first defined in 1681 by Colbert's Great Ordinance of Marine (the marine code). That regulation states that the seashore and coastal area comprise all the land that is alternately exposed and submerged, up to the line that is reached by "the great waves of March" (Valin, 1981, pp. 527–528). Within that area, construction was prohibited. This early prohibition resulted from potential dangers to the landing of ships onshore and a desire to prevent any obstructions to fishing and navigation. Although the Ordinance could be applied

Figure 9.1 Beach at Trouville, site of Council of State case 1858

Source: Thomas Ulrich. Available at: https://pixabay.com/fr/photos/trouville-plage-mer-france-66930/

to the entire French shoreline, in practice it was enforced only on the Atlantic coast. On the Mediterranean, the state originally applied old rules stemming from Roman law, which determined that the public domain was determined by the highest winter tide. This distinction arose because of eighteenth-century case law, which was regarded as a binding precedent despite its questionable legal rationale.

The rules changed in the mid-nineteenth century, when the beaches started to become centres of leisure and recreation. In 1858, the Council of State (the highest administrative authority) declared that as the seashore was part of the public domain and should be accessible to all (CE, 19 mai 1858, Vernes). The law was changed, albeit only in 1963, to include submerged lands, lands covered by the tidal reach, and any tidal deposits within the public domain. The law also allowed the designation of private land for uses that meet leisure or tourism needs.[6] In 1973, the Council of State clarified that the rules of the Colbert Ordinance applied to all shores, including along the Mediterranean (CE, 12 oct. 1973, Kreitmann: Rec. CE 1973, p. 563). In order to maximize the extent of the MPD, the Council of State has stipulated that the shoreline is to be determined according to the highest tide of the year, excluding exceptional storms and not at the highest tide of March, as was the previous rule (1973). These principles have since been adopted into law, as set out in the General Code of Public Property (CGPPP, art. L 2111-4).

The artificial MPD comprises ports and structures built to ensure public safety (CGPPP, art. L 2111-6). Such assets are State-owned, but local authorities may use them under the law. For example, all marinas have been managed by the communes since 1983.

Demarcation of the shoreline

The French MPD is not demarcated on a map. Its boundary changes according to the level of the highest tide at any given time. A rise in sea level would move land from adjacent private ownership to the MPD, automatically changing land from private to public property. Conversely, in the case of receding waters, previously submerged lands (deposits or reclaimed land) remain in the public domain. This principle has been declared compliant with the Constitution by the Constitutional Council (décision n° 2013-316 QPC du 24 mai 2013).

Although there is no general demarcation procedure for the MPD, there is a procedure for demarcation stipulated by the General Code of Public Property (CGPPP art. L 2111-6). This procedure may be implemented by the State if there is a dispute between a landowner and the State in relation to the MPD boundary. It involves local site inspections to determine tidal influence or, alternatively, scientific data which indicates the highest reach of the tides, often gathered by satellite or other photography (this may include topographical, meteorological, tidal, botanical, zoological, and historical data). This demarcation procedure is subject to a public inquiry.

Significantly, even when the above demarcation procedure has been undertaken, the boundary of the MPD is not permanent. The demarcation is valid only at the time it is undertaken to resolve a conflict.

The border between the MPD and the adjacent private properties exists regardless of whether or not it has been demarcated on a map. As such, enforcement action against illegal use or development on the MPD is not dependent on an official demarcation process. The administrative court is entitled to demarcate the MPD on the basis of the evidence provided by parties (the State and the landowner).

The MPD as protected public property

The natural MPD belongs to the State. It is inalienable (it cannot be sold) and imprescriptible (it cannot be transferred to a private party, regardless of the passage of time). While the State may permit private uses, it is never legally obliged to add a new permit or renew an existing one. The European Court of Human Rights has recently confirmed this position in a case of an existing use dating back to the nineteenth century, as follows:

In 1889, the prefect of Morbihan department (northwest France) gave a landowner permission to keep a house that had been illegally built on the MPD, subject to the payment of a fee. The permission was granted on the grounds that the occupant was a poor old sailor. The State then renewed the permission for the seaman's daughters; the house was sold in 1960 and the permission was again renewed for the new owner, three consecutive times. When in 1993, the owner applied for a fourth renewal, the prefect refused based on the provisions of the Coastal Act, which had been approved since the last renewal (1986). Nevertheless, taking into consideration the financial burden on the owner and the moral dimension, the prefect proposed a contract which would allow the owner and his wife to remain in the house but would prohibit them from selling it. The owner did not agree and took the matter to the Council of State, which rejected his claim. He then took France to the ECHR, which confirmed France's position regarding the necessity of protecting Europe's coast and its public use. The prefect therefore ordered the demolition of the house (Depalle v. France [GC], no. 34044/02, § 77, and Brosset-Triboulet and Others v. France [GC], no. 34078/02, § 80, ECHR, 2010).

Rules for use and control of the MPD

The MPD is governed by strict regulations designed to protect its public use. Case law has held that private use of the MPD can only take place if "it is consistent with the purposes for which the public is generally permitted to use the domain" (CE, 3 mai 1963, Commune de

Saint Brévin les Pins, R.D.P. 1963, p. 1174). Specifically, uses of land and sea may not hinder the public's use of the promenade or bathing activities. For this reason, some activities are always prohibited on the MPD, including the use of vehicles (C. envir., L 321-1) and overnight camping (Urban Planning Code, C. urb., R 111-33).

The principle of protecting the public recreational use is affirmed in the General Code of Public Property (CGPPP art. L 2124-1) and is the starting point for authorities evaluating proposals. For example, the Council of State has considered whether a "concession" (similar to a ground lease, described below) granted by the State for a fishery was compatible with the recreational use assigned for adjacent land (CE, 21 juin 1996, req. n° 136044 et 137008).

Anyone seeking to use the MPD for private purposes must obtain a permit (authorization for temporary occupation of the MPD). Such permits may be granted only for a limited time and authorities may revoke them at any time. They are usually granted for facilities in the public interest (recreation, piers, etc.). They may not be granted for residential use. A single use or development may be subject to several independent permit or repetitive authorization processes, as required by any relevant legislation. For example, a building permit may be required in addition to the MPD permit.

This situation obviously calls for some coordination procedures: The Grenelle 2 law exempts some marine structures constructed within the seaward part of the MPD (away from the low water mark), such as renewable energies, from the need to obtain building permits (C. urb., art. L 421-5). This measure limits the power of municipalities to hinder development projects on the State-owned public domain. It also limits litigation by reducing the number of decisions claimants can challenge. In addition, to enhance the development of marine renewable energy such as offshore wind turbines, any claims related to such developments, regardless of location, fall under the authority of the Administrative Court of Nantes, which decides both first and last instance appeals. The only means by which one may contest the Court decision is by bringing it before the Council of State (code of administrative justice, art. R 311-4).

In addition to the above unilateral permits that offer only limited legal certainty, private entities and local authorities may apply for more stable rights from the national government for the use of the MPD. Such rights are known as "concessions". They can take the form of contract (beach concession) or unilateral permits (fish farming or shellfish farming concession). They are time-limited but still provide relative legal certainty for private investors. There are several types of concessions, including for dams, for fish farming, for bathing beaches, and for marine energy.

A beach concession is a contract between the State and local authorities, or individuals (CGPPP, art. L 2124-4). The lessee operates the beach for recreational purposes and in return is entitled to charge fees for the use of public facilities. Most commonly, concessions are granted to local governments, which are then able to subcontract them to private entities. Those seeking to construct facilities related to the public use of the beach (maintenance, user safety, restaurants, and bathing facilities) compete for the available concessions. There are about 200 licensed beaches in France, primarily on the Mediterranean. Most licensed facilities sell food (e.g. restaurants or kiosks). Facilities must be removable.

Under the provisions of the Environment Code (C. envir., L 321-9), which originated from the Coastal Act, beach concessions must "... *preserve free movement on the beach and the free use by the public of a zone of significant width along the sea. Any concession contract must determine the width of this space, considering the characteristics of the place*". According to the General Code of Public Property (CGPPP art. R 2124-16), a minimum of 80%

of the shore length per beach and 80% of the beach surface must remain clear of any facility. Yet according to a State-sponsored report (Wellhoff et al., 2009), lessees do not always comply with these rules.

The beaches must remain vacant – free of any facilities – for at least 6 months a year. In some designated tourism communes, this period may increase to 8 months if the municipality agrees. In some other specific communes, the lessee (usually a commune) may request the prefect to authorize facilities to remain in place all year round. This rule which limits the use of the beach is often criticized by business owners, who argue that the disassembly of their facilities is not compatible with the level of investment required to operate them.

The Coastal Act also provides that any "substantial change" in the use of the public domain requires a public inquiry. Examples of "substantial changes" include expansion of a harbour and granting a concession for use of MPD for a fish farm.

Case law has made it clear that decisions regarding the use of the MPD must ensure consistency with municipal planning regulations (CE, 30 mars 1973, n° 88151, min. Aménag. territ., Équip., Aménag. et Tourisme c/ Schwetzoff et a.). Thus, the courts have ruled that although the State is the authority responsible for issuing permits in the MPD, the communes are the ones that have planning powers in this zone.

The protection of the MPD also includes more powerful instruments to regulate violations than other types of land use and urban planning. This will be discussed in the section on compliance and enforcement.

Right of public access

As outlined above, the laws relating to the use of the MPD consider accessibility within and along that zone. To clarify, I will collate here the points about accessibility addressed above in passing.

By law (Urban Planning Code, C. urb., art. L 121-31), a 3 m wide easement for pedestrian use must be instituted along the landward edge of the MPD (Tanguy, 1991, p. 7; Prieur, 2012). This law, developed in the 1970s (long after much of the land beyond the MPD had been developed), seeks to balance between the need for public accessibility and the impact on private property rights. As such, the easement is only 3 m wide and the law is not retroactive: Any dwelling constructed prior to 1976 within 15 m of the landward limit of the MPD is not subject to this easement requirement. The route and width of the easement may be modified where it is restricted by physical barriers, but this entails a public inquiry procedure.

If there is no public road within 500 m to access the MPD, the 3 m easement may be supplemented by an additional easement perpendicular to the shoreline, along existing private roads and paths (Urban Planning Code, C. urb., art. L 121-34). Unlike the 3 m easement, this supplementary easement does not exist as-of-right but rather is created on a discretionary basis.

Property owners must be compensated for costs incurred as a result of these easements, for example, if required to build a fence (CE, 30 septembre 2011, req. n° 336664). The addition of this easement was reinforced in 1986 by the introduction of an article to the Urban Planning Code which stipulates that uses permitted on the coast must ensure open access to the shoreline (C. urb., art. 121-7). The idea of this requirement is to prevent tourist or residential developments from further hindering access to the coast. Yet to date, its implementation has not been tested by the courts.

Figure 9.2 The coast at Nice

Source: Annie and Andrew. CC BY 2.0 license. Available at: https://www.flickr.com/photos/anwenandandrew/6065731555

Limitations on urban development in the Coastal Act

The Coastal Act has considerable legal force. It takes precedence over Territorial Coherence Schemes (SCOTs) and Local Urban Plans (PLUs) and is directly applicable to building permits (CE, 31 mars 2017, req. n° 392186). It also contributes to legal uncertainty, as the implementation of the Coastal Act through both SCOTs and PLUs can be questioned each time a building permit is challenged before the Court (Prieur, 2018). The situation could change, as a 2018 Law has strengthened the SCOT as a tool to implement the Coastal Act.[7] Significantly, however, this Law uses general concepts and standards and not precise definitions (except for the 100 me setback zone discussed below). The Coastal Act was adopted just three years after the Decentralization Act of 1983. In this context of decentralization, the idea was to empower municipalities to implement the 1986 Law's general standards in their strategic and statutory urban plans. But in practice, this idea was not realized, as jurisprudence has defined the Coastal Act concepts quite precisely, significantly reducing the role of local plans in its implementation. The Law contains several provisions that are intended to influence the urban

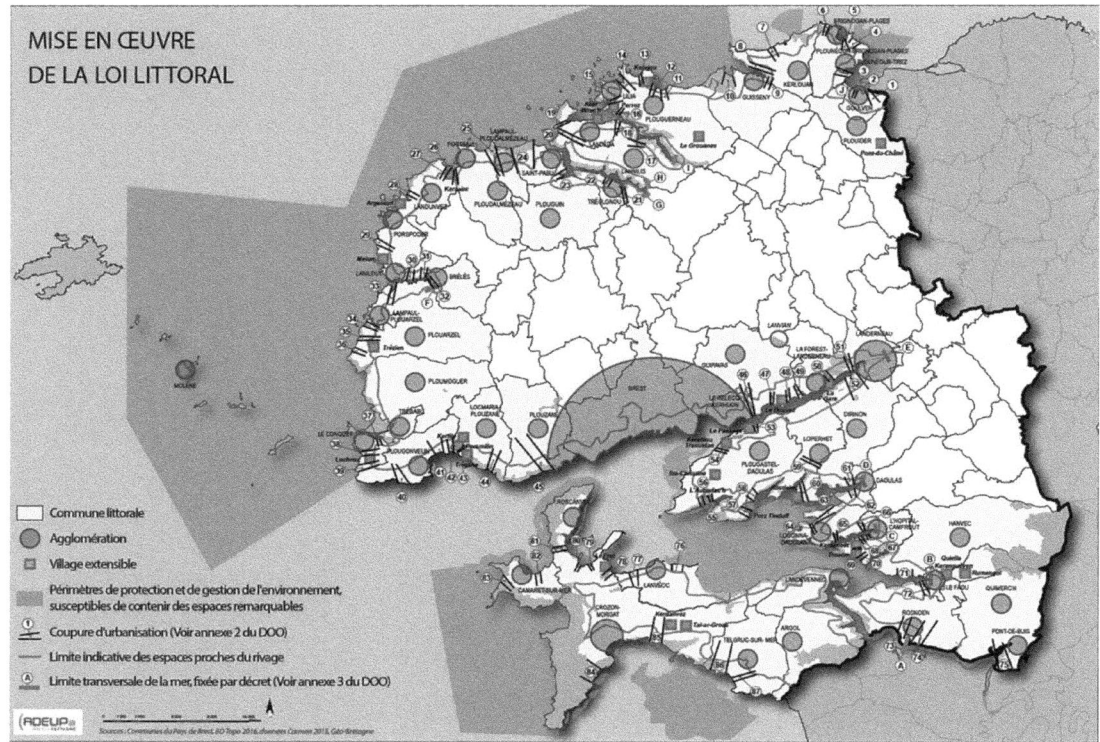

Figure 9.3 Plan for implementation of the Coastal act in the Brest SCOT

Source: Brest SCOT (public document)

structure of entire municipalities that are defined as "coastal". The Law sets several criteria that must be considered, as follows (these provisions are codified in the Urban Planning Code, C. urb., art. L 121-1 onwards):

Carrying capacity

The Coastal Act requires that a coastal city's urban planning regulations include the areas designated for urban construction according to their carrying capacity.[8] The aim is to prohibit development that would exceed the carrying capacity of local infrastructure or endanger areas with high environmental sensitivity. This is a general requirement; in practice, planners often consider the sewage system, the drinking water network, or the potential impact of a development on fauna and flora to evaluate the carrying capacity. The University of Nantes has developed a State-sponsored guide to determining carrying capacity, which is frequently use by planning agencies and municipalities (Chadenas et al., 2010). Urban plans are rarely annulled for a lack of consideration of carrying capacity.

Green buffers to avoid linear urban sprawl

SCOTs and PLUs must incorporate green buffers between nodes of development along the coast. This rule seeks to avoid a continuous built-up front along the shore.[9]

Prohibition of urban expansion beyond existing clusters

The Coastal Act requires that new development in coastal local authorities be contiguous to existing urban clusters (known as "agglomerations" or "villages"). This rule seeks to protect agricultural and open spaces. As noted, this rule is a prominent attribute of French coastal regulation in that it applies to the entire territory of the municipality, even inland far from the coast.

The compulsory contiguity rule has, to date, been by far the most contentious in the Coastal Act. It is difficult to implement and provokes the most litigation. It is regularly criticized by elected members of coastal communes. Although coastal municipalities have generally accepted the obligation to protect the most sensitive areas or those located directly on the coast, they have great difficulty prohibiting development, ostensibly based on coastal preservation, when the proposed project is located several kilometres away from the sea.

The case law has made it clear that the notion of urban clusters refers to areas characterized by a significant number and density of buildings (CE, 27 sept. 2006, req. n° 275924; CE, 9 novembre 2015, req. n° 372531). In practice, only urban development which comprises at least forty buildings can be classified either as a cluster or a village. Those with less development are characterized by the courts as "dispersed areas" and no new construction may be approved. The provision in the Coastal Act has been amended twice, in 1999 and 2015, to provide exemptions for farm buildings and wind turbines.

In response to the tension provoked by the contiguity rule, the Coastal Act was waived in 2018 through an amendment to the Urban Planning Code (C. urb., art. L 121-3 and L 121-8). Accordingly, strategic plans and urban plans may now indicate urbanized areas (usually at least twenty to twenty-five buildings) in which additional houses may be built. The perimeter of these areas must not be extended. Many plans are under revision based on this new provision. Its implementation has not yet been tested by the courts. New developments are still forbidden in dispersed areas.

Limited development in areas close to the shore

In order to protect the coastal landscape, the Coastal Act allows for only limited expansion of development "near the shore". In these areas, new planned construction is limited and must be of a similar bulk and density to neighbouring built-up areas (CAA Marseille, 6 avr. 2016, n° 15MA03273). This rule was used to prevent significant projects similar to those that had been built in the 1960s and 1970s. It does not apply retroactively to valid building permits which were issued prior to approval of the Coastal Act.

Case law has interpreted "areas near the shore" quite broadly. They should be defined as a function of the distance from the coast, of whether the area is urban or rural, and of visibility of the coast from the project site. In practice, even sites where buildings or steep slopes that prevent visibility are classified as "areas near the shore" so long as they are within a few hundred metres of the MPD. Natural open spaces or rural lands may be defined as "near the shore" even at a distance of 1.5 or 2 km of the MPD (CE, 3 juin 2009, req. n° 310587).

Coastal setback

The Coastal Act requires a 100 m setback from the landward edge of the MPD in which construction is prohibited. Only renovation or alteration of existing structures is permitted.

The mandatory setback does not apply in existing urban areas. The courts are strict in their interpretation of this exception; they consider that only land within an urban cluster as defined above is within urban areas (CE, 22 févr. 2008, req. n° 280189).

The Law also provides an exception for economic activities or public services that must be proximate to the water. This exception is used primarily to allow uses such as fish farms (CE, 11 févr. 2004, req. n° 212855) or facilities related to water safety or recreation. It may not be used for tourist developments such as restaurants or spas (CE, 9 oct. 1996, req. n° 161555). There is also an exception for the landing of communication cables for electricity from marine renewable energy.

Overall, compliance with these setback regulations is high. The necessity of protecting the 100 m strip is well accepted by the public and by municipalities. Notably, when we compare these rules to the broad list of exceptions in the Mediterranean ICZM Protocol (Article 8), we notice that the coastal setback provisions in the French law are much more stringent.

Protection of significant sites

The Coastal Act mandates that "Significant Sites" on land and in the marine environment must be protected. The types of sites that plans must identify and protect as "Significant" are listed in the Coastal Act and by a ministerial decree. They include wetlands, beaches, and forests close to the sea. In practice, case law recognizes as significant those sites which are already protected or identified through environmental legislation (e.g. "Natura 2000" sites), as well as sites of natural beauty or sites that shelter important fauna or flora, even if they are not protected by other environmental legislation.

Within Significant Sites, only light structures are permitted, as defined by decree, which is integrated into the Urban Planning Code. The rationale is to balance the objective of preservation and accessibility of the site, while at the same time allowing minimal construction ancillary to coastal or marine-related industries (fishing or farming). For this purpose, the decree authorizes unpaved parking lots, agricultural structures of less than 50 m² or any construction required for fisheries. The decree was modified in May 2019 to allow underground pipes to Significant Sites (Urban Planning Code, C. urb., art. R 121-5). This amendment was quite controversial because its purpose was to allow thalassotherapy (sea water therapy) facilities. The decree had thus been challenged before the Council of State by an environmental NGO. The Council of State has dismissed the NGO (CE, 10 july 2020, France Nature Environnement, n° 432944).

New roads

The Piquard Report (1973) pointed out the role of coastal roads in the increasing urbanization of the coastal zone. The Coastal Act addresses this issue by prohibiting new roads along the coast. It also prohibits transit routes of any kind within 2 km of the shoreline.

Camping and caravan parks

The creation or extension of campsites and caravan parks are subject to the same rules as urban development. As such, they may be developed only contiguous to existing urban clusters and villages. This rule poses difficulties for existing campsites located away from built-up clusters, which have a competitive disadvantage because they cannot expand.

Planning tools for coastal protection and development

First, we present a brief overview of two key planning documents in France: At the inter-municipal level, SCOTs, and at the local level, PLUs.

SCOTs (Territorial Coherence Schemes) are local-level plans which are developed through inter-municipal cooperation (between dozens and up to one hundred communes). SCOTs provide a general guide as to expected development outcomes. They are not mandatory, but in practice most coastal municipalities are covered by them.

SCOTs must be compatible with the Coastal Act. In effect, in the frame defined by jurisprudence, they give spatial form to the Law's provisions. Yet SCOTs may adapt those provisions to some extent, as required to cater to the local context. Once a provision of the Coastal Act is clarified or elaborated in the SCOT, PLUs (Local Urban Plans) must be compatible with the scheme.

Municipal councils may prepare and approve PLUs. These plans cover the entire territory of the municipality, including its maritime part. They are not mandatory, but most coastal cities and towns do have them.

Plans specific to the coastal zone

In addition to the above plans, coastal areas may be covered by State-approved Sea Development Schemes. These plans, introduced in 1983, may be either stand-alone documents or integrated within a SCOT. They provide an example of good integrated coastal management, as they apply both to the terrestrial and maritime areas. Unlike PLUs and SCOTs, Sea Development Schemes can regulate marine activities such as navigation or fishing. They must respect the Coastal Act but take precedence over PLUs and other local planning documents. While Sea Development Schemes are very innovative, they are, unfortunately, regarded as a failure due to the very low rate of their approval. Only four such Schemes have been adopted as standalone documents since their introduction in 1983,[10] and two have been integrated in SCOTs (one of which was initially standalone). This failure is due to the rather complex drafting procedure which requires collaboration with stakeholders with conflicting interests (fishing, industry, boating, fish or shellfish farming, etc.). The fact that Sea Development Schemes must be approved by the State is also a hindrance, as in general, planning is a decentralized power.

In 2010, another planning instrument was initiated by the Grenelle 2 Law specifically for the coastal zone. This is a regional strategic Coastal Zone Plan (in French, "sea façade" plans) which may be prepared for specific parts of the coastal zone (C. envir., art. L 219-3). Four such strategic schemes are under development, one for each of the four coastal councils introduced earlier in this chapter. The role of these plans is to give local expression to the National Strategy for the Sea and Coast (2017). The plans define regional policy for the development of marine activities, protection of the environment, and allocation of land to various uses at sea and on the coast. These plans should be approved by 2021 and will be binding on all other relevant plans and administrative actions.

Compliance and enforcement

As part of the special high protection accorded to the MPD, there are also special rules to enforce cases of non-compliance there. We first discuss these, and then enforcement issues in urban planning in the other land to which the Coastal Act applies.

Illegal use of the MPD is subject to a specific procedure known as *contravention de grande voirie* (literally, "contravention of large roads"). This procedure allows authorities to both bring criminal charge against the party which has harmed the public domain and oblige that party to restore the land to its previous state. It seems that this procedure has not been applied in a systematic way, especially with regard to beach concessions (Wellhoff et al., 2009). It is clear from the case law that the State is obliged to implement this procedure in case of illegal use of the public domain. In addition, a recent directive makes it clear to prefects that they are obligated to strictly enforce the rules for the MPD (Ministry of Ecology, Sustainable Development, Transport and Housing, 2012). Individuals and associations also have standing to ask the prefect to act and, in the event of refusal, to refer the matter to the first level of administrative court.

In general, illegal construction without any permit is not rampant in France. If development is carried out without authorization or is in violation of planning rules, this is considered a criminal offence (so are minor infringements of the permit). The Urban Planning Code authorizes the judge to impose fines of up to 6,000 euros per square metre of illegal construction (C. urb., art. L 480-4). Given the relatively low level of illegality, especially when compared to some other South European countries, such fines are rarely issued (Pelletier, 2005).

More frequent are challenges to the legality of the permits themselves. Because the legality of development permits is predicated on compliance with the Coastal Act, when issuing building permits local governments' exercise of discretion may be subject to legal challenges. The number of appeals to the court is significant even though recent laws have attempted to reduce them. The outcomes of these lawsuits can be uncertain, especially given that the rules with which building permits must comply are subject to interpretation or discretion. The wording of the Coastal Act as it applies to building permits is especially open to interpretation: As we have seen, the Coastal Act obliges local government to apply several norms (all undoubtedly based on good planning practice) that do not have a numeric or geographic definition and thus rely on a considerable level of discretion. These include carrying capacity, compact development, and even the definition of "close to the shore".

In French law, third parties, such as neighbours, nongovernment associations, and state authorities, may challenge the legality of a permit granted by a local authority. In such cases, the permit decision may be subject to administrative judicial review. If a building permit is found to be illegal, it may be voided by the administrative courts. These courts can issue injunctions to stop construction, but they cannot require demolition (discussed below). Such court challenges could take two to three years, during which the builder is in a state of uncertainty. But the situation has improved since 2018, given a decree (C. urb., art. R 600-6) which now forces the administrative tribunal to issue a decision within ten months where the case relates to a building permit for two or more dwellings. Voiding of a permit does not imply an obligation to demolish.

In France, injunctions and demolition orders entail a separate legal procedure before the civil courts, and such procedures are also drawn out. Since 2015, obtaining a demolition order after the building permit has been voided has been made even more difficult. In an attempt to enhance certainty for developers who do hold a building permit, the law limits demolition procedures by third parties only to buildings located in sensitive areas (Urban Planning Code, C. urb., art. L 480-13). These sensitive areas do include the 100 m coastal setback zone, Significant Coastal Sites, and sites marked as undevelopable in disaster prevention plans. For all other areas within the coastal zone, the legal capacity to begin a demolition procedure before the civil court has been significantly reduced. This limitation does not apply to cases of illegal construction. In such cases, the criminal court can fine the builder and order the demolition. The criminal chamber of the Court of Cassation has recently reiterated that in addition to the issue of a fine, a building built without a permit must be demolished. This came in a case in which a landowner had illegality built two villas with an area of 670 m² on a Significant Site in Corsica. The Court of Appeal of Bastia fined him 1,000,000 euros but did not order a demolition. That court's decision was this overturned by the Court of Cassation (19 mars 2019, n° 18-80869).

Public participation

French law does not require any special or enhanced public participation procedures for coastal areas. In general, French law complies with the principles laid down by the Rio Declaration and the Arhus Convention which relate to access to environmental information and public participation.

Access to administrative information is ensured by a 1978 law which sets out the rights of the public. Environmental documents may be accessed as soon as they are completed, regardless of decision-making processes of which they may be a part (art. L 300-1 onwards, Law No. 78-753).

The Urban Planning Code sets out the requirements for public participation in the preparation of planning regulations, including PLUs and SCOTs. With the exception of minor changes, the drafting process of a plan requires both consultation and a public inquiry. The aim of the consultation (C. urb., art. L 103-2) is to determine the position of the public from the beginning, and during the whole drafting process. The public inquiry (art. L 143-22 for the SCOT and art. L 153-19 and 20 for the PLU) is organized at the end of the planning process, before the final approval of the plan; public opinion is sought on the completed document.

Authorities have discretion as to the form that consultation on plans takes. In general, consultation involves a mix of public meetings, exhibition of documents, and the opportunity for the public to provide comment. Authorities must determine the consultation procedure from the start of the plan preparation process, and the consultation must last throughout the entire drafting process.

The procedure for the public inquiry is strictly defined by the Environment Code (C. envir., art. L 123-1 and on). The public inquiry is placed under the authority of a commissioner designated by the president of the administrative tribunal. This commissioner has broad powers to ensure the best information is provided to the public. They can organize public meetings, extend the duration of the inquiry (beyond the standard month), ask for any documents, and, if needed, seek the advice of an expert.

The Urban Planning Code also provide that at the initiative of the municipality or of the developer, a consultation (as defined by C. urb., art. L 103-2) may be organized for a building project. Such a consultation must be conducted before the building permit application (C. urb., art. L 300-2).

In some cases, defined by the Urban Planning Code and Environment Code, a building permit must undergo a public inquiry process. Such is the case for permits relating to exceptions in the 100 m setback zone (C. urb., art. L 121-24 and L 121-17). In addition, a building permit relating to land in a Significant Site is also subject to a public participation process, which may include a public inquiry or, more simply, public exhibition. The requirements depend on the nature of the project and are set out in the Environment Code.

Response to climate change

As it was introduced in 1986 and is primarily focused on landscape protection and public use of the beach, the Coastal Act mostly does not directly address the more recent concerns of climate change and rising sea levels. But recently, discussion of the effects of climate change on coastal areas arose in parliament (Prieur & Leost, 2015). As a result, a 2016 amendment to the Coastal Act integrated the risk of submersion into the definition of carrying capacity. This change also allows municipalities to extend the 100 m setback zone through local plans (PLUs).

The potential implications of climate change are taken into account in several pieces of French regulation. Flooding risk and sea level rise are addressed by both PLUs and SCOTs and by Natural Hazard Prevention Plans, which are specialized urban planning documents approved by the State (C. envir., art. L 562-1). These plans cover only areas where a specific risk has been identified.

PLUs and Natural Hazard Prevention Plans have the same legal weight; the law does not prioritize one over the other. Building permits must comply with both. But there is coordination, given that case law has established that a planning document may not authorize construction in an area identified as under threat in a risk prevention plan and that a plan which did so would be illegal.[11] In addition, every municipality must apply general urban rules set by the Urban Planning Code. According to one of these rules (C. urb., art. R 111-2), a building permit application may be refused in the case of natural risk.

Unfortunately, Natural Hazard Prevention Plans prepared before 2010 were based on underestimates of submersion due to sea level rise. This issue was identified in the wake of Cyclone Xynthia, which swept northwest Europe in February 2010, killing more than 40 people in France. The State has since launched a policy of re-evaluation of Natural Hazard Prevention Plans and, in 2013, released maps of areas at risk of submersion. These maps are based on a sea level calculated over a 100-year return period plus 20 cm. As such, Natural Hazard Prevention Plans are under revision or have already been revised to integrate this new data. In the meantime, or if the relevant parts of the coastline are not covered by Natural Hazard Prevention Plans, although the risk maps have no direct legal force, they may serve as ground for refusing building permit applications (C. urb., art. R 111-2).

Fiscal aspects of French coastal regulation

In this section we address fees related to occupation of the MPD and compensation for regulatory takings.

Fees

The General Code of Territorial Communities provides that any occupation (even illegal) of the public domain is subject to a fee, payable to the State. In 2013, the total sum of such fees to the State was 27.3 million euros (Charpin et al., 2014).

In the case of beach concessions, the right to occupy the land is granted by the State to the municipality or, in some cases, to private companies (e.g. the concession holder at the beach of La Baule is VEOLIA, a company specializing in public service management), who pay concession fees to the State. The beach is then sublet to operators by the municipalities. In the case of marine farm concessions or occupation permits issued by the State, the fee is paid directly to the State by the occupant.

With the exception of marine farms concessions for which the fee is defined at the national level, the amount due by the MPD occupant is determined by the State, but at the department level, which leads to significant differences. The fee can be, but is not always, calculated according to the square metreage (e.g. euros per square metre) sometimes without any consideration for the profit made by the lessee. A 2014 report on the MPD fees noted that Deauville beach was granted to the municipality for a fee of 4,000 euros but subleased by the municipality for 200,000 euros (Charpin et al., 2014, p. 17). Yet research has indicated that the fees are too low when compared with similar fees charged in other European states (Grenelle de l'Environnement, Operational Committee no. 12, 2008, p. 11).

If any construction is built on the MPD, the occupant will pay an additional development tax. This tax is collected by the municipality. The fee is determined according to the rights granted to the permit holder.

In case of illegal occupation of the MPD, a fee is due by the occupant, who can also be fined through the *contravention de grande voirie* procedure described above.

Compensation

French law explicitly prohibits compensation for regulatory takings (i.e. reduction of value of land when an urban plan is amended or cancelled for any reason; Renard, 2010). There are only three exceptions. The first two are outlined in the Urban Planning Code and apply particularly where the restriction infringes on a vested right – for example, where the classification of land is modified during the construction process. This is very rare because the Urban Planning Code stipulates that when a developer is authorized to develop a subdivision, the existing planning rules are guaranteed for five years.

The third exception was created by case law of the Council of State in 1988 in response to the provisions of the European Convention on Human Rights: Compensation is due when a restriction causes an excessive loss to the landholder which is out of proportion with the general public interest pursued (CE, 3 juillet 1998, Bitouzet, req. n° 158592). This rule is interpreted very narrowly. To date, the Council of State has granted compensation only once on this basis since 1988 (CE, 29 juin 2016, req. n° 375020). Thus, in general practice, no compensation is due when a plot of land is rendered undevelopable by the Coastal Act or local planning regulations which protect the coast.

But there is another avenue to compensation, one which is used more frequently. French administrative law allows a person who has suffered damages due to illegal decision-making by government or municipalities to obtain compensation. Members of the public regularly bring these types of liability actions in response to urban planning decisions, along the following lines – with examples related to coastal issues:

Say an urban planning regulation classifies land as developable in violation of the Coastal Act. Prior to the sale of land, a notary representing the seller will apply to the local government for a certificate of urban planning, confirming that the land area is developable. Such certificates enhance the value of land and play an important role in the land transaction market. If a new owner is later granted a building permit by the municipality and the legality of the permit is successfully challenged (by neighbours, an association, or the Prefect – the national government authority), that owner can submit a compensation claim against the municipality and, in most cases, the municipality will be required to compensate for the loss of value of the land (CAA Nantes, 10 novembre 2009, req. n° 08NT01567).

These types of disputes are more and more frequent, indicating that planning regulations do not adequately address the planning law. They are problematic because the compensation sums required are very high for municipal budgets. Some municipalities have difficulties in finding an insurance company willing to ensure against such claims.

Coordination in coastal zone management

Numerous authorities have responsibilities associated with management of the French coast. At the State level, the Ministry of Ecology is the main responsible agency. Coordination among ministers is ensured by the Inter-ministerial Committee on the Sea, which meets periodically, and by the General Secretariat for the Sea, which is a permanent body.

Local authorities have a wide range of responsibilities on the coast. The regions manage the maritime ports of commerce, government grants, etc. The Departments are responsible for fishing ports, island servicing, and sensitive environmental areas. The municipalities are responsible for local planning.

In order to ensure better coordination, a National Council for the Sea and Coastal Areas was set up in January 2014. The Council is responsible for presenting proposals to the Government for coordinated public action on the coast. It is supported by Coastal Councils, which ensure the representation of relevant stakeholders and which are in charge of preparing the strategic Coastal Zone Plans (discussed above).

Since 2006, the various environmental protection areas (Natura 2000 sites, marine parks, nature reserves, etc.) are coordinated by an agency for Marine Protected Areas under the Ministry of Ecology.

Overall assessment

French law has produced a relatively complete coastal development scheme. On some points, it is more binding than the ICZM Protocol to the Barcelona Convention. This is particularly true for the specific rules which limit urban development in the coastal zone. The instruments exist; what is required is clarification of the scope and better coordination across legislation and regulation to ensure true integration. Sea Development Schemes, which were intended to take a coordinated and integrated approach, have failed due to a burdensome and uncoordinated drafting process. Instead, the National Strategy for the Sea and Coast (2017) has taken on this role.

Notes

1. This figure does not include the territories of Antilles and Guyana, Mayotte Island and scattered islands, French Polynesia, New Caledonia, Wallis and Futuna, Artic and Antarctica, St. Pierre and Miquelon, and Clipperton Island.
2. This average figure hides significant variations. The density varies from 100 inhabitants per square metre on the island of Corsica or in the west Atlantic shore to 500 inhabitants per square metre in the southeast and southwest (ONML, n.d.).
3. The pre-emption rights were granted by Article 65 of Law no. 60-1384 (la loi n° 60-1384 du 23 décembre 1960 de finances pour 1961; JO 24 déc. 1960, p. 11628). On this question see Toulemonde (1978), p. 645.
4. In France, a *grenelle* is a negotiation process between government and the public. The term originates from the Grenelle agreements (named for the street in Paris where the Ministry of Labor is located), negotiated in 1968.
5. The decree which establishes the list of municipalities bordering estuaries was not issued until March 2004, following a condemnation of the Government by the Council of State (CE, 28 juill. 2000, req. n° 204024)

6. This provision primarily relates to the Mediterranean coastline, where the maritime public domain is relatively narrow.
7. A 2018 law (Law n° 2018-1021) provides for SCOTs to give spatial expression to provisions of the Coastal Act relating to urban clustering and green buffers (code de l'urbanisme art. L 121-3). This was common practice previously but is now clearly stipulated by law. The implications are potentially significant. Previously, the SCOT was binding only on the PLU (local plan) while applications for building permits were to be assessed directly according to the criteria in the Coastal Act, particularly if challenged in court. As a consequence of the 2018 law, once the SCOT identifies the location of the relevant development clusters, its policies may be applied directly to decisions about building permits. The Council of State recently made an important decision which supports this elevated role of the SCOTs in relation to the Coastal Act (CE, 11 mars 2020, Confédération Environnement Méditerannée, n° 41986).
8. The notion of carrying capacity is also mentioned in Article 19 of the ICZM Protocol.
9. This rule echos the ICZM Protocol's call for limitation linear urbanization (Art. 8)
10. Thau Lagoon, 1995; Arcachon Basin, 2004; Gulf of Morbihan, 2006; Trégor-Goëlo Basin, 2007.
11. The administrative court considers that zoning which is clearly unsuited to the de facto status is illegal (CE, 23 mars 1979, Commune de Bouchemaine, D 1979, p. 534, note D. Broussolle; A.J.D.A. 20 mai 1979, pp. 95 et 80, chronique O. Dutheillet de Lamothe et Y. Robineau).

References

Alterman, R. (Ed.). (2001). *National-Level Planning in Democratic Countries: An International Comparison of City and Regional-Policy Making*. Liverpool University Press.

Braud, X. (2013). La gestion intégrée des zones côtières et le droit de l'urbanisme littoral en France [Integrated coastal zone management and coastal planning law in France]. *VertigO – The Electronic Journal in Environmental Sciences*, Special Issue 18 (December). Available at: http://vertigo.revues.org/14259; doi: 10.4000/vertigo.14259

Calderaro, N. (2008). Le protocole de Madrid et la loi littoral [The Madrid Protocol and the Coastal Act]. *Bulletin de jurisprudence du droit de l'urbanisme* (BJDU) *[Bulletin of Jurisprudence of the Law of Urbanism]* 3.

Chadenas, C., Pouillaude, A., Pottier, P., & Struillou, J. F. (2010). *Évaluer la capacité d'accueil et de développement des territoires littoraux* [Assessing the Carrying Capacity and the Development of Coastal Territories]. Pays de la Loire. Available at: http://www.pays-de-la-loire.developpement-durable.gouv.fr/guide-pratique-2eme-edition-a436.html

Charpin, J., Clément, D., de Galbert, M., & Weymuller, B. (2014). *Les redevances d'occupation du domaine public naturel: Rapport de l'inspection Générale des finances* [Occupancy Fees in the Natural Public Domain: Report of the General Inspectorate of Finance]. May 2014. 78 pages. Available at: https://www.ladocumentationfrancaise.fr/var/storage/rapports-publics/174000415.pdf

Colas, S. (2015). Économie maritime et des territoires littoraux: Activités économiques littorales et maritimes [Maritime Economy and Coastal Territories: Coastal and Maritime Economic Activities]. Observatoire national de la mer et du littoral. Available at: https://www.onml.fr/articles/les-emplois-de-leconomie-maritime-donnees-2015/

Conservatoire du littoral. (n.d.). Conservatoire du littoral. [Coastal Conservatory]. Available at: http://www.conservatoire-du-littoral.fr/3-le-conservatoire.htm. [Accessed July 2020].

Grenelle de l'Environnement, Operational Committee no. 12. (2008). Report on 'Integrated management of the sea and the coast'.

IFOP. (2014). *Les Français et l'aménagement du littoral* [The French and Coastal Management]. Available at: https://www.ifop.com/wp-content/uploads/2018/03/2696-1-study_file.pdf

Le Louarn, P. (1995). Departmental policies for the protection of sensitive natural areas on the Coastline. *LPA* (1).

Ministry of Ecology, Sustainable Development, Transport and Housing. (2012). Circulaire du 20 janvier 2012 relative à la gestion durable et intégrée du domaine public maritime naturel [Circular on the sustainable and integrated management of the natural maritime public domain], 20 January. Available at: http://circulaire.legifrance.gouv.fr/pdf/2012/04/cir_35125.pdf

Ministry of Ecology, Sustainable Development and Energy. (2014). *Etat des lieux Mer et Littoral rapport Final* [State of the Sea and Coasts. Final Report], October. Office of the Commissioner General for Sustainable Development. Available at: http://webissimo.developpement-durable.gouv.fr/IMG/pdf/Rapport_-_Etat_des_lieux_mer_et_littoral_cle76f2cb.pdf

Ministry for the Ecological and Solidary Transition. (2017). National Strategy for the Sea and Coast, Decree 2017-222 of 23 February 2017. Available at: http://www.geolittoral.developpement-durable.gouv.fr/IMG/pdf/17094_strategie-nationale-pour-la-mer-et-le-littoral_en_fev2017.pdf

ONML – Observatoire National de la Mer et du Littoral [National Observatory of the Sea and Coasts]. (n.d.). Démographie, occupation du sol et logement [Demography, land use and housing]. Available at: https://www.onml.fr/chiffres-cles/cadrage-general/demographie-occupation-du-sol-et-logement/

Pelletier, P. (2005). Propositions pour une meilleur sécurité juridique des autorisations d'urbanisme: Rapport au garde des sceaux et au ministre de l'équipement [Proposals for a better legal certainty of urban planning authorizations: Report to the Keeper of the Seals and the Minister of Urban Planning], January. Available at: http://www.ladocumentationfrancaise.fr/var/storage/rapports-publics/054000147.pdf

Piquard, M. (Ed.). (1973). Perspectives pour l'aménagement du littoral français [Perspectives for the development of the French shoreline]. Doc. fr., 1974.

Prieur, L., & Leost, R. (2015). La prise en compte de la submersion marine par la loi littoral [Taking submersion into account in the Coastal Act]. *VertigO – The Electronic Journal in Environmental Sciences*, Series 21 (April). Available at: http://vertigo.revues.org/15823; doi: 10.4000/vertigo.15823

Prieur, L. (2012). L'accès au rivage [Access to the shore]. *Revue juridique de l'environnement 5*, 93–103. Available at: https://www.persee.fr/doc/rjenv_0397-0299_2012_hos_37_1_5763

— (2014). *La loi Littoral* [The Coastal Act]. Voiron: Groupe Territorial.

— (2018). La loi littoral et les outils juridiques de gouvernance des collectivités locales [The littoral law and the legal tools of governance of local authorities]. *Bulletin juridique des collectivités locales 3*, 184–190.

Renard, V. A. (2010). France. Chapter 7 in Rachelle Alterman (Ed.), *Takings International: A Comparative Perspective on Land Use Regulations and Compensation Rights*. pp. 139–148.

Tanguy, Y. (1991). Les servitudes de passage le long du littoral [Access easement along the coast]. RDI 1991 (January–March), pp. 7–18.

Toulemonde, B. (1978). Les périmètres sensibles [Sensitive areas]. *Actualite Juridique Droit Administratif* (December) pp. 645–.

Valin, R.-J. (1981). Nouveau commentaire sur l'ordonnance de la Marine du mois d'août 1681 [New comment on the order of the Navy of August 1681], t. II: éd. originale 1760, réédition Droit maritime français et *Journal de la marine marchande.*

Wellhoff, F., Allain, Y.-M., Chalvron, J.-G., & de Goulam, Y. (2009). *Les difficultés d'application du décret relatif aux concessions de plage* [The Difficulties in Implementing the Beach Concessions Decree]. Report for the General Council of the Environment and Sustainable Development, January. Available at: http://www.ladocumentationfrancaise.fr/rapports-publics/094000132/index.shtml

World Factbook. (n.d.). France. Available at: https://www.cia.gov/library/publications/the-world-factbook/geos/fr.html [Accessed September 2019]

Legislation (listed chronologically)

Urban Planning Code (C. urb.)
Environment Code (C. envir.)
General Code of Public Property (CGPPP)
Colbert's Great Ordinance of Marine (the marine code), 1681

Decree No. 59-768 of 26 June 1959 for the conservation of the coast of Provence

Law No. 63-1178 of 28 November 1963 on the maritime public domain

Law No. 78-753 of 17 July 1978 on various measures to improve relations between the administration and the public

Law No. 86-2 of 3 January 1986 for the preservation and the management of the coast (Coastal Act)

Decree No. 2006-608 of 26 May 2006 on beach concessions

Law No. 2010-788 of 12 July 2010 for a national commitment to the Environment (Grenelle 2 Law)

Conseil d'Etat (CE) [Council of State] – Cases

CE, 19 mai 1858, Vernes, Rec. p. 399, D. 1859, III, p. 51

CE, 3 mai 1963, Commune de Saint-Brévin-les-Pins, R.D.P. 1963, p. 1174, note Marcel Waline

CE, 30 mars 1973, min. Aménag. territ., Équip., Aménag. et Tourisme c/ Schwetzoff et a., n° 88151: AJDA July–August 1973, p. 366, note J. Dufau

CE, 12 oct. 1973, Kreitmann: Rec. CE 1973, p. 563; RDP 1974, p. 1150, concl. M. Gentot

CE, 20 févr. 1981, Commune de Saint-Quay-Portrieux: Rec. Conseil d'Etat 1981, p. 96; AJDA 1981, p. 476; D. 1982, jurispr. p. 351, note F. Moderne

CE, 21 juin 1996, S.A.R.L. Aquamed et autres et secrétaire d'Etat à la mer, req. n° 136044 et 137008, Rec. Tables p. 866

CE, 9 oct. 1996, Union départementale Vie et Nature 83 req. n° 161555

CE, 3 juillet 1998, Bitouzet, req. n° 158592

CE, 5 juill. 1999, Comité local pêches maritimes et élevages marins Noirmoutier et comité local pêches maritimes et élevages marins Loire-Atlantique Sud, req. n° 197287

CE, 28 juill. 2000, France Nature Environnement, req. n° 204024, Dr. env., n° 82, oct. 2000, p. 8, note L. Le Corre

CE, 11 févr. 2004, Société anonyme France, req. n° 212855, AJDA 7 juin 2004, p. 1151

CE, 27 sept. 2006, Commune de Lavandou, req. n° 275924, BJDU 2007, n° 1, p. 46, concl. C. Devys

CE, 22 févr. 2008, Bazarbachi, req. n° 280189, BJDU 2008, n° 2, p. 89, concl. Y. Aguila

CE, 3 juin 2009, Commune de Rognac, req. n° 310587, BJDU 2009, n° 3, p. 208, concl. M. Guyomar

CE, 30 septembre 2011, Lenoël, req. n° 336664

CE, 9 novembre 2015, Commune de Porto-Vecchio, req. n° 372531

CE, 29 juin 2016, req. n° 375020

CE, 31 mars 2017, Society "Savoie Lac investissement", req. n° 392186

CE, 10 juillet 2020, France Nature Environnement, n° 432944

Cour Administrative d'Appel (CAA) [Administrative Court of Appeals]

CAA Marseille, 6 avr. 2016, n° 15MA03273, SARL Chêne Roc

CAA Nantes, 10 novembre 2009, Groupama Loire-Bretagne, req. n° 08NT01567

CAA Nantes, 10 octobre 2014, Commune de Saint-Philibert, req. n° 13NT00220

Other courts

Cour de cassation [Court of Cassation], 19 mars 2019, n° 18-80869

Cons. const. (Conseil constitutionnel) [Constitutional Council] décision n° 2013-316 QPC du 24 mai 2013

Depalle v. France [GC], no. 34044/02, § 77, ECHR 2010

Brosset-Triboulet and Others v. France [GC], no. 34078/02, § 80, ECHR 2010

10 Italy

Enzo Falco and Angela Barbanente

Overview

Italy's story of coastal law and regulation reflects the country's challenges of governance and the differences across regions (sub-national authorities) in capacity to meet these challenges. The country's sunny coastal land is a magnet not only for second homes and tourists but also for illegal development. Italy also faces significant issues of institutional coordination. The high fragmentation of laws and regulations seems to be the main issue that needs to be somehow tackled if better practice for protection and management of coastal areas is to be achieved.

Given the large differences between regions, this chapter tells two stories: In addition to the national level, this chapter also focuses on a selected region – Puglia, in the south-east. This region faces major challenges in coastal preservation yet in recent years has developed ambitious regulations and statutory plans to improve the management of its coasts.

The national law defines a 300 m setback zone, but regional and local plans can override restrictions. Enforcement against illegalities is fragmented among many municipalities and differs from one region to another. In some areas, the Mafia has undue influence. Although there has been some progress, regional and urban planning regulations have not yet been able to stop the illegal construction.

PART I: The national level

The context: Introduction to Italy's coastal issues

Italy's coastline is about 7,600 km long (MATTM, 2014a; World Factbook, n.d.), making it the second longest in the Mediterranean, after Greece. As is common around the world, Italy's coast attracts a disproportionately large population: The total area of Italy's 644 coastal municipalities (illustrated at Figure 10.1) is around 14% of the total national land area, yet the total population of these municipalities represents 28% of the total national population (Istat, 2019). Furthermore, the average population density of Italy's coastal municipalities is 400 inhabitants per square kilometre, more than double the density (168 inhabitants per square kilometre) of inland municipalities (Istat, 2017).

Despite the law which sets strict rules about development within 300 m of the shoreline (Legislative Decree 42/2004, discussed below), construction within this zone has rapidly increased in the last 50 years (ISPRA, 2011) with the central regions that show rates of developed land to be over 50% of the total. To date, 34% (692 km^2) of the land has been developed

Figure 10.1 Italy's coastal municipalities and regions

Source: Image by Enzo Falco

(both legally and illegally). In addition, in the central regions, which have undergone significant development in the last fifty years, over half of the land within 300 m of the shoreline, including cities, is developed (Abruzzo, 62%; Marche, 59%; and Emilia-Romagna, 55%). Nationally, 53% of coastal land within 300 m of the shoreline is developed (ISPRA, 2011, p. 263).

Evolution of the legal framework for coastal zone management

Italy's system for safeguarding and regulating the coastal zone is quite complex. Maritime domain laws, rights of use, landscape and urban planning laws, national policies and strategies, Civil Code, and Navigation Code regulations all overlap to protect coastal areas from unregulated and illegal development, uses, and general damage. Yet, as we will demonstrate later in the chapter, enforcement of these laws is weak, leading to rampant illegal development.

In Italy, legislation for coastal protection is part of broader environmental legislation pertaining to "landscape". The foundation for Italy's environmental laws is Article 9 of the Italian Constitution, which states that as a fundamental principle, the Italian Republic safeguards its "landscape" (Amato, 2001). Legal provisions relating specifically to protection of the coast were first introduced in 1939, through the law "Protection of Natural Beauty" (Law 1497/39). More recently, two laws in the 1980s strengthened the legal protections for coastal areas: The 1982 law "Provisions for the Defence of the Sea" (Law 979/82) and the 1985 law on "Urgent provisions for the protection of areas of particular environmental interest" (Law 431/85), which established a coastal setback zone on land within 300 m of the shoreline. In addition, a general law for "environmentally protected areas" (Law 394/91) protects environmental assets across Italy.

The Law 979/82 established a framework for preparation of a national "General Mercantile Plan for the safeguard of sea and coasts", but such a plan was never prepared. The 1985 law, however, was more effective: It introduced special controls over development in a 300 m zone – described here as a "setback zone". The 1939 and 1985 laws have since been superseded, first in 1999 by a law on "cultural and environmental assets" (Law 490/99), then in 2004 by the Code on Cultural Heritage and Landscape (Law 42/2004; henceforth the 2004 Code).

Italy's Civil Code (Article 822) and the Navigation Code (Article 28) both define the sections of land along the coast that fall within the maritime public domain. The Navigation Code contains extensive provisions regarding the definition, acquisition, and use of the maritime public domain, as will be discussed below.

Until 1967, legislation which defined and regulated the use of the maritime public domain (the Civil Code and the Navigation Code) took precedence over urban planning legislation and urban plans (Casanova, 1986; Virga, 1995; Conio, 2010). But in 1967, the "Legge Ponte" (Law 765/67, bridging law) reformed the national Planning Law (1942). Since that time, public works carried out on public domain, including maritime public domain, must be in accordance with the provisions of the relevant binding urban plan (Law 765/67, Article 10). Authorization from the relevant mayor is required for works carried out by third parties within the public domain. This represents a major change from the previous regime, as it means acknowledging that public domain areas are part of the territory and therefore subject to urban planning policy and regulations.

Significantly, the 2004 Code changed the paradigm for coastal protection in Italy, as it delegated significant powers to the regional governments (but not all; e.g. environmentally protected areas under Law 394/91 are planned jointly by the relevant region and the State). While the Code still lists land within 300 m of the shoreline as protected and subject to restrictions on development, it leaves it up to the regions to regulate specific restrictions, through *pianificazione paesaggistica* (landscape planning). Under Section III of the 2004 Code, each region is required to prepare a landscape plan which should detail how natural areas, including land within the coastal setback zone, are to be protected and managed. The Code also states (at Article 143) that the regional landscape plan must identify areas where construction or other activities are permitted, based on special authorization by the responsible authority (Luchetti, 2006). Any provisions included in regional landscape plans take precedence over local urban plans. The 2004 Code has been amended twice – in 2006 and 2008. The amendments further specified the list of natural and protected areas and their protection and safeguard through *pianificazione paesaggistica.*

Italy has not yet ratified the Integrated Coastal Zone Management (ICZM) Protocol to the Barcelona Convention, which was adopted by the European Council in 2008. As far as we know, the Protocol and its ratification are not perceived as major issue on policymakers' tables, and there is no visible public discussion.

Maritime public domain – definition and permitted uses

Italy's Civil and Navigation Codes define a maritime public domain (MPD), which is coastal land owned by the State. The purposes of the MPD, and public domain land in general, is to fulfil the need and interest of the public (De Martino et al., 1976). The Civil Code defines the maritime public domain as follows (Article 822):

> The shore of the sea, the beach, the bays and the ports belong to the State and belong to the public domain.

Similarly, the Navigation Code (Article 28) lists the following as being part of the maritime public domain:

a   the shore, the beach, harbours/ports and bays;
b   lagoons, river mouths/estuaries that flow into the sea, basins of salt or brackish water that flow freely to and from the sea, at least during a part of the year;
c   canals that can be used for maritime public use.

The classifications in the two codes differ terminologically but not substantially. Scholars acknowledge that the definition found in the Navigation Code is more detailed but that all the listed elements fall within the general categories identified in the Civil Code (Avanzi, 2000; Gullo, 2006). We note that the elements (shore, beach, etc.) are not specifically defined in the law, which affects legal certainty for landowners.

Delineation of the shoreline and MPD

Italy's shoreline is defined separately from the landward boundary of the MPD. The shoreline is generally identified through the interpretation of aerial orthophotos on the basis of calm sea (it is not clear whether this refers to low tide or mean sea level, but it is not high tide).

The shoreline is delineated on the official cadastre, and its demarcation is the responsibility of the State through the Minister for the Environment. Regions may define and demarcate their shoreline through *pianificazione paesaggistica* (landscape planning) and regional landscape plans in collaboration with the Ministry for Cultural Heritage Activities and Tourism, but only for the purposes of coastal landscape protection under the responsibility of this ministry. The Puglia region discussed below is one of the regions which has elected to demarcate its shoreline.

The natural parts of the shoreline and their delineation are subject to erosion and change. As Gaeta (1965) notes, the shoreline follows the sea, taking into account tidal patterns and coastal erosion. It follows that the shoreline changes continuously. The delineation is updated at random intervals by the Ministry for the Environment, but the reassessment procedure is not set out in the law.

The demarcation of the shoreline contributes to the demarcation of the maritime public domain; anything seaward of the shoreline is "automatically" owned by the State as public domain. The technical procedures for the landward delineation of the MPD are stipulated by the Navigation Code, which states that public domain is determined on the basis of the highest water mark. In this case too, reassessment of the MPD areas happens at random intervals. Decree 78/2015 (Art. 7) provides that regions and the State should collaborate to define a periodic redefinition of the MPD, though the time periods and procedures remain undefined. As the MPD is State-owned, the power to determine its limits rests with the State (through the Ministries for Transport and Infrastructure, Economy and Finance, other interested ministries, and the maritime authorities). Even in cases where another administration (e.g. regional government) is responsible for the management of that specific part of the MPD, it is still the State that has the power to determine its boundaries. Such a delimitation power represents an instance of the exercise by the State of the self-protection power (*potere di autotutela*). In cases where the State needs to expand the MPD beyond the already identified areas, the State may expropriate bordering private properties.

Private properties which are permanently affected by flooding or erosion which causes shores and beaches to disappear become part of the public domain *ipso iure* (Querci, 1959; Gaeta, 1965). The implications on the affected property are clear: The property is automatically expropriated and transferred to the State. Private landowners have the right to appeal against a delimitation decision, either to the ordinary court (regarding suitability of the land to be included in the MPD) or to the administrative court which settles disputes between private citizens and public institutions.

Issues related to shoreline erosion and change were highlighted in the preparation process for Puglia's Regional Coastal Plan (2012, described below), where investigation indicated that the previously designated MPD had narrowed in many places, expanded in others, and, in some places, even disappeared entirely under the sea. In these cases, the regional administration must undertake a complicated and lengthy procedure for the modification of shoreline delineation, which is subject to authorization by the national government.

Status of the maritime public domain

The maritime domain falls within the category of public assets. As such, the maritime domain is inalienable: No area can be sold, and if this happens, the selling contract is to be considered null and void. The public domain is not subject to prescription rules and cannot be acquired by continued and regular use. It also cannot be expropriated by any government authority (it is already public) unless a specific State act cancels the public domain status. The public domain is generally not subject to rights that favour third parties except for specific cases, such as concessions for beach resorts.

Ownership and management of maritime public domain

The body of law regarding the owner and administrative functions related to the maritime domain is complex and has undergone numerous changes over time, especially on matters concerning delegation to the regional governments. The debate over who owns maritime goods and the responsibility to manage and administer them revolves around whether the manager of the goods can, or should, be considered the owner. Following long debates regarding delegation, the State (national government) remains the owner of all maritime goods with the exception of those in the Sicily Region, in which ownership of the goods was transferred to the regional authority through the D.P.R. (Decree of the President of the Italian Republic) 684 of 1977 (Salamone, 2004).

Prior to 1977, the maritime public domain was managed by the State. In 1977, a Decree of the President (no. 616) transferred management of tourism and recreational uses in the maritime public domain to the regional governments. The State retained management powers relating to national safety, immigration police, harbours, and areas of national navigation interest. This represented the first attempt of delegation of administrative functions from the State to the regions, but there was no real delegation of powers until almost twenty years later. In 1995, through a decree of the Prime Minister, the State and regional management responsibilities were formally clarified. Then, over 1997–1998, the functions were transferred to the regions (through Law 59/1997 and Legislative Decree 112/1998, which established administrative federalism, *federalismo amministrativo*). The purpose was to identify the functions that were of exclusive responsibility of the national government and leave all other functions to the regional and local administrations' responsibility.

In 2001, the Constitution (Section V) was amended (by Constitutional Law 3 of 2001) to assign all the administrative functions of the State to the municipalities (Article 118, Section 1 of the Constitution). Thus, all administrative functions are attributed to the municipalities except when these are more adequately exercised by a higher-tier administration, on the basis of principles of adequacy, subsidiarity, and differentiation.

Land use in the maritime public domain

Any use of the maritime public domain is subject to an authorization in the form of a "concession" (ground lease) between the managing authority and the party seeking to use the land. The Navigation Code regulates concessions and differentiates between concessions granted for different time periods (over 15 years; between 4 and 15 years; less than 4 years). The Ministry for Infrastructure and Transportation is responsible for granting concessions for a period of time over 15 years, while the other concessions are the responsibility of the Maritime Authority.

Concessions for beach resorts, commercial activities, and boat rentals generally last for a period of six years and, until 2011, were automatically renewed at the end of that period for another six years (Law 296 of 2006 *Financial and Budget Law*, which amended Decree 400 of 1993 *Provisions to determine fees for MPD concessions*). Following an infringement procedure initiated by the European Commission in 2008,[1] in 2011 the Italian authorities repealed the part of the Financial and Budget Law which provided for automatic renewal of concessions in the MPD. Thus, concessions in the maritime public domain now expire. Originally, the 2011 amendment provided a transitional period of up to 2015, before concessions expired. Another extension was granted in 2012 (Law 221/2012), allowing existing beach concessions to remain in place until 31 December 2020.

The extensions for concessions were contentious, and the debate reached the Council of State (the highest administrative court), which determined that the 2012 extension was not compatible with the European Community principles of free competition and equal opportunity for businesses. The Council of State thus referred the question to the Court of Justice of the European Union (CJEU). The CJEU (C-458/14) determined that extensions are no longer possible and private businesses that intend to use the MPD for economic reasons must submit to a tender to win a contract.

The Navigation Code and Civil Code stipulate that structures erected in the MPD must be "easily removable". After a long period of uncertainty regarding this requirement, various national and regional rules have established that "removability" does not imply that a structure must necessarily be dismantled at the end of the bathing season or when beaches are closed and that it can be kept on site for the entire duration of the concession. Structures may be built on concrete platforms or supported with concrete in the foundations (Ministero dei Trasporti e della Navigazione, Circolare no.120/2001). However, the Regions are authorized to make stricter rules, as we shall see in the Puglia case study.

In order to regulate the use of the maritime public domain for tourism and recreation activities, each regional authority must produce a "utilization plan" which specifies detailed regulations, used also to guide tenders for granting concessions for such activities (Piano di Utilizzazione delle aree Demaniali Marittime, PUD). Apart from specifying quantitative rules for permitted uses, these plans should also aim to ensure the right of public access to the shore, as discussed below. Given that the use of maritime public domain for tourism and recreation has potentially significant impacts on the coastal environment, requests for concessions for these uses are subject to environmental impact assessments (Licciardello, 2008).

When beach-bathing operators apply for permission to erect "easily removable structures" within the public domain, due to the landscape protection of the 300 m setback zone they require authorization from the local representatives of the Ministry for Cultural Heritage Activities and Tourism (known as *Soprintendenti*). Despite the fact that it is not required by law, in the sub-region of Salento in Puglia (as detailed below) *Soprintendenti* often require that structures be removed at the end of the bathing season, on the basis of impacts on the landscape values of the area.

Coastal setback zone

Italy's Navigation Code (Article 55) specifies that "new works within 30 metres of the maritime domain or from the edge of the elevated land on the sea" are subject to State authorization. These requirements may be extended to apply to land inland of the 30 m line by decree of the President. Whilst the requirement for authorization is not equivalent to an absolute restriction on construction, this provision does indicate an awareness that land in proximity to the sea requires additional protections. We refer to this 30 m strip as the "mini-setback zone".

Italy's coastal setback zone is set at 300 m from the shoreline. Within this setback, development is restricted (but not outright prohibited) and is regulated by regional plans through *pianificazione paesaggistica* (landscape planning). Since 2004, there are no longer any uniform provisions regarding permitted uses within the setback zone. As the regional regulations generally do not contain outright prohibitions against development, it is not uncommon for urban plans to zone land within the setback zone for low-density residential development while still following the requirements of the relevant regional plan. Below we will present one example of regional rules, in our discussion of the Puglia region.

Coastal zone management and urban planning

Italy has not yet ratified the ICZM Protocol and, despite having ratified the Marine Strategy Framework Directive (13 October 2010 through Legislative Decree no. 190), does not yet have a marine national strategy. These two elements are symptomatic of the overall lack of coordination in Italy's coastal management system. As highlighted in the introductory section to this chapter, powers relating to the maritime public domain are fragmented between the national government, the regional governments, and the municipalities. This institutional fragmentation may explain some of Italy's difficulties in achieving a coherent coastal policy and implementation.

Coastal zone management is implemented through landscape planning and in some regions through Regional Coastal Plans (as is the case for Puglia). The planning system at the regional level is defined through a set of strategic plans. The General Plan (*Piano Territoriale Regionale*, PTR, or *Piano di Indirizzo Territoriale*, PIT) identifies the vision, main objectives, and infrastructure projects for the region. The 2004 Code on Cultural Heritage and Landscape introduced the Regional Landscape Plan (*Piano Regionale Paesaggistico/Paesistico*, PRP), which is a regional-level plan which specifically focuses on the protection of landscape and environmental values. The PRP may replace the PTR/PIT, but where both are in place, the PRP must be in accordance with the PTR/PIT.

Given that PRPs are mandatory, all regions do have one in place, though only four regions (Friuli V.G., Puglia, Piemonte, and Toscana) have a PRP which fully complies with the 2004 Code. The recent trend across Italian regions is to substitute the PTR/PIT (General Plan) with a PRP (Regional Landscape Plan). These plans, which apply to the whole regional territory, including coastal areas, place particular emphasis on environmental values. They identify areas of environmental significance and include development restrictions. PRPs are binding and local urban plans must conform to them.

Regional Coastal Plans (*Piano Regionale delle Coste*, PRC) add an additional, but optional, layer to the already complex regional planning system. Such plans are specifically aimed at the protection of the coastal environment. All coastal regions except Friulia Venezia Giulia have a coastal plan in place. These plans are subordinate to their region's PRP.

Beyond regional planning, local authorities must each prepare a local land use/urban plan. Thus, coastal planning and management is defined through at least three plans which apply in the vast majority of local areas: The PRP, PRC, and local urban plan (as well as a fourth plan where a PTR/PIT is also in place). Furthermore, in one region, Puglia, authorities are also required to prepare Municipal Coastal Plans (*Piani Comunali delle Coste*). This adds an additional level of complexity. We explore the case of the Puglia region in detail later in this chapter.

Right of public access

In Italy, a formal right of vertical public access to the shore was introduced in 2006 (Financial and Budget Law, Article 254). This right is to be guaranteed through the regional "utilization" plan prepared specifically for the MPD areas (PUD; refer to the section on the public domain). The law states that the relevant regions and municipalities must strive to find a correct balance between beach areas whose use is granted to private third parties by means of concessions and beach areas that are to be freely accessible to all citizens. Horizontal access to the shore is also guaranteed, though in a minimal manner. The public has a right of access along the shore within 5 m of the shoreline. To that end, operators of beach resorts are not permitted to block free passage along the coast. They are also obliged to identify and mark paths of public access through their resorts to the shore. The public can register complaints and NGOs, mainly Legambiente, monitor public access to the shore.

The above legal provisions relating to access were introduced as a consequence of the proliferation of beach resorts which impeded access to the shore, but the 2006 legislation was not effective: According to WWF (2012), in 2012, across a 4,000 km stretch of bathing beaches, 12,000 beach resorts occupied a stretch of 900 km along the coast; nearly double the number of resorts as ten years earlier. A specific example is the beaches in Lido di Ostia, Rome, where in 2011, access to the shore was not available in over 90% of resorts, which collectively occupied 17.5 km of land along the coast of the municipality (Legambiente, 2011). In response, in June 2015, the relevant region (Lazio) passed a law which requires that municipalities allocate at least 50% of the length of their coastlines as freely accessible beaches.

Compliance and enforcement

Illegal construction has long been a feature of the development industry in Italy, and coastal areas are no exception. In fact, coastal areas draw more illegal construction than inland areas. Illegal development is not limited to illegal buildings, but also applies to extensions.

Without delving into the history of illegal development in Italy (for that, see Zanfi, 2013), we note that the phenomenon was particularly prominent over the three decades beginning in the 1960s, when it accounted for about 25% of total developments (Zanfi, 2013, p. 3428). This number pertains to buildings without any permit. Smaller violations are rampant. The history also includes three amnesties (*condoni edilizi*), in 1985, 1994 and 2003, which resulted in an increased amount of illegal development (Zanfi, 2013). In more recent years, the phenomenon has decreased to a national average of just over 10% – most likely primarily as a result of the reduced building activity in major cities due to the economic crisis of 2008 – but this figure is still considerable.

Specifically relating to coastal areas, every year the environmental NGO Legambiente produces a report called *Mare Monstrum* (Monster Sea) on illegalities, including illegal building activities (but also fishing, wastewater treatment, and navigation) which have taken place in the 300 m setback zone and MPD. In 2017, 3,314 building violations were reported in the coastal areas across Italy (approximately 19.5% of total reported illegalities). In absolute terms, most of the illegal building activity along the coast is located in the southern regions. In fact, the four Mafia-influenced regions (Campania, Puglia, Sicilia, and Calabria) account for 54.3% of the yearly total (see Table 10.1). However, perhaps a more relevant method of comparison across regions is the number of illegalities in the building sector per kilometre of coastline. Using that measure, Basilicata, in the country's south, has the largest number of illegal structures, followed by Campania (south), Lazio (centre), and Emilia Romagna (north), whereas Sicily and Sardinia are well below the average.

Over the years, and especially since 2009, the absolute number of building-sector-related illegalities steadily decreased until 2013, with an upsurge in the years 2015–2017 (Figure 10.2). In 2013, the number of building-sector illegalities reached unprecedented low levels for Italy, down to 2,412 from 3,954 in 2009. The reasons for this decrease are not clear, but we suggest that contributing factors include the economic crisis, a lack of demand for second homes, and more frequent demolitions, as recorded on the Legambiente website.[2] More recently, the trend has reversed.

Table 10.1 Absolute number, coastline length, and number per km of coastline of building sector illegalities in the MPD in 2017 by Region (Data source: Legambiente, 2018)

Region	Number of building illegalities	Coastline length (km)	Building Illegalities per km of coastline
Abruzzo (centre) ^	99	125	**0.80**
Basilicata (south) ^	**117**	**56**	**2.09**
Calabria (south)	478	736	0.65
Campania (south) ^	702	480	**1.46**
Emilia Romagna (north) ^	**123**	**130**	**0.95**
Friuli Venezia Giulia (north)	80	111	0.21
Lazio (centre) ^	347	290	**1.20**
Liguria (north)	150	466	0.32
Marche (centre)	93	172	0.54
Molise (centre)	1	36	0.03
Puglia (south)	417	865	0.48
Sardegna (island)	160	1897	0.08
Sicilia (island, south)	204	1623	0.13
Toscana (centre)	251	442	0.58
Veneto (north)	92	140	0.66
Average	**220.9**	**N/A**	**0.68**
^ Region with above average number of illegalities per km of coastline			

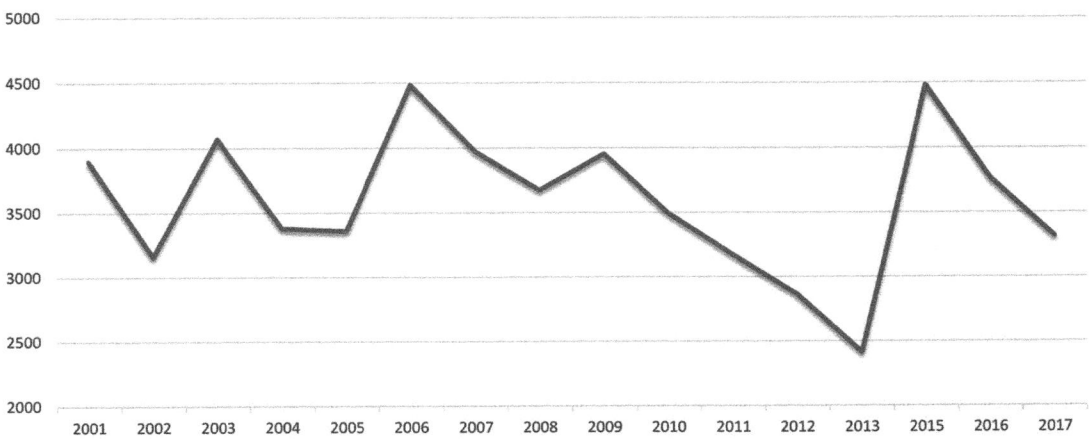

Figure 10.2 Building-sector illegalities on the maritime public domain 2002–2017

Data source: Legambiente 2002–2017. No data for 2014

We now turn to the matter of enforcement against illegalities in the maritime public domain and the setback zone.

Enforcement

Italian legislation offers a broad set of enforcement and punitive measures for the protection of the MPD. They are obviously not enough to deal with the still-extensive illegal construction. The Ministry for the Economy and Finance is responsible for enforcement within the maritime public domain. Enforcement measures available to that agency to protect the public domain include *rivendicazione* (claim), *negatoria* (denial), *regolamento di confine* (border-determination procedure), and *apposizione dei termini* (border-restoration procedure when the boundaries between public domain and private properties are certain but no longer visible). There are additional actions related to possession that are known as *reintegrazione* (reintegration) and *manutenzione* (maintenance) (Civil Code, Articles 948- and 1168-).

In addition to the above, the maritime public domain police is a body intended to guarantee order, public safety, and respect on the part of the general public of use regulations. In addition, there is a power known as *autotutela* (literally, "self-protection"), through which the public administration has the powers to modify, revoke, and render null any concessions previously granted in order to ensure that the public domain continues to be protected.

In cases of illegal use or development in either the maritime public domain or the 30 m "mini-setback zone", the public administration may require the perpetrator to demolish the illegal structure. In cases of inaction following a demolition order, the responsible administration may proceed to demolition *ex-officio* (Navigation Code, Articles 54 and 55).

Illegalities are punishable through sanctions that are also regulated through the Building Code (*Testo Unico dell'Edilizia*, 2001), under Article 35, which deals with illegal construction on land owned by the state and other public administrations. The demolition of illegal structures is the responsibility of the municipality in which the relevant public domain land is located. Costs are to be covered by the offender who is subject to potentially severe punishment – a fine of up to 51,645 euros and incarceration of up to two years. In general, not only on the MPD, demolitions of illegal development are not frequent, due to the expense. According to Chiodelli (2019), based on Legambiente data, between 2004 and June 2018 only 19.6% of 71,450 demolition orders issued were actually carried out (Legambiente, 2018).

Climate change awareness

The National Strategy for Climate Change Adaptation (NSCCA) was approved by the Ministry for the Environment and Protection of Territory and Sea (MATTM) in 2015. The Ministry began to publish related policy documents in 2013 (MATTM, 2013a) following a consultation process with the national scientific community, policymakers, and interested stakeholders. A questionnaire survey was also conducted in 2012 to collect the stakeholders' opinions and views on climate change issues and impact (Davide et al., 2013).

The policy documents on the NSCCA contain a specific section dedicated to coastal areas and the ways in which they are impacted by climate change. A series of policy documents published during 2013–2014 identifies sea level rise and resulting erosion as the main issues affecting the Italian coastal environment (MATTM, 2013a, 2013b, 2014a, 2014b; Castellari et al., 2014). They highlight that about 42% of approximately 4,000 km of beaches are subject

Table 10.2 Sandy-beach coast subject to erosion activity by region

Region	Coastline length (km)	Beach (km)	Erosion (km; %)
Sardegna	1897	459	195; 42
Sicilia	1623	1117	438; 39
Puglia	**865**	**302**	**195; 65**
Calabria	736	692	300; 43
Campania	480	224	95; 42
Liguria	466	94	31; 33
Toscana	442	199	77; 39
Lazio	290	216	117; 54
Marche	172	144	78; 54
Veneto	140	140	25; 18
Emilia Romagna	130	130	32; 25
Abruzzo	125	99	50; 50
Friuli Venezia Giulia	111	76	10; 13
Basilicata	56	38	28; 74
Molise	36	22	20; 91
Total	**7569**	**3952**	**1681; 42**
Data source: MATTM, 2014a			

to erosion, as shown in Table 10.2 (MATTM, 2014). Our selected region, Puglia, has one of the highest rates of coastal erosion.

The NSCCA identifies several adaptation measures, including an initial set that includes increased investment in ecological research and the development of a strategy to address the main risks for endangered species. The second set of measures includes adaptation of infrastructure networks, new policies for water supply, limitations, and restrictions on urban development with the introduction of new building technologies and safety measures (MATTM, 2013b, p. 44–46). The NSCCA states that implementation is to be achieved through sectoral plans. It also addresses the phasing of the implementation, monitoring and evaluation, key actors and stakeholders, and allocations of financial resources (MATTM, 2013b, p. 2).

Coordination and integration

Lack of national strategy and lack of coordination among government agencies are key issues in Italy. The State's response to the need to bridge implementation gaps in many fields appears to consist essentially of returning power and resources to the national level. This response, reinforced by the 2008 financial crisis, is based on the widespread perception that intergovernmental conflicts between regional/local and national governments reduce decision-making efficiency. Planning for the coastal zone is highly fragmented: As indicated above, several overlapping plans must be prepared to regulate the same coastal areas. At the regional level, two or three plans are expected to determine the vision, strategy, safeguards, and protections for coastal areas. A single region might even have several of the same type of plan in place concurrently. For example, the most recent Liguria General Plan (PTR), approved in 2014, replaced six PTRs, a situation which was described as *"creating difficulties of interpretation, increasing administrative discretion and reducing clarity"* (Regione Liguria, 2014).

The Ministry for the Environment and Protection of Territory and Sea (MATTM) states on its website that in order to improve the management framework and fragmentation of responsibilities in ICZM it has

> ... *activated an agreement with the other institutional partners (regional governments and municipalities), with regard to planning and management of coastal areas in view of the definition of the necessary national strategy as well as the preparation of plans/ programmes or guidelines for the ICZM Strategy.* (MATTM, n.d.)

There has been no evident follow-up to that statement.

CAMP Project

The UN has set up special programs to implement the ICZM Protocol in the Mediterranean countries. One of these is the Coastal Area Management Programme (CAMP) Italy that began in 2014, with an agreement between MATTM (Ministry for the Environment and Protection of Territory and Sea) and UNEP/MAP (United Nations Environment Programme – Mediterranean Action Plan). The project is intended to assist local-level implementation of the ICZM Protocol (despite the fact that the Protocol has yet to be ratified by Italy). The CAMP project Italy differs from CAMP projects in other countries in that it is the first multi-area project involving five different coastal areas and three regions (MATTM, 2018). The areas involved in the project include two in Sardinia, two in Tuscany, and one in Emilia Romagna.

One of the main objectives of the CAMP project is the introduction of an integrated management of coastal zones through actions intended to reduce coastal erosion, biodiversity loss, and pollution. In order to achieve this broad objective, a variety of agencies must work together on specific sub-projects. In addition, regions must work together in mapping ICZM actors; capacity building; identifying ICZM indicators and collecting data; and networking. In order to promote knowledge sharing and exchange of best-practice examples, an online platform, e-CAMP, was planned, but as of 2019 the project was no longer online.

PART II: Focus on the Puglia Region: A region with major coastal challenges yet determined to change course

Puglia as a focus region

A regional account is an important supplement to this chapter, given the extent of delegation of legal powers to regional authorities. The Puglia region provides an ideal case study: Situated in the extreme southeastern tip of the country, it is the Italian mainland region with the longest coastline (865 km, according to Castellari et al., 2014).[3] It is also a region with high rates of illegal development on the coast (see Table 10.1) and has one of the highest rates of coastal erosion (Table 10.2). At the same time, since 2005, Puglia's elected government has been determined to change course towards greater sustainability of the coastal areas, reduction of illegal construction, and increased public awareness of the importance of coastal preservation.

The region was the first in Italy to approve a regional landscape-territorial plan (PRP) that fully complies with the 2004 Code (MIBACT, 2017). As a result of its actions, Puglia has been recognized as one of three Italian "virtuous regions" in that it has implemented a coastal policy aimed at guaranteeing citizens the right of public access to beach areas (Legambiente, 2019).

Puglia is very much a coast-oriented region. It is composed of a long and narrow peninsula, bordering two seas – the southern Adriatic and the northwestern Ionian (both subdivisions of the Mediterranean Sea). It is a diverse region. A variety of physical, historical, cultural, and socio-economic characteristics and processes affects its coastal areas. Of the 258 municipalities in the region, 68 (26%) are on the coast; but those municipalities are home to 43% (1,718,759) of the 4 million in the region. Most of Puglia's coastal areas – 86% of its coastline length – are classified and used as beaches.

Various agricultural activities take place on land abutting the coast (Mininni, 2010) and over the years have preserved significant areas in the face of tumultuous development, especially post-WWII. These open spaces are of great environmental and landscape value, including vegetable gardens and the citrus groves of Gargano Park, which are now in danger of disappearing due to the abandonment of agriculture in favour of forest expansion.

Coastal areas in Puglia have been increasingly affected by competing processes and interests. These can be read as a "double movement" (Polanyi, 1944): As markets have expanded, counter-movements emerged to limit their reach and influence and to protect human beings and nature. On the one hand, socio-economic changes have led to increasing anthropic pressures on the coastal environment; on the other, social awareness has grown and the public has increasingly mobilized to prevent or minimize activities which can cause environmental damage and to implement public action for the protection of environmental assets in coastal areas.[4] In Puglia, this mobilization is expressed in the region's adoption of innovative regulatory tools to promote ICZM.

Anthropic pressures and resulting implementation gaps

Up until the end of the 1950s, over 80% of the Puglia coast was entirely free from development (Romano & Zullo, 2014). The following decades saw rapid transformation of Puglia's coastal areas, like the other Italian southern regions (also called "*Mezzogiorno*"),[5] which had historically been less developed than the north. In the 1950s, the focus of development in the region was on large infrastructural projects for the modernization of agriculture. From 1960 to 1980, development policy, organized and run by a public agency known as *Cassa per il Mezzogiorno*, was focused on large-scale heavy industry (Graziani et al., 1973). The most relevant outcomes of this period in Puglia were the establishment of highly capital-intensive large-scale state-owned firms (Partecipazioni Statali) in port cities: A giant steel-maker, Italsider (now AncelorMittal), in Taranto; petrochemical industries in Brindisi and Manfredonia. In addition, around Bari, state-owned and private firms were established but then progressively replaced by a network of small and medium-sized local firms, mostly supported by EU financing programs (Barca & Ciampi, 1998).

Today, Puglia's coastal ecosystems are under severe pressure from the impact of industrial and building activities. The price of economic growth policies, from the perspective of environmental sustainability, has been high, especially if we consider that such policies were not able to stimulate significant autonomous growth or to reduce development gaps between northern and southern Italy (Trigilia, 1992). The coastal location most under threat from environmental degradation is Taranto (Barbanente & Monno, 2004; Banini & Palagiano, 2014) but the other industrial growth poles – Brindisi and Manfredonia – have also been affected. These areas have been defined as contaminated Sites of National Interest (SIN) on the basis of the quantity and hazardousness of pollutants, the extent of health and ecological risks, and degradation of cultural and environmental heritage. They are characterized by releases of different types of pollutants (heavy metals, PCB, hydrocarbons) and industrial discharges (including cooling waters) (Shape – IPA project, 2014).

Since the 1970s, land use in Puglia's coastal zones has progressively become suburban and building development has been increasingly disconnected from the compact coastal cities, due to the growth in the number of second homes and, more recently, of recreation and tourism activities. As has occurred in other Mediterranean regions (European Environment Agency, 2006; Salvati et al., 2013), urban sprawl and sprinkling (Bonifazi et al., 2017) have been the predominant pattern of spatial transformation in Puglia's coastal areas, which are now overloaded by construction, both legal and illegal, including on dunes and cliffs, close to canals and dams (Bonifazi et al., 2016; Zanchini & Manigrasso, 2017).

These factors, together with agricultural and water interventions (irrigation, dragging, etc.), have had a huge impact on the extent of coastal erosion (Table 10.2; Sansò, 2010; Regione Puglia, 2012, 2018). Erosion has increased in recent years; the extent of affected coastline doubled between the periods 1992–2005 and 2005–2017 (Regione Puglia, 2012, 2018; MATTM, 2017). The construction of port facilities and hydraulic works at sea and along the main waterways have caused erosion, but also progradation (sediment build-up), depending on the case.

These processes have led to changes in the position of the shoreline, but authorities have failed to update data in MPD information systems (which includes cadastral information, aerial photography, and satellite images). As such there are situations in which private land and associated developments fall into the MPD in some areas and the MPD demarcation falls under the sea in others (Figure 10.3).

Figure 10.3 Irregularities in the demarcation of the MPD, Puglia (left: Marina di Lesina; right: Monte Sant'Angelo)

Source: Base map with demarcation from SID, (Ministry of Infrastructure and Transportation, n.d.), labelled by Angela Barbanente

Any steps taken to solve these irregularities will have to contend with potential significant impacts on the fisheries and tourism sectors. Both industries make significant contributions to the regional economies (Crea, 2019; Regione Puglia, 2017). In addition, bathing-beach operators are perhaps the most stubborn defenders of the status quo, as they often benefit from illegal use of the MPD.

The regional policies that will be discussed in the following sections originated from calls from the public for a change in Puglia's approach to coastal zone management, to stop the privatization of beaches and improve environmental quality and services in coastal areas. But policy proposals have been met with strong resistance from beach managers, often supported by local policymakers and professionals, who fear that the changes proposed would conflict with their own interests. This has considerably slowed down the implementation process.

Regional regulation and planning for coastal zone management

A general change in regional policies for coastal areas over the 2000s has been the shift from a focus on individual places and projects to the consideration of the coast as a complex system, made up of dynamic relationships between sea and land as well as coastal and inland areas. Actions that previously consisted of the protection of individual sites have been replaced by rules and plans for the protection and use of the entire regional coastal system. These policies have been increasingly influenced by a vision of regional development focused on the recovery and enhancement of endogenous natural and cultural resources and on local action that recognizes the value of these resources and reappropriates them for more sustainable development (Barbanente, 2011). This shift is a result both of increased public awareness of environmental issues and a change in the regional government of Puglia since 2005.[6]

Before 2005, the protection of areas of extraordinary natural value was primarily initiated within the framework of EU directives and State laws. Puglia implemented EU Council Habitats Directive (92/43/EEC), through which it identified 77 Sites of Community Importance (SCI), 21 of which are in coastal areas. Puglia is home to Gargano Park (121.118 hectares), which is a national protected area established under the law for environmentally protected areas (Law 394/91) and includes important rocky coasts and wetlands. The region also includes two nature reserves which are marine-protected areas and three wetlands of international significance, protected areas at the international level through the Ramsar Convention (Shape – IPA project, 2014). In addition, there are 18 protected natural areas established on the basis of a regional initiative (Law no. 19/1997), most of which are located along the coast, twelve of them established after 2005.

As early as 1980 (five years prior to adoption of the 1985 law discussed above), Puglia adopted a law (no. 56) which prohibited any building within a 300 m coastal setback zone. However, this law was not effective, as (a) it provided significant exemptions for development within the zone and (b) it did not curb illegal development, which was later legalized through national amnesty laws (1985 and 1994).[7] Moreover, the prohibition expired with the entry into force of the first Regional Landscape Plan (approved 2001; Law 431/1985), which paradoxically reduced the width of the strip within which development was prohibited from 300 m to 200 m.

Before 2005, public administrations carried out specific projects which, at best, solved local coastal problems for which they were responsible, ignoring the consequences that such interventions could have on neighbouring areas. The turning point of this approach dates back to 2006, when an integrated vision of the coastal zone was started as an essential prerequisite for a policy that seeks to integrate social and economic development with the protection and improvement of the coastal zone environment. The case of Puglia is interesting both for the particularly innovative policies in the national panorama promoted by the Region and for the difficulties encountered in their implementation. Not only has this clashed with established economic interests and power relations that revolve around the privatization and urbanization of coastal areas, but it has also had to address the problems of lack of cooperation and coordination between the different levels of government – central, regional, and local – that characterize the management of all Italian coastal areas (see Part I).

As explained in Part I, in Italy the protection, management, and planning of coastal areas are essentially founded on two separate legislative frameworks established at the national level: The first concerns the protection and management of the maritime public domain; the second concerns the protection and planning of the setback zone, which is under the landscape legislation. In the following sections we will illustrate how the Puglia region implemented secondary legislation and planning instruments within the abovementioned two national legislative frameworks.

Puglia Law Number 17: "Rules for the protection and use of the coast"

Soon after the election of the new government in 2005, in June 2006, Puglia adopted a regional law (17/2006) on "Rules for the protection and use of the coast". This law provides a framework for policy actions to be implemented in the maritime public domain, based on ICZM principles, with innovations aiming to ensure public access and free use of the MPD and territorial sea, and at promoting the preservation, protection, and sustainable use of the coastal environment, as well as the cooperation between different levels of government and coordination between different activities, public uses, and designations. The law outlines the rules for the exercise of administrative functions for the management of the MPD, in accordance with the Regional Coastal Plan (Piano Regionale delle Coste – PRC) and Municipal Coastal Plans (Piani Comunali delle Coste – PCCs).

Law no. 17 transcends national legislation by requiring that at least 60% of the available length of the MPD within each municipality (excluding unusable areas such as ports or cliffs) be reserved for public use and free bathing. It is worth noting that this is the highest minimum percentage required across the coastal regions: Sardinia also requires 60%, Lazio 50% and Liguria 40%, and five regions do not include this numeric requirement (Legambiente, 2019). Moreover, Law 17/2006 prohibits municipalities from granting concessions for private use in ravines areas, river mouths/estuaries, alluvial channels, areas at risk of erosion, and other sensitive and vulnerable sites.

These regulations, which inevitably required declassification of beaches, met with strong resistance, especially from operators of beach resorts, who had previously gained concessions for the use of the MPD as well as automatic renewals and had used the land as exclusive private property.

Law 17/2006 prohibits the construction of fences on the MPD and leaves it to the Regional Coastal Plan to define specific rules for concessions, which must ensure public accessibility and free use of the shore, including for people with disabilities. Fences may be authorized and, in such cases, vertical access to the shore must be guaranteed at least every 150 m. The Law also provides a more restrictive definition of the State standard for "easily removable structures", prohibiting the use of any kind of cement, and requiring structures to consist of modular elements which, after being dismantled if necessary, can then be reassembled in situ.

The Soprintendenza (see Part I) of Salento (sub-region of Puglia) often specifies on permits for such "easily removable structures" that they are valid only for the bathing season (from April to October), in order to minimize the impacts on views and on the hydro-geomorphology, especially in areas characterized by sand dunes and vegetation. If the Soprintendenza wishes to impose the requirement that such structures be disassembled in winter, they must provide adequate justification. Recently, the Council of State (no. 00738/2019) rejected an appeal brought by a beach-bathing operator in Lecce against the Soprintendenza, which had required removal of a concession. The Court ruled that such a decision by the Soprintendenza is legal assuming it is well founded in the provisions of the laws for landscape protection and has been adequately justified, which it found to be the case.

Finally, the law institutes deadlines for accomplishment of regional and municipal obligations, including adoption of rules for public works on the coast (which were previously largely unregulated) and the preparation of PCCs.

In 2015, this 2006 law was repealed and replaced (by Law 17/2015) because of two key legal innovations: The 2011 amendment to the national law which required that concessions expire (Law no. 217) and the approval of a national law (Law no. 27/2012 on competition, infrastructure development, and competitiveness) which transferred powers to regions to approve master plans for regional harbours and ports. The new law slightly modified some provisions of the old law to improve the effectiveness of regional action in monitoring and implementing coastal policy, committing the region to establish a "Regional coastal observatory for maritime conservation, development and planning" and to issue "Guidelines for the exercise of functions delegated to municipalities".

Puglia's regional coastal plan (PRC) 2012

The Regional Coastal Plan (PRC) is strictly limited to regulating the use and management of the MPD, with three primary policy aims: Safeguarding the environmental and landscape heritage, guaranteeing free access to the shore, and promoting the development of sustainable tourism and recreation activities. It sets binding rules for the grant of concessions in the maritime public domain, as well as for development of the 68 municipal coastal plans (PCCs). These plans must be based on detailed studies and conform to the regional plan. They address the protection, restoration, and monitoring of the coast, as well as the main contributing causes of degradation and morphological instability.

The PRC, prepared by an interdisciplinary group of experts from the Politecnico di Bari (Polytechnic University of Bari), was based on a strong foundation of technical and scientific knowledge of the dynamics of coastal areas. The key guidelines for coastal works or development on the coast emerge from the definition of three classes of the level of critical danger of erosion of sandy beaches ("criticality") and three classes of environmental sensitivity ("sensitivity"). Combined, these two classifications generate nine different coastal zone classes, each with different allowances regarding use and development, as well as different guidelines for minimizing the impacts of coastal activities. According to the plan's regulations for implementation (*norme tecniche di attuazione*) and recommendations for designing the PCCs, in each coastal municipality, concessions for any use in the maritime public domain (whether for a new application or renewal) may be granted only for areas included in the lowest levels of "criticality" and "sensitivity".

In other words, concessions should not be granted unless the municipality lacks less critical areas, and in such cases, the concessions should be granted gradually to ensure the coast is stable, and only after a technical assessment approved by the Autorità di Bacino dell'Appennino Meridionale (Southern Apennine Basin Authority), the authority responsible for soil protection, indicates that erosion has stabilized. In order to ensure the implementation of this rule, the Puglia region promoted several monitoring programs and recently adopted a programmatic framework for combating coastal erosion and defining priorities for action (Regione Puglia, 2018).

Similarly, in areas with highly sensitive values, concessions are usually prohibited, and if the municipal territory lacks areas with low or medium values, they should be granted only after a specific environmental assessment submitted with the application for a concession in addition to that required for environmental and landscape permits. In areas of high sensitivity, priority should be given to "free beaches with facilities" over private beaches. Moreover, in sensitive areas, concessions are limited to minimum beach services (small bar kiosks and public services).

The approval of the PCCs has been considerably delayed, so much so that in early 2018, the region appointed commissioners to take on substitutive powers in 23 defaulting coastal municipalities. The difficulties in approving PCCs primarily relate to the incompleteness and inconsistency of information on the legal status of the MPD (described above), particularly changes to the shoreline position due to erosion, as well as significant numbers of developments and concessions which do not comply with the law.

The regional landscape-territorial plan (PPTR), 2015

The Puglia Piano Paesaggistico Territoriale Regionale (Regional Landscape and Territorial Plan, henceforth PPTR), approved in February 2015, was the first Italian plan to fully comply with the 2004 Code and to apply the principles of the 2000 European Landscape Convention (ELC). It covers the entire regional territory and has a particular focus on coastal landscapes. The PPTR is binding on all land-development activities falling within the plan limits and on all other relevant general and sectoral plans at all levels – regional, provincial, and municipal.

The Puglia PPTR is extremely innovative in the Italian context: It demonstrates an evolution from a restrictive-normative tradition to a complex dynamic planning vision, based on the integration of top-down and bottom-up approaches. While the PPTR is a statutory plan, it adopts a strategic approach. This mix of statutory and strategic emerges from the two different regulatory foundations for the preparation of PPTRs: The 2004 Code gives the PPTR statutory superiority over other plans, which allows it to dictate rules to prevent the coastal landscape from being further compromised by entrenched planning practices. On the other hand, the ELC principles call on governments authorities to adopt a policy based on active landscape protection; dynamic landscape management which involves the public and their expectations; and framing of planning projects for coastal areas (Council of Europe, 2000).

The plan is organized into three main parts: (i) An Atlas of environmental, territorial, and landscape heritage; (ii) a Strategic Scenario, which includes a vision and outlines objectives and guidelines, planning projects, and actions for bringing the territory-landscape closer to the proposed vision through time; and (iii) regulations for implementation (*norme tecniche di attuazione*), which include guidance, directives, and requirements. Overall, the PPTR combines a strategy based on a selective range of objectives and issues and an open, proactive approach to plan-making and implementation, with statutory legal certainty and clear rules for the transformation of protected areas (Albrechts et al., 2020).

In relation to coastal areas, the PPTR includes an online GIS (geographical information system)-based map, indicating the limits of the 300 m setback zone, as jointly delimited by the Region and the Ministry (Figure 10.4). This map must be periodically updated by the Regional Landscape Observatory according to the results of the annual monitoring of the plan. The PPTR regulations protect the 300 m setback zone by prohibiting any plan, project, or works in a range of categories, including construction of new buildings or fences that reduce access to the coast or coastal views; removal of natural vegetation; changes in use of existing buildings for large-scale

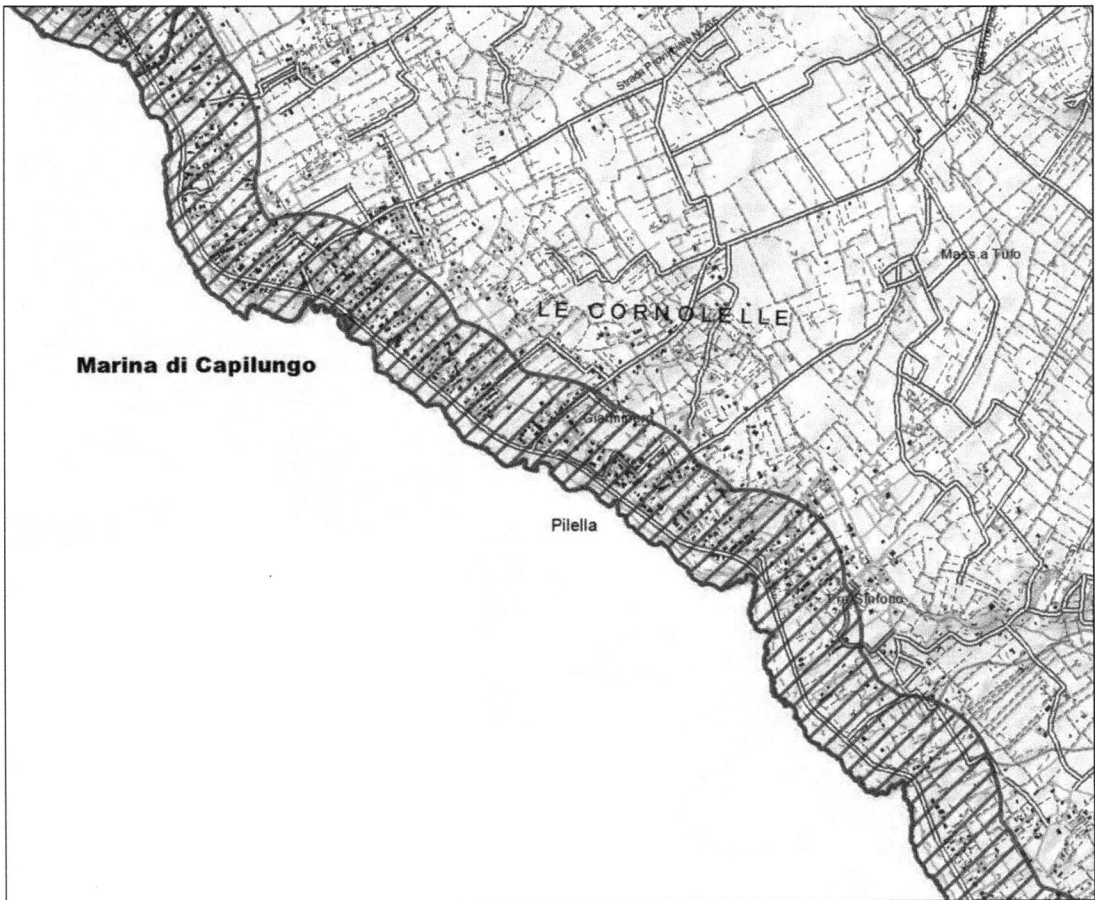

Figure 10.4 The 300 m setback zone as jointly delimited by the Region and Ministry

Data source: Regione Puglia (2015) PPTR

industrial and commercial activities; the use of materials and construction techniques that reduce soil permeability; and the construction of new roads, with the exception of those designed to improve existing settlements in ways consistent with site morphology and landscape features.

In addition, the PPTR extends the requirements of Regional Law 17/2006 and the PRC regarding "easily removable facilities" for bathing and other recreational activities to apply beyond the MPD, to the 300 m setback area, but without obliging concession holders to remove them after the bathing season. It specifies that these facilities may be permitted only on condition that they do not damage the natural landscape, alter the morphology, or reduce the usability or accessibility of the coast. In addition, they must be constructed from ecological materials.

The regulations also encourage maintenance and restoration of the coastal environment through various works and appropriate infrastructure, such as rainwater collection plants.

A key objective of the plan is to promote protection and improvement of the coastal landscape as a valuable element of the natural and historical heritage, as well as an important socio-economic asset. As a consequence, the Strategic Scenario includes a specific Regional Project (RP) for the "integrated protection and improvement of coastal landscapes".[8] The RP is consistent with the RCP and PPTR regulations but allows a more holistic approach to management of the coastal zone. It includes areas that go far beyond land affected by the PRC and PCC (Figure 10.5). The project promotes a proactive approach for ensuring that the public can enjoy the coastal areas, creating synergies with inland areas for a broader view of the coastal

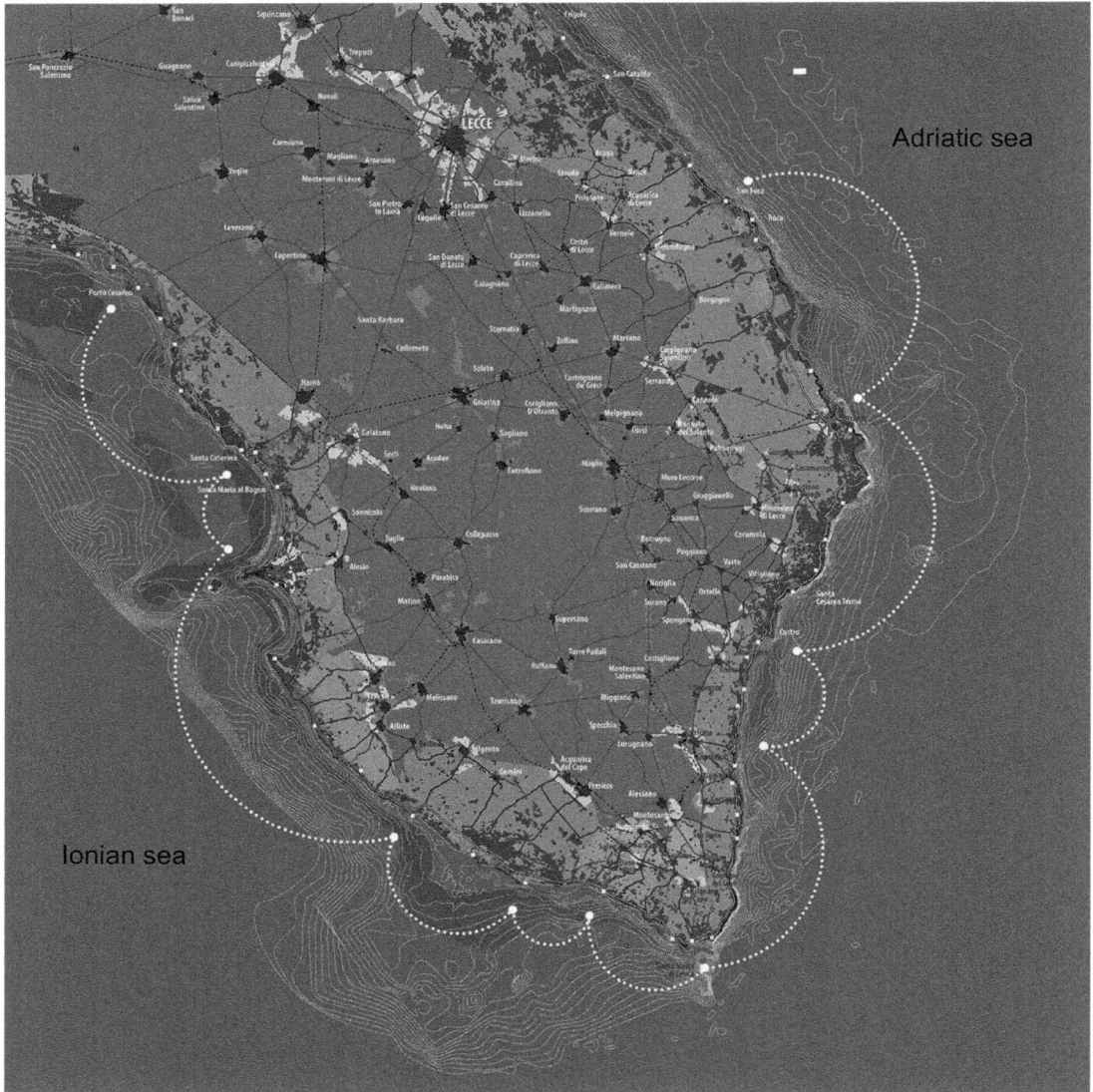

Figure 10.5 Regional project for the "integrated protection and improvement of coastal landscapes": Salento sub-region

Source: Regione Puglia (2015) PPTR

zone. It limits land take-up, thus preventing the formation of continuous linear development along the coast and protecting the immense heritage (urban, natural, and rural) which can still be found in the coastal system and its inland areas. These goals can be achieved through Regeneration Schemes aiming to improve the ecological and landscape quality of settlements, focusing on the enhancement of the large undeveloped areas as well as on urban waterfronts, suburbs, infrastructure connecting between coastal and inland areas, and low-impact navigation (Granatiero et al., 2011).

Compliance and enforcement in Puglia

Any effort to implement ICZM in Puglia is hampered by illegal activities in the coastal areas. As demonstrated in Table 10.1, the number of illegal buildings constructed in Puglia's coastal zone is high, but the number per km of coastline is lower than Italy's average. A crucial problem is the failure of municipalities to comply with the basic rules in force for illegal buildings which may not be legalized retroactively; namely, to take enforcement action through fines or demolition. As such, demolitions are rare – only just over 10% of owners of illegal developments were issued demolition orders over the period 2004–2018 (Legambiente, 2018). Demolition orders are usually issued only decades after illegal developments are detected, following extended

Figure 10.6 Illegal and legalized (after amnesty) buildings in the Lecce MPD

Source: F. Curci & C. Novak, DAStU, Politecnico di Milano, "Arretrare per riconquistare e tutelare i beni pubblici e ridare valore al patrimonio costiero", Presented at SIU Seminar Politecnico di Bari, 4 June 2019 [public domain presentation]

court battles, and rarely acted upon due to the reluctance and limited financial resources of municipalities. Most of the demolitions in Puglia are acted upon by the Prosecutor's office following criminal proceedings.

Another compliance issue relates to beaches and beach services (parking areas, kiosks, etc.) which operate without concessions or in areas where such uses are prohibited by the Law (17/2006). In addition, many beaches are not in accordance with legal obligations, particularly the required minimum levels of services (sanitation, showers, kiosk, and signage) and vertical and horizontal public access.

State legislation does not assign specific responsibilities to the regions to prevent and suppress illegal construction. Puglia Law No. 15/2012 ("Rules on regional functions of prevention and repression of illegal building"), aiming to enhance the effectiveness of the region's enforcement actions, is considered a "virtuous case" within a context in which the national parliament and some regional councils recently attempted to approve essentially what were masked new amnesties.[9] The Law is the result of a process that involved all the key actors, including the association representing municipalities in the region, prosecutors, and law enforcement agencies, as well as environmental NGOs. The Law:

- Stabilizes institutional cooperation through agreements with local authorities and judicial and police organizations operating in the field of urban planning control
- Provides a database on illegal development, integrated into the regional GIS system, in order to improve the monitoring of land use changes, information exchange, and coordination of administrative actions
- Supports the demolition of unauthorized buildings by removing key barriers to municipal implementation or lack of human and financial resources (or excuses to that effect). This involves two actions: (i) Enhancing the regional exercise of power of substitution, by appointing regional acting commissioners and involving the prosecutors for investigation; and (ii) allowing municipalities to use a regional revolving fund for demolition and reversion to the previous state. The expenditures are to be refunded by the owners of illegal buildings.
- Defines general criteria for allocation of the regional fund, including the extent of the phenomenon, the damage caused by the illegal activity, and the landscape value of the area concerned

Implementation is slow and difficult given that this law requires significant change in well-established social behaviours and political and administrative routines. The "implementation map" of this law varies according to contextual factors: If we focus on the sub-regions most affected by illegal buildings, we see some progress in Salento but stubborn inaction in Gargano. Salento has seen some good practice; it has carried out demolitions using the regional revolving fund. These demolitions have been initiated by the Prosecutor's office and, to a lesser extent, by the municipalities and result from ongoing collaboration between the region and law enforcement agencies, with four regional officials employed by the prosecution and paid by the region for monitoring and control activities. The same initiatives promoted by the regional government in Gargano failed miserably. In response, the region exerted the power of substitution, replacing officials in four municipalities with regional acting commissioners for building demolition. In Gargano, the regional government used an incremental approach, as it seemed to offer the best way to prevent paralyzing conflicts related to stubborn opposition to demolition in an area characterized by collusion between local organized crime and public administration.

The rate of illegal development in Puglia has declined since 2012. In 2017, it was estimated that for every 100 authorized buildings, there were 39.6 illegal buildings – a much lower rate than in other southern regions: 67.6 in Campania, 65.4 in Calabria, and 60.9 in Sicilia (Istat, 2018). This certainly cannot be directly attributed to the measures described above but perhaps may be an indicator of a turnaround to which regional and local governments and NGOs have contributed by their initiatives.

Public participation and proactive implementation of the Regional Landscape and Territorial Plan (PPTR)

The above plans and actions were developed with participation from the public and NGOs. The following refers specifically to the most recent plan prepared – the Regional Landscape and Territorial Plan.

Participation of local authorities, stakeholders, NGOs, and the public at large was promoted from the very beginning of the planning process and continued during implementation, using specific tools, which were tested during the plan-making stage, as part of standard practice in territory management (Iacovone, 2011).

The participation tools included in the plan are area conferences, community maps, eco-museums, and an interactive website with an online observatory. In addition, the plan includes governance tools such as agreement protocols, local territorial pacts, river agreements, awards benefits and incentives, and integrated pilot projects.

During the formal participation procedures required by law, on exhibition of the draft PPTR, the Regional Council received 2,700 formal requests for revision of the plan, mainly from landowners, but only 2% of these requests concerned coastal areas. This is due, on the one hand, to the accuracy of the delineation of the 300 m setback area (at a scale of 1:5000) and, on the other hand, to heightened public awareness of the environmental and landscape values of coastal areas and the need to preserve them for use by the public.

In addition, the plan spurred one hundred appeals to the administrative court, all concluded in favour of the region by decision of the Council of State. To prevent the opposition from getting the upper hand, the region increased its efforts, including using financial resources, to involve municipalities and other local actors in the proactive implementation of the plan.

The most innovative tools that were used during the plan-making process are "integrated pilot projects". These projects involved about 50 local authorities, together with numerous organizations and social actors and aimed to demonstrate, "live", the bottom-up approach and proactive role for local actors envisioned by the PPTR.

Five integrated pilot Regeneration Schemes for coastal landscapes were undertaken during the plan-making process. They were launched in 2012 and approved in 2013. The first included four municipalities on the southern part of the Ionian coast, led by Gallipoli, which experiences massive tourism pressure on its attractive beaches, especially in August,[10] putting unsustainable pressure on its fragile ecosystem. The four municipalities cooperated on a strategy for the regeneration of the coastal area, drawn up with the participation of residents. The Regeneration Scheme includes a range of actions for the improvement and sustainable future use of the coastal landscape (Figure 10.7). As the strategy aims to promote local development, specifically through the creation of new forms of sustainable tourism, it has been financed with European Community and national cohesion funds reserved for regions classified by the EU as "less developed". Since the approval of the PPTR, the region has continued to promote integrated projects.

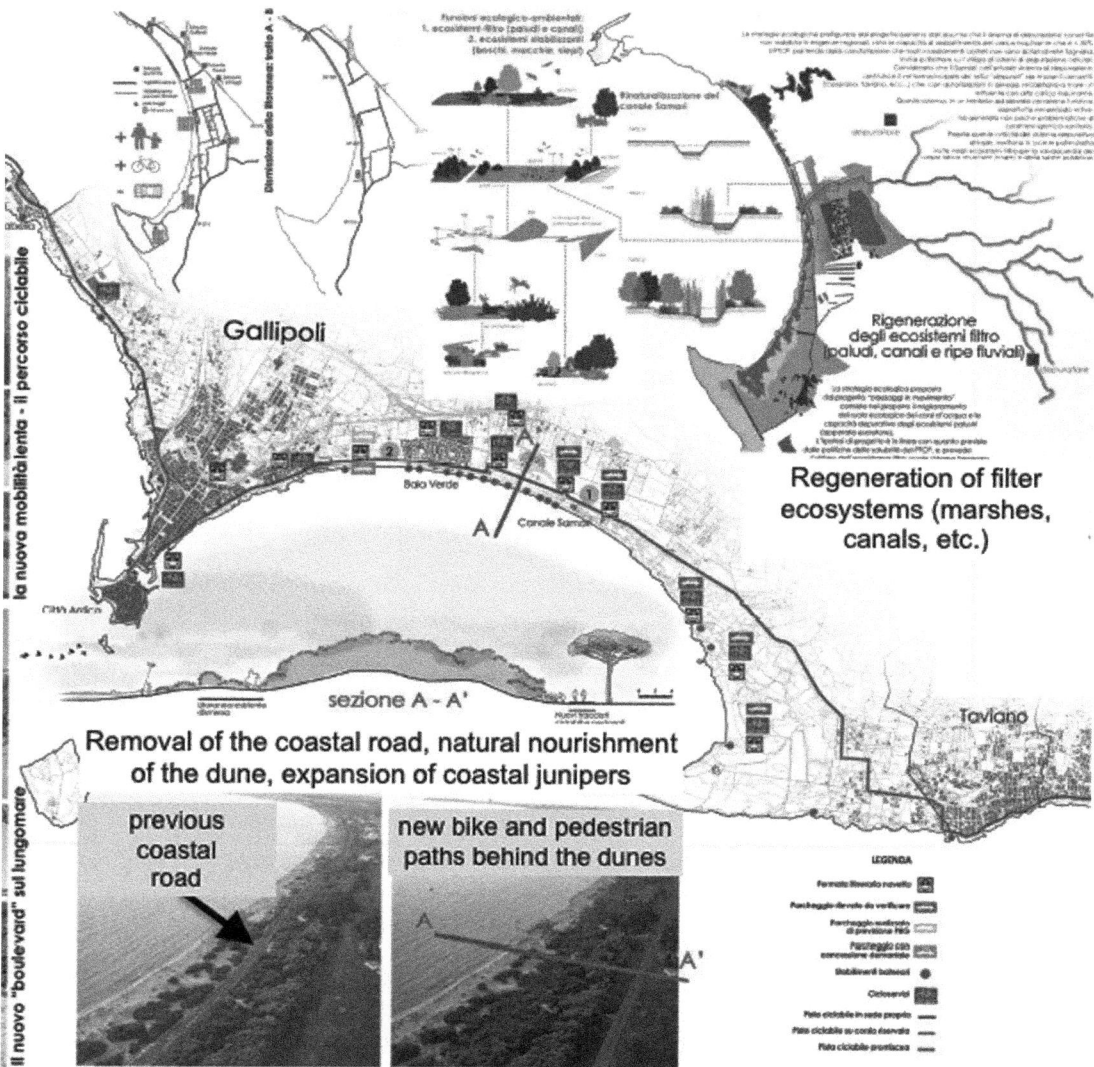

Figure 10.7 Extract from the Regeneration Scheme for the coastal area of Gallipoli and three neighbouring coastal areas

Data source: Regione Puglia, *Progetti integrati per i paesaggi costieri ad alta valenza naturalistica*, 2013 [public domain document]

Conclusions from Parts I and II

In Part I, we discussed the main features of the Italian system of planning regulations in coastal areas and laws relating to the maritime public domain. We emphasized the main peculiarities of a system that is quite fragmented in relation to management of permitted uses and concessions, construction, planning, and administrative functions. Even national strategies for coastal zone management and adaptation to climate change seem to be detached. No coordination is found between them, and implementation is lagging.

The measures and regulations found within the Navigation Code and Civil Code are consistently oriented to safeguard the public domain and minimize the impacts on it. Despite the myriad of regulations on concessions, uses, planning, and property rights, protection of coastal areas is not always successful. Illegal development is still very widespread, especially in the southern regions, and planning regulations have to date not succeeded in attempts to thwart it.

In Part II, we used the image of "double movement" to depict a region affected by increasing anthropic pressures on the coastal environment, a region which is trying to implement a more sustainable development in coastal areas through the mobilization of cognitive, social, political, and organizational resources. Both disputes and conflicts with central government and locally well-established illegal practices and behaviours complicate the path to implementation. Yet through innovative regulation and planning approaches, the Puglia region has made significant progress towards more sustainable coastal zone management and more effective preservation of its coastal landscapes.

Notes

1. Letter of formal notice dated 7 May 2010.
2. http://www.legambiente.it/abbattilabuso/abbattuti
3. 985 km according to the more accurate survey of the Regional Coastal Plan.
4. There is no space in this chapter for even a cursory consideration of all the harsh conflicts arising around the management of coastal and maritime areas in Puglia. Significant cases which have seen conflicts between the State, Puglia and others include the ongoing construction of the Trans Adriatic Pipeline (TAP) for the import of natural gas from Azerbaijan to Italy, with the landing point on southern Puglia's Adriatic coast; oil exploration and extraction all along the coast of Puglia; and offshore wind energy projects, particularly concentrated around the Gargano Park.
5. This term refers to the whole of Southern Italy, comprising 123 thousand square kilometres, with about 21 million inhabitants and eight regions out of twenty.
6. In 2005, a leader of the *Partito della Rifondazione Comunista* (Communist Refoundation Party), Nichi Vendola, won the Puglia regional primaries and then the elections for President. The region was previously governed by the centre right. He was re-elected regional president in March 2010. His government, surprisingly the most enduring in the history of the region, proposed an alternative model for development focused on the enhancement of regional resources: social capital, especially youth, and cultural and environmental "common goods" (Damiani, 2011).
7. Unlike the amnesty of 2003, which legalized only "minor illegal works" in environmentally protected areas, the laws of 1985 and 1994 allowed legalization of entire illegal buildings.
8. The other 4 projects are: The regional ecological network, the city-countryside pact, the soft mobility system, and the systems for public use of cultural heritage.
9. Draft national law AS 580-B/2016, known as "Falanga" after the first signatory senator, on the criteria for execution of demolition of illegal buildings, which would make it more difficult to perform demolitions. In addition, in 2017, the State took both Campania and Basilicata to the Constitutional Court because they introduced new proposals for amnesties for illegal development.
10. In August 2014, the number of tourists was estimated at 60,000 per day compared to a resident population of 20,000 residents.

References

Albrechts, L., Barbanente, A., & Monno, V. (2020). Practicing transformative planning: the territory-landscape plan as a catalyst for change. *City, Territory and Architecture* 7(1), 1–13.

Amato, A. (2001). The Italian coastal legislation: A European paradox. *Revue juridique de l'Environnement* 26 (1), 277–286.

Avanzi, S. (2000). *Il nuovo demanio nel diritto civile, amministrativo, ambientale, comunitario, penale, tributario* [The new public domain in civil, administrative, environmental, community, criminal, tax law]. Giuffrè Editore.

Banini, T., & Palagiano, C. (2014). Environment and health in Italian cities: The case of Taranto. In A. Malik et al. (Eds.), *Environmental Deterioration and Human Health*. Springer.

Barbanente, A. (2011). Un piano paesaggistico per la difesa dei beni comuni e uno sviluppo diverso [A landscape plan which safeguards common goods and promotes a new type of development]. *Urbanistica* 147, 60–64.

Barbanente, A. & Monno, V. (2004). Changing Images and Practices in A Declining "Growth Pole" in Southern Italy: the 'Steel Town' of Taranto. *Städte im Umbruch* 2, 36–44.

Barca, F., & Ciampi, C. A. (1998). *La nuova programmazione e il Mezzogiorno* [The new planning in Italy's southern regions]. Donzelli.

Bonifazi, A., Balena, P., & Sannicandro, V. (2016). I suoli di Puglia fra consumo e politiche per il risparmio [The land of Puglia, between consumption and preservation policies]. In *Centro di ricerca sui consumi di suolo, Rapporto 2016*. INU Edizioni.

Bonifazi, A., Balena, P., & Torre, C. M. (2017). Forme della dispersione urbana in Puglia: Land of sprinkling? [Forms of urban sprawl in Italy: Land of sprinkling]. In *Centro di ricerca sui consumi di suolo, Rapporto 2017*. INU Edizioni.

Casanova, M. (1986). *Demanio marittimo e poteri locali [The maritime public domain and local authorities]*. Giuffrè Editore.

Castellari, S., Venturini, S., Ballarin Denti, A., Bigano, A., Bindi, M., Bosello, F., Carrera, L., Chiriacò, M. V., Danovaro, R., Desiato, F., & Filpa, A. (2014). *Rapporto sullo stato delle conoscenze scientifiche su impatti, vulnerabilità ed adattamento ai cambiamenti climatici in Italia [Report on the state of scientific knowledge on impacts, vulnerabilities and adaptation to climate change in Italy]*. MATTM – Ministero dell'Ambiente e della Tutela del Territorio e del Mare.

Chiodelli, F. (2019). The illicit side of urban development: Corruption and organised crime in the field of urban planning. *Urban Studies* 56 (8), 1611–1627.

Conio, A. (2010). Il Demanio Marittimo: Titolarità e Gestione tra Stato e Autonomie Territoriali [The Maritime Public Domain: Ownership and Management of State and Territorial Autonomy]. Phd thesis in Administrative Law, XX Cycle, Università Degli Studi Di Roma Tre.

Council of Europe. (2000). European Treaty Series No. 176. Florence, 20 October.

Crea. (2019). *Annuario dell'agricoltura italiana 2017* [Italian Agriculture Yearbook 2017]. Consiglio per la ricerca in agricoltura e l'analisi dell'economia agraria.

Damiani, M. (2011). Nichi Vendola: For the new 'laboratory' of the Italian left. *Bulletin of Italian Politics* 3 (2), 371–390.

Davide, M., Giannini, V., Venturini, S., & Castellari, S. (2013). *Questionario per la Strategia Nazionale di Adattamento ai Cambiamenti Climatici: Elaborazione dei risultati* [Questionnaire for the National Strategy of Adaptation to Climate Change: Report on the results]. Rapporto per il Ministero dell'Ambiente e della Tutela del Territorio e del Mare. Roma.

De Martino, F., Resta, R., Jaricci, P., & Pugliese, G. (1976). *Commentario del Codice Civile. Beni in generale. Proprietà. Beni pubblici. Superficie (artt. 810-956 del Cod. Civ.).* [Commentary on the Civil Code. Goods in general. Property. Public goods. Surface rights. (articles 810-956 of the Italian Civil Code)]. Zanichelli.

European Environment Agency (2006). Urban Sprawl in Europe. The ignored challenge, Report 10/2006. Joint Research Centre, Copenhagen.

Gaeta, D. (1965). Il demanio marittimo [The maritime public domain]. *Novissimo digesto italiano*, 10, 918.

Granatiero, G., Maggio, G., & Migliaccio, A. (2011). Scenario strategico: Cinque progetti territoriali per il paesaggio [The strategic scenario: five territorial projects regarding regional landscape]. *Urbanistica* 147, 34–41.

Graziani, A., Del Monte, A., Piccolo, D., Giannola, A., Matrone, L. (1973). *Incentivi e investimenti industriali nel Mezzogiorno* [Incentives and industrial investments in Southern Italy]. Franco Angeli.

Gullo, N. (2006). Beni pubblici [Public goods]. In Corso, G., & Lopilato, V. (Eds.), *Il diritto amministrativo dopo le riforme costituzionali*, Parte speciale, vol. II. . Pp. 187–204. Giuffrè Editore.

Iacovone, G. (2011). L'impianto normativo del Pptr tra i limiti del vecchio Putt e nuova concezione di pianificazione del paesaggio. [The regulatory system of Puglia's landscape plan from the limitations of the former Putt to the new concept of planning laid out in the landscape Code]. *Urbanistica* 147, 56–60.

ISPRA. (2011). *Mare e Ambiente Costiero 2011* [Sea and Coastal Environment 2011]. Available at: http://www.isprambiente.gov.it/files/pubblicazioni/statoambiente/tematiche2011/05_%20Mare_e_ambiente_costiero_2011.pdf/view

Istat. (2017). *Annuario Statistico Italiano 2017* [Italian Statistical Yearbook 2017]. Available at: https://www.istat.it/it/files//2017/12/C01.pdf

— (2018). *BES. Il Benessere Equo e Sostenibile in Italia* [Fair and Sustainable Wellbeing in Italy]. Available at: https://www.istat.it/it/files/2018/12/Bes_2018.pdf

— (2019). Demo Istat [Demographics]. http://demo.istat.it/pop2019/index.html

Legambiente. (2002). *Mare Monstrum 2002*. Legambiente.

— (2003). *Mare Monstrum 2003*. Legambiente.

— (2004). *Mare Monstrum 2004*. Legambiente.

— (2005). *Mare Monstrum 2005*. Legambiente.

— (2006). *Mare Monstrum 2006*. Legambiente.

— (2007). *Mare Monstrum 2007*. Legambiente.

— (2008). *Mare Monstrum 2008*. Legambiente.

— (2009). *Mare Monstrum 2009*. Legambiente.

— (2010). *Mare Monstrum 2010*. Legambiente.

— (2011). *Mare Monstrum 2011*. Legambiente.

— (2012). *Mare Monstrum 2012*. Legambiente.

— (2013). *Mare Monstrum 2013*. Legambiente.

— (2014). *Mare Monstrum 2014*. Legambiente.

— (2016). *Mare Monstrum 2016*. Legambiente.

— (2017). *Mare Monstrum 2017*. Legambiente.

— (2018). *Mare Monstrum 2018*. Legambiente.

— (2018). *Abbatti l'abuso. I numeri delle (mancate) demolizioni nei comuni italiani.* [Demolish the abuse. The numbers of (missed) demolitions in Italian municipalities]. Legambiente.

— (2019). *Rapporto spiagge* [Beaches report]. Legambiente.

Licciardello, S. (2008). Demanio marittimo e autonomie territoriali [Maritime domain and territorial autonomies]. In A. Police (Ed.), *I beni pubblici: Tutela, valorizzazione e gestione*. Atti del Convegno di studi, Ville Tuscolane, 16–18 November 2006.

Luchetti, M. (2006). Attività edilizia dei privati su aree demaniali [Building activity of private individuals on public domain land]. *AmbienteDiritto*, 19 July. Available at: https://www.ambientediritto.it/dottrina/Dottrina_2010/attivita_edilizie_demanio_luchetti.htm

MATTM. (The Ministry for the Environment, Safeguard of Territory and Sea). (n.d.). *Verso la Strategia Nazionale per la Gestione Integrata delle Zone Costiere* [*Towards the National Strategy for Integrated Management of Coastal Areas*]. Available at: http://www.minambiente.it/pagina/verso-la-strategia-nazionale-la-gestione-integrata-delle-zone-costiere [Accessed September 2019]

— (2013a). *Elementi per una Strategia Nazionale di Adattamento ai Cambiamenti Climatici.* [Elements for a National Climate Change Adaptation Strategy]. Ministero dell'Ambiente e Tutela del Territorio e del Mare.

— (2014a). *Consultazione Pubblica. Strategia per l'ambiente marino. Programmi di monitoraggio.* [Public consultation. Strategy for the marine environment. Monitoring programs]. Ministero dell'Ambiente e Tutela del Territorio e del Mare. Available at: http://www.strategiamarina.isprambiente.it/sintesi-risultati-consultazione-2014

— (2014b). *Strategia Nazionale di Adattamento ai Cambiamenti Climatici.* [National Strategy for Adaptation to Climate Change]. Ministero dell'Ambiente e Tutela del Territorio e del Mare.

— (2017). *L'erosione costiera in Italia: Le variazioni della linea di costa dal 1960 al 2012.* [Coastal erosion in Italy: The variations of the coast line from 1960 to 2012]. Ministero dell'Ambiente e Tutela del Territorio e del Mare.

— (2018). *Il Progetto "CAMP" Italia.* [The "CAMP" Italy Project]. Ministero dell'Ambiente e Tutela del Territorio e del Mare. Available at: https://www.minambiente.it/pagina/il-progetto-camp-italia

MIBACT – Osservatorio Nazionale per la qualità del paesaggio (Ed.). (2017). *Rapporto sullo stato delle politiche per il paesaggio.* [Report on the state of landscape policies]. Ministero per i Beni e le Attività Culturali e il Turismo.

Mininni, M. (2010). *La costa obliqua. Un atlante per la Puglia.* [The oblique coast. An atlas for Puglia]. Donzelli editore.

Ministry of Infrastructure and Transport. (n.d.). Sistema Informativo del Demanio Marittimo [Information System for the Maritime Public Domain] – SID.

OECD. (2015). *Drying Wells, Rising Stakes: Toward Sustainable Agriculture Groundwater Use.* OECD Studies on Water. OECD.

Polanyi, K. (1944). *The Great Transformation: The Political and Economic Origins of Our Time.* Beacon Press.

Querci, F. A. (1959). *Demanio marittimo.* [The maritime public domain]. In Enciclopedia del Diritto, Vol. V. DeJure.

Regione Liguria. (2014). *Il Piano Territoriale Regionale: Il Piano in dieci pagine.* [The Regional Territorial Plan: A ten-page plan]. Available at: http://www.regione.liguria.it/argomenti/territorio-ambiente-e-infrastrutture/piani-territoriali-e-progetti/ptr-piano-territoriale-regionale.html

Regione Puglia. (2012). *Piano Regionale delle Coste* [Regional Coastal Plan]. Available at: http://www.sit.puglia.it/portal/portale_pianificazione_regionale/Piano%20Regionale%20delle%20Coste/Documenti

— (2013). *Progetti integrati per i paesaggi costieri ad alta valenza naturalistica.* (Finanziati con i fondi del Programma Triennale per l'ambiente. Realizzazione di Progetti Integrati di Paesaggio nell'ambito del Piano Paesaggistico Territoriale della Regione Puglia (PPTR) - DGR 2486 del 27.12.2012) [Integrated Projects for coastal landscapes of high naturalistic value (Funded by the "Three-Year Programme for the Environment. Implementation of Integrated Landscape Projects within the Landscape and Territorial Plan of the Puglia Region (PPTR)" Resolution of the Regional Government no. 2486 of 27.12.2012].

— (2015). *Piano Paesaggistico Territoriale Regionale* (PPTR). [Regional Territorial Landscape Plan]. Available at: https://www.paesaggiopuglia.it/pptr/il-pptr-quadro-sinottico.html

— (2017). *Osservatorio del Turismo.* [Tourism Observatory]. Rapporto 2017. Available at: https://www.agenziapugliapromozione.it/portal/osservatorio-del-turismo

— (2018). Indirizzi operativi per l'Azione di Contrasto all'Erosione Costiera regionale e avvio 1° Fase del Quadro Programmatico – Studi Preliminari. [Operational guidelines for the Regional Coastal Erosion Action Plan and start of the 1st Phase of the Framework Program – Preliminary Studies]. Deliberazione della Giunta Regionale 26 settembre 2018, n. 1694.

Romano, B., & Zullo, F. (2014). The urban transformation of Italy's Adriatic coastal strip: Fifty years of unsustainability. *Land Use Policy* 38, 26–36.

Salamone, L. (2004). La gestione del demanio marittimo: dallo stato, alle regioni, ai comuni: Il caso della regione sicilia. [The management of the maritime public domain: from the state, to the regions, to the municipalities: The case of Sicily]. Diritto & Diritti, 21 December. Available at: http://www.diritto.it/articoli/amministrativo/salamone10.html.

Salvati, L., Sateriano, A., & Bajocco, S. (2013). To grow or to sprawl? Land cover relationships in a Mediterranean City region and implications for land use management. *Cities*, 30 113–121.

Sansò, P. (2010). Le coste. [The coasts]. *Geologia dell'Ambiente – Periodico della Società Italiana di Geologia Ambientale*, Supplemento "Il patrimonio geologico della Puglia" (4), 95–104.

Shape – IPA project. (2014). Definition of the Adriatic ecosystem quality as basis for Maritime Spatial planning: Contribution to the initial assessment of marine Adriatic waters according to Directive 2008/56/CE, Action 4.2, Final Report; Action 3.1, Facilitating the implementation of ICZM Protocol.

Trigilia, C. (1992). *Sviluppo senza autonomia* [Development without Autonomy]. Il Mulino.

Virga, P. (1995). *Diritto amministrativo: I principi.* [Administrative law: The principles]. Giuffrè Editore.

World Factbook. (n.d.). Italy. Available at: https://www.cia.gov/Library/publications/the-world-factbook/geos/it.html [Accessed September 2019]

WWF. (2012). *Dossier Coste: Il 'profilo' fragile dell'Italia.* [Coast Dossier: Italy's fragile 'profile'].

Zanchini, E., & Manigrasso, M. (2017). *Vista mare: La trasformazione dei territori costieri italiani.* [Sea view: The transformation of the Italian coastal territories]. Edizioni Ambiente.

Zanfi, F. (2013). The città abusiva in contemporary Southern Italy: Illegal building and prospects for change. *Urban Studies* 50 (16), 3428–3445.

National Legislation (listed chronologically)

Law on "Protection of Natural Beauty" (Law 1497/39)
Civil Code 1942 (as amended)
Navigation Code 1942 (as amended)
Decree of the President of the Italian Republic 684 of 1977
Law on "Provisions for the Defence of the Sea" (Law 979/82)
Law on "Urgent provisions for the protection of areas of particular environmental interest" (Law 431/85)
Law 394/91 Framework Law on environmentally protected areas
Decree 400 of 1993 "Provisions to determine fees for MPD concessions"
Law 59/1997 Bassanini Law – Administrative Federalism
Legislative Decree 112/1998 – Administrative Federalism
Law on "cultural and environmental goods" (Law 490/99)
Constitutional Law 3 of 2001 – Changes to Title V of the Constitution
Code on Cultural Heritage and Landscape (Law 42/2004; 2004 Code)
Law 296 of 2006 Financial and Budget Law

Regional Legislation

Puglia Law "Rules for the establishment and management of protected natural areas in the Puglia Region" (19/1997)
Puglia Law "Rules for the protection and use of the coast" (17/2006; amendment 17/2015)
Puglia Law "Rules on regional functions of prevention and repression of illegal building" (15/2012)

11   Slovenia

Naja Marot

Overview

To a Slovenian, the word "coast" evokes a similar response as does "California" to many Americans: A place where life is simple and relaxing; where the sun is always shining and there is no need for snow tires. Living on the coast is a luxury, but holidays or day trips are within reach. Given that the coast is very short (the shortest coast of all the countries in this book), development pressures are high.

Slovenia still suffers from some of the aftermath of the transition from communist governance to market economy. Yet this country is one of the fastest learners and best economic performer among the post-communist countries. The country established its first Waters Act in 2002 and a Planning Act in 2003 – only five years prior to signing the Integrated Coastal Zone Management (ICZM) Protocol to the Barcelona Convention in 2008. In some ways, these recent laws appear to have benefited from the experiences of other countries and were highly impacted by EU legislation and policies. However, these laws and the restrictions only steer new development, while a relatively large proportion of Slovenia's coastal land was already developed prior to its independence in 1991.

Introduction: The context for coastal zone management in Slovenia

The Slovenian coast is on the Adriatic Sea and is a prime location for recreation and tourism for the country's two million residents, as well as home to a relatively small local population. In addition, the Slovenian coast hosts the Port of Koper – the maritime window to the economic world for Central European countries, including Austria, Slovakia, and Hungary. Thus, the three elements of tourism, residential use, and economy collide on a coastal strip which is only 46.6 km long (World Factbook, n.d.; Ogrin, 2012).

Across Slovenia, 37% of the country's land is protected under the EU's Natura 2,000 network (Marot et al., 2013). In the coastal zone (land within 100 m of the shoreline), the proportion of land which is protected is much higher – 70% (URBI & IPO, 2014). Of the remaining land (the unprotected 30%), more than two-thirds has been developed for urban purposes. Within 200 m of the shoreline, only 1.4% of land is unprotected (URBI & IPO, 2014).

In geographic terms, the Slovenian coastal zone belongs to the Gulf of Trieste; the geomorphology of the coast includes flysch (sedimentary rock) cliffs and shallow bays with salt pans. There are no sandy beaches on the Slovenian coast. Over time, human intervention has modified the natural coastline, which now features artificial concrete walls along the beach and port.

Figure 11.1 Sketch of the Slovenian coast

Source: Illustration by Barbara Kostanjšek, September 2019

In some locations, land reclamation has shifted the coastline more than 2 km seawards (Kolega, 2015). For example, Koper was an island connected to the mainland only by a causeway, but the bay was fully reclaimed by 2010 to cater to the needs of the port. Today, three-quarters of the coast is artificially fortified and there are only a few areas, such as the Mesečni Zaliv nature reserve in Strunjan Landscape Park, where the coast is in its pristine form. Human intervention in the landscape is heavily present in the two salt pan areas, including Sečovlje salt pans (Figure 11.2). To a degree, these physical characteristics of the coast affect implementation of planning law and other relevant law and policy, including the Mediterranean ICZM Protocol.

Figure 11.2 View of the Sečovlje salt pans from the hinterland

Source: Photo by Naja Marot, September 2019

The coastal area spans the administrative boundaries of four municipalities: Beginning at the northwest (the Italian border), these are Ankaran, Koper, Izola, and Piran, on the Croatian border. Population and geographic data for these municipalities can be found at Table 11.1. In total, the population of these municipalities is 86,783 (SORS, 2019) which represents 4.2% of Slovene population (2,055,279 people; SORS, 2019). Their combined population density is among the highest in Slovenia, at 384 persons per km², while the Slovene average is 102 persons per km². The population of the coastal municipalities is ageing; most

Table 11.1 Population and geographic data about Slovenia's coastal municipalities

Municipality	Population (2019)	Area (km²)	Population density (inh. per km² 2019)	Population change 2019/2015	Share of the young population (2019)	Share of the old population (2019)	Share of vacation apartments (2018)
Ankaran	3,153	8	394.1	−2.1%	13.0	21.9	10.5
Izola	15,872	28.6	555.0	0.0%	14.4	21.9	6.2
Koper	50,438	303.2	166.4	−1.0%	14.7	20.4	1.4
Piran	17,320	44.6	388.3	−3.0%	11.8	22.7	10.0
Data source: SORS, 2019							

glaringly in Piran, where the ageing index (the ratio between the population age 65+ years and that under 15 years) was 192 in 2019. Apart from low birth rates, this is likely due, in large part, to the outmigration of the young population from Piran due to low living standards encumbered by restrictions and limitations associated with cultural heritage protection (no cars permitted, old sewerage systems, and low light due to the dense urban pattern). The lowest ageing index can be found in the municipality of Koper (139 in 2019), which has the highest number of newly built neighbourhoods and urban functions important for the quality of life of younger people.

The above municipalities make up the Obalno-kraška (Coastal–Karst) region, one of the country's twelve statistical regions. The largest city in this region is Koper, which has one of the strongest regional economies,[1] partly due to the presence of the Port of Koper and tourism. In 2017, the region had the second highest GDP per capita – 21.242 euros (SORS, 2019) after the Ljubljana Urban Region (29.371 euros); the Slovene average was 20.815 euros.

The activities which drive the economy of the region have significant environmental impact on the coastal area. The Port of Koper requires land for port activities and causes pollution. Tourism, particularly in the peak summer season (Figure 11.3), has several impacts, including pollution of the sea water, water shortages in the summer, overloaded infrastructure, and car emissions (Nemec Rudež & Vodeb, 2010). In the peak month for tourism (August), the ratio of visitors to local residents is the highest for Ankaran (63 tourists per 100 residents), followed by Piran (49), Izola (16), and Koper (2). It follows that development of tourist apartments in the coastal towns and on the agricultural land in the hinterland is significant: In Piran

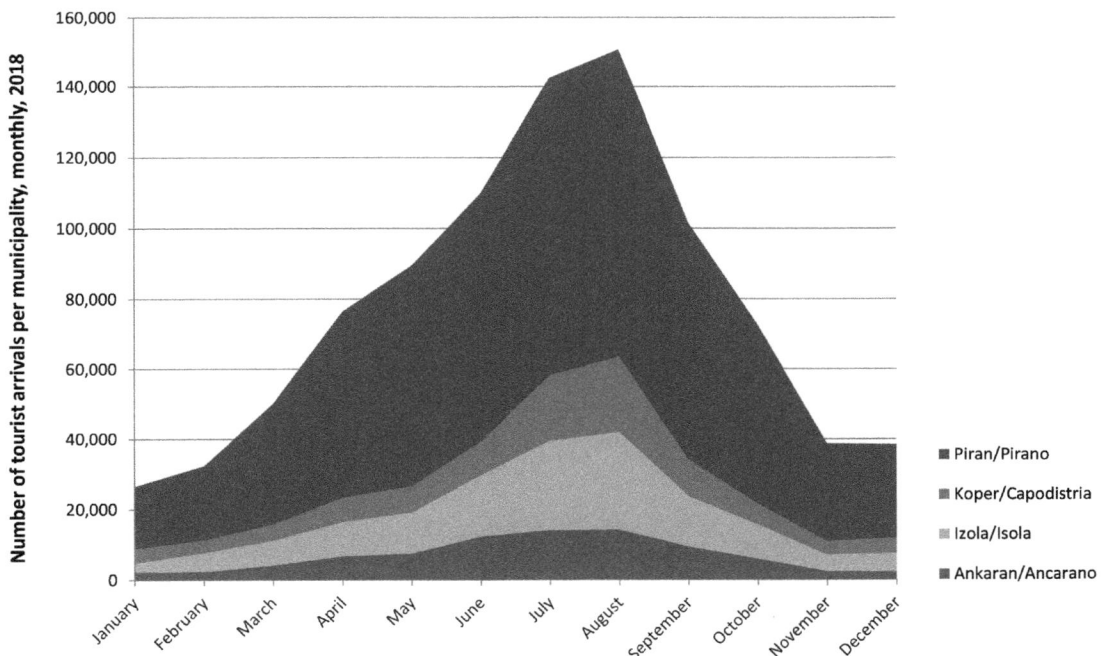

Figure 11.3 Number of tourist arrivals in coastal municipalities, monthly, 2018

Data source: SORS, 2019, Tourism statistics

and Ankaran, these apartments made up 10% of all apartments in 2018 in the official statistics; in Izola, 6%; and in Koper, 1% (SORS, 2019).

While the coast is marketed heavily as a destination, the tourism sector has many problems: It is poorly managed, hotels are old and in disrepair, parking is scarce, and public transport is inadequate. In addition, some of the public beach facilities are old and require repair and renovations, although there have been some investments (in Portorož, Piran, and Koper) in the last decade.

A 2010 study of residents' perceptions of tourism in two coastal municipalities, Koper and Piran, indicated primarily negative views, particularly regarding sociocultural and environmental impacts (littering of public areas; destruction of natural resources, including flora and fauna; impaired views; noise pollution). Residents identified only one positive outcome of tourism: Employment. Furthermore, the residents of Piran were of opinion that "tourism contributes to a decline in traditional culture and habits" (Nemec Rudež & Vodeb, 2010).

Overview of legal framework for coastal zone management

The primary pieces of Slovenian legislation relevant to coastal zone management are the Waters Act (2002) and the Spatial Planning Act (2007, updated 2017). Both are relatively recent laws, developed following the establishment of the state. The Waters Act applies to all Slovenian water bodies, with a subordinate act for each body. It defines coastal public land and guides the provision of public services and access to the water. The current Spatial Planning Act replaced the original 2003 Spatial Planning Act. Notably, in planning there is a disconnect between the national and local levels: At the local level, the coastal municipalities are guided by spatial plans which date back to the communist regime (1984, with several amendments having taken place over the years). Although the government had intended to adopt new local plans by 2014, the coastal municipalities are not actively working towards that goal with the same speed as are inland municipalities, most of which have adopted the new municipal spatial plans.

Tourism is managed through local strategic documents; examples include a tourism development strategy for the municipality of Piran (2009–2015), a strategy of the tourism development and its marketing in the City Municipality of Koper until the year 2025 (Mestna občina Koper, 2017), and detailed spatial plans, such as the plan prepared for the Sečovlje salt pans adjusted land (2010).

The Republic of Slovenia signed and ratified the ICZM protocol in 2009. However, the analysis below will show that the ratification has had little effect on land policy or law. This is unsurprising in the context of the lagging development of the country's planning and environment legislation. The EU, keen to support its members' efforts to promote ICZM, has sponsored several projects to assess the feasibility and potential impact of implementing the ICZM Protocol in Slovenia.[2]

In 2016, following adoption of the EU Directive on maritime spatial planning, the Ministry of Environment and Spatial Planning ordered a study on the implementation of that Directive and its implications for coastal zone management. However, no relevant policies or regulations have yet been adopted.

Definitions of the Slovenian coast and shoreline

Slovenia's Waters Act (2002) includes definitions for a range of different elements within the coastal zone, which affect land policy and property rights. In developing these definitions, it appears that the architects of the law drew from older laws from across Europe (such as those of France, Spain, and Greece). At first glance, the definitions appear to be based on the movement of the tides: Most significantly, the "**Shore**" is defined as *"the land between the lowest low tide and the highest high tide"*. As we will see below, however, in practice the tides do not ultimately define the landward boundary of the Shore.

Other definitions related to the definition of the Shore include:

– "**Sea-bed**" – The internal sea waters and territorial sea, seaward of the lowest low tide, which are state-owned.
– "**Sea Water Body**" – the land which was created in the sea due to sand deposits and marine regression.
– The Slovenian shoreline – the "**Shore Border**" – is defined as the highest level of the high tide.

How is "the highest level of the high tide" identified? Detailed regulations[3] stipulate that the line of the highest tide is the highest tide expected within a period of 100 years, but also follows the contour line marked at 1.73 m above sea level.[4] Thus, despite the definition found in the Waters Act appearing to rely on changing tides, the Slovenian definition of the shoreline is in fact fixed, at 1.73 m above sea level. This provides legal certainty for coastal property owners and spatial planning. Yet in determining property rights in cases where natural disasters have resulted in permanent changes to the water body, the authorities must attempt to establish where the initial shoreline lay, using the measure of the highest tide.

Significantly, the Slovenian regulations do provide some flexibility for the Shore Border to be altered in cases where there is existing construction or existing public goods. Determination of the shoreline and other boundaries in the coastal zone is the responsibility of the Surveying and Mapping Authority of the Republic of Slovenia, which utilizes survey work by the Slovenian Environment Agency. The Shore Border is delineated on the digital cadastre (with exact georeferenced coordinates) and stored by the Slovenian Environment Agency.

By 2017, Slovenia had completed the task of demarcation of the Shore Border (shoreline) across its entire coast, except for a small area at the border with Croatia (including the Sečovlje salt pans). The missing piece is the results of a border dispute between the two countries, which was in arbitration at the Permanent Court of Arbitration. In June 2017, the Court ruled in favour of Slovenia (Croatia v. Slovenia, PCA CASE no. 2012-04), but Croatia does not respect the verdict and has therefore not fully complied to date (Republic of Slovenia Government, 2019).

Slovenia's coastal setback zone

The Waters Act defines an "Inshore Belt" – a setback zone from the Slovenian shoreline where development is restricted. This zone has a width of 25 m, extending inland from the Shore Border (shoreline). Not only is this setback zone significantly narrower than the standard set by the ICZM Protocol (100 m), but the Waters Act stipulates that it may be narrowed by the government (the Spatial Planning Authority), if any of a set of fairly arbitrary situations arise:

1 There is a proposal for development on land within the area of an existing settlement
2 The proposed development within the Inshore Belt will not increase the risk of flooding or erosion
3 The proposed development will not lower the quality of the water
4 The relevant land is required for the provision of public services
5 The special regimes of the use of the water are not interrupted
6 The proposal is not contradictory to relevant water management objectives

In 2013, partners in the EU SHAPe project[5] undertook to evaluate the potential widening of the Inshore Belt to the setback width of 100 metres prescribed by the ICZM Protocol (URBI & IPO, 2014). They found that the total land area of a potential 100 m setback zone along the coast is 4.7 km². Of that land, 38% is used for agriculture, forest, or internal waters (14% agricultural use; 9% forest; 9% water surfaces; 6% open spaces, e.g. moorland). Of the remaining 62%, approximately one-third is undeveloped. The figures for undeveloped land by municipality are Koper, 32%; Izola, 34%; and Piran, 28%.

On one hand, the above figures are significant, in that they indicate the areas in which a 100 m setback zone would be irrelevant, given the presence of existing development. On the other hand, only 30% of all land within 100 m of the shoreline is not already protected from development – either by European or by domestic legislation. Examples of protections which limit development on the remaining 70% of land include Natura 2000, areas of ecological importance, nature reserves (Nature reservoir of Škocjanski Zatok, Landscape Park Sečoveljske Soline, Landscape Park Strunjan), and sites of cultural heritage.

The consensus arising from the SHAPe project is that if the setback zone were to be extended, the following land uses would be excluded from development restrictions: Land for which national detailed plans have been adopted (including developments of national importance, e.g. for the Port of Koper); developed areas (town centres, hotels, etc.); ports; and marinas. The setback zone would nevertheless protect agricultural land, forests, and dispersed settlements and would add an additional layer of protection to nature reserves.

After assessing options for implementation of an extended setback zone, the partners in the SHAPe project found that the most viable solution would be to adopt an ICZM-specific regulation. Whilst such a regulation might place additional burden in the planning process for the relevant municipalities, it could be introduced in the timeliest manner.

Public coastal land

According to the Waters Act (2002), the Shore and Sea Water Body (including the Sea-bed), as defined above, are state-owned public goods. The land may not be transferred to other parties. The local authorities are responsible for defining the specific status of these public goods and the conditions for their use.

The Sea Water Body and Sea-bed are owned and managed by the state, but the Shore and public land within the Inshore Belt are managed by the relevant local municipality. Bathing beaches and other public amenities may also be managed by local public utility companies (there are several examples of such arrangements, including Portorož beach, managed by the Piran communal utilities company Okolje).

Given Slovenia's short coast and extent of public land ownership, the authorities' task of controlling uses and development in the coastal zone is relatively simple. Coastal land use and development are thus strictly monitored and controlled.

Restrictions on land use and development in the coastal zone

By law, decisions regarding the use of the water bodies and the shore belt should take into account issues of water quality; protection against erosion; and protection of ecosystems and landscapes in keeping with nature protection legislation (Waters Act, Article 5). The law restricts development on each of the Shore, Seabed, and Inshore Belt. On this land, permanent construction is prohibited. Exceptions from this rule include public infrastructure, utilities or developments required for the protection of people, animals, or property. Developments of national importance might be permitted in cases where there is a significant financial advantage over other locations (cost saving) and on the condition that they are cleared by an environmental impact assessment.

The above restrictions on development of the Seabed and Shore existed under the former regime of Yugoslavia. In comparison, the restriction on the Inshore Belt was introduced with the Waters Act in 2002. As such, as might be expected, there is existing development within that zone. Temporary uses, such as construction of a pedestrian boardwalk (without roof or any buildings construction), are permitted on the Shore, Sea-bed, and Inshore Belt (in areas without additional environmental protection) but must be registered with the municipality or local police (for security reasons).

Notably, the Waters Act recognizes that prior to its adoption, owners of land in the Inshore Belt may have expected to use and develop their land for a variety of uses which are now prohibited. Thus, those whose use of the land is restricted may receive compensation from the State – either by payment or by compensation in kind (Article 43 of the Waters Act).

Right of public access

Accessibility is a principle identified in both the Waters Act and the Spatial Planning Act, which each state that the coast should be freely accessible to the public. These laws prohibit the development of structures that would limit or deny free passage across the Inshore Belt, Shore, and sea. Areas of the coast used for industrial purposes (e.g. Port of Koper; salt pans) are exempted from this access requirement, as are the marinas at Portorož, Izola, and Koper and other sites set aside for special uses, such as the youth resort at Debeli Rtič. In addition, some hotels have private beaches which the public may only access subject to a fee.

The beach operators (municipalities or utility companies) are responsible for ensuring that the public beaches are accessible. The twelve Slovenian Blue Flag beaches and three Blue Flag marinas (Modra Zastava, 2019) must meet the standards set by the international Foundation for Environmental Education for safe beach access.

Over time, government agencies have modified the Slovenian coastline to make it more accessible: Given the geomorphology of the coast described earlier in this chapter, it is often accessible only by stairs or other artificial paths. Further interventions have benefited those with special needs: In Izola, for example, the authorities developed a beach tailored especially to the needs of people with physical disabilities, with railing, ramps, and other tailored features, which is accessible free of charge. Also in Izola, a hotel tailored to the elderly incorporates a bespoke beach.[6] Another example of special arrangements for beach access is the Youth Health Resort at Debeli Rtič (Ankaran), a facility operated by the Slovenian Red Cross.[7] This facility provides a coastal retreat for school children, including those from lower socio-economic backgrounds, and for others from disadvantaged families who would otherwise not be able to enjoy holidays on the coast.

Municipalities, or municipal corporations, are responsible for managing bathing beaches. This responsibility comes with the cost of maintaining the beaches and related services. To supplement maintenance costs, until 2004 all municipalities charged entrance fees for most beaches. For example, managers of Portorož beach (see Figure 11.4) collected 40,000 euros in entry fees annually. However, in the 2000s, the number of beach patrons fell dramatically (from 4,000 per day to 2,000 per day in the peak season), which led to a decision to abolish the fees and instead raise the funds required for maintenance through the lease of bars, cafés, and restaurants. This management model has persisted since it was introduced.

Figure 11.4 Bathing beach in Portorož with related infrastructure, access free of charge

Source: Photo by Maša Bantan Marot, September 2019

Planning legislation and its implications in practice

The first Slovenian Spatial Planning Act was adopted 12 years after the country gained independence, in 2003. The Act divided planning responsibilities across the national, regional, and local administrative levels. On the national level, the state developed a strategic framework – the Slovenian Spatial Planning Strategy (2004, amendment pending) and a statutory framework – the Spatial Planning Order (2004), which guides development. These two documents include specific guidelines and objectives targeted to the coastal area. For example, the following is an extract from the Spatial Planning Strategy:

> *The coastal region combines the areas of high quality natural and cultural landscape features with the conurbation of Koper, Izola, Piran and Portorož. Its coastal and border position determines its orientation towards the further development of tourism, transport, industry, agriculture and fishing. The integrated spatial concept of the coast shall be ensured, by which the interests of development activities are harmonized with spatial possibilities and protection requirements. At the same time, conditions for the development of a high-quality range of tourist services and amenities shall be established and permanent public access to the seashore and beaches shall be ensured.* (Ministry of the Environment and Spatial Planning, 2004, p. 30; notably, the Strategy does not define the coast, seashore, or beaches)

Figure 11.5 Izola, one of the larger cities on the Slovenian coast. The old city core on the peninsula (left) and the modern development in the hinterland (right)

Source: Photo by Naja Marot, September 2019

Since the publication of the Strategy and to the time of writing, authorities have followed the principles of the strategy regarding protection of the coastal zone (with few exceptions). Yet the vision for the establishment of a "high-quality" range of tourist services and amenities has not been realized, most likely due to a lack of funding for this purpose.

The Slovenian Spatial Strategy is currently being renewed, and in the drafting process, a special focus group was established to deliberate on strategies for planning and development of the coastal area, including the sea, taking into account the ICZM Protocol and the EU Directive on maritime spatial planning. The outcomes of these discussions remain to be seen.

The 2003 Spatial Planning Act introduced the concept of a regional strategic planning document to guide development, but this option for strategic planning was later overwritten by the updated 2007 Spatial Planning Act. In 2006, a draft strategic plan, *Conception of the Spatial Development of the South Primorska Region and the Programme of the Measures for Its Implementation* (ACER & OIKOS, 2006), was prepared for the coastal area, but it was never officially adopted (and thus was not implemented). The 2007 Spatial Planning Act replaced the concept of the regional strategic plan with a more zoning oriented inter-municipal spatial plan, but to date, only one plan of this nature has been adopted. The idea of the regional strategic plan was again reintroduced in the new 2017 Spatial Planning Act, but has not yet been put into practice.

The 2007 Spatial Planning Act also introduced a new format for "local planning acts" (the local statutory planning framework), where local plans would ascribe specific uses to each land parcel, allowing little room for discretion. The Act stipulated that all municipalities should adopt such local schemes by 2014, but to 2017, only half had done so. The rest of the municipalities, including all four coastal municipalities, still rely on schemes from 1984 (with amendments). The new schemes are in various stages of preparation across the respective municipalities. This apparent reluctance of municipalities to update their planning schemes might stem in part from the fact that they have very limited resources for planning (Marot, 2010). In addition, they are likely concerned that the new format for local plans will limit investment within their jurisdictions, given that these plans provide less scope for ad hoc approval of development.

Public participation

Slovenia has no specific policies or practices for public participation in coastal zones. Nevertheless, the Aarhus Convention is incorporated into the Slovenian Nature Conservation Act (1999), and its principles are implemented through the planning process. Like in most countries, public participation in planning processes in Slovenia is very limited in scope: In the preparation of municipal land use plans, participation involves only consultation (through public hearings which are traditionally announced in newspapers and on billboards), though research by Marot (2010) has revealed the presence of more advanced practices of communicative planning, including workshops, public lectures, and project councils. There has recently been an increase in the number of civil initiatives which eventually impact the official planning process and dialogue between stakeholders; for example, there was a civil initiative against the enlargement of the Port of Koper.

There are NGOs addressing coastal issues, but these NGOs tend to focus on strictly environmental concerns, rather than on planning and land use–related matters (Berdavs, 2010, 2015). For example, in 2011, the association Ecologists Without Borders spearheaded a study on the deposit of waste into the sea. The findings showed that most of the waste in the sea off the coast of Slovenia is plastic and that the most polluted areas are Seča and Moon Bay – the latter being an environmentally protected area (Rajh, n.d.; Laglbauer et al., 2014).

Compliance and enforcement

Slovenians have identified the potential gain from additional development, particularly tourist accommodation, in the coastal zone and have found creative ways to satisfy their appetites for such development. The bulk of illegal development in the coastal zone is limited to private land in the Inshore Belt (setback zone) and its hinterland. Most commonly, owners (or developers) begin by enlarging, replacing, or modifying disused agricultural sheds on orchards, olive groves, or other agricultural land with sea views (Babič, 2009). At first, the modifications are minor, such that no building permit is required. Gradually, however, these sheds grow to become small-scale overnight accommodation. Such developments are not connected to local utilities (e.g. electricity and water) and their owners do not pay the municipal taxes usually required from operators of accommodation facilities. As at September 2019, it appears that these sheds are being replaced by mobile homes permanently located on the lots (Figure 11.6).

Another form of illegal development common in the coastal zone occurs where owners/developers receive building permits but diverge from the permits in the construction stage. They might use different materials than approved; develop the building in a larger form (e.g. an approved small cottage is developed as a big villa); change the use of the building (e.g. what is planned as an agricultural dwelling is developed as a spa); or develop more units than were approved.

In Slovenia, enforcement against illegal development is generally weak. While the planning legislation provides for the use of measures such as fines and demolition,[8] these are rarely practised. Cases of illegal development are identified through the Construction Inspectorate, a body within the Ministry of the Environment and Spatial Planning. The Ministry has recently reported that on the coast, such cases are generally solved by issuing a notice to the owners which requires them to return the property to its previous state (Ivanič, 2015). Such notices inform the owners that if they do not adhere to the requirement, the municipality will impose more severe measures, such as fines and demolition. These notices are effective, but only because most offenders construct small additions to existing buildings, as opposed to new buildings.

Figure 11.6 Example of a mobile home located on the agricultural land (probably replaced a shed)

Source: Photo by Naja Marot, September 2019

In one case, in Bužekijan (Municipality of Izola), the Inspectorate required that construction be halted at an advanced stage. The building remains standing and empty on a very prominent site (Figure 11.7). While development may not be completed, for unknown reasons the municipality has not issued an order for demolition. There are several other such cases where a notice or fine has been issued and the building is not in use but, similarly, the authorities have not progressed the enforcement to the point of demolition.

Based on data from all four coastal municipalities, the Inspectorate has become more active and more stringent in recent years; the number of registered offences and suggestions for control has been increasing, while the proportion of those proceedings relating to minor offences is in decline. In a detailed study of compliance and enforcement in the Municipality of Izola, Marsič (2012) found that, in that municipality, approximately 500 new cases of illegal development (including extensions, sheds, etc.) are detected in the coastal zone each year. This number pertains primarily to minor extensions where owners/developers take a chance that they will go unnoticed. In addition, in 2012, no enforcement measures had been taken against 450 existing cases of illegal development. In Izola, over the years 2011–2012, the municipality and the Farmland and Forest Fund of the Republic of Slovenia notified the Inspectorate of 79 new cases of illegal development.

Although the statistics on illegal development are vague, it is reasonable to assume that one might find a proportionally higher number of larger-scale illegalities (e.g. entire houses) in inland regions of the country where there is a lower level of scrutiny.

Figure 11.7 Half-built illegal tourist facility in Bužekija, Municipality of Izola

Source: Photo by Naja Marot, September 2019

Climate change

The Slovenian coast consistently experiences phenomena associated with climate change, such as droughts, frosts (Ogrin, 2002), and flooding. Nevertheless, the national government has invested little in the study of climate projections and potential risks. The available data is primarily derived from transnational projects, such as the EU project ClimChAlp (Climate Change, Impacts and Adaptation Strategies in the Alpine Space).

Strategies for climate change adaptation are integrated into several Slovenian policies at the national level,[9] yet there is no policy focused specifically on climate change in the coastal zone. In 2014, the government commissioned a review of existing studies about climate change in Slovenia (including climate modelling) in order to improve adaptation initiatives (Kajfež-Bogataj et al., 2014). Overall, the review revealed that there is a lack of data about climate change and how the threats of climate change might be addressed. While the risks of climate change in the coastal zone, such as sea level rise, are mentioned in regional development programmes, there are no national adaptation strategies or measures in place which address those risks. The exception is a few strategies which apply to landslide risk on agricultural land and flood risk management in the valley in the Rižana and Dragonja river region.

On the local level, the Sustainable Urban Strategy of the Municipality of Koper (2016) adopts adaptation measures via the green system concept, such as greening the city and taking care of the sewage waters (Mestna občina Koper, 2016). In the past, Koper adopted a programme for protection against natural and other disasters for the short-term period of 2006–2010. The programme defined the goals, guidelines, and strategies for protection against disasters, including flooding. It relied on up-to-date flood maps and vulnerability assessments.

Integration and coordination

There is no national framework for the integration and coordination components of ICZM in Slovenia. As we have shown throughout this chapter, much of the management of the coastal area falls to the relevant municipalities, primarily through spatial planning and strategic processes. Yet the bulk of the power in determining how the coast will be used and managed is held by the nature and cultural protection agencies, such as the Institute of the Republic of Slovenia for Nature Conservation, which are supported by EU legislation and its adoption into Slovenian law.[10] These agencies prioritize conservation and very rarely decide in favour of development, even in cases in which the proposal is justified by a need for maintenance of the property. On the other hand, on the local level, authorities responsible for planning and development tend to have a strong development agenda, and as such, the restrictive approach taken by the protection and conservation agencies acts as a counterbalance.

The distribution of EU and national funds is carried out at a regional level. Within each region, Regional Development Programmes are prepared to define the allocation of funds. The Programme for the coastal region is prepared by the Regional Council and the regional development agency (Regional Development Centre Koper). The Regional Council is a decision-making body which, together with State authorities, confirms the Regional Development Programme and supervises the work of the regional development agency. The members of the Regional Council represent a variety of sectors, including businesses, municipalities, the public sector (health, social care, and education), and civil society. Apart from this legally anchored institutional framework, several other institutions function as active stakeholders (NGOs, cultural institutions, and private companies). The Programme defines guidelines, goals, and measures for the region, as well as projects which will be funded. It lists for the coastal area a set of general priorities which take into account both economic and preservation interests. Until recently, spatial planning did not occur at the regional level, but since 2014, Regional Development Programmes must include a spatial dimension – yet to date, this requirement has not been fully implemented (Regionalni razvojni center Koper, 2015). Larger-scale change is expected in the new Regional Development Programmes for the period 2021–2027, as the 2017 Planning Act more specifically requires integration of the spatial dimension into the Programmes, as well as preparation of separate Regional Spatial Plans.

Coordination or cooperation between the coastal municipalities is rare. The four municipalities are in competition with each other. Long-standing rivalries exist between Piran and Koper regarding competition over tourism and investment. Similarly, Koper and Ankaran have an enduring dispute about the enlargement of the Port of Koper.[11]

Fiscal aspects

Potential compensation rights for the change of the value of land on the basis of planning decisions (regulatory takings) are under discussion in Slovenia (Ivanič, 2015). In the past, these were defined in the Agricultural Land Act, but this was valid only for a very short period. Apart from the compensation available to landowners within the Inshore Belt under the Waters Act (mentioned above), there are no other compensation rights specifically related to coastal land.

It should be noted that municipalities must source funds for beach management. Sources of income for this purpose include parking fees; charging for beach services, including swimming pools; and rentals of beach equipment, such as sun umbrellas. In addition, hotels maintaining private beaches must pay fees for the privilege.

Conclusion

Although the Slovenian coastline is short in length, the authorities entrusted to manage the coastal zone face challenges which mirror those in other Mediterranean countries – particularly pressure for development associated with tourism and the port. Despite the fact that the ICZM Protocol has yet to influence Slovenian law or practice in any significant way, existing measures in planning and environmental laws, together with the relative ease of monitoring a small area, have to date been generally effective in managing development pressures.

Nevertheless, the pressures continue to intensify: There is speculation about the expansion of the Port of Koper; accessibility of the coast is threatened; a gas terminal may be developed in Žavlje; additional tourist accommodation may be developed on the Ankaran peninsula; and a bypass road is proposed between Izola and Portorož and towards the Croatian border. Furthermore, local authorities continue to support development proposals in an effort to attract investment. In addition, management of the coast is characterized by fragmentation across municipalities. Increased coordination and integration of the principles of the ICZM Protocol into Slovenian law would likely assist the authorities to manage the increasing pressures.

Notes

1. Based on the Development Risk Index, which is calculated by weighing indicators of economic development (e.g. GDP per capita, gross basis for income tax per inhabitant), population (dependency ratio), education (average number of schooling years), and environment (share of population connected to public sewage system, share of territory of Natura 2000 areas, and settlement indicator) for all 12 Slovenian regions. It is used as a basis for distributing the EU funds granted to Slovenia through the Operational Programme on Strengthening Regional Development Potentials, e.g. through the Cohesion fund.
2. Including SHAPe (Shaping an Holistic Approach to Protect the Adriatic Environment between coast and sea).
3. Official Gazette of the Republic of Slovenia, 106/2004, changes, 77/2010.
4. Sea level is Slovenia's national reference level for the elevation coordinate system.
5. SHAPe: Shaping an Holistic Approach to Protect the Adriatic Environment between coast and sea.
6. The hotel is owned by the Slovenian association of the pensioners societies. ZDUS is a non-governmental umbrella organization bringing together 503 local pensioners' organizations and clubs.
7. http://www.zdravilisce-debelirtic.org/en/
8. Fines of 30,000 to 80,000 euros apply where an owner/developer carries out development without a permit or undertakes works that will change the use of the building from that allowed in the permit (Construction Act, Article 179). Fines apply to all the persons who carried out these activities – e.g. the construction site manager, planner. Demolition is an available tool, but in practice it is not applied much.
9. e.g. Resolution on the National Programme of Environment Protection for the Period 2005–2012 (2004); Action Plan for Reducing GHG Emmissions (2003), Resolution on the National Energy Programme (2003).
10. For details on the power balance, see, for example, Marot (2010).
11. Ankaran, which is against the expansion of the port, is supported by several civil organizations which focus on conservation of the beach and protection of other water resources. The relevant NGOs include one which supports the independence of the Municipality of Ankaran, the society Green Progress, the Society for the Protection and Development of the Peninsula Debeli Rtič.

References

ACER & OIKOS. (2006). Zasnova prostorskega razvoja v Južni Primorski in program ukrepov za njeno izvajanje [Conception of the spatial development of the South Primorska Region and the programme of the measures for its implementation]. Novo Mesto: ACER, OIKOS.

Babič, T. (2009). Analiza in ovrednotenje pobud fizičnih in pravnih oseb za spremembo veljavnega prostorskega plana [Analysis and evaluation of initiatives by natural and legal persons to change the existing spatial plan] (Master's thesis). University of Ljubljana, Faculty of Arts.

Berdavs, J. (2010). *Urbanizacija, meje in trajnostni razvoj: Primer Mestne občine Koper: doktorska disertacija [Urbanization, borders and sustainable development: The case of the Municipality of Koper]* (Doctoral dissertation). University of Primorska, Faculty of Humanities.

Berdavs, J. (2015). Interview about the urbanization process and management of the Slovenian coast. Ljubljana.

Ivanič, L. (2015). Interview about planning legislation and coastal management. Ljubljana: Ministry of the Environment and Spatial Planning.

Kajfež-Bogataj, L., Črepinšek, Z., Zalar, M., Golobič, M., Marot, N., & Lestan, K. A. (2014). *Podlage za pripravo ocene tveganj in priložnosti, ki jih podnebne spremembe prinašajo za Slovenijo: končno poročilo [Groundwork for Risk Assessment and Assessment of Opportunities Climate Change Can Bring Slovenia: Final Report]*. University of Ljubljana, Biotechnical Faculty.

Kolega, N. (2015). Coastline changes on the Slovenian coast between 1954 and 2010. *Acta Geographica Slovenica* 55(2), 205–221.

Laglbauer, B.J.L., Melo Franco-Santos, R., Andreu-Cazenave, M., Brunelli, L., Papadatou, M., Palatinus, A., Grego, M., Deprez, T. (2014). Macrodebris and microplastics from beaches in Slovenia. *Marine Pollution Bulletin* 89(1-2), 356–366.

Marot, N. (2010). *An Assessment of the Role of Spatial Planning Legislation in the Slovenian Spatial Planning System*. University of Ljubljana, Faculty of Civic and Geodetic Engineering.

Marot, N., Kolarič, Š, & Golobič, M. (2013). Slovenia as the natural Park of Europe? Territorial impact assessment in the case of Natura 2000. *Acta Geographica Slovenica* 53(1), 91–116.

Marsič, B. (2012). Črne gradnje so velika težava [Illegal construction is a big problem]. Regionalobala.si, 27 September. Available at: http://www.regionalobala.si/novica/crne-gradnje-so-velika-tezava

Mestna občina Koper [City Municipality of Koper]. (2016). Trajnostna urbana strategija mesta Koper. Koper. [Sustainable urban strategy of the city of Koper]. Mestna Občina Koper. Available at: https://www.koper.si/wp-content/uploads/2019/01/TUS-Koper-FEB-2016.pdf

Mestna občina Koper [City Municipality of Koper]. (2017). Strategija razvoja in trženja turizma v Mestni občini Koper za obdobje do leta 2025. [Tourism development and marketing strategy in the Municipality of Koper for the period to 2025]. Mestna občina Koper. Available at: https://www.koper.si/wp-content/uploads/2019/03/Strategija-turizma-v-MOK-do-2025.pdf

Ministry of the Environment and Spatial Planning. (2004). *Spatial Development Strategy of the Republic of Slovenia*. Ministry of the Environment and Spatial Planning.

Nemec Rudež, H., & Vodeb, K. (2010). Perceived tourism impacts in municipalities with different tourism concentration. *Turizam: Znanstveno-stručni časopis* 58(2), 161–172.

Ogrin, D. (2002). Dry and wet years in submediterranean Slovenia from the 14th to the mid-19th century. *Acta Universitatis Palackianae Olomucensis. Facultas Rerum Naturalium. Geographica* 37, 55–62.

Ogrin, D. (2012). Uvod v oceanografske razmere Tržaškega zaliva [Introduction to the oceanographic conditions of the Gulf of Trieste]. In D. Ogrin (Ed.), *Geografija stika Slovenske Istre in Tržaškega zaliva* (pp. 107–114). University of Ljubljana, Faculty of Arts. Available at: http://geo.ff.uni-lj.si/sites/geo.ff.uni-lj.si/files/Dokumenti/Publikacije/geograff_12.pdf

Rajh, E. (n.d.). Plastic in our lives and on the plates. Ecologists without borders. Available at: https://ebm.si/prispevki/plastika-v-nasih-zivljenjih-in-na-kroznikih [Accessed July 2020].

Regionalni razvojni center Koper. (2015). *Regionalni razvojni program za Južno Primorsko regijo [Regional Development Programme for the Southern Coastal Region] 2014–2020*. Available at: http://www.rrc-kp.si/sl/regionalni-razvoj/rrp-2014-2020.html

Republic of Slovenia Government. (2019). Arbitraža [Arbitration]. Available at: https://www.gov.si/zbirke/projekti-in-programi/arbitraza/

SORS – Statistical Office of the Republic of Slovenia. (2019). The demographic data. Available at: https://pxweb.stat.si/SiStatDb/pxweb/en/10_Dem_soc/

URBI & IPO. (2014). Uskladitev režimov v 100-metrskem priobalnem pasu slovenskega dela Jadranskega morja z zahtevami 8. člena protokola ICZM [Harmonization of regimes in the 100-metre coastal zone of the Slovenian part of the Adriatic Sea with the requirements of Article 8 of the ICZM Protocol]– project SHAPe. Available at: https://www.rrc-kp.si/sl/domov-slo/4-projekti/referencni/161-shape.html

World Factbook. (n.d.). Slovenia. Available at: https://www.cia.gov/library/publications/the-world-factbook/geos/si.html [Accessed September 2019]

Modra Zastava. (2019). Vse lokacije [Slovenian Blue Flag Beaches]. Available at: https://www.modra-zastava.si/vse-lokacije/

Legislation (listed chronologically) available at http://www.pisrs.si/Pis.web/#

Nature Conservation Act (1999). *Official Gazette of the Republic of Slovenia*, 96/04

Waters Act (2002). *Official Gazette of the Republic of Slovenia*, 67, pp. 7648–7680

Spatial Planning Act (2003) *Official Gazette of the Republic of Slovenia*, 110, pp. 13057–13083

Construction Act (2004). *Official Gazette of the Republic of Slovenia*, 102, pp. 12358–12407

Regulation on the detailed delineation of the Shore Border (2004). *Official Gazette of the Republic of Slovenia*, 106

Local Self-Government Act (2007) *Official Gazette of the Republic of Slovenia*, 94, pp. 12729–12745

Spatial Planning Act (2007) *Official Gazette of the Republic of Slovenia*, 33, pp. 4585–4602

Promotion of Balanced Regional Development Act (2011) *Official Gazette of the Republic of Slovenia*, 20/11

Spatial Planning Act (2017) *Official Gazette of the Republic of Slovenia*, 61/17

Court case

Permanent Court of Arbitration: Croatia v. Slovenia, PCA Case No. 2012-04, Final Award, 29 June 2017

12 Greece

Evangelia Balla and Georgia Giannakourou

Overview

Greece has the longest coastline of all states on the Mediterranean Sea and the third longest coastline of the countries in this book – after Australia and the USA. Given their attractiveness for a range of uses, Greek coastal areas have increasingly been subject to intensive pressures from human activities, including tourism, recreation, vacation homes, fisheries, and aquaculture. These pressures threaten coastal ecosystems and natural resources while also generating conflicts between incompatible land uses. The sheer length of Greece's coastline, together with its centralized system of governance and a fragile economy, has challenged coastal zone management. Greece has not yet ratified the Mediterranean Integrated Coastal Zone Management (ICZM) Protocol, and its coastal setback falls short of the standard set by that document. In addition, authorities must contend with past widespread illegal development. More recently, various measures taken during the economic crisis period (2010–2018) in order to boost the Greek economy have added additional layers of complexity. This chapter delves into these challenges at a time when the Greek public is gradually becoming more aware of the value of the coastal area as both an environmental and an economic resource.

The Greek regulatory context changes relatively rapidly. This chapter presents the state of play and data to August 2018.

The context: Introduction to the coastal issues in Greece

At 13,676 km (World Factbook, n.d.), the Greek coastline makes up almost one-third of the total coastline along the Mediterranean basin.[1] Almost half of this coastal zone is located in continental Greece, with the remaining half dispersed among Greece's 3,000 islands (or 9,800, if islets are included). This extensive resource is a key element of the Greek landscape: About 33% of the Greek population resides in coastal areas within 1–2 km of the coast (YPEN, 2018, p. 234). Located in the coastal zone are: (a) The country's largest urban centres, among them Athens and Thessaloniki; (b) 80% of national industrial activity; (c) 90% of tourism and recreation activities; (d) 35% of the country's farmland; (e) the country's fisheries and aquaculture; and (f) an important part of the country's infrastructure, including ports, airports, roads, power, and telecommunication networks (YPEN, 2018, p. 234). Additionally, Greek coastal areas are characterized by a rich biological and cultural diversity: Natural habitats and habitats of species (YPECHODE, 2006), coastal forests and forest lands, archaeological sites, monuments, and historic settlements.

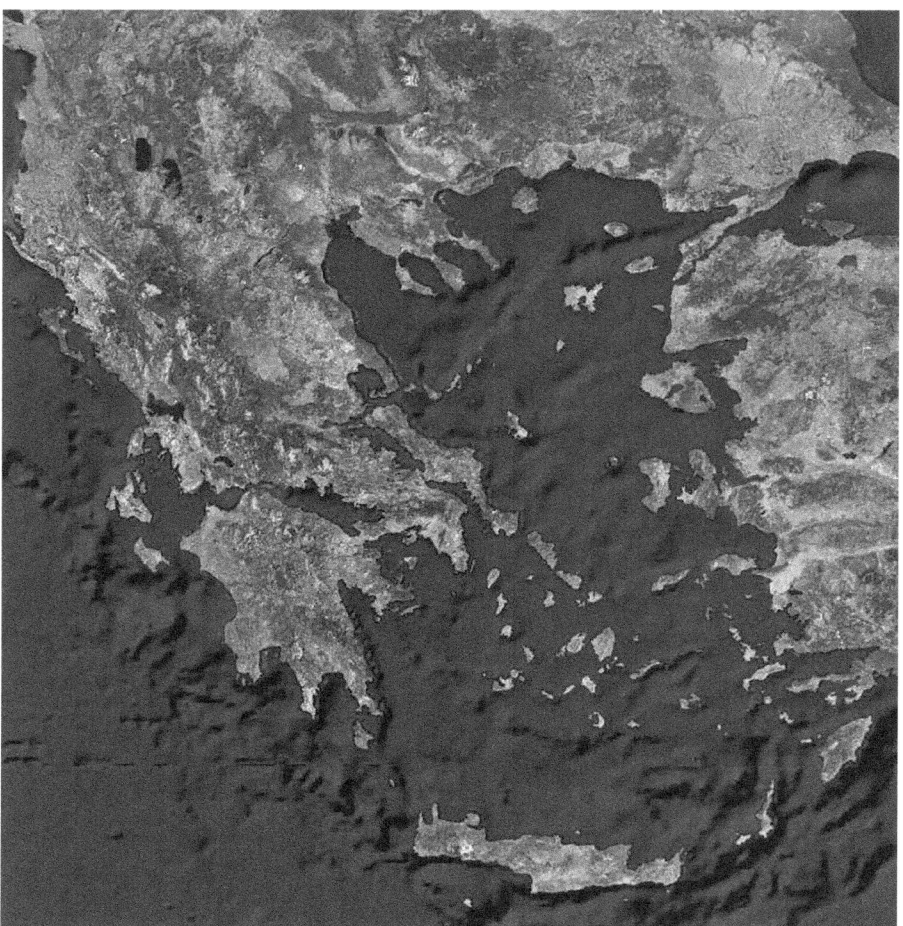

Figure 12.1 Satellite map of Greece: The longest coastline on the Mediterranean Sea

Source: NASA

Greek administrative structure

To understand Greece's coastal laws and policies, it is necessary to appreciate its administrative structure. There are three levels of governance in Greece (central, regional, and local) but four key administrative bodies:

- *Central/State/National Government*
- *Decentralized administrations* are agencies of the national government established in 2011 under a then new administrative structure (Law 3852/2010, which defines the administrative structure of Greece). They are responsible for State audit and executive tasks. There are seven decentralized administrations, all of which are on the coast: *Attica*; *Thessaly–Mainland Greece*; *Epirus–Western Macedonia*; *Peloponnese, Western Greece, and Ionian Islands*; *Macedonia-Thrace*; *Aegean*; and *Crete*.

- *Regions* (*periféreies*) are governed by a regional governor and a regional council popularly elected every five years. There are thirteen regions which are then divided further into regional units (perifereiakés enótites), usually but not always corresponding with the former prefectures. Among the thirteen Regions, twelve qualify as coastal.
- *Municipalities* (*dímoi*) are governed by a mayor and a municipal council, elected every five years. The municipalities are further subdivided into municipal units.

Within the central government, but at a decentralized level, an important group of administrative bodies which play a key role in coastal zone management in Greece are the Regional Directorates of Public Property (RDPPs). The RDPPs are regional arms of the Ministry of Finance, which manages public land. By Presidential Decree (142/2017), the RDPPs are the responsible authorities for the protection and management of the Greek coast (Article 105). We will discuss their role in greater detail below.

Overview of the Greek legal framework for coastal zone management

As early as 1940, the Greek state recognized the need to protect and manage coastal areas by legal means, and introduced special coastal legislation in the form of an Emergency Law[2] (2344/1940 – henceforth, the '1940 coastal law'). The 1940 coastal law addressed the definition, delimitation, use, and protection of the 'Seashore' and the 'Beach' as integral parts of the country's public domain. This law remained in force until 2001, when it was replaced by Law 2971/2001 on 'Seashore, Beach and other provisions' (the '2001 coastal law').

Besides the 2001 coastal law, topics relevant to coastal zone management appear in other laws, including laws addressing protected areas and nature conservation, water, regional and town planning, fishing, ports, and marinas.

The backbone for all domestic legislation for environmental protection, management, and planning is the Greek Constitution (1975, most recently amended in 2008). The Constitution stipulates that protection of the natural and cultural environments is a duty of the State (Article 24). To that end, the State has developed a special set of national rules for environmental protection and planning regulation, which cover, *inter alia*, the coast as an environmental asset and an economic good. The need for such rules was reinforced by Greece's entry (in 1981) into the European Community and its consequent obligation to adopt Community objectives and policies for environmental protection. Indeed, more than two hundred EU environmental directives have been incorporated into Greek law since 1981, covering both traditional environmental themes (e.g. protection of species, water and air quality) and new areas of environmental interest, such as climate change, resource efficiency, and biodiversity protection. Under the dual requirements of constitutional rules and Community legislation, several additional pieces of domestic environmental legislation have been enacted since 1975. The legislation affects – or should affect – both the general and special planning frameworks at the national and regional levels, land use regulation at the local level, and environmental impact assessments and licensing at the site level.

Greece's recent environmental and planning legislation provides a framework and vision for integrated coastal zone protection and management. For example, L. 3937/2011 on the 'Preservation of Biodiversity and Other Provisions' (henceforth, 'the 2011 biodiversity law') includes several provisions specific to the coast, while L. 4546/2018 on the 'Incorporation into Greek law of the Directive 2014/89/EU on maritime spatial planning' (henceforth, 'the 2018 maritime spatial planning law') provides, for the first time, for an integrated management of the coastal zone through maritime spatial planning. Although Greece has not yet ratified the Protocol on Integrated Coastal Zone Management (ICZM Protocol, which it signed in 2008), many of its objectives and principles have been substantially introduced into Greek law through recent legislation on maritime spatial planning. Past and future challenges relate to the systematic implementation of the relevant legislation.

Significantly, tensions between recent provisions and 'old-type' legislation, which focused on the administration of the coastal public domain (including the 2001 coastal law), could potentially undermine the capacity of the regulatory system to address complex coastal policy issues. Moreover, the lack of resolution on some issues generates significant gaps between policy, regulation, and implementation. A new approach is needed to secure a better balance between coastal zone preservation and development. In this chapter, we hope to contribute to the ongoing debate on the way forward for Greek coastal zone management.

Finally, we note that planning legislation plays an important role in coastal zone management, as outlined in detail at the section 'Planning policies and tools for coastal protection and development' in this chapter. The most recent Greek planning legislation is Law 4447/2016 on Spatial and Urban Planning (henceforth the '2016 planning law').

Definition and delineation of the coastal zone in Greece

Defining the coastal zone, or specific elements within the zone, is essential to understand the property rights implications of coastal law and policy. But in Greece, the legal definitions and associated procedures which were used to define areas of the coastal zone, until recently, did not provide certainty regarding the precise location of boundaries, leading to disputes and delayed implementation.

Definition of the coastal zone: From the 2001 coastal law to 2018 maritime spatial planning law

Until recently, the notion of a 'coastal zone' in Greece remained a vague geographical concept, without explicit recognition in national legislation. Under both the 1940 and 2001 coastal laws, there was no definition of the coastal zone, but the 'Seashore' and the 'Beach' were defined. The following definitions are provided at Article 1 of the 2001 law:

The term **'Seashore'** (*'aigialos'* in Greek) refers to the area of the coast which might be reached by waves in their highest point (excluding unusual storm events). The 'Seashore' also serves to define the shoreline – the line between land and sea. The shoreline is located at the 'Seashore' boundary defined by the 'usual maximum winter wave run-up'.

This definition of the 'Seashore' originates from an 1837 law on the Greek public domain. The use of the 'maximum' wave run-up might imply that the Seashore could move as high tides get higher. As we see in other countries in this book, such a reliance on nature is not unusual. However, the Greek definition is based on the word 'usual' maximum wave run-up, which could evoke an expectation for the responsible body to set some limits, by calculating what constitutes the 'usual' within determined periods of time. Nevertheless, the Greek authorities did not attempt to make a quantitative determination of what is 'usual' until they enacted the 2001 coastal law. Prior to that time, deep uncertainty was created regarding the legal status of landholders, investors, and government authorities with interests on the coast (Alterman et al., 2016). The impacts of this uncertainty have been far-reaching: As will be discussed in detail below, the legal definition of the Seashore also determines the legal ownership of the land, as the Seashore is public land; thus, many thousands of stakeholders have been affected.

The '**Beach**' ('*paralia*' in Greek) is defined as a zone adjacent to the Seashore, with a width of 'up to 50 metres'. This zone is essentially a buffer zone between land and sea. The precise width of the Beach is to be decided on a case-by-case basis, with consideration of local conditions and existing development patterns. The Beach zone is usually defined as 'open space' in spatial plans, but may be used for roads, pedestrian, and bicycle routes. Yet there is no legal requirement that the Beach be demarcated, and in many cases it is not. Where a Beach area has been defined, private property plots begin at the outer boundary of the Beach. Both the Seashore and the Beach are part of the Greek public domain, while their public use is, according to the law, permitted as-of-right. The use of the Seashore and Beach is discussed below.

The 2001 coastal law also defines the concept of the '**old Seashore zone**'; the area of land between the previously identified (historical nineteenth-century) shoreline and the newly identified shoreline. This definition pertains to locations where the sea has receded and the shoreline has shifted towards the sea: In other words, where the coastal zone has been extended by additional land which was previously under the sea. Some of the locations where this occurs have very high land values; therefore, there are significant property rights issues associated with the change. The old Seashore belongs to the State (but as private domain) and is registered as public property (Article 2). Beyond the definitions we have mentioned here, the 2001 coastal law does not define a broader 'coastal zone'.

A different, more comprehensive, approach to the notion of the coastal zone can be found in the 2011 biodiversity law. According to this law, the '**Coastal Zone**' is defined as:

> Terrestrial and aquatic sections on either side of the shoreline in which the interaction between the marine and terrestrial part acquires the form of complex systems of ecological elements and resources composed of biotic and abiotic components coexisting and interacting with human communities and relevant socio-economic activities. The coastal zone may include natural formations or small islands in their entirety. (Article 2, para. 12)

The same law introduces the notion of a '**Critical Coastal Zone**', which is defined as:

> The part of the coastal zone in which marine and terrestrial parts meet and interact... [and in which] are included geomorphological formations, areas consisting of corrosion materials from nearby areas or carried by wind, characteristic flora or land eroded at a rate that is a danger to anthropogenic facilities or activities.

These definitions reflect a more comprehensive approach to the demarcation of the Greek coastal zone, based on ecological, biological, and climatic criteria. They imply that the coastal zone may cover a wider area than the land within the 'Seashore' and the 'Beach', but these two zones are the minimum basic components. These definitions come in the wake of decisions of the Greek Council of State, which has accepted that the coasts are vulnerable ecosystems (CoS 978/2005) requiring increased protection (CoS 1500/2000) and are suitable only for minor development (CoS 1340/2007, 1790/1999, 1129/1999, 3344/1999). Both definitions, however, appear to apply only under the 2011 biodiversity law and thus do not provide a broader legal basis for coastal protection and management.

The EU Directive on maritime spatial planning (2014/89/EU) suggests that EU members take into account land-sea interactions when establishing and implementing maritime spatial planning. As such, the recent 2018 maritime spatial planning law (introduced above) opted for a unique spatial planning and management system for marine and coastal areas. The new law, besides transposing the definitions on maritime spatial planning deriving from the relevant directive into Greek law, introduced additional definitions for the coastal zone and integrated coastal zone management.

According to this law, the '**Coastal Zone**' is defined as:

> *the geomorphological area on either side of the shoreline in which the interaction between the marine and terrestrial segments takes the form of complex systems of ecological elements and resources composed of biotic and abiotic components coexisting and interacting with human communities and relevant socio-economic activities.* (Article 3, para. 5)

The same law introduces the notion of '**Integrated Coastal Zone Management**', which is defined as:

> *a dynamic process for the sustainable management and use of coastal zones, taking into account the vulnerable nature of coastal ecosystems and landscapes, the diversity of activities and uses, their interactions, the marine orientation of certain activities and uses and their impacts on the maritime and land sections.* (Article 3, para. 6)

The introductory report of this law states that '*sea and coastal areas are not two distinct zones but a "whole" that needs to be addressed through a specific methodological approach and particular management practices*', and '*the understanding and treatment of the land-sea interactions is vital for sustainable management and development of coastal areas, and for the coherent planning of land and sea activities*'.

Delineation of the shoreline and coastal zone

By 2001, following several decades in which market forces rather than planning drove development decisions in the coastal zone, there was a new approach for the demarcation of the shoreline: Authorities sought to define a permanent or quasi-permanent line. The official procedure for the delineation of the Seashore/shoreline was thus introduced by the 2001 coastal law (Article 4). That procedure involved the appointment of a committee to identify, on site, features of the landscape that would indicate the location of the 'usual maximum winter wave run-up'. The process could be initiated either by the relevant state authority (*ex officio* procedure) or following a request from an interested party, such as a landowner. However, even though a Joint Ministerial Decision was issued in 2005 (Government Gazette 595 B/2005) particularizing in detail the set of criteria to be taken into account for the delineation of the Greek shoreline, the completion of the process was delayed for several years. Furthermore, the delineation was undertaken on a case-by-case basis in what was a resource-intensive process. Thus, by April 2014, only 8% of Greece's shoreline had been officially delineated and ratified (Ministry of Finance, 2014). Areas experiencing high pressure for residential and tourism development, such as Attica and Cyclades, were amongst the regions with the highest percentage of demarcated Seashores and Beaches (Karousos, 2010, p. 41).

Given the difficulties of that method, as well as pressure from foreign institutions (troika)[3] to speed up the delineation process, a new administrative procedure for delineating the coast was adopted in 2014, through amendments to the 2001 coastal law. The new fast-track procedure was completed in 2018.

The procedure was based on photo interpretation of orthophotomaps which depict a zone at least 300 m from the shoreline (hereinafter referred to as 'basemaps'). According to this procedure, key environmental features were identified on the basemaps, to delineate a 'preliminary Seashore' line (Argyriou, 2012).[4] The orthophotomaps marked with this line, were then sent to the relevant national government agencies (Regional Directorates of Public Property – RDPPs and Hellenic National Defence General Staff – HNDGS) for approval. In areas where the Seashore had not previously been delineated, the RDPPs were required to check the 'preliminary Seashore' line against coastal conditions, using criteria established in the aforementioned 2005 Ministerial Decision (geomorphology, maximum wave run-up, ecosystems, and more) and then make a proposal for the final demarcation of the Seashore, due by end of June 2018. The maps were then approved by regional committees and ratified by the relevant decentralized administration. The new procedure resulted in a geoindex and a map with the delineated shoreline across the country.[5]

Following the completed delineation process, any party who contests the delineated Seashore can request a re-delineation of the Seashore and the Beach (Article 7A of the 2001 coastal law).

Legal status of the coastal zone in Greece

We noted above that the 'Seashore' and 'Beach' have long been defined as part of the Greek public domain. The coastal law of 2001 reinforces this designation, specifying that these areas constitute properties for public use and are owned by the State. The State is responsible for their protection and management (Article 2, para. 1).

On designation of these zones, private property rights are deemed to have been expropriated. Where private land, beyond the shoreline, is included within the Seashore and thus expropriated, affected landowners receive compensation in accordance with the general legislation on compulsory acquisition. But those whose land is expropriated for the 'Beach' receive compensation through a more demanding procedure related to the implementation of town plans. This can be a long, drawn-out process. In addition, any increase in the value of the relevant land, if resulting from improvements made following its declaration as 'Beach', is not taken into account in the calculation of due compensation (2001 coastal law, Article 7, para. 4).

Land use in the coastal public domain

In keeping with the purpose of the coastal public domain as a natural open space, permanent construction is prohibited on 'Seashore' and 'Beach' areas (2001 coastal law, Article 13). The land may be used for environmental and cultural purposes (e.g. protection of archaeological sites and monuments) or for other uses in the public interest, provided such uses do not undermine the public designation of the land and do not damage the natural landscape. The law also allows concessions on both the Seashore and the Beach for works that serve commercial, industrial, transportation, and port purposes or other purposes in the public interest (2001 coastal law, Article 14).

Temporary uses, such as those associated with bathing (sunbeds, parasols) or other recreational purposes (e.g. playgrounds, kiosks, and Beach bars), are an important feature of public use of the coastal zone. As such, the Ministry of Finance may concede to individuals or to private and public legal entities (including municipalities) the right to use the Seashore and the Beach for such temporary uses. These rights of use are known as 'concessions'. In protected areas, such as the sites belonging to the European network Natura 2000, the consent of the

Ministry of the Environment is required before any concessions can be granted. The municipalities set the cost for 'concessions' for temporary use, and the revenue generated through the
process is an important component of their budgets.

Notably, the Ministry of Finance has delegated significant powers regarding the development and use of public property to two public enterprises with large portfolios of coastal real
estate assets, namely, the Public Properties Company (ETAD) and the Hellenic Republic Asset
Development Fund (TAIPED). The former manages a large portfolio of approximately 70,000
titles of properties owned by the Greek state, among which over 2,000 plots are located in
coastal areas. The latter was founded in 2011 as part of the country's Medium Term Fiscal
Strategy, with the aim of promoting the country's privatization programme. However, its role
in land development has been weakened in recent years, and its real estate portfolio, including coastal properties, has been drastically reduced since 2016. Indeed, in that year, both
ETAD and TAIPED became direct subsidiaries of the Hellenic Corporation of Assets and
Participations S.A., a public company created in order to (a) contribute resources for the implementation of Greece's investment policy and make investments that contribute to strengthening
the development of the Greek economy and (b) contribute to reducing the financial obligations
of the Hellenic Republic.

Coastal setback rules

In our discussion of rules for coastal setbacks, we first note that no construction is permitted
on the 'Beach', as defined above. As such, where the Beach has been delineated, it plays the
role of a *de facto* setback zone. But, as we have noted, a 'Beach' zone is optional to define. The
coastal setback we now turn to discuss is beyond the Seashore and Beach zones.

The coastal setback zone widths defined by Greek legislation are well below the standard
minimum 100 m set by the ICZM Protocol. In coastal areas lying outside town plans (and outside settlements which existed before 1923), new development must be set back at least 30 m
from the shoreline (the boundary of the Seashore; Law Decree 439/1970, Article 1). Even this
modest setback rule does not apply to (a) industrial uses which must be located on the coast, (b)
significant hotel and tourism-related services (which are not further defined in the law), and (c)
public works and port and marina works. In these cases, the law provides for the issuance of
special case-specific Ministerial decisions which expound the reasons for exemption. We note
that while some exemptions may be necessary for the public good, this long list of exemptions
undermines the essence of the very public purpose of the setback regulations. This problem of
exemptions appears repeatedly in the Greek legislation, as we will see below.

Apart from these general provisions, Greece has adopted special rules for tourism and
recreation facilities developed on the 'Seashore' or 'Beach', through the 2013 tourism law
(L. 4179/2013, Article 5, para. 3). According to this law, all tourist accommodation located
in large-scale tourist resorts have a setback rule of at least 50 m from the shoreline, while
non-tourist buildings located in these resorts (e.g. holiday homes, recreation complexes, and
sports facilities), which are maximum 7.5 m high, have a 30 m coastal setback requirement.
The setback distances for tourist resorts may be further reduced when the total façade of the
land plot is at least 100 m in length along (parallel to) the Beach. In this case, restaurants,
recreation areas, restrooms, sports facilities, and playgrounds included in the resorts may be
developed at the outer edge of the Beach, or when the Beach is not defined, at a mere 10 m
distance from the Seashore/shoreline, so long as they are no taller than 3.5 m (Article 5, para. 4
of the 2013 tourism law).

Right of public access

Greek legislation explicitly requires provision of free access for the public to and along the 'Seashore' and the 'Beach' (2001 coastal law, Article 2, paras. 3 & 4). The law stipulates (Article 15, para. 3) that any 'concessions' for use or works on the 'Seashore' or 'Beach' should ensure and not impede public access to these areas, with limited exceptions (e.g. security, public health). Authorities may not grant exclusive use (where access is barred to the public) of the 'Seashore' or 'Beach', unless required for reasons of national defence, public safety (e.g. during construction works), or protection of antiquities (Article 15, para. 4).

The notion of an open and accessible coast preceded the 2001 coastal law and is certainly reflected in other laws applicable today. For example, the 1983 urban planning law (1337/1983) prohibits the erection of fences within 500 m of the shoreline (Article 23), to protect the coast and ensure access. Yet this prohibition is not absolute: A Presidential Decree (236/1984 A. 95) was published specifically to identify how the fencing prohibition is to be used and includes a long list of land uses that are exempt. The decree takes a broad stance on uses which should be protected for the benefit of the public. Among exempted uses are several kinds of agricultural installations and farms; hotels and other tourist facilities; industrial installations and mines; military installations; big transport infrastructure (airports, ports, etc.); schools, hospitals, and other buildings of social character; sports facilities; prisons; monasteries; cemeteries; natural monuments; and archaeological sites. In view of the large number of exceptions listed in the Presidential Decree, the 500 m fencing prohibition has been substantially undermined and it is questionable whether it serves a meaningful purpose in its diminished form.

Despite its limited applicability, the fencing prohibition has drawn several disputes, probably because it touches directly on private property rights issues. The topic has even reached the Greek Council of State twice. In a ruling from 1992 (CoS 3521-22/1992, plenary session), the court held that the prohibition complies with the protection of the environment required under Article 24 of the Greek Constitution without violating the constitutional right of ownership, since it applies only to areas not designated for residential use (outside approved city plans and outside existing settlements). The Court further found that, given the exemptions listed in Presidential Decree 236/1984, fencing is allowed for a wide range of uses and, therefore, the ban is enacted in very few cases – and even in these cases, fencing is permitted if landowners are growing trees or crops on the property. Under these conditions, the Court concluded, the law neither violates the core of the property or its intended use nor harms the opportunity for exclusive use (when permitted). Thus, the court considered that the law is compatible with the provisions of the Greek Constitution regarding property protection.

In 1970, the same law which set a compulsory 30 m coastal setback (L.D 439/1970) also provided for expropriation of land to be used for the construction of access roads to the coast. The minimum width required for such access roads is 10 m. Building on this provision, the 1983 urban planning law provides for authorities to create public access routes to the Beach and Seashore through expropriation of private property (Article 24). It also allows authorities to expropriate and demolish existing enclosures blocking access to the coast; to remove existing buildings on the shore; and to transfer ownership to local authorities or to public benefit organizations until demolition. Beriatos & Papageorgiou (2010) note that at the time of their approval, the access road provisions were seen to be in the public interest and to satisfy 'the sense of public justice'. However, such access roads are not common and those which were established have not been effectively monitored to keep them open and safe for use.

Overall, the specific requirements for the provision of access roads and prohibition of fencing are poorly enforced. In many areas, the public cannot access the sea due to continuous rows of private properties and hotels which lead to a *de facto* privatization of the shore. Poor administrative responsiveness and local clientelism, along with poor reception and even opposition from property owners to the access laws, are among the main factors that have led to this situation.

Planning policies and tools for coastal protection and development

Beyond the public domain and the rather narrow setback zone, the regulation of coastal development in Greece relies on the country's general planning legislation. Existing planning instruments can be utilized to achieve coastal protection and development goals. For example, planning law (the 2016 planning law) provides explicitly for the possibility of adopting special strategic guidance at the national level for coastal areas and islands. In addition, special guidelines and regulations for coastal areas may be included in regional and local spatial plans.

Reliance on local planning means that there are disparities across municipalities. It also means that there is room for positive local initiatives in coastal zone planning. There is, however, a concern amongst Greek scholars that general planning legislation might not be adequate to ensure effective coastal protection and management (Papapetropoulos, 2004; Beriatos & Papageorgiou, 2010). These scholars suggest that general planning schemes at the national and regional levels do not clearly distinguish between coastal and other areas and that the special planning schemes adopted to date are oriented towards the formulation of criteria for the siting of sectoral activities, such as tourism, aquaculture, and wind parks, rather than taking a holistic view. There is also concern regarding regulatory planning at the local scale, which, beyond some specific local setback limitations and land use restrictions, remains limited in scope and does not address integrated coastal zone management. On the other hand, there is no evidence that special coastal planning legislation could ensure a better balance between development and conservation goals in the Greek coastal zone or better outcomes in terms of coastal protection and management.

Strategic planning guidance for coastal protection and development

Greek authorities have adopted several sectoral strategic plans since the 1990s. Most recently, in 2008–2009, the national government approved the country's first national strategic spatial plan – the General Framework Plan – and three Special Framework Plans (dealing with Renewable Energy Sources, Industry, and Tourism respectively). Each of these plans contains specific provisions for coastal areas, but these provisions are very general and there may be cases in which the various policies contradict each other. There is no measure in place to prioritize or coordinate policies for the benefit of the coastal zone.

The General Framework Plan (2008) generally promotes the protection of coastal resources and increased coordination on coastal matters between responsible authorities at the national, regional, and local levels (Article 9). It stipulates that authorities should avoid siting or approving large-scale installations near the Beach (assuming, of course, that the relevant installations do not require proximity to the sea for effective operation). The Plan refers to the application of principles of integrated coastal zone management in designing policy measures and regulation for coastal areas. In referring to implementation of its general guidelines, the Plan explicitly states that there is a need to adopt a Special Framework Plan for coastal areas and islands.

Despite that statement, there is no adopted Framework Plan for the coastal zone. The authorities prepared multiple versions of such a draft Framework Plan over several years, beginning in the late 1990s. A version of the draft Plan from 2003 proposed a 100 m setback provision, which was later dropped. Another version, from 2009, responded to the ICZM Protocol to the Barcelona Convention by redefining and reclassifying the coastal zone beyond the definitions found in the 2001 coastal law. The new definition included both terrestrial and marine elements, and the Plan divided the coastal area into critical, dynamic, and other/transitional zones. Each zone was subject to different land use and development provisions (Beriatos & Papageorgiou, 2010). However, in the late 2000s, tourist and renewable energy investors became increasingly vocal and were successful in shifting national planning priorities in a more sectoral direction (Giannakourou, 2011, p. 37). Thus, the Special Framework Plan for coastal areas and islands was abandoned, while the Special Framework Plans for Renewable Energy Sources, Industry, and Tourism were approved in 2008–2009. As a result, strategic guidance for coastal protection and management is still limited to the mostly general policies found in the General Framework Plan.

The Special Framework Plan for Tourism (approved in 2009, amended in 2013) was annulled by the Council of State in 2015 for technical legal reasons.

The new provisions on maritime and coastal spatial plans

The 2018 maritime spatial planning law (discussed above) introduced two new categories of strategic spatial plans directly related to maritime and coastal areas: a) The National Maritime Spatial Strategy, which identifies the strategic guidelines for maritime areas and coastal zones at the national level and indicates the priorities for the preparation of Maritime Spatial Plans in individual spatial units; and b) Maritime Spatial Plans, which apply to marine and coastal spatial units of sub-regional, regional, or interregional character. Both documents are approved after consultation with the public and the relevant authorities, while Maritime Spatial Plans must, in addition, first be submitted for a strategic environmental assessment.

One of the most important issues arising regarding maritime spatial planning is its relationship with terrestrial spatial planning. In this respect, the 2018 maritime spatial planning law provides (at Article 15) that, when preparing and approving the National Maritime Spatial Strategy and the Maritime Spatial Plans, authorities must take into account the guidelines of existing terrestrial spatial plans. These requirements cannot, however, avoid all potential tensions between terrestrial and maritime spatial plans. Such potential tensions were the key cause of public concern which emerged during the consultation period for the draft law, both from some of the country's main economic and social partners, such as the Hellenic Industries Association, and from relevant scientific organizations, such as the Association of Greek Spatial Planning Engineers (2018). Notably, land and waters which are affected by a member state's statutory planning laws and plans are excluded from the scope of the Maritime Spatial Planning Directive. As such, we see the choice of the Greek legislator to include coastal zones in maritime spatial plans as a typical case of 'gold-plating' (over-implementation).

Regulatory planning and coastal zone management

There is no planning regulation which specifically address coastal zone management. Land use regulation is undertaken by local authorities (with oversight from the national government), through Local Spatial Plans (Article 7 of L. 4447/2016). Each Local Spatial Plan applies to the entire area of a municipality and defines detailed rules for land use and development. These plans categorize land using standardized categories. Since 2016, coastal areas may be classified either as protected areas or as areas of land use control.

At the time of writing, no Local Spatial Plan has been approved since the 2016 amendment to planning legislation which introduced the above classifications. As such, there is no evidence as to how these classifications are used in practice.

Special planning laws and the coastal zone

Apart from general planning legislation, several special planning regimes have been established since 2010 in order to promote private investments or to facilitate privatization of public properties. These regimes introduce special substantive and procedural rules for the development of private or public assets.

The law on Strategic Investments (L. 3894/2010), generally known in Greece as Fast Track law, was one of the first statutes passed after the beginning of the sovereign debt crisis in 2009. This law was intended to facilitate strategic investments – that is, investments which have a significant positive impact on the national economy in the long term. To promote such investments, the Fast Track law (L. 3894/2010, as amended by L. 4146/2013) introduced Special Spatial Development Plans for Strategic Investments (ESCHASEs), along with special land use and building rules and licensing procedures. Authorities may adopt ESCHASEs to override other relevant plans through definition of specific uses which are permitted to facilitate development. They may grant rights of use on the 'Seashore' or 'Beach' or permission for Seashore and shoreline infrastructure. Thus, the potential effects on the coastal zone are considerable. Yet the authorities may not adopt such plans without oversight: ESCHASEs can be approved only by Presidential Decrees following review by the Council of State.

ESCHASEs are based on the model of Special Spatial Development Plans of Public Estates (ESCHADAs) introduced by Law 3986/2011 (Urgent Measures for the Implementation of the Medium-Term Fiscal Strategy) in view of the privatization of State-owned public properties. These new planning tools were positively received by the Council of State, which, during 2013–2017, gave a 'green light' to ten draft Presidential Decrees approving eight ESCHADAs and two ESCHASEs respectively, nine of which concern beachfront land plots. The approval of these plans by the Council of State indicates that, despite the fears initially expressed by various actors that prioritizing investment will adversely compromise environmental protection, both ESCHADAs and ESCHASEs have been prepared in full compliance with EU and Greek environmental law and meet the required environmental and planning standards (e.g. CoS 3874/2014 plenary session, CoS 1704/2017 plenary session).

The successful implementation of these planning tools led, in 2016, to the expansion of their scope through the country's general planning legislation. The 2016 planning law introduced a plan type similar to ESCHADAs and ESCHASEs – Special Spatial Plans (Article 8). These plans provide 'tailor-made' and timely planning responses to large-scale or important development proposals in various designated zones, including coastal zones.

Compliance and enforcement

Illegal development, including on the Seashore and the Beach, is a major issue in Greece. There are no official figures regarding the extent of illegal development in the Greek coastal zone, but it includes residential buildings, port and tourism facilities, berths, and jetties.

Attempting to reign in this phenomenon, the 2001 coastal law stipulates that any illegal construction on the Seashore or Beach (once they are defined and have been expropriated, as described above) must be demolished, *regardless of construction date,* excluding only protected cultural heritage (Article 27). The RDPP (Regional Directorate of Public Property) may issue a demolition notice in such cases, and owners or developers may be subject to criminal charges or fines. Demolition notices may not be withdrawn except under certain circumstances, including hardship to the property owner, or in cases where there is ample access to the coast and the illegal building does not obstruct this access (Administrative Court of Appeal of Piraeus/Suspension Commission 8/2013, Administrative Court of Thessaloniki/Suspension Commission 33/2017).

The national government's ability to apply enforcement measures on the 'Beach' or 'Seashore' is obviously dependent on those zones being delineated. Considering the difficulties and delays that Greece has encountered in the past in relation to demarcation (described above), it is not surprising that the issue of enforcement in the extensive areas where the Seashore has not been delineated has come before the Council of State. The court held that in such cases, the responsible authorities should carry out an assessment of the limits of the 'Seashore' prior to either issuing building permits (CoS 3483/2003, 377-378/2002) or determining cases of exemption from demolition (CoS 680/2002). The Council of State has also ruled that where a building permit was issued prior to the demarcation of the Seashore, the RDPP may not issue a demolition notice unless the government withdraws the relevant building permit on the basis of the public interest (e.g. CoS 3354/2014, 3622/2014). Regarding withdrawal of building permits, the Council of State has ruled that the government must weigh its decision in light of the time lapsed since the building permit was issued and that the property rights acquired *in bona fide* (CoS 3354/2014).

Setting aside the issue of demarcation, even in cases where enforcement measures against illegal development can be fully justified, they are rarely implemented. There are several reasons for this failure, including a lack of funds and limited human resources in the decentralized administrations, who were responsible until 2017. In 2017, Law 4495/2017 conveyed the responsibility of demolition to the Regional Directorates of Development Control ('Regional Observatories'). However, the latter have not yet been enacted, due to a delay in issuing a required Presidential Act (Article 5). But the key issue is likely a lack of political will. This, along with lack of financial and material means, as well as poor administrative capacity and limited human resources in the responsible public authorities, led to poor results regarding enforcement against illegal development in the coastal zone. However, as a result of the 2018 Attica wildfires, which primarily affected the densely populated coastal village Mati of Attica in July 2018 and caused the death of 102 people (European Parliament, 2018), the Government announced its intention to demolish 700 illegal constructions in the coastal zone of Attica. To this end, it issued an Act of Legislative Content (Government Gazette 149A/2018) for the demolition of all unauthorized enclosures which prohibit access to the coast.

In the past, another key factor in the failure of authorities to implement enforcement measures was the absence of a monitoring and control authority for illegal development at the national level (Economic and Social Council of Greece, 2007, p. 28), to counter issues arising out of local clientelism. In 2010, following the 2009 Attica wildfires in Mount Parnitha, this issue came to light and a Special Inspectorate Agency for Demolition of Illegal Construction (EYEKA) was then established within the Ministry of the Environment (L.3818/2010, Article 7; L.4014/2011, Article 28). EYEKA's initial tasks included the demolition of illegal construction – either by its own means or by private operators in cooperation with the decentralized administrations. Subsequent amendments to the legislation on illegal construction, as well as on the organizational structure of the Ministry of Environment, diminished EYEKA's powers regarding the demolition of illegal constructions and coordination, and implementation of demolition was left to the decentralized administrations. However, the tragic events of the 2018 Attica wildfires, which were the second-deadliest wildfire in the twenty-first century, led the Greek government to reassign responsibilities for demolition of unauthorized developments on the Seashore and Beach back to EYEKA (now in the Ministry of Environment and Energy).

Greece recently paid a heavy price for the enforcement problems encountered in the past: Among the 102 people who lost their lives during the 2018 Attica wildfires, 26 deaths were tragically caused by people being trapped on land with illegal enclosures which prohibited access to the sea (BBC, 2018). Whether the political and administrative system will be adequately shaken by this tragedy to induce meaningful change remains to be seen.

Integration and coordination

Several Greek governmental bodies and agencies are involved in different administrative stages of coastal protection and management, with overlapping jurisdiction (Table 12.1). The resulting administrative landscape is fragmented and extremely complex, giving rise to potential tensions and even power struggles between various public authorities. The system prioritizes sectoral policies and activities as opposed to integrated coastal zone management. Parallel coastal jurisdictions and responsibilities lead to red tape, delay, and inefficiency.

To date, integration across these ministries has been limited. This has been recognized by the OECD (2011, p. 26), which has noted that the Greek central administration lacks the management, oversight, and coordination initiatives to support effective implementation and long-term management of policy measures. In cases where coordination does happen, it is usually ad hoc, based on initiatives introduced by individuals and not supported by the existing management structures.

Yet in recent years, the national government has taken steps to create institutional coordination mechanisms for the implementation of EU-related policies and laws in the maritime domain, which also affects coastal zones. For example, the National Committee of Maritime Environmental Strategy (L.3983/2011, Article 18) was established when the EU Marine Strategy Framework Directive was adopted into Greek law in 2011. In addition, another cross-sectoral Committee has been formed for the implementation of the EU Integrated Maritime Policy and the coordination of the responsible national authorities (Law 4150/2013, Article 1). The Committee is chaired by the Secretary General of the Ministry of Shipping and includes representatives from several other ministries (Foreign Affairs, Finance, National Defence, Environment & Energy, Development & Tourism, Culture & Sports, Education, Research & Religious Affairs, Agriculture & Foods and Citizen Protection). Nevertheless, it is also worth noting that the authority responsible for the implementation of the Maritime Spatial Planning Directive (2014/89/EU) is the Minister of Environment and Energy itself (2018 maritime spatial planning law, Article 14). In addition, both the Ministries of Environment and Shipping are the responsible authorities for the implementation of the Barcelona Convention and its Protocols by law (Article 3 of L. 855/1978).

On the whole, in line with the Recommendation of the European Parliament and the Council concerning the implementation of Integrated Coastal Zone Management in Europe (2002/413/ EC), Greek authorities have identified integrated coastal zone management as a matter which requires coordination of administrative bodies at national, regional, and local levels. Further work and instruments are required to establish more coordinated processes.

Table 12.1 Main fields of responsibility in the coastal zone

	Demarcation	Concessions	Planning	Protection (env. and public domain)	Granting permits (building & env.)	Imposition of sanctions
Ministry of Finance	X	X	X	X	X	X
Ministry of Environment & Energy (YPEN)	X	X	X	X	X	X
Ministry of Shipping and Insular Policy			X	X	X	X
Ministry of Economy and Development		X			X	
Ministry of Tourism		X	X		X	
Ministry of Culture & Sports		X	X	X	X	X
Ministry of Interior Affairs				X		
Decentralized administration	X	X	X	X	X	X
Regions						X
Local authorities		X			X	X
Hellenic Coast Guard				X		X
Hellenic Police				X		X

*Concessions are regulated by Articles 13 and 14 of L. 2971/2001. See also CoS 646/2015 for related responsibilities of the Ministry of the Environment

The potential negative effects of this complex administrative structure of responsibilities came sharply into focus during the 2018 Attica wildfires: The lack of coordination among the Hellenic Coast Guard, the Hellenic Police, the Hellenic Fire Department, and the Regional and local authorities, as well as the Secretary General for Civil Protection, led to the failure to make a decision to evacuate the coastal settlement of Mati by sea. Port boats reached the coast after a long delay, when Mati residents had already arrived there on their own initiative, attempting to save themselves from the flames.

Public participation and access to justice

There are no special provisions in Greek law for public participation on matters associated with coastal zone management. Yet the public can be involved in coastal protection and development decisions through standard public consultation procedures found in planning and environmental legislation.

The public can participate in coastal plan-making and in environmental permitting, by submitting, in writing, their positions on any Strategic Environmental Assessment (SEA; required by Law 4447/2016) or Environmental Impact Assessment (EIA; required by Law 4014/2011 for projects with potential significant impact on the environment). These procedures are also open to submissions from organizations representing universities, professional chambers (e.g. the Technical Chamber of Greece), and NGOs dealing with environmental and cultural issues. However, the authorities generally comply only with the minimum legal requirements, without attempting to foster productive dialogue (European Commission – MRAG, 2008, pp. 10–12).

The public may also contest planning and development decisions which result from the above processes. In accordance with the Aarhus Convention and European Directive 2003/4/EC on Public Access to Environmental Information), the Greek legal system must allow a broad range of individuals or associations to challenge land use plans, zoning regulations, and planning and environmental decisions. The Council of State has recognized that a *locus standi* may be accepted for persons other than the landowner or operator (third parties) – including neighbouring residents, local authorities, environmental NGOs, local improvement associations, etc. – if the decision might cause them injury. Examples of such injury in the context of the coastal zone include deterioration of the built or natural environment, increased risk of flooding, coastal erosion, or damage to health and livelihoods. Furthermore, in challenges of environmental decisions, including those concerning coastal areas, the Council of State has accepted standing not only for environmental NGOs but also for associations of lawyers, which might be concerned with matters of general national or social interest, such as the Constitutional protection for the natural and cultural environments (e.g. CoS 646/2015, Cos 2320/2014, 2257/2014).

All parties with legal standing may petition the court for the annulment of a spatial plan, an environmental permit, or any other permit concerned with the use and development of a coastal area.

Climate change issues

Climate change threats to Greece's coastal zone are primarily related to sea level rise and storm surge events. Both phenomena can amplify coastal erosion and coastal flooding and potentially significantly impact the built environment and coastal ecosystems.

A 2011 vulnerability assessment of Greece's coastal regions looked at the potential effects of sea level rises of between 0.2 m to 2 m by the year 2100 (BoG, 2011, pp. 156, 170; YPEN, 2018, p. 137). A total of 21% of Greece's total coastline is classified as having 'medium to high' vulnerability to sea level rise; most at risk are the deltaic areas of many Greek rivers and gulfs (YPEN, 2018, p. 236). The economic impacts of this climate change threat on Greece's shoreline are remarkable: The total cost of the impacts of sea level rise (SLR) of just 0.5 m by 2100 for Greece as a whole has been estimated at approximately 355 billion euros; in the scenario of a sea level rise of 1 m, the total cost of impacts would increase to 650 billion euros. The present values of the estimated total costs of SLR impacts by 2100, discounted in the year 2010, using appropriate discount rates, result in costs of 145 billion euros and 265 billion euros for SLR of 0.5 m and 1 m, respectively. The total costs were calculated for five land uses (housing, tourism, wetlands, forestry, and agriculture) (BoG, 2011, p. 165).

Other climate phenomena of concern in coastal areas include the anticipated increase in storms and frequency of storm surges (Solomon et al., 2007), which, in turn, may cause flooding of coastal areas, destruction of coastal infrastructure, coastal erosion, and intrusion of salt water in coastal habitats (BoG, 2011, p. 160).

To understand the potential impact of climate change on Greece's shoreline, one must consider the rate at which coastal erosion has already occurred. The estimated proportion of total coastline which has already been impacted by erosion is over 30% (EUROSION, 2004, p. 6), making Greece one of the most vulnerable countries among the twenty-two coastal EU Member States. Erosion is expected to increase in the immediate future, due to (a) the anticipated rise in mean sea level; (b) the intensification of extreme wave phenomena; and (c) the further reduction of river sediment discharge as a result of variations in rainfall and the construction of river management works (YPEN, 2018, p.235). The cost of the protection of Greece's coastline from coastal erosion has been estimated at 5.377 million euros for the period 1990–2020 (YPEKA, 2013, p. 28). Furthermore, the cost of adaptation measures for the protection of coastal systems in the years 2025–2070, which would reduce the impacts of climate change by 60% to 70%, amount to a total of 3.946 million euros (YPEN, 2018, p. 104).

Given the imminent threats of sea level rise and storm surge events, the implementation of a coordinated adaptation policy is required to ensure the protection of Greece's coastline. This has been recognized as an important policy issue in several domestic studies (YPEN, 2018; BoG, 2011), in line with the relevant EU Recommendation (2002/413/EC) and ICZM Protocol provisions. As foreshadowed by those studies, apart from the adoption of the National Adaptation Strategy, a comprehensive plan is required. Such a plan would involve elaboration of a coastal cadastre; the designation of high-, medium-, and low-risk zones depending on the characteristics of each coastal area; any engineering works required to stabilize the coastline; and setting up a permanent coastal monitoring system for each region (YPEN, 2018, p. 50; BoG, 2011, p.173).

Greek government action on climate change

The Greek National Adaptation Strategy (NAS) for Climate Change was formally endorsed by the Greek Parliament in August 2016 (Law 4414/2016, Article 45), following initial drafting by the Athens Academy and the Bank of Greece and public consultation from the Ministry of Environment. Law 4414/2016 defines the Ministry of Energy & Environment (MEEN) as the responsible authority for national adaptation policy and foresees the process for revision of the NAS along a ten-year planning cycle.

The Greek NAS (YPEN, 2016) is an overarching policy document which should be implemented at regional level through Regional Adaptation Action Plans (RAAPs). As such, the law (Law 4414/2016, Article 43) sets the minimum technical specifications for drafting the RAAPs and provides for their preparation by the thirteen Regional Authorities of Greece. RAAPs should be assessed and reviewed, if needed, within a seven-year planning cycle. The content of RAAPs is specified in a Ministerial Decision (MD 11258/2017), which also requires Regional Authorities to perform a detailed assessment of potential climate change impacts; identify and map relevant climate-related risks and vulnerabilities; prioritize adaptation action; identify synergies with other policies and regional plans (e.g. land use plans, water management, and flood risk management plans); and integrate, as required, priority measures into regional planning. Each RAAP will define priority adaptation actions based on the unique context of each Region. The development of the thirteen RAAPs is ongoing with several Regions being more advanced than others.

Law 4414/2016 also established (at Article 44) the National Climate Change Adaptation Committee (NCCAC) to act as the formal advisory body to YPEN at national level, for adaptation policy design and implementation. The NCCAC comprises representatives from all Ministries with sectoral roles in adaptation policy planning and in funding of adaptation actions, as well as representatives of other relevant stakeholder bodies and governmental authorities (Ministerial Decision 34768/2017).

In addition, climate change is addressed by some national strategic planning documents, the 2001 coastal law, River Basin Management Plans, Flood Management Plans, and Marine Waters Management Plans. For example, the General Framework Plan (GFP) suggests avoiding the siting of large-scale installations near the Beach, while the Special Framework Plan for Industry discourages the siting of industrial installations within 350 m of the Seashore (Articles 2 and 4). The majority of Spatial Plans date back to 2009. Several of these Spatial Plans are being, or will be, revised. In addition, the 2001 coastal law (at Article 12) contains special provisions for the prevention of coastal erosion, albeit by simply allowing technical works which prevent further erosion. Hard engineering structures used in Greece to protect the coast from erosion include seawalls, groynes, breakwaters, revetments, flood embankments, placement of gabions, and rock armouring.

The Greek government has also prepared (or is preparing) several plans and strategies in accordance with EU directives. These include the River Basin Management Plans 2016–2021 for fourteen territorial districts, within the framework of the EU Water Framework Directive, the Flood Management Plans, as well as the Marine Waters Management Plans. In addition, Maritime Spatial Plans, an important tool for climate change adaptation in the coastal zone, are expected to be prepared by 2021, following the recent transposition of the 2014/89/EU Directive into domestic law.

Despite the significant progress made in last years, there is still room for further improvement with regard to policy coordination, development and dissemination of good practice, and, most importantly, capacity building. In September 2017 the Ministry of Environment and Energy (YPEN) submitted a proposal for an eight-year EU project (2017 LIFE Climate Action) which includes actions to a) coordinate cross-regional and enhance national–regional–local adaptation action; b) build capacity at national and regional stakeholders; c) support cross-regional cooperation and transnational cooperation with countries from the Balkans and the wider Mediterranean area; d) develop and operate a National Adaptation Knowledge Hub; e) develop and test methodologies to monitor the progress achieved in the implementation of the NAS and RAAPs; and f) assess the existing level of mainstreaming and integration of climate change adaptation priorities to other sectors at national level. The National Centre for Environment and Sustainable Development, along with YPEN, will take over training, information sharing, and monitoring of activities after the end of the project.

All the above are expected to contribute to a better awareness at the local level of climate change issues and challenges, but this remains to be seen. In a 2016 EU research project, partners interviewed several municipalities along the Greek coast. There was little evidence that information or national policies on climate change have trickled down to local awareness or action (Alterman et al., 2016).

Fiscal aspects of Greek coastal regulation: Types and scope of compensation mechanisms

We have noted above that according to the 2001 coastal law (L. 2971/2001), land identified as part of the 'Seashore' or 'Beach' may be expropriated if it was not publicly owned prior to demarcation. Compensation for land expropriated for 'Seashore' is granted according to standard expropriation legislation, while compensation for expropriation of 'Beach' land is determined through the local planning process.

Under the 2001 coastal law, there are no compensation rights for landowners for regulatory 'takings' – land use or development-control bans and restrictions which do not result in expropriation. Thus, landowners cannot claim compensation on the basis of any additional restrictions on land in the coastal zone beyond that of actual expropriation. But in some cases, landowners consider that they have a right to compensation; thus, this issue has repeatedly been the subject of legal action which reached the Council of State. The court has ruled that planning restrictions in the out-of-plan coastal areas (non-residential areas) are compatible with Article 17 of the Greek Constitution on the protection of private property and the First Additional Protocol of the European Convention of Human Rights (ECHR), since they do not eliminate all use or render property worthless in relation to its purpose (CoS 3758/2014). Furthermore, the court found that the regulations put in place to protect the environment are appropriate in light of that objective (CoS 2923/2011, 3511/2010). The court also ruled that when environmental protection measures result in substantial limitations on the use of property for its designated purpose, the owner can claim just compensation (with consideration of the extent, duration, and intensity of the relevant 'taking') based on the principle of 'equality before public burdens' deriving from Article 4 (para. 5) of the Greek Constitution (CoS 5504/2012 para. 15, CoS 3431-2/2015 para. 5). Yet the absence of a compensation clause within the regulation which results in 'regulatory takings' does not affect the integrity or the legality of that regulation (CoS 3758/2014, 2923/2011).

At the same time, there are some environmental laws which recognize a right to compensation for owners whose land may be substantially affected by regulatory measures taken for nature conservation (Giannakourou & Balla, 2006), including coastal preservation areas. Specifically, Law 1650/1986 'On the protection of the environment' (Article 22 – the '1986 environment protection law'), as amended by the 2011 biodiversity law (Article 16), provides for affected landowners to claim compensation directly from the State if the restrictions imposed by those laws effectively nullify their development rights. This compensation mechanism relies on the issuance of a Presidential Decree, which would define the procedure and the substantive requirements for granting compensation (1986 environment law). Once issued, the Presidential Decree would allow compensation to be provided in the form of money or in kind, including land exchange (affected land goes to the State and landowners receive State land elsewhere), transfer of development rights, or subsidies or other financial aids for affected farmland. But to date, the Presidential Decree has not been issued. Despite this oversight, the Council of State has ruled that affected landowners can claim compensation directly before the court (CoS 1611/2006). Several such cases have since been heard and compensation has been granted (e.g. CoS 3432-3433/2015, 1478/2016).

The same 1986 environment protection law (Article 22, para. 9) foreshadows the State issue of another Presidential Decree which would define economic incentives for the conservation of the natural environment and biodiversity. Such incentives would encourage individuals and local communities to contribute to the law's conservation objectives. The State has not issued this Presidential Decree to date.

No preventive fiscal measures are provided to address coastal threats proactively. There are, however, special provisions in the general legislation for civil protection (L. 3013/2002) which would allow the State to introduce special compensation mechanisms in areas affected by natural disasters. Owners whose properties are damaged by, for example, sea level rise, cliff erosion, or flash flooding might then be granted loans for relocation or property restitution or provided tax exemptions during the restitution period.

Overall assessment

Many eyes are directed at the Greek coasts: Those of the local population who rely on their country's coasts for vacationing and income, as well as many of the millions of tourists from across the world who visit the Greek coasts annually. The exposure of the Greek coasts to the world is, thus, quite significant.

In this chapter, we have shown that the management and protection of the Greek coastal zone is hindered due to difficulties within a multitude of laws affecting the coastal zone and the frequently conflicting priorities of the government institutions which implement those laws. In addition, we have demonstrated that the governance system for coastal zone management is 'top-heavy', with most powers held by the central government, and that there is a chronic lack of integration and coordination between the various responsible government bodies.

On the legal level, the key issue has been various difficulties with the definition and the delineation of coastal land. Prior to 2001 the definition was vague. Since 2001, a functional definition has been in place, but there are lingering challenges in the definition of private property rights, although these will now be greatly diminished given the new fast-track delineation procedure. In addition, the definitions of 'Seashore' and 'Beach' are not adequate to represent the full 'coastal zone', which certainly reaches beyond those areas. The 2011 biodiversity law did include more extensive definitions of 'coastal zone' and 'critical coastal zone', but these are useful only in the implementation of that specific law. With the recent adoption of the 2018 maritime spatial planning law, there has been a shift. This law introduced a general definition for both the coastal zone and integrated coastal zone management, as well as special types of spatial plans for maritime and coastal areas. These spatial plans are expected to be approved by 2021, in line with the relevant provision of Directive 2014/89/EU.

On the institutional level, the main obstacle is divergent policy agendas – environmental protection and short-term economic gain. The focus of most government agencies is on limited sectoral interests, and little effort is placed on promoting coordination between those interests and broader coastal management. Another key issue is Greece's weak record of monitoring and control of illegal development practices, persisting over several decades. Both these matters might be resolved only by will of the central government. The private sector and civil society may also play a role in any reform, most likely through petitions to the court.

Key short-term challenges for coastal protection and management in Greece include the approval of maritime and coastal spatial plans by the end of 2021. In principle, the new planning instruments provided in the 2018 maritime spatial planning law can serve as a stimulus for Greek authorities to develop a more comprehensive approach to coastal protection and management. In addition, these plans may pave the way for the adoption of the ICZM principles in Greek law and practice.

Yet the challenge for Greek coastal law and policy to become more effective and integrated goes well beyond the approval of these plans or the ratification of the ICZM Protocol. The adoption of a comprehensive and integrated coastal zone management approach amounts to a paradigm shift across the country. Evidence from the recent Attica wildfires has shown that, beyond environmental threats, lack of an integrated and coordinated approach for coastal protection and management can be a serious threat to the human life and property. However, whether and how these lessons will be appreciated by the country's leaders and decision makers and Greek society as a whole remains to be seen.

Notes

1. According to several sources, the combined Mediterranean coastline is 46,000 km. See https://planbleu.org/sites/default/files/publications/soed2009_en.pdf
2. Emergency Laws were legislated during tumultuous periods in which the Parliament did not operate or did not operate normally (dictatorial periods, siege situations, etc.).
3. The term 'troika' (or later 'quadrate') has been used to describe Greece's international lenders during the sovereign debt crisis which hit the country in late 2009. The term refers to the EU Commission, the European Central Bank (ECB), the International Monetary Fund (IMF), and, since 2015, the European Stability Mechanism (ESM).
4. The preliminary shoreline was delineated according to nine thematic criteria (*vegetation borders, wave overtopping, top of ridge, construction borders, building borders, semi-urban area, river mouth, closed saltmarsh, open saltmarsh*). See Argyriou (2012).
5. Geoindexed map available at https://www1.gsis.gr/gspp/dhpe/publicgis/faces/homeShore (Accessed September 2019).

References

Alterman, R., Pellach, C., & Carmon, D. (2016). *MARE NOSTRUM PROJECT Final Report: Legal-Institutional Instruments for Integrated Coastal Zone Management (ICZM) in the Mediterranean.* Available at: https://alterman.web3.technion.ac.il/files/mare-nostrum/Mare_Nostrum_Final_Report_2016.pdf

Argyriou, A. (2012). The cartographic base map of country's shoreline and its use for the determination of the preliminary Seashore. *12th National Cartographic Conference*, Kozani 10–12 October 2012.

Association of Greek Spatial Planning Engineers. (2018). Memorandum to the standing committee on production and trade of the Greek parliament for the consideration of the draft law: Incorporation of Directive 2014/89/EU 'establishing a framework for maritime spatial planning' and other provisions into the Greek legislation. 30/05/2018. Available at: http://www.chorotaxia.gr/ftp/2018/SEMPXPA_SN_thalassios_xwr_sxediasmos_.pdf

BoG (Bank of Greece). (2011). *The Environmental, Economic and Social Impacts of Climate Change in Greece.* Bank of Greece. Available at: http://www.bankofgreece.gr/BogEkdoseis/SEESOX%2002-2011.pdf

BBC. (2018). Greece wildfires: Dozens dead in Attica region. 24 July 2018. Available at: https://www.bbc.com/news/world-europe-44932366

Beriatos, E., & Papageorgiou, M. (2010). Towards Sustainable Urbanization and Spatial Planning of the Coastal Zone in Greece and the Mediterranean Basin. In ISOCARP, *Sustainable Planning of the Coastal Zone in Mediterranean, 46th Congress Proceedings.* Available at: http://www.isocarp.net/data/case_studies/1727.pdf

Economic and Social Council of Greece. (2007). *Opinion No. 190: Urban and Regional Planning.* Available at: http://www.oke.gr/sites/default/files/op_190.pdf

European Commission – MRAG. (2008). Appendix F: Greece. In *Legal Aspects of Maritime Spatial Planning. Final Report to DG Maritime Affairs and Fisheries.* Available at: http://ec.europa.eu/maritimeaffairs/documentation/studies/documents/legal_aspects_msp_report_en.pdf

European Parliament. (2018). European Parliament resolution on July 2018 fires in Mati in the Attica region, Greece, and the EU's response (2018/2847(RSP)). 11 November. Available at: http://www.europarl.europa.eu/doceo/document/B-8-2018-0393_EN.html?redirect

Eurosion. (2004). *Living with Coastal Erosion in Europe: Sediment and Space for Sustainability. Part II: Maps & Statistics*. Available at: http://www.eurosion.org/reports-online/part2.pdf

Giannakourou, G. (2011). Europeanization, actor constellations and spatial policy change in Greece. *disP – The Planning Review*, 47(186), 32–41.

Giannakourou, G., & Balla, E. (2006). Planning regulation, property protection and regulatory takings in the Greek planning law. *Global Law Studies Review* 5(3), 535–558.

Karousos, G. (2010). Comparison of seashore delineation methods, *Thesis, School of Rural & Surveying Engineering*, National Technical University of Athens. Available at: http://dspace.lib.ntua.gr/handle/123456789/3702

Ministry of Finance. (2014). Public Consultation on the Draft Law 'Delineation, Management and Protection of the Seashore and the Beach'. Available at: http://www.opengov.gr/minfin/?p=4692

OECD. (2011). *Greece: Review of the Central Administration*, OECD Public Governance Reviews. OECD Publishing. doi: 10.1787/9789264102880-en

Papapetropoulos, A. (2004). Spatial planning of coastline and Beach. Theoretical and jurisprudential approaches. *Nomos & Physis*. Available at: http://www.nomosphysis.org.gr/articles.php?artid=3749&lang=1&catpid=1#_ftnref51

Solomon, S., Qin, D., Manning, M., Chen, Z., Marquis, M., Averyt, K. B., Tignor, M., & Miller, H. L. (2007). *Climate Change 2007: The Physical Science Basis*. Contribution of Working Group I to the Fourth Assessment Report of the Intergovernmental Panel on Climate Change. IPCC. Cambridge University Press.

World Factbook. (n.d.). Greece. Available at: https://www.cia.gov/library/publications/the-world-factbook/geos/gr.html [Accessed September 2019]

YPECHODE [Ministry of the Environment, Planning and Public Works]. (2006). *Report of Greece on Coastal Zone Management*. Athens: YPECHODE.

YPEKA [Ministry of Environment, Energy and Climate Change]. (2013). *Guidelines of Development Strategy for the Ministry of Environment, Energy & Climate Change Competency Sectors*. Athens: Greece. Available at: http://www.eysped.gr/el/Documents/120531%20%CE%9A%CE%91%CE%A4%CE%95%CE%A5%CE%98%CE%A5%CE%9D%CE%A3%CE%95%CE%99%CE%A3%20%CE%A3%CE%A4%CE%A1%CE%91%CE%A4%CE%97%CE%93%CE%99%CE%9A%CE%97%CE%A3%20%CE%A0%CE%95%CE%A1%CE%99%CE%92%CE%91%CE%9B%CE%9B%CE%9F%CE%9D%20%CE%95%CE%9D%CE%95%CE%A1%CE%93%CE%95%CE%99%CE%91%20%CE%A4%CE%95%CE%9B%CE%99%CE%9A%CE%9F.pdf

YPEN [Ministry of Environment and Energy]. (2016). *National Adaptation Strategy for Climate Change*. Available at: http://www.ypeka.gr/Portals/0/Files/Klimatiki%20Allagi/Prosarmogi/20160406_ESPKA_teliko.pdf

YPEN [Ministry of Environment and Energy]. (2018). *7th National Communication and 3rd Biennial Report under the United Nations Framework Convention on Climate Change*.

Legislation and associated documents (listed chronologically)

Law 2344/1940 – "About the Seashore and the Beach" (the 1940 coastal law)

Law Decree 439/1970 – Complementary Provisions for the Seashore

Law 855/1978 – Ratification of the Barcelona Convention

Law 1337/1983 – "Expansion of Town Plans, Residential Development and Other Provisions"

Presidential Decree 236/1984 – "On the enclosures of land plots within a zone of 500 meters wide from the coast or from the banks of public lakes, in accordance with Article 23 par. 1 of Law 1337/83"

Law 1650/1986 – "On the Protection of the Environment"

Law 2971/2001 – "Seashore, Beach and other Provisions" (the 2001 coastal law)

Ministerial Decision 1089532/8205/B0010 – "Criteria for the demarcation of the Seashore and the Beach" (Government Gazette 595 B/2005)

Law 3422/2005 – "Ratification of the Aarhus Convention on Access to Information, Public Participation in Decision Making and Access to Justice on Environmental Matters

Joint Ministerial Decision 11764/653/2006 – "Public access to public authorities for the provision of information on the environment, in accordance with the provisions of Directive 2003/4 / EC 'on public access to environmental information and repealing Council Directive 90/313 / EEC'"

Law 3818/2010 – "Protection of forests and forested lands of Attica Prefecture, the establishment of Special Secretariat for the Environmental and Energy Inspection and other provisions"

Law 3852/2010 – "New Architecture of 1st and 2nd tier Local Authorities and Decentralized Administration – Kallikrates Program"

Law 3894/2010 – "Acceleration and Transparency for the implementation of Strategic Investments" (the Fast Track law)

Law 3937/2011 – "Preservation of Biodiversity and Other Provisions"

Law 3986/2011 – "Urgent Measures for the Implementation of the Medium-Term Fiscal Strategy 2012–2015"

Law 4014/2011 – "Environmental licensing of works and activities, regulation of illegal constructions in connection with environmental stability and other provisions falling under the competence of the Ministry of Environment"

Law 4150/2013 – "Reorganisation of Ministry of Shipping and the Aegean and other Provisions"

EU Directive on maritime spatial planning (2014/89/EU)

Law 4447/2016 – "Spatial Planning, Sustainable Development and other provisions" (the 2016 planning law)

Law 4414/2016 – Law about Renewable Resources Energy and Climate Change

Law 4495/2017 – "Control and Development of the Built Environment and other provisions"

Law 4546/2018 – "Incorporation into Greek law of the Directive 2014/89/EU on maritime spatial planning"

Ministerial Decision 11258/2017– "Specification of the content of the Regional Plans for the Adaptation to Climate Change, in accordance with Article 43 of Law 4414/2016

Ministerial Decision 34768/4.8.2017 "Establishment and regulation of the operation of the National Council for Adaptation to Climate Change in accordance with article 44 of Law 4414/2016"

Act of Legislative Content of 10th August 2018 (Government Gazette 149A/10 August 2018)

Special Framework Plan for Industry (Government Gazette 151D/2009)

Council of State cases

CoS 3521-22/1992, plenary session
CoS 1129/1999
CoS 1790/1999
CoS 3344/1999
CoS 1500/2000
CoS 377-378/2002
CoS 680/2002
CoS 3483/2003
CoS 978/2005
CoS 1611/2006
CoS 1340/2007
CoS 3511/2010
CoS 2923/2011
CoS 5504/2012
CoS 2257/2014
Cos 2320/2014
CoS 3354/2014

CoS 3622/2014
CoS 3758/2014
CoS 3874/2014, plenary session
CoS 646/2015
CoS 3431-3433/2015
CoS 1478/2016
CoS 1704/2017, plenary session

Other cases

Administrative Court of Appeal of Piraeus (Suspension Commission) 8/2013
Administrative Court of Thessaloniki (Suspension Commission) 33/2017

13 Malta

Kurt Xerri

Malta is a tiny island state located south of Italy in the Mediterranean Sea. Given its size, the entire country might be defined as a "coastal zone" and, of course, Malta relies heavily on its coasts for its economic development – particularly tourism and industrial uses. The Maltese coast draws much foreign investment in housing and hotels.

In this cross-national study, Malta is the only country which is not a member of the OECD. This chapter tells the story of a country whose government policy has historically emphasized economic performance at the expense of environmental concerns and has never developed a framework for coastal management. In recent years, the authorities have, at least formally, weakened regulations pertaining to the protection of coastal areas. They have removed prohibitions on construction and specific uses on the country's beaches and withdrawn a previous commitment to bring all the shoreline into public ownership. As such, there is much legal ambiguity over the rules of coastal protection. Perhaps because of those government actions, the country has seen a rise in activism by members of civil society who are seeking better protection of the coastal environment; but their capacity to act is still limited.

The context: Introduction to Malta's coastal issues

Malta is an archipelago consisting of three main populated islands (Malta, Gozo, and Comino), together with several other small uninhabited islands. The country covers a land area of 316 km² and its coastline measures 196.8 km (World Factbook, n.d.).[1] This tiny country has a population of over 400,000, giving it a relatively high population density of over 1,000 people per square kilometre. Given its limited resources and prevailing economic interests, the Maltese government has historically prioritized development over preservation of coastal land, particularly in those zones reserved for tourism. The result is that as much as 27% of the area within 1 km of the coastline had been developed by 2005 (MEPA, 2011, p. 16). That figure has likely risen since that time, but no official updates have been released.

Malta's economy has always been strongly tied to the coast and maritime activities, but in the post-war era, coastal tourism has become increasingly significant. In the 1980s, the government gave up (through sale or perpetual lease) a considerable stretch of the coast, in order to incentivize the expanding tourism industry. Today, there is no doubt that tourism is the main contributor to Malta's market services sector; it is estimated to account for 29% of the GDP (Ministry for Tourism, 2015, p. 12). The tourism industry disproportionally affects the coast. Not only do tourists increasingly arrive by sea (cruise liners), but they come for marine activities such as diving, bathing, and water sports. In addition, 94% of new tourist accommodation constructed up to 1998 was reportedly located in coastal areas (Axiak, et al., 1999).[2]

Beyond tourism, significant pressures on the Maltese coast include fishing, aquaculture, shipping, and infrastructure. All contribute to the Maltese economy, but the social significance of fishing in the Maltese cultural landscape far outweighs its economic influence: In 2008, a conflict arose when plans for the development of the cruise liner terminal would displace the old fish market located in the Valletta Grand Harbour (European Commission, 2008, p.19). The fish market was eventually relocated to another venue on the opposite side of the harbour (Malta Today, 2011).

Administrative structure – key points

Given that Malta is a small island state, most legal and administrative decisions relevant to planning and coastal zone management take place at the national level. Prior to 2002, two key government bodies were responsible for planning and environment: The Planning Authority and the Environment Protection Department within the Ministry for the Environment. In 2002, the Maltese government amended the Development Planning Act to establish an umbrella authority for environment and planning: MEPA – the Malta Environment and Planning Authority (Act VI 2002, Article 57). In 2016, the two authorities were decoupled (Planning Authority, 2016).

Weak protection of the coast in law or policy

Malta did not have effective planning legislation or land use planning until 1988, when the government adopted the Building Permits (Temporary Provisions) Act (Scicluna, 2012). That Act provided a provisional framework, while a comprehensive strategic plan and complementary planning law were developed. In 1990, the Draft Structure Plan for the Maltese Islands was produced, with a final version adopted in 1992 (Government of Malta Planning Services Division, 1990). The Structure Plan provided a vague definition of the coastal zone and indicated that the relevant authorities should prepare a comprehensive policy for this zone. Despite various papers and reports addressing coastal issues in Malta,[3] no specific policy was ever developed.

The Development Planning Act was adopted in 1992. Malta's first environmental legislation, the Environment Protection Act, was introduced only in 2001. Neither law addressed coastal use or preservation at the time, nor has reference to such been added in subsequent amendments. In 2002, the Malta Planning Authority (PA) released a *Coastal Strategy Topic Paper* which defined the coastal zone and made some preliminary management recommendations. None of those recommendations have been formally adopted. In 2008, Malta signed the Integrated Coastal Zone Management (ICZM) Protocol to the Barcelona Convention. Unsurprisingly, given the scant attention the country had paid to coastal preservation, it did not ratify the Protocol until April 2019, when it acceded (Government of Malta, 2019). To date, Malta has not explicitly adopted any of the principles of the Protocol into law or policy.

The Malta Structure Plan (1992) was replaced with the Strategic Plan for Environment and Development (SPED) in July 2015. The new plan mentioned the vulnerability of coastal and marine areas while simultaneously stressing the importance of those areas to the country's economy. It defined the "terrestrial extent" of the coastal zone on a map, but the accompanying objectives and policies are generalized and vague. In fact, the SPED provides even less specific policy guidance on coastal issues than did the Structure Plan. For example, whilst the

Structure Plan stipulated that construction and specific uses should be prohibited on the country's beaches, the SPED is silent on this matter. Thus, it might be argued that the replacement of the Structure Plan with the SPED has taken Malta backwards in terms of the establishment of ICZM principles within the country's legal and policy framework.

In 2016, an amendment to the Malta Civil Code finally introduced legal definitions and minimal protection for the coastal zone, with a focus on public lands. As will be discussed below, the definitions are vague and are yet to be tested in practice or by the courts.

Definition of the Maltese coastal zone and shoreline

The Coastal Strategy Topic Paper (Planning Authority, 2002) defined the coastal zone as follows:

> A geographical space incorporating land and sea areas within which the natural processes interact to create a unique dynamic system; it also incorporates those activities on land and at sea where human activities are directly influenced by or can influence the quality of natural resources

This vague definition allows for the coastal zone to be identified on the basis of a mix of ecological, physical, and socio-economic criteria. The Strategic Plan for Environment and Development (SPED) differentiates between "predominantly urban" and "predominantly rural" coast. Overall, the land identified as "coast" in the Coastal Strategy Topic Paper amounts to 61.8 km²; 19.6% of the total land area of Malta (PA, 2002, p. 12).

Until 2016, there was nothing in Maltese law that defined any part of the coastal zone. Since 2016, following a move to classify coastal land as public domain in the law (see the following section), the Civil Code contains the following definitions (at Article 311(2); emphasis added):

> The "**coastal perimeter**" is that part of the land which lies fifteen metres from the shoreline inwards, whether it is foreshore, landmass or cliff or is a combination of them and, where the foreshore extends beyond fifteen metres, to the limit of the foreshore.
>
> The "**foreshore**" is that part of the coastal perimeter, including where it exceeds fifteen metres, which is normally covered by water due to the action of the waves and the use of which is restricted by this fact. The foreshore extends up to the reach of the largest wave and, even if it lies beyond the reach of the waves, to the limits of any beach:
>
> Provided that the foreshore shall not extend over or onward of a schemed public road.
>
> For the purposes of this sub-article:
>
> (a) a "**beach**" is that part of the land contiguous to the shoreline, irrespective of how far inland it extends, which is of its nature or characteristics destined for public use in accordance with its nature and in accordance with any law from time to time regulating development planning;
>
> (b) a "**landmass**" or a "**cliff**" is that part of the coastal perimeter which is elevated from the sea, is not accessible from the sea and, or is not subject to being covered by any wave; and
>
> (c) the "**shoreline**" is the land contour which is constantly in direct contact with the sea; provided that when the shoreline changes due to erosion or collapse, the baseline for calculation of the coastal perimeter shall be adjusted accordingly from time to time without prejudice to the application of any law regulating development planning.

While they provide some guidance as to the legal limits of the coastal zone, which was previously entirely absent from the law, these definitions present several challenges for those seeking to interpret the law. For example, what land is "by its nature destined for public use"? What does "constantly in direct contact with the sea" mean in the context of daily tides? Significantly, these definitions are yet to be tested in further government decision-making or by the courts.

Public domain

Maltese courts have long held (at least since the 1920s) that ports, wharfs, the territorial sea, and its shores have a special public domain status and are inalienable (may not be sold).[4] Nevertheless, this elevated status was not formally recognized in Maltese legislation until very recently. Instead, unlike the French Civil Code, for example, Maltese legislation did not differentiate between "public property" and "public domain" and thus sections of the foreshore could be transferred in the same manner as could other government property.

Maltese jurisprudence holds that coastal land is presumed to belong to the State; however, if a private individual brings proof of their ownership of relevant land (through land title), the title would be acknowledged. For example, in the late nineteenth century, a public official sought the reinstatement of the foreshore in favour of the government on the basis that the former fell within the public domain and that it could therefore not be transferred to private ownership. In this case, a private landowner who had acquired rights spanning over the coastal territory had proceeded to erect a wall that had barred access to the foreshore. The Court ruled in favour of government, but only on the basis that the original deed of transfer contained a condition that bound the owner to maintain a passage to the shore. Significantly, the ruling implied that had this condition not been included, the landowner would have been able to claim an exclusive right over the entire plot of land (Emmanuele Luigi Galizia v. Emmanuele Scicluna, 1886). This reasoning was confirmed as recently as 2009, when the government sued a private owner/developer following the latter's works of excavation on the foreshore. Upon reviewing the facts, the Court of Appeal noted that neither party could prove an absolute title over the land. Nevertheless, since the foreshore was held to fall within the public domain and the private developer was not capable of defeating this presumption, the case was decided in favour of government (Direttur tal-Artijiet v. Vincent Farrugia et, 2009).

The 1992 Malta Structure Plan contained the following policy (CZM3): "All the coastline will be brought into public ownership within a specified period" (MEPA, 1992). That policy was never implemented; due to both lack of funds required to expropriate private land and lack of political will (Axiak et al., 1999).

Paradoxically, rather than acquire more coastal land, the government continued to sell tracts of the coast to private developers until 2004. Since that time, transfer of coastal land has continued, but through perpetual leases (title of emphyteusis).[5] While there is no official position on why the government now prefers perpetual leases, it appears that while wanting to render the land economically productive, the State is wary of irreversibly relinquishing its coastal property, being a finite resource. The 2015 SPED, which replaced the Structure Plan, makes no reference to public ownership of coastal land. According to MEPA (Malta Environment and Planning Authority), the omission was intentional because "ownership is not a planning issue" (Debono, 2015).

In 2013, the Ministry for Fair Competition, Small Business and Consumers published a White Paper on the classification of Maltese land as public domain. This document clarified that the "coastal perimeter" (as defined in the previous section) is in the public domain and stipulated that property in the public domain could not be transferred unless "declassified" as such by an Act of Parliament.[6] This was eventually enacted into law. Yet existing privately owned land in the public domain remains in private ownership, with the stipulation that the owner is required to "preserve its substance with regard both to matter and to form" (Public Domain Act, Fourth Schedule, article 4(10) *et seq.*). According the White Paper,

> *The owner will not, however, be free to damage or destroy it and will be expected to enjoy his rights consistently with the special nature of the property he owns* (Ministry for Fair Competition, Small Business and Consumers, 2013, p. 13).

The Public Domain Act 2016 expressly states that the land within the "coastal perimeter" is included in the public domain. The unanimous approval of the Public Domain Act indicates that the administration was committed to protecting the coast, or at least those tracts that remained in public ownership. The Minister for the Environment at the time described the concept of public domain as essential so that the *"collective good and public interest can be safeguarded against unsustainable development, commercialisation and environmental destruction"* (Times of Malta, 2016a). In addition, the shadow minister praised the Bill as one that would prevent speculation on State-owned property. Nevertheless, the effectiveness of this law in safeguarding the public ownership of the coast is yet to be tested. In fact, although the procedure has become relatively more cumbersome, Parliament still requires only a simple majority to declassify land, meaning there is no need for bipartisan consensus in such decisions.

Permitted uses in the coastal public domain/beach

The SPED (2015) does not contain specific provisions regarding use of coastal land. Instead, it generally seeks to ensure that *"existing coastal recreational resources are protected, enhanced and accessible"* and to *"facilitate the provision of new recreational facilities which do not restrict or interfere with physical and visual public access to the coast..."* (Coastal Objective 3).

The 1992 Structure Plan took a more stringent approach, prohibiting any form of permanent construction in sandy coastal areas. Development which contravened this principle was to be removed wherever practicable (Policy RCO 16). This provision of the Structure Plan led to the development of a policy document named *Development Control Guidance: Kiosks* (MEPA, 1994), which was not repealed together with the Structure Plan and thus remains in force to this day. The Kiosks document states (at Paragraph 5.2) that kiosks or stalls are not to be permitted on sandy beaches. Exceptions may be made to allow a temporary kiosk structure in areas where no such facility exists.

In the era of the Structure Plan, the courts upheld decisions by MEPA to limit encroachment of kiosks and picnic tables on the coast on the basis of Policy CZM3 (discussed above under Public Domain), even when these uses were proposed as far as 60 m from the shoreline (in combination with the need to protect Special Areas of Conservation; Carmel Chircop v. MEPA, 2012).[7] The authorities also successfully defended the use of the policy to justify the refusal of a permit for changing the use of a boathouse to a snack bar (Georgia Cini v. Development Control Commission, 1999). Given the much more vague language of the SPED, it is questionable whether similar decisions will be upheld under this legal regime.

Besides kiosks, it appears that MEPA has largely contained development of other activities along the coast. The Development Notification Order 2007, which exempts a range of minor developments from full development permit application procedures, lays down that any tables and chairs placed on a pavement, promenade, or belvedere must be at least 1.5 m clear from the outer edge of these areas. In relation to beach facilities, these are only permitted in *designated beaches* as determined by the Malta Tourism Authority, which issues invitations to tender for the management of these beaches. For example, a 2015 tender included "beach concessions" (rights of use) for hiring of umbrellas and deckchairs at Blue Lagoon and Santa Marija Bay (Comino). The tender would also stipulate the number of deckchairs and the minimum bid for each lot (Malta Tourism Authority, 2015).

The Planning Appeals Board has been cautious in its assessment of such decisions concerning scheduled Areas of Ecological Importance, particularly when these would impact public access to the coastline.[8] In Joe Debono v. MEPA (2012) the Environment and Planning Review Tribunal denied the applicant permission even for placing tables, due to the area being earmarked by the North Harbours Local Plan for fishing-related activities and pedestrian access. Nevertheless, there were cases, including Coronato Portelli v. MEPA (2012), in which the Board gave precedence to economic and tourism considerations.

Permitted uses (or those for which a permit is granted), such as industrial uses or kiosks, may be constructed on public land by virtue of a perpetual lease (title of emphyteusis). In the case of kiosks, such leases may be granted for a 25-year period, as long as the beneficiary had a valid permit issued by the Lands Authority to operate a kiosk on the land prior to 1996 (Government Lands Act, 2017, Article 31). In addition, specifically on the seashore, lease titles may be transferred for up to 10 years if the relevant use is "a room or any other building" or caravan.

Coastal setback

In Malta, there is no defined coastal setback zone. Nevertheless, a large extent of the coastal zone (as defined by the Coastal Strategy Topic Paper, 2002) has been designated as being an Outside Development Zone (ODZ), where development is generally not permitted. The ODZ is determined by local plans which, according to the Development Planning Act, set out detailed policies for land which must be generally in accordance with the Spatial Strategy. There are exceptions to the restrictions on development in the ODZ, particularly for uses which require a coastal location (such as thermal power stations, ports, desalination plants, etc).

Right of public access

The Structure Plan (1992) policy CZM3 included the following:

> *Public access around the coastline immediately adjacent to the sea or at the top of cliffs (including in bays, harbours, and creeks) will be secured. This will include taking shorelands into public ownership, Government acquisition of illegal developments and encroachments, and suitable construction works. In the few cases where this is not practical (for example where security considerations are paramount), nearby detours will be established.*

It appears that while it applied, the relevant authorities adhered strictly to the above policy. This is illustrated in Dr. Alfred Galea nomine v. Development Control Commission (2000), in which a hotel sought the approval for the development of a yacht club which included a number of holiday apartments and berthing and storage facilities for boats in St George's Bay. The permit was rejected due to the fact that the proposed development would obstruct public access to the foreshore. The Planning Directorate justified its decision by stating that:

> *Access to the coast is becoming restricted by the demands of private development, particularly hotels and beach concessions. The coastal strip is under great pressure - a case in*

point is St. George's Bay itself and its environs. The coastal strip requires protection from overdevelopment. The major objection in this case, is related to the fact that the proposal is rather extensive considering the extent of the site.

In 2002, a hotel developer applied for retroactive approval for an existing extension to a legally constructed beach club in St. Paul's Bay. Although the owner had a legal title over the land, part of the development was not covered by a development permit (St. Paul's Bay Residents Association v. Development Control Commission, 2002). The Development Permission Application Report prepared by the Planning Authority revealed that despite the fact that the area was not defined as public land, the plan annexed to the public deed of transfer showed a setback of 4.75 m from the shoreline, having adopted the assumption that that distance should be kept unobstructed in case of government transfers of coastal land. Although the contractual obligations for public access to the foreshore were unclear, the report proposed that the permit be issued on the condition that the developer retreat landward to at least 6 m from the shoreline, in order to allow for unobstructed access. That recommendation was adopted by the Development Control Commission and the approval was granted on this basis.

More recently, in 2017, the EPRT (in Michael Stivala v. The Planning Authority) reaffirmed the Planning Authority's refusal of proposed works of a tract of rocky foreshore, in Sliema, for leisure activities. The applicant claimed that a concrete platform would improve accessibility to the coast, but the Authority held that the development would have urbanized a part of the coast that was still in its natural, pristine state. The EPRT agreed that the development would have altered the area's natural appearance. The decision was supported by the Local Plan in force for the area, though the Planning Authority also quoted policy CZM3 in justifying its decision. Interestingly, while noting that the Structure Plan (containing Policy CZM3) was no longer in force at the time of the decision, the EPRT suggested that its strategic objectives were still contained in the respective Local Plans.

Compared to the Structure Plan, the SPED (2015) is much less ambitious about expanding public access to the coast. Although its objectives include the enhancement of public use of bathing areas, as well as encouraging public access for informal recreation, its emphasis on accessibility is much less emphatic. Nevertheless, the importance of public access has been translated into area-specific local plans, which regard the use of the coastal area as a recreational space as an *"important element leading to the regeneration of the area"* (MEPA, 2002, p. 57). Notably, the language in the North West Local Plan goes beyond physical barriers to accessibility and suggests that the proliferation of illegal structures along the coast create a *"strong psychological inhibition to the public from using or gaining access to the foreshore"* (MEPA, 2006a, p. 95).

The issue of accessibility is given the greatest emphasis in the North Harbours Local Plan, since this district is under intense pressure from commercial development. Due to the concentration of tourist facilities located in the area, the plan notes that less than a third (28%) of beaches around St. George's Bay are available for public use and almost a fifth (17%) of the beaches between Tigné and Balluta Bay have restricted access to the general public (MEPA, 2006b, pp. 73–74). As such, the plan actively seeks, proposals that improve access along the waterfront (Policy 9.3.4, p. 71). In relation to tourism resorts, the plan states that proposals to upgrade such resorts will only be considered on the condition that *"access to and along the coast is safeguarded"* (Policy 15.4.15, 129). It appears these policies have been upheld to date.

Accessibility has been emphasized in various Development Briefs, which are policy documents summarizing the Planning Authority's position on development of specific land areas. For example, a key aim of the Draft Development Brief for the Regeneration of the Cottonera Waterfront (a former industrial area) was to provide public access to the waterfront; specifically, through the development of a continuous promenade along the coast (MEPA, 1997). In addition, in the approved briefs for both the Valletta Cruise Terminal Development (MEPA, 1998) and the Qawra Coast (MEPA, 2007), the government sought to enhance public access by renewing these coastal areas and increasing the potential for recreational activities within them. Furthermore, in the Fort Cambridge Development Brief, MEPA sought to return areas to the public where previously permitted "beach concessions" could no longer be justified (MEPA, 2006c, pp. 25–26).

Despite these policies, a recent court decision demonstrates the ineffectiveness of the SPED and local plans with respect to pedestrian access to the coast, in cases were land is privately owned. In Victor Borg v. Malta Environment and Planning Authority (2019), a landowner had initially been refused permission to install a timber gate on his privately owned property, since this would have barred the access to an accessway on the land which led to a nearby bay. The Local Plan (Gozo and Comino) addressed this area specifically and marked the accessway for public pedestrian access. The local authority's refusal was upheld by the Environment and Planning Review Tribunal (Victor Borg v. Malta Environment and Planning Authority, 2015a). The owner appealed on the basis that such a planning policy could not operate to create third party rights, in this case in favour of the public, on his privately owned land. The Court of Appeal upheld the owner's arguments and held that:

> no law can grant third parties rights on private property if not through the legal means which the legislator would have already put in place for such purpose. A policy certainly cannot, by itself, grant private property rights to third parties or be used to deny the development requested by an owner on his own land (Victor Borg v. Malta Environment and Planning Authority, 2015b).

The case was, therefore, sent back before the Environment and Planning Review Tribunal (EPRT) which, in this second instance, upheld the Court of Appeal's position and decided that since the government had not proceeded to expropriate the land, the owner's private property interests would override any other consideration, until any eventual transfer in favour of the public.

In all, it does appear that the Maltese government has prioritized public access to the coast in all relevant planning decisions since at least the 1990s. Although the SPED is vaguer than the previous Structure Plan, it does seek to protect physical and visual access. Significantly, the Paceville Master plan, developed since the introduction of the SPED, holds that access to the coastline is *"not just for the privileged few occupants of the new establishments but for everyone in Paceville"* (PA, 2016, p.77).

Although, formally, the government has reiterated and reaffirmed its commitment to securing public access for all, recent events have cast doubt as to its willingness to take prompt, decisive action when such rights are imperiled by private development. We describe one such event under "public participation" below.

Compliance and enforcement

Illegal development in Malta includes any works carried out after 1967 and without development permission from the relevant authority (Development Planning Act, 2016, Article 2). Local plans may include additional parameters. For example, the Qawra/Dwejra Heritage Park

Action Plan 2005 identifies as illegal any boathouses built after 1962 which were not identified in a 1965 survey and did not receive a development permit. In such cases, owners need to request planning approval to avoid enforcement action (Nature Trust Malta, MEPA, & WWF Italia., 2005, pp. 79–80).

The tools for enforcement which exist in the framework of Maltese legislation include restrain and enforcement notices, demolition, and legalization fines – a new tool in which the owners of illegal structures pay fines in order to legalize their development and its use. In some cases, such as removing illegal caravans from coastal areas, enforcement action has been effective (Times of Malta, 2009). In general, however, Maltese authorities are not rigorous in enforcement against illegal development.

One of the key reforms within the planning authority was the setting up of a specialized Enforcement Directorate (previously, enforcement functions fell under the responsibility of the Planning Directorate). Nevertheless, in a 2013 report on enforcement action in the ODZ (Outside Development Zone), the National Audit Office remarked that the Planning Authority's inability to apply a zero tolerance approach has weakened its effectiveness, given that *"[p]otential contraveners may be encouraged to commit irregularities on the premise that delayed enforcement action may render illegalities advantageous to them"* (National Audit Office, 2013, p. 63). Enforcement actions undertaken during the 2006–2012 time period were found to be minimal in the context of the number of outstanding ODZ Executable Enforcement Notices (including Notices which pertained to developments eventually removed by owners or legalized; National Audit Office, 2013, p. 57). Furthermore, the Audit Office flagged issues of transparency associated with decision-making processes (National Audit Office, 2013, p. 58).

Perhaps, the most widespread and significant type of illegal development in Malta's coastal areas is boathouses. These structures might be initially built for boat storage (legally or illegally), but often they are eventually modified and illegally used as summer homes. In the 1990s–2000s, a trend arose involving the construction of single-room structures in attractive coastal areas, followed by servicing works such as access roads and paving (MEPA, 2006a, p. 95). In this way, significant stretches of public land were illegally seized by private citizens; and large agglomerations of these structures mushroomed in Marfa Ridge, Gnejna, Marsascala, and Mellieha Bay (MEPA, 2002, p.46). The North West Local Plan pledges that MEPA will continue with the removal of illegal structures on or adjacent to the coastline (MEPA, 2006a, pp. 96–97). In addition, this plan specifically notes that although it would be politically expedient to leave these developments undisturbed, the Authority's inaction could serve to incentivize further illegal development (p. 94).

Despite the above policy, in keeping with the findings of the Audit Office (2013), government commitment to take enforcement action against illegal boathouses has been very weak; on more than one occasion the authorities have succumbed to the private interests of offenders. Both political parties have reportedly conducted negotiations which would allow illegal boathouses – or replacement holiday homes – to remain (Times of Malta, 2013), for example, in Armier Bay (Figure 13.1). Despite never publicly approving such a plan, the government has never outright condemned illegal boathouses, even providing "temporary" energy supply to occupants as recently as 2014 (Vella, 2014).

Illegal boathouses constitute one of the greatest sores of Maltese planning policy, and their continued existence, despite the wide public dissent surrounding the issue, proves the government's inability to safeguard the public interest in the face of arbitrary action by a group of private citizens. This issue exposes the ineffectiveness of local enforcement policies as well as the system's significant susceptibility to political pressures.

Figure 13.1 Coastal shanty town in Armier. Illegally erected "boathouses"

Source: Frank Vincentz. CC BY-SA 3.0 license. Available at: https://commons.wikimedia.org/wiki/File:Malta_-_Mellieha_-_Triq_ir-Ramla_tat-Torri_l-Abjad_-_Kitesurfing_05_ies.jpg

Climate change awareness

As Malta is a tiny island nation, the potential impacts of climate change, including sea level rise and associated problems of coastal inundation, erosion, migration of beaches, and damage by waves and high winds, would have a significant impact on the island and its population (MRRA & the University of Malta, 2010, p. 32). Amongst the uses that would be most significantly affected are areas protected for their environmental values (including Natura 2000 sites, Special Areas of Conservation, and Specially Protected Areas), ports, and beaches. At the national level, it is generally accepted that sea level rise will occur, and that a certain degree of adaptation will be required (Malta Resources Authority, 2014, p. 142). The vulnerability of coastal areas, both ecological and physical, is recognized in the SPED, which directs development away from areas which are under significant risk of flooding (MEPA, 2015, p. 22).

The industry which is at greatest risk is certainly tourism, since disruption in the coastal activity and environment, together with harsher temperature extremes, would likely result in lower demand for Malta as a holiday destination (MRRA & the University of Malta, 2010, p. 338). As such, the Climate Change Committee for Adaptation has recommended development of a Tourism Action and Contingency Plan, which would determine how beaches which run the risk of being eroded are safeguarded and how coastal ecosystems are to be protected (Climate Change Committee for Adaptation, 2010, p. 131). Since 2010, the Institute of Earth Sciences at the University of Malta has engaged in research on the impacts on coastal communities and adaptation measures. New technical facilities were also set up to assist students in performing research on climate change and coastal inundation (Malta Resources Authority, 2014, p. 177).

The most relevant legal instrument in this field is the European Assessment and Management of Flood Risks Regulations, which require members to assess and manage flood risks by undertaking preliminary flood risk assessments and to subsequently prepare flood hazard maps and flood risk maps. In other words, Malta is required by EU law to identify the assets and humans at risk in these areas, and to take adequate and coordinated measures to reduce flood risks (European Commission, 2007).

Malta has not adopted any national laws dedicated to climate change mitigation or adaptation.

Coordination and integration

As highlighted in the introductory section to this chapter, there are several conflicting uses along the Maltese coast: Tourism and recreation, fisheries and aquaculture, shipping and infrastructure. As such, the key players in coastal management include the Malta Tourism Authority, the Department of Fisheries and Aquaculture within the Ministry for Sustainable Development, Environment and Climate Change (MSDEC), Transport Malta, Enemalta (Malta's electricity company), the Water Services Corporation (WSC), and WasteServ Malta (waste management services).

Given these many land uses and authorities, there is a need for a coordinated approach to management of coastal land. The SPED recognizes that most of the nation's strategic infrastructure (energy, ports, desalination, and sewage treatment plants) is located along the foreshore and that the thriving local tourism industry is similarly dependent on the coastal area (MEPA, 2015, p. 15). As such, it promotes a balance between the various competing uses. Amongst its objectives are included development of a "national integrated maritime strategy" (Coastal Objective 1; MEPA, 2015, p. 26), but no further guidance about coordination is provided. The *National Environment Policy* (NEP) also refers to coastal areas and the need to reduce conflict, protect the environment, maximize access, and control development, while identifying spatial planning as the key tool to ensure protection of coastal areas from inappropriate development (Ministry for Tourism, the Environment and Culture, 2012, p. 49).

Indeed, local plans and development briefs do carry assessments of competing land uses and establish which of these uses should be prioritized over others in a given area. For example, the North West Local Plan prioritizes conservation and recreation and severely restricts new development in the coastal zone (MEPA, 2006a, p. 142). On the other hand, the Plan regulating the highly touristic North Harbours area is much more receptive to the development of new yachting and berthing facilities (MEPA, 2006b, p. 74).

A notable example of how land use conflicts are managed through local plans can be found in the Grand Harbour Local Plan, which deals with an area that accommodates an intense variety of uses (MEPA, 2011, p. 7; see Figure 13.2). In order to minimize the conflict, the Authority devised a system of prioritization and distribution of uses in such a way that the Grand Harbour area was subdivided into three zones, ensuring that the activities in each zone would be protected (MEPA, 2002, p. 63). Zone A (The Inner Harbour) prioritizes commercial, industrial, and dock uses; Zone B (Valletta/Floriana) prioritizes cruise passenger, leisure, and tourism; Zone C (Cottonera) prioritizes residential, leisure, and tourism.

Another example of the use of zones to manage conflicting uses can be found in the proposed Development Brief for Marsaxlokk Bay. Figure 13.3 shows how the area was divided into zones. The Harbour area (Zone E) was proposed to safeguard the needs of fishermen against conflicting uses (Planning Authority, 2017, p. 12).

Decisions by the Planning Appeals Board (and subsequently the Environment and Planning Review Tribunal; EPRT) have dealt with coastal land use conflicts with caution. In one case, the government had leased a property that was not fully compliant with the development permit to a local Fishing Cooperative in Marsaxlokk. The Development Control Commission then denied the Fishing Cooperative a permit for alterations and extensions, on the basis that the site fell outside the development zone and it saw no justification for intensification of urban development in this location. The Fishing Cooperative then submitted an appeal on the basis that the government would not allow alterations or extension on the premises that it had provided to the Cooperative specifically for the purpose for which those alterations were required (Publius Falzon noe v. MEPA, 2012). Recognizing the importance of planning policies that

Figure 13.2 Conflicting uses at Dockyard Creek (Grand Harbour). Local fishing boats and the touristic Vittoriosa
(Birgu) waterfront

Source: Sudika. Available at: https://commons.wikimedia.org/wiki/File:Sudika_Dockyard_Creek.jpg

promote sustainable primary industries, the Board upheld the Cooperative's appeal, albeit only while the property remained in its possession.

In a recommendation that sought to manage the conflicting interests of yachting and leisure users (EPRT, 2011), the EPRT recommended the granting of vehicular access to the Super Yacht Facility in an area that had been initially designated as strictly pedestrian. In granting time-limited access, the EPRT noted that:

> It is the considered opinion of this Tribunal that a compromise must be found in order to, on the one hand, preserve a recreational area that is clear from traffic; and on the other to allow yacht owners free and easy access to their boats

Public participation and access to justice

In Malta, public participation is mandatory in some aspects of environmental and planning decision-making. The Environment Protection Act 2016 (EPA) lists functions of the Environment and Resources Authority, which include conducting consultation with government agencies, local councils, and NGOs (Article 8(4)(c)). Any regulation made under the EPA must be the subject of a four-week (minimum) public consultation process (EPA, Article 55).

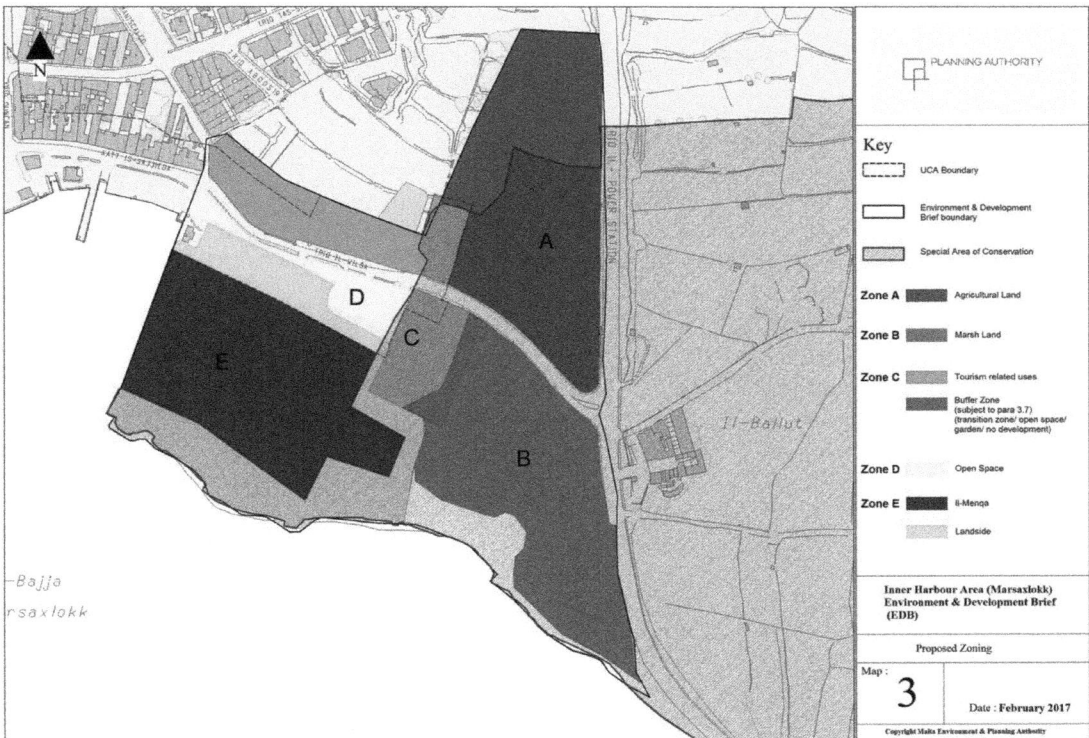

Figure 13.3 Proposed Zoning for the Inner Harbour Area (Marsaxlokk) Environment and Development Brief

Source: MEPA, Marsaxlokk Inner Harbour Area Environment and Development Brief. Approved Plan, August 2017. Reproduced with permission

The Development Planning Act 2016 (DPA) contains similar provisions. The Act lists the functions of the Executive Council of the Planning Authority, which include undertaking research and conducting consultation with government departments and NGOs (Article 38(1) (k)). The Executive Council is bound to grant organizations and individuals a minimum three-week period within which to submit their comments in relation to the SPED and any subsidiary plan or policy (i.e. subject plans, local plans, action or management plans, and local briefs; Article 53). The greatest innovation contained in the new DPA (2015) is the designation of an additional two members on the Planning Board: one representing the interests of environmental NGOs and another from the local council within whose boundaries the major project under discussion lies (Article 63(2)(e) and (h)). The local council representative varies according to the project under discussion and is selected by the relevant local council.

Interestingly, the introduction of these (relatively recent) provisions led the Planning Authority to argue that if outvoted on the Planning Board, local councils, environmental NGOs, and the EPA had no right of appeal. If this had indeed been decided to be the legal procedure, such a decision would have effectively muzzled some of the most relevant stakeholders in controversial planning decisions. This, however, did not come to pass: The EPRT (Environment and Planning Review Tribunal) ruled that each of these entities had a right of appeal, confirming that the right to representation subsisted throughout the entire planning process (Sliema Local

Council v. The Planning Authority et., 2017; Flimkien ghall-Ambjent Ahjar and Others v. The Planning Authority, 2017).

In environment and planning appeals, the rights of individuals to appeal has progressively been broadened. The DPA (2016) specifies that any person may declare an interest in a development on the basis of issues relevant to environment planning, as long as his or her written declaration of interest and representations are duly submitted to the Planning Board (Article 71(6)). The EPRTA defines a "person" as any association or body of persons, regardless of their status as a legal person (Article 2). This Act further specifies that such third parties do not need to prove judicial interest according to the traditional doctrine, but that their appeal needs to be justified on environmental or planning grounds (Article 22(1)). As stated in various EPRT decisions,[9] this change that was introduced in the EPRTA makes planning considerations the centre of appeals and emerged from the legislator's aspiration to encourage third parties to come forward with their arguments – particularly since these would often represent the interests of the wider community.

In line with these changes, any person with an interest[10] in the case, may apply to the Tribunal, to challenge the substantive or procedural legality of any decision relating to a development which is subject to an Environmental Impact Assessment or an Integrated Pollution Prevention and Control (IPPC) permit (EPRTA Article 11(1)(e)). This brings Malta in line with European Directive 2003/35/EC regarding public participation.[11]

The strengthened avenues for representation reflect an increasing public awareness on matters of environmental protection, particularly in the current climate, in which the government has recently approved extensive development on public land. Environmental activism has been on the rise following the exposure of controversial deals with private developers. Recently, a popular front (*Front Ħarsien ODZ*) arose in response to the government's announcement of its plans to allow construction of a private university on coastal land in an Outside Development Zone in Marsascala. In opposition to this plan, an estimated 3,000 citizens attended what was described as the "biggest pro-environment protest ever held in Malta" (Times of Malta, 2015a). The protest was partially successful: The government negotiated with the developers to reduce the footprint of the development (Government of Malta, 2015; Times of Malta, 2015b).

Activists claimed another partial victory in 2016, regarding public access to the coast on a small island off the coast of Gzira. The developers had barred access to the foreshore, in a clear violation of the permissions granted to them. A group of activists (the group *Kamp Emergenza Ambjent*), supported by the Local Council of Gzira and other private citizens, cut through the fences erected by the developers to make it through to the coast (Malta Independent, 2016). As a result, the public was eventually granted access to the foreshore, albeit only during the day (Times of Malta, 2016b).

The above examples are telling in that they demonstrate that the authorities have prioritized development over preservation of the coast in recent years. Not only that, but even in the last case, in which the developers were in clear violation of their permit, the government did not fully prioritize public rights over the foreshore.

Fiscal aspects of coastal zone management

The only fiscal tool used in coastal zone management in Malta is expropriation. Once private interests on coastal land are proven, government may expropriate if it can show that such a move would be in the public interest.

In 2004, a piece of coastal land was transferred to a private developer, who promptly barred public access to the surrounding shore at St. Paul's Bay. Following public protests, the government took steps to expropriate the area of the land which was used by bathers prior to its transfer to the private developer. The developer applied to the Constitutional Court (Raymond Vella et v. Kumissarju ta' l-Artijiet, 2004) on the grounds that the expropriation was not legal due to a lack of public interest (they claimed that the protesters did not represent the wider public). The Constitutional Court rejected the developer's claims in this regard, as the expropriation would allow free and unhindered access to the sea. Nevertheless, the Court did uphold the developer's claim that they were discriminated against, as the government's actions were isolated rather than part of a plan to acquire all privately owned parts of the Maltese foreshore. While this expropriation took place under the old Structure Plan regime, the court did not reference the policy which sought to bring coastal land into public owner-ship (CZM3) in its decision. There have been no similar examples since the introduction of the SPED.

In a 2011 case, the government had expropriated land for the construction of a road, but it used part of that land to erect several boathouses which it then leased to private citizens. The previous owners applied to the civil court on the basis that privately-owned boathouses do not serve any public purpose (Residual Limited v. Kummissarju tal-Artijiet, 2011). The court upheld the petitioners' claims, finding that the government had violated the Maltese Constitution (article 37) and the European Convention. As such, the court ordered the proper-ties be returned to the applicants.

Overall assessment

The coast has always been of key importance to the Maltese economy. The trend to maximize its economic potential has, however, led to the rapid seizure of public land, limited coastal access, and increased coastal erosion.

The growth of various competing uses and its impact on the coast has been acknowledged both at a policy level (local plans) and at the legislative level, with proposals that aim to reign in development and increase transparency and protect public land. In addition, environmental NGOs and politicians have increasingly pushed for enforcement action on agglomerations of illegal structures along stretches of coastal land.

The increasing pressure on the Maltese coast appears to have sensitized planners as to a need for careful management. This is evident in local plans, such as the Grand Harbour Local Plan, which carefully prioritize and zone coastal land uses.

Despite progress in planning and public awareness of coastal issues, the Maltese authorities continue to prioritize economic considerations, authorizing the intensification of development in the commercial zones on the coast and even new private developments on previously pristine coastal areas. These moves have been in line with the direction of the 2015 SPED policy docu-ment, as well as the 2016 decoupling of the environment and planning authorities, both which clearly demonstrated a push to utilize planning for economic gain, at the expense of environ-mental protection. The onus of objecting to developments which prioritize private interests at the expense of the public has, therefore, fallen on the shoulders of civil society, where activism is gaining in its significance and power. Yet to this day, the more powerful development lobby has considerable influence on decision-making bodies.

It is ultimately this asymmetry between strong economic interests and weaker mechanisms for environmental preservation that prevents Malta from developing an effective coastal man-agement strategy which meets environmental standards and the public's expectations while balancing economic aspirations.

Notes

1. According to MEPA (2011), the coastline length increased by over 30 km between 1994 and 2004 due to artificial extensions through the construction of marinas and the extension of quays.
2. The authors of the State of Environment Report 1998 did not specify how they defined coastal areas for this purpose.
3. For example, MEPA (2011).
4. See *Gustav Lapira v. Canonico Capitolare Monsignor Giuseppe Caruana Dingli et*, Court of Appeal, 10 October 1923, and *Giuseppe Cutajar et v. Giuseppe Cutajar et*, First Hall (Civil Court), 27 February 1960 (Vol. XLIV.II.524).
5. A title of emphyteusis is a perpetual ground lease which provides the lessee with extensive property rights. See The Law Dictionary (n.d.).
6. Any transfer of land must also comply with the provisions contained in the Disposal of Government Land Act (DGLA).
7. The same was decided in a case concerning a proposed snack bar in a scheduled area of ecological value (*Neville Fenech v. Development Control Commission*, Planning Appeals Board, 27 June 2003, PAB/212/02 KA).
8. For example, see *John Baptist Spiteri v. MEPA*, Planning Appeals Board, 9 January 2008, App. no. 17/07 RT, and *Kevin Fenech v. MEPA*, Environment and Planning Review Tribunal 29 November 2011, App. no. 96/10 CF.
9. For example, *Dr. Joseph Vella Briffa et v. Development Control Commission et*, Planning Appeals Board, 26 September 2003, PAB/263/02 KA; *St. Paul's Bay Residents Association v. Development Control Commission et*, Planning Appeals Board, 8 November 2002, PAB/184/01 KA.
10. Article 71(6) of the Development Planning Act states that "Any person may declare an interest in a development and, on the basis of issues relevant to environment and planning, make representations on the development."
11. The Directive is specifically addressed in the "Plans and Programmes (Public Participation) Regulations 2006" Subsidiary Legislation 546.41 (Legal Notice 74 of 2006).

References

Axiak, V., Mallia, E., Gauci, V., Schembri, P. J., Mallia, A., & Vella, A. J. (1999). *State of the Environment Report for Malta 1998*. Available at: https://era.org.mt/en/Documents/SOEReport1998.pdf

Climate Change Committee for Adaptation (Malta). (2010). *National Climate Change Adaptation Strategy: Consultation Report*.

Debono, J. (2015). Ownership of coastline not a planning issue – MEPA. *Malta Today*, 12 October. Available at: https://www.maltatoday.com.mt/environment/environment/57939/ownership_of_coastline_not_a_planning_issue__mepa#.XRFlkegzZPY

EPRT. (2011). Recommendation to the Minister responsible for Planning and the Environment by the Environment and Planning Review Tribunal. Recommendation no. 1/2012 CF.

European Commission. (2007). The EU Floods Directive. Available at: http://ec.europa.eu/environment/water/flood_risk/

— (2008). Fisheries Operational Programme. Available at: https://ec.europa.eu/fisheries/sites/fisheries/files/docs/body/malta_en.pdf

Government of Malta Planning Services Division. (1990). *Structure Plan for the Maltese Islands*. Written Statement – 1st Draft. Available at: https://www.um.edu.mt/library/oar/bitstream/123456789/34196/1/Structure_plan_for_the_Maltese_islands_written_statement_November_1990.pdf

Government of Malta. (2015). Investment Għan-Naħa T'isfel Ta' Malta [Investment for the South of Malta: American University of Malta]. Available at: https://web.archive.org/web/20160304213220/https://opm.gov.mt/en/Documents/AUM/AUM%20PRESENTATION.pdf/

Government of Malta. (2019). Malta accedes to the Protocol on Integrated Coastal Zone Management (press release). Available at: https://www.gov.mt/en/Government/DOI/Press%20Releases/Pages/2019/April/11/pr190758.aspx

Malta Independent. (2016). Manoel Island "open to the public again" as activists cut through MIDI gates and fences. *Malta Independent*, 10 September. Available at: http://www.independent.com.mt/ articles/2016-09-10/local-news/Manoel-Island-open-to-the-public-again-as-activists-cut-through-MIDI-gates-and-fences-6736163561

Malta Resources Authority. (2014). The Third, Fourth, Fifth and Sixth National Communication of Malta under the United Nations Framework Convention on Climate Change. April 2014, on behalf of the Ministry for Sustainable Development, Environment and Climate Change.

Malta Today. (2011). New fish market in Albert Town approved. *Malta Today*, 16 September. Available at: https://www.maltatoday.com.mt/news/national/12756/new-fish-market-in-albert-town-approved#. W98Z15Mzahc

Malta Tourism Authority. (2015). Invitation to Tender in four (4) Lots, Ref: MTA/878/2015, April 2015.

MEPA (Malta Environment and Planning Authority). (1992). *Structure Plan for the Maltese Islands*.

— (1994). Development Control Guidance: Kiosks, Approved Supplementary Guidance (May). Available at: https://www.pa.org.mt/General/file.aspx?f=11968

— (1997). Development Brief for the Regeneration of the Cottonera Waterfront, First Draft, June 1997, 21.

— (1998). Valletta Cruise Terminal Development, Approved Development Brief, Commissioned by the "Valletta Cruise Terminal Steering Committee", July 1998.

— (2002). Grand Harbour Local Plan, Approved Plan, April 2002.

— (2006a). North West Local Plan, Approved Plan (July 2006).

— (2006b). North Harbours Local Plan, Approved Document (July 2006), 73 (9.4.10).

— (2006c). Fort Cambridge Development Brief, Final Approved Plan, January 2006.

— (2007). Qawra Coast Development Brief, Approved Draft (May 2007).

— (2011). *Report on the Implementation of the Recommendation of the European Parliament and of the Council concerning the implementation of Integrated Coastal Zone Management in Europe* (2002/413/ EC): MALTA.

— (2015). *Strategic Plan for Environment and Development (SPED)*. Approved July 2015, 30.

Ministry for Fair Competition, Small Business and Consumers. (2013). *The Public Domain: Classifying Public Property – Achieving a Qualitative Leap in Protection and Governance* (White Paper). Available at: https://gpd.gov.mt/media/71185/public_domain__act_updated.pdf

Ministry for Tourism, the Environment and Culture. (2012). National Environment Policy.

Ministry for Tourism. (2015). National Tourism Policy: Draft National Tourism Policy 2015–2020.

MRRA (Ministry for Resources and Rural Affairs) & University of Malta. (2010). The Second Communication of Malta to the United Nations Framework Convention on Climate Change, May 2010.

National Audit Office. (2013). Performance Audit: Enforcement Action by MEPA within the Outside Development Zone. (September).

Nature Trust Malta, MEPA & WWF Italia. (2005). Qawra/Dwejra Heritage Park Action Plan. Approved Plan 29 November 2005. Available at: https://www.pa.org.mt/en/action-plan-details/file.aspx?f=205

PA (Planning Authority). (2002). Coastal Strategy Topic Paper. Final Draft.

— (2016). Paceville Master Plan. 77.

— (2017). Marsaxlokk Inner Harbour Area Environment and Development Brief. Approved Plan, August 2017.

Planning Authority. (2016). Launch of The New Planning Authority. Available at: https://www.pa.org.mt/ en/news-details/launch-of-the-new-planning-authority

Scicluna, M. (2012). Half a century of planning abuse. *Malta Independent*, 4 July. Available at: http:// www.independent.com.mt/articles/2012-07-04/opinions/half-a-century-of-planning-abuse-312475/

The Law Dictionary (n.d.). What is EMPHYTEUSIS?. Available at: https://thelawdictionary.org/ emphyteusis/

Times of Malta. (2009). Updated: MEPA moves in on Gnejna caravans. 9 June. Available at: https:// timesofmalta.com/articles/view/mepa-moves-in-to-remove-gnejna-caravans.260308

— (2013). Government reacts as Muscat "confirms" Armier boathouses agreement. *Times of Malta*, 7 March. Available at: http://www.timesofmalta.com/articles/view/20130307/local/muscat-confirms-agreement-with-armier-boathouses-company.460617

— (2015a). Massive turnout for protest against development on ODZ land. *Times of Malta*, 20 June. Available at: http://www.timesofmalta.com/articles/view/20150620/local/massive-turnout-for-protest-against-development-on-odz-land.573303

— (2015b). Update 3 – "American" University to occupy Dock 1 buildings and reduced Zonqor site. *Times of Malta*, 20 August. Available at: http://www.timesofmalta.com/articles/view/20150820/local/update-3-american-university-to-occupy-dock-1-buildings-and-reduced.581335

— (2016a). Public domain Bill approved. *Times of Malta*, 12 May. Available at: www.timesofmalta.com/articles/view/20160512/local/public-domain-bill-approved.611778

— (2016b). Manoel Island: Activists claim victory as Midi says it will grant access to the foreshore. *Times of Malta*, 27 September. Available at: http://www.timesofmalta.com/articles/view/20160927/local/manoel-island-midi-to-grant-public-access-to-the-foreshore-from-this.626304

Vella, M. (2014). ARMS to begin accepting applications for temporary energy supply to boathouses. *Malta Today*, 20 October. Available at: https://www.maltatoday.com.mt/news/national/45159/illegal_st_thomas_bay_boathouses_to_get_temporary_energy_supply#.XW07vSgzZPZ

World Factbook. (n.d.). Malta. Available at: https://www.cia.gov/library/publications/the-world-factbook/geos/mt.html [Accessed September 2019]

Legislation *(listed chronologically)*

Malta Civil Code

Disposal of Government Land Act 1977 (Chapter 268 of the Laws of Malta)

Development Planning Act 1992 (Act No. I of 1992)

Environment Protection Act 2001 (Act XX of 2001)

Cultural Heritage Act 2002 (with amendment to Development Planning Act; Act VI of 2002)

Directive 2003/35/EC of the European Parliament and of the Council of 26 May 2003: Providing for public participation in respect of the drawing up of certain plans and programmes relating to the environment and amending with regard to public participation and access to justice Council Directives 85/337/EEC and 96/61/EC

Freedom of Access to Information on the Environment Regulations, Subsidiary Legislation 504.65. 17 May 2005

European Assessment and Management of Flood Risks Regulations 2007, Subsidiary Legislation 423.41, transposing Directive 2007/60/EC of the European Parliament and of the Council of 23 October 2007

Development Notification Order 2007, Subsidiary Legislation 504.80 (Legal Notice 115 of 2007)

Environment Protection Act 2016 (Act No. I of 2016)

Development Planning Act 2016 (Act No. VII of 2016)

Public Domain Act 2016 (ACT XXV of 2016)

Court and Tribunal Cases *(listed alphabetically)*

Carmel Chircop v. MEPA (2012) Environment and Planning Review Tribunal, 8 November 2012, App. no. 738/11 CF.

Coronato Portelli v. MEPA (2012) Environment and Planning Review Tribunal, 7 February 2012, PAB/319/06 CF.

Direttur tal-Artijiet v. Vincent Farrugia et (2009) Court of Appeal, 27 March 2009, App Civ. Nr. 114/2003/1.

Dr. Alfred Galea nomine v. Development Control Commission, Planning Appeals Board (2000), 3 November 2000, PAB/293/99 KA.

Emmanuele Luigi Galizia v. Emmanuele Scicluna (1886) Court of Appeal, 30 April 1886.

Flimkien ghall-Ambjent Ahjar and Others v. The Planning Authority, Environment and Planning Review Tribunal (2017) 19 January 2017, PAB/262/16 MS.

Georgia Cini v. Development Control Commission (1999) Planning Appeals Board, 23 July 1999, PAB/350/97 KA.

Joe Debono v. MEPA (2012) Environment and Planning Review Tribunal, 31 July 2012, App. no. 200/11 CF.

Michael Stivala v. The Planning Authority (2017) Environment and Planning Review Tribunal, 4 May 2017, App. 190/14MS.

Sliema Local Council v. The Planning Authority et. (2017) Environment and Planning Review Tribunal, 19 January 2017, App. 261/16MS.

Publius Falzon noe v. MEPA (2012). Environment and Planning Review Tribunal, 27 September 2012, App. no. 656/11 CF.

Raymond Vella et v. Kumissarju ta' l-Artijiet (2004) Constitutional Court, 24 May 2004, App. Civ. Nr. 551/1995/1.

Residual Limited v. Kummissarju tal-Artijiet (2011) First Hall (Civil Court) Constitutional Jurisdiction, 19 October 2011, Rik. Nr. 69/2006.

St. Paul's Bay Residents Association v. Development Control Commission et (2002) Planning Appeals Board, 8 November 2002, PAB/184/01 KA.

Victor Borg v. Malta Environment and Planning Authority (2015a) Environment and Planning Review Tribunal, 29 January 2015, App. 289/13 MS.

Victor Borg v. Malta Environment and Planning Authority (2015b) Court of Appeal (Inferior), 20 May 2015, App. 7/2015.

Victor Borg V. Malta Environment and Planning Authority (2019) Environmental and Planning Review Tribunal, 30 April 2019, App. 289/13 LM.

14 Turkey

Fatma Ünsal

Overview

Turkish coastal laws and policies reflect this country's intermediate position between a developing country and an advanced-economy one. On the ground, Turkish coasts have drawn masses of illegal development: Permanent residential homes and condominiums, summer homes, hotels, and resorts. At the same time, the parliament has adopted a series of laws to protect the coast and to enforce measures against past and new illegal construction and the courts have issued decisions that promote coastal management.

Although the essence of the Coastal Law 1990 was to protect the natural characteristics of coastal areas and to prohibit uses that are not in the public interest, the actual pattern of development in coastal areas continues to disregard these goals. The planning process for coastal areas has not prioritized a holistic approach and as a result, the development pattern is fragmented. Plans approved by national government (Environmental Order Plans) encourage compact cities along the coast, but this principle has been undermined by the government's own project-oriented developments and local Development Plans. Furthermore, amendments to the Coastal Law have made it easier for the authorities to approve construction in the coastal zones, despite the ostensible restrictions.

The context: Introduction to the Turkey's coastal issues

This section highlights the key geographic, economic, social, administrative, and legal context pertaining to Turkey's coastal zone.

Administrative structure

Turkey's governance is two-tiered, with administration at the national and local levels. To aid national management at the regional level, the country is divided into 81 provinces. Each province is also known as a Governorship, where the Governor is the chief executive responsible for the implementation of legislation at the provincial level, as well as for monitoring government decisions. The governors are appointed by the President of the Turkish Republic based on the recommendation of the Ministry of Internal Affairs. Each province has a central city and surrounding settlements. All settlements which have a population over 2,000 inhabitants have municipal councils and locally elected mayors.

Coasts of Turkey in context

The total length of coastline in Turkey is 7,200 km – 2.5 times the length of the inland borders, which are 2,816 km long (World Factbook, n.d.). The coastline is divided across three seas: The Black Sea, Marmara Sea, and Mediterranean/Aegean Sea. The largest of these three coastlines is that on the Mediterranean Sea.

The geological and morphological characteristics of the different seas surrounding Turkey vary. Geologically, the Mediterranean Sea is one of the oldest seas in the world, whereas the Aegean Sea is one of the youngest. There are five general types of coastal morphologies in Turkey, including parallel coastlines (northern and southern coasts); perpendicular coastlines (western coasts); ria coastlines (southwestern and northwestern coasts); dalmatian coastlines (southwestern coast); and lagoon coastlines (northwestern coast).

Coastal management is a significant matter in Turkish international relations, given that 73% of the total international borders are made up of coastline. It is also significant from a domestic perspective: While the total area of coastal provinces makes up approximately 30% of the country's land area, it is home to almost 50% of the population (TUIK, 2018a). Furthermore, the average population density across coastal provinces is 251 persons/km^2, significantly higher than the average population density in the rest of the provinces – 60 persons/km^2 (TUIK, 2018b).

Even though the economic and demographic weights of Turkey's coastal areas is not as overwhelming as those of some other countries, the coastal areas do play a role of strategic importance. One would, therefore, expect more attention to improving the country's coastal zone management. Furthermore, Turkey's potential role in the context of international coastal zone management in the Mediterranean region is significant. However, as this chapter will show, there is a large disparity between the declarative planning levels and successful implementation and enforcement on the ground.

Turkey's local governments can be divided into two tiers: There are 30 greater municipalities[1] and 81 provinces. Twenty-eight of the provinces are in the coastal regions. Sixteen of those provinces are Greater Municipalities (see Figure 14.1).

Coast of Turkey in macro-economic context and population growth

There is a clear developmental gap between the eastern and western regions of Turkey (see Figure 14.2). The highest gross value added per capita is almost four times higher than the lowest (17,827 USD compared with 4,162 USD). This inequitable distribution of wealth leads to migration flows from less to more developed regions, which in turn lead to population pressures on the western and southern coasts of Turkey. As might be expected, the region surrounding Istanbul gets the lion's share in terms of migration flows. However, the net growth rate of Antalya, located on the southwestern coast, is comparable to that seen in Istanbul and Ankara.[2]

Not all coastal areas experience the same high growth rates. When the recent population growth rates and rates of urbanization of the different coastal provinces are examined individually, population growth rates vary widely across regions. The highest rates are seen in the regions adjacent to Istanbul and the southern coast. Conversely, the population growth rates in the northern coastal regions are the lowest (see Figure 14.3).

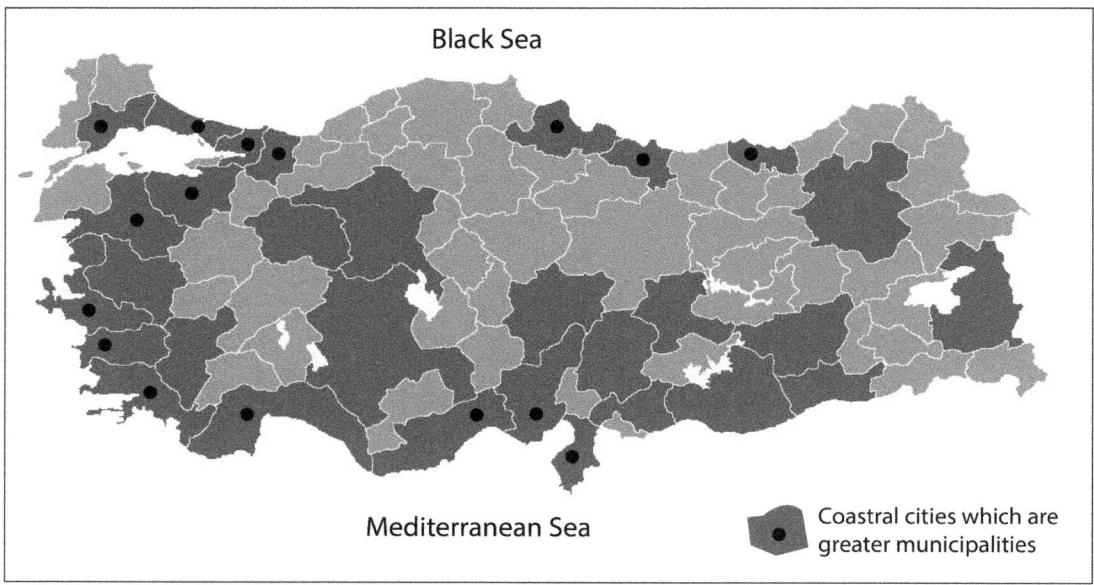

Figure 14.1 Provincial division and the Greater Municipalities in Turkey (2019)

Source: Created by author using data from Ministry of Internal Affairs (2019)

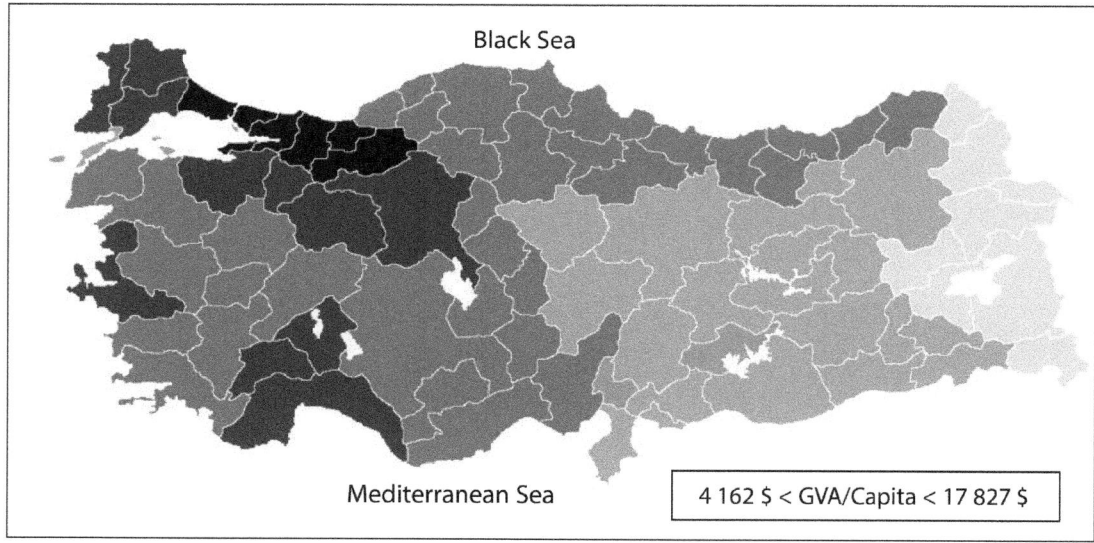

Figure 14.2 Distribution of gross value added per capita ($) (2017)

Source: Created by author based on data produced by the Turkish Statistical Institute (https://biruni.tuik.gov.tr/bolge-selistatistik/degiskenlerUzerindenSorgula.do)

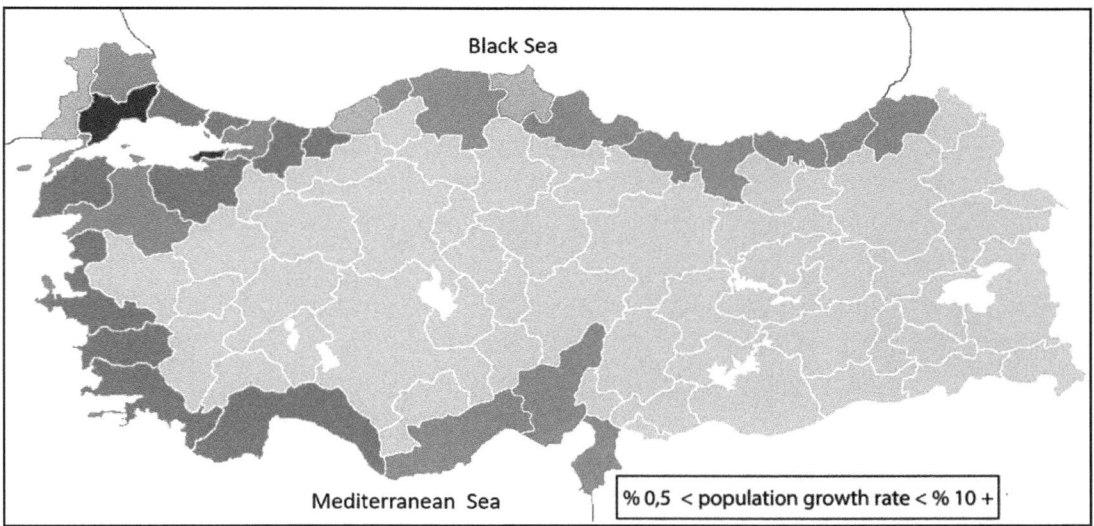

Black Sea

Mediterranean Sea

% 0,5 < population growth rate < % 10 +

Figure 14.3 Population growth rates in coastal provinces (2011–2018)

Source: Created by author based on data produced by the Turkish Statistical Institute (http://www.tuik.gov.tr/UstMenu. do?metod=temelist)

The evolution of Turkish coastal laws, regulations, and policy

Ostensibly, Turkish legislation has dealt with the pressures affecting the coastal regions since the 1970s. However, as we will see, ambiguities in the legislation, as well as rampant unenforced illegal development caused an undesired urban sprawl in the coastal areas of Turkey.

The backbone of coastal legislation in Turkey is the Coastal Law of 1990 (amended 1992). Yet the history of coastal legislation prior to the introduction of that law provides an important insight into the Turkish context and ongoing implementation challenges.

Journey to the Turkish coastal law

This section recounts the evolution of the current Coastal Law (Law no. 1990/3621). This journey has included several important junction points reflecting changes in national policy emphasis, as well as some significant court decisions.

Attention to the status of the coasts goes far back to the Turkish Civil Law of 1926. It first identified the coasts as public property and mandated that they be used only for public benefit. Notably, the Civil Law did not define the coasts in any way. However, the differentiation between the public and private properties was not sufficiently defined in this law. A quantitative measure to define the extent of the area of the coast to be protected for public purposes was introduced in 1933 with the Law of Structure and Roads. This law stated that no structure may be built within a distance of 10 m from the shoreline, but the shoreline remained undefined in the law.

The first legal provision applying to coastal areas came in the form of a 1972 amendment to the Law of Development (1956/6785) – the primary planning and development legislation. This law made it illegal to construct any new buildings or enlarge existing ones on public land within a specified distance from the shoreline. This distance was left open, to be determined by the

Ministry of Development and Settlement (now Ministry of Environment and Urbanization).[3] The former rule pertaining to the first 10 m from the shoreline was retained, and that strip was declared as public land. In the same year, the first legal definition of the shoreline appeared in a decision of the Court of Appeals (Yargıtay, E. 1970/7, K. 1972/4). The decision was based on a geomorphological approach, meaning that the shoreline was drawn at the landward edge of geomorphological features associated with the sea (Babacan Tekinbaş, 2001, p. 116).[4]

The 1972 amendment to the Law of Development was clear regarding the importance of maintaining horizontal public accessibility along the coast (seaward of the shoreline) and the fact that the coast is intended solely for the public benefit. Nevertheless, the protective effectiveness and the public purpose dimensions of the law were questionable. In fact, many commercial activities were permitted on the coast following the implementation of the law (Babacan Tekinbaş, 2008, pp. 305–307). The primary reason for these permissions was a time lag in implementation of the Law and regulations.

It appears that by 1982, the pattern of uncontrolled development which had begun along Turkey's coast in previous decades was of enough concern to warrant mention in the Constitution, as amended in that year. This amendment represented a significant turning point for coastal legislation and other legislation affecting urban development in Turkey: Public rights and social equity were to be protected as key responsibilities of the State.[5] The Constitution now emphasized, in Article 43, that the public benefit would be prioritized in determining the use of coastal areas and that decisions regarding these areas would be subject to a special law.

As a result, Turkey introduced its first Coastal Law in 1984. This Law addressed the delicate balance between the private use of coastal areas and public rights. It simultaneously prohibited private ownership and developments on the coast. The 10 m strip of public land prevailed in the existing or planned urban areas, but it was enlarged to 30 m in other areas. Exceptions to these limitations were construction of factories for water products, shipbuilders or repair shipyards, and educational, sports, and touristic facilities determined to be "for the public benefit". All these exceptions would have to be approved by a decree based on of a Development Plan (refer to the section on planning below).

That first Coastal Law was repealed by decision of the Constitutional Court in 1986: The Court found that the law allowed for private ownership and use of coastal areas for purposes which were contrary to the social equity principles established by the Constitution (AYM, E. 1985/1, K. 1986/4). As a result, a second Coastal Law was adopted in 1990. This Coastal Law increased the coastal setback in which development is prohibited, with different widths for planned and unplanned areas. The penalties for the construction of prohibited developments were also increased.

And yet these changes were not adequate to satisfy the Court, which, on appeal (AYM, E. 1990/23, K. 1991/29), repealed some articles of the 1990 Coastal Law. These repealed articles were those which allowed "exceptional uses" and acquisition of land through filling and reclamation, as they were deemed to be inconsistent with the constitutional principle of free accessibility of the coast. In addition, the Court noted that the differentiation between the planned and unplanned areas in determining of the width of the coastal setback were inappropriate. Finally, the Court made a dramatic ruling – that the minimum setback width should be 100 m from the Coast Edge Line. In the first 50 m inland from the shoreline, only pedestrian paths and recreational facilities could be built. In the second 50 m, the court allowed for construction of roads. In 1992, the Coastal Law was amended to take these considerations into account (Law no. 1992/3830). The current Coastal Law is founded on the key principles of environmental protection, public access, and social equity and on respect for the natural and cultural differences between coastal areas.

Two issues are noteworthy regarding Turkey's current coastal and planning legislation: Firstly, there is a gap between the Law of Development (planning law) and the Coastal Legislation. Even though the Law of Development, empowers the local governments in terms of making and approving Development Plans, it is clear that the central governmental institutions are the major decision-makers regarding the development of coastal areas. Secondly, although the Coastal Law is regarded as a protective law, it is certainly far from being a comprehensive coastal zone management law, as it does not address the comprehensive list of principles defined for Integrated Coastal Zone Management.

Definitions and delineation of the shoreline and coastal zone

The Coastal Law Regulation 1990 (and its minor amendments in 2014) contains the following definitions related to the delineation of the shoreline and coastal zone (see Figure 14.4):

- **Coast Line:** The natural line along which water meets land and which changes meteorologically along the coasts of seas, lakes, and rivers. Flooding conditions do not contribute to the determination of the Coast Line. This line is equivalent to the average tide line. It is not to be confused with the generic use of the term "coastline".
- **Coast Edge Line:** The natural boundary determined by the inward motion of water from the Coast Line, including the land with sand, pebbles, boulders, rocks, reeds, and marshland. This line is comparable to the "shoreline" described in many of the laws of other countries in this book, where defined on the basis of geomorphological features indicating the highest reach of the water.

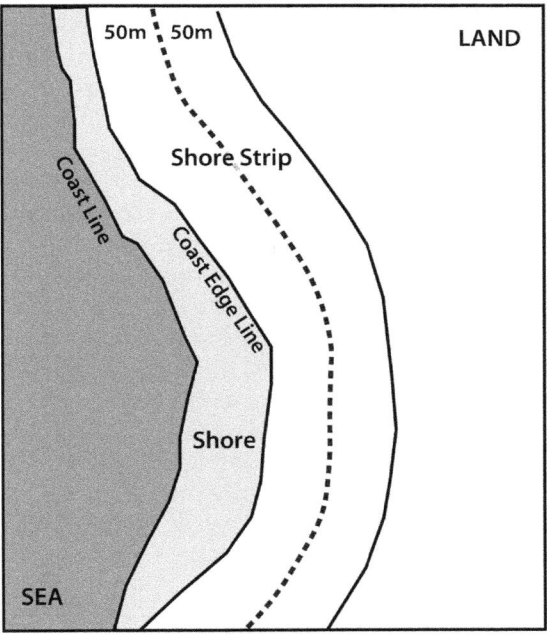

Figure 14.4 Legal partition of coastal land

Source: Created by author based on the definitions of the Coastal Law (1990/3621)

- **Coast:** The area between the Coast Line and the Coast Edge Line (not to be confused with the general use of the word "coast" throughout this book)
- **Shore Strip:** The area starting from the Coast Edge Line and stretching inwards with a horizontal width of 100 m. The Shore Strip is made up of two parts, each 50 m wide (see the section on setback from the shoreline below).

The demarcation process

While most of the Coast Edge Line (shoreline) demarcation process is now complete (98%), it is important to understand the concepts and the process. Within each province, the Coast Edge Line is determined by a committee made up of five members, reporting to the Governorship. The committee's decision is then subject to approval of the Ministry of Environment and Urbanization. The law specifies that the committee should comprise a geologist, topographic engineer, agricultural engineer, city planner, or architect and civil engineer. The process has been quite efficient: To date, 98% of the Turkish Coast Edge Line has been mapped out (Karabeyli et al., 2006). Once demarcated, the Coast Edge Line is not subject to change based on movement of the tides. Changes may only come if as a result of court decisions in cases of property disputes.

Governorships are responsible for the determination of the Coast Edge Lines, and they prepare annual programmes in order to cover all coastal areas under their jurisdiction. The process involves the use of maps or orthophoto maps, which are prepared based on identifying natural coastal characteristics.[6] The Coast Edge Line defined by the committee is then approved by the Ministry in draft format. The final line is approved after a period of public consultation (in which the public may make submissions).

Private property rights are considered in the delineation process: First, if a landowner or government entity makes a specific request for the delineation of the Coast Edge Line, this request receives priority consideration, even if it was not part of the annual programme. Second, the line may be challenged in court. If part of the Coast Edge Line is cancelled for a specific plot or plots of land as a result of a court case, the committee considers the continuity of the Coast Edge Line in the new demarcation process, without jeopardizing the acquired rights.

According to the Coastal Law Regulation (1990), the Coast Edge Line should be determined before the planning and development process starts for a given coastal area, or prior to 11 July 1992 (when the current Coastal Law was adopted). For areas where the development and implementation plans were approved before 11 July 1992, if they are fully or more than half built up, then the Coast Edge Line indicated on the approved plan is considered valid. If they are less than half built up, then the Coast Edge Line should be determined by the committee within a year following approval of the development plan, and the approved plan should be modified accordingly. However, there is an exemption for areas where the closest plots to the sea are fully or more than half developed. In those cases, the Coast Edge Line defined in the plan is taken as the Coast Edge Line.

Although to date, the vast majority of the Coast Edge Line has been delineated according to these rules, there continue to be disputes and ongoing lawsuits about its location and affected private properties. Furthermore, court and committee decisions about the Coast Edge Line are not filed correctly and conflicting decisions for the same coasts lead to confusion in plan-making (Karabeyli et al., 2006, pp. 17–25).

Notably, the Performance Audit Report of Planning and Audit of Coastal Utilization (Karabeyli et al., 2006) found that in view of the fact that demarcation has not been completed, the base and the main frame of reference for the implementation plans are inadequate. Interestingly, the Appeal Commission (TBBM, 2012) further found that Coast Edge Line disputes have been a key cause of overdevelopment of the coastal zone. That Commission recommended investigation of the disputes in order to identify ongoing problems and to train the members of the delineation committee accordingly.

Public domain

As outlined above, Turkey's coasts (vaguely defined) have been recognized as land under the control and disposal of the State since the introduction of the Civil Law in 1926. Yet the legal framework for use of the coasts in the public interest and the extent of the coast to be subject to these provisions was not defined until the 1970s. The Constitution (38th article) was amended in 1971 in order to provide for the expropriation of coastal land to serve the public interest, with compensation to be paid over 10 years. The Law of Development (1957/6785) was then amended (Law 1972/1605) to prohibit private acquisition of coastal land located within 10 m landward of the Coast Edge Line.

What was missing from the amendment to the 1972 Law of Development were provisions regarding the status of properties which were in private ownership prior to its adoption. This omission was addressed by the courts: The Supreme Court has ruled that land which was privately owned before the Law came into force (1972) should be maintained in private ownership until legitimately acquired by the state (Şimşek, 2010, p. 100).

When the Coastal Law was adopted in 1990, it mandated that private ownership was prohibited within 50 m landward of the Coast Edge Line. In addition, private ownership was prohibited on reclaimed land. These are the rules which apply to this day (Coastal Law 1992).

Following the adoption of the 1990 Coastal Law, the Treasury of the State sought to annul titles held by private entities on land within 50 m of the Coast Edge Line, without compensation. This move, however, was contrary to the rulings of the European Court of Human Rights (ECHR), which require that compensation be paid, to balance public and private interests (Şimşek, 2010, p. 87). Furthermore, some of the land set out as public in the law remains in private ownership to this day. On this matter, the Appeal Commission of the Parliament (TBBM, 2012) found that the fact that not all of the land has been brought under public ownership is a result of mismanagement rather than of any deficiency in the legislation. It is stated that there is no legal obstacle for expropriation of the relevant properties.

Coastal public land in Turkey is under the control and disposal of the Ministry of Treasury and Finance (Law 1990/3621). Thus, its status is different from other public land owned by the Treasury of the State. The land is leased to municipalities based on the agreement protocols between those municipalities and the Ministry of Finance. Although the main concern of these protocols is to enable the municipalities to audit effectively and prevent the illegal use of coastal land, most of the municipalities take the advantage of the protocols in order to use the rentals as a source of revenue and delay losing them (Karabeyli et al., 2006).

Uses permitted in the coastal public domain which forms part of the Shore Strip are outlined in the following section.

Setback from the shoreline (in which development is restricted)

The current Coastal Law (1992/3830) defines the "Shore Strip" as a strip with a width of 100 m from the Coast Edge Line. This Shore Strip is essentially a setback zone. The zone is divided into two parts, each 50 m wide, each subject to different land use and ownership rules. The first 50 m is publicly owned, as outlined above.

Permitted uses in the "Shore Strip"

Across the Shore Strip, any kind of construction or building permits are forbidden until an Implementation Plan, which defines specific permitted land use and development, is in place. An Implementation Plan may only be developed after the demarcation of the Coast Edge Line has been completed.

Uses and development which may be permitted through an Implementation Plan across the entire 100 m Shore Strip are:

- Promenades, pedestrian accessways, and open recreational facilities for public use
- Infrastructure and facilities which facilitate the public use or protection of the coast (Ministry of Environment and Urbanization, n.d.a). These include piers, ports, and supporting infrastructure; breakwaters, boathouses, and beach facilities (subject to conditions regarding maximum floorspace and distance between facilities)
- Facilities which must be located on the coastal zone by nature (Ministry of Environment and Urbanization, n.d.a). These include shipyards, marinas, fishing ports, and, since 2005, cruise facilities (following an amendment to Coastal Law 1990/3621 in the same year)
- Wastewater management facilities (Article 13/c of the Regulation of the Coastal Law)
- Sports facilities and accommodation related to the sports activities (following a 2008 amendment to Coastal Law 1990/3621)
- On reclaimed land, additional uses including structures for exhibitions, fairs, picnics, and entertainment are permitted, but must be temporary structures (portable construction) and may not be more than 5.5 m high

In addition, in the second 50 m only (between 50 m and 100 m from the Coast Edge Line), tourism facilities for daytime use (excluding accommodation facilities) may be permitted. Such facilities are subject to restrictions, including maximum floorspace ratio (20%) and maximum height (4.5 m for one-storey buildings and 5.5 m for buildings with a mezzanine). Coastal security facilities and accommodation for security personnel may also be built.

Historic buildings which are subject to the Law of Protection of the Cultural and Natural Assets (1983) are exempt from the above land use restrictions. The municipalities are responsible for inspection and enforcement of these rules. Beyond municipal boundaries, the responsibilities fall on the governorships.

Right of public access

The current Coastal Law (1992) prioritizes accessibility of the coastal zone. The Coastal Law Regulation (Article 17) clearly lays out that the first 50 m of the Shore Strip is to remain undeveloped and entirely open to the public.

Within the first 50 m of the Shore Strip (landward), structures which prevent accessibility to the coast, such as walls, fences (including wire fences), open ditches, or waterways, are prohibited. It is also forbidden to construct new motorways in the first part of the Shore Strip (50 m from the Coast Edge Line). However, on reclaimed land, connecting roads may be constructed if these are part of an approved implementation plan.

Notably, the Coastal Law did not cancel all development rights granted before it was adopted: Previously approved plans which were unrealized prior to 1992 may now be disregarded, but the buildings which were completely constructed or partially constructed to at least the plinth level prior to 1992 have their vested rights preserved. As such, there are several existing structures which present irreversible barriers to accessibility. Yet the Coastal Law Regulation does highlight (at Article 16/c) the need for accessibility in areas developed according to plans approved prior to 1992.

In addition, several historical monuments and private estates which are protected by the Law of Conservation of Cultural and Natural Assets are sometimes also obstacles to the accessibility of the coastal zone. For example, accessibility to the shores of the Bosphorus strait is very limited due to the presence of historic buildings, which are primarily private estates.

Ensuring accessibility along the coasts is the responsibility of municipalities within the municipal boundaries and governorships in rural areas.

Planning for coastal areas

To aid understanding of the story of planning for coastal areas in Turkey, a brief explanation of the Turkish planning system follows. Planning legislation is based on the Law of Development (1985/3194). There is a three-tier hierarchy of plans: Plans prepared at the national level; Local Development Plans; and Special Purpose Plans. Table 14.1 summarizes the types of plans, the institutions responsible, and the pertinent laws.

Plans prepared at the national level: Environmental order plan, regional plan, regional development plan

Environmental Order Plans, prepared by the Ministry of Environment and Urbanization, are regional-scale plans made by the central government, which guide spatial development in accordance with the national and regional socio-economic plans and set the basic land use policy for housing, industry, commerce, and more, including major infrastructure facilities.

Prior to 2006, Regional Plans were prepared by the State Planning Office (this office has since been merged into other government departments).[7] These plans utilized data on socio-economic development patterns and the development potential of the settlements in order to guide spatial development.

Since 2006 (Law 2006/5449), Regional Development Agencies have been set up (initially by the State Planning Office) to prepare Regional Development Plans, which function as action plans and resource management plans with a focus on economic development.

Development Agencies, especially those of the more developed regions, implement participative planning techniques and focus primarily on sustainable economic development and encouraging entrepreneurship. Regional Plans and Regional Development Plans are not binding, regulatory spatial plans but take a conceptual approach to spatial issues and land use decisions. Notably, there is no mechanism for coordination between the two separate planning processes established by two different ministries.

Local development plans

Development Plans are statutory binding plans prepared by municipalities or governorships (by authority of the Law of Development 1985). These plans set out land use and development provisions, similar to those found in zoning or land use plans. Particularly, in the past decade, there has been a tendency for the Turkish central government to undermine the authority of the local governments through Special Purpose Plans.

Table 14.1 Types of plans relevant to coastal areas, institutions responsible, and legal basis

Plan type	Institution	Legal basis	Purpose
Regional Plan	State Planning Office	State Planning Office Establishment Law (1960/91)	Strategic planning guidance
	Ministry of Development and Settlement	Law of Development (1985/3194)	
Environmental Order Plan	Ministry of Environment and Urbanization	Law of Development (1985/3194) Decree of the Cabinet for Establishment and Responsibilities of the Ministry of Environment (1990/443)	Highest level in the statutory spatial planning hierarchy
	Directorate of Specially Protected Areas	Decree of the Cabinet (1989)	
Regional Development Plan	Development Agencies	Law of Development Agencies (2006/5449)	Strategic plan for economic development
Development Plan and Implementation Plan	Municipalities/ Metropolitan Municipalities/ Governorships	Law of Development (1985/3194) Metropolitan Municipalities Establishment and Administration Law(1984/3030)	Local level in the statutory spatial planning hierarchy
	Ministry of Culture and Tourism (for tourism development areas)	Tourism Incentives Law (1982/2634) Decree of the Cabinet (1989)	
	Ministry of Environment and Urbanization (for the filled coastal land)	Coastal Law (1990/3621)	
	Directorate of Specially Protected Areas	Decree of the Cabinet (1989)	
Development Plan for Protection	Protection Councils for Natural and Cultural Assets	Law of Protection of Cultural and Natural Assets (1983/2863)	Statutory spatial planning for protection sites
Integrated Coastal Area Plan (Special Purpose Plan)	Ministry of Environment and Urbanization	Regulation of Making Spatial Plans (Official Gazette 29030 dated 14.6.2014)	Strategic guidance for coastal planning and management
Special Use and Management Plan	Directorate of National Parks	National Parks Law (1983/2873)	Statutory spatial planning for special uses.
	Directorate of Forest Management	Law of Forest (1956/6831)	
	Directorate of Specially Protected Areas	Decree of the Cabinet (1989)	
	Directorate of Privatization	Law of Privatization (1994/4046)	

(continued)

Table 14.1 (continued)

Plan type	Institution	Legal basis	Purpose
Infrastructural Plan	Ministry of Transportation, Maritime and Communication (MTMC)	Coastal Law (1990/3621) Executive Order of the Cabinet for the Establishment of MTMC (2011/655) Law of Establishment of Directorate for Highways (1950/5539)	Statutory spatial planning for infrastructure
	Directorate of State Water Works	Law of Establishment of Directorate of State Water Works (1953/6200)	

Adapted from PAP/RAC (Priority Actions Programme Regional Activity Centre, Split) (2005), *Coastal Area Management in Turkey*, p. 52 (original source in Turkish – Sonmez, 2002)

Special purpose plans

Integrated Coastal Zone Management (ICZM) Plans are regarded as Special Purpose Plans.

The Law of Development (1985) defines uses for which the central government has the authority to make Special Purpose Plans: Tourism development zones, special protection areas, and major infrastructure. Responsibility for these areas and works is divided across several different ministries. Special Purpose Plans may be prepared by a range of ministries and pertain to uses such as tourism, industry, ports (maritime transportation), marinas, and fisheries. These plans can be grouped into two main categories: Those for the protection of a special zone and those for a special use of land. ICZM plans fall in the first category.

The impact of planning policy on Turkey's coastal areas

Although the essence of the Coastal Law was to protect the natural characteristics of coastal areas and to prohibit uses that are not in the public interest, the actual pattern of development in coastal areas continues to disregard these goals. The planning process for coastal areas has not prioritized a holistic approach and, as a result, the development pattern is fragmented. Environmental Order Plans encourage compact cities along the coast, but this principle has been undermined by local Development Plans that do not comply with the relevant Environmental Order Plan. Although the Environmental Order Plan is binding according to the Regulation of Making Spatial Plans (2014), there are some cases in which local governments succumb to the ambitious development demands of local landowners/developers in return for their political support. Most of those cases are taken to court by government or NGOs, but long-lasting legal process in the courts and lack of enforcement actions mean that development can proceed.

For example, the demarcation of the Coast Edge Line for Ataköy (Bakırköy district, Istanbul) was approved by the Governorship of Istanbul in 2004. In 2010, a local NGO (Association for Conservation and Beautification of Ataköy District 1) appealed the demarcation on the basis of a scientific report from Istanbul University.[8] After the 9th Administrative Court rejected the case because the time limit for appeals had passed, the NGO appealed to the Council of State. In 2015, the Council of State ruled that the Coast Edge Line demarcation was indeed not

Figure 14.5 Development at Ataköy, Istanbul

Source: Photograph by Fatma Ünsal

supported by scientific data, and thus should be redetermined (Danıştay 14., E. 2014/868, K. 2015/10666). Yet in the five years between the initial appeal and the Council of State decision, permits were granted for construction of high-rise housing on land that should have been in the Shore Strip (setback zone), construction was completed and most of the properties sold (Sendika, 2017; see Figure 14.5).

Expansion of urban areas along the coast has also occurred illegally through the construction of summer homes or individual tourism projects that do not comply with the relevant tourism master plans. The developments along the coasts take advantage of ambiguities in relevant legislation. Furthermore, amendments to the Coastal Law in 2005 and 2008 facilitated construction in the coastal zones. The 2005 amendment (2005/5398 which amended Article 13 of the Law) brought a major change in that it defined cruise ports, as well as eating, shopping, and logistic facilities serving cruise passengers as exceptional structures which may be developed in the Shore Strip. The 2008 amendment (2008/5801, which amended Articles 3 and 6) further permitted sports activities and accommodation facilities serving sports activities.

The establishment of the Ministry of Environment and Urbanization in 2011 (through the amalgamation of two different ministries) led to prioritization of development over the environment. Previously, the Ministry of Environment had jurisdiction over environmental matters, without the need for consideration of the economic benefits of construction. But after the amalgamation, the new Ministry represents conflicting interests, and prioritizes the construction sector, which has been the leading sector in Turkey's economy for the last few decades. As such, development proposals are increasingly defined as "exceptions that merit national intervention". In addition, there is an increasing tendency for the central government to exercise its power to prepare Special Areas Plans. Several institutions (municipalities, governorships, Ministry of Tourism, Directorate of Privatization) may make plans and approve development in coastal areas and there is a lack of coordination between these institutions.

Nevertheless, some recent decisions of the Constitutional Court have been promising in the eyes of those concerned about conservation of the coasts. Recently, the Court repealed an amendment to the Coastal Law (Law 7162, 2019) which exempted specific ports and filled lands (Çandarlı, Rize İyidere, and Bitlis Ahlat) from development restrictions. The decision (AYM decision number 2019/53, R.G. 24.7.2019, sa. 3084) claimed that the uses which would be permitted by the amendment would not serve the public good and would disturb "sensitive areas" of the coast.

Another recent decision of the Constitutional Court is about Sivriada. Sivriada is one of the Princes' Islands of Istanbul. The island was formerly used by the Ministry of Defence but was assigned to be used by the Ministry of Culture and Tourism in 2012. Although it is a natural part of the ecological system of the Princes' Islands, its status under the Law of Protection of Cultural and Natural Assets (1983/2863) was cancelled in 2013. The cancellation was followed by a modification of the Law of Build-Operate-Transfer Model for Services and Investments (1994/3996; addition of Article 2 on 3/4/2013) by the Law of Public Finance and Liability Management (2013/6456), which allowed significant developments which were previously prohibited on the island. Recently, that amendment was annulled by the Constitutional Court (AYM, E. 2019/35, K. 2019/53), given the significant harm it has allowed to the free use of the Sivriada coasts.

Specific plans for coastal areas

The Law of Development does not contain special provisions for the planning of coastal areas. Nevertheless, if a specific coastal area is considered an exceptional case defined in the Law (such as an area earmarked for tourism development or private land), then the development and the implementation plans may be prepared by the relevant ministry. Regardless of the authority making the plan, any plan prepared must be in accordance with the Coastal Law and the Coastal Law Regulation.

A report of the Appeal Commission of the Parliament (TBBM, 2012) noted that planning is the key tool for balancing coastal protection and development. Unfortunately, authorities have tipped the balance towards development. Key problems identified include uniform regulations which disregard the diversity of the coast; disputes about delineation of the Coast Edge Line; and delays in updating spatial plans.

As the protection of the coasts is a delicate issue due to the rapidly developing dynamics of Turkey, both the coastal zone management experience of developed countries and international legislation have served as guiding examples. Even though Turkey is not a signatory to the Protocol on Integrated Coastal Zone Management (ICZM) in the Mediterranean, it began to take the initiative to develop regional ICZM plans beginning in 2007. Prior to 2014, despite the absence of a dedicated statutory plan for coastal areas, the Turkish government created draft plans for the coastal areas, especially for the excessively polluted industrial-coastal regions of

Turkey, İskenderun, and İzmit Bay. These plans were formerly called Integrated Coastal Zone Management Plans (ICZM plans), and eight ICZM plans (approved and draft) were uploaded to the official website of the Ministry of Environment and Urbanization, (n.d.b).

The year 2014 represented a turning point for planning legislation in Turkey in general, as well as for the planning of coastal areas specifically. Following critiques of the Law of Development and its deficiencies in addressing contemporary urban economic dynamics and technological developments, a new Regulation (Regulation of Making Spatial Plans) was adopted. The 2014 Regulation defines new types of plans which formally allow the central government to take over planning responsibility from municipalities, primarily for megaprojects, privatized areas, and coastal areas.

One of the new plan types introduced by the Regulation of Making Spatial Plans is the Integrated Coastal Area (ICA) Plan. These ICA Plans replace the ICZM Plans which had been previously introduced ad hoc. The primary purpose of Integrated Coastal Area Plans is the coordination of the wide variety of institutions making implementation plans for coastal areas. In other words, management issues are still the primary concern of ICA Plans, despite the new name. The Regulation and official website of the Ministry of Environment and Urbanization clearly set out that ICA Plans are not part of the hierarchy of spatial development plans but are intended only as strategic guides. There is, therefore, some ambiguity about the relationship between the different types of plans. Coastal Area plans are prepared and approved by the Ministry of Environment and Urbanization, whereas local Development and Implementation plans are prepared by local governments. The Regulation does not offer adequate tools for coordination between the different levels of government or effective implementation guidance. Furthermore, the introduction of this type of plan did not change any legal provisions relating to the use of coastal land.

At the time of writing, there are five ICA Plans on the Ministry website, one of which is a draft. The plans are for Antalya (2012), İzmit (2015), İskenderun (2015), and Bursa (2015). There is also a plan for Samsun, but this plan has not yet been approved. These plans exhibit a broad economic perspective, especially focusing on tourism.

The primary justifications for ICA plans are a deficiency in the records of the current conditions and state of coastal areas, concern for the loss of ecological values, and lack of guidance for investment on the coast. These plans lay out the strategic framework for development plans and land use decisions. They address coastal management issues, as well as the monitoring of development.

There are some ambiguities about the relationship between the conventional plan types and ICA plans. As outlined above, local Development and Implementation plans are made by local governments, while ICA plans are prepared by the Ministry of Environment and Urbanization. Tools for coordination between the different levels of government are not well defined in the new 2014 Regulation. An additional criticism relates to the scope of the ICA plans: Most are limited to a very narrow coastal area adjacent to the shoreline and disregard the socio-economic relationship between the coast and the hinterland.

ICA plans are part of the regulatory planning system and fit under the category of "Special Purpose Plans" (SPP). SPPs are under the jurisdiction of the Ministry of Environment and Urbanization, rather than local governments. As such, they are not subject to the same level of public participation as are local plans. Given that they come from above rather than the local level, SPPs are often not embraced by the public and their implementation is challenging. Thus, ICA plans in Turkey have not had a "healthy" beginning and the process of their development does not reflect the basic characteristics of existing ICZM Plans in other countries.

Compliance and enforcement

Illegal development is widespread in Turkey, and coastal areas are no exception, despite the regulatory context outlined above. Although there are no official figures on the extent of illegal development in these areas, it is accepted knowledge that much of the development in coastal areas is illegal, as outlined by non-government agencies (e.g. Chamber of City Planners and Mediterranean Conservation Society), as well as by government reviews, including the audit report of the Turkish Court of Accounts (Karabeyli et al., 2006) and various special reports of the Parliament (e.g. Parliament Report, Petition Commission Decisions, 27/6/2012). Thus, the public authorities are well aware of the significant presence of illegal development.

The extent of illegality across Turkey is a symptom of the overlap in responsibilities across institutions and lack of coordination between them (refer to the section on integration and coordination). But illegal development on the coast may also be attributed to the relatively high rates of population growth in coastal regions (refer to the introductory section), which leads to high real estate values. In addition, the complexity of regulations and exemptions, combined with the dynamic nature of the coastal zone, may contribute to the problem.

There are no official statements about the extent of the illegal developments in the coastal areas. However, the excessive amount of the illegal development along the coast not only has been subject to critical articles within the academic and NGO circles but also has been explored thoroughly by government institutions (e.g. audit report of the Turkish Court of Accounts, special reports of the Parliament). As such, the excessive illegal developments should be attributed to deficiencies in enforcement, rather than to ignorance on the part of the public authorities.

Illegal development in Turkey is a general urban problematic encouraged by development amnesties, whereby owners of illegal developments may pay to have them legalized. The latest and most comprehensive building amnesty (completed July 2019) received 10 million applications. The applicants receive a "building registration certificate" in return for a payment based on a standard calculation announced by the Ministry of Environment and Urbanization. The amnesty has served as a populist tool for politicians, as the related fees are relatively affordable. However, it also serves as a source for generating public funds, particularly given the number of applications received. The cost of these social and political gains is the destruction of natural assets, including the coasts. The only positive part of the amnesty programme is that the "building registration certificates" granted are valid only for the registered building; if that building is demolished, any new building in its place must will not automatically be considered legal.

Enforcement measures

Enforcement measures available to the authorities in cases of illegal development include fines (mesne profits) and, though rarely used, demolition. Coastal areas are not regularly monitored by government agencies and thus enforcement measures are primarily initiated by complaints by NGOs or private citizens. This complaint-based monitoring is not only irregular and ad hoc but also ineffective, as it is difficult to remove illegal developments.

Fines for illegal use of land

The law authorizes municipalities to impose penalties for illegal use and development (technically called "mesne profits"). The penalty applies to the profit made from the illegal use up to the point that the penalty was issued. Payment of the fine does not "buy" a right of use for the land or buildings illegal in the future. Some violators may have thought that payment of the fine legitimizes the illegal use and development, but a report of the Appeal Commission of the Parliament (TBBM, 2012) clarified that this is not the case.[9]

Responsibilities in enforcement

Responsibility for monitoring of and enforcement against illegal development lies with the municipalities or governorships. Profits are determined by the municipalities (for the urban areas) on behalf of the Treasury of the State. However, municipalities tend to overlook unlawful developments for the sake of encouraging investment in tourism, to enhance the competitiveness of their region. As such, disputes between the Treasury and the municipalities often arise.

On reclaimed land, monitoring and enforcement is more complex, as a third party is involved in the process. That party varies according to the land use; in the metropolitan cities, that party is the relevant greater municipality; in special cases, such as the regenerated cruise ports in Istanbul, it is the Directorate of Privatization.

The Performance Audit Report of Planning and Audit of Coastal Utilization (Karabeyli et al., 2006) found that the complaint-based monitoring of coastal developments is not only time-consuming but also insufficient to achieve the aim of establishing an equitable and sustainable development pattern for coastal areas. Furthermore, in 2012, the Appeal Commission of the Parliament reported that the monitoring and enforcement system is lacking. The Commission's report found that the government ministries involved in the process do not have enough qualified personnel (TBBM, 2012). Municipalities also claim that they do not have appropriately trained staff. In response, the Commission recommended that the Ministry of Internal Affairs explore methods of efficient monitoring and guide the municipalities accordingly.

Not only is the monitoring and enforcement system problematic but the 2006 Audit Report also found that, in some cases, the institutions responsible for monitoring coastal developments disobey coastal legislation themselves, which has a negative impact on the society's perception of protection and fair use of coastal land. The Appeal Commission (TBBM, 2012) noted that the failure of municipalities to carry out their monitoring responsibilities encourages the public to disobey the legislation.

National government reporting

Turkey's national government has carried out two reviews of the legal context and implementation of law in coastal areas: The Performance Audit Report of Planning and Audit of Coastal Utilization (Karabeyli et al., 2006, pp. 8–11) and the Report of the Appeal Commission of the Parliament (TBBM, 2012, pp. 31–38). The findings of these monitoring instruments are highlighted in the appropriate sections of this chapter. They include neglect of the public interest in development of coastal areas; mismanagement of land ownership, which in turn allows for privatization; and issues with coordination of responsible institutions.

It should be highlighted that Turkish legislation protecting the coasts was initiated relatively early in the life of the Republic and that the protection, as well as the public use of the coasts, was designated a constitutional right. The Parliament Report and the recent decisions of the Constitutional Court (described in the section on planning above) confirm the dedication of some public authorities to the issue. However, the extent of illegal development along the coast reveals the fact that in practice, the system is misused. As such, there is a need for scrutiny of the implementation process of the law, at all governmental levels. It is likely that certain interest groups have undue influence over the process.

Climate change awareness and legal aspects

Turkish law referenced climate change as early as 1983 (Environmental Law 1983/2872, Article 18), and additional laws have since addressed aspects of research, education, and awareness.[10] Although there has been an increasing awareness and government focus on climate change in Turkey over time, there is very little in Turkish law or policy which specifically addresses climate change and its effect on coastal areas. Climate change is not referenced in the Law of Development, the Coastal Law, or other laws which have a direct impact on the development of coastal areas.

Specific climate change policy emerged in 2001, when the Prime Ministry established the Coordination Committee for Climate Change (by Circular Order 2001/2). This Committee has been restructured and enlarged several times since and most recently was incorporated into the Coordination Committee of Air Management. In addition, Turkey's commitment to addressing climate change concerns has been boosted by its commitments at the international level: Turkey has been a party to the United Nations Framework Convention on Climate Change since 2004.

Turkey's Climate Change Strategy 2010–2023 was prepared in consultation with public, private and non-government institutions and universities and approved by the Prime Ministry Higher Planning Council (Ministry of Environment and Urbanization, 2010). Since the preparation of that Strategy, the Ministry of Environment and Urbanization has prepared the Climate Change Action Plan 2011–2023 (Ministry of Environment and Urbanization, 2012b) and National Climate Change Adaptation Strategy and Action Plan (Ministry of Environment and Urbanization, 2012c). The Action Plan was prepared in coordination with 500 experts from 180 institutions in 25 workshops (Ministry of Environment and Urbanization, 2012a, p. 5).

Across all these documents, reference to the coast is mostly superficial. The coast is mentioned in the "adaptation" section of the Action Plan (Ministry of Environment and Urbanization, 2012b) in the context of the objectives of "management of water resources" and "ecosystem services, biodiversity and forestry", as well as indirectly in the context of "soil management" and "protection and improvement of wetlands". A more substantial discussion of the coast and climate change comes under the objective of the Climate Change Strategy and Action Plan that is specifically dedicated to the integration of climate change adaptation into coastal zone management. In this context, the following is stated:

> The effects of human consumptions [sic] on the coastal zones where tourism activities increase due to their climatic, geographic and morphological features are combined with the negative conditions caused by global climate changes and create a constant pressure.
> … In the strategy, researching the effects of climate change on sea level rise and adaptation activities was identified as the main objective. In this context it is necessary to; i) ensure the sustainability of marine and coastal protected areas, ii) analyse the lagoon fishery in terms of the effects of climate change (extinction risk), iii) research the possible causes of salinization of drinking and domestic water and rise of seawater level, iv) map the agricultural lands with inundation risk, v) map the settlements and coastal zones that may probably be submerged, vi) integrate the research on the effects on and adaptation to the sea level rise with wetland conservation policies. (Ministry of Environment and Urbanization, 2012c, pp. 47–48)

Two actions are defined in this context: The first involves adding consideration of climate change adaptation into integrated studies of marine and coastal areas. This should then feed into Integrated Coastal Area Plans. The second action is controlling developments which reduce the resilience of marine and coastal ecosystems to climate change in shore settlement planning, implemented through zoning plans and other planning documents. The responsible authority, for both actions, is the Ministry of Environment and Urbanization.

Although there has been a remarkable increase in awareness-raising activities in the public domain and institutional recognition of climate change, the concept has not been truly embraced in planning and policy development for coastal areas. Integrated Coastal Zone/Area Plans do not mention climate change as a matter of course, and when they do, it is in vague terms, without any complementary implementation strategies.

Despite the lack of concrete steps in the integration of the climate change considerations into coastal zone management, flood legislation lays ground for avoiding risk-generating developments. Although legislation related to flood defence previously focused on the post-disaster period,[11] preventative measures have emerged in the discourse since 2006, after Turkey experienced tragic flood disasters. Two Circular Orders of the Prime Ministry (2006/27 and 2010/5) refer to floods and improvement to riverbeds. These circular orders stipulate requirements relating to approval of developments which may cause flooding, prevention of unlicensed developments on riverbeds, and other precautions.

Arguably, the implementation of flood legislation is more traceable than implementation of climate change regulations, given the strong spatial references and immediate physical impacts of the former.

Both the country's flourishing academic research and Turkey's hopes to join the EU have greatly contributed to climate change awareness and the above actions.

Integration and coordination

Coastal zone management and protection are addressed across several laws and responsibilities are shared across several institutions. Those institutions are primarily at central government level. This is demonstrated at Table 14.1 above (which highlights plan types and responsibilities for those plans) and Table 14.2 below (which highlights responsibilities beyond those related to planning).

Table 14.2 Institutional structure for coastal development and management (excluding plans)

Action	Institution	Legal basis
Permit for Reclamation of Marine Areas, Construction of Harbours	Ministry of Environment and Urbanization	Harbours Law (618)
	Governorships	
	Directorate for Maritime Affairs	Executive Order of the Cabinet for the Establishment of MTMC (2011/655)
Permit for Fishery Facilities	Ministry of Agriculture	Water Products Law (1971/1380)
Security	Directorate of Coastal Security	Executive Order of the Cabinet for the Establishment of MTMC (2011/655)
	Ministry of Defence	Law of Development (1985/3194)

Adapted from PAP/RAC (Priority Actions Programme Regional Activity Centre, Split) (2005), *Coastal Area Management in Turkey*, p. 52 (original source in Turkish – Sonmez, 2002)

Notably, until 2011, the Ministry of Environment and Ministry of Public Works and Settlement[12] were two different ministries. This led to a debate about the sharing of planning authority between the two ministries. The debate was resolved after the merging of these two ministries, but new concerns arose when the merger resulted in more intensive development outcomes and environmental degradation.

Overall, the above demonstrates the finding of the Performance Audit Report of Planning and Audit of Coastal Utilization (Karabeyli et al., 2006) that planning responsibilities for coastal areas are scattered across several institutions. In addition, that report found that some municipalities lack technical and legal competencies to achieve appropriate planning and management outcomes. Finally, the report noted the absence of holistic management model or tools for coordination between the relevant public institutions.

The lack of tools for efficient coordination is a wide-ranging weakness of planning law and implementation in Turkey. Development decisions based on and fuelled by the ambitious development targets of different economic sectors (e.g. industry, tourism, and housing) have been an obstacle to securing a holistic strategic approach and a functioning coordinated system. The lack of coordination has been overlooked not only for the sake of ambitious development decisions but also for micro benefits of local people in return for political support. In other words, those seeking to increase development opportunities and outcomes on the coast have taken advantage of the structural deficiencies which led to a lack of coordination.

In addition to this structural deficiency, competing demands, which are more amplified in coastal areas compared with inland areas, make it more difficult to develop suitable coordination mechanisms. From the economic perspective, there are certain activities which can only take place in coastal areas: Fishery facilities, ports and connecting transportation facilities, shipbuilding yards, and major type of tourism. These facilities, which contribute significantly to the prosperity of coastal regions, often cannot or will not share coastal land resources. From the ecological perspective, coasts are the transition zones between land and water ecosystems and their management has cross-border implications. The conventional struggle between conserving natural resources and the economic utilization of these resources is highly relevant to coastal zones; and the pollution of this vulnerable transition zone through waste disposal is an additional burden. Added to this struggle between environment and economy is the competing social demand for public use of coastal areas, given that free accessibility to the coasts is a constitutional right in Turkey. The harsh competition between these demands creates a challenging environment for the establishment of efficient coordination mechanisms, the absence of which only serves to maximize profit margins for private entities.

The central government, which has a broad view of the competing interests, with an eye on international relations, should play a key role in improving coordination in coastal zone management. The central government is also positioned to act on this matter, given that coastal legislation in Turkey is enacted at the central government level and is implemented by the governorships. The governorships have a view not only of the responsibilities and activities of separate ministries but also of local governmental and civic dynamics. In other words, the governorships are well placed to act to improve both vertical and horizontal coordination. Despite these advantages enjoyed by the governorships, they tend to shrink from their coordination responsibility due to pressures exerted by powerful ministries or non-governmental organizations.

The Integrated Coastal Area Plans described above can not only enhance the vertical coordination between the different levels of government but also help to improve horizontal coordination. Horizontal coordination between the different sectoral targets, public benefit and private expectations, policymakers and academics is a basic need in the Turkish planning system. ICA plans might be a remedy for the malfunctioning of the planning procedures in Turkey, if they are properly established in law and coordinated with the other types of plans, with appropriate guidance provided for their preparation.

It is worth noting that although a basic principle of integrated coastal zone management is empowerment of the public to oversee coastal planning and management, it is questionable whether Turkish society as a whole is ready to take on such a role. As such, the coordination role of government – and particularly governorships – is crucial until the consciousness of wider Turkish society further awakens to the issues of environment and sustainability.

Public participation and access to justice

In theory, public participation facilitates the balanced distribution of political power throughout the society. Yet we can differentiate between the impact of proactive and reactive participation processes and their outcomes. Turkish Planning Legislation has provided reactive participation tools such as "right to be heard" and "right to object to plans" as well as the provision of information from different institutions related to development since the Law of Development came into force. However, proactive participation mechanisms reflect perhaps a higher level of partnership between government and the public. Although there has been an increasing awareness about the importance of proactive participation over the last three decades in Turkey, such participation was not mentioned in environmental legislation until 2013, and in the context of the Law of Development or Coastal Law and related regulations, not until 2014.

During the 1990s, various attempts to improve participation and information on coastal developments were introduced and proved effective. In 1993, the Mediterranean Coastal Foundation (MEDCOAST) was established as a nonprofit scientific and environmental organization. This is one of the leading Turkish organizations contributing to coastal and marine conservation in the Mediterranean and Black Seas through improved coastal management practices. Since 1993, MEDCOAST has successfully organized international scientific meetings, training programmes, and joint research.

Awareness about public participation rose over the 2000s, and as a result, participation began to appear in the legislation. The adoption of the Regulation of Environmental Impact Assessment in 2013 was a milestone for public participation in environmental decision-making processes in Turkey. The 9th article of this Regulation is dedicated to the organization and utilization of public participation meetings.

Still, prior to 2014, public participation processes in planning took place only at the initiative of visionary public administrators or well-established and persistent NGOs. A relatively high number of lawsuits were recorded in the implementation period of plans, which indicates there was a lack of public participation in the decision-making process: In Turkey, the duty of the 6th Chamber of the Council of State is to resolve the legal disputes on planning between public authorities and private entities. In 2018, 27,188 cases (17,553 of which were carried over from the previous year) were judged and filed (Danıştay Başkanlığı, 2018, p. 23). Although there is no evidence for a direct relationship between legal disputes and a lack of public participation, the excessive number of lawsuits might be regarded as an indicator.

The Regulation of Making Spatial Plans (2014) acknowledged proactive public participation for the first time in planning legislation. Public participation and other feedback mechanisms are defined in the Regulation in the following contexts:

- The advice of related institutions should be sought through methods such as questionnaires, public inquiries or research, meetings, workshops, web announcements, or exhibition, based on the type of the plan in the decision-making phase (Article 7/1/j)
- Plans should be prepared with a multidisciplinary team, including different fields of specialization, and with the participation of institutions which will be affected by the plan, development agencies, universities, local governments, non-governmental organizations, professional associations, and representatives of the private sector (Article 14/1/e)
- A participatory management model should be developed in order to provide and facilitate strategies in making Integrated Coastal Area Plans (Article 29/1/g)

Note the last point relates specifically to ICA plans. However, in the part of the Regulation which describes the preparation of these plans, public participation is not mentioned. Apparently, the legislators thought that consultation of government bodies was enough.

In order to integrate genuine and effective proactive public participation mechanisms into the decision-making and implementation processes in coastal development, availability of and accessibility to the information about the coasts is valuable. Data about the environment is stored and published by the Turkish Statistical Institute (TUIK) but it is limited to data about air, water, wastewater, and environmental expenditures. Data about the use of the coasts is not available in this context. But under the Right of Information Law (2003/4982), public institutions are obliged to provide information requested within fifteen days or, if the information is coming from a different institution, within thirty days. The exceptions from this obligation are State secrets, economic data which will cause unfair competition, and information which will unreasonably impinge on individuals' privacy.

There is still much to be done to improve public participation in Turkey, especially on trans-boundary issues. For example, Turkey is not a member of the EU, and it follows that it has not signed on to the Aarhus Convention. Notably, however, the Convention is published on the official website of the Directorate of European Union and Foreign Relations within the Ministry of Agriculture and Forestry. (The Turkish Republic looks to EU Legislation as a guide as part of its long-lasting, but stalled, candidacy for EU membership.)

Fiscal aspects of coastal zone management

The rights of private property owners who incur a loss due to planning legislation are mainly disregarded in Turkish planning legislation. The only exception is under the Law of Development (1985, Article 9), where private properties which are defined as public service areas in the relevant Development Plan must be expropriated within five years of the approval of the Plan. However, there have been consistent delays in expropriation procedures, and landowners have been forced to file lawsuits, which eventually led to decisions in the property owners' favour.

The amount of compensation to be paid in cases of compulsory acquisition is determined with respect to the balance between the property rights (Articles 8 and 14 of the Law of Title) and the priority given to the public use of coastal areas (as defined in Article 43 of the Constitution and the Coastal Law).

Overall assessment

Turkey's framework for coastal protection and management warrants a thorough examination due to the excessive length of its coastlines and the geopolitical importance of its location. This chapter has sought not only to explore Turkey's coastal legislation but also to make sense of the management framework in the context of recent international efforts towards Integrated Coastal Zone Management.

The principles of protection and public use of the coasts appeared in the Civil Law (1926) very early in the life of the Republic and has since appeared as a feature of planning and development legislation, even prior to adoption of the dedicated Coastal Law in 1990. Yet despite the spirit of protection and social equity of the relevant laws and regulations, they could not protect the coast from inappropriate and illegal developments.

Illegal developments are a result of rapid coastal population growth, as well as of certain deficiencies in the relevant legislation and its implementation. The populist approach of the public authorities laid the ground, taking advantage of ambiguities in the law and facilitating opportunist illegal developments. The government's prioritization of development over coastal protection has also fed ambiguities and stimulated coastal deterioration. Furthermore, the development projects undermining laws designed to protect the coast have resulted in the court cancelling several legislative decisions.

Promising efforts have been made in the last decade in terms of integrating coastal legislation and the development. Although Turkey is not a part of the Protocol on Integrated Coastal Zone Management (ICZM) in the Mediterranean, the government has introduced and begun to prepare Integrated Coastal Area (ICA) Plans in the spirit of the Protocol. Nevertheless, ICA Plans are regarded only as guiding strategic documents.

A positive next step would be the integration of ICA Plans into the statutory spatial planning hierarchy. These Plans should propose management models with efficient coordination and implementation tools. A longer-term ambitious project would be a programme for increased public awareness about coastal deterioration and protection, with the ultimate goal of enhancing participatory decision-making processes.

Notes

1. Thirteen of these municipalities were established in 2012 under Law 6360: The Law of Establishment of 13 Greater Municipalities and 26 Districts.
2. It should be noted that population growth rates resulting from internal migration have an exponential impact on the social profile of the relevant cities and towns: The magnitude of the social change might be much more significant than the difference in numbers of population. For example, some of the cities which have high rates of urbanization draw unqualified labour, especially for construction projects, whereas educated people are leaving the metropolitan cities on retirement. Thus, statistics on net migration do not adequately represent the social change that these cities experience.
3. The Ministry of Development and Settlement was established in 1958. This Ministry was merged with the Ministry of Public Works in 1983 to form the Ministry of Public Works and Settlement, which in 2011 was merged into the Ministry of Environment and Urbanization.
4. Following that decision, the Ministry of Development and Settlement issued a circular order in 1976 (5.12.1976, no. 75) and a team of agricultural and topographic engineers were commissioned to identify the shoreline, which delineation was to be approved by the Ministry of Development and Settlement (Babacan Tekinbaş, 2001, pp. 117–118).

5. The 1982 Constitution came into force after a military coup. Consequently, it was highly authoritarian and restrictive in terms of democratic rights. It was subject to major changes in 2007 and 2010, by referendum. Nevertheless, the social rights and social equity had been secured (e.g. the public use of coasts by the 43rd article, the right of environmental health by the 56th article, and the right of housing by the 57th article) as the main responsibilities of the State. Although the main approach of the Constitution was not democratic and did not enhance democratic practices, it laid the ground for protecting environmental assets, including the coasts.

6. In preparing the maps for determination of the delineation of the Coast Edge Line, the geographic area covered is decided according to natural characteristics of the coast. The Regulation specifies that the area shown should be at least 50 m wide for the narrow, steep coast and 200 m wide for the low, flat coast.

7. The timeline of relevant government departments is as follows: The State Planning Office (established 1960) merged into Ministry of Development (NOT to be confused with the Ministry of Development and Settlement) in 2011. In 2018, the Ministry of Developed was re-established as Directorate of Strategy and Budget. However, in the same year, Regional Development Agencies joined the Ministry of Industry, by decree of the President (Official Gazette 30479 dated 15.7.2018).

8. Report by Prof. Dr. Ali Elmas, Department of Geological Engineering, Istanbul University.

9. The report of the Appeal Commission brings related legislation to demonstrate the idea of mesne profits. One relevant law is the Public Tender Law (1983/2886), in which the lease and mesne profit are clearly differentiated. Another is the Regulation of the Real Estates of Treasury (2007/Official Gazette 26557), which indicates that the mesne profit does not legitimize the use of the land or the building after the payment.

10. Law of the Institutional Establishment of the Directorate of Meteorology (1986/3254) promotes research into climate change in the context of education and raising awareness (Article 9/b). The Law of Energy Efficiency (2007/5627) promotes the provision of theoretical and practical knowledge to public institutions about climate (Article 6).

11. Law of Flood Defence (1943/4373), Law about the Establishment and the Duties of the General Directorate of the State Hydraulic Works (1953/6200), The Law about the Precautions and the Charity after the Public Disasters (1959/7269), Law about the Establishment and the Duties of the General Directorate of the Highways (2010/6001).

12. See note 3.

References

Babacan Tekinbaş, B. (2001). *Mekan Planlama Ve Yargı Denetimi* [Spatial Planning and Judicial Supervision]. Edited by M. Ersoy, Ç. Keskinok, & Y. Yayınevi. Yargı Yayınevi.

— (2008). *Yargı Kararlarında Planlama* [Planning and Judicial Decisions]. SPO.

Danıştay Başkanlığı, T. C. (2018). *2018 Yılı İdare Faaliyet Raporu* [Council of State Annual Report]. Available at: https://www.danistay.gov.tr/upload/2018-Yilii-Idare-Faaliyet-Raporu.pdf

Karabeyli, L., Çelebi, O., Efendi, M., Karaman, F., & Karanfiloğlu, A. Y. (2006). *Kıyıların Kullanılmasının Planlanması ve Denetimi* [Planning and Supervision of Coastal Use]. Sayıştay Başkanlığı [Turkish Court of Accounts]. Report. June.

Ministry of Environment and Urbanization. (n.d.a). Kıyıda Planlama [Coastal Planning]. General Directorate of Spatial Planning. Available at: https://mpgm.csb.gov.tr/sss/kiyida-planlama [Accessed July 2019]

— (n.d.b). Bütünleşik Kıyı Alanları Planları (BKAY) [Integrated Coastal Area Plans (ICZM)]. General Directorate of Spatial Planning. Available at: https://mpgm.csb.gov.tr/planlar-ve-projeler-i-84130 [Accessed July 2019]

— (n.d.c). Alo 181 Çağrı Merkezine Sıkça Sorulan Sorular [181 Call Centre Frequently Asked Questions]. General Directorate of Spatial Planning. Available at: https://mpgm.csb.gov.tr/sss/alo-181-cagri-merkezine-sikca-sorulan-sorular [Accessed July 2019]

— (2010). *Climate Change Strategy 2010–2023*. Available at: https://webdosya.csb.gov.tr/db/iklim/editordosya/iklim_degisikligi_stratejisi_EN.pdf

— (2012a). *Climate Change and Turkey*. Report. Available at: https://webdosya.csb.gov.tr/db/iklim/editor-dosya/BROSUR_ENG.pdf

— (2012b). *Climate Change Action Plan 2010–2023*. Available at: https://webdosya.csb.gov.tr/db/iklim/editordosya/iklim_degisikligi_eylem_plani_EN_2014.pdf

— (2012c). *Turkey's National Climate Change Adaptation Strategy and Action Plan 2011–2023*. Available at: https://webdosya.csb.gov.tr/db/iklim/editordosya/uyum_stratejisi_eylem_plani_EN(2).pdf

Ministry of Internal Affairs. (2019). Türkiye Mülki İdare Bölümleri Envanteri [Public Administration Units]. Available at: https://www.e-icisleri.gov.tr/Anasayfa/MulkiIdariBolumleri.aspx

PAP/RAC (Priority Actions Programme Regional Activity Centre, Split). (2005). *Coastal Area Management in Turkey* (original source in Turkish – R. Sonmez, 2002). Available at: https://www.medcoast.net/uploads/documents/Coastal_Area_Management_in_Turkey.pdf

Sendika. (2017). Danıştay kararı: Ataköy sahilindeki lüks konutlar hukuka aykırı [The decision of the Council of State: Ataköy coast luxury housing is against the law]. *Sendika*, 2 August. Available at: http://sendika63.org/2017/08/danistay-karari-atakoy-sahilindeki-luks-konutlar-hukuka-aykiri-437933/

Şimşek, S. (2010). Kıyılarda Mülkiyet Sorunu: Avrupa İnsan Hakları Mahkemesinin İptal Kararları Işığında Bir Çözüm Önerisi [The Problem of Ownership in the Coast: A Proposal for a Solution in the Light of the Cancellation Decisions of the European Court of Human Rights]. *Sayıştay Dergisi* 77, 87–118.

TBBM [Turkish General Assembly]. (2012). Dilekçe Komisyonu Genel Kurul Karar Cetveli Sayi: 12 [Appeal Commission of the Parliament Table of Resolutions no. 12]. Report. 27 June.

TUIK [Turkish Statistical Institute]. (2018a). Annual growth rate and population density of provinces by years, 2007–2018. Available at: http://www.tuik.gov.tr

— (2018b). Population of provinces by years, 2000–2018. Available at: http://www.tuik.gov.tr

World Factbook. (n.d.). Turkey. Available at: https://www.cia.gov/Library/publications/the-world-factbook/geos/tu.html [Accessed September 2019]

Legislation (listed chronologically)

Law of Structure and Roads, 1933

Law of Development (Law no. 1957/6785) as amended 1972 (Law no. 1972/1605) and 1985 (Law no. 1985/3194)

Constitution of Turkey 1982 (and previous version amended 1971)

Law of Tourism Incentive (Law no. 1982/2634)

Law of Protection of the Cultural and Natural Assets 1983 (Law no. 1983/2863)

Environmental Law 1983 (Law no. 1983/2872)

Coastal Law 1990 (Law no. 1990/3621) and as amended 1992 (Law no. 1992/3830)

— Also amended 2005 (Official Gazette 5398 dated 3 July 2005) and 2008 (Official Gazette 5801 dated 31 July 2008)

Coastal Law Regulation 1990 (issued on the Official Gazette 20594, on 3 August 1990), as amended 2014 (issued on the Official Gazette 29072, on 24 July 2014)

Civil Law (Law no. 2001/4721), (formerly Law no.1926/743 – repealed)

Right of Information Law (2003/4982)

Regulation of Environmental Impact Assessment 2013 (issued on the Official Gazette 28784, on 3 October 2013)

Regulation of Making Spatial Plans 2014 (Official Gazette 29030 dated 14 June 2014)

Court cases

Yargıtay, Esas No. 1970/7, Karar No. 1972/4 (Resmî Gazete, 16.4.1972, sayi 14161) [Court of Appeals Official Gazette, 16.4.1972/14161].

Anayasa Mahkemesi (AYM), Esas No. 1985/1, Karar No. 1986/4 (Resmî Gazete tarih, 10.07.1986, sayi 19160) [Constitutional Court Official Gazette, 10.07.1986/19160].

Anayasa Mahkemesi (AYM), Esas No. 1990/23, Karar No. 1991/29 (Resmî Gazete, 23.01.1992, sayi 21120) [Constitutional Court Official Gazette, 23.01.1992/21120].

Anayasa Mahkemesi (AYM), Esas No. 2019/35, Karar No. 2019/53 (Resmî Gazete, 24.7.2019, sayi 30841) [Constitutional Court Official Gazette, 24.7.2019/30841].

Danıştay 14., Esas No. 2014/868, Karar No. 2015/10666. Available at: http://vatandas.uyap.gov.tr/danistay/portal_baslangic.uyap?param=user

15 Israel

Dafna Carmon and Rachelle Alterman

Overview

Israel has by far the highest population growth rate among the countries in this book, with most of the population concentrated along the Mediterranean coast. For Israelis, beaches provide the most popular form of recreation. Beach-related issues probably draw more public and media attention than any other environmental topic in Israel.

The first national plan for the coastal zone was approved in the 1980s. The plan restricted development in a 100 m setback zone, but this was not enough to prevent overdevelopment of the coast: In the 1990s, several contentious hotel or apartment/hotel buildings were approved. As a result, environmental organizations, propelled by the general public's special concern about the coasts, fought for unprecedented parliamentary legislation – and were successful. The 2004 Coastal Law introduced a new and progressive policy and created a dedicated Coastal Committee. The law imposed binding rules to tighten up the 100 m rule and created an additional coastal planning zone with a width of 300 m.

Civic-society bodies have successfully fought several landmark cases in the courts, and these decisions have generated further preservation momentum. However, although the Israeli legislation is comparatively progressive and enforcement has significantly improved, there are still threats and battles to fight in order to preserve the limited open coastal land.

Introduction to country and coastal issues

Israel is a small country, one of the most densely populated in the Mediterranean region and has by far the highest fertility rate among OECD member countries. It also has a very short coastline – only 273 km long (World Factbook, n.d.). Most of the country's population is concentrated along the coast: Approximately 70% of 8.7 million people reside within 15 km of the coastline. Thus, the coastal area in Israel plays a crucial role and is perhaps the most highly pressured among the countries in this book.

Most of the coastal zone is already built up, with some ancient cities and many new ones. In addition, most of the country's linear infrastructure runs along the coast and there are two major international ports. The country's defence needs also take up some sites along the coast. Today, less than 7% of the coast is available for bathing or recreation. Furthermore, the presence of some unbuilt development rights, granted two or three decades ago, poses a significant legal constraint in implementing current preservation policies. Israel's coast also faces the ongoing challenge of cliff erosion along the coast. Needless to say, in the context of such

Figure 15.1 The crowded Tel Aviv beach

Source: EdoM. Available at: https://commons.wikimedia.org/wiki/File:Israel_-_Tel_Aviv_Beach_001.JPG

current and future pressures, land values in coastal areas run extremely high and preservation initiatives have faced major conflicts from other government bodies and from developers. But time after time, civil-society bodies and the general public, as well as court decisions, have propelled preservation goals, and these groups are winning major battles.

Administrative and planning structure

Some background about Israel's administration will aid the reader's understanding of this chapter. Israel is a relatively young country, having declared independence in 1948. It began as a poor developing country but today is a member of the OECD. Its governance consists of national government and municipalities. There is no general regional level. However, for planning decisions there are six statutory District Commissions, whose approval is necessary for any major local planning decisions. Overall, Israel's governance structure is highly centralized (Alterman, 2001). The highest planning authority is the National Planning and Building Board (henceforth, National Planning Board or National Board).

Israel's key planning legislation is the Planning and Building Law 1965 (with over 120 amendments). The Law stipulates a hierarchal set of plans: National Outline Plans (NOPs),

District Outline Plans (DOPs), and local plans. Each plan must be consistent with the plans above it in the hierarchy. When granting development permission, local governments must ensure that the proposal is fully consistent with the entire hierarchy of plans. NOP 35 is a comprehensive land use plan covering the entire country (and is occasionally amended). In addition, there are over 40 other NOPs for specific topics, such as national infrastructure, as well as for site-specific major facilities. For our topic, the major national plan was, until **2019**, NOP 13 – Coastal Zone Protection (discussed below). A recent amalgamation of all the NOPs, called NOP One, further builds on the contents of NOP 13.[1] The coastal protection chapter, instead of simply compiling previously approved coastal regulations, contains important improvements, and has thus drawn major public attention. All national plans are binding and relatively detailed. Israeli planning law does not recognize strategic or policy plans, although such documents are prepared from time to time.

On the local level, there are Master Plans and Detailed Plans. In addition, Local Comprehensive Plans were introduced in 2014 to replace the overly detailed patchwork of amendments to local plans and, once approved, grant local governments additional local planning decision powers. Nevertheless, the new comprehensive plan is to be prepared by the District Planning Commission, composed mainly of national-government representatives. A building permit to be granted by the local government is required for any construction, including by government bodies. The permit must strictly accord with the relevant plans (Alterman, 2020).

The bulk of Israel's coastal zone management is either part of the statutory planning system or relies heavily on that system.

Overview of Israel's regulatory context for coastal zone management

Regulation of Israel's coastal zone began as far back as 1983 with the introduction of National Outline Plan for the Mediterranean Coast (NOP 13). NOP 13 (now part of NOP One) covers all of Israel's Mediterranean coastline. The goal of the plan was to reduce land use conflicts and ensure that uses which do not require proximity to the sea are not developed on the coast. It instituted a 100 m setback zone and set out land use rules along the coast (discussed below). In 1983, Israel was still a quasi-developing country and environmental NGOs were weak, so this initiative by the national planning bodies was a landmark. It provided a foundation for coastal management in Israel and was the only dedicated coastal regulation until the introduction of the Coastal Law in 2004. However, as environmental awareness matured, the deficiencies of the plan – particularly ambiguities in land use terms – were widely decried.

The ambiguities in the plan were exploited by developers who sought to build lucrative residential real estate projects as close as possible to the sea, successfully arguing that these were "vacation apartments". Among the controversial high-end projects developed between 1983 and 2004 were (i) Herzliya "Marina", a posh area of towers and town houses, close to Tel Aviv; (ii) a resort along the coast of Hadera, midway between Tel Aviv and Haifa; and (iii) a tower complex consisting of hotel and vacation apartments in Hof HaCarmel in Haifa (Figure 15.2). In addition, there are still approximately 30 small sites with development rights granted before 2004 (Adam Teva V'Din, n.d.), as discussed below.

NOP 13 was also criticized because it maintained the previously existing institutional divide between the sea and the coast. The terrestrial zone was protected by NOP 13, while the marine environment was protected only by a dedicated national planning committee – the Coastal Waters Committee. This situation prevented a holistic consideration of plans, with both marine and terrestrial implications (Alfasi, 2009).

Figure 15.2 Hof HaCarmel hotel plus vacation apartments

Source: Meronim. CC BY-SA 3.0 license. Available at: https://commons.wikimedia.org/wiki/File:WikiAir_Flight_IL-13-02_1593.JPG

By the 1990s, the inadequacies of NOP 13 as a management tool for Israel's coasts had become apparent. By that time, Israel's environmental NGOs had gained public momentum. During this period, Israel was experiencing massive waves of immigration from Russia and Ethiopia, which accelerated demand for housing and employment. In the meantime, Integrated Coastal Zone Management (ICZM) and sustainable development had become key issues on the international environment agenda, spearheaded by the 1992 Rio Summit. In 1998, these conditions led Israel's Ministry of the Environment, together with environmental NGOs, to preparing a draft "Coastal Conservation Law". The draft law was "aimed at preserving and restoring the coastal environment and its fragile ecosystems, reducing and preventing coastal damage and establishing principles for the management and sustainable development of the coastline" (UNEP, 2001).

The Bill was not easy to pass, given the scarcity of developable land and high population growth rate noted above. However, with extensive lobbying by NGOs and several years of negotiations, consultations and hearings in the Knesset (Israel's parliament), the Protection of the Coastal Environment Law (henceforth, Coastal Law) was finally adopted in 2004. By that time, the ICZM Protocol to the Barcelona Convention was in draft form and, indeed, Israeli participants took part in its drafting.[2] The 2004 Law was a major leap for coastal conservation in Israel. It introduced innovative ideas and a new approach to managing the country's coasts and the threats posed by development.

The Coastal Law's overall objective is to "reduce damage to the coastal environment" (Section 3). As we will discuss in greater detail below, the Law defines the "coastal environment" (or coastal zone) as land within 300 m of the shoreline. The law obliges "any authority authorized to grant a license, permit… for any activity within the seacoast… [to] do so, as far as possible, in a way that is designed to reduce damage to the coastal environment" (Section 3).

One of the important innovations of the 2004 Coastal Law was the establishment – through an amendment to the Planning Law – of the National Committee for the Protection of the Coastal Environment (CPCE). This is a powerful body affiliated with the National Planning Commission. In its scope, the Committee fulfils one of the essential principles of the ICZM concept – its jurisdiction encompasses both the terrestrial and marine coastal environments. This body is charged with assessing any new project proposals within the defined coastal zone to ensure that their impact on the coastal environment is not unreasonable.

Significantly, the 2004 law did not replace NOP 13; thus, the regulatory powers remained within the planning system. This was a good decision, intended to prevent disconnection of coastal management from other urban and rural planning issues. However, the coexistence of the two legal documents left several inconsistencies. One that has recently reached the courts is the differences in the definitions for how to demarcate the shoreline (described below). Another difference is the definition of the coastal zone. While NOP 13 defines only the terrestrial part of the coast and regulates its uses, the Coastal Law defines the coastal environment in a more integrated way, including both land and sea components.

The latest major decision in Israel's coastal regulation was the almost final approval (pending cabinet decision) of National Outline Plan One (NOP One) which is intended to replace many of the sectoral national plans, including most parts of NOP 13, except those pertaining to marine spatial planning and to amendments approved for some of the major pre-existing urban areas. The preparation of NOP One, which took three years, was quite turbulent, especially regarding its coastal zone proposals. A coalition of environmental NGOs negotiated hard with the National Planning Board and eventually succeeded not only in reinstating some of the protective elements that were to be relaxed, but also in installing greater coastal zone protective framework than did the original NOP 13. NOP One regulations are now clearer and more consistent with the Coastal Law.

Definition of the shoreline, setback zone, and coastal zone

The key land use regulations pertaining to Israel's coasts rely on definitions of the shoreline, which serve as the basis for the definitions of the setback zone and coastal zone. These definitions have historically been unclear due to inconsistencies in the relevant regulations.

Definition of the shoreline and its implications: Every centimetre counts

There are two different legal definitions for Israel's shoreline – one in NOP 13 and the other in the Coastal Law (and now embedded in NOP One). Both are based on the standard mean sea level measurement:

- Clause 12(2) of NOP 13 specifies that the coastal *setback* (discussed below) will be measured from the "highest tide"; a term that, in practice, was interpreted as the point at which 0.00 mean sea level (MSL)[3] intersects with the land
- The Coastal Law adopts as its benchmark for defining the shoreline a measurement of 0.75 m above geodetic zero. This measure moves the shoreline landwards, thus providing a somewhat wider berth of protection for the coastal zone

Following approval of the Coastal Law, the 0.75 m (above geodetic zero) rule was adopted by the Survey of Israel – Government Agency for Mapping and is now considered the national measurement for defining the shoreline. Yet there was still ambiguity regarding which measurement should be used in decisions pertaining to plans which were approved under NOP 13 before the enactment of the Coastal Law: How should the shoreline be measured in such cases? The difference between the two measurements could mean 10 or 20 m. In a country where every bit of land may matter to developers, it was only a matter of time before this ostensibly small disparity would reach the courts. Developers (obviously) favour the 0.00 mean sea level rule, while environmentally aware NGOs and citizens who want to prevent any encroachment into the coastal zone prefer the more protective measure. For years the matter created uncertainty in practice.

In October 2017, the Tel Aviv District Administrative Court gave a rather dramatic ruling on this matter, given the circumstances. The case involved a local plan approved in 1999 for a hotel close to the beach in the city of Bat Yam, on the southern outskirts of Tel Aviv. At the time, NOP 13 applied, and there was no Coastal Law. Thirteen years later, the landowners and developers sought a permit to demolish the old hotel and build a larger one in its place. The local planning commission approved the proposal on the assumption that the plot of land was entirely outside the setback zone as defined by NOP 13 – that is, 100 m landwards from the point at which 0.00 MSL hits the shore.

Residents of the area partnered with a leading environmental NGO (Adam Teva V'Din) and a coastal protection NGO to appeal the decision all the way up to the courts. However, by the time they filed the petition, the hotel was under construction. In *The Forum for Saving the Beach v City of Bat Yam Planning Commission and the National Planning Board* (Administrative Petition 27857-04-14), the petitioners argued that the amendment to the previous plan was illegal because since 2004, the shoreline should be defined according to the more stringent rule of the Coastal Law (0.75 m above geodetic zero), even in decisions to amend existing plans ("grandfathered" by the earlier regulation). The Tel Aviv District Court accepted this daring argument, stating that the norms of preservation of the coastal zone and social justice are of such high public priority that they should prevail – even though the developers were relying on the demarcation rule that was in force when they built the original hotel, in the same location. Because the new building was already under construction, the District Court did not order direct demolition, but gave the developers two years to sort out the matter. The developers appealed to the Supreme Court (Administrative Appeal 9557/17). The District decision was overturned, but not the basis of substantive reasons – only due to procrastination by the initial appellants. Seeking to prevent further cases of uncertainty, the Supreme Court asked for a government declaration that the then-forthcoming NOP One would set clear rules about the measurement of the shoreline – which it did. In the meantime, the District Court's decision created waves of public support and further awareness.

Demarcation of the coastal zone (coastal environment)

NOP 13 does not define a coastal zone in terms of distance from the shoreline. Instead, it provides a map specifying areas to which the plan's various protective rules apply. The seaward boundary of the plan is the extent of Israel's territorial waters. The landward boundaries vary according to what the planners considered as areas meriting protection, taking into account various constraints such as highways. Note that NOP 13 does not draw a line between urban and rural areas per se, and applies to urban areas as well, if designated on the map. The Plan classifies all land within its boundaries according to several categories, including beaches for bathing and recreation; beaches forming part of natural reserves; national parks; and rural land (Clause 8). In some areas the map does not extend much beyond the 100 m setback zone; in other areas, it extends a few kilometres.

The Coastal Law, on the other hand, contains a quantitative definition of the Coastal Environment (in Hebrew: *sviva hofit*), as follows:

> an area extending 300 metres inland, measured from the Mediterranean coastline…as well as the area measured from the Mediterranean coastline… seaward to the limit of the territorial waters and including, on land – surface and subsurface, and in the sea – the seabed and sub-bottom, as well as natural and landscape resources, natural and heritage assets, and antiquities.

Within this 300 m zone, development plans are subject to approval by the CPCE (coastal committee).

Definitions in NOP One

NOP One, in its Coastal Chapter (expected to receive final approval in 2020) adopts the Coastal Law definitions for both the shoreline and the Coastal Environment. The plan also introduces another definition and protective rules – the Coastal Hinterland, defined as land "bordering and adjacent to" the 100 m setback zone, with some "affinity" to the sea. This definition is clearly open to interpretation but is probably inspired by the maps included in NOP 13. Finally, NOP One differentiates between urban and non-urban land – an important new policy that will be further discussed. Thus, NOP One adds additional layers of protection for the coast to those found in current regulations, but also takes a more pragmatic stance by recognizing that controls over existing urban development should be somewhat relaxed.

Public land ownership on Israel's coasts

Israel has quite a unique land regime, which has some counterintuitive aspects when it comes to coastal areas. More than 90% of the land is owned by the State and two other national bodies. All national land is centrally managed by the Israel National Lands Authority (NLA). Israel is the only OECD member country with this type of land regime. Because this pattern is the result of historical events rather than outright nationalization, national ownership does not imply any particular land use or development rules and is not primarily intended to protect public goods or services: The Planning and Building Law applies equally to both national and private land. Much housing, commercial, and industrial use is located on national land, whereas some environmentally valuable areas may fall on privately owned land (Alterman, 2003). However, due to the historical evolution of property, it so happens that almost all non-urban land along the coast is national land because the dunes were historically regarded as undesirable and left underused. Within the older cities there is some private land, and even along the non-urban coast there are small pockets of private land – today highly desirable.

Beach zones do receive high protection through the Israel Real-Property Law (1969), which generally applies to both national and private land. Article 108 states that "land *beneath* the coastal waters" is national land. Article 107 upgrades the protection for any nationally or municipally owned land on the "beach" by turning it into "public-purpose land". Any change in this designation may be made only after ministerial permission – and this is rare. Notably, the "beach" is not defined in the Israel Lands Law or any other relevant legislation, but this has not proven to be a problem.

Coastal setback zone and permitted uses

As mentioned above, NOP 13 defines a setback zone of 100 m inland from the shoreline, in which development is restricted (NOP 13, Clause 12(4)). The Coastal Law has maintained this same setback zone, calling it "Shore Area" (*techum ha yam*). The Law also tightens restrictions on development. Restrictions in the setback zone apply irrespective of whether the land is publicly or privately owned. The only facilities permitted within the setback zone are bathing facilities, some tourism, natural reserves, ports, and agricultural land.

Prior to 2004, NOP 13 allowed the National Planning Board considerable discretion to permit exceptions within the 100 m zone. The wording is quite broad – "so long as the overall objectives of the Plan are taken into account". Even though the Coastal Law did not abolish the discretionary element, it made an important institutional change: By establishing the Coastal Planning Committee (CPCE), the Law in fact created a dedicated watchdog that took over the powers of the generalist National Planning Board. Any proposed development in areas covered by NOP 13 – not only the setback zone (except within plans approved before 1983) – must first be cleared by the CPCE. Municipalities, too, must approach the CPCE for any new developments, extensions to existing buildings, and redevelopments. Even the National Planning Board cannot override the Coastal Committee's decisions. Though the Law does grant the Committee discretion, in practice, the CPCE rarely approves development within the 100 m zone.

Land designated as beaches

Where NOP 13 designates zones as beaches for bathing or recreational uses, permitted uses include only sunbeds, umbrellas, sports facilities, medical services for the beach, picnic facilities, parking, and kiosks. Operators may obtain permits for such uses from the relevant local authorities. In practice, many kiosks erected on the beach years ago, when enforcement was lax, have (illegally) been developed into restaurants; a phenomenon we will discuss below under "compliance and enforcement". Although NOP 13 does not make an overall distinction between urban and non-urban beaches, in practice, beaches in urban areas are more developed than in non-urban areas, either because the permissions predate NOP 13 or because special permission has been granted by the National Board (or some illegal extensions may not yet have been demolished).

As one may have expected, the fact that NOP 13 covers some of the built-up areas of coastal cities – including major areas of Tel Aviv – has made the planning life of these cities difficult. Originally, under NOP 13, any change in existing structures with the coastal zone would have to receive clearance from the National Board and, since 2004, from the CPCE. In recent years, three urban conurbations have pressed for an amendment to NOP 13: Tel Aviv District (covering the greater Tel Aviv conurbation) and the cities of Haifa and Netanya have convinced the National Planning Board to amend NOP 13 so that they can grant planning permission for small-scale changes to the built environment. The cities also introduced clear siting rules for beach-related facilities (bathing, kiosks, etc.), including minimum distances from the shoreline. In addition, many more local authorities have introduced bylaws to facilitate day-to-day beach management. A most recent amendment to NOP 13 now requires that the installation of amenities on the beach will be in clusters, leaving an open and free beach between these clusters.

An innovation introduced in NOP One is a differentiation between urban and non-urban beaches:

- Urban beaches are open spaces on the coast which are used as meeting places for the enjoyment of the public – for recreation, sports, tourism, and similar uses. In addition, urban beaches are gateways to their respective cities, for those approaching by sea.
- Non-urban (open) beaches are intended for preservation of the environment and heritage. By means of the non-urban beaches, NOP One seeks to preserve a stretch of open spaces along the coast.

NOP One allows a greater variety of uses on urban beaches than non-urban ones, including clusters of kiosks, a promenade, and watersports facilities.

Development restrictions beyond the 100 m setback zone

Beyond the 100 m setback zone, the Coastal Law restricts development in the Coastal Environment (land within 300 m of the shoreline): Any proposed development or use change within this zone should be in accordance with the requirements of NOP 13 (or NOP One in future) and must receive approval from the Coastal Committee.

NOP One specifies that in the urban part of the Coastal Hinterland, clusters of more intensive uses may be permitted. These may include restaurants or other public uses that are related to the use of the coast for recreation, such as watersports facilities. In the non-urban parts of the Coastal Hinterland, development is more restricted in order to maintain open stretches along the coast. NOP One also introduces new procedures for approving any development. Any proposed (minor) construction in the setback zone or the Coastal Environment will have to be advertised to the public and a policy plan should be submitted to the CPCE for approval.

The problem with "grandfathered" plans/development rights

The Achilles heel of Israel's coastal protection is that in 1983, NOP 13 "grandfathered in" all plans approved prior to that date, including those with yet-unrealized development rights. Some of these were approved before 1983, other were approved in the 1990s or early 2000s, before the adoption of the Coastal Law, under the discretionary powers granted by the NOP to the National Planning Board.

So why is this still a problem today? Under Israeli planning law, plans do not expire after a set time period, but rather remain in force unless authorized planning bodies make a specific decision to abolish them. Such decisions are seldom taken because, under Israel's planning law, any reduction in development rights – and certainly cancellation of building rights altogether – will entail payment of hefty compensation for the full loss of value of the plot created by the reduction of development rights (Alterman, 2010).[4] In coastal areas, development rights have skyrocketing value.

According to a survey conducted by Adam Teva V'Din (a leading environmental NGO), there may still be 30 such unbuilt plans for projects in various locations along the coast (Adam Teva V'Din, n.d.). Most are for hotel or resort-related projects. Most of these are located on nationally owned land, and only a few on one of the few small pockets of private land. As noted, land ownership type does not matter much, but projects on national land entail extra steps of public tender (Alterman, 2003).

One may ask: Why were these plans and development rights approved in the first place? And why did the Israel Lands Authority issue tenders for development? The answer is that they reflected the public priorities of the time. In the 1970s and early 1980s, Israel's economy was still quite weak and coastal development was regarded as an important way of boosting the country's economy. Encouragement of the still-frail tourist sector by permitting hotels was viewed as especially desirable because it would bring in crucial foreign currency which the country was lacking at the time (unlike today). For all these reasons, when NOP 13 was debated, the planning authorities elected to leave the pre-existing approved plans intact. In subsequent years, as the norms of coastal protection gained greater weight in the public eye – and as Israel's economy stepped up considerably – these grandfathered plans and their developers became the key target of criticism by environmental NGOs and even the State Comptroller (Israel State Comptroller, 2013)

We also noted earlier that plans grandfathered in by the Coastal Law (2004) benefited from the more lenient delineation of the shoreline at 0.00 MSL, rather than 0.75 m above geodetic zero. When owners of built-up areas would ask for permission to extend the building or change its use, they benefited from the more lucrative interpretation.

Given Israel's short and highly pressured coastline and the few open coastal areas left for public use, even a few more hotel or resort projects, if realized, would indeed cause major disruptions to coastal preservation. However, revision of the legislation about compensation rights or about the lifespan of plans is unlikely – especially if applied retroactively. Given the constitutional anchoring of property rights (Basic Law: Human Dignity and Liberty, Clause 3), such a revision would probably have to be accompanied by a huge budgetary allocation (an unlikely priority), and many interim court actions.

Despite the serious legal and budgetary constraints, the combination of public protests, NGO actions, the growing awareness of the planning bodies, and court decisions is collectively gradually succeeding in stalling, derailing, and even reversing decisions on major projects. Each such project is a separate case, with a different trajectory. Two of the most prominent ones are worthy of a "zoom in": One project at Palmachim open beach quashed before it was built and the partial stalling of a high-profile urban hotel complex in Haifa.

The story of the palmachim non-urban beach – unrealized development rights

The Palmachim battle became a national emblem for effective grassroots environmental action. Palmachim is one of the few relatively pristine beaches remaining in Israel, within a short driving distance from the Greater Tel Aviv conurbation (Figure 15.3). Development of land on the dunes for a "resort village" of 350 units was approved by the planning authorities in 2000, a tender was held, and a contract with the Lands Authority was signed in 2004. The developers paid approximately $3 million USD (in current value) for 7 hectares of developable land. Alerted by NGOs, the State Comptroller dedicated a special report to Palmachim back in 2009. The report criticized the project but did not find a distinct legal problem. Nevertheless, it criticized the Lands Authority's haste in tendering the project – with only a 30 m setback – before the Coastal Law would come into force (Israel State Comptroller, 2009).

In September 2007, the District Planning Commission, relying on the Coastal Law, ordered the local commission to issue the permit only for land beyond the 100 m setback. Yet, the developers appealed to the National Planning Board, still believing they could convince it to use its discretionary powers for plans approved prior to the Law. In the meantime, in early

Figure 15.3 Palmachim Beach

Source: Yuvalr. CC BY-SA 3.0 license. Available at: https://commons.wikimedia.org/wiki/File:Palmachim_beach(6).jpg

2008, the developers obtained a temporary permit to fence off the project area, beyond the 100 m setback. Presumably, the project would have been lucrative even with this setback.

But then, the tide turned. A seventeen-year-old member of a nearby kibbutz, Adi Lustig, was shocked to see the freshly installed fencing and the bulldozers ready to go. Called "the savior of Israel's coastline" (Klein Leichman, 2013), she became a national environmental-protest icon when she quickly recruited hundreds of other young protestors and extensive media coverage.[5] Environmental NGOs now gained the support of the broad public. When the developers received a negative answer from the National Board and petitioned the Tel Aviv District Court, one of the NGOs joined as respondent. In *Palmachim Resort Village Corp. v. Central District Planning Board and Adam Teva V'Din*, the Court reinforced the National Board's decision, basing its ruling on the normative *spirit* of the Coastal Law in seeking to protect the publicly valuable coast (Administrative Petition 1772/08). Although the developers had not yet given up, this decision signalled the beginning of the end of the project.

In 2013, following a government (cabinet) decision to cancel the plan, the Nature and Parks Authority submitted a plan designating the entire Palmachim beach area for a national park. At first, the District Planning Commission held off approval in fear of the compensation claims to come (Frenkel, 2013). The new plan was finally approved in 2014, even though the compensation issue had not yet been resolved (Rinat, 2015). There are two types of compensation in this case: Against the Lands Authority, to reimburse the sum paid during the tender, and against the Local Planning commission, according to the Planning Law. The former potentially has monetary resources, if it so decides, but the Local Planning Commission does not.

On the compensation issue, the Palmachim case made another piece of history – less known to the public, but perhaps legally and financially the most important: Following further NGO pressure, in 2016 the Israel Lands Authority, the Ministry of Finance, and the Ministry of Environmental Protection reached an unprecedented agreement. The national bodies agreed to indemnify the local planning commission for any compensation claim won by the developer (Ministry of Environmental Protection, 2016). Understandably, for budget reasons, this is precisely the precedent that the national authorities had tried their best to avoid. The door may now be open for more cases of rolling back development rights for environmental purposes.

The story of the Haifa "Monster" hotels complex – how legal/planning perceptions changed on the go

The earliest urban-beach project challenged in the courts – all the way to the Supreme Court – was the Carmel Beach (*Hof HaCarmel*) Towers. Popularly known in Haifa as "the monster" (Koriel, 2018). This project's trajectory best symbolizes how publicly embedded norms are changing on the go, and how potent these have become, even in the face of one of the country's most influential development corporations.

The project's detailed plan was initially approved in 1978, before any national coastal regulations were in place. At the time, Haifa was desperate for economic development, and hotels with vacation housing (usually for foreign investors) were considered highly desirable. The relevant plot of land happens to be one of the few privately owned pockets along the coast (although, as we saw, this is only a minor factor). The property exchanged hands for hefty sums, until in the early 1990s, a prominent development company decided that timing was ripe to realize the development rights. The NGOs voiced objections, arguing that in the 1970s no environmental impact studies were conducted (nor required) and that the hotel encroaches into the 100 m setback zone. However, the national planning bodies did not, at the time, see a way of cancelling the development rights or imposing updated regulations retroactively. In the first stage, a huge structure was built, blocking access and views (refer back to Figure 15.2). There were development rights for five more buildings, and the developers' vision was to build them in stages.

But life for the developer became tougher and tougher as time passed, public awareness evolved, and the courts embraced the norms of sustainability, at times beyond the letter of the law. The developer was caught by surprise time after time.

The second building was challenged, and this led to a path-breaking Supreme Court decision (Civil Appeal 1054/98). Despite the Court's strong affirmation of the importance of coastal preservation norms, it did not see a way of stopping the construction of the second tower altogether. Yet the Court did make a precedential ruling in which it defined the "vacation housing" which could be allowed under NOP 13. The court ruled that the apartments in that category could not be used for permanent housing and must enter a pool of rental vacation apartments for at least six months a year. This ruling drastically changed the economics of all such projects in Israel, including retroactively.[6]

The Hof HaCarmel corporation – headed by Israel's most famous developer – tried for several years to receive building permits for the remaining four buildings, exhausting all planning and appeal procedures. Finally, aware that norms may have changed, the developer offered to finance reclamation of a strip of land from the sea in order to create a full 100 m setback. However, as this book was going to press, even that offer was rejected by the planning bodies. To stave off unbearable compensation claims, the Israel Lands Authority and the developer are now negotiating about some alternative (less desirable) site. The story of Hof HaCarmel is likely to deter other initiatives of this kind.

Other approved plans still wait in line, with various trajectories for the future, but their prospects have changed. Even the financial constraints posed by the law's compensation duty – previously regarded as the Iron Wall – have proved to be partially surmountable.

Right of public access

In reviewing accessibility of Israel's coasts in law and practice, we divide our discussion into several aspects of accessibility: Horizontal accessibility (along the coast); vertical accessibility (to the coast); accessibility for people with disabilities; accessibility of views of the coast; and social justice in accessibility.

Horizontal accessibility – for the general public and people with disabilities

The Coastal Law 2004 introduced a requirement for right of access along the beach. Specifically, the Law requires an open pedestrian right of way along "the entire length of the beach" (Article 5). It does not specify the required width of the right-of-way. NOP One follows this principle, requiring free access along the beach, explicitly also including requirements for accessibility for people with disabilities. In practice, the width of the pedestrian access way is set according to the physical conditions of the beach. Where possible, beach amenities are to be placed further away from the shore in order to leave a relatively wide sandy beach open for access and public use.

Beyond construction that requires permission by planning bodies, the municipalities are responsible for regulating the amenities to be allowed on the beach. This includes paving and paths, permitted places for overnight camping, and the like. Many coastal cities have introduced paved promenades along the beach to allow the public to walk or cycle relatively close to the shoreline. A few cities located along coastal cliffs have sought permission to build an elevator down to the beach.

But developments of this type can also be controversial and in recent years have led to important court decisions where the pro-preservation norms have clashed with pro-accessibility norms, especially for people with disabilities. For example, in the case of the vibrant Tel Aviv beach, a coalition of NGOs and citizens petitioned the Tel Aviv-Jaffa District Administrative Court in opposition to works to upgrade the popular beach promenade to facilitate better access, including for people with disabilities (Administrative Petition 34039-05-13). In 2014, in a long and detailed decision with extensive citations about the normative value of coastal preservation for future generations, the Court dismissed the petition. The Court stressed that an important counterbalancing consideration is *distributive justice*. This norm calls for providing good accessibility and comfort in urban beaches, especially for people with disabilities. The Court also noted that the environmental impact assessment did not show any negative impact on sand replenishment. This court decisions protects access to the disabled without any explicit legislative basis. Neither NOP 13 nor the Coastal Law states this obligation explicitly. However, the new NOP One now stipulates that public access – both horizontal and vertical – should take special account of people with disabilities.

There are some exemptions from the rule of open access. The Coastal Law and NOP 13 allow for fencing, but only if permitted through a statutory plan or permit. Permission is usually granted only for major infrastructure installations. These include, as one would expect, defence, ports, power stations, and desalination plants, but also nature reserves or national parks. Due to Israel's small land size and the dependence of most of these installations on the Mediterranean coast, they do not leave long stretches of contiguous beach access. Today, planning bodies tend to require public access wherever possible.

Accessibility can also be hampered by vehicles driving on the beach. These can be dangerous and disruptive. For many years, owners of Jeep-like vehicles would drive along crowded sandy beaches or damage sandy cliffs with moderate slopes. As such, the Coastal Law (2004) introduced a legal prohibition against driving vehicles on the beach (Article 4A(a)). Enforcement of this vehicle restriction was not easy, often encountering conflicts. But, after several years of concerted enforcement and education, the use of such vehicles has become rare. If someone still disobeys, beachgoers are likely to report them.

Vertical accessibility

Vertical accessibility is not expressly required by NOP 13 or by the Coastal Law. However, awareness of this issue has risen since these plans were approved. In urban areas, the ongoing policy of the CPCE is to require clustering and avoid sprawl (Alterman et al., 2016).[7] Clusters allow interim space for access to the beach. Several local governments have incorporated rules for vertical footbath access in local plans. NOP One will now explicitly require vertical access from the Coastal Hinterland to the beach.

In non-urban areas, the CPCE occasionally requires that the relevant landowners create and pave a path to the beach. There are cases where the National Planning Appeals Committee required vertical access even when the CPCE did not.[8] Such was the case in 2006, when the local planning commission of Hof HaSharon – a quasi-rural area just north of Tel Aviv – initiated a detailed plan to extend an existing high-end villa development (known as Arsuf) located right on the coast. Despite an objection by the Green Party (an NGO), the plan was approved by the CPCE, which argued that the extension would not damage the coastal zone. The Green Party appealed this decision to the National Appeals Committee, which left the extension intact but accepted the NGO's argument that there must be a vertical public path leading to the shore as a condition for issuing a building permit. This decision had special importance because Arsuf is a notorious example of repeated attempts to illegally gate public access to the beach.

View protection

Accessibility may also refer to open view of the sea. NOP 13 and the Coastal Law do not explicitly prevent projects that obstruct the sea view. However, this consideration too is taken into account by the CPCE when it reviews proposed plans. A concrete step forward is taken by NOP One. Under that regulation, every proposed plan (building project) will be required to present an analysis of view lines to the sea. This rule will apply in both urban and rural areas, with different provisions for each category.

The issue of views could, at times, have major implications for real estate development. In 2019, the CPCE and National Planning Appeals Committee reached a dramatic decision on the basis of view protection: They did not approve a long-awaited initiative by Tel Aviv-Jaffa Municipality to finally resurrect the eyesore "Atarim" public elevated plaza and (by now abandoned) shops constructed in the 1960s, when such projects were "the last word" in urban design. Over time, the site had deteriorated into a public menace located right on the most intensively used and built-up urban beach (Figure 15.4). In order to convince the owners sitting on this extremely high-value location to cooperate, the City proposal to demolish the existing structures and build three 40-storey towers for mixed use, including commerce, hotels, and – controversially – housing (which would likely be purchased only by the extremely wealthy, including overseas investors). The project, which represented a major diversion from the previous plan, was approved not only by the Local Planning Commission, but also by the Tel

Figure 15.4 Atarim Square, Tel Aviv (left – view from within the square; right – aerial view from the sea)

Sources: Dr. Avishai Teicher CC BY 2.5 license. Available at: https://commons.wikimedia.org/wiki/File:PikiWiki_Israel_45060_Atarim_square.JPG (left) and Ron Naveh CC BY-SA 4.0 license. Available at: https://commons.wikimedia.org/wiki/File:Tel_Aviv_Marina_aerial_photo.jpg (right)

Aviv District Planning Commission, composed largely of central government representatives. Tel Aviv Municipality had already budgeted for the significant public investment, through an anticipated steep increase in local taxes.

Then came the unanticipated blow. According to the Coastal Law, such a diversion from the former plan requires clearance by the CPCE (Cohen & Melnitzki, 2019). Citing the importance of preserving an open view to the sea, the CPCE partially overruled the District Commission's decision. It cut the project down to three 25-storey towers and did not approve any of the highly lucrative housing to be mixed with commercial and hotel uses. The developers and Tel Aviv Municipality appealed this decision to the National Planning Appeals Committee, which upheld it regarding the height limitations but reversed the decision regarding housing, which would be permitted alongside commercial and hotel uses (Cohen, 2019). Since housing within the setback zone is a red flag for NGOs but important for the economic feasibility of such major projects, we conjecture that this case will find its route to the High Court of Justice.

Social justice in accessibility – the debate about financial charges

The main barrier to social justice in accessibility of Israeli beaches is entrance fees. As discussed in our introduction, Israeli beaches are highly valued by all sectors of the population as integral recreation venues. As early as 1959, a private citizen refused to pay entrance fees for access to the beach and the topic reached the Knesset (Rinat, 2016). In 1964, the Sea-Bathing Law was enacted. This law restricts municipal authorities from charging entrance fees for beach services (Article 6); they may charge fees only for beaches which have special amenities, beyond basic lifeguard services and running water. Although the Sea-Bathing law empowers the planning bodies to approve fencing, such permission is rarely granted.

But as public expectations of enhanced services and amenities increased, local governments began charging fees within the foggy scope of "special amenities" to finance beach maintenance. Following years of strong public criticism and squabbling between government levels, in 2005, Adam Teva V'Din petitioned the High Court of Justice on this matter. In *Adam Teva V'Din v The Minster of Interior et al.* (Administrative Petition 5824/05), the Court once again reiterated the norms that the beaches should be free and open to the public. The decision clarified the right to free access and services, but the burden remained with the municipalities. This ruling thus affected smaller, rural municipalities more than the larger ones. Urban beaches deliver higher tax revenues from ancillary commercial facilities, whereas rural beaches do not have the same extent of facilities. After years of public pressure and more squabbling, the national government announced in 2016 that it will share the costs of beach maintenance (Lior et al., 2016). This policy is being phased in.

At the same time, in their attempt to make ends meet, several smaller municipalities have established a side business of renting out beach spots for private events (such as weddings or company get-togethers). Until very recently, the legality of this practice was in the grey zone. The operators of such "concessions" usually do not close off horizontal beach access, nor necessarily disrupt vertical access. Both NOP 13 and the Coastal Law are silent on this issue. Nevertheless, this practice is increasingly being perceived by planning bodies as anathema to the social, cultural, and public function of Israeli beaches, and a symbol of social division.

Beaches in Israel have traditionally been the most vernacular type of recreation accessible to all. The National Enforcement Authority for Planning and Land Laws has for some years been determined to halt such practices. It draws (tentative) legal authority from a 2005 decision by the South District Administrative Court pertaining to Nitzanim Beach. The court noted that there are alternative interpretations of what the law permits, and thus ruled that the more prohibitive approach adopted in that case by the South District Planning Commission was legal (Administrative Petition 269/02). The enforcement authority's view that private commercial use is illegal has not received solid legal affirmation, but NOP One will explicitly forbid any "private" events of any kind. That regulation does allow fencing off part of the beach for public events, such as festivals, as long as reasonable physical access is assured. Without awaiting NOP One's approval, a lower court ruled, in September 2019, that the use of the beach for any private commercial events is illegal. However, we foresee further legal conflicts because the distinction between "private" and "public" is not defined.

There is another head-on conflict emerging between new forms of what might be called "beach culture" and the regulatory bodies. A recent trend in beach going is the erection of temporary "gazebos" by individual families or groups of friends. These structures are equipped not only with tables and chairs but also with kitchen facilities, sometimes even electric ovens (Figure 15.5). Some families or groups stay overnight – a practice that the enforcement authorities regard as the most offensive. There is a growing number of private businesses renting out such facilities. The line between individual or cultural habits and legitimate public use is not clear. These gazebos are an eyesore and may create barriers to pedestrian mobility on the beaches. However, due to Israel's land scarcity, there are very few alternative sites for similar uses such as caravans or camping trailers. The gazebos have not yet been challenged in court.

Compliance and enforcement

Compared with some of the other countries in this book, Israeli coasts do not have many totally illegal structures without any building permits. There are many violations, but they are usually at a smaller scale. Thanks to a combination of historic, geographic, and economic circumstances, Israel has been spared the phenomenon of popular secondary homes along the coast (or anywhere else). As seen in the other chapters in this book, summer homes can be a magnet for illegality (big or small, depending on the country). Infringements of planning law in Israel tend to be more subtle. Until recently, there was a widespread phenomenon of small kiosks with permits that somehow "grew" gradually through illegal extensions, some becoming restaurants and, in the most infamous case, at Lido Beach in Ashdod, even a four-storey

Figure 15.5 Large "gazebo" used for private recreation on the beach

Source: Rachelle Alterman

building (Figure 15.6). In recent years, the number of new illegal extensions or changes of use has been much reduced due to improved monitoring and enforcement. The major challenge is existing structures and their use. A related issue is beach facilities that gradually "creep" closer to the shoreline.

Although there is not a dedicated enforcement unit for the coast alone, coastal enforcement is a high priority of all enforcement agencies. Enforcement powers on the coast are grounded both in the Planning and Building Law and the Coastal Law. The general responsibility for enforcement of construction and land use is legally shared by all three tiers of the planning administration (local, district-level, and national). This also applies to the coastal environment. Land within the 100 m setback zone (if nationally owned) is additionally under the responsibility of the Lands Authority. In addition, the Ministry of Justice has established a dedicated unit for coordinating the scores of (outsourced) prosecutors for land and planning law violations. The Ministry of Environmental Protection, too, has an enforcement unit, for violations of environmental regulations. Thus, at the national level, there are four agencies involved in enforcement along the coast.

Originally, the Planning and Building Law placed all planning enforcement responsibility in the hands of the local planning commissions. These fell far short of the challenge, so the district level was conferred parallel powers. That did not suffice either; and in 1988, a special enforcement unit was established within the National Planning Administration.[9] Under this arrangement, the district and national levels can step in when the local level is recalcitrant or ineffective (Article 207 of the Planning and Building Law). But even this upscaling proved insufficient to deal with the many infringements of planning law – including in the coastal

Figure 15.6 Illegal "kiosk" extension at Lido Beach, Ashdod (before partial demolition)

Source: Photographer Boaz Raanan

zone. One obstacle was that offenders have many possibilities to appeal enforcement actions and, further, that the courts have previously granted offenders time to try to convince the planning bodies to legalize the offence, potentially dragging the issue on for years. Thus, very few demolitions were carried out until the late 2010s.

In 2017, a major revision of the Planning Law (Amendment 116) introduced what is effectively a new regime of enforcement. Enforcement personnel at all three tiers (local, district-level, national) were provided new, potent instruments that can (it is hoped) reduce the rush to the courts. Enforcement agents can now issue not only stop orders but also administrative demolition orders, as well as hefty fines. Before the amendment, most demolition orders had to be issued by the court. Under Amendment 116, offences on land in the coastal zone are high on the list of "violations of national importance", which means they could be categorized as criminal offences and bear higher fines. The catch is that these enhanced powers apply mostly to relatively recent construction carried out in recent months. For older violations, as in the case of the many "creeping" restaurants, a court order is still necessary. Interviews with enforcement agents conducted by Calor and Alterman (2017) confirmed that coastal areas do receive very high priority, not only by the national authorities but also by local enforcement personnel. In addition, within the coastal zone, the rate of demolitions has increased in recent years. Tougher enforcement actions are being taken, including for the notorious "kiosk"

Figure 15.7 "Kiosk" at Lido Beach, Ashdod, after illegal extension demolished

Source: Photographer Boaz Raanan

turned four-storey building, mentioned above, which was issued a demolition order, upheld by the courts, for all but the ground floor (Waizman, 2018) – and the demolition has since taken place (Figure 15.7).

Climate change awareness and special environmental issues

In general, climate change is only beginning to capture public attention in Israel (perhaps because the public agenda is occupied by geopolitical and security issues). However, government professionals, researchers, and the environmental NGOs are well aware. This concern is now expressed in NOP One, where climate change awareness is explicitly mentioned as one of the plan's objectives. Although climate change concerns can arguably be found in the Coastal Law and NOP 13 as well (in their discussions of environmental sustainability), the explicit mention of climate change represents progress. It will be interesting to follow how quickly relevant considerations find their way into concrete decisions by the relevant planning bodies and the courts. One can surmise with high certainty that citizen activist and NGOs will soon be calling upon this rationale in the many battles to come on coastal protection. One should, however, mention that sea level rise is relatively slow at the eastern shores of the Mediterranean.

Coordination in coastal zone management

Israel is not unique in that coordination across the different levels of government (vertical coordination) and across various authorities at each level (horizontal coordination) is always a challenge. As mentioned above, the country has a relatively centralized governance system, with much power assigned to the national level. Is this structure helpful for better coordination? Possibly, the national Committee for Protection of the Coastal Environment (CPCE) can be seen as a positive model of horizontal coordination in coastal decision-making, as committee members include representatives from several relevant government ministries, as well as a representative of the union of environmental NGOs, a marine academic expert, and a marine transport expert. Nevertheless, there is no single coastal authority able to amalgamate the duties and actions of the many national agencies with coast-related responsibilities.

A recent initiative which has probably made an indirect positive contribution towards horizontal coordination among national agencies is the new Israeli Marine Spatial Plan that was recently completed. The body overseeing this plan is the National Planning Board, thus the emerging marine spatial policy will be strongly linked to land planning policies. This linkage facilitates an integrated approach to terrestrial and marine spatial planning. The preparation of the new national plan has seen an unprecedented level of coordination between the broadest range of government, quasi-government, academic bodies, and NGOs ever convened for a national planning initiative.

At the municipal level, the country's "best practice" city – Tel Aviv-Yafo – has innovated in mechanisms of internal coordination for managing its beach assets. Instead of having many municipal departments involved in coastal issues, Tel Aviv created a municipal corporation that integrates most of the city's regulations and initiatives concerning its coast. As early as 1968, it founded a joint state-municipal corporation (together with the Ministry of Tourism) ("Atarim" – "sites"). The purpose was to develop the city's tourist attractions, the beach being amongst the major attractions. In 2016, Tel Aviv-Yafo municipality bought the national government's shares and thus has full control of its beach assets. Atarim is in charge of beach concessions and other local issues.

Haifa Municipality – the second largest city along the coast – has also taken some steps towards internal coordination, though more modest in scope than Tel Aviv and with an impetus from the outside: Haifa was a partner in the international Mare Nostrum research project financed by the EU (and headed by Alterman; Alterman et al., 2016). With this stimulus, Haifa took upon itself to create, for the first time, an internal interdepartmental forum to coordinate the various coast-related duties of each of many municipal departments.

So far, we have addressed horizontal coordination – at both the national and the local levels. Let us now look at the vertical coordination challenges from the municipal point of view upwards. In the absence of a national comprehensive coastal authority, each city faces vertical coordination challenges alone, interfacing with a plethora of national-level agencies. We will refer to two examples of major cities: Tel Aviv and Haifa.

The Tel Aviv professionals we interviewed[10] enumerate at least twelve such agencies, among them the Ministries of Finance (where the National Planning Administration currently resides), Environmental Protection, Transportation, Tourism, Energy and Water Resources, Defence, and Agriculture and, of course, the Israel Lands Authority. We have not undertaken an empirical assessment of the relative effectiveness of Tel Aviv compared with other cities in the vertical coordination tasks, though one can conjecture that Tel Aviv's status and resources give it some advantages. A municipality such as Haifa probably contends with more difficulties, and Haifa's challenges are especially complex, as the city is home to one of Israel's two major international ports. One could only surmise the coordinative capacities of the smaller urban municipalities and regional (rural) authorities.

Good news for both horizontal (cross-municipal) and vertical coordination may be coming from a recent bottom-up initiative for concerted inter-municipal action. Led by Tel Aviv-Yafo, in August 2015 a voluntary multi-municipal forum was initiated. The Federation of Local Authorities, the Federation of Regional Councils, and the Institute for Local Government (an academic research arm of Tel Aviv University) launched the Coastal Management Forum, comprising all twenty coastal municipalities in Israel – both urban and rural. After some years of slow progress, in 2019, the Forum began work on a policy paper for ICZM in Israel, in cooperation with Tel Aviv University, the relevant national level ministries, and the major environmental NGOs. The academic leaders of this project[11] are well aware of the Barcelona ICZM Protocol (rarely noted by any other Israeli body) and plan to incorporate it into their proposed policy.

Another development is an informal forum for horizontal coordination, formed in 2013, to coordinate the enforcement and legal prosecutor actions formally dispersed among the four national-level agencies responsible for land-related and environmental enforcement.[12] This body has been operating regularly and helps to coordinate the policies and activities of the four agencies. It provides a means to deliver government actions in an area where sensitive and often painful legal-economic issues – at times with social impact – are encountered every day.

Neither vertical nor horizontal intuitional coordination is ever achievable in full. The informal attempts to assuage the built-in cleavages are worth following.

Public participation

In Israel, formal legal requirements for public participation and information are rather lean. Happily, on this issue too, civil-society action, growing public awareness, and a few path-breaking court decisions have gradually expanded participation practices. However, legislation is lagging.

The main procedure for involving the public, mandated by the Planning and Building Law, is the right to submit an "objection" to district or local plans (Articles 89, 100). The Law grants this right to any interested party that sees itself as affected by the proposed plan deposited for public review for a preset period of time. In recent years, civil society in many cities has been successfully pressing for more involvement of the public in earlier stages, well beyond the formal right to object.

Unsuccessful objections may be appealed before at least one, often two or three appeals echelons. Legal standing before the courts is interpreted very broadly (Alterman, 2020). This also applies to decisions by the CPCE. These can be appealed before the National Planning Appeals Committee. All these layers of opportunities are mixed news: Good access to justice on the one hand, but very lengthy procedures on the other hand. Once the appeal procedures have been exhausted, Israeli law grants unrestricted right to submit a petition to the relevant district administrative court. There is also unlimited right to appeal to the Supreme Court. Petitions against state-level institutions can sometimes be brought directly before the High Court of Justice.

Formally, to date, coastal planning decisions have come under the same public participation obligations and rights as any other planning matter. But the special sizzling public-legal arena that characterizes coastal preservation issues has now led to a surprising innovation in participation requirements for the coastal zone, to be included in NOP One. This is the first time, in any statutory planning procedure in Israeli history, that local planning commissions will be assigned an active *legal* duty to reach out to the public with information and participation at an earlier stage of plan preparation, not only during the usual "plan deposit" stage. It would be a fascinating research project to evaluate how these new duties will be interpreted by the many local and district planning bodies involved in coastal issues.

Even without this innovation, we have seen how participation in coastal issues has received a special and unprecedented boost from the courts. In the case of the refurbishment of the Tel Aviv beach promenade, the District Administrative Court ordered the municipality to carry out extra public participation actions, even though these have no anchoring whatsoever in written legislation. Tel Aviv obeyed this requirement, even though it could have appealed the decision. Such "judge-made law" reflects rising public awareness and will likely further influence decision-makers in planning, well beyond coastal issues.

Fiscal aspects

Land expropriation for coastal preservation has not been exercised in Israel and is unlikely to come up, even though legally it may be possible. As elsewhere, this strategy does not come up because it is exceedingly expensive and will likely encounter opposition and drawn-out legal processes.

The major fiscal challenges affecting coastal management in Israel arise from the statutory right of landholders to demand full compensation in cases where planning decisions cause decline in property values. Israel is unique in this respect among the countries represented in this book. This "elephant in the room" and its various manifestations has been discussed above, especially in the context of the "grandfathered" plans where cancellation of development rights entails hefty compensation even if they have not been realized for many years. The issue also came up as we discussed current projects designed to be constructed in phases: The first stages, which had been approved according to conceptions valid at the time, were indeed constructed, but subsequent phases have been "caught" by the deeply altered views of coastal zone preservation. There are no elegant solutions to this lock-in, and each case is a drama with its own script, where the players are the developer, NGOs, the planning bodies, and the courts. Since policies have been rapidly changing in recent years, at present, each script has an unforeseen ending. It is difficult to guess whether there will be a major legislative change (which seems unlikely) or more ad hoc solutions.

Another fiscal aspect unique to Israel (within this book) is the well-established betterment levy. The Planning and Building Law mandates that every local planning decision that uplifts the value of the specific property entails payment to the municipality of a betterment levy of 50% of the increment. At first glance, this may seem to be the reverse of the compensation requirement that would arise if any "grandfathered" plans were to be amended. In fact, the income from the betterment levy is hardly ever a source for paying compensation because the two financial elements are not linked in sum, timing, or use. Betterment levies are a general municipal income source, rather than an earmarked possible-future-compensation fund (Alterman, 2012).

The major fiscal conflict between local and national government is about division of responsibilities for maintenance of the popular non-urban beaches. The usually budget-tight regional authorities are responsible for maintaining beaches that serve the entire nation – much beyond their own tax-paying population. As discussed earlier, this high-profile issue has been entangled within the issue of accessibility: May local governments charge entrance fees? Once again, public protest and awareness have recently succeeded in pushing the national government to chip in.

Overall assessment

We have saved for last the story of how the 2004 Coastal Perseveration Law was enacted. This was, and may still be, the most significant achievement of the environmental movement in Israel.[13] The government had no intention of proposing a bill on this topic. The prevailing institutional view was that coastal preservation is a matter for the planning bodies; if there is a need to improve or change policies, then the National Planning Board has all the necessary powers. This is indeed legally true. However, by the latter 1990s, environmental NGOs came to the conclusion that NOP 13 and the National Planning Board's policies are insufficient to halt the parade of coastal projects that managed to receive approval for perceived inappropriate uses, such as "vacation apartments" rather than real hotels. The two dozen government representatives that compose the National Board, with only a few non-government members, do not have enough political will or clout to fight the developers and local governments (and, sometimes, the Israel Lands Authority).

So in 1998, the NGOs (with the backdoor help of the Ministry of the Environment) took a daring decision: To bypass the Planning and Building Law through a new law dedicated to the planning and management of the coast. The NGOs lobbied Knesset members and gradually managed to align over twenty MKs, from both the governing coalition and the opposition, willing to sign as co-sponsors of a private bill. As the public momentum grew, the Government decided to avoid the embarrassment of opposing a bill with so many supporters (even though it had the majority to defeat it). The bill was reclassified as a Governmental bill, thus simplifying the parliamentary legislative process and assuring its passage.

Initially, the bill was criticized by some members of the National Planning Board.[14] They saw it as a dangerous precedent where direct land planning rules (the quantitative setback line and the hinterland) were imposed by primary legislation rather than by a statutory plan approved by the Board. In retrospect, it is clear that the adoption of the Coastal Law in 2004 opened a new era not only in coastal preservation but also in the role of Israeli civil society, in synergy with cases of judge-made law.

Notes

1. NOP One is an important innovation in Israeli statutory planning, both in regulatory efficiency and, one might say, even in planning theory terms: Prepared by one of Israel's leading planners – Moti Kaplan – the new national plan amalgamates most of the 40 national sectoral plans and countless amendments into a single, comprehensive document, resolving conflicts and simplifying procedures. The entire set of land-use and building regulations is rewritten in simplified, non-legal language, demonstrating that even statutory planning can become "communicative planning". The plan came into force in early 2020.
2. Conversations in 2013–2014 with Dr. Rachel Adam of the Israeli Ministry of Environmental Protection, who participated in the Israel delegation, and in 2019 with Attorney Dan Zafrir, who was at the Ministry at that time.
3. Interpretation of 0.00 MSL emerged from Supreme Court Administrative Appeal 6732/13 Guetta v The District Planning Board.
4. See Alterman (2010) for comparative analysis of compensation rights across 14 states.
5. Mostly in Hebrew. For English-language media, see Rinat (2008) and Green (2008).

6. For example, further decisions based on the original ruling led to hundreds of buyers of housing units in the "Marina" projects along the Herzliya beach abutting Tel Aviv learning that the apartments they had purchased as residential must be rented out for tourist accommodation for a good part of the year. The value of these apartments plummeted.

7. Comments about CPCE's practice are partially based on Rachelle Alterman's period of membership on the Board of Appeals of the National Planning Commission, which hears appeals over a range of planning decisions, including those of the CPCE.

8. Planning appeals committees are the address for both the initiators of plans and third parties to request administrative review of planning decisions. There are national, regional, and district-level committees.

9. This evolution is summarized in the 2013 Guidance Note of the State Attorney General on Planning Enforcement, number 8.1101, available at: https://www.gov.il/BlobFolder/policy/guidance_of_the_attorney_general/he/guidance_of_the_attorney_general.pdf

10. Interview conducted in 2016 with Suzana Kreimer, Strategy Development Director, Atarim.

11. Dr. Orli Ronen is a prominent expert in environmental research and action, head of the Urban Sustainability Lab at the Porter School at Tel Aviv University. Mr. Ophir Pines-Pass is the head of the Tel Aviv University Institute for Local Government. Based on interviews in September and December 2019.

12. Interview (2014) by the authors with Attorney Amit Ofek, the current deputy head of the State Enforcement Unit for Land-Related violations, a department in the State Attorney's office.

13. The information about the process that led to the enactment of the Coastal Law is based on Rachelle Alterman's first-hand involvement in the process. In 2000, she was invited by the Chair of the Knesset Committee for Internal and Environmental Affairs to serve as a consultant in evaluating and preparing the Coastal Bill for possible adoption. This appointment did not materialize because shortly after, the Knesset established an in-house Information and Research Center which could fulfil the need. (To the best of our knowledge, no comparative research was carried out.) Because of this request, Alterman had access to the background materials surrounding the Coastal Bill.

14. Based on first-hand knowledge on the part of Rachelle Alterman, who was a member of the National Planning Board at the time, as a representative of the Technion University (one of the statutory non-governmental members).

References

Adam Teva V'Din. (n.d.). Hofim [Coasts]. Available at: https://www.adamteva.org.il/public-space/beaches/ [Accessed September 2019]

Alfasi, N. (2009). Can planning protect the public interest? The challenge of coastal planning in Israel. *Geography Research Forum* 29, 83–102.

Alterman, R. (2001). *National-Level Planning in Democratic Countries: An International Comparison of City and Regional Policy-Making*. Liverpool University Press.

— (2003). The land of leaseholds: Israel's extensive public land ownership in an era of privatization. Chapter 6 in: C. B. Steven, & H. Yu Hung (Eds.), *Leasing Public Land: Policy Debates and International Experiences* (pp. 115–150). Cambridge, MA: The Lincoln Institute of Land Policy.

— (Ed.). (2010). *Takings International: A Comparative Perspective on Land Use Regulations and Compensation Rights*. American Bar Association Publishers.

— (2012). Land use regulations and property values: The 'Windfalls Capture' idea revisited. In N. Brooks, K. Donaghy, & G.-J. Knaap (Eds.), *The Oxford Handbook of Urban Economics and Planning* (pp. 755–786).

— (2020, forthcoming). Planning law in Israe. In R. Alterman (Ed.), *Routledge Compendium on Comparative Planning Law*.

Alterman, R., Pellach, C., & Carmon, D. (2016). *MARE NOSTRUM PROJECT Final Report: Legal-Institutional Instruments for Integrated Coastal Zone Management (ICZM) in the Mediterranean.* Available at: http://marenostrumproject.eu/wp-content/uploads/2014/02/Mare_Nostrum_Project_Final_Report.pdf

Calor, I., & Alterman, R. (2017). When enforcement fails: Comparative analysis of the legal and planning responses to non-compliant development in two advanced-economy countries. *International Journal of Law in the Built Environment* 9 (3), 207–239.

Cohen, A. (2019). [A blow for developers of a mega plan in Tel Aviv's Atarim Plaza: They will not be permitted to build 40-storey towers] (in Hebrew). *The Marker*, 31 July. Available at: https://www.the-marker.com/realestate/1.7608427

Cohen, A., & Melnitzki, G. (2019). [Towers are up in the air: The National Planning Board has not made a determination on the Atarim Plaza] (in Hebrew). *The Marker*, 13 June. Available at: https://www.themarker.com/realestate/1.7366859

Frenkel, B. (2013). [Palmachim Beach is not yet saved] (in Hebrew). *YNET*, 11 February 2013. Available at: https://www.ynet.co.il/articles/0,7340,L-4343588,00.html

Green, M. (2008). The battle for Israel's Palmachin Beach. *Green Prophet*, 17 February. Available at: https://www.greenprophet.com/2008/02/battle-beach-palmachim-israel/

Israel State Comptroller. (2009). [Development of a Tourist Resort at Hof Palmachim. Jerusalem] (in Hebrew). 18 November. Available at: https://www.mevaker.gov.il/he/Reports/Report_169/bec5241b-1288-48b0-8191-5e305c602050/6292.pdf

— (2013). [Coastal Environment] (in Hebrew). Annual Report 2012. pp. 435–456. Available at: https://www.mevaker.gov.il/sites/DigitalLibrary/Documents/63c/2013-63c-206-SvivaChofit.pdf

Klein Leichman, A. (2013). The savior of Israel's endangered coastline. *Israel 21C*, 5 February. Available at: https://www.israel21c.org/the-savior-of-israels-endangered-coastline/

Koriel, I. (2018). [Drying the sea: This is how the Carmel Beach Towers are being re-planned] (in Hebrew). *YNET*, 13 September. Available at: https://www.ynet.co.il/articles/0,7340,L-5348985,00.html

Lior, I., Spiegel, N., & Ben Zikri, A. (2016). Entry fees at 10 Israeli public beaches to be eliminated. *Haaretz*, 15 March. Available at: http://www.haaretz.com/israel-news/.premium-1.709080

Ministry of Environmental Protection. (2016). [Palmachim Beach Remains in the Public's hands] (in Hebrew). Press release. Available at: http://www.sviva.gov.il/InfoServices/NewsAndEvents/MessageDoverAndNews/Pages/2016/January2016/Palmachim-Beach-Public-Park.aspx

Rinat, Z. (2008). Who stole my beach? *Haaretz*, 17 March. Available at: https://www.haaretz.com/1.5004329

— (2015). Palmachim Beach national park plan may run aground. *Haaretz*, 23 December. Available at: http://www.haaretz.com/israel-news/science/.premium-1.693303

— (2016). Thanks to this man, you don't have to pay to go to the beach in Israel. *Haaretz*, 27 May. Available at: http://www.haaretz.com/israel-news/.premium-1.721599

UNEP. (2001). *MAP CAMP Project "Israel": Final Integrated Report and Selected Documents*. MAP Technical Report Series No. 134. Part of United Nations Environment Programme Mediterranean Action Plan.

Waizman, M. (2018). [The famous building at Lido Beach will be partially demolished according to a court order] (in Hebrew). *Kan Darom Ashdod*, 12 September. Available at: https://www.kan-ashdod.co.il/law/39367

World Factbook. (n.d.). Israel. Available at: https://www.cia.gov/library/publications/the-world-factbook/geos/is.html [Accessed July 2020]

Legislation and statutory plans (Hebrew; listed chronologically)

Sea-Bathing Law 1964
Planning and Building Law 1965 – as amended
Israel Lands Law 1969 – as amended
National Outline Plan (NOP) 13, 1983 – as amended
Basic Law: Human Dignity and Liberty 1992 (Israel). Available in English at: https://www.knesset.gov.il/laws/special/eng/basic3_eng.htm
Coastal Law (Protection of the Coastal Environment) 2004
National Outline Plan (NOP) One 2020

Court and Appeal Committee Cases

Civil Appeal 1054/98 (Supreme court). *Hof HaCarmel Resort and Tourism Corporation v. Adam Teva V'Din et al.* Decision dated 4 January 2002.

Administrative Petition 269/02 (South district court) *The Society for the Protection of Nature in Israel v. Shikmim Local Board et al.* Decision dated 1 February 2004.

Administrative Petition 5824/05 (High Court of Justice) *Adam Teva V'Din v The Minster of Interior et al.* Decision Dated 10 December 2009.

Administrative Petition 1772/08 (Tel Aviv-Jaffa District court) *Palmachim Resort Village Corp. v. Central District Planning Board and Adam Veva V'Din (NGO).* Decision dated 7 April 2009.

Administrative Petition 34039-05-13 (Tel Aviv-Jaffa District Court) *The Green Party v Atarim et al.* Decision Dated 17 November 2014.

Administrative Appeal 6732/13 (Supreme Court). *Guetta v. District Planning Board et al.* Decision dated 1 February 2015.

Administrative Petition 27857-04-14 (Tel Aviv-Jaffa District Court) The *Forum for Saving the Beach v. City of Bat Yam Planning Board and the National Planning Board.* Decision dated 24 October 2017.

Administrative Appeal 9557/17 (Supreme Court). City of *Bat Yam Planning board v. The Forum for Saving the Beach et al.* Decision dated 13 November 2018.

Country reports

Group III: Countries not subject to supranational legislation

16 Australia

Nicole Gurran

Overview

Australians have had a long love affair with the beach. More than 85% of the nation lives in coastal cities or towns, and growth in the peri-metropolitan areas, spanning six state capital cities, is predominantly along the coastline. Further afield, retirees, alternative lifestylers, tele-commuters, and economic migrants have sought refuge from urban sprawl in seaside villages and coastal towns, bringing significant environmental, social, and economic challenges akin to those reported in coastal areas experiencing growth and change in many parts of the world (Gurran, 2008).

This chapter explores the current legislative and administrative frameworks for coastal management in Australia, which has evolved through a series of national and state-level policy processes since the 1970s. The chapter highlights the tensions associated with Integrated Coastal Zone Management (ICZM) within a context of competing drivers for urbanisation (second-home tourism, retiree migration, and speculative development), and political contests over growth and environmental protection. Within this complex setting, some state and local governments have been particularly innovative in their approaches to planning and management in the coastal zone.

Introduction to coastal issues in Australia

Australia is one of the largest countries completely surrounded by water, with a coastline of 25,760 km (World Factbook, n.d.). The country's coastline stretches significantly when the many small islands within its boundaries are taken into account (Geosciences Australia, 2015). Across Australia, the coastal environment is extremely varied, comprising sandy beaches, dunes, estuaries, mangroves, salt marshes, seagrass beds, gulfs, bays, and wetlands. Many different ecosystems support numerous terrestrial and marine plants and animals.

Despite the extent of the coastline, much of the coastal environment is under pressure from urban development, agriculture, fishing, shipping, industry (including mining), and recreational activities. The concentration of urban population in the nation's coastal cities and towns, where around 21.4 million Australians reside (Australian Bureau of Statistics [ABS], 2018), exacerbates these pressures.

According to Australia's *State of the Environment Report* (2011), urban and commercial developments, as well as other industry practices, have modified coastal habitats through vegetation clearing and sometimes dredging of wetlands, changing river flows, disturbance of soils,

Figure 16.1 Beach in Sydney suburb of Bronte, NSW

Source: David Baron. CC BY-SA 2.0 license. Available at: https://www.flickr.com/photos/dbaron/42179912590/

and the intrusion of pollutants and invasive species. However, the extent of damage varies across the continent. Less than 10% of the native vegetation remains in many parts of coastal Victoria and South Australia, while up to half persists in parts of the northwest and northeastern areas, and from 71% to 100% is preserved in northern Australia (State of the Environment 2011 Committee, 2011). In 2006, it was estimated that if development trends continued on the east coast of the continent, around 42% of the coastline between the NSW South Coast town of Nowra through to the Southern Queensland city of Noosa (a distance of around 2,000 km) would be urbanised (House of Representatives, 2009).

Increasing rates of sea level rise are a perennial concern for Australia's coastal areas. On average, sea level rise has occurred at a rate of 3.1 mm per year since the early 1990s, compared to 1.2 mm per year across the twentieth century (State of the Environment 2011 Committee, 2011). Rising sea surface temperatures are also impacting marine ecosystems, affecting the distribution and abundance of coral reefs, fish species, seabirds, and sea grasses. Since the early twentieth century, sea temperatures have risen by 0.7°C (State of the Environment 2011 Committee, 2011). Sea level rise will have different impacts in different coastal areas – with soft sandy beaches particularly vulnerable to increased levels of shoreline erosion, storm surge, and flooding. Overall, the changed weather patterns associated with climate change represent significant environmental, financial, social, and legal risks to coastal populations. Significant assets are already exposed: Of the estimated 711,000 existing homes located near the water, up to 35% are at risk of inundation under a sea level rise scenario of 1.1 m, while many items of significant community infrastructure – from fire stations to hospitals, water treatment plans, and emergency services – are situated within 200 m of Australia's shore (Department of Climate Change, 2009, p. 71).

Overview of legal framework

Under Australia's federal system, the national 'Commonwealth' government has limited responsibilities for the environment but has increasingly adopted high-level policy development and environmental protection functions, while State/Territorial and local governments have struggled to integrate their various roles in relation to coastal management, urban planning, and environmental assessment. All three levels of government officially endorse principles of ICZM; however, legal and policy interpretations and implementation approaches differ (Norman, 2009).

The main responsibility for coastal management sits with the six states and the self-governing Northern Territory (an additional self-governing territory, the ACT, has no coastal land). State government 'enabling legislation' for urban planning, environmental, and coastal matters provides the administrative and legal framework for managing the coastal zone. State Ministers retain powers on major strategic decisions, such as rezoning of coastal lands from 'greenfield' rural land to urban land available for development, although these actions are often triggered and informed by local government planning processes. Local government is largely responsible for applying the legislation in local planning and development decisions, within the policy framework set by higher levels of government. Significant decision-making occurs at the local level, which, although it often applies to relatively small-scale changes, can have a cumulative environmental impact on the coast.

The national-level Commonwealth government has responsibility for maritime areas associated with national sovereignty, as well as for the very limited 'matters of national environmental significance' (usually those arising from international treaties such as the World Heritage and Ramsar conventions, as well as various international instruments relating to oceans). However, the Commonwealth has played an important role in Australia's coastal policy development since the 1970s. This has occurred through mechanisms for facilitating cooperation between the States on environmental and resource management issues, as well as through a series of policy development and funding initiatives. In 2003, the National Natural Resource Ministerial Council endorsed 'Integrated Coastal Management' (Natural Resource Management Ministerial Council, 2006) as the overall approach for managing coastal pressures. Although the framework has been endorsed by the states, definitions of the coastal zone and approaches to its management continue to differ.

National policy processes and inquiries

A major national-level coastal policy and research development process was undertaken in the 1990s (Resource Assessment Commission, 1993), although this work fell into a policy interregnum until the emergence of climate change concerns from the beginning of the new millennium. Since 2009, the Federal Government has been more active in the development of national coastal policy, influenced by a series of reports, including *Managing our Coastal Zone in a Changing Climate: The Time to Act Is Now*, known as the 'George' Inquiry (House of Representatives Standing Committee on Climate Change, Water, Environment and the Arts, 2009); the report to the Minister from the national Coasts and Climate Change

Council (Coasts and Climate Change Council, 2010); the Productivity Commission report on Adaptation (Productivity Commission, 2012); *Climate Change Risks to Australia's Coast: A First Pass National Assessment* (Department of Climate Change, 2009); and *The Critical Decade* by the Climate Commission (Steffen & Hughes, 2013). During the same period (2009–2013), a considerable body of research was undertaken into the impacts of climate change on the coast, through the National Climate Change Adaptation Research Facility (Norman et al., 2013). *The Climate Change Risks to Australia's Coast: A First Pass National Assessment* (Department of Climate Change, 2009) established some initial baseline data on sea level rise and implications for coastal vulnerability.

Definition of Australia's coastal zone and shoreline

The definition of Australia's coastal zone and shoreline is contentious. Across the Commonwealth, states, and territories, coastal zone boundaries – critical for planning, management, and property ownership purposes – differ.

The coastal zone

The Commonwealth defines the coastal zone in a very fluid and expansive sense as follows:

> the boundaries of the coastal zone extend as far inland and as far seaward as necessary to achieve the policy objectives, with a primary focus on the land/sea interface (Resource Assessment Commission, 1993, p. 2).

This implies a definition of the coastal zone which reflects ecological processes (such as water catchments), rather than administrative boundaries (between state and local government jurisdiction and local government areas). The concept of the 'catchment, coast, ocean' continuum underpins the Commonwealth's ICZM framework (Natural Resource Management Ministerial Council, 2006).

In practice, the coastal zone is primarily under state jurisdiction, aside from areas of Commonwealth land (largely defence authority sites). State jurisdiction over marine waters extends for three nautical miles seaward. The Marine boundary for the Commonwealth extends to the boundary of the Australian Fishing Zone, 200 nautical miles seaward of the low-water mark.

Formal definitions of the coastal zones are contained in state coastal policies and laws, and the implications of these designations differ. Table 16.1 summarises the different definitions of the coastal zone at the time of writing.

Within the coastal zone itself, questions of ownership and tenure are governed by laws defining land titles and coastal management. While the beach is regarded as public land, determining the boundary between the formal shoreline and private land can be complex due to the dynamic nature of the coastal environment. Site surveys are used to delineate private and public land and easements for access or other purposes. The public domain of beaches (discussed below) is generally defined as the space between the highest and lowest astronomical tides. Areas above this line (sometimes called 'dry sand') and towards vegetation are usually included in the public beach. Natural factors such as storm events, sea level rise, and erosion can affect the tidal lines, creating confusion and uncertainty about the boundaries between public and private land, and access to the beach (Cartlidge, 2011, p. 2).

Table 16.1 Definitions of the coastal zone, Australian jurisdictions

Jurisdiction	Definition of coastal zone	Source
Commonwealth	The extent of human uses and activities associated with coastal resources and process, and the extent of water catchments draining into coastal waters	Resource Assessment Commission 1993
New South Wales (NSW)	The *coastal zone* is defined in relation to legislated coastal management areas, which typically contain coastal waters, estuaries, lakes, lagoons, and land adjoining, including headlands and rock platforms; as well as land subject to coastal hazards	NSW Coastal Management Act 2016
Northern Territory (NT)	Sea, land, and waterways interacting with the coastline, including offshore islands controlled by the Northern Territory Government	NT Coastal Management Policy 1985
Queensland	Coastal waters and all areas landward where there are physical features, ecological or natural processes that affect the coast or coastal resources, including catchment areas and all coastal waters	Coastal Protection and Management Act 1995
Tasmania	Primary elements of the coastal landscape and 'associated areas of human habitat and activity'; extending inland to the extent needed to address uses and developments which may impact on the coast	Tasmanian Coastal Policy 1996
South Australia (SA)	100 m above high water (urban areas; 550 m in rural areas); 3 nautical miles seaward of mean low water. All land within any coastal waterway subject to tidal movements	Coast Protection Act 1972
Victoria	Land and waters on the seaward side of coastal watersheds, sea and seabed to 3 nautical miles from the high-water mark	Coastal Management Act 1995
	Definition of 'the coast': "'the coast' encompass coastal, estuarine, and marine environments on both public and private land. This applies to: the marine environment – nearshore marine environment, the seabed, and waters out to the State limit of 3 nautical miles (5.5 km) foreshores – or coastal Crown land up to 200 m from the high-water mark coastal hinterland – land directly influenced by the sea or directly influencing the coastline and with critical impacts on the foreshore and nearshore environment (these influences range from visual to drainage impacts) catchments – rivers and drainage systems that affect the coastal zone, including estuaries atmosphere – near, around and over the coast" (p. 6)	Coastal Strategy 2014
Western Australia (WA)	'Areas of water and land that may be influenced by coastal processes, which can be any action of natural forces on the coastal environment' (p. 1)	WA Coastal Zone Strategy 2017
Source: Updated from Gurran et al., 2005; Harvey & Caton, 2010		

The shoreline

Corkill (2012) summarises shoreline law in Australia, explaining the dynamic nature of the high-water mark, which forms the boundary between tidal waters and adjacent land. In the state of New South Wales (NSW), as in most of the other jurisdictions, this boundary is not fixed but moves in line with coastal processes. Boundary determination becomes important when land is being defended, developed, or transferred. In the case of gradual coastal processes which result in an extension or contraction of land (described as 'accretion'), the site boundaries move accordingly:

> where the boundary of land extends due to the gradual build-up of sediment, the adjoining owner gains that land. Conversely, where the boundary contracts due to erosion, the area gradually reduces and the owner loses that area of land. (Corkill, 2012, p. 17)

This means that the adjoining landowner has ownership of new land formed through accretion processes. At the same time, territory which gradually falls below the high-water mark becomes public land to be 'held in trust for public purposes' (Corkill, 2012, p. 27).

While there are no formal processes for recording this loss of ownership, Corkill notes that the record of land boundaries will be redrawn when land is sold:

> Thus the effect of the 'silent transfer' of minute sections of land to the Crown, repeated many times over a long period of time, may result in the dimensions and area of a property being significantly and suddenly reduced when a survey of the property is next prepared in readiness for offering the land for sale. (Corkill, 2012, p. 33)

This reflects the situation where land titles recognise 'fixed' boundaries. However, there may be some unusual property titles where 'ambulatory' boundaries are recognised. These 'ambulatory boundaries' move in line with the mean high-water mark, so can move seaward if sand movements result in a larger beach but can also move landward as a consequence of beach erosion. This remains an uncertain aspect of law in Australia and may be challenged in future as wealthy landowners seek to exert a right to erect structures which diminish public access to the beach or seek the right to protect their property by erecting seawalls on a public beach (which in turn may result in a loss of public access).

If the shoreline moves, affecting a property boundary, no compensation is payable for the loss or gain of land (Corkill, 2012). These principles reflect English common law and have been upheld by Australian courts. The prospect of 'losing land to the sea' has significant implications for property owners and explains tensions surrounding attempts to protect private property from coastal erosion (for which there is no inherent common law right). Unfortunately, many such attempts to protect private property interfere with coastal processes.

However, private landowners might assert that the local council (typically, by default responsible for the beach) owes them a 'duty of care' to intervene if private properties are threatened by coastal erosion (Corkill, 2012, p. 49). State laws on this point vary; however, in NSW the duty of care is limited to the period of issuing development consent for a development. Provided that the decision made by council is in good faith and consistent with provisions contained in a prescribed coastal management manual, further liability is limited. Another complicated situation can arise when property owners claim that insufficient works on public lands (i.e. beaches) have been undertaken to protect adjacent homes, and the case law on this remains complex and unclear.

Public land

All land seaward of the high-water mark (discussed above) is in public ownership (known as 'Crown land' in Australia). Further, although the States and territories oversee the policy and legal framework governing coastal lands, it is generally local government which has management of beaches. Beyond the beach, provisions for the reservation and/or acquisition of foreshore lands exist in most jurisdictions. Where such land is in public ownership, it is generally owned by local councils and managed as a 'Crown reserve'. In urban areas, these reserves will often be public parks and sometimes also include tourism uses such as camping grounds or car parks.

The other form of public land use prevalent in coastal Australia is as a national park or other conservation area managed by state or Commonwealth agencies. Subject to various state limitations, Crown land may be affected by Indigenous land rights claims (whereby traditional Aboriginal owners will seek to have their ownership reinstated as freehold title, allowing land to be developed or sold) or the more restrictive 'native' title determination under Commonwealth law (allowing traditional owners access to land for ceremonial, management, or foraging purposes). Many Crown lands in coastal Australia have been subject to native title and land rights applications, but to date, few have been granted in the populated eastern and southwestern parts of the country. The negotiation of a formal Indigenous Land Use Agreement which provides for co-management of protected areas between traditional owners and State/Commonwealth conservation agencies has become an important part of this process (Bauman et al., 2013).

Permitted developments and or activities in public coastal lands are managed by various state planning, environmental, and coastal management laws, as well as local government regulations. In general, coastal lands are able to be used for a variety of recreational purposes. Activities which might modify the coastal environment (including activities undertaken by a public authority) are subject to an environmental assessment process.

Regulations on development activities in public coastal lands are strictly enforced. However, some 'non-conforming' uses remain in various parts of Australia, particularly on lands which have subsequently been acquired for public purposes but where existing use rights have been recognised. Beach 'shacks' used by private individuals in coastal foreshore areas are an example of such non-complying uses which have been allowed to continue for a defined period of time. Shacks on public land rely on leases and are not permitted to be sold, although in certain circumstances they can be passed on to members of a family. Most structures were built by fishers or the unemployed between the 1930s and 1950s, and some have cultural heritage significance.

In South Australia, sites for beach shacks on Crown reserves were leased by State and some local governments in the 1950s and 1960s. By the 1970s, over 7,000 beach shacks had been erected in that state (Harvey & Caton, 2010). While a subsequent programme reduced the number of beach shacks, particularly in ecologically vulnerable areas, in the early 1990s the remaining shacks (around 1,600) were granted freehold title, providing ongoing, unencumbered ownership and development rights (Harvey & Caton, 2010). This policy has been criticised for undermining the wider principles of coastal planning and management in South Australia. Although new development has to comply with strict coastal management principles and legislation, lawfully erected coastal shacks are able to bypass contemporary coastal planning law (Harvey & Caton, 2010, p. 170).

Port lands, marinas, and wharves

Ports in Australia are generally owned and managed by State-owned Port Authorities. Thus, they are covered by planning law but have special provisions governing their activities. Major infrastructure development associated with Ports is subject to environmental impact assessment (or equivalent) under state planning law (sometimes triggering Commonwealth interest as well). As a quasi-public authority, Ports usually have some power to self-certify developments and activities which are related to core Port business, and these provisions will be established by the applicable planning regulation.

Special-purpose zoning designations for working waterfront and marina areas exist under most state jurisdictions. These are typically used to denote and control activities by private operators for the most part operating on land (or water easements) which have been leased from the state. Private wharves are also subject to these special leasing/licensing provisions. Development of wharves and marinas falls within the planning process, and there are provisions to integrate the environmental assessment with environmental and marine permits issued by other authorities. Considerations for assessing development of wharves and marinas are normally set out within local planning instruments, which must be interpreted in the light of applicable state policies and plans, including coastal management policies or laws. Criteria for assessment will typically include considerations relating to the impact of proposals on the marine ecosystem, public safety (arising from additional boating movements, etc.), visual impacts, and local community impacts (for instance, additional parking or traffic generated by users).

Setback from the shoreline

Coastal setback rules are set by state planning regulations, sometimes also affected by coastal management provisions. Even within each state, there is not a uniform required setback distance. Setbacks are most likely to be defined on zoning plans or similar, but in some cases specific setback distances are considered only when a landowner has requested planning permission for new development.

The overarching considerations for determining setback rules include preserving public access to the beach; managing visual intrusions; and preventing development in areas which might become subject to beach erosion in the future. Overall, Australian coastal policy seeks to preserve natural coastal processes to provide a 'buffer' for future shoreline erosion, storm surge, and potential sea level rise. However, historical planning decisions have meant that areas have been inappropriately zoned or subject to lax development controls, and it is winding back these controls which presents a significant challenge for local authorities (Figure 16.2).

In general, the amount of coastal setback required depends on:

- State laws – for instance in Western Australia, subdivision in coastal areas includes a mandatory dedication of foreshore land to the State government, to be used as reserve
- The underlying cadastral pattern and the dimensions of individual sites (smaller, shallower sites, historically created, will in general be subject to less stringent setback requirements)
- Exposure to natural hazards and storm surge
- The type of development – certain types of shorter-term uses will not face as significant setback requirements as short-term activities

The practice on private land will usually be to enforce the largest possible setback from the shoreline, depending on the depth of the lot, historical settlement patterns, and exposure to coastal hazards. For instance, when there is a proposal to demolish an existing home and build a new dwelling, the practice will usually be to require the new dwelling to be set back further from the shoreline than the previous structure, but this is usually subject to a 'merit' assessment.

Figure 16.2 Sydney Harbour, NSW

Source: Rodney Haywood. Available at: https://en.wikipedia.org/wiki/File:Sydney_Harbour_Bridge_from_the_air.JPG

A 'merit' assessment proceeds from a technical or implied permissible use (designated in the original land use zoning) but is subject to additional decision-making criteria relating to the details of specific sites or development proposals, at the discretion of the responsible authority. Property owners can and do appeal refusals of their applications, but the rights of third parties to appeal planning approvals are generally limited in most Australian jurisdictions to higher-impact developments or administrative challenges (exceptions being Victoria and Tasmania, where objectors are permitted to appeal decisions).

In case of sites where ongoing habitation remains untenable, many coastal councils are attempting to acquire these properties, providing financial compensation to owners. However, this is an expensive process and not always financially or politically feasible.

Where setback zones are defined, the extent to which landholders are able to develop within these zones varies on a case-by-case basis, depending on state and local laws and the circumstances of the site itself. In general, any development within identified areas of vulnerability would be limited to moveable structures (to enable retreat) or minor repairs to existing buildings.

Right of public access

As discussed above, since the seaward area of the shoreline is by definition in public ownership ('Crown land'), public access to all beaches is implied. However, although most coastal policy documents prepared by state governments in Australia emphasise the importance of public

Figure 16.3 Beach on the Gold Coast, a popular tourist destination, Queensland

Source: Francisco Anzola. CC BY 2.0 license. Available at: https://creativecommons.org/licenses/by/2.0/

access to the beach, preservation of access rights is not necessarily guaranteed. For instance, in the case of Queensland, it seems that public access rights are guaranteed only via marine waters (Cartlidge, 2011).

In practice, 'vertical' access points are regulated by public and private landowners. There are some instances in which certain authorities will restrict all beach or shoreline access, and these are usually related to particular activities, such as defence or port operations. In general, however, beach access is usually regulated by local authorities (via management plans for coasts or reserves) to maintain the environmental integrity of coastal systems, minimising erosion of sensitive sand dunes, and preventing intrusion of non-native plants and animals. In most cases, coastal vegetation with controlled access paths provides a sufficient barrier to manage beach access, with provision for pedestrian entry usually available every 400 m or so in built-up areas. Tighter access restrictions apply for recreational activities, including for four-wheel-drive vehicles (some beaches only) and for dogs (on and off leash).

Maintaining public access points can be difficult in the context of frequent coastal storms and erosion, and restoring beach paths and stairs can be an expensive component of local government coastal management responsibilities. Residential subdivisions are usually planned to maintain public easements for ongoing access to beaches and foreshores. In established harbourside areas and in relation to coastal lakes and lagoons, public access is less consistent.

Urban and regional planning – laws and implementation

Urban planning in Australia is primarily governed by the six States and two self-governing Territories. Urban planning laws provide for spatial plan making and the assessment of developments against these plans and specify the bureaucratic arrangements for administering the system. Overlaying these state responsibilities, the Commonwealth government has responsibility for matters of 'national environmental significance' under the *Commonwealth Environmental Protection and Biodiversity Conservation Act 1999* (the CEPBC Act). These matters include:

- World heritage properties
- National heritage places
- Wetlands of international importance (listed under the Ramsar Convention)
- Listed threatened species and ecological communities
- Migratory species protected under international agreements
- Commonwealth marine areas
- The Great Barrier Reef Marine Park
- Nuclear actions (including uranium mines)
- A water resource, in relation to coal seam gas development and large coal-mining development

Thus, in relation to coastal areas, the Commonwealth's responsibilities under the CEPBC Act often intersect with State environmental planning laws and processes. Where an action may have impacts on a matter of national environmental significance, approval from the Australian Government Minister for the Environment is required in addition to any State planning processes.

In practice, coastal planning policy in Australia is primarily articulated by the States and the Northern Territory, often through special policy instruments or documents. In turn these policies are incorporated into spatial plans (for instance, requirements about coastal zoning, setbacks, and development types/acceptable impacts in coastal areas) and are required to be considered when developments in coastal areas are assessed. In many cases, a special expert body, at arm's length from the government, will advise on – and sometimes determine – significant developments in the coastal zone and/or consider or prepare coastal planning policies

For the most part, Australia's state coastal policies seek to promote compact settlements rather than coastline 'ribbon' development (often referring to a hierarchy of coastal settlement types); maintain and enhance the environmental values of coastal ecosystems; preserve public access to beaches and foreshores; and minimise vulnerability to coastal hazards (including coastal flooding) (Gurran et al., 2005).

Contemporary coastal management and planning principles reflected in these state policies emphasise maintaining existing topographical features and ecological processes. However, it is often the case that coastal topography will be levelled, or certain areas dredged and filled, to facilitate urban development. In some states, the construction of artificial coastal waterways to provide water frontages for new housing (known as 'canal estates') continues to occur; although this has been phased out in most jurisdictions.

Much of the 'day-to-day' development in coastal areas – for instance, houses or residential subdivisions within already residential zones – falls under the jurisdiction of local government.

The local government's consideration entails an expert assessment against the applicable plans and development controls to determine the legality of the proposed development, public exhibition of the proposal, then consideration and determination by a group of elected representatives (the 'council') and/or a local expert panel.

Table 16.2 outlines the main State policy documents and laws relevant to urban planning in coastal Australia.

In Victoria, an independent, council of experts, the Victorian Coastal Council, oversees the development and implementation of the state's coastal policy. The Council has worked closely with state government in commissioning important research and policy tools relating to the management of coastal growth and change and, more recently, in relation to climate change. This includes the specification of coastal management principles in the Victorian State Planning Provisions, which must be called up within local planning instruments, and the preparation of Coastal Action Plans, on the basis of coastal catchment areas. These documents provide a basis for both planning and management of coastal areas, and are also referred to within local planning schemes.

One of the important differences between the management of Victorian coastal areas and the other states is that the majority of foreshore land (which varies in width but is typically between a coastal road and the low-water mark (Croft, 2017)) is in public ownership and managed as reserve. This has moderated development pressures and perhaps explains why the introduction of settlement limits – formal urban growth boundaries – have been more effective in reducing the tendency towards linear coastline development than is seen in the other states. These settlement boundaries have been set to enable future growth but are introduced at the same time as other accessible inland development opportunities are identified, thus ensuring a balance between settlement containment and the need for ongoing housing supply. Second-home ownership is a major policy issue affecting coastal planning and management in Victoria, given the relative proximity of coastal holiday settlements to the state capital, Melbourne.

The State of NSW has long benefited from a coastal policy, design guidance, and detailed state-issued guidelines for local governments for informed consideration of flood risk and other hazards in plan-making and development assessment. NSW has also provided financial support to local governments for coastal management activities. Under these conditions, many local governments developed their own innovative approaches to coastal planning within their local planning instruments. For instance, Byron Shire in the far north of NSW developed an early development control plan to manage the issue of coastline erosion. According to the policy, permission to develop in areas potentially susceptible to coastline erosion was subject to special requirements (such as temporary structures able to be relocated) to provide for natural retreat in affected areas. However, the policy has been difficult to implement in practice and the Council has faced ongoing legal battles with affluent property owners who are intent on protecting their properties from coastal erosion.

The NSW State government has periodically sought to clarify and standardise coastal planning and protection policy, and a new Coastal Management Act, management manual, and state planning policy were introduced progressively from 2016, replacing the state's 1997 Coastal Policy.

While there is no formal regional layer of government in Australia, in many cases regional approaches have provided important strategic frameworks for integrated coastal planning and management. These include formal and legally recognised regional plans driven by state governments, as well as less formal processes initiated by regional groups of local councils.

Table 16.2 State policy and law relevant to coastal Australia

State/Territory	Key legislation/regulations/documents (legally enforceable)	Key policies/strategies
NSW (under review)	*Environmental Planning & Assessment Act 1979* (NSW) and *Environmental Planning and Assessment Regulation 2000* (NSW) *Coastal Management Act 2016* *Marine Estate Management Act 2014* *State Environmental Planning Policy (Coastal Management) 2018* *Local Planning Direction 2.2 Coastal Management*	NSW Coastal Management Manual and Toolkit (2018)
Northern Territory	*Planning Act* (NT) Northern Territory Planning Scheme	
Queensland	*Planning Act 2016* (Qld) *Coastal Protection and Management Act 1995* (Qld) State Development Assessment Provisions *State Planning Policy* (April 2016) Erosion prone area mapping (declared under s 70 of the *Coastal Protection and Management Act 1995* (Qld)	*Coastal Management Plan (2013)*
South Australia	*Coast Protection Act 1972* (SA) *Planning, Development and Infrastructure Act 2016* (SA) *Planning, Development, and Infrastructure Regulation 2016* (SA)	*Coastline: Coastal erosion, flooding and sea level rise standards and protection policy no 26* (1992) *Policy on Coast Protection 1991* and *Coast Protection Board Policy Document 2012* *Coastal Planning Information Package: A guide to coastal development assessment and planning policy 2013* *Living Coast Strategy* (2004)
Tasmania	*State Policies and Projects Act 1993* *Tasmanian State Coastal Policy 1996* *Land Use Planning and Approvals Act 1993*	*Derivation of the Tasmanian Sea Level Rise Planning Allowances: Technical Paper* (August 2012) Tasmanian Coastal Works Manual (includes provisions for climate change) Climate Change Impact Statements Draft Tasmanian Coastal Policy Statement (2013)
Victoria	*Planning and Environment Act 1987* *Coastal Management Act 1995* *Climate Change Act 2010* (requirement to consider climate change in developing coastal strategies/actions plans) *Victoria Planning Provisions – State Planning Policy Framework* (includes coastal considerations) Municipal statements in local planning schemes	Victorian Coastal Strategy 2014 Coastal Action Plans and Coastal Management Plans (West Coast, Central Coast, and Gippsland Coast) – a mechanism for implementing the coastal strategy at the regional level
Western Australia	*Planning & Development Act 2005* (WA) *Statement of Planning Policy 2.6: State Coastal Planning Policy 2013*	Coastal Hazard Risk Management and Adaptation Planning Guidelines (2014) WA Coastal Zone Strategy 2017
Source: Adapted from Gurran & Squires, 2008; Environmental Defender's Office NSW, 2010		

Climate change awareness – legal aspects

Concern about climate change has waxed and waned in Australia. Under a (left of centre) 'Labor' government (2007–2013), significant policy commitment to climate change resulted in the establishment of a number of initiatives and research efforts, including a national Coasts and Climate Change Council. That Council delivered a number of recommendations relating to managing coastal risk; coastal policy and regulatory reform; adaptation efforts; and addressing legal implications arising from coastal climate change (Gibbs and Hill, 2011). A Climate Change Select Committee, comprising Ministerial representatives of the states and the Northern Territory, was established in 2011, and advised on roles and responsibilities for all three levels of government and the private sector in relation climate adaptation. There have also been varying levels of state and local government commitment to addressing climate change risks through the urban planning process.

Across all levels of government, the subject of climate change mitigation and adaptation efforts is politically charged. At the local level, where climate risk implies potential changes to private development rights, the topic is particularly political. A study led by the author (involving an internet survey, in-depth interviews, and focus groups with planners and councillors), across 47 coastal councils of non-metropolitan Australia (Gurran et al. 2012), found high levels of awareness about climate risks, particularly in relation to sea level rise, shoreline loss, storm surge, and coastal erosion. Respondents expressed concern that development was continuing in vulnerable locations despite adequate information demonstrating the risk of future exposure. Levels of community anxiety about climate risk were also reported, although in many areas, communication strategies focused on preparing for 'coastal hazards', recognising that the concept of climate change was not fully accepted by the community. Some respondents advised that changes to insurance policies, whereby properties at risk of coastal flooding were subject to significantly higher insurance premiums, had begun to change local attitudes towards climate risks.

Overall, decisions about appropriate development entitlements and the capacity to maintain and defend properties in exposed locations remain extremely contentious in Australia. Of the climate-change-related litigation in Australian courts to 2017 (some 80 cases) (Pain, 2018), a handful have addressed these issues. In NSW, these cases have primarily been brought by property owners appealing against local planning authority decisions to refuse development in vulnerable coastal areas. For instance, *Pridel Investments Pty Ltd v Coffs Harbour City Council [2017] NSWLEC 1042* concerned an appeal against the council's refusal of an application to develop a thirty-nine-lot residential subdivision due to high flooding risks, inconsistency with sustainable development principles in the local plan, and potential climate change impacts. The council's decision to refuse the application was upheld on appeal.

Integration and coordination

At the national level, Australia's Natural Resource Management Ministerial Council has endorsed the ICZM framework for different government roles and responsibilities in the coastal zone (Natural Resource Management Ministerial Council, 2006). In practice, the Commonwealth's limited formal responsibilities in relation to the environment and planning mean that this framework does little more than describe the overlapping roles undertaken by national, state, and local levels. As outlined earlier, the Commonwealth's primary responsibilities in the coastal zone fall within the CEPBC Act. The States and the Northern Territory, with responsibility for the environment and urban planning, administer special-purpose planning, coastal management, environmental protection, and conservation laws, all of which have implications for integration and coordination. Different state agencies typically have responsibility for urban planning, environmental protection, and natural reserves, with the coastal zone falling across these portfolios. Infrastructure provision (major roads and transport) and maritime activities are also the responsibility of discrete agencies. At the local level, the range of responsibilities relating to local land use planning, development control, infrastructure delivery, and land management do come together. However, this level of government often faces significant resource constraints, with limited budgets, few professional staff, and often extensive areas of coastline to manage.

One of the enduring criticisms of coastal zone management in Australia has been the lack of effective coordination across the three vertical tiers of government, as well as horizontally between State agencies (Norman, 2009; Wheeler et al., 2011). This is despite the existence of a strong policy commitment to integrated coastal zone management, evident in most states (Table 16.2). It likely reflects the overarching complexities associated with urban planning, infrastructure provision, and environmental protection more widely, which cut across many different policy areas and government portfolios (e.g. urban planning, transport, environmental protection, nature conservation, recreation, tourism, and economic development). Nevertheless, regional-level initiatives have appeared to have the most success in delivering an effective framework for integrated coastal zone planning and management in the Australian context (Norman, 2009).

Public participation – legal anchoring

Australia is not formally a party to the Aarhus Convention (the Convention on Access to Information, Public Participation in Decision-Making and Access to Justice in Environmental Matters, which came into force on 30 October 2001). However, the principles of this convention are consistent with those of environmental law in Australia (Dwyer & Preston, 2015).

Both formal and informal approaches to public participation underpin planning and management in the coastal zone. Almost all urban planning policies and instruments must be publicly exhibited before being adopted, with provision for public submissions to be made and considered before instruments are finalised. Most classes of development in the coastal zone will also be publicly exhibited, again with provision for formal objections to be lodged. The capacity for a member of the public (including a non-government organisation) to appeal a decision is available for matters meeting certain criteria, which differ from state to state.

While planning documents and, generally, the information on which they are based are publicly available, detailed spatial data on Australia's extensive coastal zone as a whole remains limited. Nevertheless, there are ongoing efforts to develop a national source of data and periodic initiatives to extend and disseminate coastal and climate change research (Department of Climate Change, 2009; Department of Climate Change and Energy Efficiency, 2011). There is also a strong tradition of local participation and volunteer involvement in coastal management and environmental rehabilitation efforts.

Fiscal aspects: Incentives and disincentives regarding ICZM

Financial arrangements relevant to this chapter relate primarily to questions of raising money for coastal management activities, beach protection, the provision of recreational facilities, and in some cases for land acquisition. In general, local governments are able to levy special rates (local taxes) to provide for coastal management activities and/or the provision of recreational facilities. There are also small funding programmes available (subject to competitive application) for various coastal research, planning, and infrastructure purposes.

Compensation

In general, there are no compensation arrangements for the imposition of development restrictions affecting private land. However, in practice, the tendency in Australia has been to avoid reducing existing (implied) development entitlements associated with land uses (defined by land use zones) and or controls relating to the design, bulk, and scale of a prospective buildings.

For instance, guidance for coastal planning in NSW has suggested that local governments consider reducing the range of permissible activities in coastal zone areas, in light of new environmental knowledge, but advises that they retain some possibility for economic uses of private land:

> Other rural or undeveloped land in coastal risk areas may be zoned E2 Environmental Conservation Zone which provides the highest level of protection, management and restoration for such lands, while allowing uses compatible with those values. It must be noted that the range of permitted uses should not be drawn too restrictively as they may, depending on circumstances, invoke the *Land Acquisition (Just Terms Compensation) Act 1991* and the need for the Minister to designate a relevant acquiring authority. (Department of Planning, 2010, p. 10)

Another way in which local planning authorities are restricted in their capacity to impose new constraints on the development of land is in relation to uses which have been previously approved. While development consents are time limited in most Australian states, in general once a development has technically commenced (for instance, clearing a site of native vegetation), the approval will be preserved. This has resulted in the perseverance for many years of new developments which were significantly out of step with prevailing rules. For instance, while 'canal developments' (artificially constructed waterways to provide waterfront sites for housing) were banned in NSW in the mid-1990s, they continued to occur through the early years of the new millennium due to historical approvals that were still being played out.

Finally, even where a development approval has lapsed, in practice it is difficult for a planning authority to refuse a subsequent application unless there has been a very significant change to the planning laws affecting the site.

These long-standing principles may increasingly be tested, however, as the prospect of more intense or frequent coastal storms and flooding arising from climate change begin to inform coastal planning decisions.

Forced demolition

In NSW, where there are properties located in coastal areas which are now subject to ongoing risks associated with erosion, Councils can and do issue demolition orders over properties which become a risk to the public. Some councils have developed a clear policy framework to guide this process; for example, Greater Taree Council's *Coastal Zone Management Plan, 2015* indicates that:

> Under this plan Council will determine when a structure is at risk of collapse or is a risk to beach users and will serve a Notice of Intention to serve an Order for demolition/removal followed by formal Order. If the structure is in immediate risk of collapse we will issue an emergency Order to demolish/remove the structure. (Greater Taree Council, 2015, p. 38)

These provisions are increasingly contained in local coastal zone management plans (which, once approved by state government, allow a number of activities to take place with consent, including coastal protection works for private property). A famous case involves the loss of private property through coastal erosion in the area of Old Bar Beach in the mid North Coast of NSW – within the Greater Taree Council area. In this case, the landholder lost around 40 m of land and was required to demolish structures as they became unstable. However, the Council did permit the landholder to undertake protective works to sustain the remainder of his property, subject to the criteria set out in its Coastal Zone Management Plan.

Acquisition

There are various schemes to acquire environmentally significant coastal land for public uses. In NSW, a funding programme known as the Coastal Lands Protection Scheme provides funds to bring significant coastal lands into public ownership and for their long-term management and care. It currently has an annual budget allocation of $3 million. Originally, the scheme was used to purchase lands with features such as headlands, dunes, hinterland, coastal lagoons, and lakes. Current funding criteria cover public access, scenic qualities, and ecological values.

Local government can also raise funds through charges (for instance, for parking) and sometimes for leasing reserves for the purpose of camping or caravan parks. However, areas with small base populations and subject to heavy influxes of visitors during holiday periods experience particular funding pressures and infrastructure burdens on water and sewerage systems. This remains an open problem and there have been various debates about ways to either restrict the informal conversion of residential neighbourhoods to de facto tourism uses or to impose additional levies on tourism operators through a 'bed tax', a 'toilet tax', or a differential rate for non-resident property owners. To date, none of these approaches have persisted due to strong state government constraints on local government rating and charging powers.

Overall assessment

In summary, Australia has long sought to implement the principles of ICZM through Commonwealth, State, and local policies, plans, and management practices. However, changing policy priorities, and ambivalence about the implications of climate change, have been reflected in inconsistent and ad hoc approaches to coastal planning and management law, particularly over the past decade. Furthermore, problems of vertical and horizontal integration across the different levels of government and the various agencies with responsibility for matters affecting coastal areas remain an ongoing challenge.

Nevertheless, as outlined in Table 16.3, a comprehensive approach to coastal management has been established through Australian planning law since the 1970s, and this has evolved to incorporate stronger climate change considerations over the past decade. Provision for public

Table 16.3 Summary of approaches to integrated coastal zone management in Australia

Theme	Summary description
Definition of the Coastal Zone	Varied across jurisdictions – from a broad 'ecological processes' definition (Commonwealth) to numerical definitions, usually commencing at 3 nautical miles seaward to a defined landward boundary. Beaches are delineated with reference to the high- and low-water mark.
Public land	All land seaward of the high-water mark. Provisions to reserve public space in coastal foreshore areas where possible.
Ports and wharves	Governed by state authorities; leased to private operators.
Coastal setbacks	Governed by state planning laws; somewhat bound by historical patterns of subdivision. Defined to maintain public access provision; minimise exposure to coastal hazards; and provide for planned retreat where possible.
Accessibility	All beaches are public land; access ways controlled by public authorities.
Urban and regional planning laws and implementation	Governed by States and Territories; implemented by state and local planning authorities. Coastal policy implemented through new land use plans and when proposals are assessed. Penalties, including potential criminal proceedings, for breaches of environmental planning laws. Varying levels of mandatory versus guiding considerations in planning law.
Climate change awareness	High degree of climate change awareness across public policy agencies and the general public. However, imposing development constraints to reduce exposure to enhanced climate change risk remains politically contentious.
Overall management and coordination	Australia's National Cooperative Approach to Integrated Coastal Zone Management (2006) sets out a framework for the roles and responsibilities of all three levels of government. However, in practice, vertical and horizontal coordination between and across government agencies remains challenging.
Public participation	Formal provisions for public participation in environmental plan making and development assessment, and environmental law underpinned by principles of information transparency. Local participation in coastal planning, management, and rehabilitation efforts.
Fiscal aspects	No compensation for development restrictions imposed through the planning system unless the restrictions introduce a new restriction preventing economic use of the land. Some government funding to acquire sensitive coastal sites.

access to beaches, and protection of beaches and coastal reserves from intrusive developments has remained an important element of coastal planning and policy in Australia. Overall, while the framework has been subject to ongoing criticism, in particular regarding the lack of national-level leadership for a consistent approach to coastal planning and management, elements in the Australian model may provide some lessons for other jurisdictions.

References

Australian Bureau of Statistics. (ABS). (2018). *3101.0 Australian Demographic Statistics, Population Change*. Canberra: ABS.

Bauman, T., Haynes, C., & Lauder, G. (2013). *Pathways to the Co-management of Protected Areas and Native Title in Australia*. Vol. 29, AIATSIS Research Discussion Paper No. 32. Canberra: AIATSIS Research Publications.

Cartlidge, N. (2011). *Whose Beach Is It Anyway?* Bond University.

Coasts and Climate Change Council. (2010). Coasts and Climate Change Council Report to Minister Combet. Coasts and Climate Change Council.

Corkill, J. (2012). *Principles and Problems of Shoreline Law*. National Climate Change Adaptation Research Network.

Croft, R. (2017). *Guidelines for the Preparation of Coastline Management Plans*. Environment, Land, Water and Planning.

Deboudt, P. (2010). Towards coastal risk management in France. *Ocean & Coastal Management* 53 (7), 366–378.

Department of Climate Change. (2009). *Climate Change Risks to Australia's Coast: A First Pass National Assessment*. Australian Government.

Department of Climate Change and Energy Efficiency. (2011). *Climate Change Risks to Coastal Buildings and Infrastructure*. Australian Government.

Department of Planning. (2010). *NSW Coastal Planning Guideline: Adapting to Sea Level Rise*. Sydney: NSW Department of Planning.

Dwyer, G. J., & Preston, J. A. (2015). Striving for best practice in environmental governance and justice: Reporting on the inaugural environmental democracy index for Australia. *Environmental and Planning Law Journal* 32 (3), 202–255.

Environmental Defender's Office NSW. (2010). *Audit of Sea Level Rise, Coastal Erosion and Inundation Legislation and Policy. Report prepared by the Environmental Defender's Office of NSW for the Sydney Coastal Council's Group*. Sydney: Sydney Coastal Councils Group.

Geosciences Australia. (2015). *Border Lengths – States and Territories*. Geosciences Australia.

Gibbs, M. & Hill, T. (2011). Coastal Climate Change Risk-Legal and Policy Responses in Australia. Commonwealth of Australia.

Greater Taree Council. (2015). *Greater Taree Coastal Zone Management Plan*. Greater Taree Council.

Gurran, N. (2008). *The Turning Tide: Amenity Migration in Coastal Australia*. International Planning Studies 13(4), 391–414.

Gurran, N., Norman, B., & Hamin, E. (2012). Climate change adaptation in coastal Australia: An audit of planning practice. *Ocean & Coastal Management* 86, 100–109.

Gurran, N., & Squires, C. (2008). *Meeting the Sea Change Challenge: Sea Change Communities in Coastal Australia. Update Report and Data Supplement 2008*. University of Sydney Planning Research Centre; National Sea Change Taskforce.

Gurran, N., Squires, C., & Blakely, E. (2005). *Meeting the Sea Change Challenge: Sea Change Communities in Coastal Australia*. National Sea Change Task Force and the Planning Research Centre, University of Sydney.

Harvey, N., & Caton, B. (2010). *Coastal Management in Australia*. University of Adelaide Press.

House of Representatives Standing Committe on Climate Change, Water, Environment and the Arts. (2009). *Managing Our Coastal Zone in a Changing Climate: The Time to Act Is Now*. Committee Report. Australian Government.

Natural Resource Management Ministerial Council. (2006). *National Cooperative Approach to Integrated Coastal Zone Management Framework and Implementation Plan*. Commonwealth of Australia.

Norman, B. (2009). Principles for an intergovernmental agreement for coastal planning and climate change in Australia. *Habitat International* 33 (3), 293–299. doi: 10.1016/j.habitatint.2008.10.002

Norman, B., Steffen, W., Webb, B., Capon, T., Maher, B., Woodroffe, C., Rogers, K., Tanton, R., & Vidyattama, Y. (2013). South East Coastal Adaptation (SECA): Coastal urban climate futures in SE Australia from Wollongong to Lakes Entrance. NCCARF.

Pain, N. (2018). *Update on climate change litigation – A New South Wales perspective* Brisbane: Environmental Defenders Office Queensland.

Productivity Commission. (2012). Barriers to effective climate change adaptation. Commonwealth of Australia.

Resource Assessment Commission. (1993). *Coastal Zone Inquiry Final Report.* Canberra: Resource Assessment Commission.

State of the Environment 2011 Committee. (2011). *Australia State of the Environment 2011: Independent Report to the Australian Government Minister for Sustainability, Environment, Water, Population and Communities.* DSEWPaC.

Steffen, W. & Hughes, L. (2013). The Critical Decade 2013: Climate change science, risks and response. Climate Commission.

Wheeler, P. J., Peterson, J. A., & Gordon-Brown., L. N. (2011). Spatial decision support for integrated coastal zone management (ICZM) in Victoria, Australia: Constraints and opportunities. *Journal of Coastal Research* 27 (2), 296–317. doi: 10.2112/jcoastres-d-09-00150.1

World Factbook. (n.d.). Australia. Available at: https://www.cia.gov/Library/publications/the-world-factbook/geos/as.html [Accessed July 2020]

National Legislation (for state-level legislation, see Table 16.2)

Commonwealth Environmental Protection and Biodiversity Conservation Act 1999 (CEPBC Act)

Court cases

Pridel Investments Pty Ltd v Coffs Harbour City Council [2017] NSWLEC 1042

17 United States of America

A. Dan Tarlock

Overview

The United States faces a myriad of coastal use and management issues resulting from a clash of public and private interests. The intense development permitted along large stretches of its coastlines intensifies competing demands. In the future, the threats posed by global climate change (GCC) will put large areas at an increased risk of coastal flooding, as painfully demonstrated, once again, by Hurricane Harvey in August 2017. Twenty million people along US coastlines are at risk of inundation if climate change continues unabated (Strauss, et al., 2015).

Coastal management is complex in the United States, as there is no overall federal coastal management policy. Instead, management of the country's coastal zones is fragmented across all three levels of government – federal, state, and local – often with conflicting ideologies in play. In addition, the country's strong protection for private property rights plays a significant role in the story of coastal protection. This chapter provides an overview of the issues, policy, and legislation related to coastal zone management, drawing on examples from all three levels of government.

The context: Introduction to the United States' coastal issues

The United States is bordered by two oceans, the Atlantic and the Pacific, and by one Gulf, Mexico; has a peninsula state, Alaska; and has an archipelago one, the Hawai'ian Islands. There are 12,383 miles (19,924 km; World Factbook, n.d.) of the US coastline. This figure includes the five interior Great Lakes, which are also considered part of the country's coastline. The focus in this chapter will be on ocean and sea coastal management rather than on the country's "inland seas," although many of the issues are similar.

Historically, the Atlantic coast has been classified as a submergent coast and the Pacific as emergent. Although this classification is simplistic (Finkl, 2004), the most at-risk populations do tend to be located along the Atlantic (together with Los Angeles and San Francisco on the Pacific; Strauss et al., 2012).[1] Its relatively low coastline makes the Atlantic coast vulnerable to erosion. Along the Pacific Coast, earthquakes are the major serious property damage and human life risk. No hurricane has ever made landfall in California, but southern California does face some risk of hurricanes and tropical storms (NASA, 2012).

The management challenge

Americans love to live near the water, in both the warmer southern and colder northern regions. According to the United States National Oceanographic and Atmospheric Administration

(NOAA), the primary federal agency charged with promoting coastal management, some 123,000,000 people – 39% of the country's 2010 population – live in counties[2] directly on the shoreline. Yet these jurisdictions constitute less than 10% of the total land area of the country (excluding Alaska). The population density of coastal shoreline counties is over six times greater than that of the corresponding inland counties (NOAA, 2018). The highest concentrations are along the Atlantic and the Gulf of Mexico; the main coastal population concentrations along the Pacific are in southern California. The cold Pacific is not generally swimmable except for in that southern region.

The rush of population to the coasts is projected to continue and accelerate. According to the NOAA, from 1970 to 2010 the population of coastal counties increased by almost 40% and is projected to increase by an additional 10 million people, or 8%, by 2020 (NOAA, 2018). Thus, the population density in coastal areas will also continue to increase in the future (NOAA, 2013).

The United States faces the problems that all developed coastal nations face. These include competition with private property owners for public access, erosion, marine pollution, land-based pollution, and the destruction of coastal ecosystems, especially wetlands and mangrove swamps (Titus et al., 2009). Florida, the Gulf Coast, and the Atlantic Coast up to New England are subject to hurricanes and storm surges (Pielke et al., 2008). This problem will be

Figure 17.1 Three Arch Bay, Laguna Beach, California

exacerbated by GCC as many of the country's major Eastern and Gulf population centers are expected to experience coastal flooding from sea level rise, which increases the height of daily high tides (Melillo et al., 2014). The projected increase in damage levels is a major problem because much coastal development is located in areas vulnerable to these natural hazards.

The coast and politics

In the United States, there is an active policy community concerned with ocean and coastal issues, but coastal issues are not a high political priority. There are several reasons for this. First, the United States Congress has ceased to function as a body that identifies major problems and crafts appropriate legislation. Second, federal administrative agencies increasingly lack the resources and the political support to undertake new initiates. Third, the gridlocked legislative process and the shrinking federal government reflect the deepening partisan divide in the United States. Resource management is caught between competing ideologies: The idea that government is evil and attempts to resurrect the idea that government can be a positive force. The 2016 presidential election of Donald Trump, who has rejected scientific explanations of anthropogenic climate change and is a strong proponent of increased oil and gas drilling, introduced extreme uncertainty into US coastal policy. However, many coastal states and coastal areas which are actually experiencing rising sea levels, such the Greater Miami area in Florida, have to continue to take aggressive adaptive measures (Miami-Dade County, 2016).

There is one exception to the federal government's glaringly low level of involvement in coastal issues: It takes a disaster of "biblical" proportions such as Hurricanes Katrina, Sandy, and Harvey, or a major environmental disaster such as 2010 BP oil spill, to stimulate interest in more comprehensive approaches to coastal management[3]. Climate change is a semi-exception. The Obama administration launched several climate change adaptation initiatives directly related to many coastal issues (these are discussed in subsequent sections). This said, coastal policy remains an important state-level issue in at-risk states such California, Florida, and Louisiana.

Federal legislation for coastal zone management

While environmental legislation is usually enacted at the state level, the United States has two major federal laws which deal with coastal management and planning. The Coastal Zone Management Act (CZMA) of 1972[4] and the Coastal Barrier Resources Act both selectively superimpose federal law over state and local land use decisions.[5]

The CZMA is the oldest federal program designed to check unlimited coastal development and to preserve the natural resiliency of coastal ecosystems. It acknowledges (at Section 302(c)) that intensive development has caused the loss of living marine resources, adverse impacts on coastal ecosystems, and shoreline erosion. The program was introduced in an attempt to solve problems caused by fragmented national and local controls over coastal regions (Thompson, 2012). The CZMA was designed to reflect the desire to develop a more integrated approach to coastal management that would protect federal interests while recognizing the primacy of state and local control.

> CZMA could have been integrated into a general, federal land use-planning program, but instead the United States has carved up its land base into a series of private, exclusive entitlements, exercised limited federal control to retained public lands, and enshrined the idea that land should be controlled at the lowest level of government, if at all. (Tarlock and Chizewer, 2016)

The CZM Act does not provide a precise, geographic definition of the coastal zone. Instead, it defines the zone as follows:

> ... *the coastal waters (including the lands therein and thereunder) and the adjacent shore-lands (including the waters therein and thereunder), strongly influenced by each other and in proximity to the shorelines of the several coastal states, and includes islands, transitional and intertidal areas, salt marshes, wetlands, and beaches.* (§ 1453(1))

The Act sets out a program which provides planning grants to states to develop coastal zone management programs and mandates that the federal government itself must be consistent with state-approved plans (Thompson, 2012). In exchange for adopting plans for coastal areas, states can then deny permission to federal agencies to carry out development (such as federal roads, rail, and federal public buildings) if they are inconsistent with the state's program (§ 1456). Yet the President can override a state's refusal to certify federal activities if a waiver is in "the paramount interest of the United States" (§ 1456). Congress decided to make participation in this CZMA program voluntary, but thirty-four out of thirty-five coastal and Great Lakes states have chosen to participate; Alaska withdrew its participation in 2011.

The Coastal Barrier Resources Act (CBRA), adopted in 1982, employs a creative approach to coastal protection: It prohibits federal funding for development in designated coastal areas, based on the recognition that the federal government historically permitted and subsidized development that resulted in the loss of barrier islands; in threats to human life, health, and property; and in the expenditure of millions of tax dollars each year.

To prevent further damage, the CBRA requires the mapping of coastal barrier islands and prohibits certain development and many types of federal expenditures in these protected areas. The types of prohibited federal expenses vary widely: From financing or undertaking construction of roads and airports providing access to hazardous coastal areas, to federal flood insurance, to emergency operations. The CBRA does not prohibit privately funded development but rather is founded on the hope that without the federal support, developers will be deterred. The Act initially *"designated 186 units* [of land], *comprising about 453,000 acres along 666 miles of shoreline from Maine to Texas"* and now includes 585 units and 1.3 million acres (GAO, 2007).

The CBRA is a model for curbing moral hazard behavior in at-risk areas; it has succeeded in saving significant federal dollars, according to the Fish and Wildlife Service (FWS, 2002). These savings stem from averted disaster relief costs, as well as construction costs.[6] The FWS also noted, however, *"[w]here the economic incentive for development is extremely high, the Act's funding limitations can be overcome"* (2002). Indeed, ten years after CBRA's enactment, a General Accountability Office (GAO) Report determined that the program largely failed, because nine of the thirty-four hazardous areas had undergone significant new development, with more development planned. In 2007, the GAO did a follow-up report and determined that even with limited federal financial assistance, in areas conducive and attractive to development, states or local governments that want the development provide their own subsidies (GAO, 2007). Agencies also might have had difficulty determining whether the properties in question were within the CBRS, due to mapping problems.

The ability to deter development in the CBRS depends significantly on the state and local attitude toward these lands. The CBRA experience only reinforces the need for state and local collaboration with the federal program or willingness to impose more stringent floodplain controls.

Definition of the shoreline and coastal public land

The United States has clear rules to delineate boundaries between land and sea, albeit with variations across the states. This section discusses how delineation rules are tied up with rules relating to ownership of coastal land.

Shoreline delineation rules

The definition of the line between land and sea originates from the Outer Continental Shelf Lands Act. That Act sets out that the states own submerged lands up to the dry sand area (§ 1311).[7] It defines submerged lands as follows:

> ... *all lands permanently or periodically covered by tidal waters up to but not above the line of mean high tide and seaward to a line three geographical miles distant from the coast line of each such State and to the boundary line of each such State where in any case such boundary as it existed at the time such State became a member of the Union, or as heretofore approved by Congress, extends seaward (or into the Gulf of Mexico) beyond three geographical miles...* (§ 1301(a)(2))

Thus, the shoreline is the line between submerged lands and dry land. Yet the method of identification and delineation of that line is left to the determination of each individual state, because the states, not the federal government, succeeded to the rights of the Crown of England and adopted rules before there was a national government. There are basically three rules from which states may select to mark the boundary between public submerged lands and private ownership: (1) The high tide line, (2) the low tide line, and (3) the line of vegetation. Both the high tide line and low tide line are artificial lines based on historical tidal cycles (means). The high tide line was the English common law rule.

Originally, many Atlantic coastal states interpreted the English common law to adopt the low tide line as the dividing line between public and private ownership, to promote access to commercial navigation by allowing extensive piers and harbors to be built. All other coastal states adopted the mean high-tide line (Tarlock, 1988, Section 3:35). Today, only five states use the mean low-tide line – Delaware, Maine, Massachusetts, Pennsylvania, and Virginia.

The Supreme Court adopted the rule that the seaward boundary of federal grants is the mean high tide line, which is determined by the average of the height of all tides over an 18.6-year period (Borax Consolidated, Ltd. v. Los Angeles, 1935). The mean high-water line along a beach is where a plane of an average elevation based on 18-plus years of tidal data intersects the contours of a particular beach. These rules are discussed in more detail below because they are relevant to coastal access.

Public land ownership

In the United States, coastal public land includes submerged lands and other categories of coastal land, as detailed in the following sections.

Submerged lands

State ownership of tidelands is subject to special restrictions. States own submerged lands in trust for the public. The doctrine has been traced back to Roman law, but its more immediate origins are in sixteenth-century England. After Henry VIII took England out of the Catholic Church, many church and other lands, including "waste" or lands along the sea, were forfeited to the Crown. Ultimately, the courts held that these lands were held by the Crown to protect public uses such as fishing and navigation (Royal Fishery at Banne, 1611). The doctrine allows states considerable, but not unlimited, discretion to dispose of or retain tidelands. In the nineteenth and early twentieth centuries, many states granted tideland ownership and severed these lands from the trust. Thus, in urban areas, there are many filled and privately owned tidelands. But the public trust doctrine imposes on the states substantial but varying duties regarding the use and development of non-severed tidelands.

In 1892, the Supreme Court invalidated a grant by the legislature of the State of Illinois of a large portion of the city of Chicago's submerged lands in Lake Michigan to private entities, as inconsistent with the state's public trust duty to keep these waters and lands open to use by the public (Illinois Central Railroad v. Illinois 1892). Since that time, state courts have adopted more restrictive rules for the disposal and use of tidelands. There is no uniform rule, but there are at least three restrictions which are followed in many states: (1) There is a presumption against the severance of tidelands from the trust; (2) if private tidelands have not been filled or otherwise developed, they are subject to public servitude for navigation, fishing, and recreation; and (3) tidelands can only be conveyed or leased for trust purposes, such as harbor development, energy exploitation, or even non-water-related uses such as sports stadiums (Tarlock, 1988).

Other coastal lands

In the United States, the land ownership regime along the coasts is not too different from the country's mainly private regime. Landward of the shoreline (mean high or low tide), "dry sand" is usually owned by private entities. There is comparatively little publicly owned dry sand beach or dry coastal land, and there is almost no continuous public ownership on any coast. Only about 30% of United States dry sand beaches or adjoining upland, along the oceans or Great Lakes, is publicly owned (Rowe, 2013).

Most public land is held by the states or in local-government ownership; there is very little federally owned land along the coasts. Being aware of the role of public land ownership, most coastal states have made efforts over the years to acquire land for state beach parks, but these are generally narrow strips of beach which seldom stretch for more than three miles. The largest beach state park in California, Crystal Cove State Park, has only 3.2 miles of beach plus 2,400 acres of inland wilderness. Cities and counties also own a considerable amount of beach land. These lands are primarily allocated for seasonal temporary recreational uses.[8]

The federal government does own small stretches of coastal land, but primarily along the Pacific coast (Gorte et al., 2012), with only a few national seashores on the Atlantic. It did not historically own land along the Atlantic, because federal land ownership began in 1789 (with the adoption of the US Constitution), long after private land claims were established in the east. Federal land ownership along the Pacific is the result of several small states forcing some of the large original states, which had western land claims to largely unsettled land, to cede these lands to the newly created federal government. The reason was greed; the small states wanted to open the frontier to speculation by all citizens. Yet today, land along the Pacific coast is mainly in private ownership. For example, in California, the ownership of much of the coastal land derives from Spanish and Mexican land grants which were recognized when California became a state.

Federal land ownership along the coast consists almost exclusively of forests, open range, and mountainous areas that were not conveyed to private parties during the settlement era.

There are only two large federally owned national parks along the three coasts – Everglades National Park and Redwood National Park. In general, national park boundaries have often been drawn to avoid coastal land, because of existing towns and Indian[9] reservations (Lien, 2000). The boundaries of the Olympic National Park in Washington state, for example, were carefully drawn to avoid the coast; there is only a 73-mile narrow strip along the Pacific Ocean which is now a federally owned wilderness.

The most important category of federal coastal ownership is the ten national seashores, which were created between 1953 and 1975 through purchase/eminent domain ("expropriation" in most countries). Seashores were an early, and now stalled, response to post–World War II demand for increased recreational opportunities of all types. The seashores provide the public with accessible beaches, primarily along the Atlantic Coast. (There is only one national seashore, Point Reyes, on the Pacific Ocean.) These areas have a mix of federal, state, and private ownership. The use and management problems caused by this pattern are discussed below under "urban and regional coastal planning."

As indicated throughout this section, coastal public land in the United States is limited. The net result on the country's coasts is that market forces, as regulated by state and local governments, dictate the use of the coast. This has substantial environmental, social, and economic implications. Control of coastal development has been largely left to local governments which have a long history, stretching back to the eighteenth century, of promoting extensive coastal development and transferring state owned tidelands to private ownership. This is especially true on the Atlantic Coast.

One specific outcome is that the preferred adaptation response to increased hurricanes and sea level rise is to focus on increasing municipal "resilience" (the ability to cope with climate change–induced conditions). This is done – or attempted, with varying degrees of effectiveness – through new building restrictions, seawalls, and the elevation of roads, rather than by means of a more comprehensive approach to coastal development that includes retreat from the shore. In addition, as part of the focus on "resilience," the federal government has continued to pump millions of dollars into beach restoration programs despite criticisms about the endless need to invest in post-storm beach restoration (Pilkey & Cooper, 2014). More details on "resilience" programs are outlined below.

Permitted uses on coastal public land

The public has a right to use state tidelands (submerged lands) and public beach land for recreational purposes. There are no uniform federal or state laws specifying the range of permitted uses of publicly owned beaches, but in general, unlike some other countries represented in this book, public beaches are limited to recreational access for swimming, walking, picnicking, water and beach sports, and sun bathing. The 1972 CZMA introduced the concept of water-dependent uses, and many states have developed water dependency policies to regulate waterfront development.[10] Common structures on public beaches include older fishing and amusement piers (no longer permitted), public restrooms, lifeguard stations, and boat storage facilities.

The rules relating to the definition and use of public coastal land have on the whole been strictly enforced, and in some states strict enforcement measures are specifically required by law. For example, the Texas Open Beaches Act mandates the Commissioner of the General Land office to "strictly and vigorously enforce the prohibition against encroachments" which interfere with public beach use (Section 61.011c). There are many litigated cases where a dry sand property owner's encroachment on state tideland has been declared illegal (e.g. Lechuza

Villas West v. California Coastal Commission, 1992). The enforcement of prohibitions against private encroachments on state-owned tidelands is shared between state and local governments under the public trust doctrine.

Right of public access

Given the relatively small amount of public littoral land, coastal access is a major issue in many states. Access rules are, in general, a matter of state law. But the Fifth Amendment to the United States Constitution prohibits the taking of private property without just compensation. This allows a direct judicial challenge to regulations which mandate coastal access as condition to the approval of a development permit. Two major United States Supreme Court decisions (Nollan v. California Coastal Commission, 1987; Dolan v. City of Tigard, 1994) require a nexus between the development and the need for access and impose a high burden on the state to prove the nexus. This has made it difficult for states to acquire access without compensation, unless the access is already subject to public servitude. In this section, we address states with oceanfront property (and not the laws of the freshwater Great Lakes states).

In all states, once the dividing line between public and private ownership is established, the vertical and horizontal access rules are clear: A person must be able to reach the public shoreline by a public access point or with the consent of the "dry sand" property owner. Once the public shoreline is reached, the individual has unlimited horizontal access up to the line of private ownership, since the public has a right to use public trust lands for recreation, with some exceptions.

The link between public land ownership and accessibility is a key aspect of state lawmakers' decisions regarding the definition of the shoreline (Figure 17.2). The public trust doctrine guarantees public use of state-owned submerged lands, but efforts to expand the common law rule of public ownership can be challenged as a taking of property without due process of law. Some states chose to use the low tide line as the reference, on the basis of a theory that this rule promoted water access by allowing private piers and wharves in areas covered with water part of the day. Furthermore, several states have extended (or sought to extend) public ownership in order to promote accessibility.

Oregon, Texas, and Hawai'i are the only coastal or oceanfront states that, in general, clearly allow public access of the beach up to the vegetation line, thus significantly widening the area open to public access. These three states have adopted this rule despite the fact that the official shoreline in all three states is delineated at the high tide line. In Hawai'i, however, this level of accessibility is not facilitated by the law: The state initially extended horizontal access by adopting the landward vegetation line as the dividing line between public and private ownership (County of Hawai'i v. Sotomura, 1973). However, a federal district court held that the state court's rule which allowed the extension was an unconstitutional taking, at least when applied to registered titles (Sotomura v. County of Hawai'i, 1978). Nonetheless, many beaches in Hawai'i, even those at the most exclusive resorts, are open to the public. Oregon accomplished the same result, with no exceptions, when the state Supreme Court found that since the arrival of American settlers in the 1840s, the state custom had been to allow public access of the dry sand area (Thornton v. Hay, 1969; Stevens v. City of Canon Beach, 1994). However, in other states, extensions of public ownership beyond the high water mark are open to the challenge that the state has taken private property without compensation.

The New Hampshire, Maine, and Massachusetts Supreme Courts have held that the legislative extension of public access to the area between the high and low marks would be a

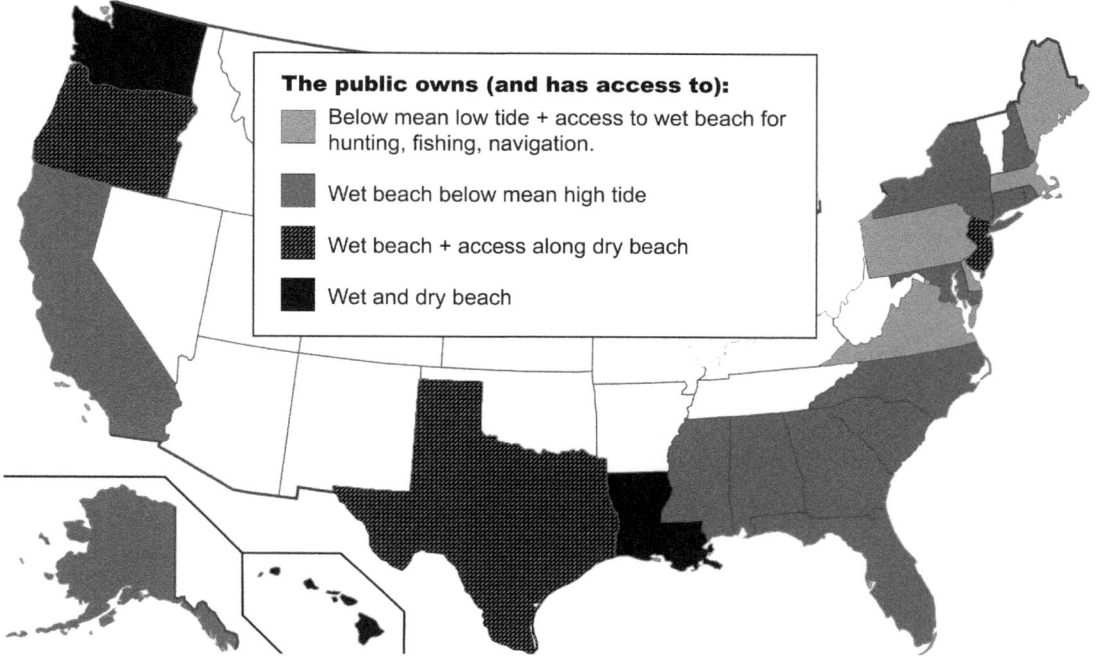

Figure 17.2 Variations in beach ownership and access among the US Coastal States

Source: Prepared by Cygal Pellach, based on image by Rick Wilson/Surfrider Foundation (2014)

taking.[11] The possibility of takings challenges has been further expanded by a 2010 United States Supreme Court decision, Stop the Beach Renourishment v. Florida Department of Environmental Protection (560 U.S. 702, 2010). Florida enacted legislation which fixes beach erosion lines – a new boundary between public and private property. Seaward of the line, the state now owns the submerged land and any beaches created by erosion. Property owners still have access to the ocean, but only as members of the public. Property owners challenged the legislation as a taking of their common law right of water access. The Florida Supreme Court held that littoral owners never had a right to receive accretions and thus there was no taking. All justices agreed that no taking had occurred.

California has the most determined legislative program to provide public access. The state's Coastal Act (§ 30211-30212) provides:

> *Development shall not interfere with the public's right of access to the sea where acquired through use or legislative authorization, including, but not limited to, the use of dry sand and rocky coastal beaches to the first line of terrestrial vegetation.*
>
> a *Public access from the nearest public roadway to the shoreline and along the coast shall be provided in new development projects except where (1) it is inconsistent with public safety, military security needs, or the protection of fragile coastal resources, (2) adequate access exists nearby, or (3) agriculture would be adversely affected.*

> *Dedicated access way shall not be required to be opened to public use until a public agency or private association agrees to accept responsibility for maintenance and liability of the access way.*

The legislation has enabled the state to acquire some 2,000 coastal access easements (California Coastal Commission, n.d.). This said, the United States Supreme Court cases discussed at the beginning of this section have allowed successful challenges to Commission demands for access (Donahue, 2016). On the other hand, in 2018, the US Supreme Court refused to hear a case that challenged the requirement for property owners to retain coastal access. In Surfrider Foundation v, Martins Beach 1, LLC (2018), a California Court of Appeal had held that a beachfront property owner who terminated previously existing coastal access must apply for a permit from the Commission in order to do so. The Supreme Court refused to consider the new property owner's taking challenges to the Commission's permit demand.

Social justice in accessibility

Social justice in accessibility is a significant issue in some areas of the United States (Kahrl, 2015). Unless a public easement exists by a judicial finding of prescription or voluntary land dedication by the upland owner, users must access the beach only through public access strips. This is a major problem, especially in affluent beachfront residential areas. Many cities allow free access to their beaches, but there are many de facto and de jure barriers. One of the major de facto barriers is the limited number of public access points in many states, especially for beaches at the base of cliffs.

Beachfront property owners in affluent areas, such as Malibu and Newport Beach in California, have actively discouraged public use, especially by Black and Hispanic users (García & Baltodano, 2005). Property owners have removed beach access signs, planted vegetation to cover them, put "No Trespassing" or "Private Property" signs on publicly owned beach property, or employed private security firms to intimidate legal beach users (Beachapedia, 2019). More subtle forms of discouragement include the common municipal refusals to provide parking near beaches, high parking fees for beachfront lots, high daily or seasonal beach fees, and charging differential rates for municipal and non-municipal residents. There are no comprehensive figures on the number of municipalities that charge beach access fees, but there is considerable evidence that many wealthy coastal communities use fees and parking restrictions to limit access by poor and racial minorities as well as non-residents from inland communities (Kahrl, 2018).

State and local setback standards

Setting development back from the coast has been widely recognized, across the United States, as an important aspect of coastal zone management. While there are no uniform federal coastal setback standards in the United States, two-thirds of coastal and Great Lakes states have adopted standards at state and local levels. These standards are a result of the federal Coastal Zone Management Act, which lists protection of beaches, dunes, and barrier islands as one of the major purposes of the Act (§ 1452(2)(A)). Almost all of the Atlantic Coast states have adopted setback regulations (Randall & deBoer, 2012).

North Carolina provides one of the best examples of setback regulation because its low-lying, heavily used coastline is vulnerable to sea level rise (Strauss et al., 2014). In addition, houses are built to the edge of private property in many parts of North Carolina, especially on the barrier islands of the Outer Banks. The state's setback standards are as follows:

> *Oceanfront construction setback is measured landward from the first line of stable natural vegetation, or a static vegetation line when applicable. Setback distance is determined by two variables; (1) size of structure; (2) a setback factor based on shoreline position change rates... As specified in Rule 15A NCAC 7H .0304(1) (a), the minimum setback factor is 2, unless the shoreline is eroding at a rate greater than 2 feet per year. Therefore, when the shoreline is accreting (moving seaward), or eroding at a rate less than 2 feet per year, the default setback factor is 2.* (North Carolina Division of Coastal Management, 2014)

The state's Coastal Area Management Act (Section 103) allows only limited exceptions for development within the setback zone, such as road and utility maintenance. There are no variance provisions for new development that falls outside these limited categories.

The setback distance is determined as the size of the structure multiplied by the relevant setback factor. Based on the author's personal visits to several of the state's beaches, it appears that the setbacks are strictly observed. Development is intense but uniform behind the dune line. This can be attributed to the fear of hurricane damage and to consensus regarding the need to protect the public's right to use the dry sand area for recreation (Nies v. Town of Emerald Isle, 2015; Slavin v. Town of Oak Island, 2003).

Significantly, the State of North Carolina presents the need for setbacks as emerging from erosion rates, while failing to recognize potential sea level rise. In 2009, the state enacted legislation which prohibits the use of any reference to sea level rise in coastal land use planning. That legislation came as a result of fierce pushback from the real estate industry, in response to a report by the North Carolina Coastal Resources Commission which projected a 40 cm rise by 2100 as certain and a 100 cm rise as likely. Thus, ironically, while North Carolina has sophisticated setback regulations, it is also the subject of ridicule among those who are convinced that global climate change is a scientific fact.

Urban and regional coastal use planning

Land use regulation is a fragmented and overlapping system. In the United States, three levels of government – the federal (national), the states, and local jurisdictions (primarily cities and counties) – share the power to regulate land. The federal government historically allowed states to regulate land under the Tenth Amendment. In turn, the states legislatively delegated this power to local governments after the introduction of zoning in the 1920s. Thus, coastal land use planning is primarily a local and state responsibility.

Although historically there has been a push for the federal government to adopt a comprehensive land use planning program,[12] the issue is now off the political agenda for the foreseeable future. Instead, the federal government has addressed specific land use problems only on a piecemeal basis. Relevant federal programs primarily deal with sensitive lands such as wetlands or attempts by local governments to block land uses, such as cell towers, that are essential to national security. For example, a federal permit is required to fill wetlands connected to navigable waters or to develop an area which is habitat for listed endangered species (McKinstry, 2006). Coastal lands fall into the former category, and it follows that coastal use planning is one of the areas the federal government has entered.

The Coastal Zone Management Act (CZMA), introduced earlier in this chapter, is the key federal legislation which guides coastal land use planning. In accordance with this legislation, several states have used federal funds to compile inventories of coastal access points among their shorelines and to make them available to the public.[13] In addition, Virginia has developed a "Living Shoreline" management program to encourage the use of alternatives to traditional hardening techniques to stabilize eroding shorelines. This concept of soft or natural shorelines has spread to states on both coasts and the Great Lakes.[14]

CZMA's biggest weakness is that it does not mandate any particular set of issues that must be addressed in the state coastal plan. However, a major section, 309, provides a powerful incentive for states to develop aggressive coastal protection policies. This section encourages states to undertake enhancement projects across certain key areas – wetlands; coastal hazards; public access; marine debris; cumulative and secondary impacts; special area management plans; ocean and Great Lakes resources; energy and government facility siting; and aquaculture (§ 1456(b)).

In June 2014, the NOAA (National Oceanographic and Atmospheric Administration) amended its Section 309 guidance to ensure greater consideration of climate change challenges in coastal management. State coastal plans must address coastal flooding as a result of sea level rise. The NOAA made available $1.5 million of competitive funding to help states and tribes make improvements to their coastal management programs, and the program has survived Trump administration efforts to roll back all previous climate change adaptation programs (NOAA, n.d.). The guidance will help state and tribal coastal managers better prepare for the impacts of climate change and improve the safety of their communities.

The states have significant power in coastal planning matters under the CZMA. This is illustrated in a case where the state of Delaware refused to certify New Jersey's approval for Crown Landing LLC to develop a Liquefied Natural Gas terminal on the bed of the Delaware River (owned by Delaware). Delaware's coastal zone management plan prohibited all industrial development. The District of Columbia federal Court of Appeals summarized the relevant powers as follows:

> *Crown Landing did not file a CZMA certification with Delaware but did request a status decision from the state (we gather that a status decision is, in effect, a preliminary, yet preemptive, decision). On February 3, 2005, the Delaware Department of Natural Resources and Environmental Control, petitioner here, issued its decision and rejected the project. On appeal, Delaware's Coastal Zone Industrial Control Board unanimously affirmed that decision. Meanwhile, New Jersey filed an original action before the Supreme Court challenging Delaware's jurisdiction to regulate the Crown Landing terminal pursuant to its authority under the CZMA. The Supreme Court confirmed that Delaware indeed possesses this authority. New Jersey v. Delaware, 128 S.Ct. 1410, 1427-8, 170 L.Ed.2d 315 (2008)...* (Delaware Department of Natural Resources and Environmental Control v. Federal Energy Regulatory Commission, 2009)

Selected state programs

Two states with noteworthy planning instruments for coastal management are California and North Carolina.

California

California's coastal zone management program, regulated through the California Coastal Act (1976), is the national gold standard. In this state, all new development in the coastal zone must both meet local land use regulations and obtain a certificate of approval from the regional coastal zone commission. Thus, the definition of the coastal zone is critical. However, there is no fixed, uniform definition of the zone because the Act uses maps approved by the legislature. Thus, the area subject to regulation can vary over time. The primary definition on which the maps are based is:

> *that land and water area of the State of California from the Oregon border to the border of the Republic of Mexico, specified on the maps identified and set forth in Section 17 of that chapter of the Statutes of the 1975-76 Regular Session enacting this division, extending seaward to the state's outer limit of jurisdiction, including all offshore islands, and extending inland generally 1,000 yards from the mean high tide line of the sea. In significant coastal estuarine, habitat, and recreational areas it extends inland to the first major ridgeline paralleling the sea or five miles from the mean high tide line of the sea, whichever is less, and in developed urban areas the zone generally extends inland less than 1,000 yards. (§ 30103(a))*

As of 2014, there had been twenty-six amendments to the Act to include or exclude land (§ 30140–30176). The Act creates a two-level review process for new development that falls within the mapped zone. The developer must obtain a permit from a regional Coastal Commission and comply with all applicable local land use ordinances (§ 36000). In addition, each local government in the zone must prepare a local coastal management plan (§ 35000). Special attention must be given to sensitive areas:

a   *The commission, in consultation with affected local governments and the appropriate regional commissions, shall, not later than September 1, 1977, after public hearing, designate sensitive coastal resource areas within the coastal zone where the protection of coastal resources and public access requires, in addition to the review and approval of zoning ordinances, the review and approval by the regional commissions and commission of other implementing actions.*
b   *The designation of each sensitive coastal resource area shall be based upon a separate report prepared and adopted by the commission which shall contain all of the following:*

   1   *A description of the coastal resources to be protected and the reasons why the area has been designated as a sensitive coastal resource area.*
   2   *A specific determination that the designated area is of regional or statewide significance.*
   3   *A specific list of significant adverse impacts that could result from development where zoning regulations alone may not adequately protect coastal resources or access.*
   4   *A map of the area indicating its size and location.*

c   *In sensitive coastal resource areas designated pursuant to this section, a local coastal program "shall include the implementing actions adequate to protect the coastal resources enumerated in the findings of the sensitive coastal resource area report in conformity with the policies of this division".* (§ 30502)

It is too early to tell whether this program is effective in protecting the coastal zone from harmful or hazardous development.

North Carolina: A good plan gone bad

North Carolina has a long, low, intensively developed coast, especially along the Outer Banks, a chain of barrier islands. In 1974, the state adopted a progressive Coastal Area Management Act. Local governments were mandated to develop coastal land use plans and development approvals had to be consistent with these plans, under North Carolina Statutes (Section 113A-111). However, in 2012, the state elected a conservative legislature, which engaged in an extraordinary act of climate change denial. North Carolina's legislature considered a widely ridiculed bill to ban all local and state entities, other than the state Coastal Commission, from determining the rate of projected sea level rise. It also required the Commission to limit its review to historical data. In 2012, a less extreme version of the bill, but one that still limits consideration of sea level rise, became law without the governor's signature (North Carolina House Bill 819).

There is increasing evidence that market correction is occurring: The value of beachfront properties is declining as buyers become more risk adverse (Urbina, 2016; Luntz, 2018). However, the North Carolina real estate industry continues to fight any "disclosure" of sea level rise (Leavenworth, 2017).

Compliance and enforcement

In general, illegal building is not a problem in the United States. Any building on private land requires a local permit, and authorities have ample power to penalize illegal building. Enforcement is relatively regular. A decision from 2013, Sansotta v. Town of Nags Head (North Carolina), is illustrative of the power of cities to prevent illegal building. After beach erosion caused six cottages to shift seaward to the line of vegetation and a coastal storm left them stranded on a public beach, the town ordered the cottages to be torn down as public nuisances. Nonetheless, the owners continued to repair the cottages. The court brushed aside a "due process" (procedural) challenge to the order and subsequent assessment of fines for violating it. The court ruled that these types of regulatory actions *"represent limitations on the use of property that inhere in the title itself, in the restrictions that background principles of the State's law of property and nuisance already place upon land ownership."*

The largest problems with private development in or affecting public protected areas occur within national seashores. Unlike most national parks, these areas are not composed of land owned exclusively by the federal government, and many are located in popular second-home areas. Thus, the designation includes a patchwork of public land, often acquired after the creation of the seashore, and private inholdings. These are privately owned lands within a national park or other publicly owned, protected area. Some inholdings have been acquired through voluntary purchases or the use of eminent domain (Dilsaver, 2004). Because each seashore has a separate federal law which delegates considerable management authority to the states, the federal government's authority differs from state to state. However, the states are usually loath to transfer such inholdings into public ownership and the federal government is constrained, for both financial and legal reasons, in its ability to acquire land.

The Cape Cod (Massachusetts) National Seashore as an example

The ongoing conflicts with inholding building on Cape Cod National Seashore illustrate the problems of managing the seashores (Lombardo, 2010). There are 600 inholdings on the 27,000 acres of national seashore at Cape Cod. The local towns have the authority to zone these areas and thus control development and redevelopment. The federal government's hook is that it can issue zoning standards. If a town's zoning bylaws conform to the federal guidelines, the federal government cannot exercise eminent domain. Furthermore, *"wealthy owners push the limits of Park Service guidelines, or ignore them altogether"* (Rozhon, 2006) and build large new houses.

A few years after the seashore's designation, the federal government began negotiating with owners of the new, but now illegal, houses, with the implicit threat that they could be seized through eminent domain. Most people either sold out to the government in the 1970s or negotiated a sale that guaranteed them life use of the property or 25-year leases (all of which have now expired, except a few that were extended due to personal hardship). Some of the houses were donated or bequeathed to the park.

Illegality also becomes a burden in case of a major disaster. In such cases, considerable disaster relief is often available for rebuilding. This lessens the incentives for illegal rebuilding. There have been federal and state efforts to purchase at-risk property and demolish it. Yet there are social equity impacts of buyouts.[15]

Climate change awareness

This section addresses policy responses to climate change on the federal and state levels.

Federal executive responses

The threats of sustained sea level rise and increased and more intense hurricanes which promise more coastal flooding are taken seriously by some states and most at-risk local governments. But the United States faces a strange situation with respect to climate change. There is an overwhelming scientific consensus that global climate change (GGC) is occurring, but there is a divergence over the causes. A majority of Americans believe that climate change is occurring, but a majority in most counties of the country also believes that it is not caused by human activity (Holthaus, 2015). A major component of the Republican Party's policy agenda is to block all climate change legislation. This became the federal government's stated policy with the election of Donald J. Trump as president in 2016. The Trump Administration, supported by the Republican-controlled Congress, has rolled back all of the Obama administration's climate change mitigation and adaptation efforts (including several Executive Orders issued between 2009 and 2015; White House, 2014).

Many agencies have crafted policies for integrating climate change adaptation into their operations in coastal areas. These include FEMA – the Federal Emergency Management Agency (FEMA, 2011) – and the EPA (Environmental Protection Agency, 2014). The US Army Corps of Engineers has issued several reports addressing climate adaptation since 2013

(USACE, 2013, 2014). In 2015, the Army Corps' North Atlantic Coast Comprehensive Study (NACCS) was prepared in response to the post-Sandy Disaster Relief Appropriations Act of 2013. That Act directed the Army Corps to *"conduct a comprehensive study to address the flood risks of vulnerable coastal populations in areas that were affected by Hurricane Sandy"* (USACE, 2015, p. i). The NACCS report provides a risk management framework and supports coastal communities in efforts to consider future sea level and climate change scenarios. The Corps assesses vulnerability, or the inability to cope with adverse effects of coastal flooding, by analyzing the nature and magnitude of the hazard and the characteristics of the community (USACE, 2015, p. 21).

During the administration of President Barack Obama (2008–2016), FEMA encouraged local governments to integrate hazard mitigation[16] analysis into land use decisions (FEMA, 2013a). FEMA justified its stepped-up role in influencing local government action relating to disaster damages on the basis that (1) hazard mitigation planning fits squarely in the local government's role in protecting the welfare of the community and (2) the economic benefits of proactively avoiding or minimizing risk through safe development practices outweigh the costs of damage and disruption (FEMA, 2013b). However, all references to climate change have disappeared from Trump Administration FEMA documents. This is consistent with that administration's rejection of the idea that climate change is caused by human activity. In August 2017, Trump led the US withdrawal from the Paris Agreement.

State responses

As noted above, the Trump administration (2016–) has withdrawn from the promotion of either climate change mitigation or adaptation. The case is different at the state and local levels. The story of the English king Canute is instructive. He initially listened to his minions, who told him that he could hold back the tides, but immediately realized that he could not (Medievalists. net, n.d.). Following the chastised king, many states, primarily along the Atlantic coast, and local governments are acting on the almost uniform and increasingly strident scientific consensus that the adverse impacts of climate are beginning to manifest themselves. States have been very proactive in dealing with hurricane winds, but much less so in dealing with increased storm surges and long-term flooding. Most coastal states have building codes that mandate the construction of buildings better able to withstand hurricane-force winds (IBHS, 2015), but several Gulf Coast states, which experience frequent hurricanes, have recently weakened their codes under pressure from the real estate industry. For example, prior to 2017, Florida adopted updated international codes without revisions for all construction, but in 2017, new state legislation required that the state only review (not necessarily adopt) the updated code. The state can adopt less stringent, alternative standards (Florida House Bill 2021 (2017)).

California, again, has the most forward-looking climate change program at a time when the federal government under the Trump administration, as well as states controlled by Republicans, is going in the opposite direction. In 2015, the Governor of Florida instituted an unwritten ban on the use of the words "climate change" or "global warming" (Korten, 2015). The North Carolina Department of Environment and Natural Resources removed links and documents about climate change from its website because it held that the state lacked "clear regulatory responsibility" to deal with global warming (Atkin, 2015).

In 2013, the California Coastal Commission issued a strategic plan for 2013–2018. The climate change section of the plan projects the development of regulatory guidance for the location of new development on sensitive bluff tops and coastal flood zones and for wetland protection buffers (California Coastal Commission, 2013, p. 22). It will also conduct *"a broad vulnerability assessment of urban and rural areas to identify priority areas for adaptation planning"* which can include higher density development to reduce greenhouse gas emissions (California Coastal Commission, 2013, p. 23).

Local governments

Miami-Dade County, Florida, which is on every map of adverse impacts from sea level rise, initiated a process to integrate potential climate change impacts into its local planning in 2010. The process first considered how hazards and climate change could impact issues relating to stormwater management and runoff, infrastructure maintenance and placement, and other planning efforts (FEMA, 2013a). Miami-Dade's Office of Sustainability then produced a strategy plan titled *GreenPrint: Our Design for a Sustainable Future* in December 2010. *GreenPrint* recognizes the importance of studying regional and local climate change trends and impacts. It emphasizes the need to *"integrate future climate change impacts into community and government decision-making for capital, operational, and land use issues"* (Miami-Dade County, 2010, pp. 76–77).

In 2012, Miami-Dade went further and prepared the Southeast Florida Regional Climate Adaptation Plan (RCAP), in cooperation with Broward, Palm Beach, and Monroe counties. The RCAP sets forth a strategy for adapting to climate change by studying and monitoring changes to the environment and community, and developing plans that factor in climate change, including sea level rise (Southeast Florida Regional Climate Change Compact Counties, 2012, p. 13). The RCAP expects the participating communities to develop new flood maps that factor in sea level rise and storm surge modeling (Southeast Florida Regional Climate Change Compact Counties, 2012, p. 17). It also promotes the integration of climate change data into its hazards emergency planning. Miami continues to take modest but concrete steps to deal with its sea level rise problems. The initial focus has been on capital improvements to protect residential properties, such as raising street levels and installing a large number of high-volume pumps to keep streets dry as the sea rises.

In the wake of Hurricane Sandy, the Obama administration launched the Rebuild by Design competition. The competition sought *"innovative community- and policy-based solutions to protect US cities that are most vulnerable to increasingly intense weather events and future uncertainties"* (OECD, n.d.). The project connected experts with local planners and citizens to help create *"environmentally- and economically-healthier"* solutions (OECD, n.d.).

The 100 Resilient Cities Campaign, launched by the Rockefeller Foundation, broadly aims to help cities become more resilient to physical, economic, and social challenges (100 Resilient Cities, n.d.). It provides financial and logistical guidance and access to expert advisors to create a network of resilient cities and a model for resilience.

New York City is a good case study in the adoption of this policy and its limits. After Hurricane Sandy substantially damaged Midtown to Lower Manhattan, New York used climate models and delineated the 500-year flood area for the year 2050 (NYC, 2013a, p. 50). This forward-looking program, part of the PlaNYC initiative, went beyond the 100-year flood Plain Maps used in the federal Flood Insurance Program and allowed New York City to benefit from federal support. New York obtained a Department of Housing and Urban Development Community Development Block Grant for Disaster Recovery and a Federal Emergency Management Agency (FEMA) Hazard Mitigation grant. However, critics of PlaNYC argue that it does not go far enough in moving citizens out of harm's way (Revkin, 2013).

New York City has taken significant action to plan for climate change through its Commission on Climate Change, its PlaNYC process, its involvement in the Rebuild by Design program, and zoning changes. The PlanYC report has led to 257-plus initiatives to improve resilience. After Hurricane Sandy, the city changed its building code to require buildings to protect to a level 1 or 2 feet higher than FEMA-designated flood elevation (NYC, n.d.). In turn, the City Council passed the Flood Resilience Text Amendment, which modifies zoning to enable flood-resistant construction (NYC, 2013b). The Amendment also introduces regulations to mitigate potential negative effects of flood-resistant construction on the streetscape and public realm.

Public participation

Public participation is an essential element of all three government layers of coastal zone planning and management, but its effectiveness is much disputed. Coastal zone planning and management remains primarily a top-down expert-driven process. This section will illustrate this point with examples from all three layers of governance; federal, state, and local.

The federal CZMA depends on the adoption of state coastal management plans implemented at the state and local levels. The Act guides state implementation by specifying several mandatory elements including the opportunity for public participation. States and local governments generally implement public participation through stakeholder workshop or task forces (e.g. Miami-Dade Sea Level Rise Task Force; Miami-Dade County, 2014) and general public hearings. The extent of opportunities and the effectiveness of public input vary widely.

California's Coastal Zone Management Act (discussed above) aims, at Section 6.C.1, to provide ample and effective opportunities for public participation in regional and local plans. However, a study of California coastal planning concluded that "*[i]n regard to public participation capacity variables, no variable made a statistically significant contribution to coastal zone land use plan quality. While public participation variables did not have a statistically significant impact on coastal zone land use plan quality, these variables have a certain influence on coastal zone land use plan quality*" (Tang, 2008, p. 553). At the local level, a recent evaluation of sea level rise adaptation planning in two of the most stressed United States cities, Miami and New Orleans, found weak public participation (Fu et al., 2017).

Liability and fiscal issues

Coastal hurricanes are Acts of God for which no one is responsible. Property owners who suffer damages have two types of recourse. First, the Stafford Disaster Relief and Emergency Assistance Act provides a wide variety of disaster relief to public facilities and private property owners. This Act is often supplemented by a special act for the damaged area which provides a combination of grants and structural measures to public governments and private individuals. Second, the National Flood Insurance Program provides reduced-rate flood insurance to residents in high-risk areas, including coastal property located in a special flood hazard area. These areas are 100-year floodplains (areas with a 1% chance of an annual flood every 100 years). The program has been criticized because it encourages building in high-risk areas at taxpayer expense. Its maps are out of date and generally do not reflect climate change risks, and the program is kept alive by borrowing from the United States Treasury and is in debt to the federal government (GAO, 2017). For example, after Hurricane Harvey in 2017, FEMA faced a $1.1 billion shortfall in payouts and revenue on top of the over $21 billion it has borrowed from the US Treasury over the years. Efforts to reform it have stalled in Congress.[17]

Hurricane flood damage can be exacerbated by public infrastructure such as dams and navigation channels. The federal government is immune from damage from the operation of flood control facilities (Flood Control Act 1944, Section 702c), but there is no blanket immunity for private and non-federal entities that may be liable under state law (Ayala et al., 2018). There is a narrow exception under federal law for non-flood-related facility operations (Central Green County v. United States, 2001), but it has proved difficult to invoke.[18]

Coordination in coastal management

Coastal management is fragmented among federal agencies, state, and local governments. The result is a fragmentation of authority which results in ad hoc and inconsistent decisions. The major federal agency, The National Oceanographic and Atmospheric Association (NOAA), part of the Department of Commerce, can foster state and local coastal zone planning, but its regulatory power is limited to overriding state vetoes of federally licensed or approved activities. Other agencies, such as the Federal Energy Regulatory Commission (FERC), can influence the coastal environment by approving energy facilities such as shipping terminals. But a state can still block FERC facilities that do not comply with state water quality law (Clean Water Act 1972, § 1341). As a result of the federal Coastal Zone Management Act, all states have coastal zone management programs, but the regulatory authority varies widely.

Overall assessment

The four United States coastlines – Atlantic, Gulf of Mexico, Great Lakes, and Pacific – are home to a growing percentage of the country's population and serve vital economic functions, from heavy industry to recreation. A maze of federal, state, and local laws governs the use of these coastal zones, but there is no coherent national policy and no prospect of such a development. Thus, coastal policy has been devolved to the states and local governments. Three trends stand out that do not bode well for the future of US coasts. First, all areas are unprepared for the consequences of global climate change, sea level rise, and more hurricanes and flooding. For example, we are still trying to preserve eroding coastlines by endlessly wasting money to rebuild beaches (Song & Shaw, 2018). Second, crucial decisions about access and the balance between environmental conservation and industrial and residential development are being made on an ad hoc basis and increasingly challenged in the courts. Third, private forces, real estate markets, and the insurance industry will play an increasingly important role in the future. The rapid increase in damages from climate change–related catastrophic disasters has already made it difficult for the insurance industry to manage these risks (Mandel, 2018).

Notes

1. Strauss et al. (2012) estimate "the contiguous US population living on land within 1 m of high tide to be 3.7 million… At the state level, Florida, Louisiana, California, New York and New Jersey have the largest sub-meter populations." See also National Research Council et al. (2012).
2. Counties are an administrative tier between state and local government.
3. A prominent example of post-disaster coastal planning and management is the Hurricane Sandy Rebuilding Strategy prepared by the Hurricane Sandy Rebuilding Task Force (2013). The Task Force was established by President Obama in 2012.
4. For a history of the Act, see Chasis (1985).

5. Cellular towers are another exception where federal regulatory programs were selectively super-imposed over them. We do have an incomplete federal program of "sensitive land" protection. Activities such as the filling of a wetland or the development of the habitat of a listed Endangered Species require a federal permit in addition to compliance with all state and local regulations.
6. The FWS estimated a saving of about $686,000,000 from 1983 through 1996 (FWS, 2002, pp. 1–3)
7. This definition allows states to claim more land. The Crown of England's claim, which is the basis for state claims, was originally measured in nautical miles, which are 3.42 geographical miles. Two states, the Florida portion of the Gulf of Mexico coast and Texas, successfully claimed that they succeeded to Spanish claims which were measured in marine leagues, giving these states submerged lands nine nautical miles seaward from the mean high-tide line.
8. For an example, see California's regulations for use of state parks, http://www.parks.ca.gov/?page_id=21301.
9. In the United States, we still use "Indian" to refer to reservations, Indian law, etc.
10. E.g. the Washington State Shore Protection Act, Revised Code Washington §90.50.20.
11. For New Hampshire, see Opinion of the Justices (Use of Coastal Beaches), 649 A.2d 620 (N.H. 1994); for Maine, see Bells v. Town of Wells, 557 A.2d 168 (Me. 1989); and for Massachusetts, see Opinion of the Justices, 313 N.E.2d 561 (Ma. 1971).
12. The National Land Use Policy and Planning Assistance Act, which provided grants to state to develop a state planning and regulatory process which included the control of "areas of critical environmental concern." The bill suffered the fate of almost all post–New Deal efforts to bring ecological and hydrological to irrational political boundaries: Intense local and state opposition. It was narrowly defeated in 1974 and any effort for general federal land use planning disappeared from the political arena, never to reappear.
13. E.g. County of Maui (2005).
14. E.g. Washington State Department of Ecology (2014).
15. For example, see New Jersey Institute for Social Justice (2013).
16. The term "hazard mitigation" means "sustained action taken to reduce or eliminate the long-term risk to human life and property from hazards" (44 CFR §201.2, *Definitions*).
17. The program must be periodically reauthorized and as of 2018 was kept alive by short-term extensions (FEMA, 2019).
18. As demonstrated in: In re Katrina Canal Breaches Litigation, 696 F.3d 4436 (5th Cir. 2012) (St. Bernard Parish Gov't v. United States, 121 Fed. Cl. 687, 718-19 (Fed. Cl. 2015), rev'd887 F.3d 1354 (Fed.Cir. 2018).

References

100 Resilient Cities. (n.d.). "About Us". Available at: http://www.100resilientcities.org/about-us/ [Accessed August 2018]

Atkin, E. (2015). Florida's mot the only state where officials censored the term "climate change". ThinkProgress, 9 March. Available at: http://thinkprogress.org/climate/2015/03/09/3631465/not-just-florida-censoring-climate-change-talk/

Ayala, D., Graves, A., Lauer, C., Strand, H., Taylor, C., Weldon, K., & Wood., R. (2018). *Flooding Events Post Hurricane Harvey: Potential Liability for Dams and Operators and Recommendations Moving Forward.* Texas A&M School of Law. Available at https://scholarship.law.tamu.edu/nrs-publications/1/

Beachapedia. (2019). Beach Access. Available at: http://www.beachapedia.org/Beach_Access

California Coastal Commission. (n.d.). *Protecting California's Coastline and Upholding the California Coastal Act.* https://www.coastal.ca.gov/enforcement/vio_pamphlet.pdf [Accessed August 2018]

— (2013). *Strategic Plan 2013–2018: Protecting California's Coasts for Present and Future Generations.* Available at: https://www.coastal.ca.gov/strategicplan/CCC_Final_StrategicPlan_2013-2018.pdf

Chasis, S. (1985). The Coastal Zone Management Act: A protective mandate. *Natural Resources Journal* 25 (1), 21–30.

County of Maui. (2005). *Shoreline Access Inventory Update – Final Report.* Prepared by Oceanit. Available at: https://www.mauicounty.gov/DocumentCenter/View/3266/Shoreline-Access-Report?bidId=

Dilsaver, L. M. (2004). *Cumberland Island National Seashore: A History of Conservation Conflict.* University of Virginia Press.

Donahue, J. D. (2016). Public access v. private property: The struggle of coastal landowners to keep the public off their land. *Loyola of Los Angeles Law Review* 49, 217–244.

EPA (Environmental Protection Agency). (2014). Climate Change Adaptation Plans. Available at: https://www.epa.gov/greeningepa/climate-change-adaptation-plans

FEMA (Federal Emergency Management Agency). (2011). Climate Change Adaptation Policy Statement. Available at: http://www.fema.gov/media-library-data/20130726-1919-25045-3330/508_climate_change_policy_statement.pdf

— (2013a). Integrating Hazard Mitigation into Local Planning: Case Studies and Tools for Community Officials. 1 March. Available at: https://www.fema.gov/media-library/assets/documents/31372

— (2013b). Building Community Resilience by Integrating Hazard Mitigation: The Role of Local Leadership. Fact Sheet #2. Available at: https://www.fema.gov/media-library-data/20130726-1908-25045-7330/factsheet2.pdf

— (2019). National Flood Insurance Program: Reauthorization. Available at: https://www.fema.gov/national-flood-insurance-program/national-flood-insurance-program-reauthorization-guidance

Finkl, C. W. (2004). Coastal classification: Systematic approaches to consider in the development of a comprehensive scheme. *Journal of Coastal Research* 20 (1), 166–213.

Fu, X., Gomaa, M., Deng, Y., & Peng, Z. R. (2017). Adaptation planning for sea level rise: A study of US coastal cities. *Journal of Environmental Planning and Management* 60 (2), 249–265.

FWS (US Fish and Wildlife Service). (2002). *The Coastal Barrier Resources Act: Harnessing the Power of Market Forces to Conserve America's Coasts and Save Taxpayers' Money.* Previously available at: http://www.fws.gov/cbra/Docs/TaxpayerSavingsfromCBRA.pdf. Available at: https://www.heartland.org/publications-resources/publications/the-coastal-barrier-resources-act-harnessing-the-power-of-market-forces-to-conserve-americas-coasts-and-save-taxpayers-money

GAO (US Government Accountability Office). (2007). *Coastal Barrier Resources System: Status of Development That Has Occurred and Financial Assistance Provided by Federal Agencies.* GAO-07-356. Available at: https://www.gao.gov/assets/260/257822.html

— (2017). *High-Risk Series: Progress on Many High-Risk Areas, While Substantial Efforts Needed in Others.* GAO-17-317. Washington, D.C.: United States Government Printing Office.

García, R., & Baltodano, E. F. (2005). Free the beach! Public access, equal justice, and the California coast. *Stanford Journal of Civil Rights and Civil Liberties* 2, 143–208.

Gorte, R. W., Vincent, C. H., Hanson, L. A., & Rosenblum, M. R. (2012). *Federal Land Ownership: Overview and Data.* Congressional Research Service, 42346.

Holthaus, E. (2015). Poll: Americans don't think climate change will affect them personally. *Slate*, 6 April. Available at: http://www.slate.com/blogs/the_slatest/2015/04/06/new_climate_change_poll_shows_americans_believe_in_global_warming.html

Hurricane Sandy Rebuilding Task Force. (2013). *Hurricane Sandy Rebuilding Strategy: Stronger Communities, A Resilient Region.* August. Available at: https://archives.hud.gov/news/2013/HSRebuildingStrategy.pdf

IBHS (Insurance Institute for Business and Home Safety). (2015). *Rating the States.* Report. Available at: https://ibhs.org/wp-content/uploads/wpmembers/files/Rating-the-States-2015_IBHS.pdf

Kahrl, A. W. (2015). Fear of an open beach: Public rights and private interests in 1970s coastal Connecticut. *The Journal of American History* 102 (2), 433–462.

— (2018). *Free the Beaches: The Story of Ned Cole and the Battle for America's Most Exclusive Shoreline.* Yale University Press.

Korten, T. (2015). In Florida, officials ban term "climate change". *Miami Herald*, 8 March. Available at: http://www.miamiherald.com/news/state/florida/article12983720.html

Leavenworth, S. (2017). Real estate industry blocks sea level warnings that could crimp profits on coastal properties. *Herald Sun*, 14 September. Available at: https://www.heraldsun.com/news/business/article173114701.html

Lien, C. (2000). *Olympic Battleground: Creating and Defending Olympic National Park*. Mountaineers Books.

Lombardo, D. (2010). *Cape Cod National Seashore: The First 50 Years (Images of America)*. Arcadia Publishing.

Luntz, S. (2018). Sea level rise is already wiping billions off property values. IFLScience, 6 August. Available at: https://www.iflscience.com/environment/sea-level-rise-is-already-wiping-billions-off-property-values/

Mandel, K. (2018). Major insurers lost billions on natural disasters in 2017, they say climate change a "serious" risk. ThinkProgress, 21 March. Available at: https://archive.thinkprogress.org/insurance-companies-lose-billions-hurricanes-wildfires-3d70c86782a2/

McKinstry, R. B., 2006. *Biodiversity Conservation Handbook: State, Local, and Private Protection of Biological Diversity*. Environmental Law Institute.

Medievalists.net. (n.d.). The changing story of Cnut and the waves. Available at: http://www.medievalists.net/2015/05/the-changing-story-of-cnut-and-the-waves/ [Accessed September 2019]

Melillo, J. M., Richmond, T. C., & Yohe, G.W. (Eds.). (2014). *Climate Change Impacts in the United States: The Third National Climate Assessment*. US Global Change Research Program.

Miami-Dade County. (2014). *Sea Level Rise Task Force Report and Recommendations*. Available at: https://www.miamidade.gov/planning/library/reports/sea-level-rise-report-recommendations.pdf [Accessed August 2018]

— (2016). Sea Level Rise Task Force. Available at: http://www.miamidade.gov/planning/boards-sea-level-rise.asp

Miami-Dade County Office of Sustainability. (2010). *GreenPrint: Our Design for a Sustainable Future*. December. Available at http://www.miamidade.gov/GreenPrint/pdf/plan.pdf [Accessed August 2018]

NASA. (2012). Could a hurricane ever strike Southern California? Available at: http://www.nasa.gov/topics/earth/features/earth20121017a.html

National Research Council, Committee on Sea Level Rise in California, Oregon, and Washington, & Board on Earth Sciences and Resources and Ocean Studies Board, Division on Earth and Life Studies. (2012). *Sea Level Rise for the Coasts of California, Oregon, and Washington: Past, Present, and Future*. Consensus Study Report.

New Jersey Institute for Social Justice. (2013). *Hurricane Sandy Aftermath: Rebuilding with Social Justice*. Available at: http://www.njisj.org/wp-content/uploads/2013/05/HURRICANE-SANDY-AFTER-MATH-Rebuilding-with-Social-Justice-in-New-Jersey.pdf

NOAA (National Oceanic and Atmospheric Administration). (2007). Ocean & coastal management: Construction setbacks. Previously available at: http://coastalmanagement.noaa.gov/initiatives/shoreline_ppr_setbacks.html

— (2013). *National Coastal Population Report: Population Trends from 1970 to 2020*. Available at: https://aamboceanservice.blob.core.windows.net/oceanservice-prod/facts/coastal-population-report.pdf [Accessed August 2018]

— (2018). What percentage of the American population lives near the coast? Available at: https://oceanservice.noaa.gov/facts/population.html

— (n.d.). National Coastal Zone Management Program: Coastal Management Program Guidance. Available at: https://coast.noaa.gov/czm/guidance/. [Accessed July 2020]

North Carolina Division of Coastal Management. (2014). Oceanfront Construction Setback & Erosion Rates. Available at: https://deq.nc.gov/about/divisions/coastal-management/coastal-management-oceanfront-shorelines/oceanfront-construction-setback-erosion-rate

NYC (New York City). (n.d.). Zoning for Flood Resiliency (web information page). Available at: https://www1.nyc.gov/site/planning/plans/flood-resilience-zoning-text-update/flood-resilience-zoning-text-update.page [Accessed August 2018]

— (2013a). *PlaNYC: A Stronger, More Resilient New York*. Available at: https://www.nycedc.com/resource/stronger-more-resilient-new-york

— (2013b). Flood Resilience Zoning Text Amendment. Available at: https://www1.nyc.gov/assets/planning/download/pdf/plans/flood-resiliency/flood_resiliency.pdf

OECD. (n.d.). Observatory of Public Sector Innovation: Rebuild by Design. Available at: https://www.oecd.org/governance/observatory-public-sector-innovation/innovations/page/rebuildbydesign.htm [Accessed August 2018]

Pielke, R., Jr., Gratz, J., Landsea, C. W., Collins, D., Saunders, M. A., & Musulin, R. (2008). Normalized hurricane damage in the United States: 1900–2005. *Natural Hazards* 9 (1), 29–42.

Pilkey, O. H., Jr., & Cooper, J. A. G. (2014). *The Last Beach*. Duke University Press.

Randall, M., & deBoer, H. (2012). *Coastline Construction Restrictions*. Research Report 2012-R-0046, 2 February. Connecticut Office of Legislative Research. Available at: https://www.cga.ct.gov/2012/rpt/2012-R-0046.htm

Revkin, A. C. (2013). Can cities adjust to a retreating coastline? Dot Earth (blog), *New York Times*, 22 August. Available at: http://dotearth.blogs.nytimes.com/2013/08/22/can-cities-adjust-to-a-retreating-coastline/?_php=true&_type=blogs&_r=0

Rowe, J. (2013). *Our Common Wealth: The Hidden Economy That Makes Everything Else Work*. Berrett-Koehler Publishers.

Rozhon, T. (2006). In Cape Cod's dunes, something's growing besides scrub pines. *New York Times*, 6 November. Available at: http://www.nytimes.com/2006/11/09/garden/09cape.html?pagewanted=all&_r=0

Song, L., & Shaw, A. (2018). "A never-ending commitment": The high cost of preserving vulnerable beaches. ProPublica, 27 September. Available at: https://www.propublica.org/article/the-high-cost-of-preserving-vulnerable-beaches

Southeast Florida Regional Climate Change Compact Counties. (2012). *A Region Responds to a Changing Climate: Regional Climate Adaptation Plan*. October. Available at: http://www.southeastfloridaclimate-compact.org/wp-content/uploads/2014/09/regional-climate-action-plan-final-ada-compliant.pdf

Strauss, B. H., Kulp, S., & Levermann, A. (2015). Carbon choices determine US cities committed to futures below sea level. *Proceedings of the National Academy of Sciences* 112 (44), 13508–13513.

Strauss, B. H., Tebaldi, C., & Kulp, S. (2014). *Climate Central, North Carolina and the Surging Sea: A Vulnerability Assessment with Protection for Sea Level Rise and Coastal Flood Risk*. Available at: http://sealevel.climatecentral.org/uploads/ssrf/NC-Report.pdf

Strauss, B. H., Ziemlinski, R., Weiss, J. L., & Overpeck, J. T. (2012). Tidally adjusted estimates of topographic vulnerability to sea level rise and flooding for the contiguous United States. *Environmental Research Letters* 7 (1), 014033.

Tang, Z. (2008). Evaluating local coastal zone land use planning capacities in California. *Ocean & Coastal Management* 51 (7), 544–555.

Tarlock, A. D. (1988). *Law of Water Rights and Resources*. Clark Boardman Co., Ltd.

Tarlock, A. D., & Chizewer, D. M. (2016). Living with water in a climate-changed world: Will federal flood policy sink or swim? *Environmental Law* 46, 491–536.

Thompson, B. H., Jr. (2012). A Federal Act to Promote Integrated Water Management: Is the CZMA a useful model? *Environmental Law* 42, 201–240.

Titus, J. G., Hudgens, D. E., Trescott, D. L., Craghan, M., Nuckols, W. H., Hershner, C. H., Kassakian, J. M., Linn, C. J., Merritt, P. G., McCue, T. M., O'Connell, J. F., Tanski, J., & Wang, J. (2009). State and local governments plan for development of most land vulnerable to rising sea level along the US Atlantic coast. *Environmental Research Letters* 4 (4). doi: 10.1088/1748-9326/4/4/044008

Urbina, I. (2016). Perils of climate change could swamp coastal real estate. *New York Times*, 24 November. Available at: http://www.nytimes.com/2016/11/24/science/global-warming-coastal-real-estate.html?_r=0

USACE (United States Army Corps of Engineers). (2013). Coastal risk reduction and resilience: Using a full array of measures. US Army Corps of Engineers Institute for Water Resources, 16 September. Available at: https://www.iwr.usace.army.mil/Media/News-Stories/Article/481104/coastal-risk-reduction-and-resilience-using-the-full-array-of-measures/

— (2014). *Climate Change Adaptation Plan*. Available at: http://www.usace.army.mil/Portals/2/docs/Sustainability/Performance_Plans/2014_USACE_Climate_Change_Adaptation_Plan.pdf

— (2015). *North Atlantic Coast Comprehensive Study: Resilient Adaptation to Increasing Risk*. January. Available at: http://www.nad.usace.army.mil/Portals/40/docs/NACCS/NACCS_main_report.pdf

Washington State Department of Ecology. (2014). *Soft Shoreline Stabilization: Shoreline Master Program Planning and Implementation Guidance*. Available at: https://fortress.wa.gov/ecy/publications/documents/1406009.pdf

White House. (2014). Fact Sheet: The President's Climate Data Initiative: Empowering America's Communities to Prepare for the Effects of Climate Change. 19 March. Available at https://obamawhitehouse.archives.gov/the-press-office/2014/03/19/fact-sheet-president-s-climate-data-initiative-empowering-america-s-comm

World Factbook. (n.d.). United States. Available at: https://www.cia.gov/Library/publications/the-world-factbook/geos/us.html [Accessed September 2019]

Legislation (listed chronologically)

Flood Control Act 1944 – 33 USC Ch. 15 § 701-709c
Outer Continental Shelf Lands Act (OCSLA) 1953 – 43 USC Ch. 29 § 1301-1356b
Texas Open Beaches Act 1959 (amended 1991)
Coastal Zone Management Act (CZMA) 1972 – 16 USC Ch. 33 § 1451-1466 16
Clean Water Act 1972 – 33 USC Ch. 26 § 1251-1388
North Carolina Coastal Area Management Act 1974 – North Carolina General Statutes
California Coastal Act 1976 – Cal. Public Resources Code
Stafford Disaster Relief and Emergency Assistance Act – Public Law 100-707 (23 November 1988)
North Carolina House Bill 819, 2011 Sess. § 2.(a)-(b) (N.C. 2012)
Disaster Relief Appropriations Act 2013 – Public Law 113-2 (29 January 2013)

Court cases

Borax Consolidated, Ltd. v. Los Angeles, 296 U.S. 10 (1935)
Central Green County v. United States, 531 U.S. 425 (2001)
County of Hawai'i v. Sotomura, 517 P.2d 57 (Haw. 1973)
Delaware Department of Natural Resources and Environmental Control v. Federal Energy Regulatory Commission, 558 F.3rd 578 (D.C. Cir. 2009)
Dolan v. City of Tigard, 512 U.S. 374 (1994)
Illinois Central Railroad v. Illinois, 146 U.S. 387 (1892)
Lechuza Villas West v. California Coastal Commission, 60 Cal.App.4th 218 (California Appellate Court, 4th District 1992)
Nies v. Town of Emerald Isle, 2015 North Carolina App. 2015 LEXIS 958, 5 (N.C. Court of Appeals), appeal pending North Carolina Supreme Court
Nollan v. California Coastal Commission, 483 U.S. 825 (1987)
Royal Fishery at Banne (The Case of), 80 Eng. Rep. 540 (Kings Bench 1611)
Sansotta v. Town of Nags Head, 724 F.3d 533 (4th Cir. 2013)
Slavin v. Town of Oak Island, 160 North Carolina App. 57 (North Carolina Court of Appeals 2003)
Sotomura v. County of Hawai'i, 460 F. Supp. 473 (H. Haw. 1978)
Stevens v. City of Canon Beach, 854 P.2d 449 (1994), cert. denied, 510 UI.S. 1207 (1994)
Surfrider Foundation v, Martins Beach 1, LLC, 14 Cal.App.5th 238 (1st Dist. 2017), reviewed denied, ____Cal.3d____ (2017), cert. denied, ___U.S.___ (2018)
Thornton v. Hay, 462 P.2d 671 (Or. 1969)

Part III

Comparative analysis and evaluation

18 Comparative analysis I: Introduction and the concept of the coastal zone

Cygal Pellach and Rachelle Alterman

Following the fifteen country reports, the final part of the book is devoted to the cross-national comparative analysis. Each country chapter has been devoted to a single country, thus enabling contextualization of ICZM-related laws and regulations within the unique attributes and complexities of that specific country. In this chapter and the next two, we take a systematic cross-national view of the country reports, with the purpose of exposing the variety of laws and practices. The readers are invited to review their own countries' parallel laws and regulations and to draw any relevant lessons. The caveats about policy transfer should of course be taken into account (see Chapter 1).

The rationale and method of comparative analysis were discussed in Chapter 1. As explained, our structured analysis is based on ten predefined "parameters" that guided the contents of all country chapters. Chapter 2 presents each of these parameters and, where relevant, indicates whether they are also reflected in one or both of the two supra-national documents – the 2008 Mediterranean ICZM Protocol and the 2002 EU ICZM Recommendation. We grouped the parameters into two sets. For convenience, we repeat them in Box 18.1.

The first parameter should stand alone, as it addresses the underlying conception of the coastal zone. This parameter will therefore be discussed first, in the present chapter. The remaining four parameters in the first set are discussed in Chapter 19, and the second set of five parameters, in Chapter 20.

We remind the readers that the comparative chapters are based on facts sourced almost entirely from the country chapter reports. Unless indicated otherwise (with specific citations), we did not undertake additional research.

Parameter A: Conception of the coastal zone

The starting point for comparing approaches to coastal zone management is to find out how (or whether) that coastal zone, as a whole, is legally defined in each jurisdiction.

Is there a legal definition of the coastal zone?

Do all the jurisdictions studied define their coastal zone, and if so, where is the definition located? Table 18.1 divides the set of jurisdictions into three groups: Those where the definition of the coastal zone is anchored in legislation (the largest group); those where such a definition is found in "soft law" (policy documents; another large group); and those without any formal definition (a smaller group).

Box 18.1

The parameters for comparison

Land demarcation and property rights: *Discussed in this Chapter (18):*

A. Conception of the coastal zone

Land demarcation and property rights: *Discussed in Chapter 19:*

B. Shoreline definition and delineation
C. Coastal public domain – extent and rules
D. Coastal setback zone – extent and permitted uses
E. Right of public access – to and along the coast

Institutions and governance: *Discussed in Chapter 20:*

F. Land use planning – institutional aspects and dedicated instruments
G. Climate change – awareness and regulatory actions
H. Public participation and access to justice
I. Integration and coordination
J. Compliance and enforcement

Table 18.1 Locus of definitions of the coastal zone across jurisdictions

Coastal zone defined in laws or regulations	Coastal zone defined in "soft law" (policy) documents	No official definition of the coastal zone
Australia (NSW, QLD, SA, VIC)	Australia (national level, NT, TAS, WA)	Denmark**
Greece	Germany (one state – Schleswig-Holstein)	France**
Israel	Malta	Spain**
Netherlands*	Portugal	Italy
USA (federal level, California and some other state laws)	UK	Slovenia
		Turkey
* Defined only in policy documents, but precisely mapped in accompanying regulations ** These countries define a broad zone to which special coastal planning rules apply (see Chapter 20)		

In the discussion of the other parameters we will learn whether or to what extent the definition of the coastal zone (or lack thereof) has implications for the regulation of coastal land. Apparently, declaration of public domains, setback zones, or planning controls can be introduced without a legal definition of the coastal zone. For example, in Denmark, France, and Spain, where coastal zone regulation is quite ambitious, there are no official definitions of the coastal zone.

The tension between the dynamics of the coast and legal certainty

In nature and in the world of environmental science, the boundaries of a coastal zone are fluid, ever-changing. As such, they often do not match political-legal boundaries. Beatley et al. (2002) have put this well:

Natural systems have transient and often fuzzy boundaries that rarely, if ever, correspond to political boundaries. This makes delineating the extent of the management area difficult. Coastal regions are dynamic interface zones where land, water and atmosphere interact in a fragile balance that is constantly being altered by natural and human influence. (pp. 13–14)

Can the biophysical dynamics of the coastal zone be translated into a legal definition? Attempts to provide a legal definition of a coastal zone will face the inherent tension between the desire to reflect the fluidity of the natural systems (sometimes also social systems), and the need for a reasonable degree of certainty that usually characterizes the world of law. The legal emphasis on certainty is especially strong in real-property law. Coastal zones are both environment and land. How does each of the fifteen jurisdictions reconcile this built-in dilemma?

A two-dimensional conceptual framework for classification

Given the tension between the dynamics of nature and the reasonable degree of certainty usually sought by law, we thought at first that we could classify the range of conceptions of the coastal zone along a single dimension – from nature-led to implementation-led (see also Kay & Alder, 2005). At one extreme, a coastal zone would be defined based entirely on natural features and processes, and at the other extreme, it would be defined based entirely on political-legal boundaries, such as municipalities, land use plans, or land ownership categories.

However, analysis of the full set of definitions across the fifteen jurisdictions indicated that a single dimension would not capture their variety. We therefore created a two-dimensional conceptual framework: One dimension addresses the *contents* of the definitions, according to the scale of "nature-led" to "implementation-led", as discussed above. The second dimension addresses the extent of room for interpretation by decision-makers or the courts. This dimension ranges from broad wording to specific wording that does not leave much leeway for interpretation. The result is a schematic two-dimensional space where one can "plot" any legal definitions of the coastal zone, as illustrated in Figure 18.1. The vertical axis is *nature-led to implementation-led*, and on the horizontal axis is *broad to specific wording*.

This framework is not normative or evaluative – it is factual-descriptive. We are not implying that one definition is better than another. This kind of determination would require a very different comparative research framework that would try to evaluate how different definitions affect decision-making – outputs and outcomes.

Juxtaposing the national definitions against the supra-national law

We first discuss the placement in the chart of the definitions found in the Mediterranean ICZM Protocol (the EU Recommendation on ICZM does not provide any definition). Here is the wording of the Protocol, which is expected to be legally binding:

"Coastal Zone" means the geomorphologic area either side of the seashore in which the interaction between the marine and land parts occurs in the form of complex ecological and resource systems made up of biotic and abiotic components coexisting and interacting with human communities and relevant socio-economic activities. (UNEP, 2008)

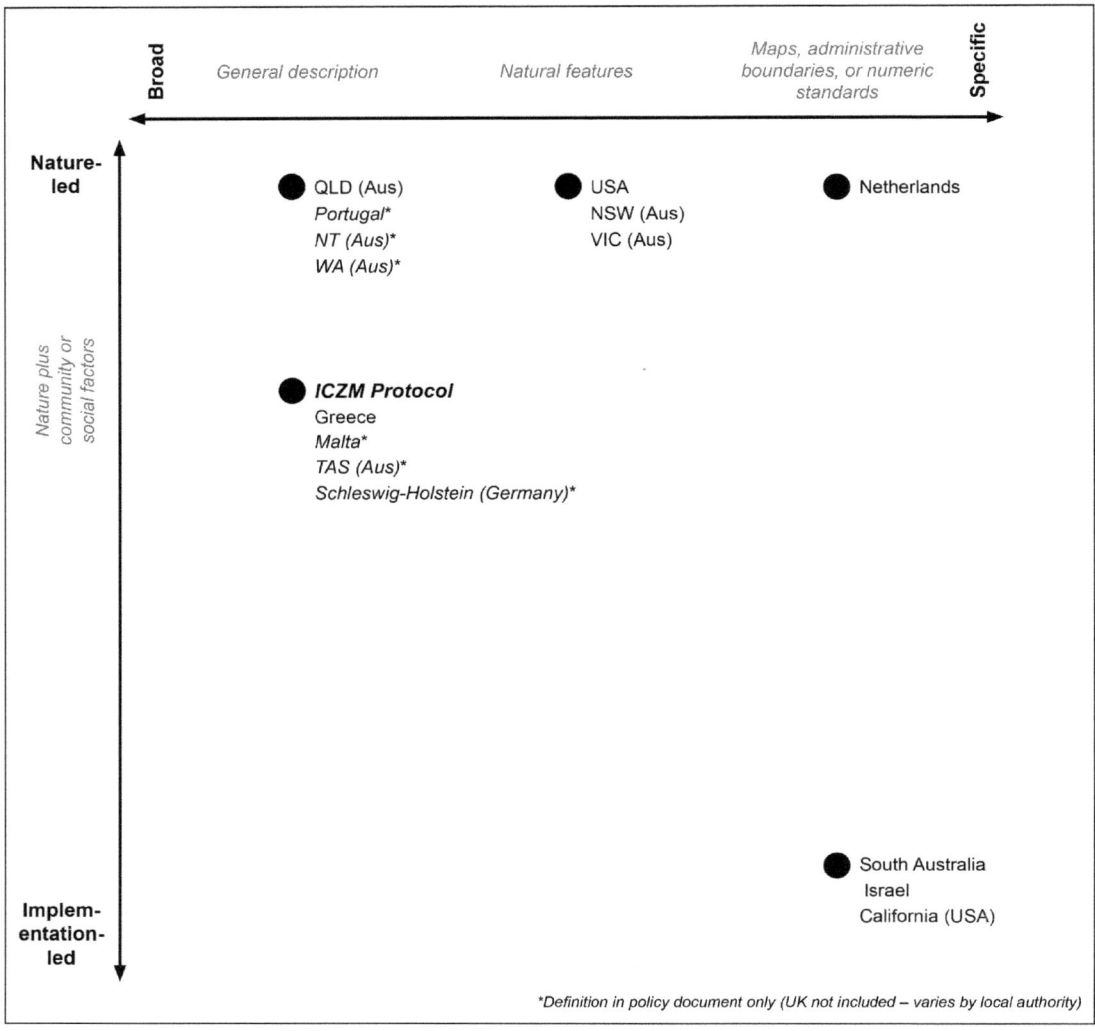

Figure 18.1 Legal and policy definitions of the coastal zone – Along two dimensions: *Nature-led to implementation-led* and *broad to specific wording*

On the vertical dimension, we plotted the Protocol's definition close to the "nature-led" edge, but not at the furthest extent, due to the reference to social communities, which, we conjecture, would entail some administrative discretion. On the horizontal dimension, we situated the Protocol's definition quite close to the *broad* end because phrases such as *complex ecological and resource systems* or *relevant socio-economic activities* could be interpreted in many ways.

An obvious question is whether the Protocol's conception of the coastal zone is in fact reflected in the definitions adopted by the eight Mediterranean nations in our set. The answer is that only Greece has adopted the Protocol's wording almost verbatim. Malta's definition is similar, but predates the Protocol.

The Greek definition (as translated by Balla and Giannakourou in the Greece chapter) is:

Terrestrial and aquatic sections on either side of the shoreline in which the interaction between the marine and terrestrial part acquires the form of complex systems of ecological elements and resources composed of biotic and abiotic components coexisting and interacting with human communities and relevant socio-economic activities. The coastal zone may include natural formations or small islands in their entirety (2011 biodiversity law, Article 2, para. 12).

This definition is very broad and open to interpretation, regarding both the natural and the social environment. We should, however, note that in the case of Greece, even though this definition is anchored in legislation, it does not carry direct legal implications.

Malta's definition is located in a "soft-law" document – its Coastal Strategy Topic Paper (Malta PA, 2002). It says that the coastal zone is:

A geographical space incorporating land and sea areas within which the natural processes interact to create a unique dynamic system; it also incorporates those activities on land and at sea where human activities are directly influenced by or can influence the quality of natural resources.

Most of the remaining Mediterranean countries have not adopted a legally anchored conception of the coastal zone. Israel does have one but, as discussed below and apparent from the chart, its definition is quite different from the Protocol's.

The definitions of the coastal zone viewed through the conceptual framework

A view of all our jurisdictions, not only the Mediterranean ones, shows much variety. Figure 18.1 places the set of definitions of the coastal zone within our two-dimensional conceptual framework. The variation among the definitions is larger than we had anticipated. The country chapters present a total of *fifteen different definitions of coastal zones*. In this number we include all the national definitions as well as selected US and Australian coastal states. There is no discernible pattern or set of variables that could "explain" the differences. One can only conjecture about the total number of differing definitions across the globe.

A broad look at Figure 18.1 shows that most definitions are placed towards the top edge of the vertical axis, meaning that they are more nature-led than implementation-led. However, there is variation along the horizontal axis – the broad-to-specific dimension. This means that some definitions refer only to general natural features or processes, while others do specify particular indicators. Broadly worded reference to natural features still leaves it up to administrative bodies to decide on the specific attributes that will be taken into account. Only three countries are classified in the implementation-led edge of the scale and another three countries are intermediate.

Let us now take a closer look. In the top left corner of the scheme are the four jurisdictions with the most nature-led and broadest definitions of the coastal zone. The group includes Portugal and three Australian states (QLD, NT, WA). Their definitions refer only to general natural processes associated with the coastal zone and are thus wide open to interpretation. For example, the Queensland (QLD) definition refers to "ecological or natural processes that affect the coast or coastal resources" (Coastal Protection and Management Act 1995).

Portugal's definition differs from the others in this group in that it is focused on future risks rather than on current natural processes. The coastal zone is:

> *the buffer zone which protects land from sea advance and climate change, and which should be considered as legally superior to spatial land use planning instruments, and abide by the principle of a [construction free] zone. (Portuguese government, 2009)*

Interestingly, even though this definition is part of soft law – the Portuguese National Strategy for ICZM – its authors nevertheless recommended that it should be legally superior to spatial planning.

Further down in the chart, in approximately the same position as the ICZM Protocol discussed above, we also included two jurisdictions not yet mentioned: The Australian state of Tasmania (TAS) and the German state of Schleswig-Holstein. Their definitions too are largely nature-based, but because they also refer to social and economic factors, we assume that in practice there would be some implementation-based criteria. The Schleswig-Holstein definition is one more indication of the many ways in which the natural coastal environment can be depicted:

> *… the coastal zone marks the border between sea and dry land. In every single case, its relevant extent is defined by the area in which terrestrial and maritime processes (economic, ecologic and socio-cultural) depend on – or influence – each other (zone of problems and potentials). (guidance document on ICZM; Ministry of the Interior, 2003)*

In the bottom-right corner of Figure 18.1 are the most "implementation-led" and "specific" definitions. Their wording is based on administrative rules and does not leave much room for interpretation by decision-makers. In this group of three we find South Australia, Israel, and California (United States). South Australia and Israel define their coastal zones according to a prescribed numeric distance from the shoreline that may remain unchanged for many years. In South Australia, the landward distance which defines the coastal zone is 100 m (but may extend up to 500 m in some cases). In Israel, the landward limit is 300 m. These distances delineate the coastal zone. They should not be confused with setback distances, which are determined separately (discussed in the next chapter).

California has chosen to adopt a definition of its coastal zone dependent on maps attached to the state's Coastal Act:

> *that land and water area of the State of California from the Oregon border to the border of the Republic of Mexico, specified on the maps identified and set forth in Section 17 of that chapter of the Statutes of the 1975–76 Regular Session enacting this division, extending seaward to the state's outer limit of jurisdiction, including all offshore islands, and extending inland generally 1,000 yards from the mean high tide line of the sea. In significant coastal estuarine, habitat, and recreational areas it extends inland to the first major ridgeline paralleling the sea or five miles from the mean high tide line of the sea, whichever is less, and in developed urban areas the zone generally extends inland less than 1,000 yards. (California Coastal Act, Section 30103(a))*

At the top-right corner of the chart is the definition adopted by the Netherlands. It stands alone, possibly as a reflection of the Netherlands' unique history in contending with the sea.

Although the Dutch definition is nature-led, being based on flood risk it is also highly specific in using technical, numeric criteria and precise maps. The text says:

> *The Coastal (Foundation) Zone consists of the whole of coastal sea, beaches, sea dikes, dunes and sea dikes and the landward strip with a functional or cultural relationship with the coast.* (Coastal Policy; Dutch government, 2007)

The technical criteria specify that the Coastal Foundation Zone includes all dunes and sea flood defences (both "soft" and "hard" defences) and land to be required in anticipation of a 200-year sea level rise. The maps attached to the Dutch General Spatial Planning Rules precisely delineate the Coastal Foundation Zone. Thus, even though the definition mentions "culture", the technical criteria and maps leave no room for discretion on this matter.

The four jurisdictions at the most "specific" end of the chart – South Australia, Israel, California, and the Netherlands – all have definitions which have direct legal expressions: They determine the land areas to which further regulations for coastal land use and development apply (see the land use planning parameter in Chapter 20).

Denmark, France, Spain, Italy, Slovenia, and Turkey are not in the chart because none of these countries have defined their coastal zones. The UK does not appear on the chart because its coastal zone definition is to be determined not by the national government but by local authorities. The national UK guidelines are very general, stipulating only that the local authorities should take into account the "direct physical, environmental and economic linkages between land and sea". These broad guidelines suggest that the local authorities should define the coastal zones taking into account both nature-based and implementation-based considerations – perhaps midway on the vertical dimension of our chart. Decentralization of the authority to determine the coastal zone is unique among our set of jurisdictions. Usually, this matter is reserved for the national or state level. This subject is worthy of further comparative research.

What can be learned?

The first parameter – the conception of the coastal zone – is a preliminary one. Our findings show that in many of the jurisdictions studied, this definition is not much more than an attempt to translate a complex multidisciplinary conception of the coast into a few lines of official text. Yet this text could be expected to convey what is perceived as the essence of the coastal zone that is worthy of management and preservation.

Our findings indicate that many decades of international discourse on ICZM have not yet produced much consensus over how the coastal zone should be defined. The differences are not trivial. In order to uncover their underlying conceptual difference, we developed a two-dimensional scheme. It highlights two fundamental axes of disagreement: First, should the official definition of the coastal zone be entirely nature-based, reflecting the ever-changing dynamics of the coast, or should it incorporate a degree of legal certainty and stability? And second, should the definition be worded in general language, leaving much room for interpretation in concrete situations, or should it offer specific rules to be applied across the board?

We were also curious to know whether the supra-national level of law would create greater convergence among the signatory countries. It turns out that the Mediterranean ICZM Protocol has not had much impact towards adoption of a consensual definition of the coastal zone among the Mediterranean countries in the book. Only Greece adopted a new definition (or amended an earlier one) in the spirit of the Protocol. Most of the other Mediterranean countries did not adopt any formal definition. Perhaps they did not see the need (legal or otherwise) to follow in the Protocol's footsteps.

Thus, in surveying the first of our ten parameters, we already have a preview of two lessons: The great variety of conceptions and approaches across jurisdictions and the limited influence of international ICZM law and policy on national legislation.

References

Beatley, T., Brower, D., & Schwab, A. K. (2002). *An Introduction to Coastal Zone Management*. Island Press.

Kay, R., & Alder, J. (2005). *Coastal Planning and Management*. Taylor and Francis.

International law and policy

European Parliament (2002). Recommendation of the European Parliament and of the Council of 30 May 2002 concerning the implementation of Integrated Coastal Zone Management in Europe. Official Journal L148, 06/06/2002 pp. 0024 – 0027. Available at: https://eur-lex.europa.eu/legal-content/EN/TXT/?uri=CELEX%3A32002H0413

UNEP (United Nations Environment Programme), MAP (Mediterranean Action Plan), PAP (Priority Actions Programme) (2008). Protocol on Integrated Coastal Zone Management in the Mediterranean. Split, Priority Actions Programme. Available at: http://iczmplatform.org//storage/documents/sewmrX-IR9gTwfvBgjJ4SAjhvqsLrBF6qB0B89xK8.pdf

National policy documents

Dutch government. (2007). Beleidslijn Kust [Coastal Policy]. Official Publications of the House of Representatives, 2006–2007, 30 195, no. 22.

Malta PA (Planning Authority). (2002). Coastal Strategy Topic Paper. Final Draft. Available at: https://discomap.eea.europa.eu/map/Data/Milieu/OURCOAST_032_303_MT/OURCOAST_032_303_MT_Doc2_MTCoastalStrategy.pdf

Portuguese government (2009). National Strategy for Integrated Coastal Zone Management (ENGIZC). Available at: https://dre.pt/application/conteudo/489264.

Schleswig-Holstein Ministry of the Interior. (2003). Integrated Coastal Zone Management in Schleswig-Holstein. Kiel. Available at: www.zeeland.nl/digitaalarchief/zee0701277

(This list includes only policy documents specifically cited in this chapter. Refer to individual country chapters for full lists of relevant legislation).

National Legislation

California Coastal Act 1976 – Cal. Public Resources Code

Greek Law 3937/2011 – "Preservation of Biodiversity and Other Provisions"

Queensland (Australia) Coastal Protection and Management Act 1995

(This list includes only legislation specifically cited in this chapter. Refer to individual country chapters for full list of relevant legislation).

19 Comparative analysis II: Land demarcation and property rights

Cygal Pellach and Rachelle Alterman

In the previous chapter, we commenced our comparative analysis of the fifteen country reports with a discussion of parameter A – the concept of the coastal zone. The group of parameters in this chapter – parameters B to E – deal with the down-to-earth laws and regulations concerning land: Its demarcation, ownership, and right to access. As a reminder – these are the parameters:

B. Shoreline definition and delineation
C. Coastal public domain – extent and rules
D. Coastal setback zone – extent and permitted uses
E. Right of public access – to and along the coast

The first parameter (B) takes the lead because the other three parameters often refer to the shoreline as their benchmark. Discussion of the delineation of the shoreline inevitably involves use of some technical terminology from fields other than our own, such as coastal hydrography, morphodynamics, and geodesy. For the comparative analysis below, we have done our best to place all the country reports on a shared terminological platform by relying on sources from the relevant literature and on consultation with experts.[1] We are aware that there may not be full consensus on all terms across disciplines or countries.[2]

Parameter B: Shoreline definition and delineation

In order to enter the realm of land-related law and administration, and thus to ICZM, coastal land management usually requires an official delineation of the shoreline, regarded generally as "the boundary between land and sea at the local scale" (Oertel, 2018). Unlike the legal conception of the coastal zone discussed in the previous chapter, a legal definition of the shoreline is prevalent among the jurisdictions in our study. Other definitions of the shoreline, without legal force, are sometimes used for scientific or other purposes. In almost all our jurisdictions, a legal definition of the shoreline is necessary for the determination of additional rules, including the coastal public domain, setback zones, and rules of accessibility. Since we are focusing on the implications of shoreline delimitation on real property, the comparative analysis will look only at the landward (rather than seaward) direction from the shoreline.

Different tide-related reference lines

Delineation of the "boundary between land and sea" may seem to be a matter of physical and natural sciences, not law. However, we encountered several different rules used in practice, even when the physical attributes may be similar. The variety of legal definitions surveyed here are drawn from different scientific disciplines. Most rely on tide-related reference lines, which are illustrated at Figure 19.1. Some of these reference lines are commonly used in hydrography – mean high water (MHW; mean high tide), mean sea level (MSL; mean tide), or mean low water (MLW; mean low tide). In addition, we encountered countries that use variations of "highest tide" (or highest reach of the waves). These, as we show below, may be based either on hydrography or coastal morphology.

The legal and public policy implications of the use of different tidal reference lines, on their own, can be huge. For example (given the same geomorphology of the littoral area and the tidal regime), where the "highest tide" rather than, say, "mean low water" line is applied, the legal shoreline might be located much further landward than if the mean low water reference line had been adopted. Since, as we shall see, the land seaward of the shoreline is (in our set of jurisdictions) always in the public domain, a shoreline based on mean low water would mean that the public beach would almost always be under water. Unless the public domain is extended landward of the shoreline – as it is in some jurisdictions (see below), the public's right to access the beach will be hampered. Furthermore, a demarcation based on the "highest tidal reach" would mean that even without an extension of the public domain beyond the shoreline, in our set of countries, private property would not be permitted on the beach. The following section addresses the interrelationship between the shoreline definition and the extent of public domain in greater detail.

For illustrative purposes, Figure 19.1 is drawn to apply only to low gradient beaches, not to coastal cliffs. As we will see below, none of our sample countries' laws seems to adjust the shoreline demarcation rules according to coastal morphologies. (But one country does distinguish between beaches and coastal cliffs when defining coastal public domain.) Across

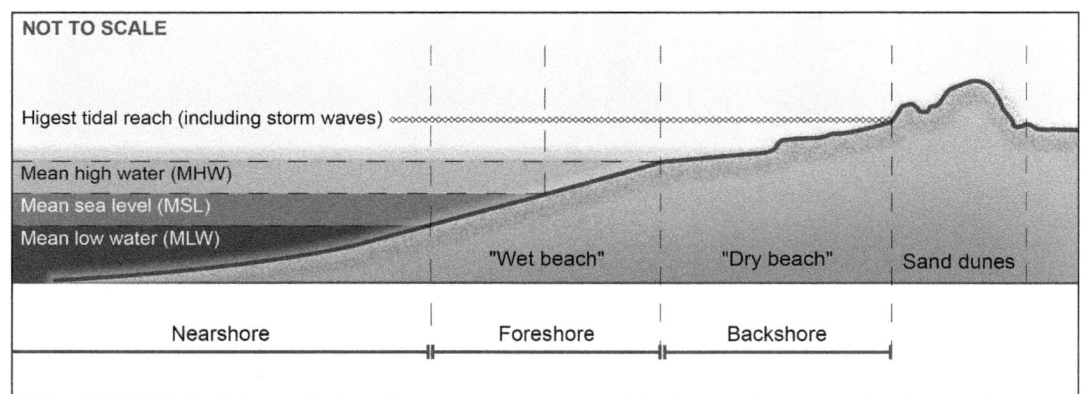

Figure 19.1 **Schematic illustration of a littoral zone: Sea level reference lines and other coastal features** (the somewhat steep topography and sandy beach are for illustrative purposes)

Source: Illustration by Cygal Pellach

coastal areas, the size and extent of the foreshore (the area between mean high tide and mean low tide; also known as "wet beach") will vary. In some locations, the extent of differences between mean high and mean low tide will be larger than in others due to different geographical settings.

Shoreline definition and supra-national law or policy

The advent of supra-national law and policy concerning coastal zones may have introduced a new legal realm of shoreline definition. The Mediterranean ICZM Protocol – applicable to seven of the countries in this book – specifies a shoreline rule: When the Protocol mandates that every signatory country must establish a coastal setback distance (discussed below), it stipulates that the distance should be measured from the "highest winter waterline".

According to Rochette et al. (2010, p. 10) the definition relates to "… the precise point reached by the highest winter tides". But interpretations, as well as methodologies for determining this line may differ across jurisdictions, and rocky shores or cliffs will be subject to different methodologies (Rochette et al., 2010; Sylaios et al., 2015). Below, we will try to answer whether all the Mediterranean countries in our group indeed abide by the Protocol's definition, however interpreted.

The authors of the ICZM Protocol apparently assumed that uniformity in the reference point for measuring setbacks is both desirable and feasible. In international law, Article 8-2, which introduces this reference line, (probably) obliges all Mediterranean parties to the treaty to adopt it. The wording clearly conveys mandatory status (Rochette & Bille, 2010):

> *The Parties: a)* **Shall** *establish in coastal zones, as from the* **highest winter waterline**… (emphasis added)

The obligatory purpose behind this wording is further implied by the fact that the Protocol predicates its most prominent and only measurable rule – the 100 m setback zone (discussed below) – on having a shared benchmark for measurement. Note, that even though the Protocol does allow the signatory states to adjust the 100 m setback to local conditions, its wording still means that the *general* principle is obligatory, and thus also the shoreline delimitation rule (Rochette & Bille, 2010).

The fundamental question in our "reality check" is whether it is indeed realistic to expect that nations will change their shoreline definitions, where relevant, and adopt the *highest winter waterline*. Since we have seven signatory Mediterranean countries, we can ask how many of them already had the Protocol's definition in place in 2008, and whether any have adjusted their definition since then.

Comparing the specific shoreline definitions across countries

Table 19.1 indicates that our set of jurisdictions has "representatives" from each and every category of tide-based definitions of the shoreline. Some of the shoreline definitions match up entirely with the reference lines in Figure 19.1, while others use general or vague wording that require additional technical guidelines to be legally operational. In total, there is a spectrum of shoreline definitions. The rationales for the different definitions may have reflected the natural geomorphological or hydrological attributes of each jurisdiction's littoral zone.

Table 19.1 Definitions of the shoreline – listed from furthest landwards to furthest seawards

Reference line	Jurisdictions and specific definitions
Highest tidal reach by exceptional storm waves + coastal features	**Spain** ^ – 5 highest storms average in 5 years **AND** sand dunes are included seaward of shoreline
Highest tidal reach (includes storm waves, but excludes exceptional storms)	**Denmark** – Vegetation line (for setbacks) high water mark (for public domain) **France** ^ – "highest tide of the year, excluding exceptional storms" **Greece** ^ – "usual maximum winter wave run-up" (measured according to geomorphological features) **Portugal** – equinoctial high tide (MSL + 2 m*) **Slovenia** ^ – "the highest level of the high tide" (MSL + 1.73 m*) **Turkey** – "the natural boundary determined by the inward motion of water" (geomorphological definition)
Surrogate for tidal reference line	**Israel** ^ – geodetic zero + 0.75 m
Mean high water (or surrogate)	**Australia** – mean high water **Germany, North Sea Coast** (Lower Saxony, part of Schleswig-Holstein) – mean high water **USA (most states)** – mean high water
Mean tide or mean sea level - MSL	**Germany, Baltic Sea Coast** (Mecklenburg-Western Pomerania, part of Schleswig-Holstein) – "Mean Tide" **Italy** ^ – Defined on the basis of "calm sea"
Mean low water	**Malta** ^ – Contour "directly in contact with the sea" **UK** – mean low water **USA (Delaware, Maine, Massachusetts, Pennsylvania, Virginia)** – mean low water

^ Mediterranean countries that are signatories to the ICZM Protocol
* according to national technical guidelines

Explanatory notes:

DENMARK – The shoreline for the purpose of demarcating the coastal public domain is not formally defined by law, but has traditionally been measured according to the "high water mark" where relevant. The precise meaning of the "high water mark" in this context is unclear, but the vegetation line is apparently used to define the setback zone
ISRAEL – The definition of the shoreline cannot be matched with any tidal reference line. It is currently located well above the "highest astronomical tide" (HAT), but its relationship with tidal measures will change as sea levels rise
NETHERLANDS – The country chapter does not report on any legal definition of the shoreline

Otherwise, they may derive from a longstanding legal tradition or be related to other aspects of public policy.

Spain's shoreline delineation, adopted in 1988, stands out as the most protective (assuming similar geomorphological conditions). It is based on the tides reached during the *highest storm events that recur at least five times within the five years* prior to delineation. In addition, Spain's shoreline is drawn based on further criteria, that bring it even landwards of the sand dunes, at least to some extent. Thus, it is uniquely higher even than the "highest tidal reach" category. As we shall see below, this is significant because Spain's shoreline defines both the landward extent of its coastal public domain and the starting point for measuring the coastal setback. However, as recounted later, this most landward delimitation of the shoreline has come at a social price.

The second most landward shoreline definition we found – the *highest tidal reach* – is adopted by six jurisdictions (the largest group), with variations (as indicated in Table 19.1). The *highest tidal reach* includes land affected by storm waves,[3] but excludes land affected by exceptional storms.[4] In all of these jurisdictions, as we shall see, there is also a coastal setback zone, so adoption of the *highest tidal reach* reference line protects more of the littoral zone.

The use of the *highest tidal reach* reference line matches up with the shoreline definition adopted by the Mediterranean ICZM Protocol – highest winter waterline. Thus, of the seven countries that are signatories to the Protocol, the majority (Spain, Greece, France, and Slovenia) have adopted a compliant shoreline definition. Turkey too – not yet a signatory state – complies with the shoreline rule. Israel's shoreline definition is not directly comparable with the Protocol definition, as it is not based on tidal reference lines. Each of these countries also has a setback zone based on this shoreline definition. Italy and Malta fall short in their shoreline definitions and of the setback rule defined by the Protocol, as we see below.

At the lowest extreme – definitions based on the mean low tide – we find the UK, five US states, and Malta.[5] As we will see below, unless the public domain is extended landward of the shoreline, or a strict setback zones is in place, this definition is, potentially, the least protective of the coastal zone.

Other jurisdictions use a variety of wordings, which match up with mean high tide or mean seal level. The Italian regulations are somewhat vague, but the language most closely fits with mean tide/mean sea level. Germany, which borders two seas with different tidal regimes, applies two different definitions for determining its shorelines: The mean tide line applies to the Baltic Sea shore, and the mean high tide holds at the North Sea shore, which has greater tidal variations.

Notably, Israel is the only jurisdiction in our set that has altered its shoreline definition in recent decades. The change was driven by environmental policy, tailor-made for the goals of the 2004 Coastal Law. In replacing the earlier rule (MSL), a compromise had to be drawn between the desire to enhance environmental protection and the legal and financial realities. In Israel, there is an obligation to compensate landowners for any reduction in development rights even if not realized for many years (Alterman, 2010a). A study conducted by the Survey of Israel initially recommended adoption of a 1.5 m increment above the *geodetic zero,* to accommodate anticipated climate change effects. However, the National Planning Administration expressed concern about compensation claims by landowners whose pre-existing development rights would be compromised if a setback line based on this criterion would be pushed further landwards. The compromise was a 0.75 m increment above geodetic zero. Thus, unlike the reference lines in the other jurisdictions, Israel's line is not anchored in tidal data, but in the country's cadastre system. Geodetic zero (the "geoid") approximates MSL, but is not quite the same measure (Fraczek, 2003). This measure provides more legal certainty than those based on tidal data, because it is not necessarily updated when MSL is updated (Survey of Israel, n.d.).[6] Given Israel's very high property prices coupled with excessive compensation rights, legal certainty was a significant consideration.

As far as we can ascertain, Israel is the only country in our sample whose shoreline definition may have been inspired by the ICZM Protocol. Even though the decision to amend the former delineation was made in 2004 – four years prior to Protocol's approval – we have evidence that Israeli representatives who were part of the international preparatory team negotiated some of the ideas.[7] Nevertheless, as noted, Israel's shoreline definition is not directly comparable with the Protocol's.[8]

Methods of demarcation and updating

In the natural world, the shoreline changes perpetually. How is this dynamic mediated into the legal-administrative world? The answer depends on the information bases and methods for the demarcation and updating.

Shoreline definitions based on mean, mean high, or mean low tides are delineated according to long-term retroactive data, using accepted measurement methods. These allow more certainty than where the legal definition uses language denoting the *highest tidal reach* but does not express how this reference line is to be identified (e.g. Denmark's law is clear that the setback should be measured from the vegetation line). In those cases, some jurisdictions use technical guidelines, such as a numeric increment above MSL or natural markers created by the highest reach of the waves. Thus, Slovenia and Portugal – where the formal definitions both refer to "highest tides" – have in fact adopted technical guidelines that grant greater certainty by converting *highest tide* to mean sea level plus a prescribed numeric increment (1.73 m and 2 m respectively).[9] By contrast, Greece and Turkey's guidelines refer to natural indicators of the waves' reach, such as vegetation and geomorphology.

Once the shoreline is determined, there are different rules about updating its delineation. Those definitions based on the tidal reference lines of mean high water, mean low water, or mean sea level are updated every 18.6 (or 19) years according to the moon's nodal cycle (Oertel, 2018). In the interim, the shoreline delineation stands. In Spain, where the definition is partly based on the tidal reach during extreme storm events, Lora-Tamayo et al. (Chapter 8) report that more frequent reviews of tidal and storm surge data are mandatory – every five years, beginning in 2013 – but the first review process has not been completed. The other countries which do not rely on tidal means take different approaches: In Denmark and France, there is no specific process for updating the shoreline demarcation, as it is settled on a case-by-case basis. In Greece and Turkey, the shoreline is mapped once demarcated, and the authors of those chapters have not reported on any process for updating the shoreline. Notably, the Greek chapter reports that the mapping procedure originated from a perceived need for a "permanent" or "quasi-permanent" shoreline demarcation to better manage development pressures.

Conflicts over property rights during the delineation or updating processes

Delineation of the shoreline can lead to real-property conflicts, whether during the initial delineation or during updates. Disputes may arise about pre-existing property boundaries or property-development rights. Several of our jurisdictions have had to adopt policies for resolving property boundaries during or after the delineation process.

Greece stands out in this book as the country that has experienced the greatest difficulties, conflicts, and delays in delineating its shoreline. We learn from the Greek chapter that until 2001, the shoreline definition – "usual maximum winter wave run-up" – was not supported by clear legal identification or demarcation procedures. The official procedure introduced in 2001 required site-by-site identification of the shoreline by an appointed committee, usually to settle property disputes. Specific technical criteria that could be considered by these committees were added only in 2005. The onerous and conflict-laden process meant that in the late 2000s, only a minority of Greece's (very long) shoreline had been officially demarcated. In 2014, a new procedure,[10] based on analysis of aerial photographs, allowed authorities to greatly speed up the process, which is now completed at the technical level. However, not all the property disputes have yet been resolved.

Spain, too, has encountered difficulties in shoreline delineation, but of a different kind. The 1988 law that originally defined the shoreline was followed by a nationwide shoreline mapping process. It lasted some time but was completed well before the Coastal Law was amended in 2013. The amendment changed the criteria and thus, the authorities were required to revise the delineation. This complex process is currently (2020) only in its initial phase. This change in shoreline definition is encountering major property rights issues, to be discussed under the public domain parameter – the topic of the next section.

Parameter C: Coastal public domain – extent and rules

The implications of the differing shoreline demaraction rules reported in the previous section will now become apparent: In most cases, the extent of the public domain is dependant on the shoreline, but the type of dependence varies across jurisdictions.

Imposed public ownership on (formerly) private, mixed tenure, or contested land is potentially the most politically sensitive issue among the ten parameters. Not all the socio-political stories behind the establishment of public domain zones are captured in the country chapters because most were established long ago. The more recent stories are woven into the more factual comparative analysis in this section.

The principles

As outlined in Chapter 2, the ethos of public land ownership stems not only from the well-known Roman-law tradition, but also from many other legal cultures around the world (Ryan, forthcoming 2020). The underlying rationale is that well-managed public land ownership could serve as a more potent tool for protection of the coastal zone and for assurance of public access, rather than relying solely on regulation of private property. Yet coastal public domain is far from universal. For example, in Finland – an EU and OECD member country not included in this book – private land ownership is permitted not only along the dry beach, but also in the foreshore area, and even seaward of mean low water (Nordberg, 2001, p. 165).

In our review, we would like to know not only about current land ownership along the coast, but also whether there has been any legal change in recent years. Have there been recent initiatives to introduce public land ownership where there is none, or to extend its span? This is important for the pursuit of better ICZM, especially in the era of climate change and projected sea level rise. One can conjecture that, with a greater extent of public domain, governments would be better able to prevent settlement in danger zones, and thus to avoid the difficult scenarios of planned or emergency retreat.

However, public land ownership on its own does not necessarily guarantee that land will remain in public ownership permanently. The question is whether the ownership status may be changed, and by what legal authority. In most of our jurisdictions where there is a coastal public zone, it enjoys a further special protected status and may never be transferred ("alienated") into non-public ownership, as the original public trust doctrine had envisaged.

Comparative analysis of the (landward) extent of the public domain

It is not simple to compare the geographic extents of public domain. A large public domain zone that is submerged most of the time does not fulfil some of its public functions of public accessibility or protection of the beach from development. Therefore, in order to compare the land areas of the public domains, one must take into account the differences in shoreline definitions.

In all our jurisdictions (but not globally), a public domain zone does exist, at least from the shoreline seaward. In many of the jurisdictions, the landward limit of the public domain is the shoreline. In such cases, the reference line used in defining the shoreline is the all-important factor that determines how much of the public domain, if any, will be on dry or partially wet beach, as discussed in the section above.

However, in some of our jurisdictions, the legal definition of the public domain extends beyond the shoreline. In some jurisdictions, such extension can "compensate" for shoreline definitions based on lower tidal reference lines by bringing the public domain well into the intertidal area or even the dry beach (Figure 19.1). When comparing the public domain area across jurisdictions, it is therefore essential to indicate the relationship with the shoreline definition.

Figure 19.2 illustrates schematically the landward extents of the coastal public domains in all jurisdictions. We cannot depict the precise relative extents of the public domain zones

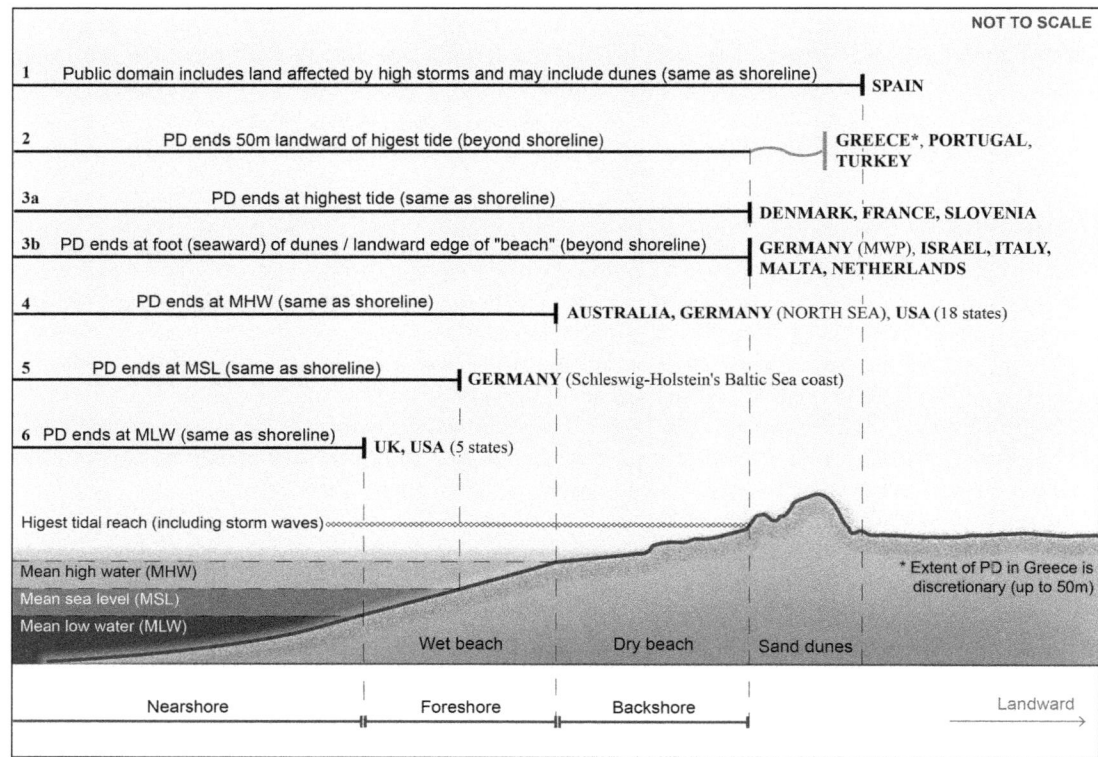

Figure 19.2 The landward extent of the public domain in relation to the shoreline definition: Schematic comparative diagram

Source: Illustration by Cygal Pellach

across the jurisdictions because the geomorphology and tidal regimes would vary locally. Yet we attempt to offer a rough indication of the relative reach of the public domain zones. We have arranged the jurisdictions roughly in rank order, each tier being represented by a horizontal line. The top line, numbered 1, indicates the presumed furthest landward reach and, thus, relatively larger public zone of land. The sixth line indicates the least landward reach. In reality, there might be some variation in the rank order; for example, depending on geography and geomorphology, the second line might overtake the first.

Importantly, Figure 19.2 illustrates the relationship between the shoreline definition and public domain. In many of the schematic tiers, the public domain does not extend landward beyond the shoreline demarcation. This applies to the jurisdictions listed along lines 1, 3a, and 4–6. Their rank order is the same as the rank order of their shorelines indicated in Table 19.1 and does not require further explanation. This means that Spain, with its unique shoreline demarcation, once again ranks the highest, even though its public domain does not extend to land beyond its shoreline. At the lower part of the scheme, along lines 4–6, are the jurisdictions with shoreline definition based on lower tidal reference lines and without any landward extension of their public domain zones. The implications are clear: The public domain, only seaward of the shoreline, will not be very functional in preventing development and allowing public access along the beach.

Now to the set of jurisdictions where the public domain does extend landward of the shoreline. The countries along line 2 – Greece, Portugal, and Turkey – all share a shoreline definition of "highest tide". To this relatively high shoreline definition, they have added a further extension of the public domain, based on a set number of metres from the shoreline. This "implementation-based" rule (according to the terminology of Chapter 18) implies that it would apply uniformly, regardless of geomorphological conditions. Portugal and Turkey use a measurement of 50 m. In practice, this means that the public domain may extend into the sand dunes (as illustrated at Figure 19.2; see also Chrzastowski, 2005). Greece adopted an unusual rule – a *maximal* extension of 50 m. On its face, this notion seems at odds with the rationale of the public domain. Perhaps it reflects the many conflicts that have surrounded the demarcation of the shoreline in Greece and the desire to give adjacent landowners greater certainty.

Line 3b encompasses five jurisdictions. Their shorelines are lower than "highest tide", yet their public domain reaches landward as far as the "highest tide". Instead of numeric criteria, these jurisdictions adopted one or more nature-led criteria to determine how far landward would be their public domain. The wording used to describe the natural features that define the extent of each jurisdiction's public domain varies: In the Netherlands and the German state of Mecklenburg-Western Pomerania (MWP), the public domain extends "to the foot (seaward) of the dunes". In Israel, Italy, and Malta the public domain includes the "beach". We have grouped these jurisdictions together because according to prevalent scientific definitions, the beach extends to the foot of the dunes (Kraus, 2005; Cornell et al., n.d.) and these are also the limit of the reach of storm waves (Chrzastowski, 2005). The quantitative distance covered will, of course, differ depending on the geography of each specific coastal region.

Malta – the tiniest and most dense country in our set – deserves special attention on two counts. First, Malta recently introduced legislation to clarify the status and extent of publicly owned land along the coast, filling a legislative vacuum that had earlier been addressed by a few court decisions. In this respect, Malta is unique, because in all other jurisdictions, the coastal public domain has been institutionalized for a long time. Second, recent Maltese law prescribes a nature-based criterion for the public domain: Wherever there is no beach (such as coastal cliffs), the public domain should extend 15 m from the shoreline. None of the other jurisdictions in this book are reported to have a geographically tailored public domain rule. However, Malta's recent rule does not apply to pre-existing privately owned land.

The idea of publicly owned land along the shores is sometimes adopted well beyond the traditional public domain. In the UK, McElduff and Ritchie (Chapter 3) report, two-thirds of the intertidal area (between mean low tide and high tide lines) has in fact come into public ownership. In Australia, which also does not extend its public domain landward of the shoreline, many large national parks are located adjacent to the shoreline. In Israel, where the formal public domain is limited to the beach, in fact most of the coastal zone happens to be nationally owned, as is much of Israel's land in general. However, the legal protection of "inalienability" does not apply to public land beyond the beach.

Property-rights pains in creating a public domain

Creation of a public domain might encounter a head-on clash with private property rights. However, as noted, not all our country chapters report on such clashes in recent years. This may be due to the long-standing existence of the public domain in many countries, coupled with reliance on tide-based shoreline demarcation rules without significant sea level rise. But where the public domain was established or expanded in recent decades, we do learn about the almost inevitable conflicts with landowners. These stories should be heeded as lessons for the likely challenges of sea level rise, which might, in some locations, push the shoreline – and thus the public domain – further inland.

As is typical of real property law, the traces of disputes over property rights can last for generations. There may be legal challenges about the right to take the land, or lingering disputes on the level of compensation. Since private land in coastal zones is likely to be very valuable, the amount of compensation due in case of fair expropriation might be prohibitive. What approaches have the various jurisdictions taken regarding such property conundrums? What legal instruments did they adopt: Expropriation with full compensation? Expropriation with low compensation? Cancellation of rights with no compensation? Procrastination? Circumvention?

Several of the country chapters provide fascinating examples of what happened when governments attempted to create public domain zones or to extend them. Although the basic issues are similar, the approaches adopted across jurisdictions differed widely.

Before we proceed, a legal distinction should be made between three basic situations that often affect legal eligibility to claim compensation when government converts private land into public ownership (not necessarily on the coast): Privately owned land that is already built up; undeveloped land without development rights; and undeveloped land with development rights that have not yet been realized. The latter category especially presents major legal differences across jurisdictions – regardless of location. In the coastal zone context, the question will be whether private holders of approved but unbuilt development rights will be eligible for full compensation. In some contexts, especially concerning high-value coastal land, the sums could be huge.

There are major legal differences among OECD countries on the issue of compensation rights, as shown in Alterman's (2010b) comparative analysis of fourteen OECD-member jurisdictions. Within our book's set of jurisdictions, most do not grant compensation for the value of unbuilt development rights, and certainly not for sheer expectations of development. However, in Israel and the USA, such claims might come up (and, in theory, in the Netherlands too;

Hobma, 2010). A landowner's mere threat of submitting a compensation claim and adjudication in the courts can deter public initiatives.

Three countries in our sample – the Netherlands, Portugal, and, very recently, Malta – permit private owners of land in the coastal public domain to remain in place so long as they can bring proof of ownership. But how far in history must ownership go back? In Portugal, that proof must date as far back as the 1860s. To date, about 500 private properties, equating to about 30% of Portugal's mainland coastline, have been recognized in this process. In Malta, ownership claims have not yet been tested.

Among our set of countries, Malta is the only one that has recently taken some steps – though modest – towards enhancing its public domain. However, the main function of the new legislation is to provide legal certainty to coastal land that is already regarded as de facto public. The law declares as public land Malta's beach areas or, depending on coastal geomorphology, a 15 m strip landward from the shoreline. This new type of public domain does not entail taking of privately owned land. The newly declared public domain is to be inalienable, except through a Parliamentary decision. These steps may seem as almost negligible in the context of ICZM, but in a tiny country such as Malta, with the highest Coastal Population Pressure Index among our fifteen countries (see Chapter 1), one can appreciate that existing property rights constrain establishment of a broader public domain zone. Yet the fact that a public domain is declared only now, and is of modest geographic extent, means that Malta's protection of its coastal zone is rather weak from a comparative perspective.

As reported by Ünsal (Chapter 14), only Turkey is currently in the midst of actions to implement decisions on public coastal domain, but for a decision made back in 1926 which did not set a landward extent. The government is now trying to implement a regulation that in the 1990s established the extent of coastal public domain. At first, the government attempted to simply abolish private titles without compensation (somewhat similarly to what Spain did in 1988, though less drastic). This action was later deemed contrary to the principles established by the European Court of Human Rights. A Turkish parliamentary commission has since found that the land designated as public domain has not yet been expropriated due to "mismanagement".

Israel – second only to Malta on our Coastal Population Pressure Index and likely to soon have the highest score due to its high birth rates – is currently contending with a special version of this issue, unique to Israel's land law. As Carmon and Alterman (Chapter 15) recount, in Israel, most of the land along the coast has a long history of national ownership, but its status is not different from the extensive national land holdings throughout the country. A few years ago, the National Lands Authority, following a tender, signed several contracts with developers to build hotels just landward of the inalienable public domain (inland from the beach, on or near the dunes). There was no distinct legal fault with these contracts.

However, public environmental protests that lasted several years finally convinced the authorities that national land ownership should, in special cases, be leveraged for extra protection of the coast, even if not legally mandated. The government planning bodies were ready to cancel the development rights but were deterred by the huge compensation sums to be incurred by the public pocket. Under Israeli law, a decision to reverse development rights would mean huge sums of compensation to the developers, even if they have not yet invested in construction. There is no difference in this legal rule between private land and nationally owned land leased out on a long-term lease. On national land, the developers are eligible to receive compensation not just for the amount they paid for the lease contract, but also for the loss of value due to reduction in development rights – the "unearned increment"! In the case of this extremely controversial project, the planning bodies finally did decide to abolish the development rights.

The compensation issue lingered on, until in 2019 several government bodies joined forces to allocate budgets to pay the hefty compensation sum. It is difficult to guess whether this case will become a precedent for others.

The Spanish saga

The most dramatic story about the clash with private property rights is told in the Spanish chapter. Spain's story is the most extreme example of the painful consequences of establishing public domain where there were had been extensive private land and property rights. This situation arose when Spain adopted the most environmentally ambitious definition of its shoreline and public domain, to extend the farthest landwards compared to the other jurisdictions (Figure 19.2). However, this environmental gain became the nightmare of thousands of landowners and residents. Following the approval in 1988 of the Coastal Law (not many years after the termination of the Franco era), large tracts of land were "automatically" converted from private to public, without any expropriation procedures and with no rights to compensation. Instead of their previous private property, the former owners were issued time-limited ground leases ("concessions"), which could not be sold. The ground leases did allow the former owners to remain on the land and use the pre-existing structures, but under highly restrictive conditions. They were not allowed to renovate their homes or to undertake any coastal defence works against possible storms. The owners included some foreign investors and owners of summer homes, but there were also many local residents, some not well-off.

These actions sparked protests and a conflict that reached all the way up to the European Parliament, which delivered scathing criticism of the ground leases and the denial of compensation. In 2013, the Spanish Parliament decided to amend the Coastal Law. It extended the time period for the ground leases and somewhat relaxed the restrictions on home repairs, on coastal defence works, and transfer of concessions to other parties. However, the other limitations remained. Public protest is still percolating.

This saga has a paradoxical sequel, embedded in the notion of public domain: In addition to the small changes in the ground leases, the 2013 amendment also introduced some modifications to the nature-based criteria for demarcation of the shoreline and thus the public domain. Whereas before, the shoreline extended to the landward side of all sand dunes, the amended law called for redrawing the line to include only those sand dunes required to ensure "stability of the beach". Locally, the new rules should lead to the release of any reclassified land from its public domain status.[11] However, former landowners who tried to claim land back discovered that they were caught in a legally circular argument: Because the original coastal law had declared the public domain as "inalienable", perhaps the land is "trapped" in its public status?[12] The re-demarcation process is still young. It will be interesting to follow the script of the second sequel of the story, which will presumably emerge through court challenges, a new group of protestors, and perhaps more legislative changes.

Permitted land use and construction on coastal public land

Public land is just a type of ownership. The important question for coastal zone management is what type of land use or development is allowed on the public domain. Comparative analysis reveals that the permitted land uses differ somewhat in practice. Some of these differences may reflect the physical attributes of the public domain. There is one common denominator: Coastal public land is much more highly regulated compared with the urban or rural zones in its hinterland. In general, only low-impact uses are permitted. These typically include bathing, hiking, and sometimes also hunting, fishing, and navigation. However, new uses sometime arise, presenting regulatory challenges. For example, in Israel, a new type of lifestyle use has appeared in recent years: Makeshift temporary vacation facilities on the beach, fitted with temporary kitchens, in large tents or gazebos. Although this use does not involve any permanent construction, it presents a challenge to the regulatory definitions of what constitutes recreation, what is temporary, and what is the dividing line between public and commercial use (where these facilities are rented out commercially). Other countries and cultures probably face additional unanticipated demand for new types of land use.

In our jurisdictions, there is also wide consensus about forbidding permanent construction on coastal public land (except some infrastructure or sea-related facilities). However, the conceptions of what is temporary differ greatly. In all the Mediterranean countries, private actors may apply for certain "concessions" (such as ground leases) for a limited period of time – in some cases for several months, in others only a few months. The structures built must be compatible (variously defined) with the public use of the coast. Some jurisdictions permit only temporary or "removable" structures, that in theory could be removed at the end of the bathing season (Greece, Slovenia, Malta, Italy, and Spain) but do not necessarily require their removal in practice. Spain's regulations are especially detailed, and include prescriptions for siting, maximum number of permitted beach concessions, and maximum floorspace and height; the Autonomous Community of Valencia even issues permits that require that structures be removed at the end of the bathing season. Israel is an exception, in that the regulations focus more on type of use and intensity, and less on permanency of the structures – perhaps because beaches are popular year-round.

The Puglia Region in Italy serves as an example of how coastal policies can be reformed within a relatively short learning time. This region has innovated in designing a sophisticated set of rules for granting concessions according to a comprehensive analysis of environmental sensitivity and danger of erosion. In addition, a cumulative limitation was adopted, so that at least 60% of the area of the Maritime Public Domain would remain free of any structures and open for public use.

So far, the picture of planning regulations over the public domain looks quite rosy. Yet one should keep in mind that similarities in planning regulations should not imply that the rules are similarly implemented and enforced. In fact, there are dramatic differences in degrees of enforcement across the sample countries, as discussed in Chapter 20.

The supra-national rules about coastal public land

When addressing the supra-national level, we ask throughout about the extent to which the prescribed rules are actually taken up by each nation. In the case of public land ownership, our findings bring us to a critical view of the supra-national documents as well.

First, let us recall what the two relevant international documents about ICZM say about public land ownership (see Chapter 2). In both, the idea of introducing or increasing the coastal public domain has an ambivalent presence. This is not surprising because intervention in land ownership is one of the most difficult ICZM-related instruments to implement. The ICZM Protocol to the Barcelona Convention avoids the term "public domain" (or "public ownership") altogether, stating only that parties to the treaty "may, inter alia, adopt mechanisms and institute easements on [private] properties" (Article 20(3)). The wording of this specific paragraph gives it advisory status only. The EU Parliament's Recommendation concerning ICZM (2002) makes a clearer statement in favour of public ownership. It recommends that member states adopt "… land purchase mechanisms and declarations of public domain to ensure public access for recreational purposes without prejudice to the protection of sensitive areas" (paragraph 3(b)(2)). However, this entire document is "soft law".

Our comparative analysis of current public coastal land ownership indicates that both documents may have missed "the elephant in the room". In all our jurisdictions, there is a public domain. The main question is the extent to which it extends landward from the sea. In many jurisdictions, this depends on the definition of the shoreline, usually based on tide-based reference lines. Neither the ICZM Recommendation nor the ICZM Protocol consider how far inland coastal public land should stretch. The latter does prescribe adoption of the shoreline based on the *highest tide*, but this is done in a separate clause, unrelated to public land ownership.

Going forward, future endeavours at supra-national legislation or policy about the land-ownership and rights components of ICZM would do well to tailor policies and priorities to the current legal contexts. Special attention should be directed at jurisdictions whose public coastal land does not extend to the "dry beach" – that is, land that is almost permanently under water or is exposed only during short periods due to the shoreline definition adopted (Figure 19.2).

Yet any jurisdiction seeking to increase the extent of its coastal public domain should heed the Spanish story and proceed with caution regarding private property rights. Apparently, adequate funding mechanisms for fair compensation are currently not in place, neither on the national level nor internationally.

Parameter D: Coastal setback zone – extent and uses

Another important instrument for coastal zone management is the coastal setback zone. In Chapter 2, we defined setbacks as designated zones in coastal areas, intended to serve as an intermediate buffer between the littoral zone and the inland areas beyond the coastal zone, where development is prohibited or restricted. Although some setback zones were in existence long before the rise of climate change awareness, they could be especially important today. Setback zones could play an important role in areas anticipating sea level rise. If well-implemented and enforced, a wide enough setback buffer could mitigate the risks to human lives and property and, at the same time, conserve the coastal environmental assets. As noted in the previous section, setback zones should not be confused with the coastal public domain. They are blind to ownership and could be delineated on land in public, private, mixed, or contested ownership. They can fully or partially overlap with public land or extend beyond it.

In this section, we first reintroduce the relevant supra-national rules about setback zones prescribed by the Mediterranean ICZM Protocol, and thus relevant to seven of our fifteen countries (or eight, if Turkey were to sign the Protocol). We proceed to survey and compare the setback regulations across all research jurisdictions, and then return to the Protocol to gauge its possible degree of de facto influence.

The setback provision in the Mediterranean ICZM protocol

As discussed in Chapter 2, among the Mediterranean ICZM Protocol's best-known rules is the setback zone, addressed in Article 8 (2). The setback rule's prominence may be due to the fact that it is the only quantitative norm in the Protocol, and thus (ostensibly) easy to recognize and measure for assessing compliance.[13]

The article says:

> 8. *Protection and sustainable use of the coastal zone*
>
> 2. *The parties...*
>
>> a   *shall establish in coastal zones, as from the highest winter waterline, a zone where construction is not allowed. Taking into account, inter alia, the areas directly and negatively affected by climate change and natural risks, this zone may not be less than 100 meters in width, subject to the provisions of subparagraph (b) below. Stricter national measures determining this width shall continue to apply;*

The Protocol does give room for national governments to adapt the setback zone's 100 m width to specific local conditions (8(2)b), but that does not detract from the obligation on all Mediterranean signatory countries to adopt it as the basic norm. This means that by now, all seven signatory countries in our set should have taken steps to adopt the 100 m setback rule, as far as possible, unless it is already part of their law and practice. Once they adopt this rule, the Protocol allows national governments to make adjustments justified by local conditions (Rochette & Bille, 2010). Let us now survey the rules about setback zones adopted by our fifteen countries and some states within.

The different definitions of setback zones and their implications

Setback zones, like public domain zones, are dependent on each jurisdiction's definition of the shoreline.

As shown in Table 19.2, ten of our fifteen countries have indeed adopted a national specified setback distance (or distances, as discussed below) from their shoreline. Three more countries leave this determination to the discretion of local or regional governments, and one, Malta, does not prescribe any setback zone. The USA is a special case, as two-thirds of its coastal states do prescribe setback rules. The remaining one third of US coastal states leave the determination of setback rules to local government discretion.

Setback zones and the coastal public domain

What is the interrelationship between the public domain and the setback zones (where both exist)? In six jurisdictions, the setback zone overlaps, or may overlap, with the coastal public domain (Table 19.3). Given that the setback zones are measured from the shoreline, the disparity between the countries on this matter is derived from whether a given country designates its public domain landward of the shoreline or only seaward, and whether the landward extent of the public domain is based on a set distance (Portugal, Turkey, and Greece) or geomorphology (Israel, Italy, Germany's Mecklenburg Western-Pomerania).

Setback zones and property rights

Because setback zones are intended to impose stringent controls over land use and development, they might, in principle, collide with property rights. None of this book's chapters report on such conflict, for three probable reasons: First, in some jurisdictions, the setback zones

Table 19.2 Types of rules regarding setbacks*

Government level of decision	Obligatory setbacks	Discretionary setbacks
National / State	Denmark France Germany Greece Israel Italy (minimum setback) Portugal Slovenia Spain Turkey 2/3 of US coastal states	N/A
Regional (significant independence)	Italy (extended setback)	
Local	N/A	Australia Netherlands UK 1/3 of US coastal states

* Malta has no setback rules at national level, nor delegation of planning powers to local authorities. In theory, setbacks may be included in "local plans" prepared by the national Planning Authority.

were established long ago, and whatever issues may have arisen then are no longer relevant. Second, where setback zones have been established more recently, or are declared by local planning authorities on an ongoing basis (where authorized), these zones usually exempt built-up areas and "grandfather in" unrealized development rights. Third, many jurisdictions may be sidestepping potential conflicts with property rights by simply not introducing a setback zone where there is none, and not extending an existing but insufficient one.

In those six jurisdictions where there is (or may be) an overlap between the setback zone and public domain, a question that comes to mind is whether there are differences in the rules applicable to the public and private sections. In fact, none of the relevant country chapter authors has expounded on the policy justification or legal implications of the degree of overlap between the setback zone and the public domain. Only Turkey has explicitly defined separate

Table 19.3 Different interrelationships between coastal setback zones and coastal public domain

Setback zone fully overlaps with coastal public domain	Portugal Turkey
Setback zone overlaps with coastal public domain only where the coastal public domain extends landward of shoreline	Greece
Setback zone may overlap with coastal public domain, depending on coastal geomorphology	Israel Italy Mecklenburg Western-Pomerania, Germany
Setback zone does not overlap with coastal public domain (public domain is only seaward of shoreline; setback zone is landward of shoreline)	Denmark France Germany (two states) Slovenia Spain

rules for use of the public and privately owned parts of the setback zone. In our view, public domain is the dominant tool of the two. Although both types of zones have a similar function in protecting the environment, people, and property, the public domain conveys an additional social and symbolic value of assuring permanent public enjoyment of the coastal zone.

Comparative setback distances

Figure 19.3 illustrates the comparative setback zones relevant to the ten countries that use distance measures. The illustration also shows wherever there are two or three sets of distances (some discretionary, some for special types of land use). However, this diagram must be viewed with caution since it does not show the differences in the shoreline definitions, being the starting points for measuring the setback distances.

Table 19.4 compares setback distances across jurisdiction within each category of shoreline reference line. This table focuses on "standard" setback distances prescribed by the national governments.

Before turning to the detail of the setback rules, we ask whether there is a dominant setback distance signifying some cross-national policy convergence. As discussed, the Mediterranean ICZM Protocol suggests that the setback distance should be 100 m, measured from the "highest

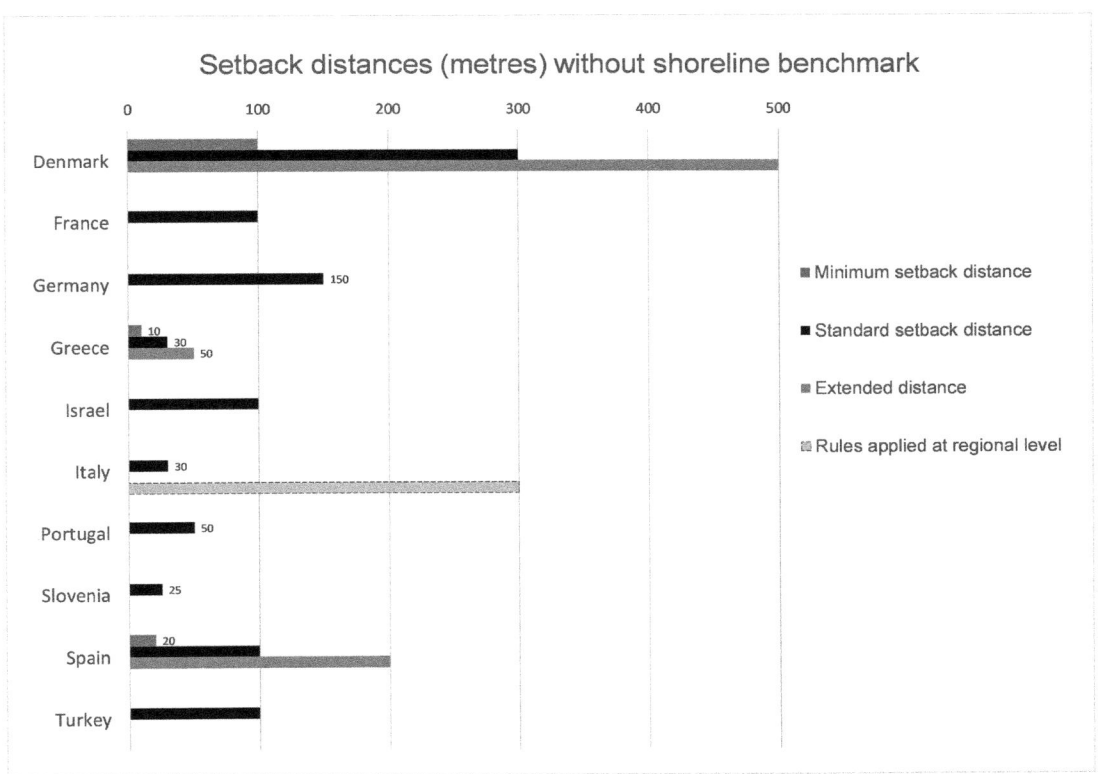

Figure 19.3 Coastal setback distances (should not be compared without the shoreline reference used as benchmark for measurement)

Table 19.4 Standard setback distances by shoreline reference line

	Standard setback distances					
	Less than 100 m			100 m or more		
Shoreline reference line	25 m	30 m	50 m	100 m	150 m	300 m
Highest tidal reach by exceptional storm waves + coastal features				**Spain** ^		
Highest tidal reach (excluding exceptional storms)	**Slovenia** ^	**Greece** ^	**Portugal**	**Turkey France** ^		**Denmark**
Surrogate for tidal reference – geodetic zero + 0.75				**Israel** ^		
Mean high water (or surrogate)					**Germany (North Sea)** *	
Mean tide or mean sea level – MSL		**Italy** ^			**Germany (Baltic Sea)** **	**Italy** ^

Jurisdiction in **grey**: Rules applied at regional level

^ Mediterranean countries that are signatories to the ICZM Protocol
* North Sea Coast states: Lower Saxony, part of Schleswig-Holstein
** Baltic Sea Coast states: Mecklenburg-Western Pomerania, part of Schleswig-Holstein

winter waterline". Do our Mediterranean signatory countries have a setback zone that is at least 100 m wide? Four do – France, Spain, Israel, and Italy (in the latter, rules vary region). But only France and Spain use the *highest tidal reach* for their shoreline reference (or further land-ward), as prescribed by the ICZM Protocol. Israel's setback zone, installed relatively recently, is measured from further seaward (geodetic true zero + 0.75 m). Our interpretation of Italy's shoreline definition takes it even further seaward, to the mean sea level mark. Furthermore, Italy has two setbacks: A small 30 m zone where there are strict national regulations, and a 300 m zone where the rules are at the discretion of the regions (we do not have information about each region). Greece and Slovenia fall far short of the 100 m norm, and Malta has not adopted any setback distance. However, Malta's extreme "Coastal Population Pressure Index" reflects the objective difficulties of introducing a significant setback zone.

Did the ICZM Protocol influence the creation or updating of the setback zones in any of the seven signatories in our sample? The answer is that although four of the signatories do have at least a 100m setback in place, in three, this is unrelated to the Protocol. These countries' setback rules preceded the Protocol's adoption by many years. In fact, the Protocol was partly influenced by the then-existing norms (Sanò et al., 2011). One notable success, where the Protocol did have a distinct influence, is Israel's adoption of the 100 m setback zone in 2004. At that time, the Protocol was in the drafting process, and the Israeli delegates to that process brought the idea back to the team drafting the new Israeli coastal law.[14] This achievement is notable in view of Israel's extremely high "Coastal Population Pressure Index", for now, second only to Malta (Chapter 1).

Let us now look at the setback rules in countries which do not follow the 100 m norm. In the following discussion, we begin with the jurisdiction with the most extensive setback distances applied at national level, then turn to those with the shortest setbacks. We focus on the "standard" nationally prescribed setback distances but also refer to minimum or maximum distances required for special circumstances (Figure 19.3). We follow with an example of a setback rule that is not based on a set distance from the shoreline. Finally, we take a broad cross-national look at the differences in the rules about permitted land use and construction in the setback zones.

Denmark's setback rules are particularly noteworthy for both distances and stringency. The Danish standard coastal setback zone has a width of 300 m, measured from the vegetation line (usually identified at the foot of the sand dunes).[15] This is the longest standard setback measured from the second-most landward shoreline reference point in our set. In some areas, the Danish setback distance extends as far as 500 m. Furthermore, in Denmark, the 100 m setback is a special minimum that applies only to built-up areas of vacation homes. Development in any other built-up areas must adhere to the standard 300 m distance or more. Within any setback zone – 100, 300, or 500 m – most forms of development and even ground works (other than those tied to the sea) are prohibited. The rules are strictly enforced.

Yet, without diminishing Denmark's leadership on the setback parameter (and some others), one should recall that this country does not have a high Coastal Population Pressure Index score (Chapter 1). Its score of 122, while not among the lowest, is much lower than the Netherlands' 284, Israel's 914, or Malta's 1288. Furthermore, it should be noted that the setback distances in Denmark were instituted as early as 1937, when, presumably, the coastal zone had still lower developmental pressures.

Four jurisdictions have setback distances of less than 100 m: Portugal (50 m), Italy (30 m), Greece (30 m) and Slovenia (25 m). Italy appears to have a larger setback distance of 300 m, but this is a special distance where the rules about permitted use or development are set at regional level and are apparently often more lax than in the standard zone. In Italy's standard 30 m setback zone, any proposed development is subject to approval by the State. Furthermore, Italy's shoreline is based on the mean sea level reference line, as opposed to the *highest tide* reference used in the other three jurisdictions.

Greece, too, has a standard setback distance of only 30 m. This standard is applied in non-urban areas, while in urban areas setback distances are to be set in local plans. The 30 m standard seems meagre given that Greece has the longest coastline among our set of jurisdictions and one of the lower scores on our "Coastal Population Pressure Index" (Chapter 1). Furthermore, Greek law does not provide a more stringent setback norm for higher-pressure types of development, even in tourist resorts. There, Greek law prescribes an even smaller setback of a mere 10 m for some uses – restaurants, recreation areas, restrooms, sports facilities, and playgrounds. On the other hand, tourist accommodation facilities in resorts do require a larger setback, of 50 m. While this distance is not large in comparative terms, in Greece it is the largest.

Slovenia has the narrowest standard setback of only 25 m. However, the objective geographic context matters here: Slovenia has the shortest shoreline among our set of countries. In 2013, the EU SHAPe project assessed the potential to widen Slovenia's setback zone to 100 m. The study found that of the potential 4.7 km² of land, 38% is currently protected for agriculture, forest, or internal waters and about 42% is built up, leaving only about 20% (less than 1 km²) which would be protected from development by an increased setback.

Setback rules are not always based on measurable, preset distances, although these dominate our set of jurisdictions. Tarlock reports (Chapter 17) about a different approach taken in North Carolina, USA. There, the setback requirements are calculated based on both the height of the proposed development and the rate of erosion in the relevant coastal location. In the author's words,

> *The setback distance is determined as the size of the structure multiplied by the relevant setback factor. Based on the author's personal visits to several of the state's beaches, it appears that the setbacks are strictly observed. Development is intense but uniform behind the dune line.*

Beyond the size of the setback zone, a big question is what land uses and development densities are permitted. In general, most jurisdictions allow only bathing facilities, pedestrian promenades, kiosks, and other amenities that support the recreational use of the beach. An exception worth noting is Turkey, where, since 2008, construction of sports facilities and related accommodation may also be permitted in the setback zone. Infrastructure specifically linked to the seafront, such as ports and marinas and associated facilities, will also be allowed in prescribed locations.

Parameter E: Right of public access – to and along the coast

In introducing the public access parameter in Chapter 2, we pointed out that in this book, we devote greater attention to this aspect than it is usually given in books about ICZM. The reason is that the public's right of access to the coast has deep philosophical and legal anchors, as an offshoot of the public domain concept. In some jurisdictions, this special right overrides private land ownership. In this chapter, we use the term "right of access" in an even broader sense than the right to physically access the coast. As noted in Chapter 2, we distinguish among five types accessibility:

a. Horizontal accessibility – walking, playing, swimming along the shoreline
b. Vertical accessibility – reaching the shoreline
c. Accessibility for people with disabilities
d. Social justice in accessibility – for the poor and special sociocultural groups.
e. Visual accessibility – ability to view the coast from a distance.

The right of access to and along the coast cannot be absolute, even in the most progressive coastal laws. Exercise of this right may be qualified by physical formations in the natural environment and by passage restrictions in areas classified for strict environmental preservation, or by closed-off built-up zones such as infrastructure installations, ports, army facilities, or industrial complexes. In some jurisdictions, the right of access clashes with private property rights – whether the property is built up or still vacant.

In jurisdictions where private property may reach all the way to submerged land, the law sometimes nevertheless grants public access as a type of easement (passage rights that override ownership's "right to exclude"). Even where there is a public domain zone landward of the shoreline, accessibility might be restricted in various ways, including by means that are illegal or in the legally grey area. Such phenomena might include hotels with "private beaches"; gated marina zones for members only; beach areas closed off for private events; gated residential communities close to the coast; or apartment and office buildings in the hinterland designed to maximize their own exposure to sea views, thereby blocking public access to views.

Our comparative findings show that in most jurisdictions, at least the minimal right of horizontal access is viewed as integral to coastal zone management. Beyond this common denominator, we see a surprisingly large variation in approaches to the right to access. Some of the country chapters recount stories about heated debates and public actions to gain one or more aspects of the right of access.

Horizontal accessibility

Horizontal accessibility – along the shoreline – is perhaps the most basic tenet of the public right of coastal access. Although the distinction between horizontal and vertical accessibility is not always clear in the wording of the laws, the primary reference to horizontal access is often implied. On this aspect of accessibility, there is "good news": In the majority of jurisdictions discussed in this book, the laws and regulations do stipulate that at least the coastal public domain should be accessible to the broad public. Only two countries lack any direct mention of the legal right of access in national (or state) coastal legislation: Australia, where accessibility is only implied, and the UK, where it is not addressed at all. However, in both jurisdictions, local-level policies may fill in this gap. The extent to which this is done in practice is beyond this book's scope.

Needless to say, the right of access within and along the "dry beach" (refer Figure 19.2) depends on whether the public domain extends to a dry or semi-dry beach during a reasonable period of time in the year. This in turn is linked with the different landward demarcations of the public domain. Thus, in twelve jurisdictions in this book (eleven countries and one German state), the public may freely access the dry beach, at least up to the foot of the dunes (Figure 19.2). However, in the remaining jurisdictions, accessibility of the dry beach is limited because those jurisdictions' public domains are demarcated according to one of the lower tidal reference lines. Thus, in eighteen of the twenty-three US coastal states and the German states of Lower Saxony and Schleswig-Holstein, accessibility is guaranteed only along the wet beach.[16]

Worse yet is the state of the right of access in five US states. There, even the "wet beach" is not in the public domain. In those states, minimal access is granted only up to the mean high water mark, for hunting, fishing, and navigation purposes. It does not extend to the dry beach. Amongst the states where the public domain does include at least the wet beach, six have alleviated the accessibility limitations by extending access also into the dry beach areas. They have done this either through other forms of public land ownership (such as national parks) or by imposing specific obligations on private landowners to permit public access through their private plots.

The French and Spanish legislation grants the right of horizontal access even beyond their already generous extents of coastal public domain. This right entails 3–5 m easements landward along the public domain. Malta's former Structure Plan would have also enhanced public horizontal access to reach "around the shoreline immediately adjacent to the sea or at the top of cliffs", but it was repealed (for other reasons). Nevertheless, Malta's planning tribunal (EPRT) has suggested that this policy is still reflected in local planning. On this basis, the Tribunal upheld a local authority's refusal to grant a permit for development on the shore. We remind again that Malta has the highest population pressure index score among our jurisdictions, so this decision might be seen as an achievement.

Vertical accessibility

The information presented in the country chapters indicates that the right to vertical access (within reasonable bounds) is, comparatively, less protected by law than horizontal accessibility. Vertical access rights are more complex to regulate than horizontal access rights because the former entail access from the urban or rural hinterland, where there are likely to be invested property rights. Existing local road networks and alignment of buildings often do not prioritize access to the coast. Ports and industrial complexes are notorious barriers preventing not only horizontal but also vertical access. Retrofitting existing built-up areas for vertical access is not simple.

Legally, vertical accessibility is highly reliant on planning regulations, urban design, and the layout of existing or planned infrastructure. These are all necessarily based on site-specific discretion. The clash with lucrative property interests may be inevitable. We were interested to learn from the comparative analysis what legal approaches our fifteen countries, and some states within, have adopted to contend with this conundrum.

Table 19.5 summarizes the extent to which vertical accessibility is required by national-level legislation. These findings are only partially encouraging. Six countries do not protect vertical access to the shore in national legislation. Interestingly, this group includes countries with a broad range of scores along the Coastal Population Pressure Index – from Slovenia at the very low end to the Netherlands and Malta at the higher end. Thus, there are no clear factual common denominators, such as existing urban density. However, vertical accessibility can, of course, be achieved without national legislation through socially embedded norms to guide planning and other authorities. We learn from the Australian and German chapters that many of the relevant authorities at both state and local levels have successfully ensured a reasonable level of vertical accessibility. We have no systematic comparative evidence on de facto accessibility.

Two countries have adopted an interesting approach intended entirely to override local planning and urban design discretion over vertical access. Spain and Greece have translated

Table 19.5 National-level legal requirements for vertical accessibility to the shoreline or the coastal public domain

No national legal rules for vertical accessibility	Australia Germany Malta Netherlands Slovenia UK
General (discretionary) requirement for vertical accessibility	Denmark France Israel (in draft regulations; earlier in some court decisions)* Italy (Puglia Region)* Portugal Turkey USA
Numerical standards for vertical accessibility	Greece (10 m wide coastal access roads) Spain (Roads every 500 m, pedestrian paths every 200 m)
* Also, specific provision or court decision(s) requiring accessibility for people with disabilities	

vertical access into obligatory standards based on maximal distance between public routes enabling access from the hinterland to the sea. (It is not clear to us whether these standards clash with environmental considerations that would seek to minimize fragmentation.) Once again, Spain stands out; its somewhat ambitious requirements stipulate that the distance between roads to enable vertical access must not exceed 500 m. In addition, there should be pedestrian paths laid out every 200 m. Greece's standards are also numeric, but their purpose and function are indirect. The legislation says that local authorities may expropriate land for coastal access roadways as long as they are at a minimum width of 10 m. However, achievement of these substantial requirements is apparently not easy. The authors of both the Spanish and the Greek chapters report that implementation of these standards is poor. The key obstacles are lack of funds and political will. In both countries, some local governments have adopted their own vertical access standards through their planning and executive powers.

Fences, too, might block vertical access. Fences are relatively easy elements to regulate compared with the broader issues of urban development. At the same time, fences, especially in housing areas, answer to issues of local politics and economic interests. So regulation of fences is a topic that several countries have deemed important enough to "scale up" from the local discretionary planning permission arena to the national or regional levels. These jurisdictions include Spain, Greece, Israel, and Italy's Puglia region, where fencing is prohibited or highly regulated within a specific distance from the shoreline (500 m in Spain and Greece, 300 m in Israel[17] and Puglia). Yet in Greece, the law allows for so many exceptions that the rule becomes almost an empty shell.

Figure 19.4 Even foldable structures, if unregulated, might block both horizonal and vertical access. Taken from a (illegally extended) restaurant on the beach south of Alexandropoulos Greece

Source: Photo by Rachelle Alterman

Finally, the right to vertical access sometimes rouses underlying ideologies of property rights. Two contrasting examples within our sample are Malta and California. In Malta, accessibility of all types has been significantly threatened by aggressive private development and a conservative interpretation of property rights by the courts. Xerri (Chapter 13) reports that in a 2015 decision, the planning tribunal (EPRT), while expressing some sympathy for public access, saw no way of ensuring it under the existing legal framework:

> *no law can grant third parties rights on private property if not through the legal means which the legislator would have already put in place for such purpose. A policy certainly cannot, by itself, grant private property rights to third parties or be used to deny the development requested by an owner on his own land.* (Victor Borg v. Malta Environment and Planning Authority)

By contrast, in California, the Coastal Act specifically provides that "development shall not interfere with the public's right of access to the sea". Even though the Californian law enables property owners to apply for a special permit to terminate a previously existing public access right through their property to the shoreline, such permits are legally difficult to obtain.[18] The contrast between Malta and the US demonstrates the significance of revisiting the deeper layers of private property rights and their limits when they conflict with major public goals of coastal zone management, such as public access.

Accessibility for people with disabilities

People with physical disabilities obviously encounter difficulties in accessing the beach area or moving along the beach. The laws and regulations in most of our sample countries have overlooked this issue. It may also be that the legislators and decision-makers preferred to leave the notion of accessibility broad and vague, so that lower-level agencies would have to encounter the reluctance of governments or entrepreneurs to finance access facilities for people with disabilities. Furthermore, provision of access to physically challenged persons often requires some form of construction, which might clash with principles for the protection of the natural environment. Be as it may, the topic of access for persons with disabilities is not adequately addressed by national level laws. As with the other types of accessibility, it may be that the access for persons with disabilities is partially addressed by local-level authorities.

The respective chapter authors highlight Italy's Puglia region and Israel for their special attention to accessibility of the coast for people with disabilities. Puglia Law No. 17 places a responsibility on government to assure that access for people with disabilities be provided. In Israel, this topic is not explicitly addressed by the Coastal Law, but court decisions, prompted by NGO action, have harnessed the notion of "distributive justice" to interpret the wording of the legislation to encompass requirements for special facilities such as elevators or special accessible paths. In one decision, the court overruled environment-focused planning regulations that disallowed such facilities. A key decision became "judge-made law" that has recently been incorporated in the new coastal planning regulations in Israel National Outline Plan One (2020).

Although this book does not address local practices systematically, some of the country chapters report about special practices. One such example is brought in the Slovenian chapter by Marot (Chapter 11). Although Slovenia does not have specific laws mandating accessibility for people with disabilities, the city of Izola has specifically designed one of its beaches to ensure access for them free of charge, even though the city might have charged for "special facilities".

This brings us to the issue of entrance fees in general and their socio-economic impacts.

Social justice in accessibility: Removal of socio-economic barriers

Beyond physical barriers, a hidden obstacle to accessibility might be entry fees for beaches and various related facilities. A "paywall" for beach access or use can lead to exclusion of lower-income groups.

Maintenance of beaches costs money, and the higher the number of users, the more expenditures will likely be necessary. If entry to beaches and other coastal facilities is free, the costs will have to be borne by some other budget source. In such cases, maintenance costs compete with other public needs. As long as the legal responsibilities for maintenance and the powers to levy the fee lie with the local jurisdictions, major issues of distributive justice might arise. If many of the beach users reside in other local jurisdictions, they may become "free riders". We did want to learn whether the social-distributive issues have surfaced as a major policy topic in coastal zone management in each of the reporting countries.

In most countries in this book, the socio-economic aspects of accessibility apparently have not surfaced as a major national-level issue in coastal zone management. Broadly, our authors report that the legal norm (whether explicitly stated or implied) is that access to beaches should be free of charge. However, the interpretation of this general norm probably varies across jurisdictions.

The issue of whether beach access and use should be free has drawn high public attention in Israel. Perhaps this reflects the fact that beaches are the main recreation space due to this country's exceedingly high score on the Coastal Population Pressure Index. In Israel, the question of free access has been high on the public debate agenda for decades, well before the rise of environmental awareness. A series of court decisions, including by the High Court of Justice, has reaffirmed the free access norm but has left room to charge for "special amenities". The definition of this term will likely continue to be debated in the media and legal arenas. The topic arises annually in heated public debates when summertime arrives.

Alternative approaches to socio-economic accessibility are reported by Schachtner in the German chapter (Chapter 6). In the states of Mecklenburg-Western Pomerania and Schleswig-Holstein, the law stipulates that entry to, swimming at, and hiking along beaches is free of charge. Authorities may thus charge for other uses of the beach, including sitting on the sand. But an interesting and legally challenging normative rule holds in Mecklenburg-Western Pomerania, where the authorities are required to retain a "reasonable balance" between free and paid parts of the beach. The courts have already allowed that there is some discretion to determine what that "reasonable balance" may be. It will be interesting to see whether any additional court decisions will further clarify this matter. However, these topics may draw less public attention in Germany than in Israel, due to the high reliance on beaches as a major mode of recreation in Israel.

A different aspect of socio-economic barriers to accessibility is reported in the US chapter, where private property rights reach the shoreline. In California, for example, where the law does provide for public access on privately owned beaches, private property owners sometimes actively discourage public access across their property by hiding "Open Beach Access" signs or by replacing them with "No Trespassing" signs. Because properties along the beach are often very expensive and there are many gated communities, blockage of access often correlates with social exclusion.

Visual access

Our final category of accessibility refers to unhindered visual lines towards the coast. Visual access has implications for urban design and architecture, and thus legislation seeking to protect visual access would likely be addressed to urban planning authorities. In our comparative analysis, we are asking which of the jurisdictions in the study regard visual access as a public right to be addressed by legislation or policy. The findings show that the right to visual access is not widely acknowledged. There are, however, some interesting exceptions, and perhaps signs that the legal status of visual access may be on the rise.

Three jurisdictions do have rudimentary provisions about protection of visual access to the coast. These are Italy's Puglia region (Regional Landscape and Territorial Plan), the Netherlands (General Spatial Planning Rules), and Spain (Coastal Law). They all use broad language to say that visual access to the coast should be provided but leave the implementation of this rule to the discretion of local statutory plans and building controls. In a fourth jurisdiction, Israel, court decisions have recognized visual access to the coast as a legitimate planning consideration, and thus one that might justify rejection of development proposals. The new Israeli National Outline Plan One (2020) incorporates this "judge-made law". It requires that proposed projects within the Coastal Environment (300 m from the shoreline) be accompanied by analysis of view lines.

Some interim observations

In this chapter we delved into the set of four ICZM parameters directly related to land and property rights. Our comparative analysis went into many details, some of which may have seemed a bit technical. In fact, ostensibly minor details about the legal contexts can make large differences when they apply to land and property rights.

In view of the caveats of comparative legal and public-policy research discussed in Chapter 1, we refrain from giving any cumulative grades to our research countries across this set of parameters. Instead, we leave it up to each reader to decide what insights are "take-away knowledge" relevant to specific countries. Here we share some observations.

The overall findings about the degree to which the research countries stand up to the ICZM principles represented by these four parameters are not very encouraging. If ICZM is to be implementable on the ground, especially in the face of sea level rise and increasingly frequent extreme weather events, major changes of direction will be necessary. (Our findings in the next chapter regarding the governance-related instruments are a bit more encouraging.)

An especially discouraging finding is the modest progress over time. Half a century after the concept of ICZM was first introduced, only a few jurisdictions in our study have taken significant steps to change their land-related laws and practices to come closer to ICZM principles. Most of those jurisdictions that today demonstrate relatively good laws and practices have inherited them from past generations. Countries that did not take such steps long ago are likely to encounter major problems in attempting them today.

Yet there are a few positive exceptions. These did not entail outright revisions of legislation but, rather, retroactive implementation of past decisions – such as demarcation of the shoreline or implementation of historically declared public domain. Even such modest actions, when attempted in recent years, have turned out to entail further legal and political stumbling blocks and delays. Progress has also been made in the realm of accessibility. Several jurisdictions have expanded the types of public access, though only modestly, shunning direct intervention in property rights.

Of all the countries and states in our sample, Spain stands out in changing its laws and practices dramatically in recent generations. In 1988, Spain took some (comparatively) extreme steps towards coastal zone preservation that involved direct intervention in private property rights. These steps were probably home-grown. They preceded widespread international concern with climate change. How were such drastic actions possible at that point in time? This enigma deserves in-depth analysis by political scientists. We conjecture that the opportunity may have been part of a "window" created a few years earlier by a dramatic change of political regimes. The take-home lessons from Spain, however, are not very encouraging for other jurisdictions. The Spanish story is a live lab demonstration of the socio-political repercussions that occur when governments take extreme steps of intervention in private property rights, even during political transition times. The conflicts continue to this very date in the form of social protests and court actions.

In structuring this book, we put a special focus on the opportunity to evaluate the degree of influence of supra-national policies and legislation. Could international law or policy push countries to adopt better coastal zone management policies and instruments? On this question, our findings are only somewhat encouraging.

The effect of the 2002 EU ICZM Recommendation about the land-related parameters has been difficult to gauge. Recall that the EU parliament voted to reject the idea of turning that document into a binding Directive. By contrast, the Mediterranean ICZM Protocol of 2008 is binding on seven (potentially eight) of the fifteen countries in this book. Yet it is not simple to attribute direct influence. Only two land-related rules in the Protocol are mandatory: The delineation of the shoreline with a relatively high reference line, and a setback distance of 100 m. The other rules are more like soft law. Among the Mediterranean countries that comply with the prescribed rules, most had these in place long before the Protocol was drafted. No country has attempted to change its shoreline demarcation law to fit the Protocol's requirements. However, at least one country – Israel – was inspired by the Protocol and did change its law to adopt the required 100 m setback zone. Two more countries have attempted to create at least some setback zone.

* * *

Implementation of the legal parameters about land demarcation and ownership analysed in this chapter is dependent on the quality of planning and governance institutions. These are discussed in the following chapter.

Notes

1. Special thanks to two experts in water- and marine-related disciplines who kindly helped us out with some of the unavoidable concepts and terms related to shorelines: **Dr. Dov Zviely**, an expert in coastal morphology and related aspects of morphodynamics, hydrography, paleogeography, and sedimentology; Head of the MA program in Marine Resource Management at Ruppin Academic Center, Israel. **Dr. Roey Egozi**, hydrologist, Research Station for Erosion Studies, Israel Ministry of Agriculture and Rural Development.

2. For example, we found several conflicting definitions of the backshore and littoral zones. Oertel (2018) indicates that the backshore comprises all sand dunes, but for our diagrams we adopted the position taken by several others, who indicate that the dunes begin landward of the backshore.

3. This is explicit in Greece, Turkey, and Denmark, which identify the shoreline using geomorphological features which are reached only by storm waves: "The landward limit of the beach, which is the limit of influence of storm waves, generally is marked by a change in material, a change in morphology, or a change to a zone of permanent vegetation" (Chrzastowski, 2005, p. 145).

4. As is explicitly stated in the French definition.

5. In the latter, the language used in the law is somewhat vague, but it appears that mean low tide is the best fit.

6. In Israel, MSL has overtaken geodetic zero by several centimetres, and this gap will grow as sea levels rise, unless geodetic zero is updated (according to Dov Zviely, as above).

7. Interviews with two representatives of the Israeli Ministry of Environmental Quality who participated in the Mediterranean ICZM Protocol preparation process. Interviews held: With Dr. Rachel Adam, 2014; with Att. Dan Zafrir, 2019.

8. Israel's shoreline definition is based on forecast sea level rise rather than on any tidal measurement. It also does not consider extreme weather events, which are less significant in the Mediterranean than in other seas.

9. Thus, accepted hydrographic measurement methods are used to interpret the legal definition. Interestingly, there is a justification for the use of a greater added increment in Portugal than in Slovenia: Portugal's tidal regime is subject to much greater natural variation (according to Dov Zviely, as above).

10. This new procedure was likely a response to pressure due to Greece's severe economic crisis.

11. By 2020, the process of revising the line is still far from completed, so we cannot say how much of the dune area (if at all) would be removed from the public domain.

12. Based on an updating interview with Pablo Molina Alegre, co-author of the Spanish chapter, December 2019.

13. See, for example, Rochette & Bille (2010); Sylaios et al. (2015).

14. See note 7.

15. See Oertel (2018), pp. 324–325; Titus (2011), p. 16.

16. On Schleswig Holstein's Baltic Sea coast, the public can access only on that part of the wet beach under mean sea level.

17. In Israel special restrictions pertain to the entire coastal zone (within 300 m of the shoreline), and exceptions (rarely granted) must obtain permission from the national level.

18. The United States chapter describes the well-known US Supreme Court decision on this matter and its impacts.

References

Alterman, R. (2010a). Israel. In *Takings International: A Comparative Perspective on Land Use Regulations and Compensation Rights* (Chapter 16, pp. 313–341). APA Press.

—— (2010b). *Takings International: A Comparative Perspective on Land Use Regulations and Compensation Rights*. APA Press.

Chrzastowski, M. J. (2018). Beach features. In Finkl C., Makowski C. (Eds.). *Encyclopedia of Coastal Science. Encyclopedia of Earth Sciences Series. Springer, Cham. https://doi.org/10.1007/978-3-319-48657-4_34-2*

Cornell, S., Fitzgerald, D., Georgiou, I., Hanegan, K. C., Hung, L.-S., Kulp, M., Maygarden, D., Retchless, D., & Yarnal, B. (n.d.). Nearshore, beaches, and dunes. Earth 107: Coastal Processes, Hazards, and Society. Penn State University. Available at: https://www.e-education.psu.edu/earth107/node/584

Fraczek, W. (2003) Mean sea level, GPS, and the geoid. Esri Applications Prototype Lab. Available at: https://www.esri.com/news/arcuser/0703/geoid1of3.html

Hobma, F. (2010). The Netherlands. In R. Alterman (Ed.), *Takings International: A Comparative Perspective on Land Use Regulations and Compensation Rights* (Chapter 16). American Bar Association.

Kraus, N. C. (2018). Beach profile. In Finkl C., Makowski C. (Eds.). *Encyclopedia of Coastal Science,*. Encyclopedia of Earth Sciences Series. Springer, Cham. https://doi.org/10.1007/978-3-319-48657-4_37-3

Nordberg, L. (2001). National report: Finland. *Revue juridique de l'Environnement* 26(1), 163–175. Available at: www.persee.fr/doc/rjenv_0397-0299_2001_hos_26_1_3855

Oertel, G. F. (2018). Coasts, coastlines, shores, and shorelines. In Finkl C., Makowski C. (Eds.). *Encyclopedia of Coastal Science. Encyclopedia of Earth Sciences Series. Springer, Cham. https://doi. org/10.1007/978-3-319-48657-4_94-2*

Rochette, J., & Billé, R. (2010). *Analysis of Mediterranean ICZM Protocol: At the crossroads between the rationality of provisions and the logic of negotiations.* Institute for Sustainable Development and International Relations (IDDRI), SciencePo. Available at: http://www.cirspe.it/gizc/Pubblicazioni/ Pubblicazioni%202/4-%20ICZM_Med_IDDRI.pdf

Rochette, J., du Puy-Montbrun, G., Wemaëre, M., & Billé, R. (2010). Coastal setback zones in the Mediterranean: A study on Article 8-2 of the Mediterranean ICZM Protocol. Institute for Sustainable Development and International Relations (IDDRI), IDDRI SciencePo.

Ryan, E. (2020). Dueling forces within water law: The public trust and private allocation coctrines. In E. Ryan, *The Public Trust Doctrine, Private Rights in Water, and the Mono Lake Story* (Chapter 2). Cambridge University Press. Manuscript in preparation.

Sanò, M., Jiménez, J. A., Medina, R., Stanica, A., Sanchez-Arcilla, A., & Trumbic, I. (2011). The role of coastal setbacks in the context of coastal erosion and climate change. *Ocean & Coastal Management*, 54(12), 943–950.

Survey of Israel. (n.d.). Objectives. Available at: https://www.mapi.gov.il/Research/sea_level/Pages/ objectives.aspx

Sylaios, G. K., Lalenis, K., Anastasiou, S., Papatheocharis, I., & Kokkos, N. (2015). A tool for coastal setbacks demarcation over rough, impermeable shores: The test case of Kavala coastline (Northern Greece). *Coastal Management* 43(5), 519–538.

Titus, J. G. (2011). *Rolling Easements. Climate Ready Estuaries.* EPA – Environmental Protection Agency. Available at: https://www.epa.gov/sites/production/files/documents/rollingeasementsprimer.pdf

International law and policy

European Parliament (2002). Recommendation of the European Parliament and of the Council of 30 May 2002 concerning the implementation of Integrated Coastal Zone Management in Europe. Official Journal L148, 06/06/2002 pp. 0024 – 0027. Available at: https://eur-lex.europa.eu/legal-content/ EN/TXT/?uri=CELEX%3A32002H0413

UNEP (United Nations Environment Programme), MAP (Mediterranean Action Plan), PAP (Priority Actions Programme) (2008). Protocol on Integrated Coastal Zone Management in the Mediterranean. Split, Priority Actions Programme. Available at: http://iczmplatform.org//storage/documents/sewmr XIR9gTwfvBgjJ4SAjhvqsLrBF6qB0B89xK8.pdf

National legislation and policy

(Refer to individual country chapters for full listing of relevant legislation and court cases)

20 Comparative analysis III: Governance, planning, and climate change awareness

Rachelle Alterman and Cygal Pellach

This chapter continues the comparative analysis presented in Chapters 18 and 19, where we discussed Parameters A through E about land demarcation and property rights. We called these the "hardware" of the kit of tools of ICZM related to real-property law. In this chapter, we review the second set of parameters, which are related to governance – institutional setups, planning, and more. These aspects are based largely on public/administrative law – the "software" of the ICZM kit of tools. Without good governance, the implementation of the property rights–related parameters will fall short.

The five governance parameters discussed here are numbered in sequence (following parameters A to E in the previous chapters):

F. Planning institutions and instruments
G. Public participation and access to justice
H. Integration and coordination
I. Compliance and enforcement
J. Climate change awareness

We introduced these parameters in Chapter 2. There, we also quoted the relevant articles from the two international documents: The binding Mediterranean ICZM Protocol and the advisory EU ICZM Recommendation. However, unlike the land and property rights parameters, where degree of compliance with the supra-national rules could be determined (to some extent), norms of governance are broad and open to interpretation. There is a lack of accepted international standards to gauge what is good governance or good planning. Thus, we assume that if ever brought before the courts, the governance parameters are likely to be regarded more like "soft law" than binding international law.

Parameter F: Land use planning – dedicated institutions and instruments

When discussing the parameters regarding coastal zones, public domain, setback zones, and accessibility, we also mentioned the variations in the specific land use and development regulations applied to these zones. We did not focus on the institutional and governance aspects of planning. The policies and regulations implemented by the planning bodies can be very significant for the prospects of sustainable management of coastal zones.

The Mediterranean ICZM Protocol (directly relevant to seven of our eight Mediterranean countries) relates thus to land use planning:

> For the purpose of promoting integrated coastal zone management, reducing economic pressures, maintaining open areas and allowing public access to the sea and along the shore, Parties shall adopt appropriate land policy instruments and measures, including the process of planning. (UNEP, 2008)

Although the Protocol uses the word "shall", the wording leaves the determination of what is "appropriate" to each country. And as we shall see, the approaches adopted do differ considerably.

Legally empowered ("statutory") land use planning systems anywhere in the world are complex institutions. They differ considerably across jurisdictions, including among OECD member countries (OECD, 2017). In our comparative analysis, we first ask whether the planning law in each jurisdiction designates special planning institutions or instruments for coastal zone regulation. We then discuss the major dedicated instruments across our fifteen jurisdictions.

Are there special planning instruments for coastal zones (beyond regular instruments)?

In principle, land use planning powers can be generic and regulate any area in a country, including coastal areas. In many of our jurisdictions, this was the situation some decades ago, before awareness grew of the special challenges of ICZM. Today, the picture is the reverse: Only four countries – Germany, Greece, Malta, and Slovenia – lack dedicated institutions or instruments for coastal zone planning beyond public land ownership and setback zones (see Table 20.1). This is an important and encouraging finding of the comparative analysis.

The absence of dedicated coastal planning institutions and instruments does not necessarily indicate that the planning policies and regulations implemented by the regular planning bodies cannot perform good coastal zone management. However, the highly specialized environmental knowledge about natural processes occurring in coastal areas, coupled with the managerial challenges necessary for good ICZM coordination and integration, probably merit dedicated planning bodies and instruments. Indeed, in surveying our set of country reports, one observes a clear trend whereby more jurisdictions are recognizing the merits of establishing a dedicated body for coastal zone planning, reinforced by special procedures and instruments.

Table 20.1 summarizes which jurisdictions have dedicated planning institutions or specialized planning regulatory instruments beyond the strict regulations that apply to public domains and setback zones.

Dedicated coastal planning bodies/authorities

Does good ICZM indeed depend on the establishment of special planning institutions for the coastal zone? Our findings do not answer this question directly but look at what exists in current laws and practices.

In our large sample of fifteen countries (and some states within), only five have established dedicated bodies to oversee coastal planning and management. These are France, Israel, the Australian states of South Australia and Victoria, and the US state of California. In only three of these jurisdictions – California, South Australia, and Israel – do these bodies have legal powers related to land use planning. The other two are advisory. These five institutions, each

Table 20.1 Special planning institutions or instruments for coastal areas

Country	Dedicated coastal planning body/authority	Special regulatory instruments beyond the setback zone	Dedicated plans for coastal areas
Australia	(Victoria, advisory & South Australia, regulatory)	–	–
Denmark	–	X	–
France	X advisory	X	X
Germany	–	–	–
Greece	–	–	–
Israel	X regulatory	X	X
Italy	–	–	X
Malta	–	–	–
Netherlands	–	X	–
Portugal	–	–	X
Slovenia	–	–	–
Spain	–	X	(Catalonia)
Turkey	–	–	X
UK	–	–	X
USA	(California – regulatory)	–	X
Jurisdictions without any special institutions or instruments are marked in bold			

with a different composition and powers, deserve a closer look (and further in-depth research about their degrees of impact):

Advisory:

- The French National Council for the Sea and Coastal Areas (sometimes translated as the National Coastal and Ocean Council) is charged with overseeing and promoting national strategies and Coastal Zone Plans for Coastal Councils. It also serves as a consultative body for coastal planning and management. Its members include representatives of national and local governments, the private sector, civil society, and experts (RISC-KIT, n.d.).
- The Victorian Marine and Coastal Council is an advisory body set up to provide guidance and advice directly to relevant State Government ministries. Interestingly, all Council members are experts rather than government officials. They are selected for their expertise, collectively spanning a range of subjects, including marine ecology, sustainable fisheries, the environment sector, governance, and law (Victorian Marine and Coastal Council, n.d.).

Regulatory:

- The California Coastal Commission plans and regulates the use of land and water in the coastal zone. In some (but not all) cases, it is the authority responsible for issuing permits for development in the coastal zone. The Commission is a quasi-judicial body made up of six locally elected officials, six appointed members of the public, and three ex officio (non-voting) members who represent the Resources Agency, the California State Transportation Agency, and the State Lands Commission respectively (California Coastal Commission, n.d.a).

- The South Australian Coast Protection Board is a statutory body formed through the Coast Protection Act 1972. Its functions include protection of coastal land from erosion, damage, or misuse; restoration of damaged coastal land; and management and maintenance of coastal facilities. This body consists of six members: Three representatives of government ministries and three experts – in local government, technical coastal protection, and environmental protection respectively. By law (Development Act 1993), planning authorities must refer to the Board development applications pertaining to land in the coastal zone (generally within 100 m of the shoreline (mean high water) but may extend to up to 500 m; not to be confused with a setback distance, which is absent in Australia). The Board will comment, and in some cases, it may direct the relevant planning authority to refuse permission or impose conditions (South Australia Department for Environment and Water, n.d.).
- Israel's National Committee for Protection of the Coastal Environment (CPCE) is a statutory planning body established by the Coastal Act in 2004. It is in charge of the Coastal Environment Zone. The coastal zone (not to be confused with the setback zone) is defined as 300 m inland from the shoreline. Due to Israel's small size and very high density, with the second-highest score on the Coastal Population Pressure Index in our sample (see Chapter 1), this span covers major parts of existing cities, villages, and infrastructure. Any proposal for development – even a small variation from a pre-approved permit – must first receive the CPCE's clearance before it can be approved by a local or district planning commission. Some major urban areas have special statutory plans that exempt them. The Committee's members include representatives of several relevant government ministries; a representative of the Union of Environmental NGOs; a marine academic expert; and a marine transport expert.

We see that in the majority of the national jurisdictions there are no dedicated regulatory bodies for the coastal zone. Good planning can probably be carried out also by the regular planning institutions.

Special planning rules for land beyond the setback zone

Although good coastal zone management could conceivably be carried out without dedicated institutions, it is likely to require special legal instruments to control the challenges posed by development pressures in coastal zones. Such pressures can be generated by land development as distant as several kilometres inland. In assessing proposals to introduce additional controls beyond the public domain and setback zones, parliaments or government bodies are likely to encounter objections from land and infrastructure development interests. In land-scarce jurisdictions, such conflicts are likely to be more intense.

Nevertheless, the findings do show signs of progress. In seven of our jurisdictions, there are special planning rules to control development beyond the setback zone (or, in the case of the Netherlands, in place of such a zone). A summary of the relevant provisions can be found in Table 20.2. Most of these rules are formulated to protect the coastal zone and its hinterland from excessive development.

Table 20.2 Special planning regulations for land beyond the setback zone

Country	Name/Description	Distance from shoreline	Summary of special planning rules (beyond setback zone)
Denmark	Coastal Planning Zone	3 km	Planning authorities should justify any significant changes in the height or volume of buildings; new urban nodes must be explicitly justified. Accessibility rules also apply.
France	Coastal municipalities	Variable (up to approximately 2 km)	Coastal municipalities in their entirety (even beyond view-obstructive mountain ridges) must exercise special planning controls against sprawl; must take account of carrying capacity in urban plans.
Israel	Coastal Environment	300 m	Any new or amended plans or permits must receive clearance from the dedicated national coastal committee (CPCE).
Netherlands	Coastal Foundation Zone	N/A (see definition in Chapter 4)	In urban areas, development is subject to assessment by municipalities. Outside urban areas, new development is not permitted, with some small exceptions.
Portugal	Coastal protection zones	500 m	Building permits must be referred to the APA before they can be approved.
Spain	Zone of (Coastal) Influence	500 m	Coastal Law defines that: (a) Development that is inappropriate for the coastal area in terms of form or density "should be avoided"; (b) In areas with road traffic to the beach, land reserves "shall be made" for car parking.

Dedicated types of plans for coastal zones

How prevalent is adoption of dedicated forms of plans for regulating the coastal environment (built or open)? The comparative analysis, summarized in Table 20.3, brings to light a potentially optimistic finding: More than half the jurisdictions in this book have chosen to adopt a special type of land use plan for their coastal zone (or subzones). As one would expect, these planning instruments are not uniform in terms of legal force or scope.

All but two jurisdictions have adopted legally binding plans, but "legally binding" is not a binary variable. In some jurisdictions, a plan can be legally planning yet strategic (not detailed). Furthermore, one cannot say a priori which type of plan – advisory or legally binding – is more appropriate for coastal zone management in specific contexts. As with land use planning in general, the effectiveness of plans depends on many variables, some unknown, and on complex decision-making processes that differ across jurisdictions and over time (Alterman, 2020). The plans also differ in geographic coverage. Some of the plans specify geographic coverage, and in others this is implied through each jurisdiction's initial definition of the coastal zone (see Chapter 18).

Two jurisdictions – France and the Spanish Autonomous Community of Catalonia – stand out in adopting especially stringent planning policies and regulations to protect their coastal zones from development pressures. In both jurisdictions, dedicated coastal plans give shape to the special planning regulations for land beyond the setback zone, (refer Table 20.2). There are two ambitious Catalonian coastal plans, both relatively new. The PDUSC (Urban Director Plan

Table 20.3 Dedicated plans for coastal zones: Legal force, scope, and current status

Country	Plan name	Legal force	Scope: Applies to	Status
France	Sea Development Scheme	Regulation of land and marine activities. Legally binding	Land and sea in coastal municipalities	Optional – currently in force for some areas
France	Coastal Zone Plan	Strategic, yet binding (not detailed). By region	Land and sea in "Coastal Councils" (not to be confused with coastal municipalities)	Under preparation for all four Coastal Councils
Israel	National Outline Plan 13 (to become part of NOP One)	Regulations for land use and development. Binding	Relevant zone defined by the plan – includes at least the setback zone and in some areas, beyond	In force. Is amended as needed Currently major update pending
Italy	Regional Coastal Plans (PRC) (Legal authority by the Regions)	Regulate use and management of coastal land. Binding	Maritime Public Domain (MPD)	Optional. In force in most regions
Portugal	Regional Coastal Zone Plan (POOCs)	Regulation and action plans. Binding	Land and sea, including all coastal waters and up to 2 km landward of the shoreline	In force. Prepared at national level but applied regionally
Spain – Catalonia	PDUSC (Urban Director Plan for the coast)	Binding supra-municipal land classification plans prepared at Autonomous Community level	Zone of Influence (between setback zone and 500 m inland from shoreline). Only in Catalonia	In force. Prepared at Autonomous Community level
Spain – Catalonia	Since August 2020 (Law 8/2020) – plans for the coastal influence area	Binding supra-municipal detailed land use plans prepared at Autonomous Community level	Up to 1 km inland from the edge of the public domain. Only in Catalonia	Not yet prepared at time of writing
Turkey	Integrated Coastal Area Plan	Strategic guidance for coastal planning and management. Not binding	The specific area defined by the plan – may be any size	Plans prepared at national level for selected areas
UK	Shoreline Management Plans (SMPs)	Non-statutory, high-level guidance plans for coastal management	The specific area defined by the plan. Includes flood risk areas	In force
USA	Coastal Zone Management Program*	Optional state-level regulatory plan. Binding if adopted	Coastal Zone (as defined by each state) in the program	In force in most coastal states, prepared at state level, approved at national level
USA	Special Area Management Plan**	Optional. Binding	The specific area defined by the plan, within the state-defined coastal zone	In force in some states for some areas, prepared at state or local level
USA California	Local Coastal Program – mandated by state for local level	Local policy plan. Binding	Coastal Zone (as defined by the state)	In force, prepared and updated at local level

* See, for example, New York State (n.d.)
** See, for example, City of Superior (n.d.)

for the Coast) classifies which areas within the "Zone of Influence" (within 500 m from the shoreline, excluding the setback zone) may be developed for urban purposes and which must be preserved. The demarcation lines are specific, down to individual plots. The second type of plan is a more detailed land use plan, introduced by a law approved in August 2020. Both plan types leave very little "wriggle room" for municipal discretion and both reflect the strong Catalan environmental protectionist outlook. It will be interesting to follow these planning innovations.

Unlike in Catalonia, France's detailed and regulatory Sea Development Schemes were to be prepared and applied at the municipal level. But Prieur (Chapter 9) reports that these plans turned out to be overly ambitious, and not many municipalities in fact adopted such plans.

Another interesting type of initiative in coastal planning is reported in the Italian chapter for one of the country's regions. In Italy in general, Regional Coastal Plans are binding, but they apply only to the coastal public domain. Much is left to the initiatives of the Italian regions. The Italian chapter includes a detailed account of the initiatives undertaken by the Puglia region to fill in this planning void.

To summarize – planning institutions

Within the scope of this book, we are unable to evaluate the *contents* of the coastal zone decisions made by the planning institutions. However, based on the formal decisions taken, one can conclude that the planning scene surrounding ICZM is encouraging. Many jurisdictions in our set have in recent years adopted new planning institutions or instruments. This momentum holds the promise of enhancing the capacity and quality of planning and land use regulations of coastal regions.

Parameter G: Public participation and access to justice

Almost every book or policy document on Integrated Coastal Zone Management mentions public participation as an essential ingredient. In Chapter 2 we cited the references to participation in both the ICZM Protocol and in the EU Recommendation about ICZM. However, participation in general is a rather elusive norm in planning, as Arnstein (1969) taught us long ago. The outcomes of participation are not necessarily supportive of ICZM. The purpose of our comparative analysis is to show how or to what extent public participation regarding coastal issues is grounded as a legal right and what are some of the key differences across our jurisdictions.

Land use planning and environmental laws generally provide at least a minimal public right to receive information and to express opinions for or against specific planning proposals regarded as injurious or undesirable (OECD, 2017). When it comes to coastal land regulations, public participation is likely to fall in the midst of tension between opposing forces: On the one hand, ICZM proponents would like to expand participation rights with the assumption or hope that this would give greater voice to supporters of sustainable environmental practices. On the other hand, stakeholders who oppose coastal zone protection due to economic or other interests may also employ their rights to public participation to increase their influence. We are interested in comparing how the different jurisdictions handled this paradox.

We first look at what our country chapters report about the general legal context for public participation and whether there are special rules for the coastal zone. Then we collate examples of the "softer" aspects of participation linked with civil society action.

Legal requirements

In order to survey the legal requirements for participation, we should differentiate between two sets of countries in this book: The eleven that are members of the EU and the four that are not.

All EU member states are party to the Aarhus Convention on Access to Information, Public Participation in Decision-Making and Access to Justice in Environmental Matters.[1] The reference to "environmental matters" includes planning and coastal regulation. Although Israel, the USA, and Australia are not party to the Aarhus Convention, the authors of the relevant chapters report that these countries' norms of public information and participation do meet similar standards. Turkey may be the exception.

Legally grounded participation does not end there. Beyond the planning and environmental bodies, the role of tribunals or the courts is crucially important. Our jurisdictions diverge significantly on this issue, which divides EU-member countries too. Some jurisdictions, most notably the UK, do not allow for "third-party appeals" (Buitelaar et al., 2013). This means that only the applicant may appeal a planning or environmental decision. Most jurisdictions in the book do allow third parties to appeal; the arena of tribunal or court appeals encompasses neighbours and NGOs, thus a much broader range of interests or views may come before the courts.

In this book we are especially interested in knowing how the legislators approach public participation regarding coastal regulation. Have they granted broader or narrower public participation rights compared with on other topics? The tentative answer surprised us. Only three of our countries – France, Israel, and the USA – are reported to have special participation procedures in decisions concerning coastal zones. Each of these three countries has a different story.

In France, within the 100 m setback zone, where construction would usually be forbidden, there is a possibility of requesting an exception. In that case, the authorities must hold a public inquiry before considering such a request. This is a more demanding procedure than the consultation and hearing required in regular planning procedures. The apparent purpose is to make it more difficult for the authorities to grant such exceptions.

In the US, the federal Coastal Zone Management Act (CZMA) says only that states should provide the opportunity for public participation. The Act does not include specific requirements, leaving the format to the discretion of state and local governments. Formats used in practice vary greatly and may include stakeholder workshops, task forces, and public hearings. The US chapter cites two research reports about the outputs of public participation in coastal regulation: A Californian study did not find any statistically significant impact of participation on outcomes; and a Miami and New Orleans study discovered that the participation processes concerning adaptation to sea level rise were rather ineffective. We do not have information on parallel studies in other countries. Yet the studies cited are important reminders that, in any country, there is no guarantee that the participation process will affect the course of government decision-making.

The Israeli chapter directs attention to the important role of the courts in enhancing legal opportunities for participation on coastal issues. Since Israel is a common law country (along with three others in this book), decisions by higher-level courts could become binding precedents. A recent court decision about construction of a beach boardwalk went so far as to oblige the local government to conduct a public participation meeting also at the permit-granting stage, where the law does not prescribe any participation obligation. The court's rationale for this precedential decision was that coastal areas are of unique public interest. This court decision paved the way for formalisation of higher participation obligations regarding coastal areas – now embedded in the new National Outline Plan One.

Civil-society action

Several of the country reports provide examples of the potential impact of environmental activism on coastal planning and management. Within the scope of this book we cannot provide a systematic comparative assessment of these actions but can provide some examples. In Malta, the Netherlands, Portugal, Spain, and Israel, civil-society actions are reported to have successfully influenced coastal planning outcomes. In each of these countries, citizens and NGOs have staged protests and at times have taken legal action against both government and developers who were planning to build within the coastal zone. In three countries – the Netherlands, Spain, and Israel – civil-society actions have not only influenced specific decisions but have had far-reaching effects on coastal law, regulation, or policy.

The Dutch chapter describes the *Baywatchers* case, in which several environmental NGOs rose up in strong opposition to draft regulations (General Spatial Planning Rules) released in 2015. These would have removed the general prohibition on development in the Coastal Foundation Zone. The *Baywatchers* action not only contributed to the shelving of these draft regulations but also led the Minister to initiate a consultation process with environmental NGOs, municipalities, and provinces. Results of that consultation included a new pact between the parties which sets out core values for coastal zone management.

On the opposite side of the debate, in Spain, there have been decades-long intensive protests by citizens and foreigners who were former owners of coastal land converted to public domain without compensation. These protests commenced following the adoption of the 1988 Coastal Law, as reported in the previous chapter. An NGO representing affected landowners petitioned the European Parliament, leading to a Parliamentary resolution in 2009 that called on the Spanish government to find a solution to the property rights issues. That petition was a key driver behind Spain's 2013 amendment to the Coastal Law, which softened some of the original restrictions but did not resolve the significant property rights issues. As such, the property owners' NGO is continuing its actions.

The Israeli chapter offers several accounts of the contribution of civil-society action to coastal policy, some of which have been mentioned earlier in our comparative analysis. The 2004 Coastal Law itself was the direct outcome of the initiative of a consortium of environmental NGOs. When the NGOs first suggested the idea several years earlier, the national government objected to it, arguing that the legal instruments for coastal protection already in place were adequate. Through systematic lobbying of Knesset (Parliament) members, the NGOs recruited enough supporters willing to submit a private bill. When the government realized the extent of public momentum, it decided to take the bill over as a government initiative, thus enabling smooth passage in the Knesset. Thanks to the Coastal Law, Israel's highly valued and extremely pressured coastal environment has gained more effective protective tools.

To summarize – public participation

As always, participatory efforts do not constitute an insurance policy for government authorities or for environmental NGOs that the inputs from the public will necessarily be supportive of ICZM policies. The "public" also includes landowners, developers, infrastructure proponents, and other conflicting interests. Our overall impression from the country reports is that in most cases, the formal requirements for public participation have not been reformatted or enhanced for specific issues related to coastal zone management. The positive aspect is the actions of NGOs, sometimes in collaboration with specific government bodies. These have, in some countries, been successful and led to government or court decisions that have pushed ICZM further. Such outcomes, however, are not predictable and vary greatly across societies, legal systems, and modes of governance.

Parameter H: Integration and coordination

Among the tenets of ICZM are integration of relevant subject areas and coordination among institutions. A high level of integration would see institutions and legislation that seek to encompass the full range of issues associated with coastal management (Portman, 2016, pp. 61–69). A high level of coordination would see institutions working in tandem towards management goals, both horizontally (between parallel levels of government) and vertically (between the national, regional, and local levels).

An integration issue unique to ICZM is integration across the land–sea divide (see, for example, Kerr at al., 2014). This divide pertains to much more than just the general, and chronic, issue of institutional coordination. In all countries, the physical division between sea and land is accompanied by legal and economic separations. Land and sea are regulated according to different legal regimes, and they often fall under the responsibility of different government offices with conflicting interests. Everywhere, the sea is also regulated by international law and treaties, whereas the terrestrial part is highly resistant to international legal interventions, as discussed in Chapter 1.

The legal divide between land and sea is exacerbated by politics, history, and culture. As recounted in the introductory chapter, the EU attempt to issue an integrated sea–land coastal directive failed due to the objection of most MEPs – even those from countries that had earlier agreed to come under an international treaty (the Mediterranean countries). The hope that an EU binding directive would enhance land–sea integration had to be put on hold. The 2014 Maritime Spatial Planning Directive was finally adopted with jurisdiction over the sea only.[2] Land–sea integration is thus left to each EU member country's desire and capacity for achieving it, similar to the situation in non-EU countries.

In reality, full integration and full coordination on any public-policy topic are insatiable ideals. In coastal matters, the plethora of issues and interests are especially challenging. The breadth of topics will always involve many government and non-government bodies with conflicting agendas. Capacity to coordinate across institutional boundaries depends much on governance culture. Given that neither the authors of the chapter reports nor we as editors have conducted empirical analysis with comparative criteria for assessing the degrees of coordination or integration in practice, we rely on the insights of each of the chapter authors. These are likely to reflect each author's expectations to improve their own country's quality of governance, including coordination. Each author's benchmark is likely to be different.

Understandably, the authors of all the country reports – except the Dutch – lament the state of integration, of coordination, or both. Most are concerned with horizontal and vertical coordination and note the fragmentation caused by the number of institutions involved in coastal matters. Only the authors for Denmark, the UK, and Germany seem to be more occupied with the need for integration of terrestrial and marine policies and regulation. These differences could simply be reflections of subjective expectations, but it may well also be that these three countries have achieved a culture of governance with a satisfactory level of institutional coordination that allows them to focus on the substantive questions of land–sea integration.

We are not surprised that the Netherlands again stands out – this time in its high level of coordination and integration. Jong and van Sandick (Chapter 4) report that the Delta Programme displays a unique broad-ranging approach. The Delta Commissioner has direct access to all cabinet ministers involved in coastal zone management. In addition, the Netherlands is currently in the final stages of a ten-year project – probably globally leading – to collate and integrate all of its environmental and planning legislation – not only regarding the coast – into a single all-encompassing Environment and Planning Act. This ambitious initiative has been resource-intensive but will lead to better integration among the various topics related to spatial and environmental planning and regulation. Coastal land planning issues are among them.

As outlined under Parameter F (planning institutions) and Table 20.1, France, Israel, the state of California in the USA, and the states of Victoria and South Australia in Australia have all established designated bodies charged with overseeing coastal planning and management. The existence of these bodies probably also contributes to coordination in state-level decision-making. In France and Israel, these institutions are relatively new, demonstrating the role of learning in improving coordination over time.

France's special attention to coordination is worth highlighting. This country's concern about coordination has led it to establish more national-level coordinative bodies than elsewhere. In addition to the national coastal planning body already mentioned, France also has an Inter-ministerial Committee on the Sea and a General Secretariat for the Sea. At the regional level, France has instituted Coastal Councils, designed to bring together a range of stakeholders to inform regional-level coastal management policies and plans.

Israel is currently in the process of establishing a new land–sea integrated body at the national level. This institution is to be one of the outputs of the recently completed national marine spatial planning project. This project was undertaken with the involvement of the broadest range of government, quasi-government, academic, and NGO bodies ever convened for a national planning initiative. The statutory National Planning Board, which is in charge of all terrestrial planning, will also be overseeing the Marine Spatial Plan, once approved. However, it remains to be seen to what extent this impressive institutional and legislative foundation will indeed succeed in enhancing land–sea integrative management.

A final example of a nationally led initiative is reported in the German chapter. An advisory council on coastal issues was formed in 2008 as a pilot initiative. It has representatives from the relevant federal ministries, the five coastal states, and three local authority associations. Unfortunately, the pilot did not continue due to funding constraints. It will be interesting to research the extent to which this pilot institutional innovation has left a legacy for improved terrestrial and marine integration.

Now, let us look at the local level. In terms of ICZM principles, horizontal inter-municipal coordination and vertical coordination between local and national governments should be just as important as at the national inter-ministerial level. In some of the countries in the book, these types of coordination may be part of existing governance culture, so they are not highlighted in the respective country reports. In the Italy and Israel chapters, the authors do direct special attention to this type of inter-scalar coordination, perhaps reflecting its current weakness in these countries.

In Italy's Puglia Region, four municipalities on the southern part of the Ionian coast, led by Gallipoli municipality, cooperated on a strategy for the regeneration of the coastal area. This strategy also encompassed enhanced modes of public participation.

In Israel, central–local cooperation is a generally weak point in the governance structure (OECD, 2017; Alterman, 2020). As noted in this and previous chapters, Israel has several notable achievements along other parameters, and in implementing some of the rules of the ICZM Protocol. Yet this country's over-centralized mode of governance makes Israel an underachiever in vertical coordination. Nevertheless, the unique exigencies of coastal zone management have led to a unique bottom-up initiative in Israel too: Establishment of a voluntary Coastal Management Forum comprising all twenty coastal municipalities. The Forum is currently negotiating with a reluctant national government to secure some municipal representation on the new inter-departmental coordinative body for coastal and marine issues.[3]

To summarize – coordination and integration

Improvement of norms of governance such as coordination and integration depend, first and foremost, on each country's current administrative culture and modes of governance. These can only change gradually and are difficult to compare. Yet there are indeed signs of progress, especially in new institutional initiatives established to improve coordination. Several countries have made concerted efforts towards improving these ICZM governance norms.

Parameter I: Compliance and enforcement

Wonderful laws, regulations, and plans are not enough. Even good records of implementation and coordination may not be sufficient. The "bottom line" of laws and regulations is compliance by the general public. Because planning laws are rarely sufficiently obeyed by individuals through social norms, all planning laws call for some means of enforcement and sanctions. There are usually administrative units dedicated to this task, but these are often short of resources and with limited legal powers (Calor & Alterman, 2017). Neighbours' expectations are also known to be important factors in compliance, and enforcement authorities often rely on citizen complaints (Harris, 2011).

Insufficient attention to compliance and enforcement

Unfortunately, the topic of noncompliance with planning laws in advanced-economy countries has drawn very little attention from scholars (Alterman & Calor, 2020). Data about violations of land or planning laws in general are often unavailable. Only a few countries reported in this book have recorded specific figures of illegal uses or construction in coastal zones. Beyond this, we have not found any published research on the specific topic of the attributes of noncompliance in coastal zones.

The degree of compliance with planning and land laws varies considerably across the world. In this book we use the terms "illegality" and "noncompliance", despite the increasing popularity of the term "informal" as an ostensible synonym. We adopt Alterman and Calor's (2020) distinction of the term "informal" as one to be reserved for jurisdictions in developing countries where the land-related legal system is grossly dysfunctional, or for special economic, social, or cultural exigencies of specific individuals or groups.

Our comparative analysis brings to light a unique characteristic of planning violations in coastal areas. Many of the country chapters report that coastal areas tend to draw more violations of rules about permitted land use or construction than inland regions. Some jurisdictions also report that government authorities have had to introduce special bodies and adopt more stringent enforcement rules for their coastal zones.

Comparative ranking

Despite the difficulties in obtaining data, most of our contributing authors have been able to gauge the broad-brush levels of noncompliance in coastal areas and to report about enforcement policies. Based on their reports, in Table 20.4 we classify the degrees of noncompliance into four admittedly rough groups along a compliance–noncompliance scale. Note that since all our jurisdictions are part of the Global North and have advanced economies, we do not encounter the most extreme types of noncompliance typical of many developing countries in the form of large-scale squatting (Alterman & Calor, 2020).

In the first group of countries we include Australia, Denmark, Germany, the Netherlands, the UK, France, and the USA. In these jurisdictions, compliance is relatively high, probably reflecting socially embedded norms. A good example is Denmark, where social norms of compliance are especially strong. Anker (Chapter 5) suggests that some minor violations in Danish coastal areas might in fact occur where homeowners and their neighbours are simply not aware that minor construction or gardening works permitted elsewhere may not be allowed within the setback zone.

Nevertheless, even in the high-compliance jurisdictions, their coastal zones apparently attract more violations than inland areas. For example, we learn from the German report that many garages attached to residences in the coastal zone have been converted into holiday apartments. In the Netherlands, almost the converse situation is noted: Apartments permitted for use only as vacation homes are being used as permanent residences. The enforcement responses differ significantly: In Germany the use was required to cease, while in the Netherlands the national government created a path to legalize the permanent occupation of vacation apartments under certain conditions.

Table 20.4 Countries grouped according to rough scale of degrees of compliance with planning and development restrictions in the coastal zones

Degree of compliance with planning regulations	
1 High level of compliance Isolated incidents of minor or very minor infringements	Australia Denmark Germany Netherlands UK France USA
2 Significant improvement in enforcement have reduced noncompliance Minor infringements still common	Israel Spain Slovenia
3 Occasional cases of major non-compliance Distinct pockets of illegal buildings inherited from the past; occasional new infringements	Malta Portugal
4 High levels of noncompliance Illegality is rampant; need for repeated amnesties, but some regions have improved enforcement	Greece Italy Turkey

Enforcement as a learning process in mid-range countries

In our second tier on the compliance scale, we have grouped together countries where, after years of poor enforcement, there has been significant improvement in recent years. This group of countries are the "learners". Major violations no longer occur, though some under-the-radar ones may still persevere. The countries in this group – Israel, Spain, and Slovenia – are, today, especially diligent in monitoring illegalities in the coastal zone.

An example of concerted action to improve enforcement along the coast is found in the Israel chapter. On the positive side, Israel has been historically spared the phenomenon of coastal summer homes (legal or illegal) characteristic of many other countries in this book. General enforcement levels in the country have also prevented the construction of entire buildings without permits. However, the commercial attractiveness of Israel's crowded beaches has been associated with violations such as permitted kiosks that "expanded" illegality into restaurants. In recent years, enforcement has targeted such phenomena. A special inter-ministerial and multi-scalar enforcement committee dedicated to coastal areas now coordinates monitoring and enforcement actions. Where planning permission is not possible, demolition orders are carried out today more than in the past. Enforcement action can now shift focus to lighter infringements such as temporary use of the beach for private events.

Spain too has recently made significant progress in enforcement along its coasts. This followed years of notorious examples of blatant violations, even within the Maritime Terrestrial Public Domain (MTPD). Furthermore, the courts have declared that there is no time limit for the authorities in demolishing illegal construction. Nevertheless, the issue of what to do with private homes predating the establishment of the MTPD and the setback zone has yet to be resolved. In addition, some Spanish local authorities have been issuing permits illegally for development within the MTPD and the setback zone. To contend with this type of government-generated illegality, the legislation was amended in 2013, so that the State may take away local authorities' powers to issue planning permits. Yet execution of demolition orders is still not easy. Spain's trajectory has certainly been towards better enforcement and higher levels of compliance – it will be interesting to see how the lingering issues are resolved.

Slovenia, as typical of many post-socialist countries, experienced significant amounts of noncompliance with planning laws during the transition period. Owners of sheds in the rural parts of the small coastal hinterland still attempt to convert them into tourist accommodation. When discovered, construction is halted, but demolition is not always carried out. However, enforcement actions have been significantly increased. Marot reports (in Chapter 11) that in recent years, the level of illegalities along the coasts had been generally lower than inland because enforcement action on the coastal zone has been increased.

The third group of jurisdictions are also "learners" but perhaps learn more slowly than the second group. In the third group there are still pockets of major illegalities in the coastal zones, occasionally even including entire buildings without permits. In Malta and Portugal, enforcement efforts have improved only mildly. In Malta, the key problem is boathouses, approved only for boat storage but sometimes converted into summer homes. The problem persists because the authorities do not demand that the illegal use cease; they only issue fines that are too low to serve as a deterrent, while refraining from demolition.

As we see from the report of Correia and Calor (Chapter 7), Portugal exhibits a mixed picture. On the one hand, new illegal construction along the coasts is not common. But on the other hand, Portugal is the only country in our sample where there are pockets of illegal development that violate not only planning law but also property law. Portugal has several squatter settlements along its coast, especially at its southern tip. They are inhabited by a mix of fishers, permanent residents, and vacationers. The Portuguese chapter recounts the story of the Farol settlement (Culatra island) in the Algarve region, where there are still some squatter settlements. These contravene almost every imaginably property, planning, or environmental regulation. While some demolition orders have been executed, others were stalled legally and politically under various pretexts (see also Alterman & Calor, 2020).

Rampant illegal development perseveres

In the fourth and final category, illegal development is rampant and may include large clusters of housing or major projects – even commercial ones – without planning permission. This group includes Italy, Greece, and Turkey. There, authorities in some regions turn a blind eye to illegal building activities. To contend with the massive cumulative phenomenon of illegality, these jurisdictions have periodically issued general amnesties, whereby development was legalized in exchange for fees or fines. Each of the three countries has its own context and trajectory.

In Greece, an amnesty was declared as recently as 2009 (Karadimitriou & Pagonis, 2019), but this time the fines were high and enforcement strict. This measure was partially propelled by Greece's massive economic crisis, which led to the appointment of international agencies to monitor the country's financial recovery. The fines are delivering significant sums of money to the national treasury.[4] Balla and Giannakourou (Chapter 12) report of another step taken in 2018 towards enhanced enforcement, especially along the coasts. Following the tragic deaths of persons trapped in illegally walled-off properties during wildfires, demolition responsibilities in the coastal zone were transferred from the *decentralized administrations* back to the national Special Inspectorate Agency for Demolition of Illegal Construction (EYEKA).

In Italy, as reported by Falco and Barbanente (Chapter 10), illegal construction is still rampant, and more so in attractive coastal areas. The Italian phenomenon is partly connected to persistent Mafia affairs (Chiodelli, 2019). The Italian Parliament has enacted a series of amnesties in the past. Overt amnesties seem to be shunned today, but in 2016, some politicians unsuccessfully sought to reinstate a de facto amnesty in a disguised format. Enforcement policies have improved where some regions, such as Puglia, adopted special initiatives. There, a 2012 law stipulating "Rules on regional functions of prevention and repression of illegal building" clarified the previously unclear roles and responsibilities of the various institutions. That legislation also established a GIS database for monitoring; created a fund for enforcement purposes; and assigned criteria for the use of the fund. While implementation of this law is not easy, particularly given deeply ingrained cultural and institutional habits that support illegal construction, the law appears to have contributed to declining rates of illegal development in the region.

Finally, in Turkey – the only country in our set where there is still large-scale migration into major metropolitan areas – illegal construction is still rampant. Enforcement encounters recurring social challenges. An amnesty was implemented unabashedly in 2019.

To summarize – compliance and enforcement

We view socially based compliance and government enforcement as key variables in ICZM, ones deserving more research attention. Our comparative analysis shows that there are still major gaps among the countries in degrees of noncompliance. However, in some of the middle-range countries, the gaps are gradually being reduced through concerted enforcement efforts. There are still, however, two or three countries where illegal construction along the coastal areas is still a significant obstacle to improving ICZM.

Parameter J: Climate change: Awareness and regulatory practice

As a response to the international initiatives to contend with the global impacts of climate change, most countries in this book have presumably fulfilled their commitments to adopted national level policies to prepare for climate change (for an international review, see Nachmany et al., 2019). However, there is a great distance between policy declaration and on-the-ground implementation.

In this parameter, we focus on the degree to which the special challenges of climate change in coastal zones have led to adoption of legal and institutional instruments. Some of the country chapters provide examples of risks already materializing, such as accelerated cliff or beach erosion, endangered properties and even lives. In the absence of adequate nature-based adaptation and mitigation measures, such cases may require large-scale public investment in engineering works. In extreme cases, planned or emergency retreats might be necessary.

One would expect that by now, general national declarations about awareness of the impact of climate change in coastal zones would have been translated into concrete laws and regulations (Peterson, 2019). Examples might include special obligations imposed on planning bodies or developers to provide impact analysis of climate risks, requirement for adaptation or mitigation measures linked to planning permissions, or specific instruments for planned retreat if necessary (Sheehan et al., 2018). Disappointingly, our overall findings show that in many jurisdictions, even such measures are lacking.

The degree to which measures to adapt to climate change are likely to clash with legally protected property rights may vary considerably across countries. This may depend on the extent to which some of the controls discussed under previous parameters – e.g. public domain, setback zones, or planning controls – have succeeded in preventing construction close to the shoreline (and, of course, the definition of the shoreline itself). Other factors relate to socio-political aspects.

Ranking the fifteen nations on coast-related climate change legislation

Because awareness of climate change is an especially broad and open-ended topic, without firm indicators, the authors of the country reports might have applied somewhat different criteria to what is to be considered climate change awareness. The comparative analysis offered here should therefore be seen as very tentative – an appetizer for more detailed research.

Based on the country reports, we have broadly classified the set of research jurisdictions into five groups along a proposed five-tiered scale, as shown in Table 20.5. This ranking reflects only the laws and policies, and not their degree of effectiveness. Our admittedly subjective ranking suggests that the countries on the higher tier have adopted laws and regulations that address issues of coastal climate change more specifically than those on the lower tiers.

Table 20.5 Jurisdictions grouped and ranked according to degree of specificity of the regulatory frameworks addressing climate change risks in coastal zones

TIER	Description		Countries
1	**Specific regulations addressing concrete climate change impacts on land (including coastal zone)**		Netherlands* Denmark Germany* France UK Spain (one topic only) Some local jurisdictions in the USA
2	**Only general reference to climate change in coastal policy or regulation**	**Some court decisions set criteria**	Australia Israel
3		**No major court decisions**	Greece Italy Portugal
4	**No reference to climate change**		Malta Slovenia Turkey
5	**Some regressive actions**		USA, at federal level and several states – especially Florida and North Carolina

* Significant government decisions and actions beyond what is required by law

Tier 1: Specific regulations addressing concrete climate change risks

The jurisdictions grouped at the highest tier deserve special attention, and their policies are summarized in Table 20.6. These jurisdictions include the Netherlands, Denmark, Germany, France, the UK, Spain, and some better-practice states or localities in the USA. They have adopted regulations that require identification and mapping of areas prone to risk of flooding or erosion, and they prescribe that these risks should be taken into account in local land use decisions. To be effective, any regulations for adaptation or mitigation of climate risks should be based on continually revised information, as recognized by Germany and France – both currently engaged in updating their maps. Recently, New York City, too, undertook comprehensive flood risk mapping and updated its building code regulations accordingly.

Among this group of six countries, we would like to elaborate on four jurisdictions (without detracting from the others): The Netherlands, Germany, California, and Spain.

It is not surprising that the Netherlands is ranked high. For several hundred years, this country's very existence has depended on excellent water management policies and practices. These preceded current legal-regulatory regimes, so the Netherlands does not have (or need) the type of specific legislation that emerged much later in the other countries (Van Rijswick et al., 2012, pp. 251–268). In the Netherlands, management of land subject to flooding – including sea level rise – is embedded in strongly institutionalized national policies and regulatory planning practices. Currently, the major policy packages at the national level are the Delta Programme and Fund. The Delta Programme includes specific plans to protect the country from flood events.

Germany too stands out in the top tier. Its government has taken significant proactive steps to address climate change risks well beyond the legislative requirements. A national (federal)

Table 20.6 Tier 1 jurisdictions: Summary of regulations addressing climate change risks on land/coastal zone (see Table 20.5)

Jurisdiction	Law/Regulation	Specific requirements
Netherlands	Delta Act	Hundreds of years' tradition of sea and flood management. Currently, national Delta Programme, Delta Fund, Delta Commissioner, Delta Decisions. Programme includes plans to protect the country from high water.
Denmark	Coastal Protection Act / Flood Risk Act	Municipalities must prepare Flood Risk Plans. These binding plans must be considered in the drawing up of Municipal Plans or Local Plans under the Planning Act.
	Planning Act	Municipalities must mark (additional) areas prone to flooding or erosion in their Municipal Plans. When planning for urban development in these areas, must include appropriate mitigation measures.
France	Urban Planning Code	Natural Hazard Prevention Plans must be prepared for areas where a specific risk has been identified. Building permits must comply with these plans.
	Coastal Law	Climate change must be taken into account as a factor of carrying capacity when planning for new development in the coastal zone.
Germany	Federal Water Resources Act	Requires the development of risk maps and restrictions for the designation of building areas in land use plans, especially within flood plains.
	Mecklenburg-Western Pomerania Water Act	New buildings must be prohibited if they would be threatened by coastal erosion.
New York City (as a US local example)	Building code	Requires buildings to protect to a Level One flood elevation (based on city-wide flood risk mapping).
	Flood Resilience Text Amendment	Modifies zoning to enable flood-resistant construction (NYC, 2013b). Regulations to mitigate potential negative effects of flood-resistant construction on the public realm.
Spain	Coastal Law	If, due to sea level rise, the water reaches concession (ground lease) areas within the public domain (MTPD), all concessions will be cancelled, and the structures built on that land must be demolished. Decision-making regarding concessions must take climate change considerations into account.
UK	Flood and Water Management Act (England and Wales)	Several requirements, including the preparation of local flood risk management strategies, and local registers of structures which might affect flood risk.

Strategy for Adaptation to Climate Change and its accompanying Adaptation Action Plan have laid out specific targets and actions to be undertaken by the Federal government. The Action Plan sets out the ambitious principle that climate change impacts must be integrated into all policies, regulatory plans and implementation decisions. In both the German and Dutch cases, these policy documents place specific onus on government bodies to ensure that climate change adaptation would be a key aspect of decision-making.

Although the USA as a whole is not a candidate for the first category, among this country's fifty states there are some good practices. California is the leading state-level example. The California Coastal Commission – a statutory body – is actively working to ensure that climate change risks are appropriately considered in the planning and management of coastal zones. The Commission addressed climate change in its 2013–2018 Strategic Plan and has since adopted policy guidance about sea level rise, including recommended regulations (California Coastal Commission, n.d.b).

We have also included Spain within this higher category, though hesitantly. Spain's coastal legislation features an obligation on the authorities to take sea level rise into account when considering a request for "concessions" on the public domain. Even though broader climate change concerns are not addressed in legislation or binding policy, we regard Spain as a relatively high achiever on climate change preparedness and adaptation because its definitions of the shoreline, public domain, and setback zone reach furthest inland among our set of jurisdictions. Indeed, Spain has been applying the "highest storm" reference since 1988 – well before widespread global awareness of sea level rise. Spain's harsh measures against buildings in the coastal zone that existed prior to 1988 could be regarded as gradual "planned retreat" from the entire coastal zone (see Chapter 19). However, these measures were not motivated by climate change and still do not differentiate among subzones with higher or lower sea level rise or extreme storm risks.

Tiers 2 and 3: General reference only to climate change

The second and third tiers in the table encompass five jurisdictions – Australia, Israel, Greece, Italy, and Portugal. All have adopted legislation that refers to climate change as an important consideration in regulating coastal land but there is no reference to specific criteria or actions to be taken. We have divided this set of countries into two tiers. In Tier 2 are Australia and Israel – both common law countries – because jurisprudence ("judge-made law") has fortified their legislation about climate change. The authors of the remaining three country chapters – Greece, Italy, and Portugal – do not report of major court decisions that have helped to fill in the gap left by vague regulatory language. We thus classified these countries in Tier 3.

The role of court decisions in Australia and Israel deserves further discussion. In Australia, Gurran (Chapter 16) reports that the courts have recognized the planning bodies' authority to deny development proposals if deemed to be inappropriate in the context of climate change. For example, in 2017, the NSW Land and Environment Court upheld a local council's refusal to permit a thirty-nine-lot residential subdivision due to flooding risks associated with climate change. In Israel, the courts have for some years been taking a proactive stance regarding environmental protection, including sea level rise. With this inspiration, the National Planning Board has recently inserted a broad reference to climate change into the coastal chapter of the new National Outline Plan One. The concrete import of this reference will await interpretation by the courts.

Tier 4: No relevant reference to climate change – only general policy

Malta, Slovenia, and Turkey apparently do not refer to climate change in their laws or regulations pertaining to coastal zones. This does not mean that concern for climate change is entirely absent; there are likely to be various international commitments and national policy documents. These, though, have apparently not yet been translated into coastal land law and regulation. Malta and Slovenia, as EU members, are expected by EU directives to undertake flood risk mapping. Both countries do conduct background studies addressing climate change risks. Slovenia's regional development strategies and some national policies address the risks of climate change, but specific data about those risks is lacking. Turkey, partly spurred by its past bid for EU membership, has adopted a Climate Change Strategy and Action Plan and has also issued circulars about building in flood risk areas.

Tier 5: Regressive actions

Within our set of countries, the USA as a whole is a standalone, where the national level and several states have taken regressive actions by removing climate-oriented regulations or reducing their potency, for political reasons. The Trump administration has repealed several Obama-era regulations for adaptation and mitigation, including those designed to reduce carbon emissions. And even before the Trump administration, the North Carolina Department of Environment and Natural Resources symbolically decided to remove any links and documents about climate change from its website. The author of the US chapter also recounts how, in 2015, the Governor of Florida instituted an unwritten ban on the use of the terms "climate change" or "global warming". In 2017, that same state decided to downgrade its obligations relating to previously adopted international standards for hurricane-proof construction, requiring that the standards be only reviewed and not necessarily adopted. These backwards-march policies have relevance to coastal laws and regulations too, since these involve high-value private property rights.

In Australia too, though to a lesser extent than in the USA, some politicians continue to debate the causes of climate change and the necessity for action. The Australian federal government has made some contentious decisions in recent years, though less blatant than in the USA. Such decisions include approval of the Adani Carmichael coal mine in Queensland in June 2019 (Cox, 2019). The mine has potential negative impact on the valuable and endangered Great Barrier Reef (marine area). Yet despite these setbacks at the national level, both Australia and some US states also offer some positive examples of climate change awareness and regulation at the state and local levels.

To summarize – climate change

The overall picture is not very encouraging. Many of the countries in this book have not yet incorporated climate change in explicit and significant ways into their coastal land regulations and policies. In some cases, the coastal regulations offer only a general statement that climate change should be taken into consideration, but the specific measures – if any – are left to other agencies and regulations. In a few of the jurisdictions, issues of coastal climate change do not receive any special attention within amorphous climate change policies.

On the positive side, in all our jurisdictions (perhaps except the federal USA) we do observe a trend of increased references to climate change risks in formal documents related to coastal zones. However, national and international declarations and commitments will not mean much if they do not translate into specific regulations and policies to protect the coastal zones and their inhabitants. In most countries covered in this book, there is yet a long way to go.

Concluding thoughts

Following the fifteen country reports, written by leading authors from each country, we as editors presented three chapters of comparative analysis. The comparative findings of the land-related parameters were presented and summarized in the two previous chapters. Since this is the concluding chapter of the book, we first summarize the findings presented in this chapter, and then share some overall observations. Readers are reminded again that in view of the limitations of comparative legal and public-policy research, we refrain from pointing out overall "best practices". Each reader is encouraged to decide what insights are gained from the opportunity to observe one's own country from an external, comparative perspective.

Regarding the *planning* parameter, we showed that several of the jurisdictions in this study have in recent years adopted new planning institutions or instruments designed for coastal zone management. In many jurisdictions, special planning controls are applied to urban or rural areas well beyond the public domain or setback zones. These specialized institutions may increase the capacity to find proper balances between urban or rural development and protection of the coastal zone.

The findings regarding *public participation* are more ambivalent. In most jurisdictions, the regular formal rights and obligations for public participation in planning have not been enhanced or adjusted for coastal zone management. However, in some countries, civil-society NGOs have successfully influenced government or court decisions. The political and legal weight of civil society seems to be an important determinant of future progress in ICZM in those jurisdictions that still lag behind. Unfortunately, no national or international law can engineer civil-society action – it must emerge "bottom up".

Coordination and integration are core objectives of ICZM but are difficult to assess, much less compare cross-nationally. Yet the findings do show progress. Many countries have established special institutional setups to reduce inter-institutional fragmentation and enhance integration across topic areas.

Especially challenging among all the parameters is the rampant *noncompliance* in buildings and land use in coastal areas and the difficulties of *enforcement* . Without adequate compliance, even the best plans and regulations will not achieve their goals. The findings show that this issue is relevant to most of the Mediterranean countries in our sample and that there are signs of progress.

The final parameter in this chapter is *awareness of climate change*. The findings show an increase in references to climate change risks in legislation or policy documents. However, it is not clear how much of this increase remains on paper only. Preparation for climate impacts such as sea level rise is likely to require major interventions in land and property rights. And these, as we saw in the previous chapter, fall much short of current and anticipated challenges.

The findings in this chapter related to governance – the "software" instruments – show distinctly more progress than the findings of the previous chapter related to the "hardware" instruments. In the governance parameters, there is more evidence of progress over time than in the land-related parameters. This disparity is due, we conjecture, to the inherent differences between the realm of real-property law and the realm of administrative law.

There are four key conclusions to the comparative analysis in this book. First, laws related to real-property rights are extremely obstinate to change. Property rights are sometimes centuries old. They are often protected through public registration and complex legal rules and procedures. Thus, property law is not very amenable to the concept of "adaptive law", recommended by environmental law scholars (Arnold, 2013).

The second conclusion is that even international law (the Mediterranean ICZM Protocol), which has some obligatory clauses about land demarcation and property rights, has had only minor influence among the relevant countries in our sample. We are not aware of any major example among the seven Mediterranean signatory countries in our sample where the Protocol served as the basis for domestic court decisions.

Third: In the reported cases (not many) where more ambitious changes in property rights were attempted, there was apparently no accompanying financial scheme for reasonable compensation of the landholders. The major socio-political conflicts that ensued surrounded issues of perceived fair financial compensation for real property expropriated or extensively regulated. Locked-in legal doctrines caused major delays and, in some cases, public protest.

Our last conclusion is that due to known climate change risks, most countries urgently need to review their current land-related laws and regulations pertaining to the coastal zone. These include (variously in each jurisdiction) shoreline demarcation; expansion of the public domain landward of the shoreline; setback zones and other means of distancing development; re-conceptualization of private property, including "regulatory takings"; and broadening the rights of public access. Legislation and implementation of such drastic changes will also require appropriate funding for fair compensation – as noted, a topic ignored by all international policies to date. Within this policy domain, there is much room for innovative legal approaches.[5] It would be a pity to await major climate crises to make such adaptations politically feasible.

Notes

1. All the EU countries in the book have ratified the Aarhus Convention.
2. https://www.eea.europa.eu/policy-documents/directive-2014-89-eu-maritime
3. Updated information: Conversation with Mr. Ophir Pines Paz, Head of the Institute for Local Government at Tel Aviv University, who co-initiated the Coastal Municipalities Forum.
4. Based also on an interview by Alterman with a government officer in charge of this policy at the Greek Ministry of Treasury, August 2015. (See also Lalenis & Papatheocaris, 2013).
5. See for example, Norton (2020) about "rolling zoning" – development rights that would roll back (or forward?) with sea level rise etc.

References

Alterman, R. (Ed.). (forthcoming). *Handbook on Comparative Planning Law*. Routledge.

Alterman, R., & Calor, I. (2020). Between informal and illegal in the Global North: Planning law, enforcement, and justifiable noncompliance. In U. Grashoff (Ed.), *Comparative Approaches to Informal Housing around the Globe* (pp. 150–185). UCL Press.

Arnold, C. A. (2013). Resilient cities and adaptive law. *Idaho Law Rev* 50, 245–264.

Arnstein, S. R. (1969). A ladder of citizen participation. *Journal of the American Institute of Planners* 35 (4), 216–224.

Buitelaar, E., Galle, M., & Salet, W. (2013). Third-party appeal rights and the regulatory state: Understanding the reduction of planning appeal options. *Land Use Policy* 35, 312–317.

Calor, I., & Alterman, R. (2017). When enforcement fails: Comparative analysis of the legal and planning responses to non-compliant development in two advanced-economy countries. *International Journal of Law in the Built Environment* 9 (3), 207–239.

California Coastal Commission. (n.d.a). Our Mission. Available at: https://www.coastal.ca.gov/whoweare.html. [Accessed July 2020].

California Coastal Commission. (n.d.b). Sea Level Rise Adopted Policy Guidance. Available at: https://www.coastal.ca.gov/climate/slrguidance.html. [Accessed July 2020].

Chiodelli, F. (2019). The dark side of urban informality in the Global North: Housing illegality and organized crime in Northern Italy. *International Journal of Urban and Regional Research* 43 (3), 497–516.

City of Superior. (n.d.). Special Area Management Plan (SAMP). Available at: https://www.ci.superior.wi.us/565/Special-Area-Management-Plan-SAMP

Cox, L. (2019). Campaigners criticise "reckless" approval of Adani mine in Australia. *The Guardian*, 14 June. Available at: https://www.theguardian.com/environment/2019/jun/14/campaigners-criticise-reckless-approval-adani-mine-australia

Harris, N. (2011). Discipline, surveillance, control: A Foucaultian perspective on the enforcement of planning regulations. *Planning Theory & Practice* 12 (1), 57–76.

Karadimitriou, N., & Pagonis, T. (2019). Planning reform and development rights in Greece: Institutional persistence and elite rule in the face of the crisis. *European Planning Studies* 27 (6), 1217–1234.

Kerr, S., Johnson, K., & Side, J. C. (2014). Planning at the edge: Integrating across the land sea divide. *Marine Policy* 47, 118–125.

Lalenis, K. & Papatheocaris, I. (2013). Greece. In Alterman, R., Adam, R., Fox, J., & Pellach, C. (Eds.), *Mare Nostrum Project First Interim Report: Existing Knowledge on Legal-Institutional Frameworks for Coastline Management, The International, EU and National Levels.* https://alterman.web3.technion.ac.il/files/mare-nostrum/Mare_Nostrum_project_First_Interim_Report.pdf

Nachmany, M., Byrnes, R., & Surminski, S. (2019). *Policy Brief: National Laws and Policies on Climate Change Adaptation: A Global Review.* Grantham Research Institute on Climate Change and the Environment and Centre for Climate Change Economics and Policy.

New York State. (n.d.). New York State Coastal Management Program. Available at: https://www.dos.ny.gov/opd/programs/WFRevitalization/coastmgmtprog.html

Norton, R. K. (2020). Dynamic coastal shoreland zoning: Adapting fastland zoning for naturally shifting coastal shores. *Zoning Practice* (American Planning Association) 37 (3).

OECD. (2017). *Land Use Planning Systems in the OECD: Country Fact Sheets.* Paris: OECD.

Peterson, J. (2019). *A New Coast: Strategies for Responding to Devastating Storms and Rising Seas.* Island Press.

Portman, M. E. (2016). *Environmental Planning for Oceans and Coasts.* Springer.

RISC-KIT. (n.d.). France. Available at: https://coastal-management.eu/governance/france [Accessed July 2020].

Sheehan, J., Kelly, A. H., Rayner, K., & Brown, J. (2018). Coastal climate change and transferable development rights. *Environmental and Planning Law Journal* 35 (1), 87–101. Available at: https://ro.uow.edu.au/lhapapers/3458/

South Australia Department for Environment and Water (n.d.). Coast Protection Board. Available at: https://www.environment.sa.gov.au/topics/coasts/coast-protection-board. [Accessed July 2020].

Van Rijswick, M., van Rijswick, H. F. M. W., & Havekes, H. J. (2012). *European and Dutch Water Law.* UWA Publishing.

Victorian Marine and Coastal Council (n.d.). About us. Available at: https://www.marineandcoastalcouncil.vic.gov.au/about-us/who-we-are. [Accessed July 2020].

International law and policy

European Parliament (2002). Recommendation of the European Parliament and of the Council of 30 May 2002 concerning the implementation of Integrated Coastal Zone Management in Europe. Official Journal L148, 06/06/2002 pp. 0024 – 0027. Available at: https://eur-lex.europa.eu/legal-content/EN/TXT/?uri=CELEX%3A32002H0413

UNEP (United Nations Environment Programme), MAP (Mediterranean Action Plan), PAP (Priority Actions Programme) (2008). Protocol on Integrated Coastal Zone Management in the Mediterranean. Split, Priority Actions Programme. Available at: http://iczmplatform.org//storage/documents/sewmrX-IR9gTwfvBgjJ4SAjhvqsLrBF6qB0B89xK8.pdf

National legislation and policy

(Refer to individual country chapters for full listing of relevant legislation and court cases)

Index